TAKE CHARGE OF YOUR BODY

A WOMAN'S HEALTH ADVISOR

Revised Sixth Edition, July 1996. Includes Index.
ISBN 0-9694766-1-2

First edition March 1989
Second edition March 1990
Third edition May 1991
Fourth edition June 1992
Fifth edition January 1994
Sixth edition July 1996
Revised Sixth edition May 1997

Copyright Carolyn DeMarco M.D.

Canadian Publication Data:
DeMarco, Carolyn
Take Charge of Your Body, A Women's Health Advisor
1. Women, Health and Hygiene, Popular Works.
2. Holistic Medicine. 3. Self-Care, Health. I. Title.
RG121-D45-1995   613'.04244   C95-900213-8

Published by: **The Well Women Press.**

Formatted, Typeset and Indexed by Douglas Toner.

For Retail Orders Call:
Supplements Plus: 1-800-387-4761.

For Wholesale Orders (5 or more copies) Call:
R&R Book Bar, 14,800 Yonge St, #195, Aurora, ON. L4G 1N3.
Tel: 905-727-3300 Fax: 905-727-2620.

The opinions expressed in this book are strictly those of the author and in no way represent those of the medical profession or any medical association.

The information contained in this book is not intended to replace supervision by a doctor for medical or health related problems. Readers are urged to obtain medical supervision for health problems in addition to self help measures.

Cover Design by **Tim Kleinsteuber**, Art Director AV International.

Cover Photograph taken by **Kaloust Babian**.

Printed in Canada

TAKE CHARGE OF YOUR BODY
A Woman's Health Advisor

Carolyn DeMarco M.D.

May this book stand as a tribute and a testimony to the strength and courage of all women everywhere who are claiming back their bodies, their health and their right to a healthy environment for themselves and their children.

DEDICATION

With gratitude and appreciation
this book is dedicated to Douglas Toner
who devoted so much of his time and energy
to bring this book into fruition.

Table of Contents

Section 1: Women And Stress In The 1990's

Fading Fast: Women And Chronic Fatigue 2

Are You Doing More Than Your Fair Share?* Time Off Is As Important As A Healthy Lifestyle* Are You Torn Between Home And Office?* Emotional Conflicts Can Drain You* Additional Tests May Show Medical Cause* Biology And Hormones Play A Big Role* Here's How You Can Re-energize Your Life* Disabling Fatigue That Will Not Respond To The Above Measures* Defining Chronic Fatigue And Immune Dysfunction Syndrome (CFIDS)* A Brief Survey Of Treatments For Your Physician:* Resources

How Much Stress Are You Under? 11

Women Face Unique Stresses* Relationship And Family Stresses* Money Stress* Work Stresses* Life Stresses* How To Interpret Test Results* The Impact Of Stress* Profiles Of Women Under Stress* Conclusion* Resources

How To Cut Down On Stress 16

Analyze Your Life* Learn How To Say No* Get Help When You Need It* Arrange Private Time For Yourself* Eat Well* Exercise Regularly* Arrange A Massage Or Body Work* Learn The Art Of Relaxation* Easy Self-hypnosis:* Imagery:* Alternating Relaxation And Contraction:* Releasing Reoccurring Thoughts And Worries:* Don't Let Frustration Build Up* Never Hesitate To Get Professional Help* Develop A Support System* I Forgive Myself For Everything* Laugh A Lot* The Ten Commandments For Reducing Stress* Resources

The Sexes Aren't Equal When It Comes To Booze 22

Are You Drinking Too Much?* Women For Sobriety Acceptance Program* Alcoholics Anonymous (AA)* Women For Sobriety* Suggested Reading And Resources:

Are Computers Hurting Your Health? 28

Ergonomic Effects* Eyestrain* Musculoskeletal Problems* Stress* Electromagnetic Radiation And Its Effects* Elf Waves* Vlf Waves* Shielding For Radiation* The Question Of Cataracts* X-rays* Ultraviolet, Infrared And Visible Light* Electrostatic Charges* What About Children* What You Can Do* Conclusion

Grief Is Hard Work 38

A Society That Denies The Experience Of Loss* Dealing With Your Grief* Guidelines For Grieving* Preparing For Loss* Resources* Other Books On Grief And Loss* When A Child Or Baby Dies* Helping Children Cope With Death* For Widows* Dealing With Suicide* Where To Get These Books:* Helpful Organizations

Section 2: Birth Control And Infections

No Magic Pill 46

Blood Clots, Heart Attacks And Strokes* The Pill And High Blood Pressure* Effects Of Pills On Blood Lipids (fats)* Liver And Gallbladder Problems* The Thorny Question Of Cancer* Infertility After The Pill* Pregnancy, Lactation And The Pill* Teenagers And The Pill* The Pill And Women Over 35* Thyroid And Adrenal Effects* Infections* Depression* Metabolic Changes* Other Side Effects* Advantages Of The Pill* New Pill Developments* The New Progesterones- Hope And Hype* New Dutch Research* Other Means Of Birth Control* Conclusions* For Further Reading* Chances Of Death In A Year

Cervical Cap Makes A Comeback 57

Resources

Permanent Birth Control: The Facts 59

Vasectomy Or Tubal Ligation?* Chances For Reversal* Important Considerations Before Tubal Ligation* How A Tubal Ligation Is Done* After Surgery* Other Types Of Tubal Ligation Surgery* Long-term Complications* Tubal Ligation And Premature Menopause* Resources

Know Your Body's Cycles - To Get Pregnant Or To Avoid Pregnancy 64

How The Egg Meets The Sperm* The Two Tools Of Mucous And Temperature* Natural Birth Control* One In Seven Couples Have Trouble Getting Pregnant* Age Makes Pregnancy More Challenging To Achieve* Timing Is Everything When You Are Trying To Get Pregnant* What Makes Urine Lh Detection Possible* Five Different Lh Test Kits* How Lh Test Kits Work* Using Lh Kits As An Aid In Treating Or Diagnosing Infertility* How To Buy Lh Tests* Conclusion* Further Information* Addendum

The Yeast Among Us **70**

Predisposing Factors That Affect The Whole Body* Predisposing Factors That Affect The Vagina Locally* Symptoms Of A Yeast Infection* What You Can Do At Home* What Your Doctor Might Prescribe* Persistent Reoccurring Yeast Infections* Education Is The First Step* The Ground-breaking Work Of Dr. Orian Truss & Other Pioneers* Don't Be Confused With Vaginal Infections That Are Not Yeast* Treatment Of Chronic Yeast Infections* For More Information

Bladder Blues **78**

Symptoms Of Chronic Cystitis - Ic Type* Ic Can Begin With An Infection* The Perfect Design Of A Woman's Urinary System* What Happens In Ic* Antibiotic Usage* Serotonin Makes It Worse* Viral Infection* Hidden Bacterial Infections* Other Environmental Factors* Yeast Infection* Hormonal Factors* Psychoneuroimmunolgy* Chronic Cystitis - The Infective Type* Not Enough Good Bacteria In The Vagina* Testing Proceedures If You Suspect You Have Infectious Cystitis* Pointers On Treatment Of Infectious Cystitis* Pointers On Diagnosis And Treatment Of Interstitial Cystitis* Resources* Addendum

Chlamydia -The Greatest Threat To Reproductive Health **87**

Chlamydia A Serious Problem* What Is Chlamydia?* How Can You Test For Chlamydia?* Who Is At Risk For Chlamydia?* Protecting Yourself* When Your Doctor Should Suspect Chlamydia* How Often Should You Get Checked?* Symptoms And Complications Of Chlamydial Infections* Chlamydia And Pregnancy* The Liver, The Pap Smear And Men* Treating Chlamydia* Partners And Follow-up* Conclusion

Section 3: Making The Most Of Your Pregnancy

Favourite Childbirth Books **94**

Choice In Childbirth* Pregnancy And Childbirth Preparation* Nutrition For Mother And Child* Using Herbs, Homeopathy And Nutrition Wisely During Pregnancy* Choosing To Birth Outside A Hospital* Breast-feeding* Exercise And Yoga* Emotional And Mental Care* After The Birth* Where To Get These Books

The Amazing World Of The Unborn Child **98**

Sound And The Unborn* Sleep, Activity And Playing* How Your Feelings Affect The Baby* Connecting With Your Unborn Child* Dealing With Your Emotions

Should Every Pregnant Woman Have An Ultrasound? **101**

What Is Ultrasound?* The Debate On Routine Versus Selective Use Of Ultrasound* What The Experts Say* Selective Use Of Ultrasound* Deciding On Whether To Have An Ultrasound* Some Questions You May Want To Ask Yourself* Risks Of Ultrasound* Vaginal Ultrasound* Dangers Of Doppler Ultrasound* Women's Reactions To Ultrasound In Pregnancy* Summary* For Further Reading* Addendum On Electronic Fetal Monitoring* What Is EFM?* The Disadvantages Of EFM* Other Options Of EFM

Testing The Waters - All About Amniocentesis **108**

Who Should Consider Amniocentesis?* Medical Reasons* Who Should Not Have Amniocentesis* What Amniocentesis Can't Tell You* What Are The Risks* Genetic Counselling Necessary* Where To Have Amniocentesis* The Decision To Terminate* Chorionic Villi Sampling* An Ethical Dilemma* Further Reading

The Challenge Of Pregnancy Over Thirty Five **112**

High Risk?* Birth Defects And Age* Get All Your Questions Answered Before Testing* Alpha Fetal Protein Testing* Alpha Plus Or Triple Screening* Folic Acid Can Prevent Structural Birth Defects* Nutrition And Health* Gestational Diabetes* Coping With Fatigue* Changes In Lifestyle* Resources

Keeping Fit While Pregnant Is Good For You And Your Baby **117**

Benefits Of Exercise* The Ideal Pregnancy Exercise Program* Stretching Exercises* Aerobic Exercises* Specific Exercises For The Child-bearing Years* Breathing And Relaxation* Summary* For Further Reading

Dealing With The Discomforts Of Pregnancy **121**

Constipation* Heartburn* Morning Sickness* Stretch Marks* Backache And Hip Pain* Resources

Section 4: Satisfying Childbirth

How Painful is Childbirth? **126**

What Is The Pain Like?* Active Labour And Birth* Two Essential Characteristics* Breathing* Relaxation* Position* Vocalization* Emotional Expression* Support Systems* Pain Relieving Medications* The Best Laid Plans** Visualization: Can You Handle It?* Natural Pain Relief* In Summary* Resources

The Unkindest Cut: Are Episiotomies Really Necessary *130*

How The Routine Episiotomy Came Into Fashion* The First North American Episiotomy Trial* Alternatives To Episiotomies* Prevention During The Pushing Stage Of Labour* Prevention Before Birth* There Is No Need For An Episiotomy In A Normal Birth* Arroll's Advice To Doctors* Tears Heal Quickly* Episiotomy Does Not Prevent Later Problems* For Further Reading

Once A C-Section, Always? *135*

Sixty To Seventy Percent Of Repeat Cesareans Are Unnecessary* Reasons For Sections* Incisions And Scars* Advantages Of VBAC* Not Enough Doctors Follow The Guidelines* Getting More Support* Resources:* Useful Addresses

Miscarriage: The Need For Support *139*

Stages Of The Grieving Process* Guidelines For Grieving* Recommended Reading

The Thyroid Gland Acts Up After Pregnancy *141*

Trudi's Story* Postpartum Thyroiditis* Underactive Or Overactive Thyroid?* A Typical Case* How Often Does This Occur* For Further Reading* Taking Your Basal Temperature* Basal Temperature Chart

Section 5: Satisfying ChildbirthSpecific Women's Problems

PMS - Strength Or Weakness? *146*

How Many Women Have PMS?* What Is PMS?* Positive Aspects Of PMS* How Our Culture Contributes To PMS* Do You Have PMS?* Nutrition And Vitamins* Other Natural Treatments For PMS* Reducing Stress And Getting Support* When Should You Use Drugs For PMS?* In Summary* Menstrual Symptom Diary* Prism Calendar* References

New Hope For Lumpy Painful Breasts *155*

What Is Fibrocystic Breast Disease* Treating A Puzzling Disease* Making The Iodine Connection* All About Iodine* Getting More Iodine* Ghent And Eskin At The New Frontier* Mechanism Of Action Of Elemental Iodine* Side Effects Of Elemental Iodine Treatment* Meanwhile* Iodine And Breast Cancer* Resources* References

Pelvic Inflammatory Disease *167*

Introduction* What Is Pelvic Inflammatory Disease (PID)?* What Causes PID?* How Does PID Affect A Woman's Reproductive Organs?* Common Complications And Consequences Of PID* How Can A Woman Tell If She Has PID?* Techniques To Clinically Diagnose PID* Promptness Of Diagnosis And Treatment* Symptoms Of PID* Treatment Of PID* Special Treatment Considerations* Prevention* Special Topics* For More Information

Endometriosis - A Disease Of The 90's *173*

Symptoms Of Endo* Diagnosing Endo* Treatment Of Endo* Hormonal Treatments* The Gnrh Drugs* An Approach To Using Hormonal Treatments* Surgical Treatments* Approach To Surgical Treatments* New Evidence Emerges On Endo And The Environmental Connection* How To Avoid Exposure* Addresses

A New View Of Endometriosis *180*

Five Common Cliches About Endo* Diagnosing Endo* What Are The Symptoms Of Endo?* Where Is Endo And What Colour Is It?* Endo Does Not Progress* Dr. Redwine's Method Of Surgery* Response To Dr. Redwine's Work* Consumer Power* Alternative Treatments For Endometriosis* Specific Natural Therapies For Endometriosis* Conclusion* Useful Resources* The Most Useful Books* Other Books On Endometriosis

Section 6: Growing Older Getting Better

The Major Milestone Of Menopause *188*

Menstrual Changes* Hot Flashes* Vaginal Dryness* Other Symptoms Of Menopause* Mental And Emotional Changes* Depression, Self-esteem And Unrewarding Roles* Is Menopause A Disease?* Should I Or Shouldn't I Take Hormones?* The Down Side Of Synthetic Progesterone* The Benefits Of Natural Progesterones* Hormones And The Heart: The Pros* Are You At High Risk For Heart Disease?* Hormones And The Heart: The Cons* Hormones And Bone Loss* Hormones And Breast Cancer* Weighing The Risks Versus The Benefits* Fifty Something In The Nineties* A New Way Of Looking At Menopause* Natural Alternatives To Hormones* Menopause Specifics: Hot Flashes* Menopause Specifics: Mood Swings, Irritability And Insomnia* Vaginal Dryness* Rejuvenating Methods* Lifetime Risks Of Death For 50 Year Old Women* Relative Risk Of Selected Conditions For A 50 Year Old White Woman Treated With Long-term Hormone Replacement:* Highly Recommended:* Menopause Support Groups* Suppliers Of Natural Hormones And Vitamin Supplements

Preventing And Treating Bone Loss 205

Preventing Osteoporosis* Calcium Supplements* Calcium Supplements Useful Even After Menopause* Boron Also Is One Of The Key Minerals For Bone* Eating Well And Not Absorbing What You Need?* Folic Acid, Homocysteine And Bone* Are You At High Risk For Bone Loss?* Women Who Don't Have Regular Periods At Risk For Bone Loss* Estrogen And Progesterone - Which One Is Most Important For Bone Health?* Other Drugs For Osteoporosis* New Research On Progesterone Alone Preventing Bone Loss* Resources:* Products* Laboratories* The Daily Perimenopause Diary:* Perimenopausal Menstrual Cycle Symptom Diary Form* Osteoporosis Risk Profile* Assess Your Risk According To The Following:

How To Save Your Uterus 218

Hysterectomy Rates Vary Across The Country* Unnecessary Hysterectomies* Myths About Hysterectomy* Laparoscopic Hysterectomy* Regrets After A Hysterectomy* Valid Reasons For A Hysterectomy* Possible Conditions That May In Some Situations Warrant A Hysterectomy* What To Do About Fibroids* More About Moderate To Heavy Bleeding* A Word About Subtotal Hysterectomy* Never Have A Hysterectomy For The Following Reasons* What You Can Do To Save Your Uterus* Two Stories* Resources:* Essential Addresses

The Great Debate Over Breast Cancer Screening 227

Screening For Breast Cancer* How Useful Are Screening Mammograms?* Not All Mammograms Are Created Equal* Mammography Can Be Used For Two Purposes* How Often Should I Have A Screening Mammogram?* What Other Screening Techniques Are Available?* New Techniques* So What Do The Studies Show So Far?* Favourable Studies* What Does A 30 Percent Reduction In Breast Cancer Death Rate Really Mean?* Unfavourable Studies* The National Breast Screening Study In Canada* The Advantages Of Routine Mammography* The Disadvantages Of Mammograms* What Are The Critics Of Routine Mammography Saying?* Another View* The Large Screening Program In Ontario* The Politics Of Breast Cancer Research* What's A Women To Do?* Future Trends* Suggested Reading* Breast Cancer: What Are The Risks?

Section 7: Vital Women's Problems

Life Can Be A Drag Without Enough Iron 244

How Iron Is Taken Into The Body And Stored* Symptoms Of Iron Deficiency Or Anemia* Reasons For Iron Deficiency* Not All Anemias Are Caused By Low Iron* The Normal "Anemia" Of Pregnancy* Tests For Iron Deficiency Anemia* Dietary Sources Of Iron* Other Natural Sources Of Iron* Natural Iron Supplements* Synthetic Iron Supplements* The Dangers Of Too Much Iron* Conclusion* Resources

Exploring The Inside Of Your Uterus 249

For Diagnosis* For Treatment* Preparation For A Diagnostic Or Simple Operative Hysteroscopy With No Or Local Anesthetic* Preparation For An Operative Hysteroscope Or A D-and-C Under General Anesthetic* At The Hospital* In The Operating Room* The Operation* After Surgery* Complications

Those Annoying Varicose Veins 254

What Are Varicose Veins?* Diet And Varicose Veins* Symptoms Of Varicose Veins* Vitamins And Varicose Veins* Self-Help For Varicose Veins* Constipation And Varicose Veins* Conservative Treatment* Surgery And Sclerotherapy* Prevention Of Varicose Veins* Further Info

Beauty With Conscience 258

The Draize Eye Irritancy Test* Dermal Irritancy Test* The Lethal Dose Fifty Percent Test* What You Can Do:* Resources

The Good News About Gallstones And Women 261

What Does Your Gallbladder Do?* What Gallstones Are Made Of* Serious Complications Of Gallstones* How To Diagnose Gallstones* Cutting Out The Gallbladder, The Old Way* Cutting Out The Gallbladder, The New Way* Non-Surgical Treatments* Dissolving The Stones* Shattering The Stones* Losing Weight Too Quickly?* Hormones And Gallstones* Side Effects Of Gallbladder Surgery* Diet And Gallstones* Prevention Of Gallstones

Lesbian Health Care 267

General Quality Of Health Care* How To Increase Your Chances Of Getting Better Health Care* Health Differences Between Lesbian And Heterosexual Women* Differences In Experiencing The Health Care System* Specific Ways Lesbians Get Sub-optimal Health Care* Parenting* Emotional Aspects* Resources

Reading List and Organizations 273

Index 277

Ordering Information 297

Foreword

Reflecting on my (blessedly few) encounters with the medical profession, I realize from the vantage point of an "older woman," that the advice these male doctors gave me was uniformly harmful to my health and unborn child.

When pregnant, monthly visits to the obstetrician mainly consisted of lining up to be weighed by the nurse, who cast a baleful eye on any among us who had gained a few pounds. Incredible as it sounds, during the 1950s, doctors warned against normal weight gain as increasing the risk of toxemia. This same obstetrician, also espousing the view that formula was superior to breast milk, did his best to dissuade me from breast feeding. ("Your breasts will look like shrunken sacks!").

Later, developing amenorrhea (cessation of menstruation), I allowed an endocrinologist to pump me full of hormones which made me so jittery I couldn't sleep at night. (This endocrinologist never addressed me by name or asked me about my diet, which, at the time, barely sustained me let alone a baby.) Years later, after finally calling a halt to these shots, my periods resumed, and I gave birth to twin daughters.

Today, with doctors promoting the hysterectomy, and other operations that are, in most cases, unnecessary, and prescribing a dizzying number of drugs from tranquilizers to hormone replacement therapy, women are at even greater risk of being victimized by the medical profession.

If you feel cowed by the medical "experts," are dissatisfied with the medical care you've received or have even been harmed by certain aggressive treatments, you need help from a compassionate woman doctor who understands your needs, can give you the facts about your body, advise you about conditions that worry you, and give you confidence in your powers as a woman.

That individual is Dr. Carolyn DeMarco, a "woman's health advisor," whose remarkable book, Take Charge of Your Body, you hold in your hands.

I have read and reread Dr. DeMarco's book and, with each reading, I am struck by the wealth of information contained in this beautifully organized, highly readable book which covers every stage of a woman's life. Here is information you're not likely to find elsewhere . . . about women and alcohol, depression as related to low self esteem, the bladder condition that's often diagnosed incorrectly, current research on electromagnetic radiation, postpartum thyroiditis, a unique treatment for cystic breast disease, and natural alternatives to hormone replacement therapy.

DeMarco asks questions that other doctors should be asking and rarely do such as, is ultrasound really beneficial for the baby or the mother? As an advocate for her sisters, she scorns diplomatic docterese and gives us the facts. ("Episiotomy is an unnecessary procedure.") Some of my favourite sections are those that go beyond health issues such as women's work, and the very moving discussion of grief.

As a veteran health writer, I'm accustomed to doctor books in which the author reminisces about his favourite cases that may have little relevance to the reader's problems. Not this one. DeMarco, who is unbelievably free of ego, not only provides matchless advice in each chapter, but refers you to other authorities and books.

Furthermore, she is a consummate researcher providing information on the latest studies and treatments, consumer information and self-help groups, so you have at your finger tips a list of invaluable resources, replete with telephone numbers, addresses and product costs.

This is a book to treasure but I don't recommend sharing it with others--you may never get it back. Instead, buy copies for your daughters, your women relatives, your best friend, and give them the tools to reclaim our heritage as wise women and healers.

Jane Heimlich

*Author, **What Your Doctor Won't Tell You***

Introduction

Over the last twenty years of medical practice, I have seen many women suffer needlessly because their doctors did not really listen to the; or told them their complaints were all in their head or treated normal stages in a woman's life as if they were diseases. More recently, I have seen many women pay a heavy price for the careless prescription of tranquilizers, birth control pills, hormones and antibiotics. I have seen many women suffer because they do not understand how their body worked, had not had their treatment options explained or did not understand the side effects of drugs.

Women are hungry for reliable information explained clearly and practically. For eight years, I wrote a column **For Women Only** for **Today's Health**, a magazine which was distributed with **The Globe And Mail** to a million and a half readers across Canada in addition to 40,000 copies to doctors' and dentists' waiting rooms. During that time, I photostatted so many copies of my column for patients and doctors alike that I decided to compile them into a book so that more women could take advantage of this information. Since that time, I have completely updated, rewritten, and revised every chapter and added many new topics.

This Book Is Built On The Following Beliefs:

1. You are the most reliable expert on your body and your health care.

2. Your body is perfectly constructed for your enjoyment and benefit, whether you decide to have children or not.

3. Your first period, dealing with your fertility, being pregnant and having a baby, experiencing the monthly fluctuations of the menstrual cycle and the changes of menopause are all normal processes for which a woman's body is well designed.

4. You have innate and wondrous healing powers which can be supported and encouraged rather than suppressed and denied. Natural healing methods are often beneficial and can stimulate your body's healing capabilities without harmful side effects.

What You Can Do

1. You can help yourself a lot through regular exercise and relaxation, as well making certain that you eat as well as possible.

2. You can help yourself through reducing your work load. Too many women these days are just plain overworked, even more now since they often end up working outside the home as well as shouldering the main responsibility for the family and the house.

3. You can help re-educate your doctor on what best serves your needs.

4. You can insist that your doctor adhere to the bill of rights outlined in this book. Otherwise it is best to find a more supportive doctor.

5. You can write your MP requesting that more emphasis be put on education and prevention in the health system and that your doctor be paid for such activities.

6. You can support the rights of chiropractors, naturopaths, homeopaths and other alternative health practitioners to offer their services and be covered by medical insurance.

Dr. Carolyn DeMarco

A Woman's Health Bill Of Rights And Responsibilities

1. I have a right to be treated as an equal human being.

2. I have a right to be listened to and have my problems taken seriously.

3. I have a right to an explanation that I can understand in my native language (using a translator if necessary) on any questions concerning my health care.

4. I have a right to know the choices I face in getting treated for any health problem, and to have the possible side effects of any drugs or surgical treatments clearly explained.

5. I have a right to choose the types of treatment I prefer from among the options offered to me by my doctor.

6. I have a right for normal events in my life, such as pregnancy and menopause, not to be treated as diseases requiring treatment.

7. I have a right to choose natural therapies and not be ridiculed for doing so.

8. I have a right to request a second opinion on any major surgery or health decision.

9. I have a right to refuse any drug or surgical treatment.

10. I have a responsibility to become knowledgeable about my body and how it works.

11. I have a responsibility to learn as much as possible about my health problems so I can make informed choices.

12. I have a responsibility to look after my diet, reduce stress, exercise and relax on a regular basis.

13. I have the responsibility to avoid pressuring my doctor into giving me drugs when I don't need them.

14. I have a responsibility to prepare my questions for my doctor beforehand and schedule adequate appointment time to discuss them.

15. I am ultimately responsible for my own healthcare, using my doctor as a resource rather than an authority.

Guidelines For Combining Scientific And Natural Treatments

I have put together some guidelines for women who want to approach natural medicine, but don't know where to start.

1. Use your doctor as a resource rather than as an authority.

It is essential to knock the doctor or naturopath or chiropractor off their pedestal and establish an equal relationship. If your doctor doesn't listen or treats you in a patronizing manner, then change doctors or at least get a second opinion.

2. Educate yourself about the problem. My favourite type of therapy in my practice is bibliotherapy.

Read everything you can get your hands on, ask a lot of questions, find out, listen to tapes, go to courses, talk to as many women as you can, make use of local experts.

Educate your doctor as well. Bring him or her appropriate reading materials, especially articles from the medical literature or newsletters from self-help organizations.

3. Seek out and create support for yourself.

Solidify your network of family and friends. Women with health problems, chronic illness, pain, or disability have to learn how to say no, to delegate tasks to other family members, to know how to communicate their needs and how to ask for help. Most of all, women have to put their own health needs first.

Join a self-help group or form your own branch. Many groups have accumulated more research than most doctors will ever find time to read and offer the invaluable support of other women with the same problem. They also investigate the natural alternatives as well unusual or innovative treatments.

4. Experiment with safer, cheaper and more sane methods of therapy.

When women turn to alternative therapies, they are using systems of healing that work to stimulate the body's own natural healing abilities. They are working with a system that assumes that normal biological milestones in a woman's life are a healthy and even enjoyable part of life. They learn to listen to and trust their bodies. More importantly, they take control of their health and put it into their own hands.

Remember the following when seeking alternative care:

1. If it works for you and has no side effects then use it.

2. Trust your own perceptions about natural remedies and whether they are working for you. Trust your perceptions about your alternative practitioner.

3. Ask your friends. Ask around. Find out who is the best. Consult your local women center, health networks, women's clinics or publications.

4. Choose your alternative health care practitioner as you would any other service. By quality, experience, reputation and lack of sexism.

5. Herbs, vitamins, homeopathic remedies rarely have severe side effects. It is possible, but difficult, to overdose on vitamins or herbs. Most vitamins are safe even in high doses. You have to take a large amount of herbs to overdose on them.

About The Author

For over twenty years, Dr. DeMarco has been championing the cause of women's health. She was among the first to advocate the pro-active take charge approach to health care that is now so popular. She is a pioneer in natural childbirth and a leading advocate for midwives. Dr. DeMarco takes her message to the media through her many television, radio and newspaper interviews and her nationally syndicated newspaper column.

Dr. Carolyn DeMarco is one of only a dozen medical doctors in Canada that write regularly for the lay public. She is one of four doctors writing columns for **Lifelines** which is syndicated in all major newspapers across Canada, with an estimated readership of over two million. She is a medical advisor and major contributor to **Health Naturally** (705-342-1360). She is also featured in **Health Counselor** (414-499-2995 or 1-800-477-2995), an American self-help magazine with a readership of one million.

She has specialized in women's health issues since obtaining her medical degree from the **University of Toronto** in 1972. She works as a consultant in complementary medicine in both the city of **Toronto** and in rural **British Columbia**. Complementary medicine means combining the best of scientific medicine with the best of natural medicine. She lectures on women's health and complementary medicine throughout Canada and the United States.

For eight years, she wrote the **For Women Only** column for **Today's Health**, a magazine distributed inside 350,000 copies of **The Globe and Mail**, with an estimated readership of over one million. She is also the medical advisor and a major contributor to **Wellness MD** a magazine focusing on complementary medicine and distributed to Canadian doctors.

Her article, **Medical Malepractice**, is a chapter in the book **Misdiagnosis: Woman As A Disease**, published by the **People's Medical Society**. Her article on menopause is also a chapter in the book **On Women Healthsharing**.

She is also featured in the **National Film Board's** documentary **Born at Home**, a film about natural childbirth.

Her media work includes the **CBC** television programs **The Journal**, **Prime Time News**, **Marketplace**, **Midday**, **Alive** and **The Best Years**. In addition she taped thirteen segments for **CBC TV's** morning series **What On Earth** which is now re-broadcast on the **LIFE** channel.

Currently, she is a regular guest on **Marilyn Dennis**'s live **CITYLINE** show on **CITY-TV** broadcast nationally which introduces the concepts of holistic health to the public, and the weekly health columnist for the **Women's Television Network**.

Her book, **Take Charge of Your Body** has been widely acclaimed by women's groups across the continent. It provides a gold standard for women's health information. It is the best selling book on women's health in Canada.

What People Say About This Book

JANINE O'LEARY COBB, **Founder/Editor, A Friend Indeed and Author of Understanding Menopause.** "Take Charge Of Your Body is a great place to start. It provides short articles on many, many aspects of women's health, each one providing clear information and additional resources. An ideal book to have around the house whether you're fifteen or seventy-five."

MIKE MILNE, **The C.M.A. Journal**. "The Canadian doctors who do practise "journalistic medicine" are a long way from fitting any soap-opera mould. Dr. Carolyn DeMarco, with regular medical columns in newspapers and magazines, has a reputation based on content and comment, not on image."

EDITH AUGER, **Reader, Sault Saint Marie, Ont.** "Real practical knowledge. A handbook every woman should have. Very reassuring and practical. Makes me feel proud to be a woman."

DR. GUYLAINE LANCTÔT, **Author, Activist, Physician and Co-founder of Les Femmes D'Affaire.** Are you a woman? Are you concerned with your health? If so Dr. Carolyn DeMarco's book is what you need. If you have a question, she has the answers. Dr. Carolyn DeMarco is unique. She gathers information from all over the world, selects the best and serves it up on a platter for us to choose from. She is a remarkable physician with tremendous knowledge and passion in her quest for truth. She is devoted to the cause of empowering and informing women. Dr. DeMarco makes me proud of being both a medical doctor and a woman.

REBECCA WIGOD, **The Vancouver Sun.** "Dr. Carolyn DeMarco believes the predominantly male medical establishment deprives Canada's women of appropriate treatment for their special needs."

MARILYN MOYSA, **Edmonton Journal**. "Dr. DeMarco says self-education is the key to women taking charge of their own health care."

JOCELYN ARGUETHE, **Star Phoenix Saskatoon**. "DeMarco recommends people take charge of their own health by using a combination of western and natural medicine. Although she believes western medicine proves useful for emergency operations, diet and herbal treatments may be more effective when treating chronic ailments."

LUANNE ARMSTRONG, **Book Review, Healthsharing**. "This is a wonderful book... it contains an enormous amount of factual, well researched and often quite new information in several key areas... The perspective is refreshing. I had never before read a book written by a doctor which didn't have a slightly patronizing edge to it. There is none of that here."

THE SOJOURNER, **Boston, Mass. U.S.A.** "Take Charge Of Your Body provides women with the information they need to make empowering, personal health care decisions. The topics discussed in the book are of equal concern to all women."

DR. CAROLYN DEAN, holistic physician and author of **When You Can't Reach The Doctor.** "I have always been impressed by the amount of time, effort and energy that Dr. DeMarco puts into her work. Her writings are meticulously researched and presented in an extraordinary readable and informative manner. Required reading for any women interested in taking responsibility for her own health."

ZELDA ABRAMSON, College Street Women's Centre. "In my experience, women love this book. It is full of not readily available information on every aspect of a women's heath."

SYLVIA PLOTNIKOFF, reader, Nelson B.C. It is a rare pleasure to hear a doctor admitting that women have knowledge of their bodies and should be taken seriously ...I hope that many more women and doctors develop a more responsible point of view.

WOMEN'S NETWORK, Charlottetown P.E.I. "A wonderful resource for any women who wants to take control of her life."

DR. ANETTE GRUNDHOLM, Family Physician, White Rock, B.C. Dr. Carolyn DeMarco has researched a great deal of information on health topics of interest to women of all ages. She has synthesized this material into an easily readable form. Conventional medical wisdom, newer and alternative thinking and approaches to treatment are addressed. An excellent list of recommended reading and references complement each article. This book is highly recommended to women who wish to take an active role in their own health care."

Book Review by Zoltan Rona, MD, MSc

There are few good authors on women's health issues. Carolyn DeMarco is perhaps the best known, writing prolifically for medical journals like **Wellness Medicine** and for the general public via **The Toronto Star, Today's Health, Health Naturally** and many other publications. Given that the system conspires against any deviation from the dogmas of medical orthodoxy, Carolyn's achievements in the grossly neglected area of women's medicine are truly remarkable. When going through medical school, Carolyn DeMarco and I were soundly indoctrinated with the following "facts" about women's health:

1. Hysterectomies are the preferred treatments for endometriosis and fibroids, offering sound preventive medicine. After all, beyond childbearing age, the uterus is an unnecessary organ. Removing the uterus may well be a good way to help prevent uterine cancer.

2. Episiotomy at childbirth is a routine procedure to ensure the safety of normal deliveries.

3. All women entering the menopause must be put on synthetic female hormones to prevent osteoporosis and other effects of aging.

4. Nutrition has nothing to do with most gynecological problems.

5. The birth control pill is the safest and most effective form of birth control. Natural methods are next to worthless.

6. Once a Cesarean section, always a Cesarean section.

7. PMS is not a real clinical condition. Most women can be told, "It's all in your head." It should be treated symptomatically with psychotherapy, salt restriction, diuretics, tranquilizers and antidepressants.

8. Due to the availability of the most modern equipment and highly skilled obstetricians, the use of midwives and home births is both dangerous and irresponsible. The pursuit of natural childbirth is a myth promoted by quacks. Midwifery is outdated and potentially as harmful as the use of chiropractic treatments for back pain.

9. All women should get ultrasounds when pregnant and mammograms once they reach the age of 40.

In the sixth edition of **Take Charge Of Your Body**, Dr. Carolyn DeMarco tackles all these issues and many more. With direct reference to medical and scientific literature, she dispels all these cherishly held lies by a male-dominated profession. The underlying theme of taking more responsibility and action for one's health is in itself a step towards greater wellness. Two unique aspects of this book include "A Woman's Health Bill of Rights and Responsibilities" and "Guidelines for Combining Scientific and Natural Treatments." The book is easy reading for even the most uninitiated in wellness medicine. In researching any health problem, women should consult this book first.

This new edition is almost completely revised with over 100 pages of new information, a complete index and a new foreword by Jane Heimlich, author of **What Your Doctor Won't Tell You.** Some of the many topics covered include chronic fatigue, the yeast syndrome, endometriosis, natural birth control, natural approach to the menopause, new treatments for endometriosis and fibrocystic breast disease (benign breast lumps), how to deal with PMS naturally, and much more. Dr. DeMarco provides a list of names and addresses of organizations and resources for women for further support.

The jacket cover claims, "This book empowers every woman." I think this is far too modest. **Take Charge Of Your Body** should be read by every male and especially by every male doctor. Dr. DeMarco's book is a rare opportunity to learn the truth about women's health--no myths, dogmas or superstitions--just the facts and how to act on them to achieve higher levels of wellness. This book is a necessity in every person's home health library.

Zoltan Rona is a well known holistic physician, nutritional consultant, writer, lecturer and author of The Joy of Health (Hounslow Press, 1991) and Return To The Joy of Health (Alive, 1995).

*Published with permission of **Health Naturally**, Box 149, Nobel, Ontario P0G 1G0. 705-342-1360.*

Special Acknowledgements

With many thanks to my mom and dad, Vicky and Vince DeMarco for their warm support and encouragement; and to my sisters, Kathy Burroughs, Andrea DeMarco, Mary Sutton, Rosemary Marziliano; and my brothers Vincent, Joseph, Paul and Lawrence DeMarco, for their ongoing enthusiasm and unqualified support.

With warm appreciation for the conscientious and knowledgeable assistance of Linda Einblau, senior librarian at the B.C. Medical Library.

With much thanks and appreciation for the hard work and dedication of our proofreaders, Paul DeMarco, Daisy Kaschte, Mieke Fleck and Victoria DeMarco.

With many thanks for the constant enthusiasm, original ideas, wise advice and general all around support of Estelle Gee.

With gratitude to Stewart Brown and the staff at Supplements Plus for their dedication to women's health.

With gratitude to Sam and Elvira Graci for their gracious assistance in promoting this book and the cause of women's health.

With appreciation for the dynamic support and creative genius of Mariella Rowan, Vice-President, AV International.

A special acknowledgement to Dr. Guylaine Lanctot for her support and passionate commitment to the book.

With heartfelt thanks to Jane Heimlich for her strong support and encouragement and taking time out of her busy schedule to write the forward for this book.

With appreciation of the ongoing and enthusiastic support of Dr. Carolyn Dean.

With thanks to my former editors, Heather Howie at Today's Health, Gorden Bagley at Wellness MD, and my present editors, Laurie Imbert at Health Naturally, Karolyn Gazella at Health Counselor, and Catherine Farley at the Toronto Star and Lifelines.

Much thanks to Christina Hartling, Luanne Armstrong, Andrea Wright, Robin Wiseman, Lance Barham, Cheryl Curtis, Roger Dee, Liz Braun, Judi Jessen, Joanna DeMarco, Lynn Hamilton, Darrell Wolfe, Carol Yipp, Catherine Gabriel, Vere Shute, Healthy Horizons, Health Action Network, Consumer Health, Libby and John Gagnon, Mary Sutherland, Citizens For Choice, Harvey Diamond, Dr. Jan DeVries, Dr. Anette Grundholm, Dr. John Brighton, Gayle Brighton, Dr. Mary Doherty, Dr. Filip Vanz Hov, Dr. Donna Schoales, Dr. Richard Pragnall, Dr. Donald Gay, Dr. Tris Trethart, Dr. Verna Hunt, Dr. Pat Wales, Dr. Benjamin Foo, Dr. Stephen Aung, Dr. Emil Iliev, Dr. Will LaValley, Zelda Abramson, Margaret Tessman, The Toronto Women's Bookstore, Elizabeth Irwin, Sue Skinner, Marilyn Dennis, Bruce Steele, Bruce Edwards, Michael Snook, Clarke Donnelley, Lilli Fournier, Joyce Resin, Elizabeth Roux, Olenka Demianchuk, Alison Hancock, Trudi Pizak, Sid Tayal, Murray Cooper, Guy Krouse, Marilyn Linton, Janice Dineen, Elsa Franklin, Sharon MacFarland, Hazelle Palmer, Daniela Curk, Maureen McGuire and many others.

With gratitude to Amy Lee and the Sisterhood of the Shields.

Acknowledging the whole hearted support and inspiration of Harley Taylor and Millie Anderson.

With appreciation for the life and work of **Claude Dosdall** (1936-1993) whose book **God, I Thought You Died,** continues to be an inspiration to many and exemplifies the principles of self help and health activism.

Special thanks to all the women who have read the book and recommended it to their family and friends.

With much gratitude to all my patients over the last twenty years, who have taught me so much, and who have allowed me to participate in their journey to health.

Section One:
Women And Stress In The 1990's

Fading Fast: Women And Chronic Fatigue 2

How Much Stress Are You Under ? 11

How To Cut Down On Stress 16

The Sexes Aren't Equal When It Comes To Booze 22

Are Computers Hurting Your Health ? 28

Grief Is Hard Work 38

Fading Fast: Women And Chronic Fatigue

Over the last five years, the number of women coming into my office complaining of being drained or exhausted most of the time has dramatically increased. Few statistics have been compiled on the incidence of this important problem, but I would estimate that between 20 to 40 percent of women suffer from chronic fatigue.

Fatigue is usually defined as weariness after exertion or work. But a more useful definition coined by **Dr. Holly Atkinson**, author of **WOMEN AND FATIGUE**, says fatigue is a symptom of having too many demands placed on your body and mind. Fatigue is a vital warning signal that your body gives you that the load is simply too great. Long-term fatigue can weaken your immune system and makes you more susceptible to accidents or illness.

Some women fail to recognize how really tired they are. They start to accept chronic fatigue as a way of life.

Fatigue is a complex interplay of many factors. These include physical, emotional, psychological, social, economic, and cultural aspects.

Although some women are told fatigue is "all in your head," in at least 25 to 30 percent of cases, a medical condition is found that accounts for the fatigue. Another 25 percent of women have physical co-factors that are major contributing causes to fatigue. These physical co-factors can be easily missed or overlooked by a doctor. These include poor diet, eating disorders, use of tranquilizers and other sedatives, alcohol use, lack of regular exercise, and unfavourable working conditions.

Let's look at some of these co-factors of fatigue.

ARE YOU DOING MORE THAN YOUR FAIR SHARE ?

Overwork is probably the leading cause of chronic fatigue in women. Women have always done more than their share of work but these days women are working harder than ever.

Studies show that a typical working woman spends anywhere from 15 to 50 hours a week performing household and child care duties on top of a forty hour work week. Another study reported that working women with preschool children put in an average 77 hour total work week. The same study showed that in the last ten years, men had increased the amount of time they spend doing housework by less than half an hour per week.

Women who are full-time homemakers spend about 100 hours a week at 12 different labours. Several studies have shown that modern conveniences have not eased the burden; instead they have increased it due to higher standards of housekeeping and new functions that women are now expected to perform.

TIME OFF IS AS IMPORTANT AS A HEALTHY LIFESTYLE

The second area to take a good look at is how your lifestyle contributes to your fatigue.

Of fundamental importance to your energy level is the amount and quality of food that you put into your body. Too many women are eating inadequately, or on the run, with heavy ingestion of sugar and junk foods as well as fast foods. Too many others are dieting or agonizing about their weight. An estimated 50 percent of women suffer from some form of eating disorder and at least as many are dieting or will soon start dieting.

Coffee and black tea give a temporary energy boost, but in the long run make you more tired. Heavy smokers often experience fatigue as a side effect of smoking.

Regular exercise at some activity you enjoy, preferably outside, can produce a striking increase in your energy levels once you are in condition. Studies show that sedentary people complain of fatigue a lot more than those who are physically active.

A lot of women are not aware of how much they are drinking. Alcohol consumption makes things tolerable for a short while but in the long-term takes a heavy toll on the body and causes chronic fatigue and premature aging. Living with an alcoholic is also a very draining experience.

Some women are addicted to tranquilizers or sleeping pills without realizing it. Women are prescribed two to three times more tranquilizers than men. These drugs can cause feelings of lethargy, drowsiness and disinterest in life. Moreover, the effects of these drugs can stay in the blood stream long after they are taken and they can also be additive.

Other over the counter medicines used for colds and allergies can cause drowsiness and fatigue. Prescription drugs, such as those taken for high blood pressure, may have drowsiness as a side effect. Some drugs interact with each other, which can increase the side effects even more.

Another potential source of fatigue is the type of work that women do outside the home and the conditions under which they work. Although some women now have high paying jobs, many women are still working at low paying jobs in the service industry, in offices, and in factories.

At work, women may face both sexual discrimination and sexual harassment. Other problem areas include poor lighting, poor posture, lack of ventilation, improperly designed computer work stations, health hazards of computers, boredom, lack of daycare facilities, and exposure to noise, chemicals, and toxins.

One of the worst health habits that women have is not taking enough time for themselves. This means at least an hour every day strictly for yourself. Women often deny themselves even this small amount of time. Nobody can function optimally without this small break in the day. This is not the time to catch up on household chores or prepare an assignment for work but time to day dream, read, take a hot bath or go for a walk.

Some women do not allow themselves adequate time for rest and recreation. On a vacation, a woman can sometimes get stuck serving the other members of her family and returns home feeling anything but rested. As difficult as it may be to arrange, it is very rewarding for a woman to get away from family duties and/or work for short periods of time during the year on a regular basis.

ARE YOU TORN BETWEEN HOME AND OFFICE ?

Role conflict is another energy drainer for women who stay at home as well as those who work. Women are struggling with what it means to have a career in a work world largely controlled by male values, and what it means to be a mother and homemaker or both.

Full-time homemakers face different stresses than working mothers, and some studies show that they are actually under more stress that those who leave the home to work. Some women are completely comfortable with being at home. Increasingly, however, women may feel trapped in the home with no adult company or outside stimulation. They may feel conflict over whether to pursue a career. They may feel a need for more control over their lives and meaningful work outside the home that gives them a sense of mastery and self-fulfilment.

Single mothers struggle with an even greater burden. Sharing accommodations and child care with another single mother and her children is sometimes a workable solution than can decrease the work load of both mothers.

EMOTIONAL CONFLICTS CAN DRAIN YOU

Emotional sources of fatigue are crucial. Nothing can drain your energy more than unresolved conflicts with your mate, children, boss, co-workers, etc. Conflict over money or sex disrupts many relationships and may sometimes require expert help.

Grieving for the death of a loved one takes a lot longer than most people suppose. A grief stricken person uses up most of her energy mourning the loss and struggles just to get through the day. The first year after a major loss is the most difficult. After that, it will take another couple of years to integrate the loss into your life.

Other losses may also be mourned, although for shorter periods of time depending on the magnitude of the loss. These losses may include divorce or separation, the death of a dream, the loss of youth and child-bearing potential, and the loss of a grown child leaving home.

Staying in a job that you hate or putting up with an abusive partner can cause extreme fatigue.

ADDITIONAL TESTS MAY SHOW A MEDICAL CAUSE

Medical causes of fatigue should be carefully sought after. A detailed history of your fatigue and a thorough physical examination by your doctor are more important than lab tests in determining the causes of your fatigue. However, lab tests should also be done when appropriate.

Due to the monthly blood loss, women are particularly vulnerable to iron deficiency anemia. A hemoglobin or complete blood count may not reveal decreased iron stores or decreased iron levels in the blood. These additional tests should be requested if an iron deficiency is suspected and especially in the case of heavy or prolonged menstrual bleeding.

Other causes of fatigue may be an underactive thyroid or a hidden urinary or pelvic infection. Less obvious but very important causes of chronic fatigue are delayed food allergies, environmental allergies, hypoglycemia, intestinal parasites, chronic yeast infections and chronic fatigue syndrome.

Sometimes fatigue may be the first sign of diabetes and hypertension. Other medical diseases such as chronic emphysema and rheumatoid arthritis have fatigue as a direct result of the disease.

Fatigue following major surgery and lasting one to three months afterwards is quite common. Fatigue following hysterectomy may last a much longer time. Many cancer treatments have fatigue as a side effect. Chronic pain problems are almost always accompanied by chronic fatigue.

BIOLOGY AND HORMONES PLAY A BIG ROLE

Menopause and childbirth are pivotal events in a woman's life, and are often accompanied by fatigue, probably due to fluctuating hormonal levels. While raising small children, plain old lack of sleep is the principal cause of fatigue. Premenstrually, women may also find their energy levels fluctuating, especially if adequate attention is not given to proper nutrition, rest and stress reduction.

HERE'S HOW YOU CAN RE-ENERGIZE YOUR LIFE

When your bank of energy is depleted, you have to start making regular deposits. Then if another health crisis or major life trauma should develop, your bank will not go bankrupt.

The first step is to recognize that you are fatigued. The next step is to visit your doctor for a thorough check up and lab tests. Then go over all the possible causes of fatigue in your life and draw up a plan to overcome them.

Reduce your work load as much as possible. **Recognize** your limits. **Learn** how to say no without feeling guilty.

Work out with your partner and children a fair division of household labour. At the same time lower your standards of housekeeping as much as possible. Leave some things undone and don't worry about it. Delegate as much as possible to other members of the family.

Avoid all diets and stick to nutritious meals emphasizing fresh fruits and vegetable and whole grains. Try not to go for long periods of time without eating.

Avoid energy traps like coffee, tea, soft drinks, junk foods, sugar and sugar substitutes.

Cut down on alcohol and cigarette consumption.

Recognize if you or any member of your family has a problem with alcohol or drug addiction and get help to deal with it.

Find an exercise that you really enjoy and do it three to five times a week.

Assert yourself in the work place in order to improve conditions for yourself and other women.

Take at least one hour a day for yourself.

Learn how to take short cat naps of ten to 30 minutes throughout the day when necessary.

Address and attempt to resolve the major conflicts in your life.

Allow yourself the time and space to grieve.

Eliminate any unnecessary stresses, schedules or deadlines from your life, especially those that are self-imposed.

Learn a good relaxation technique and practise it every day.

Plan regular and restful vacations, by yourself or with your partner.

Examine your life to see if there are any major decisions you are avoiding.

Get professional help from a minister, counsellor or psychiatrist, if the problems you are dealing with are simply too great. Share your problems with a trusted friend.

DISABLING FATIGUE THAT WILL NOT RESPOND TO THE ABOVE MEASURES

Now known as **Chronic Fatigue Syndrome (CFS)** or **Chronic Fatigue and Immune System Dysfunction Syndrome (CFIDS)**, this is a very real and very disabling physical illness that causes profound fatigue and muscle weakness following a viral illness. This syndrome is also known as **Myalgic Encephalitis (ME)**, post-infectious neuromyasthenia, post-viral syndrome, yuppie flu, or formerly chronic **Epstein Barr** virus. CFIDS can cause injury to the brain, immune system and muscles of the people who suffer from it.

CFIDS was formerly thought to be caused by the Epstein Barr virus, but this has not been proven. Other viruses may also be associated with this syndrome, including herpes 6 virus, enteroviruses (coxsackie B virus, poliovirus, echovirus, etc.) hepatitis virus, influenza virus, adenovirus, and cytomegalovirus. For the viral infection to take hold, the immune system is usually already weakened by a number of causes, including the overuse of antibiotics and cortisone, major stress, poor diet and chronic yeast infections.

Dr. Byron Hyde, a leading Canadian CFIDS researcher, notes that like poliomyelitis, the incidence of CFIDS goes up after immunization, and also in late summer and early autumn. He strongly recommends that "individuals do not go to work in third world countries or start work in hospitals or schools during the first four weeks after immunization."

DEFINING CHRONIC FATIGUE AND IMMUNE DYSFUNCTION SYNDROME (CFIDS)

The long awaited case definition of CFIDS was published in the Dec 15/94 issue of, **Annals of Internal Medicine** (121;953-959). It recommends that a "thorough medical history, physical exam, mental status exam and laboratory tests be done to exclude other underlying or contributing conditions that require treatment. Diagnosis or classification cannot be made without such an evaluation."

It goes on to say that clinically evaluated and unexplained chronic fatigue cases can be classified as CFIDS if the patient meets both of the following criteria:

1. Six months or greater duration of clinically evaluated, unexplained persistent or relapsing chronic fatigue that is of new or definite onset (ie not lifelong), is not the result of ongoing exertion, is not substantially alleviated by rest, and results in substantial reduction in previous levels of occupational, educational, social or personal activities.

2. The concurrent occurrence of four or more of the following symptoms: substantial impairment in short term memory or concentration; sore throat; tender lymph nodes; muscle pain; multijoint pain without joint swelling or redness; headaches of a new type, pattern or severity; unrefreshing sleep; and post-exertional malaise lasting more than 24 hours. These symptoms must have persisted or recurred during 6 or more consecutive months of illness and must not have pre-dated the fatigue.

Dr. Hyde emphasizes the muscular component of the chronic fatigue syndrome. He defines the condition as, "a chronic illness of at least six months in duration, that develops after an acute infectious disease, in a well and physically active person. In this disease, the patient develops an unusual form of muscle failure experiencing fatigue, pain, or exhaustion in the exercised muscle."

Other important features of this illness, according to Dr. Hyde, are sleep disturbances, variability and fluctuations of symptoms, serious difficulty processing information (memory loss, lack of concentration, slurred speech, disorientation, loss of coordination) and generalized malaise.

Fibromyalgia, the "sore all over" syndrome may be part of CFIDS, with pain being a more prominent symptom than fatigue. In this condition, which affects mainly women in their late 30's and 40's, there is generalized pain and aching throughout the body, morning stiffness, fatigue, disturbed sleep, and multiple tender spots on the body.

Specialized types of brain scans have shown decreased blood flow to the brain of CFIDS patients. After exercise, brain scans also clearly show even more drastic decreases in blood flow and brain function. In addition, some researchers have noted white abnormalities in certain areas of the brain.

Most blood tests are normal in CFIDS, but there may be abnormalities of immunoglobulins and T-cell function. In particular, there may be a decrease in natural killer cells, or an increase in helper cells and an increase in the ratio of helper cells to suppressor cells.

Treatment of CFIDS requires a multi-pronged approach. It may involve gentle exercise and massage as well as nutritional and vitamin supplements to stimulate the immune system. A high quality diet with emphasis on fresh fruits and vegetables, whole grains and beans, supplemented with chicken and fish, is essential. Proper rest and balancing of activities with rest is mandatory. This illness also requires a complete change of attitude and lifestyle as well as elimination of all major stresses. Small doses of anti-depressant drugs at bedtime may be helpful for some people.

If chronic yeast infection is present, treatment is essential for recovery. **Dr. Carol Jessop**, **Assistant Professor of Medicine** at The **University of California**, treated 900 of her CFIDS patients with a strong anti-yeast drug known as ketoconazole, and a sugar free diet. Results were impressive. Eighty four percent recovered to a level at which they could remain working 30 to 40 hours a week. Of those, almost 30 percent still had a reoccurrence of their symptoms with infections, surgery or other stressors. Thirty percent fully recovered to their previous level of health.

Dr. Jessop found that 80 percent of her CFIDS patients gave a history of recurrent antibiotic use. Also, most of her patients had a history of serious sugar addiction. Eighty percent of her patients had recurrent ear, nose and throat infections as children, acne and recurrent hives as adolescents, anxiety attacks, headaches and bowel problems, and had to stop drinking because it didn't agree with them.

Dr. Jessop's current treatment of choice is fluconazole, 100mg daily combined with some form of grapefruit seed extract.

Several studies have shown that evening of primrose oil may be helpful for CFIDS. The usual dosage suggested is four capsules combined with two cod liver oil capsules (containing vitamin-A 1,250 IU and vitamin-D 100 IU) taken with breakfast and lunch but not at bedtime.

Magnesium also plays a crucial role in the treatment of CFIDS. The suggested dosage is 300mg to 500mg in liquid or capsule form, usually with an equal amount of calcium, taken at bedtime. Other important supplements include zinc, vitamin-E, mega B50, betacarotene, and vitamin-C.

A six week trial of co-enzyme Q-10 in doses of 90 to 200mg daily is recommended by American CFIDS expert, **Dr. Paul Cheney**, particularly for improving fatigue, thought processes, muscular weakness and associated heart problems.

Some doctors have found that daily or bi-weekly injections of vitamin-B-12 are helpful. A small study, published in a British medical journal (**Lancet**, Mar 30/91), showed the benefit of weekly intramuscular infections of magnesium sulphate.

Dr. Hyde also suggests a choline citrate and vitamin-C liquid mixture to be taken three times a day. "This classical treatment has been used since the 30's... it is harmless, pharmacologically sound, inexpensive, tastes good and appears to increase energy levels."

DHEA or dehydroepiandrosterone has been called the mother of all hormones. It is a steroid hormone secreted by the adrenal gland, and a precursor for estrogen and testosterone. Its functions are currently being investigated. It is a biomarker for aging and declines progressively with age. Nutritionally orientated medical doctors in the States have begun giving DHEA to selected CFIDS patients whose total serum levels are low normal or below normal. (best measured between 8:00 and 9:00am). A typical dosage is 5 to 25mg, half at 8:00am and half in the late afternoon to match the diurnal rhythm. DHEA capsules made with methylcellulose act like time release capsules. A recent study found that DHEA aids the production of T-helper lymphocytes, and enhances the availability of the T and B-lymphocytes to defend the body against infection. DHEA can produce improvement in energy level, stamina and general well being.

For all CFIDS patients, it is important to support the adrenal glands, which are often exhausted, through taking extra vitamin-C, pantothenic acid, and adrenal glandulars 2 to 3 times a day. Support of the liver through supplements and herbs is also essential. A course of immune stimulating herbs like echinacea, astralagus or cat's claw may also be necessary.

For the sleeping problems of CFIDS, tryptophan can be useful. Tryptophan is an amino acid, one of the building blocks of protein and is available only by prescription. In doses of 2,000 to 4,000mg it helps you to sleep without a hangover effect. It is not yet officially approved for this usage. In the U.S. tryptophan is available by prescription as 5-hydroxy-tryptophan (50mg of 5-hydroxy-tryptophan equals 500mg of tryptophan).

If you suspect you have this severe condition you may have to educate both yourself and your doctor. Women with this problem have tended to be dismissed by their doctors, told their problem was all in their head, or referred to a psychiatrist.

Chronic fatigue syndrome patients may be like the canary in the coal mine. They are warning us that the overuse of drugs and the onslaught of chemicals into our food, air and water, are taking a heavy toll on our health.

"Having worked with CFS patients for almost ten years, I believe this illness may simply represent the ten to 15 percent of our species, who have not yet adapted to the rapid and startling changes in the environment, and the subsequent changes in our intestinal environment." Says Dr. Jessop in her introduction to **Dr. Crook**'s book, **CHRONIC FATIGUE SYNDROME AND THE YEAST CONNECTION**.

Chronic fatigue must be taken seriously by physicians and women alike. Chronic fatigue is, I believe, another 20th century disease. It is the result of women living in a world where the food, air and water is heavily polluted, where they are burdened with ever increasing work loads and higher standards of housekeeping; where they are caught in a conflict between the roles of motherhood and career and between nurturing and self-fulfilment; and where they are living in a world where they are anything but equal.

A BRIEF SURVEY OF TREATMENTS FOR YOUR PHYSICIAN:

Dr. Paul Cheney: Two windows of recovery 2 to 3 years and 4 to 5 years.

1. Use an elimination diet to identify food allergies.

2. Digestive Enzymes with meals three times a day.

3. Activity limited: Essential to pace, avoid overheating, including saunas and hot baths.

4. Exercise prescription: Anaerobic training, submaximal aerobic training; walking, swimming, cycling.

5. Multivitamin and multimineral: High quality, hypoallergenic in capsules, plus the major antioxidant vitamins: Ester-C 1 gram; vitamin-E 400IU and betacarotene, 10,000 units daily (to destroy "neurotoxic free radicals").

6. Injectable B-12: 2500 to 5000 micrograms two to three time a week for two weeks S.C. if no response then give monthly or bi-monthly.

7. Co-enzyme Q-10: 200mg sublingual lozenges daily.

8. Magnesium citrate liquid or capsules: 250 to 500mg a day combined with at least 500mg of calcium.

9. Flax seed oil or EPO as above.

10. Hormone and DHEA replacement, as necessary.

11. Antiviral regimen: Ampligen, recently approved by the FDA for CFIDS, is given by injection. It is a mismatched double stranded RNA, and a known biological response modifier with anti-viral properties, and immune enhancing properties.

12. Hydrotherapy to improve lymphatic flow.

13. Clonazepam: .5mg to 2mg combined with doxepin one half 10mg capsule up to 20mg at night. This combination is well tolerated by CFIDS patients.

14. Topographic Brain Mapping (TBM) and Neurotherapy.

Dr. Cheney found 95 percent of 1,200 CFIDS patients had abnormal TBM's. TBM is a specialized EEG that can demonstrate subtle asymmetries, lateralization, and localization effects more efficiently than a standard EEG.

Neurophychophysiologist **Dr. Myra Preston** discovered what she believes is a sensitive and specific marker for CFIDS using the TBM, which is a predominance of delta waves and theta waves in cognitively challenged CFIDS patients, and lack of appropriate shifting to higher frequencies. Through neurotherapy (her method is patented) she trains patients to increase the frequency of their brain waves, which seems to improve cognitive functioning and other symptoms. More study is needed.

Dr. Susan Abbey, Toronto psychiatrist: According to Dr. Abbey, "Helping CFS patients learn new coping skills is the most successful treatment. Cognitive behavioural therapy is the most promising and effective rehabilitation model. It breaks the vicious cycle of learned dependency and helplessness."

Cognitive therapy aims to change habitual and repetitive thought patterns that produce habitual and repetitive emotional reactions. Founded by psychiatrist **Dr. Albert Ellis**, one of the basic premises is that feelings are determined by thought patterns and not by events. Highly recommended are two books by **Dr. David Burns**, **FEELING GOOD AGAIN: THE NEW MOOD THERAPY**, and the **FEELING GOOD AGAIN HANDBOOK**.

Dr. Majid Ali: Associate Professor of Pathology at **Columbia University** in New York. Dr. Ali believes that CFIDS is the result of accelerated oxidative injury at the cellular level triggered by infectious and chemical agents. He has treated thousands of chronic fatigue patients using a comprehensive program involving detecting and treating food and environmental allergies, oral and intravenous supplements, restoring the normal ecology of the gut, and reducing load of toxic chemicals and heavy metals. In addition, he teaches patients autogenic training for stress management, and a special form of daily and slow sustained exercise. He claims that intravenous vitamin protocols substantially speed recovery time. He stresses that he is not using nutrients to correct vitamin deficiencies, but rather to correct redox dysregulations that occur in the body as a result of oxidative injuries to enzyme systems, and to avoid the use of drugs, to which these patients are often overly sensitive, and which further damage their weakened immune systems.

Dr. Alison Bested: A hematological pathologist, Dr. Bested has seen a large number of chronic fatigue patients in her Toronto practice. Dr. Bested believes that CFIDS has a multifactorial etiology including overuse of antibiotics and steroids; infectious agents (viral, bacterial, fungal, parasitic); physical trauma of surgery or auto accidents; genetic predisposition and major psychological traumas or stressful life events. Dr. Bested also emphasizes treating co-existing problems as well, such as chronic urinary infections, chronic sinusitis, inflammatory bowel disease and interstitial cystitis.

In addition, she has found that some patients demonstrate an overgrowth of candida and parasites in their fresh stool samples and subsequent cultures, which she then treats with the appropriate oral medications. The overgrowth of candida and parasites reflect an altered immune status.

Other pointers offered by Dr. Bested includes:

1. Attention to diet especially eliminating sugar, lowering fat and increasing fibre.

2. Progressive exercise program, regular rest periods and pacing throughout the day. She tells patients the story of the bricklayers. One group of healthy young brick layers worked full steam without any breaks. They lasted for only six hours. The second group worked forty-five minutes at a time with fifteen minute breaks, and were able to last for ten hours.

3. Rest means lying down and shutting your eyes with no music, no TV, and no distractions.

4. The single most important thing for GP's, she feels, is to ensure that the patient has a good night's sleep. After trying tryptophan, she uses 10mg to 25mg of amitriptyline at bedtime for muscle aches and pain and insomnia. If this is not enough, she adds Cheney's clonazepam-doxepin combination above with good success.

5. Psychological counselling and stress management is important.

6. Relaxation or meditation technique should be practised on a daily basis.

RESOURCES:

WOMEN AND FATIGUE, by **Dr. Holly Atkinson**. Highly recommended, this book is thorough and very practical, and covers the general topic of fatigue.

CHRONIC FATIGUE SYNDROME, by **Dr. Jesse Stoff** and **Charles Pellegrino** (Random House, 1988). This is one of the best books on how to deal with CFIDS using a holistic approach. It offers a clearly described program of gentle exercise, visualization, vitamins, herbs and homeopathy to rebuild the immune system. Dr. Stoff also suggests natural support of the liver and thyroid and adrenal glands.

RECOVERING FROM CHRONIC FATIGUE SYNDROME, A Guide To Self-Empowerment, by **Dr. William Collinge** (Putnam, 1993). This highly recommended book focuses on recovery and taking an active role in your healing. Private consultations by phone. 1-800-745-1837.

TIRED OR TOXIC, A Blueprint For Health, by **Dr. Sherry A. Rogers** (Prestige Publishers, 1990). This is a thorough and well-illustrated guide to help people adjust to the chemical onslaught in our environment without getting sick. Available from Box 3161, 3502 Brewerton Rd, Syracuse, NY, 13220.

THE CANARY AND CHRONIC FATIGUE by **Dr. Majid Ali** (Lifespan Press, 1994, 201-586-9191 or 1-800-633-6226). This 580 page book covers all aspects of CFIDS treatments including detecting and treating food and environmental allergies, reducing the toxic load, restoring bowel function and using oral and intravenous vitamin and mineral supplements.

CHRONIC FATIGUE SYNDROME AND THE YEAST CONNECTION, A Get Well Guide For People With This Often Misunderstood Illness, and Those Who Care for Them. (Professional Books, Box 3246, Jackson, TN, 38302, 1992) by **Dr. William Crook**. Dr. Crook is an expert on this topic and offers a great deal of concrete information about natural and medical treatments in a format that is clear, well-illustrated and easy to understand.

FULL OF LIFE, How to Fight Epstein Barr Virus, Candida, Herpes and Other Immuno-depressive Disorders (formerly called **PEAK IMMUNITY**), by **Dr. Luc DeSchepper**, 2901 Wilshire Blvd, #435, Santa Monica, CA, 90403. This book provides valuable information about how to build up your immunity using diet, supplements, acupuncture and homeopathy.

DETECTING YOUR HIDDEN ALLERGIES, by **Dr. William Crook**. This well illustrated and practical book tells you how to play detective and find out your food as well as environmental allergies.

COPING WITH YOUR ALLERGIES, by **Natalie Golos**, and **Frances Golbitz** (Simon and Shuster, 1986). This book helps you diagnose allergies and environmental illnesses and gives practical advice on how to deal with each type of allergy.

REVIEW OF MAINSTREAM CFIDS LITERATURE (1990-1992), by **Kendra Dayger**. This review contains review of major CFIDS research to date, contact: **CFIDS Rochester Research Project**, 1200 Edgewood Ave, Rochester NY, 14618. An excellent book to give your doctor.

> **DR. PAUL CHENEY**, 10620 Park Rd #234, Charlotte, NC, 28210. 704-542-7444.

> **THE CFIDS ASSOCIATION**, PO Box 220398, Charlotte, NC, 28222-0398. Phone (Canada): 704-362-2343 Fax: 704-365-9755. In the U.S. 1-800-442-3437 or 1-900-988-2343

THE CFIDS ASSOCIATION, is a non-profit organization that publishes a comprehensive journal, **CFIDS CHRONICLE**, distributes educational material, funds CFIDS research and does advocacy for CFIDS.

> **THE NIGHTINGALE RESEARCH FOUNDATION** (**NFR**), 383 Danforth Ave, Ottawa, ON, K2A 0E1. 613-729-9643.

NFR was begun by **Dr. Bryon Hyde** to provide information and support for people with CFS. It also actively supports research on CFS and publishes a quarterly newsletter. Membership is $35.00.

Recently, NFR published the first comprehensive textbook called, **THE CLINICAL AND SCIENTIFIC BASIS OF ME/CFS**, which is a 750 page compilation of all the latest research and information. In addition, NFR has published an excellent, illustrated pamphlet which you can provide for your doctor or workplace entitled, **A PHYSICIAN'S GUIDE TO MYALGIC ENCEPHALOMYELITIS/CHRONIC FATIGUE SYNDROME**, available for $2.00 each with a minimum order of ten.

NATIONAL ME/FM ACTION NETWORK, 3836 Carling Ave, Hwy 17B, Nepean, ON, K2H 7V2. 613-829-6667.

This is the largest group of chronic fatigue support networks in North America. There are 325 groups in Canada and 425 in the United States linked together to provide support and contact people. The national director is **Lydia Neilson**. The group puts out a monthly newsletter.

THE M.E. ASSOCIATION OF CANADA, 400-246 Queen St, Ottawa, ON, K1P 5E4. 613-563-1565.

This Association produces an excellent newsletter called **THE MESSENGER**, published monthly, and offers information and support to people suffering from Chronic Fatigue Syndrome. It can also provide guidance on financial and legal problems related to the illness.

HALTON HAMILTON WENTWORTH SUPPORT GROUP, 762 Upper James St, Box 143, Hamilton, ON, L9C 3A2. 416-383-4431.

This is an umbrella group for a number of groups in Ontario and puts out a newsletter called **KEEPING IN TOUCH**. The Oakville branch is run by **Paul Beatty** from 121 Lakeshore Blvd, Oakville, ON, L6K 1E2. 416-849-1674.

Paul Beatty has helped many CFIDS sufferers with accurate information on efamol and magnesium as well as other proven treatments. Mr. Beatty will provide a large and detailed information package to the public and doctors alike. The suggested donation is $20.

THE MYALGIC ENCEPHALOMYELITIS ASSC. OF ONTARIO, 90 Sheppard ave. East, #108, North York, ON, M2N 3A1. 416-222-8820 Fax: 416-224-2181.

Since 1990, this organization has offered support, information, public education and fund raising for research.

EFAMOL RESEARCH INSTITUTE, PO Box 818, Kentville, NS, B4N 4H8. 902-678-3001.

Dr. David Horrobin is one of the leading researchers on evening of primrose oil and his institute will provide detailed scientific information to your doctor on request.

ONTARIO FIBROSITIS ASSOCIATION, c/o The Arthritis Society, 250 Bloor St East, #410, Toronto, ON, M4W 3P2. 416-967-1414.

FIBROMYALGIA ASSOCIATION OF BC, PO Box 15455, Vancouver, BC, V6B 5B2.

The U.S. address is: **FIBROMYALGIA NETWORK**, PO Box 31750, Tuscon, AZ, 85751-1750. 520-290-5508 Fax: 520-290-5550.

NATIONAL INSTITUTES OF HEALTH BACKGROUNDER ON FIBROMYALGIA. 301-494-4484.

These groups assist people with fibromyalgia in getting proper diagnosis and treatment.

PHYSICAL MEDICINE RESEARCH FOUNDATION, 510-207 West Hastings St, Vancouver, BC, V6B 1H7. 604-684-4148 or 604-684-5345.

This non-profit organization is committed to assisting people with chronic pain from injuries and other sources.

SMITH'S PHARMACY, 3463 Yonge St, Toronto, ON, M4N 2A3. 416-488-2600 or 1-800-361-6624.

SUPPLEMENTS PLUS, 451 Church St, Toronto, ON, M4Y 2C5. 416-962-8269. Canada wide mail order: 1-800-387-4761.

Bulk evening of primrose, co-enzyme Q-10, sublingual B-12, and other vitamins can be obtained through these two stores.

How Much Stress Are You Under ?

Dr. Hans Selye, a leading Canadian expert on stress once said, "Complete freedom from stress is death." But in the 1990's women are being bombarded by stress.

As well as the stress of fulfilling the traditional role of wife, mother and homemaker, women are expected to make their mark on the world, in a career, profession, business or trade. Contrary to popular belief, women working outside the home most often do so out of economic necessity. Single mothers are often the sole support of their families. In the working world, women face problems of discrimination and sexual harassment as well as lack of daycare facilities. And after work, women are still too often saddled with the main responsibilities of running the household and looking after the children.

On top of this, society gives women conflicting messages about their roles. On the one hand, women are expected to be in the home. On the other hand, the complexity of skills required to manage a household and raise children is seen to have no value either financially or on a resume.

On the other side, the women's movement has pressured women to get out of the house and into the job market. And women themselves are conditioned to blame themselves if they can't easily combine all these roles and satisfy everybody's needs. As a result of all these factors, many women face the conflict of whether to stay at home, go to work or try to do both part-time.

Lesbian couples face continuous discrimination, possible harassment and persecution as both workers and parents, as well as the difficult decision of whether to reveal their true identity to families, friends, and co-workers.

WOMEN FACE UNIQUE STRESSES

To this picture, add the unique and important stresses that women experience as they menstruate, become pregnant, and go through menopause. Each of these biological events is associated with a major life change and its accompanying emotional, psychological and hormonal upheavals.

Some of the unique stresses that women face are:

Becoming a woman with the first period.

Coping with hormonal fluctuations and bleeding every month.

Deciding whether to mother or not.

Finding the best birth control method to control fertility.

Dealing with the many pressures of unwanted infertility.

Adapting to the enormous changes of pregnancy and birth.

Facing the challenges and responsibilities of motherhood.

Coming to terms with menopause and the years leading up to it.

Coming to terms with the unpleasant prospect of aging in this society.

All these events are powerful milestones in a woman's life which are only partially acknowledged by society.

RELATIONSHIP AND FAMILY STRESSES

Relationship and family stresses loom large in the lives of most women. Women seem more sensitive to and concerned with the quality of relationships with their mate or children. Women tend to devote a lot of emotional energy to maintaining their intimate relationships.

In spite of this, with the divorce rate soaring at around 50 percent, many women also have to cope with the highly stressful events of marriage breakdown, separation, divorce, child custody disputes, possible remarriage and step-parenting. In addition, after divorce, women face a lower standard of living as compared to their ex-partner whose standard of living usually goes up.

Nothing can be as detrimental to a healthy sex life as one or both partners being under a lot of stress. Then the lack of a satisfying sex life itself becomes a stress factor.

MONEY STRESS

However, in today's uncertain economy, money problems are often a greater source of conflict and marital problems than sex.

Journalist **Geoffrey York** says in his article, **FAMILY LIFE; NOT ENOUGH MONEY, TOO MUCH STRESS**, (**Globe and Mail**, Jan 3/92):

"For most families, two jobs are now a basic necessity of life. The earnings of most Canadian workers have stagnated or declined in the past 15 years... In almost two thirds of Canadian families today, both partners are working outside the home... Some experts have estimated that a family must work 65 to 80 hours a week to maintain the same income that a single breadwinner could obtain from 45 hours of work in the 1970's."

Two income families are under tremendous stress as they work longer hours than ever for less money. Parents become exhausted as they try to look after children and perform their household duties with less and less time to do so.

Two income families are often economically insecure and thus vulnerable to unexpected events such as, "a layoff, illness, a disabling accident, unplanned expense, or loss of baby sitter or daycare center." In addition, the uncertainties of this time in history with all the unknowns about the economy and job market take a toll on both women and men.

In fact, a national mental health survey in Canada in 1992 showed that close to **fifty** percent of those surveyed felt "really stressed" three times a week, and "really depressed" at least once a month. The majority were stressed about work and money issues.

WORK STRESSES

Other work factors may also be stressful. As **Graham Lowe** says in **WOMEN PAID/UNPAID WORK AND STRESS**.

"Jobs characterized by little opportunity for decision making, repetition, machine pacing, close supervision, and under-utilization of skills and abilities will damage a worker's health, regardless of their sex."

Women also make up 70 percent of all part-time workers in Canada. Part-time employees are often treated as second class employees with lower wages and minimal benefits.

Women make up the majority of employees in health care, social services and education where job burn out is common. "What makes these jobs universally stressful," says Lowe, "is responsibility for the welfare of patients, clients or students with limited resources to deal adequately with their needs."

LIFE STRESSES

In later life, women, with their longer life expectancy, may well outlive their partners and face the prospect of the sometimes not-so-merry life of a widow with its loneliness and economic stress.

In addition, it is often women who shoulder the burden of life crises and look after the dying, the sick and the handicapped. The grief reaction, which in its acute form lasts at least a year, is often misunderstood and pushed away by family and friends alike.

In fact, any major change, whether it is home, job, spouse, lifestyle or financial status, is a stress to both women and men.

Thus, both winning the lottery and losing the lottery are considered stressful. Researchers have studied major life events and generally agree on events almost everyone finds stressful. They find that the more stress you have, the greater your chance of developing an illness in the next 24 month period.

However, the usual stress scales do not take into account stressors that are unique to women. That is why I have revised the usual male-orientated stress test.

Take five minutes now and see where you rate on the stress scale for life events.

WOMEN CENTRED STRESS TEST

DIRECTIONS: Think over what has happened in your life in the past two years, especially the last six months. Jot down the point values for events that apply to you in the column in the center.

If you feel the point scoring is under or overestimating the impact of the event on your life, you may adjust the points upward or downward as necessary. For example, the death of a beloved parent versus an abusive parent may have different effects on you. The first may produce a prolonged mourning periods, the latter a sense of relief and freedom.

	LOW	YOU	HIGH
Death of a child	75		100
Death of a spouse, partner, close friend, or lover	75		100
More than one loved one dies within short time	75		100
Home destroyed by fire, earthquake or flooding	75		100
Serious personal injury resulting in paralysis	75		100
Suicide attempt	63		84
Death of a close family member	63		84
Rape, sexual abuse, battering	63		84
Divorce or end of long-term relationship	63		84
Discovering you have cancer or AIDS	63		84
Caretaking seriously ill spouse, lover, family member or child	63		84
Jail term	63		84
Survivor of political torture or genocide	63		84
Marital or long-term relationship separation	51		70
Chronic illness like heart, kidney or lung disease	51		70
Chronic pain	51		70
Chronic fatigue syndrome	51		70
Major disability	51		70
Personal injury or major illness	51		70
Single mom with inadequate finances or support	45		63
Memories of sexual abuse surface	45		63
Declaring bankruptcy, large financial losses	45		63
Alcoholic spouse or partner	44		62
Hysterectomy, mastectomy or other major surgery on female organs	44		62
Traumatic delivery, C-Section, miscarriage	44		62
Complicated pregnancy, difficult menopause, severely incapacitating PMS	44		62
Chronic sleep lack	44		62
Chronic yeast, bladder, pelvic or other infections	44		62
Women having two full-time jobs, both inside and outside the home	37		53
Major unresolved conflict(s) in family or personal relationship	37		53
Major financial difficulties	37		53
Fired from work or laid off	37		53
Revealing lesbian sexual orientation to family, friends or workplace	37		53
Discrimination due to age, sex, race or sexual preference	34		50
Fearful of going out at night after dark, fear of being raped and/or beaten on the way to work, at bus stops, or in the streets	37		50
Dieting, bulemia, anorexia	34		50
Abuse of prescription and non-prescription drugs or alcohol	34		50

Ongoing illness or health problems of son or daughter	34	_____	50
Son or daughter having serious relationship, school or work difficulties	34	_____	50
Son or daughter gets in trouble with the law	34	_____	50
Getting married	34	_____	50
Being on welfare or unable to find a job	34	_____	50
Data entry computer operator with closely monitored work	30	_____	45
Sexual harassment or discrimination at work	30	_____	45
Unhealthy working conditions	30	_____	45
Low paid service industry job	30	_____	45
Low paid part-time work at home	30	_____	45
Low paid clerical work	30	_____	45
Stressful health care, social work or teaching job	30	_____	45
Retirement	30	_____	45
Foreclosure of mortgage or loan	30	_____	45
Change in residence	30	_____	45
Recovering from alcoholism or drug addiction	29	_____	44
Lack of daycare facilities	29	_____	44
Settling the estate of a mate or parent	29	_____	44
Change in health of family member	29	_____	44
Marital reconciliation	29	_____	44
Mate going through major stress, trauma or loss	29	_____	44
Close friend or relative diagnosed with cancer or other terminal disease	29	_____	44
Dealing with infertility issues	29	_____	44
Pregnancy, menopause	26	_____	40
Sexual difficulties	25	_____	39
Very large mortgage	25	_____	39
Gain of a new family member	24	_____	39
Change in financial state	22	_____	38
Starting a new business	21	_____	36
Car accident, major car repairs	21	_____	36
Change to different line of work	21	_____	36
Living in heavily polluted industrial area or smoggy city	21	_____	36
Buying a new house or doing major renovations	21	_____	36
Change in amount of arguments with mate	19	_____	35
Change in responsibilities at work	15	_____	29
Tax audit, or preparing taxes	15	_____	29
Marriage of son or daughter	15	_____	29
Son or daughter leaving home	14	_____	29
Trouble with relatives	14	_____	29
Positive mammogram or highly abnormal Pap smear	14	_____	29
Outstanding personal achievement	13	_____	28
Spouse or partner begins or stops work	12	_____	26
Begin or end school	11	_____	25
Poor diet high in sugar, caffeine and junk food	11	_____	25
Returning to school after many years away	11	_____	25
Revision of personal habits	10	_____	24
Trouble with boss or co-workers	9	_____	23
Change in sleeping habits	8	_____	21
Change in work hours or conditions	8	_____	20
Change in social or recreational activities	7	_____	19
Change in church/temple activities	7	_____	19
Change in social, political or community activities	6	_____	18
Small mortgage or personal loan	6	_____	17
Change in number of family meetings	5	_____	15
Change in eating habits	5	_____	15
Vacation	4	_____	13
Large Christmas/Hanukkah or other celebration	4	_____	12
Minor violations of the law	3	_____	11

Total Score _____

HOW TO INTERPRET TEST RESULTS

If your total is less than **175**, you probably won't have any adverse reactions to your stressful experiences.

A point total of **175 to 230** indicates a possible problem, with about a one-third chance you'll feel the impact of stress through physical symptoms.

A total of **230 to 350** indicates a moderate problem, with a 50-50 chance of experiencing a stress related change in your health.

A score of over **350** promises a real threat to your well-being.

If you scored high, don't be alarmed. Although you can't erase those events or changes which have already occurred in your recent past, you can take steps to minimize their stress impact on your health. For example, you can begin a stress relief training program, in which you learn, first, how to relax profoundly as a physical skill and then, how to use that skill to reduce or eliminate your stress responses to events in your life. You can also talk over your problems with a good friend, counsellor, minister or therapist

THE IMPACT OF STRESS

Stress can take the form of a variety of physical symptoms such as headaches, heartburn, backache, fatigue, sleep problems, loss of appetite and dizziness, menstrual difficulties, and shoulder and neck pain. Prolonged stress can contribute to high blood pressure and ulcers. It may also contribute to heart disease.

On an emotional level, stress can manifest as depression, agitation, anxiety, irritability, mood swings, outbursts of anger, and uncontrollable rages.

Other consequences of stress include accident proneness, increased smoking, alcohol or drug use, increase in family fights and family violence.

PROFILES OF WOMEN UNDER STRESS

Most stress problems are multifaceted, that is, they originate from more than one source.

For example, Rosemary, 23, came into my office three weeks after her first baby was born, complaining of feeling depressed, irritable and having difficulty sleeping between the baby's waking periods. Suffering from sleep deprivation, a colicky baby, a critical mother, a partner impatient for sex, fluctuating hormone levels and unrealistic expectations about motherhood, she sometimes felt like flinging the baby out the window. But this thought made her feel even worse.

As **Dr. Witkin-Lanoil** says, "Expectations about motherhood are often no closer to reality than a cartoon is to life." In fact, this new mother needed to know that many mothers feel this way, that her stresses were coming from identifiable sources, and that with understanding, rest, and physical help, she could reduce her stress to manageable levels.

Women are not always aware of how many stressors are present in their lives. They seem to be able to endure a large amount of stress and pressure before it begins to wear them out. I often marvel at how the women in my practice continue to function under such conditions.

Christine, a 28-year-old woman, came into my office wondering why she felt tired, run down and depressed. She was pregnant with her third child, still nursing her second, working as her partner's receptionist three days a week and caring for an invalid house guest.

Joan, a 38-year-old woman, complained of chronic fatigue, low energy and persistent vaginal infections. Her 10-year-old son had been killed in a car accident less than a year before, and she went right to a full-time job. Everyone commented on how strong she was, but underneath she was barely hanging on. She was also in the midst of a difficult child custody case over her remaining daughter, marital problems with her new mate, and trying to decide whether to move to another city.

My last example is Beth, a 53-year-old woman, with disabling hot flashes, a dwindling sex life and a bad case of "nerves". Her husband had to retire early and is unhappy and listless at home. Her 17-year-old son is her last child at home and they can't seem to agree on anything. Her son's behaviour constantly upsets her husband. Her daughter just went through a traumatic marriage breakdown. She finds herself spending a lot of time baby-sitting her daughter's two-year-old or trying to help her daughter sort out her life. In addition, she has just started a small crafts business from her home.

CONCLUSION

Stress is not always harmful. It is the amount of stress and the way you handle it that can have a negative effect on your health. Dr. Selye defined stress as the "rate of wear and tear within the body". When we are confronted with stress, the body goes into a "flight or fight" response. This stimulates a whole set of chemical, physical and psychological changes in the body that prepare it to cope with a threatening situation. This response is fine if you have just met a mother bear with cubs while on a camping holiday, but not if you are caught in bumper-to-bumper traffic and late for an important appointment.

In the last case, it is impossible for you to act to avoid the situation but your body is still geared up for action. In the case of repeated or prolonged stress, the body's functions never go back to the normal non-stressed level. It is this kind of stress which produces wear and tear in the body and predisposes you to stress-related diseases. It is also this kind of stress response that, with practice, you can learn to modify or alter.

But the first step in dealing with stress is to recognize that you are under stress. Look at your life realistically and identify all possible sources of stress. Look at how you handle stress, and whether this is a problem for you or not. Look for obvious causes of stress as well as the more subtle, like unspoken expectations, guilt and self-blame.

Remember, that stress is a fact of life, but doesn't have to be a way of life.

RESOURCES:

THE FEMALE STRESS SYNDROME, How To Be Stress-Wise In The 90's, (Newmarket Press, 1991), by **Dr. Georgia Witkin-Lanoil** is a highly practical and readable book.

WOMEN PAID/UNPAID WORK AND STRESS. This excellent booklet is available free from **The Canadian Advisory Council on the Status of Women**, Box 1541, Stn B, Ottawa, ON, K1P 5R5, by asking for No. 89-S-155 in your request letter.

THE JOY OF STRESS, by **Dr. Peter Hansen**. A practical and humorous book on how to handle stress.

LIFE 101, by **Peter McWilliams and John Roger** (Preludc Press Inc. 1991), Subtitled "Everything We Wish We Had Learned About Life in School- But Didn't." An excellent and entertaining book loaded with useful and practical information. Can also be ordered by calling 1-800-LIFE-101.

How To Cut Down On Stress

Managing stress requires that you not only recognize and respect the stresses in your life but also that you take steps to reduce stress and achieve some control over it.

ANALYZE YOUR LIFE

The first step is to analyze your life and figure out all possible sources of stress, big and small, obvious and subtle, trivial and major. Also examine how you react to those stresses in your life. Some you may breeze through. Others consistently present real difficulty to you.

Figure out which stresses can be eliminated right away and then do so without delay. Next, figure out which stresses can be eliminated or at least reduced over the next weeks, months, and year. Some stresses may be entirely outside your control. You can learn either how to change your response to such stresses or how to accept what you can't change. Resolve not to place yourself in unnecessarily stressful situations by taking on too much, improper planning and not knowing when to say no.

LEARN HOW TO SAY NO

The second step is to learn how to say no without apology or guilt, whether to your lover, child, employer or best friend. Women have been trained to be obliging and accommodating and find it difficult to say no when asked to help others and/or assist in community events, even when they are already overburdened.

Forcing yourself to say no is a useful tool especially if you often find yourself taking on too much and regretting it later. An assertiveness training course may assist you in developing this skill. The more you practice saying **NO** firmly, and confidently, the easier it will get.

GET HELP WHEN YOU NEED IT

The third step is to get help when you need it. Enlist the help of your mate, friends and relatives. Don't be embarrassed to admit that you can't do everything. You can't fulfil everyone's needs all of the time. If you and your partner are both working, make sure there is a fair division of labour when you both come home from work. Too often, women do a full day's work and then run themselves ragged doing the lion's share of the house work and being the main person responsible for the kids.

Lower your standards of housekeeping. Having a house that looks like a page out of **Good Housekeeping** may not be worth the price of your sanity. Let some chores go undone. Let the kids pull their own weight. If you can afford any help, even a few hours a week, don't feel guilty about hiring someone.

ARRANGE PRIVATE TIME FOR YOURSELF

The fourth step is to arrange some private time for yourself every day for half an hour, and every week for at least half a day. Women, especially those with small children, sometimes don't have a moment to themselves and need to make a concerted effort to arrange a little time for themselves. This time is not for paying the bills or catching up on household chores. Instead take a hot bath, read a magazine, daydream, get a massage, or visit a friend.

EAT WELL

The fifth step is to make sure you are eating as well as possible. Avoid junk food and fast food. Emphasize fresh fruits and vegetables and whole grains, fish and chicken. In times of stress, your body needs an abundant supply of good nutrients.

High potency mega B-50 with vitamin-C taken three or four times a day may help alleviate stress for some women. Calcium-magnesium capsules or liquid in a one-to-one ratio are useful to take at bedtime. Where possible, purchase high quality natural supplements from a health food store.

EXERCISE REGULARLY

The sixth step is to exercise regularly but not obsessively. Choose a physical activity that you enjoy doing. Don't make the obligation to exercise into a stressful situation. In addition to being a good safety valve for letting off steam, exercise helps you resist the effects of stress and makes you feel good, look better and sleep well.

ARRANGE A MASSAGE OR BODY WORK

The seventh step is to arrange for a regular massage if you face chronic stress. Massage not only helps tense muscles relax, it also makes you aware of where you carry tension in your body and how to prevent the build-up of more tension.

For chronic muscular tension, you may want to explore one of the different forms of body work which teach you how to retrain the circuits between your brain and muscles. Examples of such methods are the **Alexander** technique, **Feldenkrais** method, **Trager** therapy and **Somatics**.

LEARN THE ART OF RELAXATION

The eighth step is to learn the fine art of relaxation. Learning how to relax deeply is a skill that anyone can learn.

There is a variety of techniques from meditation to biofeedback to self-hypnosis. Here are three different types of relaxation exercises to experiment with. As you try these methods, you may find at first that you don't relax and thoughts and worries distract you. Acknowledge these thoughts and then let them go. You can also make an audiotape of these exercises and play it back to yourself.

Here are some relaxation techniques you can use.

EASY SELF-HYPNOSIS:

1. Sit comfortably in a chair facing a wall about eight feet away. Pick a spot or an object on the wall that is about one foot above your sitting level. This is your focal point.

2. Look at your focal point, and begin counting backwards from 24, one number for each breath you exhale.

3. As you count and continue to concentrate on your focal point, imagine yourself floating, floating down, down through the chair, very comfortable.

4. As you stare at your focal point you will find that your eyelids feel heavier and begin to blink. When this happens, just let your eyes close.

5. While your eyes are closed, continue to count backward, one number for each time you exhale. As you count, imagine how it would feel to be totally relaxed and floating in a safe, comfortable space.

6. As that safe, comfortable feeling comes over you, you can stop counting and just float.

7. If any disturbing thoughts enter your space, just let them flow out again, continue to feel safe and relaxed.

8. When you're ready to end the session, either let yourself drift off to sleep, or count from one to three and exit using the following steps. At **one** let yourself get ready, at **two** take a deep breath and hold it for a few seconds, and **three** exhale and open your eyes slowly. As you open your eyes, continue to hold on to that relaxed, comfortable feeling.

IMAGERY:

Sit or lie in a comfortable position, and make sure you have a blanket or sweater in case you get cold.

Just focus on your breathing and allow your breathing to become deeper and deeper and slower and slower. When you are ready, allow your eyes to close. Then imagine yourself in your favourite place in nature.

Images can be faint or unclear or just a hint of a feeling or a thought and still be very effective. Imagine what your favourite place looks like, sounds like, smells like, and feels like...

Imagine that your inner self or spiritual guide appears to you in the form of a person. Imagine that you can ask questions and receive answers from this person. The answers may be in the form of a thought, feeling or symbol.

After you have finished the questions and answers, you may spend as long as you want in your special place in nature, drift off to sleep, or open your eyes and come back to the room.

ALTERNATING RELAXATION AND CONTRACTION:

This exercise involves tensing and then relaxing each part of your body for ten seconds each, and then tensing and relaxing each part of your body more quickly to become aware of the tension and relaxation contrast.

1. Frown as hard as you can for ten seconds; then relax those forehead muscles for ten seconds. Now repeat this more quickly, frowning and relaxing for one second each and becoming aware of the different feelings of each movement.

2. Squeeze your eyes shut for ten seconds. Repeat quickly.

3. Wrinkle your nose hard for ten seconds; then relax for ten seconds. Repeat quickly.

4. Slowly press your lips together; then relax. Repeat quickly.

5. Press your head back against the wall, floor, or bed (real or imaginary), then relax. Repeat quickly.

6. Bring your left shoulder up in a tight shrugging motion, relax. Repeat quickly.

7. Do the same with your right shoulder. Repeat quickly.

8. Press your straightened arms back against the wall, or floor, or bed. Repeat quickly.

9. Clench your fists tightly for ten seconds. Relax your hands and let the tension flow out through your fingers. Repeat quickly.

10. Contract your chest cavity for ten seconds and release. Repeat.

11. Press your back against the wall or floor. Repeat quickly.

12. Tighten your buttock muscles for ten seconds; relax. Repeat quickly.

13. Press your straightened leg against the wall, or floor or bed; relax. Repeat quickly.

14. Slowly flex your feet, stretching your toes as far back towards you as possible; relax and let tension flow out through your toes. Repeat.

15. Check for tense spots and repeat the exercise where you find any.

Soon you will begin to recognize muscle contractions caused by tension, and be able to release them at will.

RELEASING REOCCURRING THOUGHTS AND WORRIES:

While in one of the relaxed states induced by one of the above exercises or your own methods, try the following:

Imagine writing your thoughts on a big black board and then erasing them.

Imagine saying your thoughts aloud into a tape recorder and then erasing the tape.

Locate the feeling in your body and change its texture, colour or location.

It is essential to practise at least ten minutes every day whatever method seems best for you. After you have become skilled at relaxing, practice every time you are confronted with a stressful situation.

If none of these techniques works for you, figure out what does, whether it's sitting quietly, reading, gardening, doing a crossword, listening to favourite music, singing in the shower, walking, stretching, dancing, or just puttering about. Become your own relaxation expert.

DON'T LET FRUSTRATION BUILD UP

The ninth step is to avoid letting frustration build up. Devise your own methods of release. Write in your journal, arrange a family meeting, plan an evening for just you and your partner, take up your grievances with the boss, get together with an old friend and talk it out, and if all else fails, beat a mattress with a baseball bat. Stuffing your feelings down (the old grin and bear it routine) contributes to ulcers, high blood pressure and asthma as well as premenstrual syndrome, depression, infertility and eating disorders.

Respect your feelings and don't judge them. You might not want to acknowledge strong or unpleasant feelings, but they are yours and if you are friendly to them they won't overstay their welcome.

NEVER HESITATE TO GET PROFESSIONAL HELP

The tenth step is never hesitate to get professional help if nothing else is working for you and you don't know where to begin to sort out your life. Make sure the person is someone you trust and feel comfortable with.

DEVELOP A SUPPORT SYSTEM

Nourish your friendships, especially with other women. Make sure you set up a support network of friends, family, co-workers and neighbours that you can call on for help without feeling the least guilty. Arrange to share household tasks, cooking and child care with other parents. Arrange for friends to take the kids for a week or weekend and do the same for them.

I FORGIVE MYSELF FOR EVERYTHING

The eleventh step is to repeat to yourself everyday, "I forgive myself for everything" and mean it. Trying to be the perfect wife, mother and wage earner, and look like Jane Fonda too, is a sure path to insanity.

LAUGH A LOT

Cultivate a sense of humour. When all else fails laugh at yourself. Humour provides instant relief and gives you a different perspective of the situation.

THE TEN COMMANDMENTS FOR REDUCING STRESS

1. Thou shalt **NOT** be perfect, nor even try to be.
2. Thou shalt **NOT** try to be all things to all people.
3. Thou shalt leave things undone that ought to be done.
4. Thou shalt **NOT** spread thyself too thin.
5. Thou shalt learn to say "**NO**".
6. Thou shalt schedule time for thyself, and thy supportive network.
7. Thou shalt switch off, and do nothing regularly.
8. Thou shalt be boring, untidy, inelegant and unattractive at times.
9. Thou shalt NOT even feel guilty.
10. Especially, thou shalt **NOT** be thine own worst enemy, but be thy best friend.

By **Mary Gibson** of Victoria, Australia reprinted from the newsletter of
THE M.E. ASSOCIATION OF CANADA.

RESOURCES

THE FEMALE STRESS SYNDROME, How to Recognize and Live with It (revised 1991), by **Dr. Georgia Witkin-Lanoil**, is a highly practical and readable book by a woman psychologist.

PSYCH YOURSELF IN, by **Dr. Marlene Hunter** (Seawalk Press, 1984), is an excellent book on how to use self-hypnosis in an easy and practical way in everyday life.

TRAGER MENTASTICS, by **Dr. Milton Trager** (Station Hill Press, 1990). A beautifully illustrated book about effortless movements that relax and heal.

RELAXERCISE, by **D. and K. Zerach-Bersin** and **Mark Resse** (Harper and Rowe, 1990). Based on the work of **Dr. Moshe Feldenkrais**, these wonderful exercises promote improvement of posture, flexibility and release of tension.

SOMATICS, by **Thomas Hanna** (Addison-Wesley,1980). The book describes a simple five to ten minute stretch that releases tension, promotes greater flexibility, and prevents pain and stiffness.

LIGHTEN UP, by **C.W. Metcalf** and **Roma Felible** (Addison-Wesley, 1992) Subtitled, "Survival Skills for People under Pressure." This book gives you simple everyday techniques on how to stay cool, calm and creative using humour.

THE LAUGHTER PRESCRIPTION, by **Dr. Lawrence Peter and Bill Dana** (Ballantine Books, 1982). Practical pointers for how to make more use of humour in your life.

THE DANCE OF ANGER, by **Harriet Goldhor Lerner** (Harper and Collins, 1989). A book about how to express anger constructively and how to improve communications in your relationship.

THE SEVEN HABITS OF HIGHLY EFFECTIVE PEOPLE, Powerful Lessons in Personal Change, by **Stephen Covey** (Simon and Shuster, 1989). This book provides a holistic, integrated and principled approach for solving personal and work related problems.

The Sexes Aren't Equal When It Comes To Booze

All alcoholics are not the same. In fact, although they have usually been lumped together, the reasons women drink, the way they drink, the way it affects their bodies, and the way they recover is completely different than for men.

To begin with, a woman's body handles alcohol very differently from a man's. The female body breaks down alcohol more slowly. A woman's body also contains less water. Therefore there is less dilution of the alcohol. That means that on the average a woman gets drunk faster and on fewer drinks than a man.

During the premenstrual period and near the time of ovulation, the absorption of alcohol is accelerated even more. At such times a woman may get drunk on fewer drinks than usual.

For women, alcohol has a much quicker and more devastating effect on their health. Women develop cirrhosis of the liver and mental deterioration at about **half** the alcohol consumption of men.

More women die as a result of their alcoholism than men. Alcoholic women have a death rate three to seven times that of women who don't drink. On the other hand, alcoholic men have a death rate only twice than of non-drinking males.

Recent studies have linked alcohol to the development of breast cancer. The studies seem to indicate that there is a 50 to 100 percent increase risk in breast cancer for one or two drinks per day (**Comprehensive Therapy**, 14(5)/88).

Heavy drinking also affects the whole hormonal and reproductive system of women. Menstrual periods and ovulation can become more erratic. The production of various types of female hormones is also altered.

Pregnant women who drink can cause serious damage to their babies. The risk to the baby is directly proportional to the amount of alcohol consumed.

No one knows for sure how many drinks per week is safe for the baby so it is probably wisest for a woman not to drink at all once she has confirmed her pregnancy.

Anemias, especially those due to deficiencies of iron and folic acid, are much more common in women drinkers than male drinkers by a ratio of three to one. Women alcoholics are also at a much higher risk for osteoporosis.

Women drinkers are more prone to nerve inflammation caused by lack of vitamin-B-1. Women are also more likely to develop the shakes or DT's during alcohol withdrawal. Mental deterioration from alcohol is **three** times as prevalent in women as in men.

In contrast, women drinkers are less prone than men to problems such as stomach ulcers and inflammation of the pancreas.

When a woman finally goes to her doctor for help, the chances are that he won't recognize that she is an alcoholic. He is also likely to prescribe tranquilizers, thus causing a dual addiction.

Women drinkers have a different drinking style than men. Women drinkers are usually secretive, most drink at home, most drink alone and only two percent drink in public places.

Studies have shown that women drink less but are more likely to drink every day or in binges. Women seem to prefer wine or hard liquor to beer. The total amount of alcohol consumed by women is less than male drinkers.

Women alcoholics usually start off as casual drinkers in high school or drinking socially with their partners. They proceed to heavy drinking later in life than men but progress more rapidly to the advanced stages of alcoholism.

Women drinkers are more likely to suffer from depression than male drinkers. There is a higher rate of suicide attempts in women drinkers. Women also feel a more guilt, anxiety and depression about their illness then men.

Dr. Jean Kirkpatrick, author of **GOODBYE HANGOVERS, HELLO LIFE**, feels that depression is more prevalent in women because most have not learned how to express their anger or it has not been socially acceptable to do so. And underneath the depression, there is often a lot of anger.

Being the victim of incest or rape has only recently been identified as a major factor in the development of alcoholism in women. Between 30 to 70 percent of women alcoholics are thought to have been sexually abused as adults or children.

"I am repeatedly appalled at the incidence of sexual abuse among the women I see," says **Caroline Mossman**, a counsellor at an alcoholic treatment program sponsored by the Albertan government. "I always encourage women to discuss their sexuality and often, even during an initial interview, painful long submerged stories of sexual abuse come pouring out... It is important that women clients have access to a female counsellor with whom to share such intimate feelings (**Healthsharing**, fall, 1984)."

Lesbian women appear to have an increased risk of developing drinking problems. Also being without a partner is a significant factor in alcohol abuse. Women who work outside the home are two to three times more likely to develop problems with alcohol. Women who stay at home are more likely to become addicted to tranquilizers.

Women from families where one or both parents are alcoholics are four times as likely to become alcoholics as women from non-alcoholic families. Unfortunately, a woman alcoholic is also likely to marry an alcoholic. But chances are that she will end up alone. One study showed that nine out of ten women stayed with their alcoholic husbands, while only one of ten husbands stayed with their alcoholic wives.

Linda Beckman, of the **Department of Psychiatry**, at **UCLA**, has done extensive research on women and alcoholism. Comparing alcoholic men and women, she found that men were likely to drink for escapist reasons while women drink to overcome feelings of powerlessness and inadequacy (Healthsharing, fall 1984).

Women alcoholics almost always have a low sense of self-esteem and negative self-image. They often have problems with relationships with men, often have a history of sexual abuse and feel guilty, isolated and depressed about their drinking.

To truly recover from an addiction to alcohol, a woman has to change how she thinks and feels about herself. She needs to build her confidence and self-esteem.

ALCOHOLICS ANONYMOUS (AA) has helped countless numbers of women and has been indispensable to their recovery. AA has a 12 step program which is practical and widely available in both rural and urban areas. It also offers ongoing support and companionship to women.

But AA does not always address the special needs of women or the fact that they are living in a world where they are anything but equal.

AA may stress being humble and admitting your faults over and over and staying connected to your past. This may be important to the recovering male alcoholic.

However, a woman alcoholic needs to go in the opposite direction. She needs to develop a stronger sense of herself and overcome feelings of worthlessness and humility. She also needs to re-examine her past relationships. Yet intimate details of incest, abuse and sexual problems are unlikely to come out at an AA meeting where there are always men present. But these issues must be talked about in a supportive atmosphere if a woman is to completely recover.

Dr. Jean Kirkpatrick was an alcoholic herself for 20 years and she found no help for herself in AA. In 1975 she founded **WOMEN FOR SOBRIETY (WFS)** a self-help group specifically designed for female alcoholics. AA and WFS have the same goal, but they approach it from a very different perspective.

"And because WFS and AA are so different, they don't conflict, says Dr. Kirkpatrick. "In fact 80 percent of our members use both. Actually it's amazing that AA has worked so well for thousands of women, because it was never intended for women. It's based on the consciousness of men, and in the first year of its existence, women were never permitted to join."

Sonia Johnson, a feminist writer, in commenting on AA and similar groups, puts it this way, "A lot of us know women in our communities who have been in recovery groups for years... whose lives revolve around their addiction... who align themselves with the most negative aspects of their lives by defining themselves AS it. "I am an alcoholic, I am a co-addict... I am an incest survivor."

In such groups, says Johnson, to be a "good" and accepted member one must always assert one's illness, one's pain and one's inability to recover.

"We women alcoholics," says Kirkpatrick, "have more severe and complicated problems than male alcoholics; we have a higher rate of recidivism [relapse]; we are more physically deteriorated by the time we get help, because we drink longer before we are identified, and we are usually dually addicted."

The double standard, according to Kirkpatrick, is particularly damning for women since the female alcoholic is condemned not only for her dependence on alcohol but for her immorality.

"A man can get up at an AA meeting and talk about the time he got bombed out of his mind and woke up in a motel room to find himself with two beautiful women. Everyone will think it was too bad he was drunk, but there's also a feeling of, 'Hey, how about that, two gorgeous broads.' If a woman got up and told about the time she woke up in a motel room, drunk with two gorgeous men, people would be appalled."

Men arc usually confronted with their alcoholism earlier by their bosses, wives, or friends. On the other hand, says Kirkpatrick, women have to overcome their own denial syndrome and then try to prove to everyone else that they are indeed addicted to alcohol.

Dr. Jean Kirkpatrick spent almost a year in a psychiatric hospital where she received many kinds of drugs and shock therapy. Her alcoholism was never mentioned. When she left the hospital, she wasn't only an alcoholic, she was also addicted to tranquilizers.

A staggering 40 percent of admissions to mental hospitals are alcohol related and most of these are women. After discharge, many of these women subsequently end up addicted to both tranquilizers and booze.

If a woman recognizes her addiction and then goes to her family doctor there is a good chance that he will not take her addiction seriously. An estimated ten percent of doctors are addicted to alcohol or drugs themselves.

The problem, says Kirkpatrick, is that male physicians often don't like women alcoholics and this makes it difficult for them to treat them properly.

There has also been an alarming increase in younger women drinkers. A recent study of 598 treatment centers across Canada and the U.S. showed that 50 percent of women seeking treatment were between age 18 and 34 years.

Older women are not immune either. An estimated one to two percent of women over 60 has a serious drinking problem. The elderly, says **Dr. Sarah Saunders**, a sociologist at the **Addiction Research Foundation** in Toronto, often begin drinking to ease their grief over a lost spouse or to ease their feelings of isolation and they usually drink alone.

Dr. Colette Lundy, a sociologist at **Carlton University** in Ottawa specializes in women and addiction. She says that to treat women alcoholics, there must be an awareness of the social and political world in which women live, and it must be stressed that there is both an outer and an inner reality that must be considered. The outer reality consists of political, social economic and legal structures, many of which discriminate against women. In treating women alcoholics, she says, one must be prepared to look at more than just the abuse of alcohol or drugs and look at a whole series of other issues including domestic violence and sexual abuse.

Other aspects of alcoholism that are often ignored is proper nutrition and vitamin supplementation which are crucial to lasting recovery.

One of the founders of AA was said to have admitted in his later years that one of his biggest mistakes was leaving sugar, nicotine, and caffeine in AA.

Dr. Janice Phelps, author of **THE HIDDEN ADDICTION AND HOW TO GET FREE**, believes that addictions are caused by an interplay of biochemistry and genetics. She has observed that addicts of every kind have a problem with sugar metabolism. Phelps believes that the underlying depression that she sees in all addicts is an inherited, biochemical, and pervasive depression that must be treated before an addict can recover.

Dr. Phelps feels that the knowledge that addictiveness is a **highly treatable** chemical imbalance in the body allows patients to take responsibility for their own recovery. She says that much like a diabetic who has learned to control her health by diet and lifestyle, an addict who understands the physiological basis for her problem can take steps to correct it.

When a person is going off booze, Dr. Phelps uses up to 4,000mg of vitamin-C every two to three hours during the detox period. She also uses an individualized nutritional program as part of a comprehensive program for recovery including acupuncture, hypnotherapy and massage. She also uses the amino acid glutamine for alcoholic craving; the amino acid tryptophan and niacinamide for depression; and calcium magnesium preparations for anxiety.

Dr. Carolyn Dean, a Toronto physician, stresses that alcoholism is a physical addiction as well as a psychological addiction and thus it must be treated in a whole person way. She suggests that an excellent diet of grains, vegetables, fish, chicken and fruits with avoidance of refined food, sugar, coffee and tea, helps to prevent cravings for alcohol. She also recommends high doses of vitamin-C, niacinamide, and mega B-50's as well as extra zinc and a good multivitamin to assist the recovering alcoholic.

The effects of alcohol on women are much more serious than on men. And to recover from alcohol addiction, a woman must build her self-confidence and develop a new image of herself. She must also change her diet and lifestyle. She must explore past sexual trauma in a supportive atmosphere. The WFS group is one that provides women with this kind of support and the practical tools to make a change. Hopefully, this group and other women centred groups can serve as a much needed adjunct to AA.

SAFE DRINKING GUIDELINES: Problem drinkers outnumber alcoholic drinkers four to one and would benefit greatly from cutting down on drinking. A programmed developed by the **College of Family Physicians of Canada** helps men and women become low risk drinkers by following the **0-3-4-12 RULE**: On some days, no drinks, on any day, a woman should have no more than 3 drinks and a man no more than 4 drinks; with no one consuming more than 12 drinks a week. Have your physician call 1-800-387-6197 for more information.

ARE YOU DRINKING TOO MUCH ?

The Brief Michigan alcohol screening test:

1. Do you feel that you are a normal drinker? — YES - 0, NO - 2. — Score _____.
2. Do friends think that you are a normal drinker? — YES - 0, NO - 2. — Score _____.
3. Have you ever attended a meeting of AA? — YES - 5, NO 0. — Score _____.
4. Have you ever lost friends, girl/boyfriend because of drinking? — YES - 2, NO - 0. — Score _____.
5. Have you ever gotten into trouble at work due to drinking? — YES - 2, NO - 0. — Score _____.
6. Have you ever neglected your obligations, your family or your work for two or more days in a row because you were drinking? — YES - 2, NO - 0. — Score _____.
7. Have you ever had delirium tremens, heard voices, or seen things that were not there after heavy drinking? — YES - 2, NO - 0. — Score _____.
8. Have you ever gone to anyone to help stop your drinking? — YES - 5, NO - 0. — Score _____.
9. Have you ever been in a hospital because of drinking? — YES - 5, NO - 0. — Score _____.
10. Have you ever been arrested for drunk driving or driving after drinking? — YES - 2, NO - 0. — Score _____.

Total Score: _____.

NOTE: Alcoholism is indicated by a score of greater than 5. Test scores are determined by tallying values for answers which are on a progressive scale of 0, 2 and 5. * From Scientific American, Medicine, Section 13, Subsection 3(5).

WOMEN FOR SOBRIETY ACCEPTANCE PROGRAM*

1. **I have a drinking (life-threatening) problem that once had me.** We now take charge of our life and our disease. We accept the responsibility.
2. **Negative emotions destroy only myself.** Our first conscious sober act must be to remove negativity from our life.
3. **Happiness is a habit I will develop.** Happiness is created, not waited for.
4. **Problems bother me only to the degree I permit them to.** We now better understand our problems and do not need substances as coping mechanisms.
5. **I am what I think.** I am a capable, competent, caring, compassionate woman.
6. **Life can be ordinary or it can be great.** Greatness is mine by a conscious effort.
7. **Love can change the course of the world.** Caring becomes all important.
8. **The fundamental object of life is emotional and spiritual growth.** Daily I put my life into proper order, knowing which are the priorities.
9. **The past is gone forever.** No longer will I be victimized by the past. I am a new person.
10. **All love given returns two-fold.** I will learn to know that others love me.
11. **Enthusiasm is my daily exercise.** I treasure all moments of my new life.
12. **I am a competent woman and have much to give life.** This is what I am and I shall know it always.
13. **I am responsible for myself and for my actions.** I am in charge of my mind, my thoughts, and my life.

ALCOHOLICS ANONYMOUS (AA)*

1. Philosophy is to "Turn over" our will and our lives.
2. Higher Power concept.
3. Emphasis on alcoholism. "My name is Jean and I'm an alcoholic."
4. Keep the past vibrant in order to stay sober.
5. AA program based on religious philosophy from the Oxford Group.
   The Oxford Program:
   a. Admitted powerlessness.
   b. Made continuing moral inventories.
   c. Confess shortcoming to another and make amends.
   d. Pray for the power to carry this out and help others.
6. A meeting a week for a lifetime or will be drinking.
7. Emphasis on humility and dampening down ego.
8. Opposed to chemicals of all kinds, asking persons to give up medications. Not opposed to coffee.
9. Often urge members to eat candy when wanting to drink.

WOMEN FOR SOBRIETY*

1. We take charge. "Our bodies ourselves."
2. Emotional and spiritual growth are fundamental.
3. Emphasis on recovery. "My name is Jean and I'm a competent woman."
4. Put past behind us to stay sober.
5. WFS program based on metaphysical philosophy, our thoughts create our world. Philosophy of WFS is also that of reality therapy.
6. Once we learn how to cope with the problems of life, we won't need a group any longer.
7. We must overcome humility and learn to find ego strengths.
8. Opposed to coffee in excess of one or two cups a day.
9. Sugar detrimental to alcoholics. Urge use of vitamins and learning about nutrition.

*Taken from Women For Sobriety lierature

The CAGE Test: Although less specific, shorter and less threatening, this test has a comparable sensitivity.

The four basic CAGE questions are:

1. Have you ever felt that you should cut down on your drinking?

2. Have people annoyed you by criticizing your drinking?

3. Have you ever felt badly or guilty about your drinking?

4. Have you ever had a drink upon wakening to steady your nerves or to relieve a hangover?

Two Positive responses are suggestive of alcoholism, and three or four are diagnostic.

SUGGESTED READING AND RESOURCES:

1. **Dr. Janice Phelps and Dr. Alan E. Nourse**, **THE HIDDEN ADDICTION AND HOW TO GET FREE**, (Little Brown and Company, 1986).

The authors believe that addictiveness is something you are born with, a matter of genetics and biochemistry, a fundamental inborn problem with handling sugar. The good news is that this book outlines a practical program for overcoming addiction using diet and vitamin supplements. One chapter is addressed to physicians to give them additional tools in handling addictions.

2. **ALCOHOLISM - THE BIOCHEMICAL CONNECTION**, by **Joan Matthews-Larsens** (Random House 1992). This book outlines a program of nutrition and vitamin supplements that eases the transition into a alcohol free life. The author claims a 75 percent success rate with her program.

3. **Ruth Fishal, THE JOURNEY WITHIN**. Highly recommended, a practical guide to recovery using meditation, visualization and affirmations.

4. **Dr. Jean Kirkpatrick, GOODBYE HANGOVERS, HELLO LIFE**. This book addresses the special needs of women alcoholics and outlines her innovative program.

5. **WOMEN FOR SOBRIETY**, PO Box 618, Quakertown, PA, 18951. 1-800-333-1606.

This toll free number can be used in Canada and the United States. For information, books and tapes and how to start your own group, please send $4.00 to cover postage and other costs for this non-profit organization. WFS groups are already found in BC, Alberta, Ontario, Manitoba, PEI, and the Yukon. For further information on Canadian groups or starting your own, contact Elizabeth Simpson, the Canadian Co-ordinator, 44 Cavalier Place, Waterloo, ON, N2L 5K7. 519-884-2395.

6. **COPA** (Community Older Persons Alcohol Project) C\O **Dr. Sarah Saunders**, **Addiction Research Foundation**, 33 Russell St, Toronto, ON, Canada, M5S 2S1. 416-595-6106.

7. **Anne Wilson Schaeff, WHEN SOCIETY BECOMES AN ADDICT**.

8. **Lynne Namka, THE DOORMAT SYNDROME** (Health Communications, 1989).

9. **The Canadian Association for Children of Alcoholics** 102 Wychcrest, Toronto, ON. 416-533-6293.

10. **RECOVERY INC, Self-help for Nervous Symptoms and Fears**, 802 North Dearborn St, Chicago, IL, 60610. 312-337-5661 Fax: 312-337-5756.

This is a community mental health organization that offers a self-help method of will training at weekly group meetings throughout Canada, the U.S., and Great Britain. Since 1952, all groups have been run by members, not healthcare professionals.

11. **ALCOHOLICS ANONYMOUS (AA)**, is the most well known 12 step self-help program. It has branches throughout Canada and the U.S. Check the phonebook for the group near you.

Are Computers Hurting Your Health ?

Within ten years every clerical worker in the U.S. and Canada will likely be working in front of a computer. Women now hold the majority of jobs that involve full-time computer use. At least half of these women are of child-bearing age.

Contrary to government and industry reassurances, working in front of a **VDT** screen (video display terminal, the viewing screen of the computer) is not the same as using an electric hair dryer.

The health issues around computers are complex and strike at the heart of some of our basic assumptions about this electric age.

According to a **Canadian Labour Congress Report**, women whose jobs require intensive use of the computer, such as data entry and word processing operators, are two to four times as likely to experience health problems as women who use their computers part-time or in a professional or technical capacity.

There are two broad categories of possible health effects. One is the interaction of the worker with her environment called ergonomics. The other is the effects of the invisible radiation given off by a computer.

ERGONOMIC EFFECTS

This first category results from unfavourable working conditions at both the physical and psychological level. A new field of study called ergonomics has sprung up which examines the worker's interaction with her work environment.

In this case, ergonomics includes such factors as the design and adjustability of computer work stations, proximity to other computers, office lighting, quality of air, noise levels, spacing of breaks from the computer, how the computer work is paced and monitored, the total time spent at the computer and overall stress levels.

EYESTRAIN

Eyestrain refers to a number of conditions which can have one or more causes. Eyestrain includes complaints of sore, burning, dry, itchy, tender, watery, or irritated eyes. It also includes the sensation of heavy or twitching eyelids or pulling or drawing of the eye muscles. Other common eye complaints include difficulty focusing, double vision, blurred vision and seeing coloured fringes or a pink after image.

To find the cause of the eye strain you have to look at three factors in your work environment: VDT screen design, office lighting and work regimens.

VDT SCREEN DESIGN: The bottom line is that the characters on the screen should be easy to read. Character readability, brightness and contrast, and amount of flicker are all important.

Studies have shown that workers reporting flickering or blurred characters on the VDT screen are twice as likely to experience eye problems as those not reporting these conditions.

OFFICE LIGHTING: The importance of proper office lighting and absence of glare on the screen cannot be overemphasized.

Dr. Helen Feeley, an Ottawa optometrist, has seen a lot of people with VDT-related eye problems. She says glare and uncorrected vision problems are the two main causes of eyestrain.

WORK REGIMENS: Eye problems tend to increase with the amount of time spent continually at the screen. There is less eyestrain if VDT work is alternated with other types of work and VDT continuous usage is limited to four or five hours a day.

MUSCULOSKELETAL PROBLEMS

The most common complaints are neck, shoulder or back pain. To prevent strain on these areas, you have to be in a comfortable position at work and have an adjustable work station.

Another frequent complaint is wrist or arm pain. This is caused by repetitive wrist movements while typing at the keyboard. This can result in inflammation of the wrist tendons (tendonitis) or injury to the median nerve in the wrist (carpal tunnel syndrome). Carpal tunnel syndrome can cause numbness or tingling of the fingers and wrist as well as severe wrist pain and weakness of the wrist muscles. Pain in the arm, neck and shoulder all at the same time can be caused by fast paced work with prolonged muscular contraction of the hand and arm.

The **Washington State Department of Labour and Industries**, according to the VDT NEWS (Sept/Oct/91), forbids VDT workers to type for more than an hour at a stretch and for more than five hours a day, to prevent repetitive strain injuries.

Sitting for long periods of time can also cause fatigue of leg and back muscles and predispose to varicose veins, phlebitis and hemorrhoids.

The **U.S. Bureau of Labour Statistics** reported that repetitive strain injuries accounted for nearly half of the illnesses reported by U.S. businesses in 1988, and more than 80 percent of the total increase in illness from 1987 through 1988. The 1988 survey included 280,000 businesses and more than 90 million workers (**VDT NEWS** Jan/Feb/90).

The **U.S. National Institute of Occupational Safety and Health (NIOSH)** has just completed a study of repetition strain injuries involving 530 employees in three cities reported in the **VDT NEWS** (Sept/Oct/92). The study confirmed a high rate of injury for VDT workers. The study noted **one** in **five** was injured.

STRESS

NIOSH also studied a group of VDT operators in the **San Francisco Blue Cross** office and found that they had higher stress levels than any other group of workers, including air traffic controllers.

A 1984 study of telephone staff in North Carolina showed that 20 percent of the women developed angina (chest pain caused by insufficient blood supply to the heart) after working more than four hours at a VDT terminal. This is ten times the normal rate of occurrence of this type of chest pain.

A research team from the **University of Bologna** found that VDT operators who worked more than four hours a day had higher levels of the stress hormones (catecholamines).

Having no control over your working conditions is extremely stressful. Several studies show that stress related health problems were highest among VDT workers whose work is both paced and monitored by the computer. For example, telephone operators and airline reservation agents are expected to process a certain number of calls per hour and this is strictly monitored by computer. Data entry operators may have their keystrokes per hour monitored. In some work places, women are forbidden to talk during work hours and have to put up their hand if they want to go to the bathroom or get up from their desks.

A recent union management study of **Bell Canada** operators showed alarming levels of stress related to VDT monitoring. As a result, Bell Canada may soon stop individual monitoring and replace it with office wide monitoring so no individual can be singled out.

Stress symptoms include headache, heartburn, backache, generalized fatigue, depression, anxiety, loss of appetite, insomnia, dizziness and sexual problems. Stress-related illnesses include ulcers, high blood pressure, and heart disease.

Bob DeMatteo, author of **TERMINAL SHOCK** (NC Press, 1986), notes in his book that symptoms similar to those caused by stress could also be caused by the very low frequency electromagnetic field emitted by the computer.

ELECTROMAGNETIC RADIATION AND ITS EFFECTS

The second category of health effects has to do with various kinds of invisible radiation given off by the computer. These include very low levels of X-rays, visible light, ultraviolet light, infrared light and electromagnetic fields.

PCBs can be released by VDTs, especially the older models.

Ultrasound, other noises, photochemical oxidants and a large electrostatic field are also generated by a computer.

ELF WAVES

Extremely low frequency (**ELF**) electromagnetic waves are produced by high voltage power lines, neighbourhood transformers, and from the front, sides, and back of the VDT screen.

Electrical appliances also give off ELF waves which drop off rapidly within a short distance of the appliance. Most appliances are only used for a short period of time. However, hairdressers who use blow dryers for hours at a time maybe at increased risk. It may be helpful to point the back of the dryer away from the user's body.

In contrast, electric blankets and electrically heated water beds as well as ceiling cable electric heat expose people to continuous ELF electromagnetic fields whose effects could be harmful (in one study causing increased miscarriage rates). Certainly it would not be advisable to add this exposure to that of full-time work on the computer.

Most recently, concern has focused around the long-term health effects of ELF electromagnetic waves on body structure and function since these waves can penetrate to the cell level. Studies done to date show that chronic exposure to ELF waves may cause lowered immunity and adverse effects on the nervous system, blood cell growth, and fetal growth.

A comprehensive three part article on the possible effects of ELF radiation on the human body appeared in **THE NEW YORKER** magazine (June 12, 19, and 26, 1989). Written by **Paul Brodeur**, author of **CURRENTS OF DEATH: Power Lines, Computer Terminals and the Attempt to Cover Up Their Threat to Your Health** (Simon and Shuster, 1989), the series details the results of studies done so far and how this information has been kept from the public.

Dr. Samuel Becker is one of the world's leading researchers in electricity and regeneration. He has written an excellent overview of the effects of electromagnetic radiation on your health, entitled, **CROSSCURRENTS; THE PERILS OF ELECTROPOLLUTION AND THE PROMISE OF ELECTROMEDICINE** (St. Martin's Press, 1990). This book not only details the risks and benefits, it also gives concrete suggestions on how to reduce exposure in your home and office.

Researchers at **John Hopkins University's School of Public Hygiene and Health** reported recently that preliminary results of a study involving more than 50,000 linemen at the **New York Telephone Company** showed increased rates for all cancers, especially leukemia. In 1992, a Swedish study showed that men exposed to high levels of electromagnetic fields at work had three times the expected rate of leukemia.

MICROWAVE NEWS, a newsletter that specializes in the health effects of electromagnetic fields and edited by **Dr. Louis Slesin**, reported in its May/June/90 issue that top officials at the **Environmental Protection Agency** (**EPA**) in the United States deleted a staff recommendation that ELF electromagnetic fields be classified as probable human carcinogens after a **White House** briefing. According to Microwave News, "Their recommendation was based on a two year review of the health effects literature. By designating ELF fields as probable human carcinogens, the EPA staff would have put them in a general class with PCBs, DDT and formaldehyde." The final report was issued without any recommendations.

Currently more than 22 studies are underway in 12 different countries on the potential link between ELF fields and cancer.

The largest occupational health study in the world on ELF effects, was done at **McGill University** in Montreal, Canada. The study was funded by **Ontario Hydro**, **Hydro-Quebec** and **Electricite de France**, and involves 52,000 workers in 600 different jobs. The study, published in March 1994, showed a link between ELF exposure and an increased risk of leukemia. A further study on Quebec and French utility workers showed a strong association between pulsed electro-magnetic fields and lung cancer.

Another study funded by Ontario Hydro and **Health and Welfare Canada**, under the direction of **Dr. Rosemonde Mandeville**, is looking at the role of ELF in initiating and promoting cancer in rats. Other researchers are studying the effects of ELF on human cell cultures.

M. Granger Morgan, head of the **Department of Engineering and Public Policy** at Pittsburgh's **Carnegie Mellon University**, put it this way: "There is clear evidence that ELF fields can produce hormonal and other changes in living things. It is not yet clear if these changes can result in risks to public health."

In fact, until more definitive studies are completed, the final answers will not be in for many years to come. Meanwhile, I believe it is wise to avoid unnecessary or prolonged exposure to ELF fields whenever possible.

VLF WAVES

Very low frequency (**VLF**) electromagnetic waves are also emitted by the computer and have been linked to numerous health problems. As Bob DeMatteo says, the large majority of Soviet studies have shown significant biological effects produced by the VLF on the central nervous system, the autonomic nervous system, and the cardiovascular system. These include alterations in blood chemistry, increased blood pressure, behavioral changes, metabolic effects on the brain, liver and muscles as well as structural changes in the reproductive organs.

In fifteen different locations in Europe and North America, there have been groups or clusters of VDT workers who reported an increased rate of miscarriage and birth defects.

Usually, the VDT machines used by these women were not checked for ELF or VLF emissions; in fact, in most cases, the machines were not checked at all or checked with inadequate equipment.

In one of the most recently reported studies, **Dr. Marilyn Goldhaber** and her colleagues studied 1,538 women attending **The Kaiser Clinic** between 1981 and 1982. These researchers found that women who worked with VDT screens more than 20 hours a week experienced a risk of early and late miscarriage, 80 percent higher than women doing non-VDT work.

A large Canadian study under the direction of **Dr. Alison McDonald** in Montreal interviewed 56,012 women in maternity wards. It showed that part-time VDT users (between seven and 29 hours per week) had an increased miscarriage rate compared to non-users. However, full-time VDT workers did not show any increased miscarriage rate. Actual levels of exposure to electric and magnetic fields were not measured, yet this study is often cited as proof that computers are safe for pregnant women.

Dr. Alexander Martin of **Western University** in London, Ontario, was part of a six center study that demonstrated an increase in birth defects among chick embryos exposed to VLF electromagnetic fields.

In December 1983, **Dr. Marha**, a scientist and expert in occupational health and his colleague, electrical engineer **David Charron**, suggested that although no demonstrable link between VLF and pregnancy outcomes had yet been proven, the government should start discussion about the feasibility of shielding VDT users from VLF waves. Computers are now partially screened for VLF radiation. In Sweden, the government has issued strict guidelines for VLF and ELF radiation levels allowable for computers.

Dr. Maria Stochly of Canada's **Bureau of Radiation and Medical Devices**, reported that rats exposed to magnetic fields, "showed some evidence of a toxic response to the magnetic fields."

At the second International VDT Conference held in Montreal in Sept/89, **Dr. Michael Wiley** of **The University of Toronto Medical School** reported on the results of his study which was funded by Ontario Hydro and **IBM**. He found no discernable effects on mouse embryos exposed to pulsed magnetic fields.

At the same conference, **Dr. Hakow Frulen**, a Swedish VDT radiation expert, found in his research that pulsed magnetic fields could harm the developing mouse embryos, especially in the first nine days after conception.

A 1991 study, directed by **Dr. M. L. Walsh**, studied VDT workers at Ontario Hydro and reported no evidence of hazardous exposure to VLF and ELF electromagnetic fields but noted "substantial discomfort from ergonomic factors."

In the US, NIOSH has been studying the effects of VDT's on the reproductive health of women. However, the questionnaire used for the study deleted references to both fertility and stress and this may weaken the credibility of the final outcome.

One part of that outcome was published in the **New England Journal of Medicine** in 1991. A study of 882 pregnant women found no association between VDT use and miscarriage rate. A British study reported in 1992 found no difference in miscarriage rate between 150 women exposed to VDT's compared with 297 women not exposed to computers during pregnancy.

However, as Dr. Louis Slesin points out, neither study group measured the total electromagnetic exposure, and there may well be other sources of such exposure in the modern office besides the computer.

The most important recent study on the relationship between strong magnetic fields and miscarriage was reported at a conference in January, 1992. This Finnish study showed that women who use VDT's that emit strong magnetic fields may have a risk of miscarriage rate three and a half times greater than women who use VDT's with lower magnetic fields. **Dr. Maila Hietanen** of the **Institute of Occupational Health** in **Helsinki, Finland** said, "The study did not reveal a miscarriage risk when women were classified according to the number of hours they worked at a VDT. It's only when exposures were classified according to actual magnetic field exposures that you see an effect."

At present, there is no agreement as to what levels of exposure to electromagnetic radiation might be considered safe. Certainly the safety of unborn children especially in the first three months cannot be guaranteed.

SHIELDING FOR RADIATION

One way to shield both VLF and ELF waves is through the use of **MU metal** but this is technically difficult.

Several companies, including IBM and **JVC**, have manufactured computers that shield VLF radiation for sale in Sweden where the government regulations require it. Recently the Swedish government issued a new protocol for VDTs which includes shielding for ELF as well as VLF exposure. Late in 1989, IBM made these VLF shielded computers available for sale in the U.S. Another company, **Digital Equipment Corp**. of Maryland, has been selling VLF shielded VDT's for a few years.

Paul Brodeur told **VDT NEWS** (Jan/Feb/90): "IBM's move is a half measure because it does not deal with 60 Hertz [ELF] fields that are emitted by VDTs. The studies of 60 Hertz radiation done in the last ten years clearly show that these fields suppress the immune system, affect cells, and promote cancer, especially leukemia, lymphoma and brain cancer. Since it is known that 60 Hertz fields are the dominant radiation emitted by computer terminals, IBM's failure to acknowledge this hazard seems irresponsible."

Because the electromagnetic fields decline with distance, and are larger at the back and sides of the computer, the most sensible solution is to make sure that you do not sit too close to your own computer or someone else's. All VDT operators should be at least 28 inches from their own terminals and 40 inches from other terminals.

THE QUESTION OF CATARACTS

Radiation induced cataracts have been reported among VDT operators in North America.

In 1981, a 54-year-old bank secretary won a **Workman's Compensation Board** appeal for compensation for cataracts of this type in New York. So far in Canada no awards have been made for this type of eye injury.

To date studies have not revealed an increased incidence of cataracts among VDT users. But definitive studies have not yet been done.

X-RAYS

Weak X-rays are generated from the impact of high speed electrons on the screen and most of them are absorbed by the screen.

The ones that are not absorbed by the screen are usually at very low or undetectable levels.

Higher levels of X-rays can be produced when the VDT unit is faultily constructed, improperly maintained or worn out.

Chronic exposure to even low level sources of X-ray radiation can cause the body to age prematurely as well as causing changes in the immune system, genetic damage and cancer.

If you are working on an older machine, especially those built before 1970 or one where the picture tube is breaking down, make sure your company checks the amount of X-rays being emitted or if necessary, hire a reputable company to do it for you, at least once a year. Do not use the computer at all if the picture tube image collapses and fails to fill the entire picture area.

The use of lead aprons, which protect against X-ray radiation, is not recommended. Wearing a lead apron can cause postural problems. In addition, **The Canadian Center for Occupational Health and Safety (CCOHS)** advised that "if a pregnant women wears a heavy lead apron, this could be dangerous for the fetus because of the additional pressure exerted on the abdomen."

ULTRAVIOLET, INFRARED AND VISIBLE LIGHT

Overexposure to infrared light (**IR**) can result in skin and eye burns and over the long-term cause cataracts. Most tests indicate that IR from VDT's are about one-tenth of the standard allowed.

Ultraviolet (**UV**) radiation and visible light (**VL**) are also given off from the screen. But measurements of UV and VL are well below the recommended maximum exposures set for North America.

Rarely, in one in 5,000 or 10,000 people (adults or children), pulsating visible light from the screen may trigger an epileptic seizure.

At present, it seems that these three forms of radiation do not pose any major health risk.

ELECTROSTATIC CHARGES

A large static electric field can build-up in front of a screen and is loaded with positive ions. This can be detected by a build up of dust on your VDT screen, glasses, synthetic clothes, carpeting and chair coverings. These high static fields can cause charged air pollutants to be attracted to the face and eyes of the operator. Itching and rashes on the face, neck and checks as well as eye irritation can result. The depletion of negative ions in the body caused by these high static fields in turn produces biochemical changes in the body. These changes can cause symptoms of fatigue, headaches, nausea, dizziness, muscular aches and anxiety.

Dr. Alan Hedge recently led a **Cornell University** research team that surveyed more than 4,400 workers in 27 buildings about job satisfaction, stress, VDT use and work environment. Air quality tests were normal. However, the team found that there was a direct correlation between workers' complaints and the concentration of mineral fibres in dust samples taken from computer screens.(VDT NEWS Scpt/Oct/92) As a result, Dr. Hedge concluded that complaints of sick building syndrome may have more to do with VDT use than with indoor air quality.

WHAT ABOUT CHILDREN

Children's systems are more susceptible to the effect of electromagnetic radiation. In addition, children often work on cheap computers that are poorly shielded and sit too close to them. They are also exposed to ELF radiation from sitting too close to TV sets and video games.

Several studies have linked an increase in childhood leukemia to proximity of high voltage power line or community distribution lines, both of which emit ELF radiation. VDT's also emit ELF waves as well other forms of radiation. But, fortunately, there is not the continuous exposure that occurs with power lines.

Most recently, after the September 1992 release of two major studies, the Swedish government formally announced that from now on it "will act on the assumption that there is a connection between exposure to power frequency magnetic lines and cancer, in particular, childhood cancer (Microwave News, Sept/Oct/92)." The Swedish government is planning to limit exposure to magnetic fields from new power lines, but no decision has been made on how to handle exposure from existing power lines in Sweden.

"The new studies go a long way toward resolving some of the ambiguities that have prompted doubts about the cancer-ELF link," comments Dr. Slesin. "Most notably, they identify dose response relationships between cancer and ELF exposure."

One of the Swedish studies showed that children with higher exposures to magnetic fields had close to **four** times the expected rate of leukemia. A Danish study showed **five** times the risk of lymphoma in children living near high voltage power lines with high magnetic field exposures when compared to children without such exposure.

Other studies are in progress to investigate the link between childhood leukemia and exposure to ELF. One study is being conducted in several major Canadian cities which is examining the ELF exposure of 400 children newly diagnosed with leukemia, and comparing that exposure to that of 400 children of the same age who do not have leukemia. Exposure will be measured using a Canadian designed device worn by the children. The results of this study should be ready in 1995.

Until more is known about the long-term effect of ELF waves on a child's biological rhythms, I recommend that parents limit the amount of computer time and make sure that children are not sitting too close to the computer (see below) and at least ten feet from the TV. Parents should also make sure that children are not being constantly exposed to high magnetic fields near neighbourhood transformers or near the main power source for their house.

WHAT YOU CAN DO

1. Make sure **YOU** and **YOUR CHILDREN** are at least 28 inches from your computer screen and at least an arm's length or 36 to 40 inches from any other computer terminal. Monitor the total amount of time your children spend in front of a video screen (computer, TV and video games) and make sure they take frequent breaks.

For those who want to sit farther away from their VDT screens but cannot see the screen clearly at a distance, a new combination glare screen magnifier may be the answer. This **COMPU-LENZ** screen can increase character size three to four times and is available for $204.95 US from: **New Concepts**, 6710 Embassy Blvd, #204, Port Richey, FL, 43668. 813-845-7544.

2. **Make sure that you are comfortably seated at your work station** while entering data on the computer. This may mean any or all of: an adjustable chair, arm or elbow rest, a copy holder and a small foot rest. The top of the screen should ideally be at eye level.

It is crucial to have a screen that is clear and easy to read with proper lighting and absence of glare. Work stations suitable for typing are completely inappropriate for computers. Windows should be at right angles to the screen, lighting should be assessed and not direct, and all surfaces around the computer should be free of glare.

3. **Work practices are extremely important.** There should be regularly scheduled breaks for ten minutes for every hour of visually demanding work (columns, figures, rapid entry of data) and 15 minutes minimum for every two hours of less demanding work.

During these breaks it is important to leave the computer, stretch, gaze into the distance and drink lots of water. Breaks should never be skipped.

Intensive VDT work should be limited to 50 percent of the work day. Four to five hours of VDT work is what many feel is the most that should be allowed. VDT work should be interspersed with other types of work.

4. **Pregnant women should be advised of the potential risk** and be given the option to work at non-VDT work or use liquid crystal screens (as in the lap top computer) throughout their pregnancy.

In fact, the **Canadian Labour Law** was amended July 1, 1993, to give pregnant and nursing women the right to ask for other work if they believe the task endangers their children. This law will cover the estimated 700,000 women working at computer terminals in banks, airline offices, telephone companies as well as the federal government.

It is unfair to make pregnant women guinea pigs for our experiments on the effect of ELF or VLF radiation on the fetus.

5. **Electromagnetic radiation can affect the biorhythms of the body**, sleep and menstrual cycles, intestinal functioning (either diarrhea or constipation) and nervous system functioning (headaches, dizziness, lack of concentration, behaviour changes, depression, memory loss).

All these symptoms can be caused by many other things. Notice if your symptoms diminish or change after a time spent away from the computer. Get a complete check-up from your doctor to see if you have a medical cause for your symptoms.

6. **Every computer emits different levels of radiation.** So if you suspect a problem, especially with an older computer, your computer should be tested individually. However, standards have not yet been established for ELF or VLF exposure.

Dr. Rosalie Bertell suggests that you outline the electromagnetic fields for yourself using a hearing aid which emits a high pitched sound when in the field. In this way, you could figure out the best distance to sit from your computer and from any other co-worker's computer near you.

In Ontario, you can obtain a list of companies that do accurate testing from the **Ontario Ministry of Labour** c/o **Radiation Protection Branch**, 81 Resources Rd, Weston, ON, M9P 3T4. 416-235-5922, Fax: 416-235-5926.

In her article **TRUST YOUR BODY BEFORE THE EXPERTS**, Dr. Rosalie Bertell also notes that, "The most sensitive measuring device to detect radiation is a simple plant, the spiderwort. There are spiderworts which have genes for blue and pink flowers. The blue gene is dominant and the flowers are therefore blue. But, radiation knocks out the blue gene and the recessive pink gene comes through. You can actually measure the amount of radiation a spiderwort has received by determining how far it has moved in its switch to pink."

Dr. James DeMeo, in his book **THE ORGONE ACCUMULATOR HANDBOOK** (available from **Natural Energy Works**), points out that electric and magnetic fields can be inexpensively detected. Electric fields can be detected through purchasing a cheap AM transistor radio, the kind with a plastic case and no external antenna. You then set the dial above 1600 kilohertz per second. You will hear a slight hissing or background static. These are the electrical fields translating into the crackling static. The magnetic fields can be detected by using a cheap telephone amplifier turned to full volume.

There are a number of devices on the market now that accurately measure electric and magnetic fields. One such device can fit in a pocket and costs $175.00 US. It can be obtained through **TRA INSTRUMENTS** in Salt Lake City, Utah. 1-800-582-3537. **Safe Computing Company** also has excellent quality field monitors in the same price range. If you wish to acquire a list of reputable dealers of magnetic field monitors send $2.00 and a self-addressed envelope to Dr. Louis Slesin care of VDT News.

7. **If you notice a build up of static electricity** in front of the screen, buy a good screen that can ground the charges. Proper ventilation of air to remove pollutants and proper humidity of that air is equally important.

The **Tesslar Watch** is supposed to protect you from such radiation, but its use has not been proven. This device and others like "pulsors" or "cocoons" are available through **New Dimensions**, 416-488-6330 or 514-426-2590, or **Essentia Communications Inc.** 613-238-4437.

The **AC Field Cancellation System** cancels out 75 to 95 percent of electromagnetic fields and costs $500.00 US. It can be obtained through **Ed Leeper, Monitor Industries** in Boulder, CO. 303-442-3773.

There are many other types of shields and devices on the market. One of the best I have seen is the **Eye-Guard Radiation Shield**, which apparently reduces the entire electrical magnetic component passing through it to one ten thousandth of the unfiltered level. This shield costs $179.00 U.S. For more information contact **Natural Energy Works** PO Box 864, El Cerrito, CA. 94530. 510-526-5978.

The **NO-RAD** radiation screen blocks 99.9 percent of electric radiation and 50 to 90 percent of higher frequency magnetic radiation. It also eliminates glare and static electricity. The **NO-RAD ELF PROTECH** shield reduces ELF magnetic field emitted by VDTs by 40 to 70 percent. Information is available from **NoRad Corporation**, 1549 11th St, Santa Monica, CA 90401. 313-345-0800. In western Canada call **Ideal Computer Environments**, 306-584-2262. In eastern Canada call **The Computer Shield Group**, 416-971-4242.

8. **If you are buying a new computer**, consider buying the new liquid crystal display terminals. They now have better resolution than the earlier models.

A new LCD line manufactured by **The Safe Computing Company**, based in the Boston area, has gone to the trouble of shielding against the small amounts of ELF radiation produced by the power transformer and cable. IBM has just brought out a new generation of VDT's that are shielded for VLF radiation.

9. **Educate yourself on the health effects of computers.** Get a copy of **TERMINAL SHOCK**, by Bob DeMatteo (NC Press, 1986), still the best overview on the subject.

The Canadian Center for Occupational Health and Safety has been responsible for increased public awareness of computer hazards and operates a prompt and courteous information service. Their booklets including **HEALTH HAZARDS OF RADIATION FROM VIDEO DISPLAY TERMINALS** and **ERGONOMICS FOR WORKPLACES WITH VDT'S** are available free from CCOHS, 250 Main St East, Hamilton, ON, L8N 1H6. Toll free 1-800-263-8276 or Fax: 416-572-2206.

An excellent synopsis on the topic is **THE HANDBOOK ON VDT HAZARDS**, available for $8.00 U.S. prepaid from **Natural Energy Works**.

Dr. Feeley has written a quick and easy to use trouble shooting manual for health and eye problems entitled, **THE VDT OPERATOR'S PROBLEM SOLVER**. This is available for $12.95 from **The Planetary Association for Clean Energy**, 100 Bronson Ave, #10001, Ottawa, ON, K1R 6G8. 613-238-4437.

Every office should subscribe to **VDT NEWS: The VDT Health and Safety Report**. (PO Box 1799 Grand Central Stn, New York, NY, 10163. 212-517-2800) Edited by Dr. Louis Slesin, a pioneer in the field, this newsletter provides up-to-date info on all aspects of the health effects of VDT's, including the latest research.

VDT NEWS also publishes the **ANNUAL VDT PRODUCT DIRECTORY** (available for $17.00 Cdn from the same address). This is an indispensable guide to computer health and safety products and services. The listing of almost 200 companies includes low ELF monitors, vision aids, radiation meters and ergonomic accessories.

Dr. Slesin is also the editor of the meticulously researched **MICROWAVE NEWS** available from the same address. MICROWAVE NEWS documents the latest on the health effects of electromagnetic fields. MICROWAVE NEWS has just published the **EMF RESOURCE DIRECTORY.** This 80 page directory contains more than 400 listings of research organizations, citizen groups, lawyers, consultants, labour unions, electric utilities, and government agencies.

10. **Talk to your union** about the recommended standards for work on VDTs.

For women interested in an illustrated practical guide to taking more control over their work environment, the book **TAKING CONTROL OF YOUR FUTURE**, by **Cohen and White**, is highly recommended (available for $15.00 from **Women And Work Research and Education Society**, 4340 Carson St, Burnaby, BC, V5J 2X9. 604-430-0458. The excellent book, **PLAYING WITH OUR HEALTH: HAZARDS IN THE AUTOMATED OFFICE** is also available from the same address for $10.00. The same group has just published a booklet on repetitive strain injuries. It contains information on how to identify this type of injury, what to do next, your legal rights, and issues around workers' compensation claims.

11. **An annual eye exam** should be required for all full-time VDT workers.

12. **Workers who develop wrist pain**, back pain, neck or shoulder pain should be checked by their doctors right away and the design, work habits, lighting and glare of their workplace improved.

In Jan/93 the Ontario government brought in a rule requiring five minutes rest for every hour at the keyboard. According to Toronto **Globe and Mail** medical reporter **Paul Taylor**, repetitive strain injury (**RPI**) is difficult to diagnose and treat properly. The diagnosis involves a specialized form of electromyography to test each individual muscle. Taylor says the problem usually starts in the neck and upper back muscles. Treatments involves a combination of modalities including muscle re-education, massage, and acupuncture needles applied to trigger points. He found no clinic that provided a totally integrated approach. However, effective clinics are found in Calgary, Vancouver, Toronto and St. Paul's Minnesota. In addition, the **Ford Motor Company** in Philadelphia has set up a specialized clinic for RPI's.

If you develop a repetitive strain injury, I suggest a video which can help you retrain the way you use your muscles. The video is called, **SELF HEALING BODY MOVEMENT**, and is available from **Lora Byxbe, Willow Productions**, 677 West 23rd Ave, Eugene, OR 97401 for $30.00 US.

RELAXERCISE, by **D. and K. Zerach-Bersin** and **Mark Resse**, is an excellent book with easy to do exercises to relieve neck, shoulder, arm and back pain.

Another recommended book is **THE HANDBOOK OF SELF-HEALING**, by **Meir Schneider** and **Maureen Larkin** (Penguin, 1994).

13. **To protect your eyesight**, some suggest that yellowish green letters on a darker green background are easier on the eye. Some find the contrast of white on black helpful for long periods of work. It is also important to do other work 30 minutes before quitting if possible to allow the eyes to adjust before driving home.

Most of all, every 15 minutes it is important to focus into the distance. Look at your hand and then at a distant object, back and forth 15 times. During breaks, you can rest your eyes by rubbing your palms together vigorously and cupping them over your eyes, while visualizing a peaceful scene in nature or just pitch blackness. This should be done for two or three minutes and is very restful for the eyes. Blink often during breaks. Practise moving your eyes through the whole range of movement five to ten times a day.

14. **M. Granger Morgan**, has written a booklet called **ELECTRIC AND MAGNETIC FIELDS FROM 60 HERTZ ELECTRIC POWER (ELF FIELDS) WHAT DO WE KNOW ABOUT POSSIBLE HEALTH RISKS?** This booklet is available free from both Canadian and American electrical companies. This booklet advises "prudent avoidance" of ELF fields which means limiting all avoidable exposure. This can be done with only small investments of time and money.

Examples are turning the heater for your water bed off at night. Use your electric blanket to warm up your bed but turn it off for the night. Move a clock radio from the head of the bed to a dresser across the room.

CONCLUSION

For women in the workplace, computers have been a mixed blessing. Full-time VDT workers do face increased health risks. In my opinion, the safety of VDT usage for pregnant women has not been adequately proven and I would not recommend taking that chance.

Lastly, I am seriously concerned about the overexposure of our children to VDT screens, especially when the answers to some very troubling questions about the effects of electromagnetic radiation may not be in for many more years.

Dr. Rosalie Bertell, author of **NO IMMEDIATE DANGER**, put it this way:

"Unfortunately, technologically-induced illnesses are denied in the late 20th century with the same vehement resistance which met theories of invisible germs and viruses in earlier decades... There are two tragedies here: the first is that a TV screen is not really necessary to enjoy the computer capabilities of word processing, the second is that health effects are almost always discovered by workers and the general public and not by the experts."

Grief Is Hard Work

Anthropologist **Margaret Mead** once said, "When a person is born we celebrate, when they marry, we jubilate, but when they die, we act as if nothing has happened."

Grief is a normal and natural reaction to the death of a loved one or to a major loss in your life. Grief is also experienced with divorce, miscarriage, relocation, the loss of a major dream, the loss of a limb, the loss of your health, and the loss of a beloved pet.

In addition, say grief experts **James** and **Cherry**, "Dealing with addictions to alcohol, drugs, food, and so on, can lead to monumental grief."

When a loved one dies, most people who experience grief are unprepared for the floodgate of emotions that sweeps over them and alters their life irrevocably. They feel devastated, crushed, flattened, disorientated, and confused. They have great difficulty even getting through the ordinary tasks of daily living.

Bella Azbug, a prominent feminist politician, had a very close and loving relationship with her husband until his death. In an excerpt from her book quoted in **Ms. Magazine** (July/Aug/90), she describes how this loss affected her:

"My reputation is that of an extremely independent woman and I am. But I was dependent, clearly, on Martin. He would embrace me in his furry chest and warm heart and protect me from the meanness one experiences in the kind of life I lead... These past three and a half years have been the most difficult period in my life. I still have this tremendous pain. And the guilt that I wasn't there when he died... There's a great loneliness... nothing substitutes."

People who have not experienced a major loss can simply not imagine how overwhelming this loss can feel to you.

Friends and relatives sincerely want to help, but they often don't know what to say. They may try to comfort you with empty platitudes and dumb cliches that only make you feel worse.

Loving, patient, and non-judgmental support is the greatest gift you can give people experiencing a major loss in their lives.

After a death or major loss, you may begin to question your religious beliefs. You may feel angry at the higher power for allowing such a thing to happen. Even if you are able to find comfort in your religion, you will not be protected from the intense and, at times, overwhelming emotions of grief.

Some clergy have no idea how to assist a grieving person. Others are very experienced. Some churches and synagogues have excellent support groups for grieving persons.

On a physical level, the most common symptom you are likely to experience after a major loss is profound fatigue, especially in the first year. Forgetfulness and sleep problems are also very common after a death. Other symptoms include headaches, joint pains, back pain and recurrent infections. You may develop a mysterious ailment for which your doctor can find no answers.

An unrelated TV program or a person in the street may trigger a flood of tears. Between three and six months after the loss, when all your friends think you should be over this now, the full and devastating emotional impact of the loss hits you in full force like a tidal wave. It feels like you have been numb before that time.

Commonly a whole year goes by in which you walk about like a zombie, barely able to keep up the pretence of functioning. One day you wake up and know you will recover. But then it will still take another one or two years before you have fully accepted the loss and made it a part of your life.

One of the most important things to remember is that you don't get over your loss, you learn to accept it, work through it, and make peace with it.

A SOCIETY THAT DENIES THE EXPERIENCE OF LOSS

It's not surprising that most of us don't know how to comfort others or handle our own loss. As James and Cherry put it in their excellent book, **THE GRIEF RECOVERY HANDBOOK**:

"Simple first aid gets more attention in our world than death and loss... We're taught how to acquire things, not how to lose them... the process of losing something feels wrong, unnatural or broken."

Early on, we learn ways of coping with loss that are detrimental to our well-being. Common ones outlined in the Grief Recovery Handbook include:

1. **Bury your feelings.**
2. **Replace the loss.**
3. **Grieve alone.**
4. **Just give it time.**
5. **Regret the past (different, better or more).**
6. **Don't trust.**

Another major pitfall is feeling pressured to pretend we have recovered. James and Cherry call this the **Academy Award Recovery**. They go on to say:

"A false image of recovery is the most common obstacle all grievers must overcome if they expect to move beyond their loss... It could be called, the I'm fine phase, the put on your happy face phase or the be fine for my family and friends phase."

In the end it is much kinder to ourselves to deal with our grief instead of avoiding it.

DEALING WITH YOUR GRIEF

Grief expert **Bob Deits** in his book, **LIFE AFTER LOSS**, outlines four key points to remember when you are grieving:

1. **The only way out of grief is through it, because there is no way around it.**
2. **There is only one very worst kind of grief and that is yours.**
3. **Grief is hard work.**
4. **Effective grief work is not done alone.**

Deits maintains that grief is an honourable emotion, not something to hide and be embarrassed about. He says that grief is both a testament and tribute to the loved one who has died or left.

"Your grief," he says, "is a symbol of your caring and a tribute to the quality of that which is lost. I encourage you to wear your grief as if it is a badge of honour."

Stephen Levine, in his wonderful book, **HEALING INTO LIFE AND DEATH**, says that we all have grief. And, "grief is that insistent mercilessness with ourselves and a world which we hardly let within. But if we allow our hearts to open to our pain," says Levine, "they will expand into more compassion and openness than we ever thought possible."

Grief pushes you to greater depths, understanding and compassion. It gives you a higher level of "bullshit" detector.

You are more experienced.

You no longer put up with superficial or inconsiderate friends.

You learn to say no to things that are not nourishing for you.

You get a clear view about what's really important in life.

You value your own life more and that of your loved ones who are still alive.

You develop a new, deeper and more realistic spiritual understanding of life.

And of course, although you wouldn't choose to go through the loss if you could help it, afterwards you are able to understand and assist others who grieve.

GUIDELINES FOR GRIEVING

1. Give yourself as much time as you need to work through your grief.

A public poll once asked how long should it take to mourn the death of a loved one. Most thought 48 hours to two weeks. According to grief experts it takes at least two to three years.

For example, if your husband of 50 years dies, this could reasonably be expected to completely shatter your life. Widows usually have to deal with financial stress as well as the incredible loss of a lifelong companion, for which there will never be a replacement.

Deits in his book quotes a long-term study that shows that the death rate among widows and widowers is about **two to seventeen times higher** in the first year after the death of a spouse.

The death of a child is the worst experience that any parent can face. Parents commonly become divorced or separated if they do not take the time to work through the grief.

2. Cast your pride to the wind and ask for help from your friends and family.

Make yourself a supportable person by expressing clearly what this loss means to you and telling friends specifically how they can help you.

3. You have a right to remember the one who has died in any way you see fit.

This may include anything from holding a funeral for a miscarried, stillborn or premature baby, to creating a special place for mementoes of the loved one, to wearing clothes of the loved one who has died, to leaving the person's room untouched for a year or more until you are ready to deal with it, to designing a memorial ceremony a year after the fact. Others are not good judges of what is right and appropriate for you. Others may feel that some of these things are morbid, but in fact, these remembrances can help you work through your grief.

James and Cherry give a very practical "**pile plan**" of disposing of the possessions of a dead person. You simply put everything into three piles:

Pile A contains the things that you are certain you want to keep.

Pile B contains the things that you are certain you want to dispose of.

Pile C contains all those things you are not sure about yet.

4. Let yourself cry. Have compassion for yourself. Let your grief out. Be gentle with yourself if you can't cry.

If you want to let out the tears, you can promote crying in a safe atmosphere. Bob Deits recommends and describes this "programmed cry" exercise in his book.

It is very important to be able to talk freely about the person who has died or the major loss that you have experienced. It is important to be able to confide your feelings in someone who will not judge you negatively or expect you to be over everything in a month. You will also experience other emotions beside sadness, especially anger and guilt.

5. Make a conscious effort to work through the grief. Do the written exercises in **LIFE AFTER LOSS** or **THE GRIEF RECOVERY HANDBOOK**. It is best to share these exercises with a close friend or partner.

By all means attend a grief group as soon as possible if one is close to you. Your funeral home may be able to direct you to the nearest group. Even while grieving, you can start your own grief group. Even though it is hard to listen to other people's grief, their support is invaluable, as well as the knowledge that you are not going crazy and that others are having the same feelings as you.

Never hesitate to seek out the help of a professional skilled in grief counselling, if you are not getting the help you need from other sources or if you just would like help in working through grief.

Dr. Edward Pakes, psychiatrist and Director of the **Bereavement Clinic**, at **Mount Sinai Hospital**, in Toronto, believes that guidance and support of families through the grieving process is good preventative medicine. It can prevent more serious psychological problems from developing in the future.

6. **In the case of the death of a baby, child or adult, it is advisable to see, touch, hold and say good bye to the body if possible, if you want to.**

This allows the family to start to grasp the reality of the death and will help prevent emotional trauma at a later date.

7. **During the grieving process it is very important to treat your body well. Eliminate sugar, junk food, fried food, and caffeine from your diet. Avoid alcohol and tranquilizers as well.**

At the wake, eliminate sugary desserts. All the above foods and drinks can contribute to mood swings and increased depression.

It is essential to attend to your diet and maintain regular exercise throughout the whole two to three year grieving period.

Researchers have found that your chance of illness or accidents is increased after grief. The risk of diseases such as high blood pressure, skin problems, arthritis, diabetes, heart disease and thyroid disease is increased.

You also risk alcohol and drug abuse, depression, migraine headaches, low back pain and blood chemistry abnormalities.

8. **Pay attention to rest and getting enough sleep.**

If you are having a lot of trouble sleeping, you may require a sleeping pill for a couple of months.

I have found that the amino acid tryptophan in dosages of two to four grams at bedtime to be useful for insomnia, although it has not been recognized for this usage. It is only available through prescription from your doctor. It has the advantage of being safe, naturally based and causes no drowsiness. It has few side effects at that dosage.

9. **Use humour to heal yourself.**

Read funny books and watch funny movies. It provides one of the best respites from grief. Humour also provides a change of perspective and boosts your immune system.

10. **Know what to expect.**

At anniversaries, birthdays, Christmas or special feast days, you are likely to have a flare-up of grief. You can plan ahead for this by getting extra rest, massage, time off, etc.

SIX TO NINE MONTHS: You may experience a worsening of grief related symptoms. **Dr. Glen Davidson**, a leading grief expert, found that 25 percent of people went through a diminishing of their natural immune system at that time.

Deits suggests that you schedule a doctor's or counsellor's appointment at that time.

THE FIRST YEAR ANNIVERSARY: It is important to take the day off to remember the loved one or do something special for yourself.

THE EIGHTEENTH MONTH: Suddenly, it seems like you are back at the beginning of your grief. It is important to remember when you have a setback like this that it just shows you how far you have come, and that it won't last long.

PREPARING FOR LOSS

1. **Allow yourself to talk about what would happen if someone close to you died.** Talk it over with your loved ones. As Deits says, all marriages end either in death or divorce.

Women are statistically very likely to outlive a male partner. All women, especially older women, should learn how to manage household, maintenance, and financial matters well before such a loss occurs.

2. **Make out your will and have your partner do so as well.** Designate a guardian for your children if you both should die. Make out a living will, if that is your desire, and make it known how you would like your remains disposed of.

These are not morbid activities, just common sense preparation which eases the burden of those left behind. It is surprising how many families and older couples have not dealt with these basic issues.

3. **Good physical health is good preparation for the inevitable losses that we must all face.**

Keeping fit, eating well and getting proper rest and relaxation are the basic elements of your health.

4. **Learn how to finish your grieving for the losses you have already experienced.**

Go through the exercises in **LIFE AFTER LOSS**, or **THE GRIEF RECOVERY HANDBOOK**, or **HEALING INTO LIFE AND DEATH**.

Practise working with your grief on smaller issues. As Stephen Levine says, you don't go to the gym and start lifting a 500 pound weight. First you get good lifting a five pound weight, then build up slowly.

5. **If someone near you has a major loss, let them talk freely and do not judge.**

Acknowledge how devastating the loss is to them. Do not try to console. Such remarks are meaningless and the truth is that the loved one can never be replaced. Also immediately after a death, inconspicuous practical help with meals and housework are sometimes very much needed.

Remember grief is hard work and takes a long time. But the rewards of truly opening to our pain and then letting go of it are many. They include a renewed enthusiasm and keener appreciation for life and a heart with more room for compassion and kindness.

RESOURCES

If you are only going to get one book it should be one of the following:

1. **LIFE AFTER LOSS**, A Personal Guide Dealing With Death, Divorce, Job Change and Relocation, by **Bob Deits** (Fisher Books, 1988).

2. **THE GRIEF RECOVERY HANDBOOK**, A Step By Step Program for Moving Beyond Loss, by **John W. James** and **Frank Cherry** (Harper and Row, 1988).

OTHER BOOKS ON GRIEF AND LOSS

HEALING INTO LIFE AND DEATH, by **Stephen Levine** (Doubleday, 1987). Highly recommended, this book offers "original techniques of working with pain and grief, and discusses the development of a merciful awareness as a means of healing as well as how to encourage others to do the same."

LIVING THOUGH MOURNING, Finding Comfort and Hope When a Loved One Has Died, by **Harriet Schiff** (Penguin 1986). Schiff discusses in detail the gradual process of grieving, offers specific comfort for different groups of mourners, stresses the need of survivors to share their emotions, and provides information on starting self-help groups.

UNDERSTANDING MOURNING, by **Glen W. Davidson**, (Ausbery Publishing 1984).

COMFORTING THOSE WHO GRIEVE, by **Doug Manning**.

THE SPIRAL OF GRIEF, by **Diana McKendree** is an excellent 24 page booklet published by the **National Selected Morticians**, and usually available without charge from your funeral home.

WHEN A CHILD OR BABY DIES

ENDED BEGINNINGS, Healing Child-bearing Losses, by **Claudia Panuthos** and **Catherine Romeo** (Begin and Harvey, 1984).

WHEN A BABY DIES, A Handbook for Healing and Helping, by **Limbo and Wheeler** (1986).

THE BEREAVED PARENT, by **Harriet Schiff** (Penguin 1977). Well written, practical and easy to read, a must for any parent whose child has died.

HELPING CHILDREN COPE WITH DEATH

EXPLAINING DEATH TO CHILDREN, by **Earl Grollman** (McClelland and Stewart, 1988).

WHEN A PARENT IS VERY SICK, by **Eda LeShan** (Little Brown, 1987).

LEARNING TO SAY GOODBYE, a book for children when a parent dies, by **Eda LeShan** (MacMillan, 1976).

HELPING CHILDREN COPE WITH SEPARATION AND LOSS, by **Claudia Jewelt** (1982).

FOR WIDOWS

BEGINNINGS, A BOOK FOR WIDOWS, by **Betty Jane Wylie**, (McClelland and Stewart, 1977).

BEYOND WIDOWHOOD, by **Robert DiGiulio**, (The Free Press, 1989).

DEALING WITH SUICIDE

AFTER SUICIDE, by **John Hewett** (Westminster Press, 1980).

SURVIVORS OF SUICIDE, by **Rita Robinson**.

WHERE TO GET THESE BOOKS:

Parentbooks has over 160 books on grief and a list of these titles is available on request. All of the books above can be obtained in person or by mail order from:

PARENTBOOKS, 201 Harbord St, Toronto, ON, M5S 1H6. 416-537-8334.

HELPFUL ORGANIZATIONS

COMPASSIONATE FRIENDS, is an international self-help group for bereaved parents with 42 groups throughout Canada and about 600 in the U.S. which also offers a supportive newsletter.

COMPASSIONATE FRIENDS, 685 William Ave, Winnipeg, MB, R3E 0Z2. 204-787-2460.

BEREAVED FAMILIES OF ONTARIO, is a self-help organization that offers education, counselling, support groups, speakers' bureau and a library for parents who have lost a child.

BEREAVED FAMILIES OF ONTARIO, 214 Merton St, #204, Toronto, ON, M4S 1A1. 416-440-0290.

L.I.F.T. (Living is For Today) is a Toronto network of self-help groups for those struggling with the grief that follows death.

BEREAVEMENT SERVICES AND COMMUNITY EDUCATION, 1403 Bayview Ave, Toronto, ON, M4G 3A8. 416-485-6415. Toll free number 1-800-268-2787.

DYING WITH DIGNITY. This society is committed to the right to self-determination for Canadians concerning their own death. It offers educational services, documents including living wills, counselling on options for the terminally ill and library services.

DYING WITH DIGNITY, 600 Eglinton Ave East, #401, Toronto, ON, M4P 1P3. 416-486-3998.

Section Two:
Birth Control And Infections

No Magic Pill 46

Cervical Cap Makes A Comeback 57

Permanent Birth Control: The Facts 59

Know Your Body's Cycles -
To Get Pregnant Or To Avoid Pregnancy 64

The Yeast Among Us 70

Bladder Blues 78

Chlamydia -
The Greatest Threat To Reproductive Health 87

No Magic Pill

SPECIAL NOTE: Much of the information contained in this article is taken almost verbatim from the **Canadian Federal Government's 1985 Report on Oral Contraceptives**. However, most of the research on which the report was based was done on birth control pills that contained a much higher dose of both estrogen and progesterone than are contained in the pills commonly used today.

The previous pills contained up to 100 or more micrograms of estrogen, which has now been reduced to between 30 and 40 micrograms. The progesterone has been reduced less than the estrogen; from one to one and a half milligrams to a half milligram; or varied between a half to one and a quarter milligram, to mimic the natural cycle.

For years women have dreamt of the perfect method of birth control. That would be a method that is 100 percent effective, easy and convenient to use, 100 percent safe with no side effects and completely reversible.

Amazonian jungle shamans and North American Indian medicine people may have had knowledge of plant combinations which accomplished this feat, but modern medicine does not.

As **Dr. Charles Dodds**, the British physician and biochemist who was the first to synthesize estrogen once said, "We should always be humbled by what we do not know about the female reproductive cycle... Until we know the mechanism that selects one Graafian follicle (that is one egg) out of perhaps thousands to mature each month, we still have to proceed with caution on any long-term hormonal treatment of the human female."

The female body and the intricate and complex interactions of hormones and chemicals that are responsible for reproduction are still imperfectly understood.

In 1960, when the pill first came on the market, it seemed like the answer to many women's prayers. However, it soon became evident that the pill had not been properly tested and evaluated before its release and that serious and even life threatening side effects were possible.

Over thirty years later, even though the estrogen content of the pill has been reduced by at least 50 percent, we can still say that the birth control pill is a very powerful medication to be used only after carefully weighing their risks and benefits for each woman. We know that the pill affects every system in the body and that some of the risks from taking the pill seem to persist indefinitely, even after the pill is stopped. The risks for women over 35 who smoke are substantial. The long-term effects on the risk of getting or enhancing a tendency towards cancer are simply unknown. It is still too early to be certain of the latent carcinogenic potential of the birth control pill.

Every woman on the pill should be fully aware of the risks she is taking and potential side effects. She should also be aware that there are other safer and highly reliable methods of birth control.

BLOOD CLOTS, HEART ATTACKS AND STROKES

To place this risk in perspective, the risk for blood clots for a woman not using the pill is about one in 30,000. Users of high dose birth control pills (any pill containing more than fifty micrograms of estrogen) face a risk of about one in a 1,000. Users of low dose birth control pills have a risk of clotting of about 21 in 30,000.

Blood clots are the most common serious side effect of the birth control pills. The risk of blood clotting is related to the estrogen in the pill, and is dose related. This means that the lower the estrogen content of the pill, the lower the risk of blood clotting.

The clotting complications of the birth control pill may also be related to the amount of progesterone contained in the pill. A British study found that the incidence of blood clotting complications was more related to the variation in dosage in progesterone than to the estrogen dosage.

Clots can form in the brain, eyes, lungs, heart, arms or legs. If the clot is in a blood vessel leading to an arm or leg, it can result in damage or even loss of a limb. The risk of blood clotting in a limb is three times higher for pill users than for non-users; about half this risk for the lower dose pills. If you have varicose veins, this does not increase your risk of this complication. However, smoking will definitely increase your risk of blood clotting.

If a clot forms in the legs or pelvis and breaks off and travels to the lungs, this results in a pulmonary embolus, which can be a life-threatening emergency. The risk of this happening is four times higher in pill users than in non-users (again less for lower dose pills).

For women on the higher dose pills, this risk of blood clots to the lungs was significant enough that women planning to have major surgery were advised to discontinue the pill four to six weeks prior to surgery and not restart until two weeks after surgery. It is unclear whether or not similar advice should be given to women on the lower dose pill.

If the clot is in a blood vessel to the heart, then a heart attack may result. Users of the high dose pills have double the chance of heart attacks as non-users. The risk of heart attack increases with age and heavy smoking. Pill users who smoke are about ten times more likely to have a heart attack than non-users who do not smoke. Women over 35 who smoke should choose another form of birth control.

Heart attacks and strokes are normally very rare for women under 50. The 1985 government report on the birth control pill cites research that says that women who have ever used the higher dose pill continue to experience a higher risk of heart disease than women who have never used the birth control pill. This means even if you stopped using the high dose pill, you may be four times as likely to die from heart disease as someone who has never used the pill. This finding has recently been disputed, with new analyses of the old studies.

According to **Dr. Stanley Brown**, **Associate Professor of Gynecology at Western University** in London, Ontario, (**Treating the Female Patient**, Sept/92) previous research was re-analyzed and showed that the death rate from heart disease was significantly increased only in women over 35 who smoked, or who had other independent risk factors, such as high cholesterol or diabetes.

If a blood clot to the brain develops, a stroke may develop. The risks of strokes in women who used the high dose pill is significantly higher than for non-pill-users and this risk is further increased by smoking. Just as for heart attacks, the risk of strokes was reported as being higher for women who have ever used the higher dose pill compared to those that haven't.

Studies have shown that women taking the high dose pill are twice as likely as non-users to have a rupture of a blood vessel in the brain.

THE PILL AND HIGH BLOOD PRESSURE

Blood pressure is very slightly increased in all women on the pill. A small percentage of women develop a marked increase in blood pressure, which usually goes back to normal within three months after the pill is discontinued.

According to **Dr. Wilfred Steinberg**, **Director of the Women's Health Center at St. Michael's Hospital** in Toronto (**Diagnosis**, July/87), studies published in 1982 linked progesterone to the development of high blood pressure and changes in blood lipids. "In some cases," says Dr.Steinberg, "these changes were dose related; in others, changes in lipid profile seemed related to a specific progesterone."

EFFECTS OF PILLS ON BLOOD LIPIDS (FATS)

The pill increases the amount of fatty substances in the blood.

Estrogen causes a mild rise in cholesterol and a moderate rise in triglycerides in the blood; while progesterone causes a rise in cholesterol and no change or a fall in triglyceride levels. What this adds up to in terms of contributing to the risk of hardening of the arteries is not known, but it is thought that the estrogen and progesterone risk cancel each other out.

Experts believe, but have no proof, that the combined effect of estrogen and progesterone is to protect against heart disease.

Pills that contain the new types of progesterones may have a more neutral effect on blood lipid levels.

LIVER AND GALLBLADDER PROBLEMS

Women on the pill have a greater risk than non-users of having gallbladder disease requiring surgery. The increased risk appears within one year of use and may double after four or five years.

Although very rare, both short term and long-term use of the pill has been linked to benign and cancerous growths of the liver. The risk of liver tumours may increase in women who have been taking the pill for more than seven years. The benign liver tumours do not spread, but they may rupture and produce internal bleeding which can cause death.

THE THORNY QUESTION OF CANCER

When certain animals are given estrogen hormone for long periods of time, cancer may develop in the breast, cervix, vagina and liver. However, studies to date have not definitely confirmed that the pill causes cancer.

Since anywhere from five to 30 years can pass between exposure to an agent that causes cancer and detection of the cancer, the most accurate thing we can say at present is that it is too early to rule out a relationship between cancer and the pill.

Recently, there have been reports that women who develop breast cancer before menopause, and who had used the pill early on, especially for four years or more before their first pregnancy, have a poorer five year survival rate than women who weren't using the pill.

CERVIX: Several studies have shown that precancerous changes in the cervix are increased in women on the pill. Other studies have not confirmed this finding.

Recently, experts have speculated that there may be an interaction between the wart virus (human papillomavirus) and the birth control pill. The wart virus is a major risk factor for cervical cancer.

A 1988 update of a study that has been going on in Britain for the last 20 years links the pill with cervical cancer. The incidence of cervical cancer in women who had taken the pill for more than ten years was four times greater than for women who had not. The overall incidence of cancer of the cervix was increased in women who had used the pill.

This study has been ongoing since 1968 and does not provide information on the sexual practices of women in the study (the number of sexual partners and the frequency of sex) which are considered to be important factors in the development of cervical cancer. In addition, the women in the study were using the higher dose pill.

Nonetheless, this study is still cause for serious concern. Results from new long-term studies that are better designed may not be in for another 20 years.

Folic acid (an important co-factor needed by the enzymes that make DNA and one which is often deficient in pill users) can protect against precancerous changes in the cervix, and it is advisable for all women on the pill to take folic acid supplements, at least .8mg once a day.

Dr. Tori Hudson, **Medical Director of the Portland Naturopathic Clinic** in Oregon, has devised an effective herbal treatment that is applied directly to the cervix, for women with abnormal Pap smears and early cervical cancer. Some naturopaths have been trained in these techniques. Diet change and vitamin and herb supplementation are also involved in her treatment program.

Folic acid taken in dosages of five to 10mg daily can also reverse abnormal Pap smears on its own.

UTERUS AND OVARIES: Use of the pill seems to decrease a woman's risk of cancer of the womb for up to 15 years afterwards. Some studies have also shown a lowered rate of ovarian cysts and ovarian cancer in pill users. All these studies were on the high dose pill, and at this time we do not know whether the low dose pill provides the same protection.

BREAST: The jury is still out about whether the pill causes breast cancer.

In February 1989, an updated report of a Boston study showed that pill users under age 45 had twice the incidence of breast cancer as non-users. The risk of breast cancer was doubled for women who had used the pill for less than ten years, and quadrupled for women who had used the pill for ten years and over.

The 1988 update of the 20 year study of 46,000 women by the **Royal College of General Practice** in England showed that women who used the pill had a slightly increased rate of breast cancer showing up before age 35. This meant that for every 7,000 women who had taken the pill under age 35, there would be one extra case of breast cancer per year when compared to 7,000 non-users.

In other words, the rate of breast cancer in women aged 30 to 34 who were former pill users was three times as high as those who had never used the pill. For pill users aged 30 to 34 who had one child, the breast cancer risk was five times as high as non-users.

Also in 1988, the **Cancer and Steroid Hormone Study** of the **Center for Disease Control** and the **National Institute of Child Health and Human Development** in the U. S. updated their study of the relationship between the pill and breast cancer. This study showed that in women who menstruated before age 13 years, who never had a child and who used the pill for eight years or longer, there was a fourfold increase risk of developing breast cancer before age 45.

A Swedish study reported in 1986, showed a twofold increased risk of breast cancer for women who ever used the pill for eight years or more, or eight years or more before their first pregnancy.

However, the majority of studies done on the pill do not show any connection between the birth control pill and breast cancer. Recently, the **Food and Drug Administration** in the U.S. met to review the evidence for the pill being related to breast cancer. The **F.D.A.** concluded that there was not enough evidence to warrant a change in pill prescribing, but admitted that the issue was not settled and called for further research.

In Canada, the **Special Advisory Committee for Health and Welfare** said no new warnings will be issued to pill users.

But as **Judy Norsigian**, of the **Boston Women's Health Collective** comments, "It's not clear the Pill is not associated with breast cancer." She feels that women should be warned that the long-term safety of the pill is still in question.

Toronto physician, **Dr. Carolyn Dean**, asks, "Since one in nine women will develop breast cancer, how can you know in advance if you are one of these women? Because one thing is known for sure and that is the pill will worsen breast cancer and may well cause a precancerous growth to turn into cancer."

Dr. Dean also adds that no one has considered what the cumulative long-term effects might be of years of pill use followed by years of hormone replacement for menopause. As a result, she feels that she cannot in good conscience continue to prescribe either the pill or hormones for menopause.

In any case, although doctors are uncertain what the new studies mean, most will continue to prescribe the pill as usual. Women will have to decide on their own whether to take the possible risks, or wait ten to 20 years to find out the link in retrospect.

Many studies have shown that pill users have a lesser risk of cystic breast disease. However, women who have had two or more biopsies for cystic breast disease, women who have a strong family history of breast cancer, and women exposed to **DES** in the womb should not use the pill.

Breast self examination and regular breast check-ups from your doctor are absolutely essential for women on the pill.

OTHER CANCERS: One study reported that urinary tract cancer, thyroid cancer and one type of skin cancer (malignant melanoma) occurs more often in pill users than non-users.

INFERTILITY AFTER THE PILL

Usually monthly periods return within three months of discontinuing the pill. However, it may take a longer time for periods to return to normal if a woman had irregular periods before going on the pill. Overall only one percent of pill users have not had their periods return after six months or longer.

PREGNANCY, LACTATION AND THE PILL

The pregnancy rate in birth control users is about one to two percent. It is frequently due to not taking all the pills, or taking the pills incorrectly. Some studies have found a small, but not significant increased risk of chromosomal birth defects, and heart and limb birth defects, in babies conceived while their mothers were taking the birth control pill. **The World Health Organization** report also noted a slight increase in the risk of miscarriage in these women.

In 1990, **Dr. Bracken**, a **Yale** professor of epidemiology, published two studies in which he found no association between birth control pills and birth defects or infertility. Dr. Bracken also believes that there is no increased risk for birth defects in women who conceive right away after coming off the pill.

Dr. Diane Millar, a Vancouver gynecologist, feels that the progesterone only pill is the best birth control choice for breast-feeding women.

On the other hand, Dr. Steinberg refers to two recent studies that show that low dose combination pills do not interfere with breast-feeding, and claims that the pill does not alter the quality or volume of breast milk. "At present," he says, "There are no recognized long-term effect on the neonate." (**Diagnosis**, July/87).

However, The Boston Women's Health Collective maintains that the pill decreases the amounts of protein, fat and calcium in breast milk and that some estrogen will come through the milk and be absorbed by the baby.

Until the long-term safety of the birth control pill has been proven for babies, I would be seriously concerned about recommending its use to breast-feeding mothers.

TEENAGERS AND THE PILL

According to Dr. Steinberg, "Once menstruation has begun, the growth spurt in adolescents is usually completed. Therefore, (the birth control pill) can be safely used without fear of growth inhibition." (**Diagnosis**, July/87).

However, the main risk for teenage women is the serious risk of chlamydial infection and sterility. Since the pill makes the teenage user more susceptible to chlamydial infections, and provides no protection against chlamydia or other sexually transmitted diseases, including AIDS, barrier methods are the preferred method for teenagers who can reliably use them.

THE PILL AND WOMEN OVER 35

The birth control pill is now being recommended for women over 35 who do not smoke or have other risk factors. Taking the pill may mask the beginning of menopause. Women over 35 should be followed in the first six months for blood lipids and blood pressure levels, and possibly fasting blood sugar levels as well.

Dr. Diane Millar suggests the use of the mini-pill or the progesterone only pill for older women. It has a slightly higher failure rate than the combination pill, but it may be safer overall. However, there may be an increased risk of tubal pregnancy with this pill.

Dr. Steinberg notes that older women who come off the pill may develop problems, "including menstrual irregularities, which may require surgical treatment or hormonal intervention." (**Ontario Medicine**, Sept/92).

However, at present there are no well designed studies that establish the safety of continued use of birth control pill past age 40. These studies may not be available for another ten years.

THYROID AND ADRENAL EFFECTS

The pill alters thyroid function blood tests, but this is not thought to be significant. In addition, it also alters adrenal function tests but this is not thought to pose any risk to health.

INFECTIONS

Pill users definitely have an increased risk of getting persistent and difficult to treat yeast infections. The pill is a definitive causative agent in the developing of chronic candida syndrome, a widespread infection of candida that involves every organ system in the body. Although some doctors still do not believe this syndrome exists, many women have been enormously helped by treatment of this condition. It is usually necessary to go off the birth control pill before treatment is started.

Some studies have shown a reduced incidence of pelvic inflammatory disease. However, according to **Jill Weiss**, of the **Canadian PID Society**, "There is disagreement about whether birth control pills really provide protection against pelvic inflammatory disease (PID). There is evidence to suggest that chlamydial infections of the cervix are enhanced by the pill. Also, women who use birth control pills have higher rates of chlamydial infection than women using barrier methods of birth control or no birth control. Some experts believe that pill use may increase the risk of chlamydia caused PID and the risks of developing silent pelvic infection which is more difficult to treat."

The cervix shows distinct changes for those on the pill, becoming redder in appearance and the cervical mucous more sticky and opaque. This is called "the pill cervix" and goes back to normal after the pill is stopped.

One study found an increase of urinary tract infections on the pill, while another study did not.

GUM DISEASE: Has been shown to increase with the use of the pill.

DEPRESSION

The link between the pill and depression has been known by women for a long time. Pill use substantially increases the chance of depression. Nine major studies have shown an incidence of depression in pill users ranging from 16 to 56 percent. Three major studies showed no connection between pill use and depression. Two other recent well designed studies showed a ten to 15 percent increase in depression in pill users.

Most long-term pill users tend to develop vitamin-B6 deficiency while on the pill, and this is often helpful in treating pill-related depression. Therefore, as a preventative measure women on the pill should take extra B6 in the form of one or two mega B tablets that each contain 50mg of all the B vitamins daily. It is also a good idea to take 500 to 1,000mg of vitamin-C along with the B vitamins. In addition, some experts also suggest vitamin E 200 IU a day and chelated zinc 25mg a day.

EYE CHANGES: The pill may cause a need for a change in contact lens prescriptions or the inability to wear contact lenes at all. The pill can rarely cause sudden blindness (due to clotting in the blood vessel leading to the eye) and cataracts.

METABOLIC CHANGES

The way sugar is handled in the body is markedly affected by the pill. The amount of sugar in the blood is increased as well as the amount of insulin and growth hormone. The long-term effects of these changes are not known.

Liver function can be altered in pill users and this can show up in altered levels of liver enzymes as measured in the blood. Only rarely (1 in 10,000) do pill users develop hepatitis with yellow jaundice. This jaundice usually subsides after the pill is discontinued.

Most blood clotting factors in the blood are also increased with use of the pill.

OTHER SIDE EFFECTS

Pill users may experience side effects that are not hazardous to their health, but are nonetheless very annoying. These include tenderness of the breasts, nausea, vomiting, weight gain, and swelling of the ankles. A spotty darkening of the skin, especially the face, may occur and, in some cases, becomes permanent. Other skin problems may occur such as eczema and hives or other skin rashes. These side effects are increased with higher doses of the pill.

On the lowest dose pills, breakthrough bleeding throughout the month is quite common, but usually disappears after three months of use.

Some studies have shown an increased incidence of chicken pox and other viral infections. The pill has also been linked to arthritic symptoms, ulcers in the mouth, hair loss and hair growth, sunlight sensitivity, bruising, lupus (a connective tissue disorder) and non-cancerous growths of the muscle tissue.

Other serious side effects include worsening of migraine, asthma, epilepsy, kidney or heart disease caused by the tendency for water to be retained when the pill is used.

Other occasional side effects include nervousness, dizziness, an increase in or loss of hair, an increase or decrease in sex drive, and appetite changes.

ADVANTAGES OF THE PILL

It enables regular predictable periods of bleeding every month. These are not true periods but really withdrawal bleeding after the pill is stopped for a day or two. The pill usually eliminates menstrual pain and prevents anemia from excessive menstrual bleeding. Certain kinds of pills cause an improvement in acne.

As mentioned previously, the high dose pill may reduce the incidence of cystic breast disease, pelvic inflammatory disease, and the incidence of tubal pregnancies. It may also reduce the risk of ovarian cysts and ovarian cancer as well as reducing the risks of uterine cancer.

Evidence is inconclusive about whether the pill has a protective effect on thyroid disease, rheumatoid arthritis, peptic ulcer, uterine fibroids or bone mass.

The pill is also a highly reliable form of birth control with a theoretical effectiveness of 99.5 percent. In practice, the actual rate of effectiveness due to forgetting pills or other errors is more like 98 percent.

Every woman on the pill should study the insert and the information booklet that is included in every package of the pill to understand thoroughly the risks she is taking. If you have questions about the side effects, your family doctor is the ideal person to consult.

NEW PILL DEVELOPMENTS

During the 1980's, new bi-phasic or tri-phasic pill formulations were introduced that mimicked the natural cycle a little more closely. The estrogen content of each pill remained the same throughout the cycle, but there were two or three different doses of progesterone mirroring the normal rise and fall in each cycle. The overall dose of progesterone per month was less.

The latest development in birth control pills involves the introduction to the market of three new and improved types of progesterone. These new progesterones have been on the European market since 1986.

"We're talking here about the first major change since the 1960's," said Dr. Steinberg, (**Ontario Medicine**, Sept/92) who teaches on the new progestins (another term for progesterone).

THE NEW PROGESTERONES- HOPE AND HYPE

NEW BIRTH CONTROL PILL HAILED AS A HEALTH AID trumpeted a July 1993 front page headline in the **Toronto Star**. The article announced the arrival on the market of the pill **MARVELON** (which contains a new progesterone called desogestrel).

"The last time a new class of progestins was introduced was during the age of Aquarius," says an ad announcing the arrival of Ortho's **ORTHOCEPT** pill containing exactly the same ingredients as marvelon. At the same time, Ortho also brought out the first triphasic pill containing a new progesterone known as **TRICYLCEN**. All the products are being marketed primarily for the new user.

The year before, Ortho had brought out **CYLCEN** which contains a new progesterone called norgestimate. CYLCEN now accounts for one in ten of new prescriptions for birth control pills in Canada.

The three new progesterones are norgestimate, desogestrel and gestodene. These new progesterones have been shown to have less androgen activity compared to the old progesterones (androgens are like male hormones but are normally present in a woman's body). This means that the new progesterones bind more specifically to progesterone receptors, whereas the older progesterones bind more frequently to androgen receptors.

But whether this means less androgen type side effects, or even if these side effects are linked to androgens, is unclear.

At a 1991 symposium on the new progestins, **Dr. David Upmalis, Associate Research Director** at **R.W. Johnson Pharmaceutical Research Institute** said, "Although definitive clinical studies have yet to be done, it is thought that androgenic activity may contribute to side effects such as acne, hirsutism [excessive hair growth on the face, breasts, etc.] and weight gain." Androgenic side effects may also contribute to breakthrough bleeding and mood swings.

An interesting study of 11,605 women taking the desogestrel pill, of whom 1,021 had pre-existing acne, showed that 80 percent of them had the acne disappear. In the same study, of 499 women with excessive hair growth before they start taking the new pill, almost 50 percent had it disappear.

Is the overall side effect picture better than the old progestin type pills? According to Belgian professor **Dr. Theo Brat** from the **University of Brussels Department of Obstetrics and Gynecology**, clinical trials to date show **no significant difference in side effects** (emphasis mine) between OC's currently in use and those based on the new progestins.

The most recent review of the effects of the new progestins was published in the June 1993 issue of **Obstetrics and Gynecology**. (Vol 81-6) **Dr. Leon Speroff** and **Dr. Alan DeCherney** and others reviewed approximately 100 studies.

They note less breakthrough bleeding and better cycle control with the desogestrel pill. However, they also note that larger trials comparing the old progesterones with new ones have not been done, and that lack of standardization in reporting and analysis "prevents meaningful comparisons of the new formulations from one study to another."

On the question of changes in blood sugar levels, the authors concluded that the new progesterones cause less changes than the old progesterones.

However, one of the main reasons doctors are being sold on these new progestins is their apparent beneficial effect on the HDL cholesterol ("good cholesterol").

Dr. Upmalis stated that the lipid effects of the new lipids are at least neutral "with a potential for lipid effects which could be beneficial."

Dr. John Collins, Professor of Gynecology and Epidemiology at **McMaster University** in Hamilton, Ontario, reviewed 40 studies involving over 100,000 women, on the new progesterones (**Journal SOGC**, Oct/91). Seventy percent of the studies did not extend past nine months. Only two studies extended follow-up for two years.

Dr. Collins concluded that the new progesterones have better effects on the levels of fatty substances in the blood than the old progesterones. They increase HDL levels and decrease LDL levels ("bad cholesterol").

However, as Dr. Collins points out, although higher HDL blood levels in women aged 50 to 70 are associated with a lower risk of heart disease, no statistics are available for younger women. Moreover, he says that studies done on men, which show that lowering the cholesterol leads to a reduction in heart disease, cannot be generalized to women particularly in the age group of pill users. Still Dr. Collins concedes that it "does make sense to prescribe birth control pills that are associated with the optimal lipid profile..."

Dr. Speroff and Dr. DeCherney reviewed 40 studies on blood fat levels and the new progesterones. Observed drawbacks included the facts that most studies lasted only six months or less, that changes in blood fats may not appear until after six months, and that in none of the studies were the treatment group compared to a non-treatment group to account for lifestyle effects like weight change, exercise and environmental changes.

In his review, Dr. Collins found that no single study evaluated a comprehensive set of metabolic and clinical effects of the new progestins.

Dr. Collins also noted that studies on blood clotting were limited to small numbers of patients, and there had been no orderly studies on the frequency of minor side effects in these new products, and how these compared to the old progestins.

Dr. Speroff and Dr. DeCherney concluded in a similar vein saying that many of the studies in this review reported laboratory data collected over a relatively short period. They recommended larger follow-up studies.

Since low dose pills are already associated with no increased risk of heart disease for women under 35 (who have a low risk of heart disease anyway) how much advantage will be gained by having these women switch to these new progestins? Does raising HDL and lowering LDL in young women result in a later reduction in heart disease? For non-smoking women over 35, and women of any age starting the pill for the first time, perhaps the new progestins will prove to be advantageous.

Meanwhile, if you are looking just at the hard scientific facts, you would have to say that all the fuss over the new progestins is premature. Again, we will have to wait for well designed studies and long-term follow-up.

NEW DUTCH RESEARCH

An entirely different approach is being taken by Dutch researchers who noted that the breeding season in animals is regulated by the hormone melatonin, which is secreted by the pineal gland in response to light. A January 1993 report in the **Medical Post** noted that the Dutch have been testing a completely new type of birth control pill since 1987. The new pill contains melatonin and progesterone, but no estrogen.

Dr. Michael Cohen, of **Rotterdam University** in Holland, reported his findings to a 1993 breast cancer symposium held in San Antonio. He said that breast cancer risk increases in direct proportion to the number of times a woman ovulates in her lifetime. The new pill has now been tested on 1221 women, with a breakthrough bleeding rate of six percent and a 93 percent ovulation inhibition rate. Dr. Cohen feels that this new pill may protect against breast cancer and other estrogen related side effects. Further studies on all aspects of this new pill are needed, but it looks promising.

OTHER MEANS OF BIRTH CONTROL

The lowest risk of death is associated with barrier or fertility awareness methods of birth control backed up by abortion in the case of failure.

BARRIER METHODS OF BIRTH CONTROL:

The condom is an excellent method of birth control and also protects both men and women from chlamydia, gonorrhea, herpes, AIDS, and other sexually transmitted diseases.

If used correctly and every time you have sex, it is 97 percent reliable. Rarely does a condom break. If a condom breaks, the morning after pill can be used to prevent pregnancy. Condoms do not have any known risks to a woman's health. Rarely, a woman may develop an allergy to the latex rubber used in the manufacture of condoms. Ultrathin condoms are now on the market, including a selection from Japan, where thinner condoms have been in use for some time.

The diaphragm with spermicidal jelly is another excellent method that offers 97 percent reliability, if it is used correctly before every love-making session.

This time-honoured method requires that a woman be properly instructed on how to place the diaphragm and apply the jelly. This is easy to learn and the diaphragm can be put in place two hours before sex.

The cervical cap is like a thick rubber thimble that fits snugly over the cervix.

It requires a lot less jelly than the diaphragm, and can be left in for a few days at a time. Some women find it more convenient than a diaphragm. However, it takes more time to fit and learn how to use than the diaphragm. It is just as effective as the diaphragm in preventing pregnancy (see chapter on cervical cap).

Both the diaphragm and cervical cap pose absolutely no risk to the woman's health and in addition protect a woman from cervical cancer and sexually transmitted diseases.

THE IUD: The main problem with this method is that it can cause pelvic infections that can make a woman sterile. It is not advised for women who have never had children. For some women who have had children, no history of pelvic infection, and a stable relationship, the IUD may be a satisfactory alternative. It is about 97 percent effective.

FERTILITY AWARENESS: This method teaches women how to determine their fertile days through observation of cervical mucous and temperature changes. If correctly taught and understood, this method can be highly effective (see chapter on knowing your body's cycles).

THE MORNING AFTER PILL: This consists of two birth control pills (50mg ovral pills are usually used) taken right after unprotected sex, and two taken 12 hours later. The pills prevent implantation of the egg in the womb in 95 to 98 percent of the cases. Used as an emergency method, it is reasonably safe. Side effects include nausea in 40 percent of the cases, and vomiting in 15 to 20 percent. Withdrawal bleeding should occur within two to three weeks after taking the morning after pill. If it does not, a pregnancy test must be done.

CONCLUSIONS

Robyn McKenzie, a medical journalist, puts it this way: "I was amused at the recent press coverage of **Ben Johnson**'s steroid use. The side effects include decreased testicular size and lowered sex drive. The general opinion was that no **man** in his right mind or who was not **misled** would subject himself to this hormone horror. Why is it O.K. to let millions of women be subjected to poorly understood hormone treatments?"

Mr. Percy Skuy, the president of **ORTHO Pharmaceutical**, a large manufacturer of the pill, said in an interview in the **Globe and Mail**, "I'd be happy to see the pill knocked off the pedestal that it's on. People have lost sight of the fact that it is a drug."

In a court ruling in January 1986 awarding damages to a 22-year-old woman who had suffered a stroke while on the pill, the judges noted that the pills "have presented society with problems unique in the history of human therapeutics... At no time have so many people voluntarily taken such potent drugs over such a protracted time for an objective other than the control of disease."

According to the Boston Women's Health Collective (**Our Bodies, Ourselves**, revised 1992), "**The National Women's Health Network** cautions that although pills with lower dosages of estrogen do seem to be **safer** than the pills used in the 1960's, there are no data to support the claim that pills in current use have all the **positive effects** and none of the negative effects of higher dose pills."

Between one million and one and a half million women in Canada use the birth control pill, a steroid medication, with serious and proven risks believing that they have no choice. Of course pregnancy itself is risky. In many cases, it is much riskier than being on the pill. But the choice is not between pregnancy and the pill, but between the pill and safer methods of birth control that also offer much more protection against sexually transmitted diseases.

FOR FURTHER READING

THE NEW OUR BODIES OURSELVES by the **Boston Woman's Health Collective** (revised, Simon and Shuster, 1992). This book is an indispensable guide for women, which I suggest that every woman should have in her home reference library.

Boston Women's Health Book Collective, PO Box 192, West Somerville, MA 02144. 617-625-0271.

This well known public information center contains national and international publications concerning women's health and other issues pertaining to women. **NATIONAL WOMEN'S HEALTH NETWORK**, 1325 G St NW, Washington, DC, 200003. 202-347-1140.

This is a national organization devoted exclusively to women and health. It publishes a newsletter as well as special news alerts concerning issues requiring immediate attention.

THE MONTREAL HEALTH PRESS INC. PO Box 1000, Stn La Cite, Montreal, PQ, H2W 2N1.

This press has an excellent fifty page booklet entitled **A BOOK ABOUT BIRTH CONTROL** for $4.00 from that address. It also has excellent booklets on sexually transmitted diseases, and sexual assault.

You can obtain a copy of the **1985 REPORT ON ORAL CONTRACEPTIVES**, free, by writing to:

HEALTH AND WELFARE CANADA, Publications, Health and Welfare, Brook-Claxton Buildings, Tunney's Pasture, Ottawa, ON, K1A OK9.

A newly revised report on oral contraceptives will be available in 1993/94.

HERBAL TREATMENT FOR CERVICAL CANCER AND ABNORMAL PAP SMEARS. For further information, and a copy of the treatment plan, write to:

DR. TORI HUDSON, Portland Naturopathic Clinic, The Teaching Clinic of The College of Naturopathic Medicine, 11231 SE Market St, Portland, OR, 97216. 503-255-7355.

The following table is taken from the publication, **THE NEW OUR BODIES OURSELVES**, written by the **Boston Woman's Health Collective** (page 224, Simon and Shuster, 1984).

CHANCES OF DEATH IN A YEAR.

Birth Control Methods:
Birth control pills (nonsmoker) .... 1 in 63,000
Birth control pills (smoker) .... 1 in 16,000
IUD's .... 1 in 100,000
Barrier methods .... none
Natural methods .... none

Sterilization:
Laparoscopic tubal ligation .... 1 in 10,000
Hysterectomy .... 1 in 1,600
Vasectomy .... 1 in 300,000

Pregnancy:
Continuing pregnancy .... 1 in 14,300

Terminating Pregnancy:
Illegal Abortion .... 1 in 3,000

Legal abortion:
Before 9 weeks .... 1 in 500,000
Between 9 to 12 weeks .... 1 in 67,000
Between 13 to 16 weeks .... 1 in 23,000
After 16 weeks .... 1 in 8,700

Cervical Cap Makes A Comeback

Years ago, the ancient Sumatrans of Indonesia knew about barrier methods of birth control. They fashioned caps made of opium to fit around their cervixes. Women in the Orient moulded oiled silk paper over their cervixes. And in Hungary, women used beeswax to make their caps. The modern world has been slow to catch up.

Finally, in Germany, **Dr. Adolphe Wilde** rediscovered the cap in 1838, 44 years before the diaphragm was discovered. Dr. Wilde took an individual impression of a woman's cervix and then created a custom-fitted cap made of rubber. At about the same time, a New York physician named **Dr. E.B. Foote** invented his own version of the cap. Since then, although the cap remained popular in England and central Europe, and was even manufactured in the U.S. until the 1960's, the cap never caught on well in the U.S. and Canada, particularly with the advent of the pill and the I.U.D.

The cap is a thimble-like rubber object that fits snugly over the cervix and is held in place by suction. It works by blocking sperm from going into the uterus. Actually, it is a more versatile birth control method than the diaphragm, and one with an equal success rate. But until recently few women had even heard of the cervical cap.

The great advantage of all barrier methods of birth control, whether the cervical cap, diaphragm or condom, is their safety and lack of side effects. This, combined with the fact that if used correctly and consistently, they are 95 to 97 percent effective in preventing pregnancy, make them a highly attractive choice for some women.

Perhaps because doctors receive little training in diaphragm fitting, and usually none in cervical cap fitting, and because both are time consuming to fit and to instruct women how to use properly, both the diaphragm and the cervical cap have been overlooked in spite of many excellent attributes. And of course until the last 25 years, women were more squeamish and less knowledgeable about handling their bodies.

In the last decade, women's clinics, in their search for safe and reliable alternatives to the pill and IUD, have rediscovered the cervical cap, and have started to fit caps and make them available to women in the U.S. and Canada. However, the caps still have to be imported from England, as there is no U.S. or Canadian manufacturer yet.

The main advantage of the cervical cap over the diaphragm is esthetics. The caps are smaller (one and a half inches long and about one inch wide), use far less spermicide, are therefore less messy, and best of all, can be left in place up to 48 hours at a time, allowing for more spontaneous sex. Since the cap can be inserted up to 40 hours in advance, it also means that birth control can be separated from actual love making.

Usually the cervical cap is used with spermicidal jelly. At present, it is recommended that the cap always be used one-third to one-half filled with spermicide and left in place eight to 12 hours after the last episode of sex. If the cap is left in place longer, up to three days, no further spermicide need be used. Some women feel so confident with their caps that they use no spermicide at all. This may be possible because the cervical cap functions mainly by means of the suction or surface tension that adheres it snugly to the cervix, and not so much as a holder for spermicide as the diaphragm does.

To date there are no known side effects of the cap but several studies are presently in progress. **The Canadian Cancer Society** in Vancouver believes that the cap, like all barrier methods, provides some protection against cervical cancer. And like condoms, the cap offers some protection against sexually transmitted diseases like gonorrhea and chlamydia.

In 1986, an **F.D.A.** sponsored study in the United States concluded that the effectiveness of the cervical cap and the diaphragm was identical. The effectiveness rate of the cap varied from 83 percent to 94 percent. The lower rates occurred for women who did not use their caps faithfully every time they had sex. Failure rates were also higher in women who had sex more than three times a week.

Women who have cervical infections or inflammations, abnormal PAP smears, herpes, or active pelvic inflammatory diseases should not use cervical caps. Certain shapes of cervices, either very short or very long, and cervices that have been severely injured, cannot be easily fitted.

Learning to insert and remove the cap requires practice and patience. Like any new skill, it takes time to master. Some women catch on immediately and others take longer to learn. Some women find it difficult to insert at first and others find removing more difficult. Before learning how to use the cap it is important to learn how to feel your own cervix. The cervix feels somewhat like the end of your nose, only softer, and is located far back in the vagina.

After choosing from one of four possible sizes of cervical cap for a particular woman, I have her put it in and take it out at least three times, checking each time to see that she has correctly placed it over the cervix. The key to successful use is to make sure that the cervix is covered at all times. Failure of the cap results from incorrect placement (the cap can stick to the vagina wall) or the cap not being used at all, or the cap becoming accidentally dislodged during sex.

Disadvantages of the cap include being harder to insert and remove than the diaphragm, at least initially, and requiring, like all barrier methods, conscientious use every time you have sex. Also the cervical cap cannot be used during menstruation, as the menstrual blood may break the suction. Thus, during menstruation, another method of birth control has to be used such as condom or diaphragm. Occasionally, a man can feel discomfort during sex at certain times of the menstrual cycle, if his penis hits the rim of the cap.

In Chicago, a doctor and dentist are working with the idea of a custom-made cap with a one-way valve that allows cervical secretions to drain and that can be left in place for long periods of time. This could be a promising development for the future.

If you are considering a cervical cap, you have to know yourself and your sexual lifestyle well enough to be certain that you are the type of person who will actually use the cap every time you have sex.

The cap is not always easy to obtain, except in major centers. Contact your nearest women's center or **Planned Parenthood Center** to get a list of practitioners and clinics that fit cervical caps. The cap costs about $35.00, roughly the same as the diaphragm.

RESOURCES

THE COMPLETE CERVICAL CAP GUIDE, by **Rebecca Chalker** (Harper and Rowe 1987). This book is a practical and well illustrated guide on how to use the cap and how to make sure it is properly fitted.

In the United States, you can contact the **CONCORD FEMINIST HEALTH CENTER**, 38 South Main St, Concord, NH 03301. 603-225-2939, for a list of practitioners and clinics that fit the cap.

Permanent Birth Control: The Facts

When a woman or a couple becomes certain they want no more children, or no children at all, they may want to consider the option of permanent birth control or sterilization.

The next major issue is who should get sterilized, the man or the woman?

VASECTOMY OR TUBAL LIGATION ?

There is no doubt that sterilization for men, or vasectomy, is a much simpler operation than female sterilization or tubal ligation. During a vasectomy, the vas deferens, which normally carries the sperm from the testicle to the penis is cut on each side. This operation is not only safe and uncomplicated, but it can be done under local anesthetic and takes only half an hour. Although vasectomy is essentially irreversible, if reversal is desired, it is easier to do than after female sterilization. The vas can be put back together or re-anastomosed in 40 to 90 percent of cases with pregnancy resulting in 18-60 percent of those successful operations.

Although both are very low, the pregnancy rate after vasectomy is somewhat lower than after a tubal ligation. And there isn't the problem of a tubal pregnancy after a failed tubal ligation, which can pose a serious health threat to women.

Furthermore, following vasectomy, complications are infrequent and of a minor nature. No long-term side effects from vasectomy have as yet been proven.

The female procedure has a **five** times greater incidence of major complications than vasectomy.

In female sterilization or tubal ligation, the fallopian tubes that connect the ovaries to the uterus are cut, burned or blocked so that the egg cannot travel to meet the sperm in the vagina. Tubal ligation requires the use of an operating room, sophisticated medical equipment, the services of an anesthetist and a gynecologist trained in the use of the laparoscope. Like vasectomy, tubal ligation is best considered irreversible.

However, with recent advances in microsurgery, in anywhere from between 30 and 60 percent of cases, the tubes can be successfully sewn back together or reconstructed. But only 40 percent of women with successful tubal reconstruction will go on to become pregnant. This means your overall chance of becoming pregnant after a reversal is really only 12-20 percent.

CHANCES FOR REVERSAL

Your chances for reversal depend on the type of operation that was done and how much of the tube was destroyed.

Where the tubes are burned or cauterized (the most common operation) the tubal ligation is more difficult to reverse. Where clips, bands, or rings are used, less tissue is damaged and the operation can be reversed a little more easily. Also these reversal rates apply only to a large medical center where the operation is performed by a gynecologist experienced in tubal reconstructions.

The reversal procedures itself is a lengthy operation involving major abdominal surgery unlike the original tubal ligation. With any major abdominal surgery, the risk of complications and length of recovery period increases.

The cost of the surgery is not covered by medical plans and must be paid by the patient. Currently a reversal operation costs about $2,000 in Canada. With anesthetic charges and hospital costs, this may add up to between $3,200 and $6,000 in some provinces.

The possibility of reversal should definitely not be counted on in making the decision in favour of either male or female sterilization. Success rates vary widely from center to center, and even if your operation is successful technically, there is no guarantee that pregnancy will follow. And if you happen to be unsuccessful after a long and costly operation, statistics will not be comforting.

Some women will consider tubal ligation as an option if they have been unable to find any safe and/or satisfying method of birth control. For example, a good candidate for tubal ligation is Sally, 36 years old, who had her first pregnancy with an IUD in place and her second while using a diaphragm. She can't use the pill because of troublesome side effects. Her partner feels threatened by the idea of vasectomy and dislikes condoms. She is also certain that she doesn't want any more children.

IMPORTANT CONSIDERATIONS BEFORE TUBAL LIGATION

Other important considerations before tubal ligation include:

1. The degree of certainty that you will never want to have another child under any circumstances.

2. Your physical, emotional, mental and spiritual ability to care for and guide the children that you already have; your children's attitude to having a new family member.

3. Your financial resources; your support network of family and friends; the amount of support you can realistically expect from your partner in raising the kids and in sharing household chores.

4. The level of co-operation of your partner in birth control matters and his feelings about vasectomy.

5. Your level of energy, major health problems, and your age.

6. Your feelings about yourself as a woman and the role of children in your life.

7. Your goals for work, schooling or training.

8. Your religious beliefs and your personal feelings about birth control and abortion.

Further, you must also ask yourself how you would feel if one of your children died; or if your partner died and you remarried; and exactly how you would respond to a pregnancy at this point in your life and later on.

Occasionally, tubal ligation is performed immediately after childbirth, Cesarean section or therapeutic abortion. I don't recommend this timing for tubal ligation for several reasons. After childbirth, you are in vulnerable state emotionally and psychologically. At this time also, your body's tissues are more delicate and prone to bleed. In addition, there is a slightly higher failure rate of the operation than when it is performed between pregnancies. Moreover, some serious health problems with babies do not develop until after birth, and this could greatly affect your decision.

Having said all this, if you have carefully considered the decision before childbirth or abortion, tubal ligation performed at the same time can still be a good choice for you.

Having a tubal ligation is an important turning point in a woman's life marking the end of her reproductive potential. It changes how she thinks of herself as a woman and her orientation in the world. It may signal her going back to school or her re-entry into the work force. It frees a woman to develop other aspects of herself besides mothering, without the fear of unwanted pregnancy or the burden of birth control. The decision is a crucial one and should not be taken lightly.

Of course, with vasectomy, a woman reaps the same benefits without taking on any additional risks to her health.

At least one woman in 200 will end up changing her mind about tubal ligation and seek a reversal of the operation. Some studies indicate that almost 30 percent of women express some regrets after the operation.

You are more likely to regret your decision:

If you undertake the tubal ligation with doubts in your mind.

If you are younger than 27 years old.

If your religion or culture has strong beliefs about the fertility of women.

If someone else has pressured you into it as your only choice.

If the operation was done at the time of childbirth or abortion.

If you strongly associate your identity as a woman with your fertility and have not worked out your feelings about this ahead of time.

HOW A TUBAL LIGATION IS DONE

In the past, tubal ligation required major abdominal surgery, but this is almost never necessary now. These days, the operation most favoured is the laparoscopic sterilization. This operation has a relatively low complication rate, a short recovery period and two very small scars.

After you are under a general anesthetic, your bladder is emptied, and your abdomen and vagina are cleansed with an antiseptic soap. Two tiny incisions are made into the abdomen, one just above the pubic bone and the other just below the belly button. These incisions are 1/4 to 1/2 inch long. The abdomen is then inflated with gas so that the tubes may be more easily seen. Next the laparoscope (a slender light-containing telescope) is inserted into the upper incision, and the instruments for blocking the tubes into the lower incision.

While looking through the laparoscope, the doctor uses the instruments to block the tubes. He or she can use a variety of means including cautery, clips, rings or band, with or without a section of the tube being removed. Cautery means burning with an electric current. Clips, rings or bands block the tubes by squeezing them together. You should know ahead of time exactly what method your doctor is using and the chances for reversal.

AFTER SURGERY

After the surgery is completed, only one to two stitches are required to close each incision. The incisions can then be covered with a small dressing or bandaid (hence this type of tubal ligation is sometimes known as bandaid surgery). The operation lasts about 30 minutes.

After tubal ligation of this type, a woman can usually go home the same day and resume her normal activities within a week or even a few days. I usually suggest five to seven days to recover from the effects of the general anesthesia, even longer if necessary. You should allow some flex in your schedule post-operatively as women vary in the amount of recovery time their bodies require, and this is not always predictable ahead of time. It is also wise not to do any heavy lifting or strenuous physical work in the first week following surgery.

The ability to become pregnant ends immediately with the operation, and unlike vasectomy, there is no three-month waiting period during which birth control is still required.

The complications rate after laparoscopic sterilization is extremely low, about six in a 1,000 cases. The most common complication is that of bleeding into the abdomen, which can require hospitalization and further surgery.

Pregnancy, although rare, is a surprising complication of tubal ligation. Two to three women in a thousand operated on will become pregnant after tubal ligation.

If pregnancy does occur, it is more likely to occur in the tubes. A tubal pregnancy can bleed or rupture, which is a serious medical emergency requiring immediate surgery.

The nature of your menstrual periods may change, with heavier bleeding, or may stay the same. The usual cycle continues every month with an egg being produced. The difference now is that the egg is reabsorbed by the body and pregnancy cannot occur.

Women are usually told that tubal ligation does not affect other body functions. This may not always be true. In theory, your hormone secretions should also remain unchanged. However, some women may have their hormonal balance altered after tubal ligation. Premenstrual symptoms may intensify. Some women go into premature menopause immediately following surgery or within two to four years following surgery.

Some women become depressed after tubal ligation, especially if they were uncertain about their choice beforehand. However, most women experience a great deal of relief at the loss of their fertility. In one study, 50 percent of couples reported an enhanced sex life after tubal ligation, and 75 percent after vasectomy.

OTHER TYPES OF TUBAL LIGATION SURGERY

As mentioned earlier there is really no reason to have a laparotomy for tubal ligation. A laparotomy, which means cutting into the abdomen, is major surgery as compared to the laparoscopic sterilization. There are significantly more risks with the procedure itself as well as more pain, a longer recovery period and a longer hospitalization. The incision in a laparotomy is four to six inches long.

There is also the minilaparotomy where the incision is smaller, about one or two inches long. This is a big improvement on the laparotomy, but it still requires a somewhat longer recovery period with more pain and cramping. However, this may be the only type of procedure available in smaller centers, and for this reason it can be very useful, especially in regions far from a major center.

Research is under way for a much less invasive operation, using a lighted tube (hysteroscope) with a video camera attached, that is inserted through the cervix and involves no cutting. One possibility being explored is the insertion of a nylon plug with a coil at each end into the tubes. These plugs can later be removed. This operation, when available, will require a skilled and experienced surgeon.

LONG-TERM COMPLICATIONS

Long-term complications of tubal ligation have not been fully studied. Some women experience heavier menstrual periods and increased menstrual pain following a tubal ligation. This can lead to repeated D-and-C's and an increased risk of hysterectomy. One study found that tubal ligation leads to a higher incidence of hysterectomy for women who were in their 20's when their tubes were tied.

The reason for menstrual complications are not understood, but they could be the result of interference with blood supply to the ovary during the operation, which then alters hormonal blood levels.

One English study showed that there was an incidence of painful periods following tubal ligation of 39 to 49 percent. Another study of 200 women two years after tubal ligation showed that 34 percent had longer periods, 32 percent had heavier periods and 20 percent had shorter or lighter periods. Of the women reporting problems, most had previously been on the pill.

For women who have been on the pill, a heavier flow can be expected because the pill normally decreases menstrual flow.

After tubal ligation scar tissue can form in the pelvic area. These bands of fibrous tissue known as "adhesions" can cause recurrent abdominal pain, which is difficult to treat.

TUBAL LIGATION AND PREMATURE MENOPAUSE

While practising obstetrics in the Melbourne area, **Dr. John Cattanach** began to notice "a disturbingly large number of young women" being admitted to hospital for hysterectomy. The usual reason given for the hysterectomy was heavy menstrual bleeding appearing several years after tubal ligation.

"Unlike abnormal uterine bleeding from other causes, the post-tubal ligation form usually failed to respond to progesterone therapy. It was also observed that many seemed to develop early estrogen deficiency [menopausal] symptoms within about four years of tubal ligation. Low grade arthritic and ligamentous symptoms and signs, particularly referable to the lumbar spine and shoulders, were observed, together with early atrophic vagina [dry vagina], skin deterioration, and complaints about loss of libido [sex drive]." (**Medical Journal of Australia**, March 3/84).

In 1988, Dr. John Cattanach studied the hormone levels of 112 women who had undergone tubal ligation at least two years previously. He found that women who had been sterilized by tying, burning or clipping their tubes had a 40 percent lower production of estrogen and a 20 percent lower production of progesterone than women who had been using natural methods of birth control (**Medical Post**, Feb 14/89).

Problems reported by women in the Australian study following tubal ligation included heavy menstrual bleeding, pain in the low back, shoulders, elbows and knees, gastritis, irritable bowel syndrome, urinary problems, excessive growth of breast tissue, heart and blood vessel problems, as well as psychological problems. Dr.

Cattanach successfully treated those problems by giving affected women a combination of estrogen and progesterone replacement hormones.

Dr. Cattanach believes that the lowered hormone levels may have been the result of damage to the blood supply to the ovary during the operation, which may occur more often with certain surgeons and certain surgical techniques.

Critics of Dr. Cattanach say that the studies he did were too small to warrant any definitive conclusion. They also point out that a review of well designed studies involving 5,000 women with tubal ligation showed no increase in health problems when compared to a group of women who didn't have a tubal ligation.

Meanwhile, Dr. Cattanach has started **DCAHS, Doctors Concerned About Human Sterilization**, to promote research into premature menopause following both tubal ligation and hysterectomy. He says there is no way of knowing which women will be most affected after surgery. However, certain surgical techniques, such as electrocautery, seem to cause more damage.

Janine O'Leary Cobb, author of **Understanding Menopause** (Key Porter, 1988), comments in her newsletter (Feb/92), "There are a number of procedures used to sterilize women and some seem less harmful than others; even so it is rare to find a physician willing to acknowledge such consequences, or indeed, warn about potential long-term effects."

RESOURCES:

DCAHS, Doctors Concerned About Human Sterilization, c/o Dr. John Cattanach, 37 Vista St, Bulleen, Vic 3105, Melbourne, Australia. 03-852-0644. Fax: 03 852-0096.

Know Your Body's Cycles - To Get Pregnant Or To Avoid Pregnancy

The true mark of a modern woman is to be in control of her own fertility. Getting to know your body's monthly rhythms is the first step to taking charge of your body. This information can be used both if you are trying to get pregnant or to avoid pregnancy.

In addition, if you are missing your period or having irregular periods, it is essential to know if you are ovulating. **Dr. Jerilynn Prior**, a BC endocrinologist, and other researchers, have found that irregular cycles, or cycles with no periods, may lead to bone loss, due to the lack of the hormone progesterone. One woman athlete developed stress fractures of the small bones of the feet after one year of no periods.

Women can inexpensively chart their cycles using mucous and temperature observations. In addition, some new tests can assist women in making these observations.

Recent developments in medical technology have also made it possible for women to accurately predict ovulation 12 to 36 hours **before** it happens.

HOW THE EGG MEETS THE SPERM

"Every 28 days or so, from puberty until menopause, one solitary egg from a woman's store of a half million goes forth to mate," as **Globe and Mail** reporter **Frann Harris** puts it (Apr 10/90). Each egg is the size of the head of a pin and is housed in a little sac known as the follicle, which is located in the ovary.

Harris reports on the work of **Dr. Roger Pierson** of the **Reproductive Biology Research Unit** at the **University of Saskatchewan**. He has been recording ovulation on videotape using vaginal ultrasound. He has observed the rhythmic pumping of the follicle as it squeezes the egg out of the follicle and propels it toward the tubes.This whole process takes about three minutes and is known as ovulation.

A complex set of hormonal events trigger the egg being released. One of the key events is the release of a hormone known as luteinizing hormone (**LH**) from the pituitary gland in a woman's brain. This so-called LH surge triggers ovulation, and is present 12 to 36 hours prior to ovulation. Using sophisticated technology, this LH can now be detected in the urine before ovulation.

Prior to ovulation, the cervix produces a special mucous for about three to nine days, for an average of four days. The presence of cervical mucous is as crucial to fertility as ovulation. Without mucous, the sperm can not survive nor be transported to the fallopian tubes to fertilize the egg. When mucous is present, it nourishes and protects sperms allowing them to live for three to five days. Mucous appears prior to ovulation as nature's way of guaranteeing that sperm are readily available to fertilize the egg before their short life-span is over.

As **Geraldine** and **Elaine Matus** explain in their book, **THE JUSTISSE METHOD FOR FERTILITY MANAGEMENT**, "The cervical mucous act as a gate. The gate is open when the mucous is flowing and the sperm can enter the uterine cavity. The gate is closed when the mucous stops flowing and forms a mucous plug. This blocks the sperm's entry into the cervix and thus the uterine cavity."

After ovulation, the egg begins its journey down the fallopian tubes, perhaps to meet a sperm. The tiny egg lives for only 12 to 24 hours and is able to be fertilized by the sperm for only half that time. Right after ovulation the basal body temperature, taken vaginally or orally, rises .2 to .5 degrees centigrade.

THE TWO TOOLS OF MUCOUS AND TEMPERATURE

MUCOUS: Stretchy clear fertile mucous is noticeable three to nine days before ovulation. Normally, a woman will notice an abundance of mucous after her period is over, especially when she wipes herself before or after going to the bathroom. At first the mucous is pasty, sticky and cloudy in colour, progressing to a wet, slippery, stretchy and transparent mucous. This stretchy clear mucous is the most fertile mucous. However, it is possible to get pregnant on any "wet" or mucousy day before ovulation. After ovulation, the so called "dry" or safe days begin. Although it takes practice to be able to detect the mucous changes, after a while the procedure becomes easy and automatic.

Another new way to check your mucous is using the **PG-53** fertility tester. This is a small pocket microscope to examine the mucous with. During ovulation the clear stretchy mucous will crystallize forming a beautiful fern-like pattern under the microscope. This method has apparently been used in Europe for a decade. It may be most useful for women who have trouble interpreting their mucous pattern.

Drawbacks include inconsistent or confusing results from the microscope reading, and lack of availability except in Europe.

BASAL BODY TEMPERATURE (BBT): BBT is the body's baseline resting temperature, best measured first thing in the morning after at least five hours of restful sleep unaffected by eating, excitement or activity. The body's hormones cause the BBT to rise by at least 0.2 to 0.5 degrees centigrade at the time of ovulation. The temperature will remain elevated until the period begins.

The most convenient way to measure BBT is using a digital basal body thermometer that reads to at least two decimal points. This thermometer costs about twenty dollars and gives its reading in only 30 seconds.

BBT records for at least three cycles are required for any woman going to a fertility clinic. They are also recommended for women who have irregular or absent periods. Irregular cycles or even cycles which appear normal, but where there is no ovulation, can lead to bone loss in women of any age. In particular, women in their forties should be aware of whether or not they are ovulating. Bone loss at this time may lead to a higher risk for fractures at menopause. Charts for this purpose have been included in the chapter on menopause.

Another way to accurately record the BBT is to measure urine temperature from a first morning urine sample. Studies have shown that urinary temperature taking is as accurate as rectal or oral temperatures and as quick as a digital thermometer. **OVUDATE-BBT** kit contains 28 styrofoam cups, a chart and instructions.

Starting on the fifth day of your cycle, you urinate into one of the cups, and let it stand for at least a minute. The heat of the urine activates a heat sensitive sensor strip at the bottom of the cup. After you empty the cup, you can read the exact temperature from the bottom of the cup. Completed charts can be faxed to the manufacture who will do a computerized analysis of it and send a copy of the chart along with the interpretation to your doctor.

The kit has been modified so that only one reusable polystyrene cup is used and the temperature strip changed daily.

BIOSELF is a small hand held instrument that is a combined computer and BBT thermometer. It keeps track of a woman's cycle lengths and BBT curves and calculates probable times of fertility and infertility. After you take your temperature, a red, green or yellow light will flash on to let you know what phase of your cycle you are in. The information on your cycles can also be printed out, but only on a special printer at a Bioself outlet.

Although BBT is a very useful tool in determining if ovulation is indeed occurring, for the most accurate results it is essential to combine it with checking your mucous discharge. Temperature readings can be inaccurate during times of illness, excessive alcohol intake, travelling, or not enough rest. By contrast, mucous readings are more dependable throughout the cycle.

NATURAL BIRTH CONTROL

Charting your mucous and temperature will enable you to tell which days in your cycle are the most fertile. Then you can avoid sex altogether on peak fertile days. An alternative is to use one of the barrier types of birth control, such as the condom, diaphragm, or cervical cap on those days. However, barrier methods have to be used very carefully at the most fertile times since failure rates at that time are higher.

According to the **NEW OUR BODIES OUR SELVES** (**Boston Women's Health Collective**, 1984), this method can be "extremely effective when taught carefully, understood thoroughly, and used correctly." The collective estimates that the theoretical failure rate of the method is between .5 to 13.1 percent, with the actual failure rate ranging from 4.5 to 34.4 percent. The higher failure rates are due to either not using the method or using it incorrectly. This method of birth control is of course 100 percent natural with no side effects and minimal costs.

Some women find it difficult to detect their mucous changes or to be disciplined enough to chart their temperature daily. It is important to know yourself well and to have the co-operation of your partner before you rely solely on this method of birth control. In addition, in order to learn this method well, it is usually necessary to have a good teacher or group of women to learn from.

ONE IN SEVEN COUPLES HAVE TROUBLE GETTING PREGNANT

Under ideal conditions, with a normal fertile couple, only 42 percent of a woman's cycles will result in pregnancy. This means **58 percent** of her cycles won't result in pregnancy.

Infertility or difficulty conceiving after one year of sex without the use of birth control now occurs in one in seven couples. In the past, infertility investigations were not even begun until a couple had been infertile for five years.

Ninety percent of the time the cause is a physical one. Thirty five percent of the time the cause is found in the man, 35 percent in the woman and 20 percent of the time the cause involves both partners. In the remaining ten percent the cause is unknown.

Among the 35 percent of infertility due to the female component, 20 percent are due to irregular ovulations, which are often accompanied by limited or poor quality cervical mucous. Charting mucous and temperature, as well as attention to nutrition and vitamin supplementation may be very helpful for this group of women. Other natural treatments such as acupuncture or homeopathy may also increase fertility in some women. Ovulation prediction tests that pinpoint ovulation can be used as additional aids.

If a woman is not ovulating at all, she may have to undergo treatment with certain drugs or hormones to induce ovulation.

The other 80 percent of female causes of infertility are due to damage to the tubes or ovaries caused by infections such as gonorrhea and chlamydia or conditions like endometriosis. The use of IUDs has substantially increased the risk of serious pelvic infections with resultant scarring and infertility. For women under 25 who have more than one sexual partner, chlamydia is the number one cause of scarring of the tubes and infertility.

Infertility resulting from damage to the tubes may necessitate some form of corrective surgery. Infertility due to male causes is more difficult to treat, but can occasionally be helped by leading a more healthful lifestyle, by vitamin supplementation and by improving the diet. Surgery may also be helpful for some men.

AGE MAKES PREGNANCY MORE CHALLENGING TO ACHIEVE

Women over 35 who are having difficulty getting pregnant may find charting their cycles particularly useful. After 35, depending on general health, diet, and lifestyle, a woman's fertility may begin to decrease by up to 30 to 45 percent. Women with decreased fertility may have less mucous or more irregular ovulations.

Men over 35 may have a reduced sperm count or poor motility of sperm. For older couples, a good understanding of how their fertility works is very helpful for proper timing of sex, as well as reassuring, because they know more of what is going on and feel more in control of the situation.

TIMING IS EVERYTHING WHEN YOU ARE TRYING TO GET PREGNANT

If a man doesn't have enough sperm or the sperm he has are slowly moving ones, and/or a woman has little or poor quality mucous, then it may be helpful to know the precise time of ovulation.

Ovulation prediction home test kits that detect the luteinizing hormone (LH) surge are a helpful addition to BBT and mucous observations.

To maximize your chances of getting pregnant, it is best to have sex on the most fertile days as indicated by your mucous and temperature charting. However, the ovulation test kits go one step further by allowing the couple to determine exactly when ovulation is going to occur 12 to 36 hours **before** it happens.

Knowing the exact time of ovulation is also helpful in cases where a man has to abstain from ejaculation in order to conserve sperm.

The time of ovulation can vary from one cycle to another in the same woman. Even a variation of a few days can cause a couple using past cycle history alone (calendar rhythm method) to miscalculate their timing. The ovulation prediction kits will objectively let a woman know whether or not her calculations are correct, or if she needs to wait a few more days before planning to have sex.

WHAT MAKES URINE LH DETECTION POSSIBLE

Ovulation prediction home test kits to detect LH use specially designed artificially produced antibodies (monoclonal antibodies) to detect LH in the urine.

LH is present in the blood throughout the whole menstrual cycle, but usually in very small amounts. Prior to ovulation the amount of LH suddenly increases. This increase is called the LH surge. The LH surge usually appears in the blood during the early morning hours between 5 am and 9 am. The LH surge then remains in the urine for about 24 hours after LH blood levels peak. Ovulation takes place 12 to 36 hours after the LH surge. The home test kit can pick up this LH surge in the urine accurately predicting ovulation within 36 hours.

Monoclonal antibodies are antibodies made from one cell line that produces the same precise antibody in an indefinite and invariable supply. These monoclonal antibodies are highly specific and can detect even minute amounts of LH in the urine, causing the urine to turn a specific shade of blue.

FIVE DIFFERENT LH TEST KITS

OVUQUICK SELF TEST FOR OVULATION PREDICTION can detect ovulation 24 to 36 hours before it takes place. It takes five minutes to perform. **CONCEIVE** is a one step urinary kit to detect ovulation. Results can be read in three minutes. Both are distributed in Canada by **PHARMASCIENCE**. Their toll free information number is 1-800-363-8805. **PHARMASCIENCE** also distributes the **BIOSELF** computer.

FIRST RESPONSE OVULATION PREDICTOR TEST detects ovulation 12 to 24 hours before it takes place. This test uses first morning urine and takes three minutes to complete. **FIRST RESPONSE** is distributed by **CARTER PRODUCTS** at 1-800-268-3186.

CLEARPLAN is a one step easy to use urinary test, which takes five minutes to perform. It pinpoints ovulation 24 to 36 hours in advance. **CLEARPLAN**, is from **FISONS CORPORATION**, Markham, Ontario at 1-800-268-1121.

OVUDATE LH KIT. This is another one step test that takes only three minutes to complete. **OVUDATE** urinary thermometer and **OVUDATE-LH** ovulator test are available through **CADNA MEDICAL DIAGNOSTIC INC.** at 1-800-561-2520 Fax 416-752-2021. In the U.S. contact **FRANKLIN DIAGNOSTICS**, PO Box 246, Morristown, NJ, 07960. 1-800-OVUDATE, Fax: 201-285-0564. A new test using a combination of urinary temperature and LH testing will soon be available from this company.

HOW LH TEST KITS WORK

All five tests are started approximately 14 to 16 days before the expected date of your next period. Charts contained in each kit tell you when to begin testing based on the average length of your past cycles, using calendar rhythm calculations.

If the woman is charting her mucous symptoms, she may start testing using the kit's suggested dates. However, if there is an onset of clear stretchy mucous before her calculated date to start, it will be more accurate to start testing with the onset of this mucous. Using mucous charts in conjunction with calculations may actually decrease the number of tests necessary, so one kit may be enough for two cycles, and the woman will save money.

The tests are all used in basically the same way. After collecting your urine, you drop it on a test pad which contains a small amount of monoclonal antibodies that act like a sponge and soak up LH. Next, reactive agents are added to the pad in timed succession, taking five minutes to complete. If LH is present, the testing spot on the pad will turn a certain shade of blue, which becomes darker as the amount of LH increases. The test result is compared to the reference spot, and recorded. The test is repeated every day until the LH surge is detected.

The **CONCEIVE**, **THE CLEAR PLAN** and **OVUDATE LH** are based on the same principles but are one step tests where you just add urine and read after three minutes, with nothing else to do.

USING LH KITS AS AN AID IN TREATING OR DIAGNOSING INFERTILITY

These kits can be used to test the effectiveness of fertility drugs that are used to bring on ovulation. The kits also allow women advance warning in order to plan for artificial insemination or in vitro fertilization.

As well, some infertility clinics use these tests to plan the timing of diagnostic procedures in the investigation of infertility such as vaginal ultrasound, hormonal blood tests, uterine biopsy, examination of cervical mucous, and the post-coital test, which tests activity of the man's sperm in the vagina after sex.

HOW TO BUY LH TESTS

The tests are available without a prescription, but are sometimes kept behind the counter. In smaller centers the tests will have to be ordered. The tests may be cheaper with a prescription. Check with your local pharmacist. All five tests cost about the same, $40.00 to $60.00 for five day tests.

CONCLUSION

In spite of these technological advances, babies continue to confound the best laid plans. Women who don't want to get pregnant seem to get pregnant a lot easier than women who desperately want to conceive.

For women who are dealing with the difficult problem of infertility, temperature and mucous observations can help some pinpoint the cause of the problem. For certain infertility problems, ovulation prediction kits can help women detect ovulation accurately 24 to 36 hours before it happens.

Sometimes it is better for infertile couples to wait longer than the usually recommended one year of trying to get pregnant, before going through expensive and invasive infertility investigations. This will allow them more time to become more familiar with their cycles and to improve their overall health.

For women wanting a safe natural method of birth control, temperature and mucous observations are the key. And for women with irregular cycles, knowing whether they are ovulating will enable them to find out whether they need medical help to keep their bones healthy.

FURTHER INFORMATION

YOUR FERTILITY SIGNALS (Smooth Stone Press, 1989), by **Merryl Weinstein**. This book has lots of drawings, with step-by-step instructions. It is also easy to understand.

THE JUSTISSE METHOD FOR FERTILITY MANAGEMENT (1988), by **Geraldine** and **Elaine Matus**. Counselling and training in this method are provided by:

   THE JUSTISSE GROUP, PO Box 441, Stn P, Toronto, ON, M5S 2S9. 416-656-7659.

Copies of their book as well as telephone consultations are available. In addition, the group offers detailed information on how to enhance fertility through the use of diet, vitamins and herbs.

INFERTILITY - PROBLEMS GETTING PREGNANT, by the **Vancouver Women's Health Collective** (1989). #302-1720 Grant St, Vancouver, BC, V5L 2Y7. 604-736-5262. A very clear and easy to understand manual with a lot of drawings on all aspects of infertility. The collective also offers a selection of books on birth control and fertility awareness.

MISSED CONCEPTIONS, by **Anne Mullens**. This is a clearly written book on all issues surrounding infertility and outlines exactly what your medical and surgical options are.

GETTING AROUND THE BOULDER IN THE ROAD: USING IMAGERY TO COPE WITH FERTILITY PROBLEMS, by **Aline Zoldbrod** (1990). This can be ordered from Dr. Zoldbrod for $8.00 from 12 Rumford Rd, Lexington, Mass, 02173.

FERTILITY CONTROL, THE NATURAL APPROACH, by **Dr. Zoltan Rona**.

This 31 page booklet is mostly about the PG 53 but also explains vitamin supplementation for impotence and infertility. It can be ordered through Dr. Rona's office at #305-1466 Bathurst St, Toronto, ON, M5R 3J3. 416-534-8880. PG 53 is currently available only in Europe.

INFERTILITY AWARENESS ASSOCIATION OF CANADA, 104-1785 Alta Vista Dr, Ottawa, ON, K1G 3Y6. 613-738-8968.

This is a non-profit organization that provides assistance, support and education to those with infertility concerns. A newsletter entitled **INFERTILITY AWARENESS** is published five times a year.

FERTILITY AWARENESS NETWORK, PO Box 1190, New York, NY, 1009.

For an information packet on fertility awareness methods and a counsellor/teacher referral list for North America, send $3.00 U.S. and a stamped self-addressed envelope to them.

OVULATION METHOD TEACHER'S ASSOCIATION, PO Box 101780, Anchorage, Alaska. 99510-1780.

This group will provide information on qualified fertility awareness teachers and groups.

FERTILITY AWARENESS SERVICES, PO Box 986, Corvalis, OR. 97339.

This group specializes in compiling all available information on fertility awareness. They will provide a free list of all fertility awareness books and groups if you send a stamped self-addressed envelope to them.

ADDENDUM

On January 23, 1996, **NU-FOCUS** introduced North America to an innovation in contraception and fertility detection called the **PC-2000 FERTILITY TESTER**.

The PC-2000 is a simple, easy to use, inexpensive and reliable method of ovulation detection. This mini-microscope enables a woman to perform saliva testing in the privacy of her own home to accurately determine her fertile period.

In 1969, a doctor named Cassals discovered that not only cervical mucous, but also the saliva of a woman produced a fibrous, vein-like structure when veiwed under a medical microscope. This crystallization, caused by hormonal changes in the body, only occurs during the woman's fertile period (which usually lasts 6-8 days). The PC-2000 Fertility Tester allows women to quickly and easily test their saliva for the crystallization pattern to determine their fertile period.

Clinical tests have proven that the PC-2000 is highly accurate. A recent study determined that, with proper use, this device is over 96 percent effective.

The PC-2000 Fertility Tester is available through most pharmacies across Canada.

The Yeast Among Us

In 1973, on my first day of work as a medical doctor, a woman walked into my office having suffered from vaginal itching for 20 years. She turned out to have a chronic yeast infection, which eventually she was able to overcome.

At various times throughout their lives, many women experience one or more vaginal infections. These highly annoying and even painful infections usually clear up rapidly with treatment. However, an estimated 20 percent of women go on to develop persistent and recurrent yeast infections.

Vaginal yeast infections are usually caused by a yeast known as candida albicans. **Candida albicans** is the name of a family of one cell fungus which belongs to the plant kingdom. Under normal circumstances, candida is present in your vagina, mouth and digestive tract and also on your skin. Some researchers even suggest that candida, in its one cell form, may be involved in a beneficial role in the hormone regulation of humans.

But under certain conditions, candida can change from its harmless one cell form into a long microscopic tube (hypha) which puts out branches (mycelia). In this form, as a mass of branches or long root-like structures, it can penetrate into cell walls and cause infection in various parts of the body.

Of course, the female body has its own defences against invading yeast cells. The vagina itself is a balanced ecosystem. It is an efficient, self-maintaining and dynamic environment with natural defence mechanisms that keep it healthy, moist and clean. The two most important defence mechanisms are the acid base balance and the cervical secretions. The healthy vagina is slightly acidic, ranging from about four to five on the PH scale (that runs from one, most acidic, to 14, most alkaline). This acid condition of the vagina discourages infections by bacteria and other organisms. Friendly bacteria called lactobacillus acidophilus help also help keep the vagina acidic and resistant to infections.

The mucous secretions which come from the cervix bathe and lubricate the vaginal walls. The amount of cervical secretions are affected by hormonal changes during the menstrual cycle. The vagina can also produce its own secretions during sexual excitement. Normal vaginal secretions have a mild, pleasant odour and fluctuate between a clear egg white consistency and a milky white creamy consistency depending on the phase of the menstrual cycle. Anything that can disturb the overall condition of your health or the natural balance of your vaginal environment can predispose you to yeast infections.

PREDISPOSING FACTORS THAT AFFECT THE WHOLE BODY

THE BIRTH CONTROL PILL: The pill changes the environment of the vagina just like pregnancy does and makes pill users more susceptible to persistent and recurrent yeast infections. Choosing another form of birth control may be necessary.

PREGNANCY: Pregnancy makes the vagina less acidic and increases the amount of sugar stored in the vaginal cell walls. This sugar can provide great fuel for the rapid growth of yeast cells. Yeast infections during pregnancy must be treated or the mother can pass on the infection on to her baby at birth.

PROLONGED OR REPEATED USE OF ANTIBIOTICS: A common example of this is the long-term use of tetracycline for the treatment of acne. Other examples are repeated courses of antibiotics for ear infections or bronchitis.

Some women get a yeast infection every time they use an antibiotic. Antibiotics kill harmful bacteria, but they also kill the good bacteria, the protective lactobacilli that live in the vagina.

A good preventive measure for women who need to go on antibiotics is to take high quality lactobacillus powder or capsules (available at any health food store). The dose is one-quarter teaspoon of powder or two capsules twice a day with meals throughout any course of antibiotics and for two weeks afterwards. Avoiding unnecessary antibiotics in the first place is always a good idea.

STEROID DRUGS OR ANTI-CANCER DRUGS: These decrease or destroy the body's natural immune systems. Even repeated or too frequent use of cortisone skin creams may predispose you to yeast infections since some of the cortisone is absorbed into the blood stream.

DIABETES: Sometimes the first sign of diabetes is a yeast vaginal infection that stubbornly won't go away or that keeps coming back. All women with recurrent yeast infections should have a blood and urine screening test for diabetes at least once.

THE OVERALL STATE OF YOUR HEALTH: Stress, fatigue, overwork, lack of sleep, and a poor diet high in sugars and refined foods can make you more vulnerable to yeast infections. Anemia, low levels of thyroid hormones in your blood, and other diseases or infections present in your body can do the same thing.

MENOPAUSE: During and after menopause, with its hormonal changes, the cells of the vagina may become thinner and cervical secretions may become less. This may make women a little more susceptible to yeast vaginal infections.

PREDISPOSING FACTORS THAT AFFECT THE VAGINA LOCALLY

WARM AND MOIST CONDITIONS: Just before or during the period, the menstrual blood is alkaline, and the moist, warm conditions are favourable to yeast growth. This is why anti-yeast medications must be continued throughout menstruation.

TIGHT CLOTHING: Tight-fitting pants, nylon panty-hose, and synthetic underwear don't allow the vagina to breathe properly. One hundred percent cotton underwear and pants of at least 60 percent natural fibres are recommended.

DEODORANTS AND SPRAYS: Vaginal deodorants and sprays are not only useless, they disturb the natural balance of the vagina. Perfumed tampons, coloured or perfumed toilet paper and bubble bath should also be avoided. Some women develop severe allergic reactions to the perfumes or chemicals used in these products. All of these products can irritate and inflame the vagina and make you more prone to vaginal infections.

DOUCHING: Douching is generally unnecessary and too much douching can be harmful. If you are going to douche, a dilute vinegar douche (two tablespoons of white vinegar to a quart of lukewarm water) is suggested once or twice a month, preferably just before menstruation. Vinegar douches can be used as an initial treatment at the first sign of a vaginal infection. Pregnant women should never douche.

TOILET HABITS: Toilet habits can also contribute to an increased chance of infection. In wiping with toilet paper, women should always wipe from front to back and not the other way around. This avoids the spread of yeast and other germs from the rectum to the vagina.

CUTS AND ABRASIONS: Vaginal cuts and abrasions can occur while inserting tampons or while making love, especially if the woman is not well lubricated.

MEN AND SEX: An intense period of sex after a long period of abstinence may be a factor in recurring yeast infections. Some men get an irritation around their foreskin area, which is usually treated with an anti-yeast skin cream. Oral-genital sex may spread yeast from mouth to vagina.

Yeast probably can be sexually transmitted, but this has yet not been proven. However, in a large percentage of cases, yeast can also be cultured from the penises of men whose partners have recurrent yeast infections. In these cases, the men may need to take oral anti-yeast medications while their partners are being treated.

Even for simple yeast infections, condoms should be used until the woman has completed her treatment.

SYMPTOMS OF A YEAST INFECTION

The main symptoms of yeast infections are usually vaginal discharge and itching of the genital area. The discharge is usually white and varies from being a little to a lot;, from being thin and mucousy to thick, curdy and cottage cheese-like (with anything in between being possible). The amount of itching also varies but can be severe enough to interfere with sleep and normal activities. Some women notice a characteristic odour suggestive of bread dough or the fermenting yeast smell of beer being brewed.

Other frequent symptoms are swelling, redness and irritation of the outer and inner lips (the labia), painful sex and painful urination due to local irritation of the urethra.

A woman with a full-blown yeast infection is acutely uncomfortable and requires immediate treatment if possible. If you suspect that you have a yeast infection see your doctor as soon as possible in order to get cultures of the vaginal secretions taken. Other vaginal infections can co-exist or produce a similar picture of signs and symptoms.

WHAT YOU CAN DO AT HOME

After you have had yeast infection confirmed by culture, or while waiting to see your doctor, you can begin treatment right away with some simple over-the-counter remedies.

Boric acid is an effective, inexpensive treatment for yeast infections. It costs $2.50 for a small bottle. Boric acid can be put in 00 gelatin capsules and inserted high into the vagina once or twice a day for seven days. As an alternative, a douche can be made using two tablespoons of boric acid to one quart of lukewarm water. This can be used daily for a week.

Another over-the-counter drug is betadine douche or suppository. Betadine is a concentrated antiseptic iodine solution that kills yeast, trichomonas and gardnerella. It is used daily as a douche or twice daily as a suppository. It has several disadvantages. It stains everything bright brown. It cannot be used for pregnant women or those allergic to iodine (test first with a small amount of the solution on the vagina). It costs $8.50 for a ten-day supply of the douche and $14.00 for a package of 14 suppositories.

One percent gentian violet is one of the oldest treatments for yeast infections and actually works well, but is messy and stains everything bright purple. Gentian violet is painted onto the vagina with a Q-tip. Remember to include the nooks and crannies of the vaginal walls when painting it on and be sure to test for possible allergic reaction first. A two-ounce bottle costs $8.00.

Another old remedy that is effective against both yeast and trichomonas is the use of a whole clove of garlic. The garlic is peeled but not nicked, and wrapped in gauze making a kind of tampon with a gauze tail. The whole thing may be dipped in vegetable oil to make insertion into the vagina easier. Leave the garlic suppository in place for 12 hours, then douche with dilute vinegar solution. This treatment usually goes on for three days. You can get an unpleasant garlicky taste in your mouth as a side effect, but otherwise this works well.

For the relief of unbearable itching try one of the following:

Witch hazel compresses.

Warm water baths with epsom salts or baking soda.

Or a poultice of cottage cheese on a sanitary napkin.

Afterwards, keep the area dry, if necessary use a hair dryer, and dust with cornstarch.

WHAT YOUR DOCTOR MIGHT PRESCRIBE

Three main types of prescription drugs are used to treat yeast infections.

The first is nystatin (mycostatin, nilstat) which was the original drug used to treat yeast infections. It comes in the form of vaginal tablets which are inserted into the vagina twice a day for seven days (this is one of the least irritating forms of treatment), and also in the form of vaginal creams which are inserted into the vagina with an applicator once a night for seven to ten days. It is safe, easy to use and cheap. It is about 70 percent effective. It costs $12.50 for a course of treatment with the tablets and $20 for the cream. Nystatin also comes in a pure powder form, which is sometimes necessary in resistant cases of yeast infection.

The second and newer family of imidazole drugs include miconazole (monistat), clotrimazole (canesten), and econazole (ecostatin). Monistat is a very effective drug for simple yeast infections. It is about 88 percent effective and comes in vaginal suppositories, and creams. A large size of monistat cream costs $38. Three and seven day courses of treatment cost about $29.

Canesten and ecostatin are more effective than nystatin but a little less effective than monistat. Canesten has both a one and three day course of treatment. Both cost about $26.00. A three-day course of ecostatin also costs about $29.00. Occasionally the one and three dose treatments can cause more burning and stinging than longer courses of treatment with lower doses.

The newest classes of drugs are the triazoles (fluconazole, itraconazole and terconazole). They are highly effective because of their ability to penetrate the cell wall of the yeast cell. Only one, terconazole, is available in vaginal creams and suppositories. Terconazole costs about $30.00 per course of treatment.

During any course of treatment it is advisable to cut out all sugars, and avoid excess dairy and bread.

PERSISTENT REOCCURRING YEAST INFECTIONS

Persistent reoccurring yeast infections are more challenging to treat. Recurrent yeast infections mean you have four or more confirmed episodes of yeast infections every year. At this stage, I might recommend monistat vaginal cream every night for seven days; then every other night for four weeks; then monthly at the time of menstruation. Boric acid capsules or nystatin vaginal tablets may be used as an alternative if the person has a sensitivity to monistat.

Recently it has come to light that recurrent yeast infections may be part of a larger picture involving widespread overgrowth of yeast organisms in the whole body. This may cause symptoms affecting every system of the body.

Symptoms include:

Fatigue.

Depression, anxiety and other mental and emotional illnesses.

Digestive difficulties, of all sorts, including indigestion, bloating, gas and diarrhea alternating with constipation.

Menstrual problems including premenstrual syndrome.

Sexual difficulties and **infertility**.

Arthritis.

Chronic skin problems.

Repeated urinary and **vaginal infections**.

Asthma and other respiratory illnesses.

Allergic reactions and **chemical sensitivities**.

Candida overgrowth may also be suspected when a person feels very ill and no cause can be found for his or her problems. He or she may have been written off as a hypochondriac.

Women are particularly susceptible to candida overgrowth, especially if they have been exposed to tetracycline for treatment of acne or long-term use of the birth control pill.

Children can also be affected if they have been overexposed to antibiotics. A baby can get thrush if her mother had a yeast vaginal infection at birth. Pregnant women with yeast infections should be treated promptly.

In children, a chronic yeast infection can show up as hyperactivity, learning disabilities, or even, in a few cases, autism. In adolescents, candida can cause depression and severe mood swings. A typical story is a top student who suddenly becomes unable to think clearly or learn, and who becomes suicidally depressed. In one teenage girl these symptoms appeared after just a two-month course of tetracycline for acne. Candida has also been implicated in some cases of teenage anorexia.

EDUCATION IS THE FIRST STEP

If you suspect this generalized type of candida problem, the first step should be to visit your doctor for a complete history and physical examination including appropriate blood tests to rule out other possible causes of your symptoms as low thyroid function, other glandular abnormalities, anemia, low blood sugar, viral infections or parasitic infections. It is important to remember that each of these conditions can mimic chronic yeast infections or co-exist with them.

The next step involves educating yourself about candida in its many and varied manifestations.

Seven books are recommended:

THE YEAST CONNECTION AND THE WOMAN, by **Dr. William Crook** (Professional Books Inc, 1995). Highly recommended. 901-423-5400.

BACK TO HEALTH, by **Dr. D.W. Remington** and **B.W. Higa** (Vitality House, 1987).

THE YEAST SYNDROME, by **Dr. J.P. Trowbridge** and **M. Walker** (Bantam 1986).

THE MISSING DIAGNOSIS, by **Dr. C.O. Truss** (1985), Box 26508, Birmingham, Alabama 35226.

CANDIDA, by **Dr. Luc De Shepper** (1986), 2901 Wilshire Blvd, #435, Santa Monica, CA, 90403.

WHO KILLED CANDIDA? by **Vicki Glasburn** (1991), Teach Service, Brushton, New York, NY, 12916.

THE BODY ECOLOGY DIET: Recovering Your Health And Rebuilding Your Immunity, by **Donna Gates** (BED Publications, 1993). Call 404-352-8048.

If the problem is detected in its early stages, treatment is much more successful. Treatment involves dietary and lifestyle changes as well as the use of either prescription or non-prescription anti-yeast medications (taken by mouth) on a long-term basis.

THE GROUND-BREAKING WORK OF DR. ORIAN TRUSS & OTHER PIONEERS

Dr. Truss, author of **The Missing Diagnosis**, is an internist in Birmingham, Alabama. He has had more than 20 years of clinical experience with over 3,000 candida patients. He is convinced that yeast is implicated in a wide variety of human ills, from depression and hormonal disturbances to allergic reactions and auto-immune diseases. Chronic yeast infections, he believes, may be a causative factor in diseases such as multiple sclerosis, Crohn's disease, schizophrenia, myasthenia gravis and lupus.

Truss feels one of the most important questions a doctor can ask is, **"When did you last feel well?"** Truss then tries to figure out if the onset of symptoms coincided with the use of antibiotics, birth control pills, steroids, other drugs or medical procedures, and/or repeated pregnancies.

The candida diagnosis, he believes, has been often missed due to two factors. The first factor is that, "This yeast lives in virtually every human being," making it difficult to track down.

The second factor is that depression, agitation, loss of memory and concentration are "almost always prominent." This combined with the multitude of symptoms can easily lead to the convenient label of psychosomatic illness. A woman may then be prescribed tranquilizers or referred to a psychiatrist. A thorough case history combined with a high index of suspicion will help a physician make the proper diagnosis.

According to Truss, the most frequent manifestation of chronic yeast are:

Mental depression, anxiety, hyperactivity and hyper-irritability.

Recurrent urinary tract symptoms usually diagnosed as cystitis.

Increased susceptibility to allergic reactions to inhaled or injected chemicals, including food or drugs.

Many indications of interference with hormonal functions like acne, rough dry skin, almost any type of disturbance of the menstrual cycle, decreased or absent libido, decreased breast size, and progressively more severe premenstrual tension. Miscarriages and endometriosis were common.

Since 1983, at the **Critical Illness Research Foundation**, Dr. Truss has been conducting candida research in the hope he can produce enough concrete evidence to persuade more of his colleagues of the yeast connection.

Dr. William Crook, a pediatrician and a leading expert in yeast infections, was the first to make the problem widely known to the public. He founded **International Health Foundation** and has authored 12 very accessible books on the topic.

In Toronto, **Dr. Carolyn Dean**, a family physician, wrote a paper on her clinical findings of 2,000 patients diagnosed with chronic candida. Dr. Dean used a blood test for candida antibodies as well as a complete history and physical to make the diagnosis of candida. Unfortunately, the test for candida antibodies is not widely available at present and is not covered by most government medical plans.

Dr. Carol Jessop, Assistant Professor in the **Department of Medicine**, at the **University of California**, treated 1,100 patients for chronic fatigue syndrome. Of these, 900 had a history suggesting chronic yeast infections so she treated them with ketoconazole, a strong anti-yeast prescription drug, for an average of five months. She was surprised by the results. Of the 900 patients she treated, "529 returned to their previous health and 261 reported significant improvement."

Dr. Jessop's current treatment of choice for severe yeast infections is fluconazole 100mg a day for three to six weeks. She believes this drug is highly effective and improves mental symptoms more quickly. She also uses grapefruit seed extract for her patients. This is a natural product available without a prescription and taken for five to nine months.

DON'T BE CONFUSED WITH VAGINAL INFECTIONS THAT ARE NOT YEAST

TRICHOMONAS is another common cause of vaginal discharge. It is caused by a tiny pear-shaped parasite. It is usually sexually transmitted but can also be passed on in whirlpools, bathtubs and through wet towels and washcloths. The discharge from this infection can be whitish, yellowish, or greenish-yellow in colour and foamy or frothy in consistency. It can also be foul-smelling and cause itching of the labia and painful urination. Both partners should be treated.

BACTERIAL VAGINOSIS. This refers to a condition in the vagina in which there is an imbalance of the normal beneficial vaginal bacteria, with an overgrowth of several other types of bacteria. The good lactobacilli are reduced, and other bacteria that grow without oxygen are found in their place. One of these is a rod-shaped bacteria called gardnerella vaginalis (also hemophilus vaginalis or corynebacterium vaginale).

Symptom-wise, there can be a greyish-white discharge with a fishy odour. Sometimes it just causes a whitish discharge with no odour.

Treatment is recommended for both partners, although it has not been proven to be sexually transmitted. The presence of bacterial vaginosis may be one factor that increases the risk of pelvic inflammatory disease, but this has not yet been proven.

Some gynecologists recommended vinegar douches for woman with mild cases. Sometimes the infection will clear up on its own. Lactobacillus powder in 00 capsules and placed in the vagina every second night for two weeks may also be tried (this is sometimes irritating to the vagina).

GONORRHEA usually causes no symptoms. Occasionally, if the cervix is involved, it may cause a thick yellow discharge which may be foul-smelling and cause burning and irritation of the vagina and labia. All sexually active women should be routinely checked for gonorrhea at every PAP test and pelvic exam.

CHLAMYDIA is another recently discovered organism which causes infections similar to gonorrhea and is thus very serious. If it causes any vaginal symptoms at all, these will be similar to those described under gonorrhea. Chlamydia cultures are now available in most cities and should be done routinely in sexually active women.

HERPES is usually easy to tell from yeast because it causes painful clear blisters in the genital area and in the vagina which can usually be seen. However, when blisters form on the cervix, which are not possible to see, herpes can cause a copious white discharge which can be confused with yeast.

Still, it may take years before the mainstream medical profession catches on to this serious problem, which has left many women without proper diagnosis and treatment. Only public pressure can speed up this process.

TREATMENT OF CHRONIC YEAST INFECTIONS

The following outline was adapted from the one developed by Dr. Carolyn Dean.

DIET: Diet is the most important contributing factor and must be changed in order to begin treatment. There should be noticeable improvement after being on the diet for four to 12 weeks. Diet must be individualized but in general, the main foods to avoid are sugars, bread with yeast, dairy, fermented foods, dried fruits, canned and processed and mouldy foods especially over-ripe fruits.

ACIDOPHILUS: At the same time, high quality dairy free lactobacillus acidophilus one-quarter teaspoon powder or two capsules should be taken by mouth, twice a day with meals for six months to a year.

PSYLLIUM SEED POWDER OR METAMUCIL WITHOUT SUGAR: These maybe necessary to help cleanse the colon and get rid of the yeast. If you are constipated, you should take metamucil or psyllium first thing in the morning and last thing at night.

NATURAL ANTI-YEAST PREPARATIONS: These include caprylic acid (made from coconut oil), mycocidin (made from the castor bean oil) and garlic in capsule form or fresh. A new and highly effective preparation, that is effective against both yeast and parasites, is grapefruit seed extract in doses of five to 15 drops three or four times a day. **Tannelbit**, a product consisting of natural tannins combined with zinc, three capsules three times a day, has been used successfully for chronic yeast, where the yeast growth is predominate in the intestines. A Peruvian plant called cat's claw is also effective against yeast and parasites.

ANTI-YEAST MEDICATIONS: If the above preparations are not effective, then you may have to resort to drug treatments.

Nystatin powder or tablets may have to be taken by mouth for an extended period of time varying from one month to six months.

Another drug being used for long-term treatment is ketoconazole (nizoral) a powerful anti-yeast drug, taken once or twice daily for one to six months. Ketoconazole may affect liver function, (about one in 10,000 cases, according to Dr. Crook) and this must be checked regularly throughout treatment.

Two new drugs, fluconazole (diflucan) and itraconazole appear to be more effective than ketoconazole. Both are exorbitantly expensive ($373.00 for three weeks of diflucan). Dr. Jessop now uses fluconazole or diflucan for treatment of her patients with chronic candida. "If they have a yeast overgrowth, my treatment of choice is three weeks of diflucan 100mg daily for three weeks."

Dr. Jessop says that her patients report improvement of mental symptoms like "brain fog" on diflucan. Some side effects have been reported in 16 percent of persons using the drug, and liver function can be affected.

On the other hand, itraconazole appears to have the least side effects of all three drugs, and does not appear to affect the liver.

CONCLUSION: The vagina has a wonderful built-in defence system. But in today's fast-paced lifestyle, with its over-reliance on drugs, poor diet and environmental stresses, natural defence systems may be overwhelmed. A simple yeast infection now and then is easy to treat but a chronic yeast infection requires a more thoughtful and thorough approach.

FOR MORE INFORMATION

INTERNATIONAL HEALTH FOUNDATION, PO Box 3494, Jackson, TN 38303. 901-423-5400.

This research foundation was founded by **Dr. William Crook** and will provide books and articles for the public and physicians. Dr. Crook has been largely responsible for educating the public about candida.

DR. ORIAN TRUSS, CRITICAL ILLNESS RESEARCH FOUNDATION, 2614 Highland Ave, Birmingham, AL. 35205. 205-326-0642.

CANDIDA RESEARCH AND INFORMATION FOUNDATION, PO Box 2719, Castro Valley, CA. 94546.

This American group has done outstanding work in educating doctors and women about this chronic illness.

YEAST CONSULTING SERVICES, PO Box 11157, Torrance, CA. 905010. 310-375-1073.

Dr. Margorie Crandall is a medical researcher, consultant and expert in the area of candida infections. Her helpful ten page booklet, **HOW TO PREVENT YEAST INFECTIONS**, is available for $4.00 U.S. from the above address.

CANDIDA RESEARCH AND INFORMATION FOUNDATION (CRIF), C/O The Canadian Schizophrenic Foundation, 17 Florence Ave, Toronto, ON, M2N 1E9. 416-733-2117. Fax: 416-733-2352.

This non-profit organization provides a resource library for the public as well as an information package on candida. The group was originally founded by **Maggie Burston** who collected more than 1,700 scientific articles on candida.

CANDIDA RESEARCH INFORMATION SERVICE (CRIS), 41 Green Valley Court, Kleinburg, ON, L0J 1C0. 416-832-0789.

Also founded by **Maggie Burston**, this new organization functions as a resource for studies, educational material, doctor referral and new research into old diseases. Maggie has put together an advisory board of prominent doctors and researchers which she can call on at any time for further expertise. Private consultations are available in person or by telephone.

SUPPLEMENTS PLUS, 451 Church St, Toronto, ON, M4Y 2C5. 416-962-8269. Canada wide mail order: 1-800-387-4761.

Books on yeast, natural anti-yeast preparations, and a comprehensive selection of vitamin and nutritional supplements can be ordered through this outlet.

SMITH'S PHARMACY, 3463 Yonge St, Toronto, ON, M4N 2A3. 416-488-2600 or 1-800-361-6624.

KRIPP'S PHARMACY, 994 Granville St, Vancouver, BC, V6Z 1L2. 604-687-2564.

Pure nystatin in powder or capsule form (prescription only) as well as a complete line of natural products can be ordered from either of these pharmacies.

KENT MACLEOD, C/O NUTRICHEM PHARMACY, 1303 Richmond Rd, Ottawa, ON, K2B 7Y4. 1-800-363-6327 Fax. 1-800-465-2965.

This pharmacy has a complete line of anti-yeast products including nystatin powder in capsules in doses of 500,000 to 2,000,000 IU per capsule, as well as time release nystatin capsules and nystatin mixed with grapefruit seed extract or caprylic acid. They also have a very good acidophilus product called **Nutridophilus Rx**.

Bladder Blues

So many women suffer from repeated episodes of bladder problems that until recently it was considered part of the fate of women. The female urethra (the tube that connects the bladder to the outside) was thought to be too short and close to the rectum, thus making it susceptible to repeated infections.

Pamela Sue Martin, who in the world of television played the character **Fallon** in **Dynasty**, in real life suffered from reoccurring disabling bladder pain for which no doctor seemed to offer any lasting solution. She took hundreds of antibiotic pills, often without a urine culture being done first. She abstained from sex. She had a D-and-C done by one doctor and a series of painful urethral dilations done by another.

Finally, after 12 years of trying unsuccessfully to deal with this problem, Pamela found out she was being treated for the wrong condition. She was not having repeated bacterial infections of the bladder. Rather she was experiencing a condition of the bladder known as interstitial cystitis (**IC**).

For **Dr. Vicki Ratner**, now an orthopedic surgeon, who developed an intensely painful bladder condition as a medical student, it took 11 months of desperate search and visits to ten urologists and two allergists before the diagnosis of IC was made. Along the way Dr. Ratner was also referred to a psychiatrist, an all too common experience for women who suffer from IC.

Cystitis is a confusing term, which can mean either a infection or inflammation of the bladder. Cystitis can be acute, which usually refers to an infection of the bladder that comes on suddenly, lasts for a short time and does not tend to reoccur. Chronic cystitis, on the other hand, may start off with a short bouts of cystitis, but then goes on to become a frequently reoccurring problem over a period of years.

It now appears that there are two distinct types of chronic cystitis. One is due to reoccurring bacterial infections of the bladder, which can happen for all sorts of reasons. The other is due to IC, which results from the interplay of numerous different factors.

SYMPTOMS OF CHRONIC CYSTITIS - IC TYPE

IC is caused by the inflammation of the interstitium, which is the space between the bladder lining and the bladder muscle. IC is still thought of by many urologists (a specialist in the urinary tract of both men and women) to be a very rare disease, which ends up with a woman having chronic pelvic pain, urinary frequency, and a shrunken ulcerated bladder.

Recently however, the innovative research work of a Californian woman urologist named **Dr. Larrain Gillespie** and the educational campaign waged by Dr. Vicki Ratner and **Dr. Kristene Whitmore** of the **Interstitial Cystitis Association**, (**ICA**) has made the public aware that IC is in fact very common among women who suffer from chronic bladder problems.

An estimated 450,000 people in the U.S. and 50,000 in Canada have IC. Ninety percent are women. The average age of onset is 40 years old, but 25 percent of these women are under 30.

A 1987 survey of IC sufferers by the **Urban Institute of Washington** showed that 40 percent were unable to work; 27 percent were unable to have sex due to pain; 27 percent had marriage breakdown; 55 percent contemplated suicide as a result of living with this disease and 12 percent had actually attempted suicide.

You might by now already suspect you have this problem if your symptoms sound similar to Pamela Sue Martin's. Typically, a woman who has this problem has recurrent bladder pain and urinary frequency, but her urine cultures keep coming back normal showing no signs of bacterial infection.

During these painful episodes, a woman can feel a painful burning sensation when she passes urine. She can also have urgency which means the urgent need to go to the toilet to urinate, but little result when she does. She usually has urinary frequency, that is, she has to urinate more frequently than normal and often during the night as well.

Her bladder pain characteristically feels worse before and after she urinates. She has a few moments of relief only when actually urinating. Her pain may be like electric shocks to the bladder area. She may also get referred pain, either shooting needling type pains in her urethral area or a bruised aching sensation in her clitoral area, or both.

She may have also noticed that acidic foods as well as foods such as chocolate, red wine, old cheese, nuts, yogurt, avocados and bananas make the pain worse.

Repeated courses of antibiotics do not help her. In fact, if an infection is not present, she might have noticed that antibiotics make the pain worse.

She could be told the problem is all in her head and psychiatric help recommended.

IC CAN BEGIN WITH AN INFECTION

In fact, the majority of women with IC did start off at the beginning with bacterial infections of their bladders. At first, these infections would be treated with antibiotics and clear up right away. After a while however, there would be no bacteria present in the urine and the antibiotics would not help.

Bacteria seem to pre-sensitize the bladder, making it more vulnerable, especially if certain other agents or promoters are present. These promoters include certain foods, drugs, chemicals, viruses, hormonal influences, chronic yeast infections and stress.

THE PERFECT DESIGN OF A WOMAN'S URINARY SYSTEM

A woman's urinary tract is designed very efficiently but quite differently from a man's. The main function of the urinary tract is to transport urine (which is the body's liquid wastes) from the kidneys and safely out of the body.

Urine travels from the kidneys to the bladder, which is a collapsible bag for holding urine. The bladder functions like a holding tank for urine. From the bladder the urine flows through the urethra to the outside.

A woman's urethra is two inches long while a man's is ten inches long. The woman's urethra is like a corrugated tube with a large surface area that can stretch and flatten out during childbirth to allow the baby's head to pass through.

Women have a muscle or sphincter located in the wall along the whole length of the urethra which acts like an on/off valve. This muscle allows control over the timing of urination. Urologists used to think that women didn't have this external sphincter and unknowingly ruptured this muscle by performing urethral dilations to stretch open the urethra. These days, this operation is rarely required.

When a woman urinates, the urethra is placed perfectly so that the urine streams over the outer and inner vaginal lips, over the area between the vagina and the rectum (the perineum), and finally over the rectum itself. As the urine streams over these areas, it thoroughly cleanses them.

The urine also cleanses the bladder as well, washing out the bacteria that normally accumulate inside it. In fact, bladder infections are not so much a matter of bacteria getting in, as they are a matter of the bacteria not getting out.

To wash the bacteria out of the bladder, it is necessary to have a good strong stream of urine flowing out. The force of a normal stream of urine should be able to "move dirt on the sidewalk," according to Dr. Gillespie. If a woman's urinary stream is sluggish and doesn't empty her bladder completely, this will predispose her to repeated bladder infections.

WHAT HAPPENS IN IC

The bladder itself is lined with a protective layer that is secreted, like mucous, by the cells that line the bladder. This protective layer protects the inside of the bladder from the acids and toxins in the urine and it also prevents bacteria from adhering to the bladder wall.

When this protective layer is damaged, it may cause the cells to leak, and exposes the small blood vessels in the bladder wall to urine, causing them to become overgrown. In addition, the urine can trigger nerve networks that are present in the deeper layers. As a result, burning, pain and frequent urination can result.

Dr. Gillespie discovered that IC was the result of a myriad of different factors, which resulted in damage to the lining and cells of the bladder.

ANTIBIOTIC USAGE

Dr. Gillespie postulated that certain antibiotics might, if no bacteria were present, end up attacking the bladder tissue itself. This could damage the all important protective layer of the bladder as well as the deeper layers, and cause the body to form antibodies to the altered bladder tissue.

In fact, Dr. Gillespie did biopsies of bladder tissues in women with IC and found that in one group of women the immune defence system of the body had been activated. A certain antibody pattern was found in bladder tissues if the woman had used nitrofurantoin, and another distinct pattern was found if erythromycin or tetracycline has been used. A third pattern was found if a combination of these drugs was used.

And as in other auto-immune diseases, where antibodies are formed against the body's own tissues, antibody formation can cause symptoms in a woman's joints, lungs and bowels.

In fact, as Dr. Kristene Whitmore, **Associate Professor of Urology** at the **University of Pennsylvania**, points out in her excellent book,**OVERCOMING BLADDER DISORDERS**, "Although it is a singular disease in many respects, interstitial cystitis has some striking similarities with certain other {auto-immune} diseases... such as lupus erythematosus, rheumatoid arthritis, asthma, allergic rhinitis (nasal congestion due to allergies) and polyarteritis (inflammation of the smaller arteries)."

SEROTONIN MAKES IT WORSE

Another piece of the puzzle fell into place when Dr. Gillespie realized that many of the foods that bothered her patients with IC contained tryptophan, tyramine or tyrosine. These substances are amino acids which are the building blocks of proteins. They stimulate the production of serotonin and norepinephrine.

Serotonin and norepinephrine are made in the brain from food and transmit messages between nerves. Recently these neurotransmitters were discovered to be present in the bladder and the gut.

Increased serotonin production could account for the electric shocks that some women experience. Increased serotonin and norepinephrine could also cause referred pain to the urethra and the clitoris.

Serotonin could cause blood vessels in the bladder to narrow and go into spasm, resulting in the throbbing bladder pain or "migraine" of the bladder that some women experience.

Over the counter cold medicines, some cough syrups and diet pills make IC worse because they increase the production of norepinephrine.

VIRAL INFECTION

IC can be caused by the **Epstein Barr** virus or other viruses. Some women with IC may also have chronic fatigue and immune system dysfunction (**CFIDS**). Fibromyalgia, now recognized as part of CFIDS, has also been associated with IC.

Viruses can be activated in the bladder by many factors, including a group of chemicals known as the phorbol esters. This group of chemicals is found in paints, lacquers, solvents, industrial chemicals, and in certain glues and polishes used by manicurists.

HIDDEN BACTERIAL INFECTIONS

Dr. Paul Fugazzoto is a microbiologist who has worked in the field over 50 years. He maintains that IC is caused by bacteria not found by the currently used methods of culturing urine specimens. By using different culturing techniques, he has found two predominant bacteria he believes are responsible for IC. The bacteria are known as enterococcus and gaffyka. Dr. Fugazzoto treats IC with long-term antibiotics, after he finds out exactly which organisms are causing the problem. **Ruth Kritz** did a small pilot study on Dr. Fugazzoto's patients, which found that 79 percent of those studied reported improvement on long-term antibiotic treatment. Since long-term antibiotic treatment may lead to chronic yeast infections, it is important to take acidophilus and other precautions to prevent this complication.

More recently, in October 1993, **Dr. Gerald Dominque**, **Professor of Microbiology and Immunology**, at **Tulane University**, in New Orleans, reported at the Interstitial Cystitis Association's seventh national meeting that his research has shown persistent bacterial DNA fragments in the bladder tissue os IC patients but not in patients without IC. Dr. Dominque believes he is months away from identifying the elusive bacteria.

OTHER ENVIRONMENTAL FACTORS

Although as yet unproven, it appears that pesticides in ground water, proximity to toxic waste sites, household cleaners, poor quality of indoor air, and other sources of environmental pollution can precipitate attacks of IC in some women.

YEAST INFECTION

Once the lining of the bladder is altered, yeast can penetrate bladder cells and break down the bladder defences further. Women can also have the yeast growing throughout their whole digestive tract. Women with these chronic yeast infections have to be treated specifically for this problem as well as for the IC. Many women do not begin to get better until their yeast infection is properly treated. The chapter on yeast infections outlines the types of treatment that are required including diet, acidophilus and anti-yeast preparations.

HORMONAL FACTORS

The female hormone progesterone tends to inhibit the formation of the protective lining of the bladder while the hormone estrogen increases it. Women on progesterone-estrogen combinations for menopausal symptoms may notice worsened cystitis symptoms. The birth control pill has also been linked to an increased incidence of bacteria in the urine and an increased incidence of bladder infections.

PSYCHONEUROIMMUNOLGY

This fancy term just means that your mind affects your body's resistance to illness. As with any chronic illness, emotional stress can bring on or worsen an episode of cystitis.

Researchers have clearly demonstrated that your thoughts and emotions can cause chemical changes in the brain which affect how your body works (the basis on which such techniques as self-hypnosis and imagery work).

Negative emotions such as anger and depression do hinder your recovery, but at the same time need to be expressed and released.

Beliefs are also important. You can't get better when you strongly believe you have an incurable condition.

CHRONIC CYSTITIS - THE INFECTIVE TYPE

If bacteria is repeatedly found in your urine then you have the infective type of chronic cystitis. This can be caused by a structural problem, such as an inherited malformation of your urinary tract, which prevents normal bladder or kidney function. These abnormalities are usually diagnosed in childhood.

Most often, however, repeated bladder infections are not caused by structural problems but by functional problems. This means the structure of your bladder and the rest of your urinary tract is normal but for some reason, they are not functioning up to par.

Reasons for this include the following:

AN OBSTRUCTION or blockage anywhere along your urinary tract, such as that caused by a stone, can be responsible for your repeated infections. This blockage would show up on an IVP or kidney X-ray.

LOW BACK PAIN: According to Dr. Gillespie, this is a leading cause of this type of urinary tract infection in women. Injury or damage to your low back area can damage the nerves that go to your bladder. This damage causes your bladder not to empty completely, so that some urine is always left. This predisposes you to repeated infections. Once the pressure on these nerves is relieved, your infections will clear up.

PELVIC SURGERY: During hysterectomy or other pelvic surgery the nerves to the bladder can also be damaged. In this case, you would notice that your bladder symptoms began right after the surgery.

BIRTH CONTROL: Diaphragms that are too large can alter the angle of the bladder neck, making it difficult to empty the bladder completely. You can avoid this problem by making sure your diaphragm fits right, and by urinating before you put it in and six hours later, after you remove it.

Tampons can also cause the same problem. Women with chronic cystitis should remove tampons before they urinate, or use sanitary napkins. They should also use unbleached tampons and pads.

Excess spermicide, foam, or lubricant can also irritate the urethra and predispose you to infections. According to **Dr. Gregor Reid** (**Globe And Mail** May 15/93), spermicides destroy a woman's helpful bacteria and increase the risk of bladder infections by as much as four times.

SEXUAL PRACTICES: Too much sex, too little sex or oral sex do not cause cystitis. However, after sex it is important to urinate, but only after you have waited long enough to build up a good forceful stream to wash out the bacteria that have accumulated in the bladder.

NOT ENOUGH GOOD BACTERIA IN THE VAGINA

Dr. Andrew Bruce, **Chief of Urology**, and **Dr. Gregor Reid**, **Director of Urology Research**, at **Toronto General Hospital** have been studying women with chronic bladder infections.

"When we looked at the two groups of women, those who did not have infections, had beautiful growths of lactobacilli," Dr. Bruce commented in the **Toronto Star** (Apr13/92). "The lactobacilli seem to have a protective effect. A significant number of women who had repeated infections had a poor population of lactobacilli."

As a result, Dr. Bruce and his research team developed an experimental vaginal suppository called **Restoration Plus**. It contains two key strains of lactobacilli called lactobacillus casei and lactobacillus fermentum.

In the study, one group of 28 women with four proven bladder infections within the past 12 months, was treated with the acidophilus suppositories; the other group with inert suppositories. Another arm of the study treated 40 women with acute bladder infections with a three-day course of antibiotics followed by a three-month course of Restoration Plus, and compared it to results with 20 women treated with antibiotics followed by three months of placebo.

The results of this study have shown Restoration Plus to be a very effective preventative treatment for bladder infections. Acidophilus suppositories seem to stimulate the normal growth of lactobacilli in the vagina. The treatment is given once a week for six to 12 months. Dr. Reid estimates that the new treatment could save the North American health care system $150 million a year.

TESTING PROCEEDURES IF YOU SUSPECT YOU HAVE INFECTIOUS CYSTITIS

1. Always give a urine sample before starting on antibiotics.

You can also purchase urine dipsticks at any drug store, or through your doctor, that can screen for urinary infections. If there are no bacteria found in your urine, stop taking the antibiotic right away. If there are usually no bacteria found in your urine, you may suspect that you have IC.

2. Also make sure your urine has been examined under the microscope to check for blood and pus cells and help make a more accurate diagnosis.

3. If bacteria repeatedly show up in your urine, you should have an IVP or X-ray of your kidney done at least once.

An IVP is an X-ray of your kidneys and urinary tract taken after an iodine dye is injected into your veins. The dye makes your kidneys and whole urinary tract visible on the X-ray.

4. You should have a pelvic exam and make sure cultures are done for yeast, trichomonas and chlamydia. These can cause vaginal infections that can cause burning when you urinate.

POINTERS ON TREATMENT OF INFECTIOUS CYSTITIS

If you have a proven infection, try to avoid taking the antibiotics tetracycline, nitrofurantoin and erythromycin. Sulfa drugs, cephalosporin, ampicillin or amoxicillin are preferable.

A one to three-day course of treatment is usually all that is necessary for a simple bladder infection that doesn't involve the kidneys. In most cases, this shorter course of treatment has been found to be just as effective as the longer ten-day course of treatment.

1. After you finish your antibiotics, you should always return with another sample of urine to make sure your infection has cleared up.

2. Women with repeated bladder infections should have urine cultures done on a regular basis even if they don't have symptoms.

3. Drink plenty of fluids, especially water.

4. When symptoms first start drink one teaspoon of baking soda in a glass of water, one time only.

Alternatives are **TUMS**, or one teaspoon of potassium citrate four times a day to help make the urine more alkaline.

5. Avoid acid foods and large doses of vitamin-C.

Dr. Whitmore notes that foods can affect the urine within 20 minutes. Use only buffered vitamin-C.

6. If you have repeated infections, you may want to try acidophilus suppositories placed in the vagina every night for a week, then once a week for six months to a year.

You can use a high quality dairy free acidophilus powder available in any health food store, and put it in 00 gelatin capsules.

POINTERS ON DIAGNOSIS AND TREATMENT OF INTERSTITIAL CYSTITIS

1. A urine culture will usually be negative. A complete blood count, a thyroid function test and a test for EBV and other viruses should also be done.

2. Diagnosis is usually made through ruling out other causes and performing a cystoscopy examination under a general anesthetic. Cystoscopy is usually too painful to perform under a local anesthetic.

The cystoscope is a lighted instrument that illuminates the inside of your bladder. The bladder is checked to see if its holding capacity is reduced, and for an over-growth of tiny blood vessels, pinpoint bleeding sites, and ulcers, which point to a diagnosis of interstitial cystitis. A biopsy can be also be taken to see if antibodies have developed to bladder tissue or if there is a high mast cell count which indicates inflammation.

3. Dr. Whitmore also suggests that you have **urodynamic studies.**

These types of studies will show how much urine your bladder holds and whether the bladder is emptying completely. They will also measure the flow of urine and test the function of muscles needed to urinate normally.

4. If you suspect IC, educate yourself and your doctor about the problem.

I suggest you present your GP and/or urologist with copies of the latest medical research on IC (available through the Interstitial Cystitis Association) and a copy of Dr. Whitmore's book, Overcoming Bladder Disorders. More resources are listed below.

5. Treatment of IC requires the help of a sympathetic doctor.

Fortunately more urologists are becoming aware of this complex problem. Dr. Gillespie found that IC was not really one disease but many, all resulting in damage to the bladder wall. Thus treatment must be highly individualized according to the specific causes and stages of the disease.

DIMETHYL SULFOXIDE (DMSO): This is the most common treatment used. DMSO is a liquid anti-inflammatory agent that is instilled in the bladder (through a catheter) once a week or so. The patient holds the medication in her/his bladder for up to a half an hour (although you can ask the nurse to leave the catheter in and clamp it off). This drug leaves a strong garlic-like odour on the skin and breath for about 24 hours after treatment. An odour-free type of DMSO called DMSO-2 is being developed.

Studies have shown that 50 to 90 percent of women with mild to moderate interstitial cystitis get improvement with DMSO. Fifty to 70 percent of women with severe IC get good to excellent results with DMSO.

For some, Dr. Gillespie instills a "cocktail" of DMSO, sodium bicarbonate, and steroids directly into the bladder, under general anesthetic every week for six weeks or until the bladder starts to heal. In severe cases of IC, she also uses the drug angiostat, which stops the tiny blood vessels in the bladder from overgrowing.

Dr. Whitmore uses a cocktail including all the above ingredients, but substitutes a local anesthetic for DMSO. This mixture seems to offer relief to half the people who have tried it. Studies are under way to further evaluate this treatment.

DIET: For some women, a restricted diet, low in acid as well as low in tryptophan and tyrosine may eliminate most of the burning sensation. If chronic yeast infection is present, a short-term diet with no sugar, fruit, yeasted bread, or dairy may be optimal. Food allergies can be tested through an elimination diet. Foods to which a person is sensitive can sometimes trigger a bladder attack.

It is very important to avoid artificial sweeteners like cyclamates or aspartame (nutrasweet). These not only irritate the bladder, they cause sugar cravings and fluctuations of blood sugar levels.

MOOD-ALTERING DRUGS: If diet alone does not control the burning sensations, some women have been helped by very low doses of elavil (an anti-depressant medication) in the range of ten to 40mg a day, usually taken at bedtime.

ANTIHISTAMINES: While over the counter anti-histamines (H1 blockers) may help, more effective are H2 blockers, drugs normally used to treat ulcers, like tagamet, zantac, and pepsid.

TENS UNIT: "Transcutaneous electrical nerve stimulation" involves using electrical stimulation of acupuncture points to reduce pain. A minimum of a four to six week trial should be tried.

ELMIRON or sodium pentosanpolysulfate is an expensive oral medication that is believed to coat the bladder and protect it from irritants. This drug may take up to three months before improvement is noticed. In April 1993, elmiron was approved for the Canadian market and in March 1996 for the U.S. It is available by prescription.

The major side effects are diarrhea and gastrointestinal problems. Preliminary studies show that this drug helps between 25 and 50 percent of those who tried the medication. More research is under way.

Dr. Ramon Perez-Marrero believes that elmiron is like heparin (a drug that decreases blood clotting) that you can take by mouth. Since heparin is far cheaper, Dr. Perez-Marrero feels it might make more sense to put heparin into the bladder. In his experience with severe IC, instillation of heparin into the bladder helped 40 to 50 percent of people with severe IC. Dr. Perez-Marrero also warns that elmiron use may lead to the development of osteoporosis, but heparin will not.

NALMEFENE: This new drug is believed to help IC by stopping the release of histamine and other substances which may be released within the bladder wall. Histamine is produced by cells in allergic or inflammatory reactions. A well designed study of this drug is now taking place at **McMaster University**.

BLADDER DISTENTION: This consists of filling the bladder with water for varying amounts of time, from a few minutes to several hours. According to Dr. Whitmore, "About 30 to 50 percent of people who undergo this procedure experience a lessening of symptoms for up to six months or longer."

LASER TREATMENT: Women with severe IC with pain and bleeding from ulcers in the bladder wall, may obtain some relief from having these ulcers burned with a laser. This must be done by an experienced surgeon as there is a danger of burning through the bladder wall.

BLADDER RETRAINING: This consist of very gradually training the bladder to stretch more, thus enabling a woman to urinate less frequently. Dr. Perez-Marrero describes it as "you get to know your bladder, and it gets to know you." Dr. Whitmore has found that after the pain of IC is controlled, bladder training has been very useful in reducing urinary frequency.

OZONE TREATMENTS: Dr. Frank Shallenberger, in Minden Nevada, 702-782-4164, has had excellent results using ozone inserted into the bladder through a catheter. This treatment is still experimental. Anti-oxidant supplements must always be taken with any ozone treatments. Contact **Maggie Burston** of **PICI** for more information.

CHIROPRACTIC ADJUSTMENTS: Studies have shown abnormalities of the fourth and fifth lumbar vertebrae in women with IC. Dr. Gillespie now works with a chiropractor who corrects the alignment of these vertebrae. This can result in improvement of pain and frequency of urination.

HARMFUL TREATMENTS: Certain treatments appear to do more harm than good. This includes the instillation of silver nitrate to burn out ulcers from bladder tissue. Surgical remedies, such as cutting off the top of the bladder, known as "bladder augmentation" are not useful. Urethral dilations, where the urethra is stretched open with a series of thin metal rods, worsen IC. No studies have demonstrated the benefit of any of these treatments.

6. Some women have obtained excellent relief from chronic bladder problems using a combination of diet, herbs, vitamins and homeopathic remedies.

Chinese medicine in the form of acupuncture and herbs works well for some women. Good results for all these methods usually depend on the supervision of an experienced practitioner who can individualize your treatment program.

According to **Dr. Matthew Lee**, who has done extensive research on acupuncture, "If you are going to get results from acupuncture, 50 percent of patients will do so within three sessions, and 90 to 95 percent will do so within six sessions (ICA update, summer 1992)."

Treatment of chronic yeast infection, if present, can result in marked improvement in both types of chronic cystitis. Emotional stresses, food allergies and environmental factors will also have to be examined closely.

It is important to remember that while there is still a lot we don't know about IC, much can be done to bring the problem under control and allow a person to lead a normal life.

SPONTANEOUS REMISSION: Dr. Perez-Marrero has reported that some women get diagnosed with IC, and then within two to five years get completely better, "without the help of anyone except themselves." In addition, he says, "I think that you can go into remission for a long time; whether you get rid of it forever or not, I don't know, because we haven't followed enough patients long enough to find out."

Why some people get better on their own is unknown, but a major life change or change in attitude may be a key factor.

RESOURCES

Highly recommended is **OVERCOMING BLADDER DISORDERS**, by **Rebecca Chalker and Dr. Kristene Whitmore** (Harper and Rowe, 1991). This is an excellent well written overview by a sympathetic doctor. It provides some discussion of natural treatments. Dr. Whitmore has also made a video entitled, "**MANAGING IC**" available from ICA Canada (see address below).

Dr. Gillespie's clear and practical book called, **YOU DON'T HAVE TO LIVE WITH CYSTITIS**, published in 1986 by Macmillan Canada, and now available in Avon paperback is also highly recommended. **THE INTERSTITIAL CYSTITIS FOUNDATION**, which supports research in the field, has a quarterly newsletter, and publishes a cookbook of bladder-proof recipes. There address is:

THE INTERSTITIAL CYSTITIS FOUNDATION, 120 South Spalding Dr, #210, Beverley Hills, CA, 90212.

UNDERSTANDING CYSTITIS, A Complete Guide to Overcoming Thrush and Cystitis, by **Angela Kilmartin** (Arrow Books, 1989) Angela Kilmartin is a world authority on self-help for chronic cystitis.

Although she doesn't distinguish between the two different kinds of cystitis, her book is loaded with practical information. Even more exciting, is the fact that since 1971, she has been able to help countless thousands of women for whom the medical profession could do nothing. She emphasizes proper hygiene as well as consideration of a multitude of factors including hormones, sexual activity and yeast infection. At the end of the book, she has developed a check-list and concrete plan of how to deal with episodes of pain and disability.

THE INTERSTITIAL CYSTITIS ASSOCIATION (ICA), PO Box 1553, Madison Square Stn, New York, NY, 10159.

The **ICA** was founded in 1984 by **Vicki Ratner**, a New York physician, and other patients in California. The Association has three main goals:

1. To provide support for IC patients and their families through support groups and telephone and mail support networks.

2. To disseminate information about the disease to patients, medical professionals and the general public.

3. To support and lobby for funding for research into IC.

The Canadian address is:

THE INTERSTITIAL CYSTITIS ASSOCIATION: PO Box 5814, Stn A, Toronto, ON, M5W 1P2. 416-920-8986, Fax: 416-968-9081.

In British Columbia there is the **BCICA**, a non-profit society providing support and information for people with painful bladder syndrome. There addresss is:

THE INTERSTITIAL CYSTITIS ASSOCIATION OF B.C., 1204-2024 Fullerton Ave, North Vancouver, BC, V7P 3G4.

In Canada, **Maggie Burston** of the **Candida Research Information Service** has done extensive research on IC as well as chronic yeast infections. She runs a patient information service for these problems called:

Patient Information on Chronic Illness (PICI), 575 Avenue Rd #601, Toronto, ON, M4V 2K2.

Private consultations are available in person or by telephone.

Dr. Paul Fugazzoto, Director Urinary Research Center, 624 6th St, Rapid City, SD, 57701. 605-343-9495.

Dr. Fugazzoto will give you a sample bottle and instructions on how to take the sample and mail it correctly. The cost of mailing is about $6.00 and the suggested donation for the analysis is $15 to $20 U.S. funds. It takes five days for the culture process and another four to five days for results to come back to you. You can call the lab for faster results.

ADDENDUM

In February 1995, **Bioniche Inc**. of London Ontario announced a new treatment for IC called Cystistat. It is installed directly into the bladder and acts as a membrane replacement. Cystistat, marketed as a medical device, is actually a solution of sterile sodium hyaluronate, a natural substance found in the body which is an acid mucopolysaccharide present in the ground substance of connective tissue that acts as a binding and protective agent. It is also found in the synovial fluid (fluid between the joint surfaces) and vitreous and aqueous humors (in the eye). The theory is that the drug will act as a temporary replacement for the defective mucosal lining.

A preliminary study of 21 patients, who previously failed to respond to all other treatments, showed that with Cystistat 70 percent experienced significant relief and 30 percent had some improvement. Further studies are underway at various medical centers across Canada. The best results appear evident after at least 16 weeks on the treatment.

Chlamydia - The Greatest Threat To Reproductive Health

Do you have a new lover in your life? Getting vague low abdominal pains and your doctor doesn't know why? Does it hurt when you urinate but your urine cultures always come back negative? Do you have a pelvic infection that doesn't clear up with the usual antibiotics?

You may have chlamydia (pronounced kluh mid-DEE-uh) the most common sexually transmitted disease in the U.S. and Canada.

"Sure", says **Dr. Philip Hall, Professor and Chief of Obstetrics and Gynecology** at **St. Boniface Hospital** in Winnipeg, "AIDS is a lethal and devastating disease, but undiagnosed chlamydia can cause terrible damage. Yet all the publicity goes to the human immune virus."

Dr. Hall represents a group of concerned physicians who say that the chlamydia problem remains unacknowledged and unrecognized by patients and health care professionals alike, obscured by the undeserved degree of panic about AIDS. "The good news," says Dr. Hall, "is that chlamydia is simple to test for and easy to cure."

CHLAMYDIA A SERIOUS PROBLEM

Every year in Canada an estimated half a million women will become infected with chlamydia, yet 60 percent of them will have no symptoms. In the U.S, in one year, at least four million women will be infected with chlamydia, and the disease is probably more prevalent than that because if is often missed and often under reported.

"It's an insidious disease and the leading cause of sterility in women," says **Dr. William Bowie**, faculty member of the **UBC Division of Infectious Diseases** and a leading chlamydia researcher in Canada.

For over ten years Dr. Bowie has been attempting to get doctors and health officials across Canada to pay attention to this important infection. Fortunately, chlamydia testing is now available in most doctors' offices, and physicians are starting to realize how prevalent chlamydial infection is.

Chlamydia may travel up into the womb and tubes causing scarring and even permanent closure. Some experts estimate that chlamydia causes 50 percent of pelvic infections and 25 percent of tubal pregnancies.

WHAT IS CHLAMYDIA ?

Chlamydia is neither a typical bacteria nor a virus. It is very small, much like a virus in size. It has some characteristics of a bacteria but it cannot manufacture its own energy. It therefore acts like a parasite, entering cells and using their energy. It starts off as little contagious particles (called elementary bodies or EB's) which attach to the cell and then duplicate inside the cell. Within 72 hours a whole bunch of EB's are then expelled from the cell, and the cycle continues.

Unfortunately, chlamydia can persist for a long time unsuspected and produce low grade inflammation. As Dr. Bowie explains, "Chlamydia is well adapted to infect women but not make them sufficiently sick that they are aware of the problem. Yet unrecognized chlamydia infection can make women sterile. The burden falls most heavily on young women."

Besides frequently not producing any symptoms, chlamydia is very difficult to culture. These two factors make it very challenging to track chlamydia down.

HOW CAN YOU TEST FOR CHLAMYDIA ?

Chlamydia cultures have only been widely available in Canada since the mid 1980's. Unfortunately, this type of cell culture is expensive, labour intensive and time consuming. However, this culture, (if performed in a reliable lab) is still the most sensitive test for chlamydia. It takes three to four days to complete. It should ideally be used for screening low risk groups, such as university students or women with only one steady sexual partner. Practically speaking, this culture is not widely available due to expense.

About eight years ago two other screening tests were put on the market. These other tests are quicker and less expensive but not as accurate as the cell culture test. In the first test the direct fluorescent antibody test (**DFA**), a specially prepared slide is examined under the microscope for EB's. In the second test the **ELISA** test (enzyme-linked immunoabsorbent assay) the presence of chlamydia is measured using a colour meter.

Both tests are only 75 to 80 percent accurate in detecting chlamydia. This means there can be both false negatives and false positives. A false positive can cause a lot of havoc in a relationship. If you have a positive test, and you are in a low risk group, you should remember that a positive test indicates a heightened risk rather than proving conclusively that you have chlamydia. Also chlamydia can be carried for a long time, certainly more than a year, and the infection could have been acquired in the past and gone unrecognized.

A false negative can cause chlamydia to go untreated and be passed on to other people. **Dr. James McSherry**, **Medical Director of Student Health Services** in Kingston, Ontario, feels that these two tests still have an unacceptably high false negative rate.

He feels that it makes sense to treat contacts of people with chlamydia infections even without taking cultures, certainly whether cultures are positive or not.

Both tests are constantly being improved, so these tests may become more accurate in the future.

The DFA test can also be used to test urine (urinary test kits for chlamydia are now available in larger cities). Because of their low sensitivity, urine tests are probably only useful to confirm infection in men who have symptoms. So far the urine tests have not been very valuable as a screening test.

However, a completely new approach for urinary testing is being developed that is much more sensitive; it can measure tiny DNA fragments of the chlamydial cell wall. This testing method is not yet widely available. However, it may end up being useful for testing both men and women who have no symptoms.

WHO IS AT RISK FOR CHLAMYDIA ?

Studies of risk profiles show the highest risk if you are under 24, have had a new sex partner within six months and are using no birth control or a non-barrier method of birth control.

When doctors say that sexually active women with many partners are at risk for chlamydia, what this means for all practical purposes is that any woman who has had more than one sexual partner, or whose sexual partner has had more than one sexual partner is at risk.

If you have just been diagnosed with herpes, gonorrhea or another sexually transmitted disease, you have a 30 to 60 percent chance of also having chlamydia.

Says **Dr. McSherry**, "Widespread use of the pill has set the scene for wholesale spread of chlamydia." The pill causes changes in the cervix that make it more susceptible to chlamydia infection as well as other sexually transmitted diseases. In addition, **Dr. Richard Boroditsky**, a Winnipeg gynecologist and researcher, points out that breakthrough bleeding while on the pill may be caused by chlamydia and easily missed.

PROTECTING YOURSELF

Condoms afford the best protection against chlamydia as well as against gonorrhea, herpes, venereal warts and AIDS. The diaphragm and cervical cap do provide more protection against chlamydia than the pill, but it is not yet certain that their level of protection is as high as the condom.

However, a new study of women with sexually transmitted diseases conducted in Denver, Colorado, showed that women who used diaphragms (or cervical caps) had 65 percent less gonorrhea and 72 percent less chlamydia compared to women who used no birth control. For women whose partners used condoms, chlamydia was reduced by three percent and gonorrhea by 34 percent. In all likelihood, condom use was inconsistent, and the spermicides used with caps or diaphragms may have provided added protection.

Surgical procedures such as IUD fitting, abortion, D-and-C, fetal monitoring, salpingography (a procedure where the tubes are outlined with a dye to check for blockage) can cause chlamydia to spread higher and affect the lining of the uterus and the tubes. Therefore it is preferable to have a negative chlamydia culture confirmed before these procedures and at the first prenatal visit.

WHEN YOUR DOCTOR SHOULD SUSPECT CHLAMYDIA

The doctor herself should be on the look-out for chlamydia if she notes a heavy yellowish greenish discharge from the cervix, and a stain of cervical cells shows more than ten pus cells per high power field. She may also be suspicious if the cervix bleeds easily while taking the PAP smear. Sometimes there is also a characteristic yellow or yellow-greenish colour on the white swab used for taking the culture.

There are certain signs of infection in the PAP smear itself that could provide clues to chlamydia, but these are not present enough of the time to make this a reliable screening test.

Your doctor should also suspect chlamydia if you complain of urethral and or bladder irritation and pus cells are found in the urinalysis but nothing is grown on the culture.

Dr. H. Hunter Handsfield of the **Seattle King Department of Public Health** and his colleagues did a study of just over 1,000 women and found that if women had two or more of the following factors, this would predict 90 percent of chlamydial infections. These factors were: age 24 or less, sex with a new partner in the preceding six months, internal exam showing yellow-green discharge from the cervix; bleeding from the cervix caused by taking the culture, and finally no birth control or non-barrier birth control method.

HOW OFTEN SHOULD YOU GET CHECKED ?

Most of the time there are no symptoms, so a sexually active woman has to insist to be checked routinely at least once a year and once for every new sexual partner. When you go to your doctor for a check-up, a sample will be taken from the cervix during an internal exam.

It is especially important that women under 24 be checked every year and frequently throughout the year if they have made love with a new person. The highest incidence of chlamydia is highest in women 15 to 19 years.

SYMPTOMS AND COMPLICATIONS OF CHLAMYDIAL INFECTIONS

The main symptoms of the women who are fortunate enough to have warning symptoms are increased or abnormal vaginal discharge, lower abdominal pain, and pain on urination. There can also be irregular vaginal bleeding and upper abdominal pain.

The most serious complication of chlamydia is acute or chronic pelvic infection, which if left untreated or if treated incorrectly, can lead to permanent infertility, painful disabling periods and possible hysterectomy.

After one episode of PID, says the **Canadian PID Society**, a woman's chance of becoming infertile is 15 percent, after three episodes of PID, the risk of infertility is over 50 percent. Furthermore, after only one episode of PID, a woman has a tenfold increased risk of ectopic pregnancy (a tubal pregnancy that has to be ended surgically). Tubal pregnancies can rupture and bleed thereby causing a life threatening emergency.

Women with IUDs have a much higher risk of PID than women not using IUDs. For this reason, I do not advise IUDs as a form of birth control, especially in women who have never had any children.

The **Canadian PID Society** lists the following symptoms of PID: lower abdominal pain, lower back pain, fatigue, fever, vaginal discharge, vaginal bleeding, abdominal swelling and increased sedimentation rate (a general blood test which suggests inflammation). Some women also experience painful sex and painful periods. However, few women experience all these symptoms. Most experience only one or two.

The first symptom that women usually experience is low mild dull bilateral pelvic pain.

Recent studies suggest that chlamydia is a major cause of infertility in women. Infertile women, who in the course of investigations were found to have scarred or blocked tubes, were often not aware that they even had PID. Researchers confirmed that chlamydia was the most likely cause of these silent pelvic infections.

Chlamydias may attach themselves to sperm and travel on to the uterus and tubes on them. Women undergoing artificial insemination or IVF should make sure that their sperm donor has been tested for all sexually transmitted diseases, especially chlamydia. Some doctors recommend that women take two weeks of antibiotics, as a preventative measure, before undergoing these procedures.

"It is interesting to note that the current interest in IVF," says **Dr. King Holmes**, Chief of Medicine at **Seattle's Harbour View Medical Center**, "is in some part a reflection of previous damage caused by chlamydia and gonorrhea. If the costs currently being put into treating people who already have tubal scarring were even partially put into early diagnosis and treatment of these diseases, the cost effectiveness of our research efforts to prevent infertility would be much greater. That's the bottom line."

Since chlamydia and gonorrhea often co-exist, anti-chlamydial treatment should be included in the treatment regimens for gonorrhea.

CHLAMYDIA AND PREGNANCY

Chlamydia can also complicate pregnancy and be transmitted to the baby during birth.

Chlamydia is the number one cause of conjunctivitis (infection of the white part of the eye) in infants in the U.S. and Canada. It is usually causes a mild infection but occasionally causes severe damage and even blindness.

But by far the most serious outcome of chlamydial infection of pregnant women is that their babies can get pneumonia. Chlamydia is the leading cause of pneumonia among infants in the first six months of life.

The pneumonia is usually mild and can be treated at home. However, 25 percent of the time, it is serious enough to require hospitalization and intensive monitoring. As such, chlamydia pneumonia can be life-threatening and it can also lead to long-term respiratory complications.

One study showed that infants exposed to chlamydia at birth had a higher incidence of ear infections in the first three years of life.

Several studies have shown that a higher incidence of stillbirth prematurity and infant death among women who have chlamydia, but more recent studies show no evidence to support this association.

Dr. Bowie feels that chlamydia infection in pregnant women can affect the pregnancy and the baby's outcome, but only very infrequently.

THE LIVER, THE PAP SMEAR AND MEN

As well as causing an inflammation of the tubes (PID) chlamydia can also cause perihepatitis at the same time. Perihepatitis is an inflammation of the liver capsule and the surrounding tissues. It causes the sudden onset of severe right upper abdominal pain, worse with deep breathing or coughing.

Several studies have found chlamydia cervical infections in a large percentage of women with abnormal Pap smear results.

In men, chlamydia can cause painful urination and painful swollen testes. Occasionally, chlamydia can cause sterility in men. It is also known to cause a rare type of arthritis in men. "The main problem with an infection in men," says **Dr. Robert Jones** of the **Indiana University Center**, "is that they will continue to infect women."

TREATING CHLAMYDIA

The most common treatment for chlamydia is tetracycline or erythromycin, given for at least seven days. Tetracycline comes in two forms: plain tetracycline, which costs about $16.00 per prescription and doxycycline which cost about $36.00. Doxycycline 100mg only has to be taken twice a day. Plain tetracycline 500mg has to be taken four times a day, on an empty stomach one hour before meals or two hours after meals.

In my experience, most people end up taking two or three pills instead of the four tetracycline per day essential for proper treatment. Therefore, if you know you are one of these people, then probably you should consider taking the more expensive form of tetracycline.

Side effects of tetracycline include stomach upset, alteration of the normal bacteria in the gut, photosensitivity and yeast infections.

Neither form of tetracycline can be taken by pregnant women. For pregnant women erythromycin is considered the best alternative. Erythromycin 500mg four times a day for seven days is the usual dosage. An alternative is erythromycin 250mg four times a day for 14 days. Directions must be carefully followed as some forms of erythromycin must be taken on an empty stomach to be effective.

For women with chronic yeast infections or those with bad reactions to tetracycline, the alternatives are either erythromycin for seven days as above or sulfamethoxazole one gram twice a day for ten days.

Women with a chronic yeast problem should take acidophilus capsules and possibly an anti-yeast medication such as oral mycostatin tablets along with their treatment.

It is of vital importance to take the whole seven or ten days of medication even if you feel better and hate to take pills.

Dr. Philip Hall recommends treatment for at least ten days instead of seven. He feels the risk of sterility is too great to take any chances. However, Dr. William Bowie feels that there is no proven advantage to taking the medication for longer than seven days.

The incubation period of chlamydia ranges from ten days to several months. It is easier to get rid of chlamydia if the infection is confined to the cervix and has not yet spread up to the uterus and tubes.

PARTNERS AND FOLLOW-UP

Both you and your partner and all your sexual contacts must be treated. Some doctors have considered making it a reportable disease and it is already in three provinces and nineteen states. Fortunately, to date there have been no cases of chlamydia that are resistant to either tetracycline or erythromycin.

Repeat cultures for chlamydia are suggested four to six weeks after treatment is completed, especially for women who may have not taken all their pills or whose partner did not take all his pills. If you and your sexual partner(s) have all taken the treatment faithfully, then retesting may not be necessary.

TREATING PID: Acute PID caused by chlamydia is a very serious infection and it must be treated promptly and thoroughly. For women with PID treated at home, you need an injection of a drug called cefoxitin or its equivalent, followed by 14 days of doxycycline by mouth. In the hospital, PID caused by gonorrhea and/or chlamydia should be treated with a combination of doxycycline and cefoxitin intravenously for ten days, followed by doxycycline by mouth for ten to 14 days.

The Canadian PID Society stresses bed rest as an important part of treatment. They refer to the work of two world authorities on PID who recommend bed rest and antibiotics as the most effective treatment. Complete bed rest helps to keep the infection from spreading.

In addition, sex will also make the infection much worse, so you must refrain from sex until the infection has completely cleared up.

CONCLUSION

The best weapons against the insidious chlamydia are information, prevention, proper treatment and correct follow-up.

Any woman with a new pelvic pain or new vaginal discharge or burning on urination should get herself tested for chlamydia right away.

All women at high-risk should be checked routinely, especially teenagers and women under 24. Chlamydia should be part of the routine prenatal work-up and should also be performed prior to the insertion of an IUD. A woman should also be checked again every time she has a new sexual partner.

This seems like the least we could do to help prevent the chlamydia epidemic that is causing painful and disabling disease and wreaking havoc with women's future ability to have children.

THE CANADIAN PID SOCIETY, PO Box 33804, Stn D, Vancouver, BC, V67 4L6. 604-684-5704.

Their highly recommended booklet entitled, **PELVIC INFLAMMATORY DISEASE**, was written to provide information for women who have PID, their families, and health care professionals. PID is the leading cause of infertility and hysterectomy in young women, yet it is preventable.

THE MONTREAL HEALTH PRESS INC. PO Box 1000, Stn La Cite, Montreal, PQ. H2W 2N1.

This press has an excellent 50 page booklet entitled, **A BOOK ABOUT SEXUALLY TRANSMITTED DISEASES**, for $4.00 from that address. It also has excellent booklets on birth control, sexual assault and menopause.

Section Three:
Making The Most Of Your Pregnancy

Favourite Childbirth Books 94

The Amazing World Of The Unborn Child 98

**Should Every Pregnant Woman
Have An Ultrasound?** 101

Testing The Waters - All About Amniocentesis 108

The Challenge Of Pregnancy Over Thirty Five 112

**Keeping Fit While Pregnant Is Good
For You And Your Baby** 117

Dealing With The Discomforts Of Pregnancy 121

Favourite Childbirth Books

Pregnancy, birth and the beginning of motherhood represent one of the major life transitions you will experience as a woman. In fact, childbirth offers you an unparalleled opportunity for personal growth and change.

The more you know about every aspect of childbirth, the more options you'll have for you and your baby. Such a remarkable rite of passage should be faced with as much knowledge and foresight as possible.

At the same time, it will be important to know when to lay aside the advice of the experts and when to pay attention to your own body's responses and your own feelings.

To help you select from among the hundreds of childbirth books now available, I have selected some favourite books for your personal library. At the end of the chapter, I have listed book stores which also carry a good selection of books on a wider variety of topics including fathering, child development, high risk pregnancy, pregnancy loss and grieving, twins, and Cesarean births. It is a good idea to make sure that your local library stocks a good selection of these books as well.

CHOICE IN CHILDBIRTH

THE RIGHTS OF THE PREGNANT PARENT, revised 1980, by **Valmai Elkins**, is a well organized and clearly written consumer guide for parents who want to have choices in how their baby will be born in the hospital.

YOUR BABY, YOUR WAY: MAKING PREGNANCY DECISIONS AND BIRTH PLANS 1987, by **Sheila Kitzinger** is an excellent and supportive guide to help you choose from among the many birthing alternatives available to you.

PREGNANCY AND CHILDBIRTH PREPARATION

WHAT TO EXPECT WHEN YOU'RE EXPECTING, by Arlene **Eisenberg**, revised 1991, is a reassuring and informative month by month guide to pregnancy and childbirth.

PREGNANCY, CHILDBIRTH AND THE NEWBORN, THE COMPLETE GUIDE FOR EXPECTANT PARENTS, revised 1991, by **Penny Simkin** and others. This book gives up to date and thorough information on all aspects of pregnancy and childbirth so that parents can develop their own way of giving birth. It also offers strategies for dealing with the new technologies.

THE EXPERIENCE OF CHILDBIRTH 1984, by **Sheila Kitzinger** is written by one of the world's foremost childbirth educators, also a respected anthropologist and mother of five daughters. In her book, a classic in the field, she integrates the physical, social and psychological aspects of giving birth in a positive, realistic and highly readable style. She also describes the breathing and relaxation exercises that provide such a useful tool during labour and delivery.

THE COMPLETE BOOK OF PREGNANCY AND CHILDBIRTH, revised 1989, by **Sheila Kitzinger**. This book is a comprehensive and extensively illustrated guide to every aspect of pregnancy and birth. Highly recommended.

In fact, if you could only buy two books during your pregnancy, I would suggest these two books by Sheila Kitzinger.

THE BIRTH PARTNER: Everything You Need To Know To Help A Woman Through Childbirth, 1989, by **Penny Simkin**. On every childbirth educator's "most recommended" list.

BIRTH REBORN, revised 1995, by **Michael Odent** contains remarkable photographs of birthing women.

Written by the French doctor who created a model of safe and harmonious birth, it is based on the belief that the woman herself knows best how to birth.

BIRTH OVER THIRTY-FIVE, revised 1995, by **Sheila Kitzinger** thoughtfully and reassuringly reviews the joys and challenges facing the older mother.

MIND OVER LABOUR; USING THE MIND'S POWER TO REDUCE PAIN IN CHILDBIRTH, 1987, by **Carl Jones** is an eight step method using mental imagery to prepare for birth.

THE WELL PREGNANCY BOOK, 1986, by **Mike** and **Nancy Samuels** is a large, illustrated, comprehensive, well written guide for pregnancy including the emotional, physical and psychological aspects. A very worthwhile book, reasonably priced.

NUTRITION FOR MOTHER AND CHILD

AS YOU EAT, SO YOUR BABY GROWS, 1980 and now revised, by **Nikki Goldbach**. This 16 page booklet contains, in concise form, all you need to know about nutrition in pregnancy. It provides an easy-to-follow plan for getting optimum nutrition during pregnancy, as well as a discussion of essential nutrients and the foods they are found in, and advice on weight gain, diet and food related problems.

WHAT TO EAT WHEN YOU'RE EXPECTING, 1986, by **Arlene Eisenberg**, is a guide to eating nutritiously at home, at work and while travelling.

MOTHER AND BABY BOOK, 1993, by **Rose Elliot**, is a complete guide to nutrition and diet during and after pregnancy.

FEEDING YOUR BABY IN THE 90'S: From conception to age two, revised 1992, by **Louise Lambert-Lagace**, is a practical, highly readable book on how to feed your baby including recipes. **THE NUTRITION CHALLENGE FOR WOMEN**, by the same author is the best overall book for women on nutrition and specifically addresses their special needs.

Also remember to visit your local public health unit to obtain their excellent pamphlets on prenatal nutrition.

USING HERBS, HOMEOPATHY AND NUTRITION WISELY DURING PREGNANCY

HEALING YOURSELF DURING PREGNANCY, 1987, by **Joy Gardner**. A clearly written guide to herbs, vitamins and nutrition offering a holistic approach to pregnancy from inception to nursing the newborn baby.

ALTERNATIVE MATERNITY, revised 1995 by **Nicky Wesson** This book was written by a British woman who was forced to learn about alternative medicine when her two young children were sick and unable to be helped by conventional medicine. This book provides a comprehensive guide to alternative therapies, including acupuncture, homeopathy and herbs.

CHOOSING TO BIRTH OUTSIDE A HOSPITAL

HOMEBIRTH, THE ESSENTIAL GUIDE TO GIVING BIRTH OUTSIDE THE HOSPITAL, 1991, by **Sheila Kitzinger.** Kitzinger feels that choosing your own birthplace, one in which you feel most secure, is a fundamental right of women. She gives a thorough scientific backing to her assertion that home is a safe place for birth. "At present," she says, "saying "no" to a hospital... is for most of us, the only way to reclaim the experience of childbirth for women." Kitzinger herself birthed her five daughters at home in England.

THE BIRTH CENTER, by **Victor** and **Sallee Berman**. A physician and nurse-midwife detail their experiences at their birth center.

HEART AND HANDS, 2nd edition revised 1992, by **Elizabeth Davis**, is a comprehensive guide to the art and science of midwifery.

WATERBIRTH, THE CONCISE GUIDE TO USING WATER DURING PREGNANCY BIRTH AND INFANCY, by **Janet Balaskas**, 1992. This book explains how water can be used in the pregnancy and birth process and also gives information on baby massage and teaching babies to swim.

BREAST-FEEDING

THE COMPLETE BOOK OF BREAST-FEEDING, by **Marvin Eiger** and **Sally Olds**. This is a comprehensive and easy to read guide to breast feeding.

THE NURSING MOTHER'S COMPANION, by **Kathleen Huggins**, is a clear trouble-shooting aid for the new mother learning how to nurse.

WORKING WOMAN'S GUIDE TO BREAST-FEEDING, by **Dana** and **Price** is a guide for the woman who want to nurse her baby and work outside the home.

SUCCESSFUL BREAST-FEEDING, also by **Dana** and **Price**, is an excellent, well laid out book with an easy to use and positive format on how to enjoy the breast-feeding experience.

THE WOMANLY ART OF BREAST-FEEDING, by **La Leche League**. This book is the bible of breast-feeding. It is a comprehensive practical manual by the acknowledged experts in the field and also offers lots of instructions and supportive advice.

BREAST-FEEDING YOUR BABY, by **Sheila Kitzinger**. Once more the great childbirth educator excels in expert common sense advice and insight for breast-feeding mothers in a book with outstanding photos and illustrations, including the great differences in the size and shape of normal breasts.

THE NURSING MOTHER'S GUIDE TO WEANING, 1994, by **Kathleen Huggins** and **Linda Ziedrich**. Huggins, who mindfully excluded weaning issues from her earlier **THE NURSING MOTHER"S COMPANION**, has now provided a most comprehensive and practical exploration of the issues.

EXERCISE AND YOGA

ESSENTIAL EXERCISES FOR THE CHILD-BEARING YEAR, 3rd edition 1988, by **Elizabeth Noble** focuses on the key muscles involved in pregnancy and delivery and the exercises necessary to tone them. Ms. Noble's emphasis is on prevention of abdominal and perineal problems before they happen and the restoration of these muscles back to normal after the birth. She also has a special section on Cesarean birth and exercises with partners.

POSITIVE PREGNANCY FITNESS, by **Sylvia Klein Olkin**, is a practical guide that shows women how to get the most out of their pregnancy and birth through a total yoga and relaxation program for mental, physical and spiritual adjustment.

ACTIVE BIRTH, The New Approach to Giving Birth Naturally, by **Janet Balaskas**, revised 1992, is a well written encouraging guide to exercise and movement during pregnancy with an easy to follow program. It helps women develop all their bodily resources for labour and birth.

Also, make sure you obtain an excellent booklet available from **Fitness Canada**, 365 Laurier Ave West, Ottawa ON, K1A 0X6, entitled, **FITNESS AND PREGNANCY**.

EMOTIONAL AND MENTAL CARE

An often neglected aspect of pregnancy but one of the most crucial is emotional and mental care. The attitudes and feelings of the pregnant woman or couple will tell me the most about whether or not complications are likely to occur. Pregnancy can be a time of great emotional upheaval. The intensity and range of emotions experienced do not matter as much as a willingness to look at yourself and an acceptance of the validity of your feelings.

BIRTHING NORMALLY, by **Gayle Peterson**, 1984. This is the first book of its kind to explain how a woman's beliefs, attitudes, lifestyle and environment affect the outcome of labour and delivery. Ms. Peterson has a discussion of pain that is the best I have read as well as visualization exercises to promote positive outcomes for childbirth.

AN EASIER CHILDBIRTH, A Mother's Workbook for Health and Emotional Well-Being during Pregnancy and Delivery by **Gayle Peterson**, 1991. This excellent workbook enables a mother to sort out her emotions, beliefs and expectations around birth, and create a supportive environment for herself as well as a personalized birthing plan.

TRANSFORMATION THROUGH BIRTH, 1983, by **Claudia Panuthos**, is an unique and readable book that offers great insight into the emotions and psychology of the pregnant woman and how she can create a healthy and rewarding birth experience. Temporarily out of print, it will probably be reprinted soon.

PREGNANT FEELINGS, 1986, by **Rahima Baldwin** and **Terra Palmarini**, is a workbook for pregnant women and their partners to use in exploring the psychological and emotional issues associated with pregnancy, giving birth and being parents.

AFTER THE BIRTH

The first three months after the birth of a baby are often the most difficult for both the mother and father.

THE YEAR AFTER CHILDBIRTH, Surviving And Enjoying The First Year Of Motherhood, by **Sheila Kitzinger** (Harper Collins, 1994).

POSTPARTUM DEPRESSION AND ANXIETY, 1987, is a practical self-help guide for helping mothers understand what is happening and what can be done. Available for $5.00 from **Pacific Postpartum Support Society**, 1416 Commercial Dr, Vancouver, BC, V5L 3X9. 604-255-7999.

AFTER THE BABY'S BIRTH, A WOMAN'S GUIDE TO WELLNESS, 1991, by **Robin Lim**. Highly recommended, this book helps women and their families have a healthier, saner postpartum experience.

WHERE TO GET THESE BOOKS

1. Your local bookstore if they don't carry them, order them. With enough demand, your bookstore will begin stocking these books.

2. Mail order: For special interest areas or hard to obtain books.

    PARENTBOOKS, 201 Harbord St Toronto, ON, M5S 1IIS. 416-537-8334. Fax: 416-537-9499.

Parentbooks has over 10,000 books on pregnancy, childbirth, parenting, education and family health. You can send for a free book list and order by mail, phone or fax.

BIRTH AND LIFE BOOKSTORE, 7001 Alonzo Ave NW, PO Box 70625, Seattle, WA 98107-0625. 206-789-4444.

This bookstore offers an extensive selection of books and tapes on childbirth and related areas, and fills orders promptly. They also publish an excellent newsletter and catalogue called **IMPRINTS** which is available on request.

The Amazing World Of The Unborn Child

Over ten years ago, the first world conference on pre and perinatal psychology was held in Toronto with leading experts from all over the world. This new science brought forth evidence of the startling mental, physical, and emotional capacities of the unborn child.

When a child is born, it is called a "new" baby and its parents "new" parents. Actually, the parent-child relationship began at conception, if not before, and had nine months of interplay.

Evidence presented at the conference suggested that the events of pregnancy and birth can be recalled in adult life.

Dr. David Cheek, one of the speakers, was an experienced obstetrician as well as a skilled hypnotist. He regressed hundreds of adults back to their prenatal and birth experiences and was able to verify details of events remembered during hypnosis with hospital records.

Another speaker, **Dr. David Chamberlain**, a leading researcher in the field of prenatal and perinatal psychology, found that his clients were spontaneously recalling their births in great detail, and wondered how he might prove the validity of these memories. He finally managed to select ten mother-child pairs in which the mother said she never told the child anything in detail about the birth, and the child said she had no memories of the birth. He regressed both the mother and the child separately using hypnosis and found that memories matched very well.

In his own words: "The memories dovetailed on as many as 22 points in the story. You could just look through the stories and see them saying the same thing. Sometimes the same statements were quoted verbatim, sequences were right, the children were able to describe things like the mother's hairdo in the delivery room, or arrangements of the furniture in the mother's room after the delivery. So many details, that I just thought it was impossible to explain it as any kind of imagination."

So it seems that during prenatal and postnatal life a physiological and/or emotional imprint of events occurs which has not previously been acknowledged by medical science.

SOUND AND THE UNBORN

The unborn child can also remember sounds and respond to them. From 20 weeks gestation onward, the unborn hears sounds of low vibrational frequency. Studies have shown that if the mother or father hums the same tune to the child every day while it is in the womb, after the baby is born, it will immediately stop crying if it hears the tune again. The baby is also attuned to the voices of mother and father.

In addition, the baby can respond to external music while still in the womb. As many mothers know, the baby will kick with glee or make contented movements in response to music it likes, or squirm in response to music it dislikes. Mothers learn to distinguish the two types of movements.

Recently, researchers at the **University of Southern California** (USC) listened in to babies in the womb. By using specially designed microphones, they were amazed at the intensity of sounds they heard.

"In fact," says **Dr. Jeffery Phelan**, associate professor of obstetrics and gynecology at **USC**, "I couldn't believe what a baby is subjected to... I had to turn down the volume because my ears couldn't stand the noise." **Dr. Phelan** had been monitoring the exact sound levels as experienced by the baby.

"We heard almost everything," said co-researcher, **Dr. Satt**, "from people talking twelve feet away, to a door opening in another room, to a cart going down the hall, with the door closed."

Dr. Phelan admits their work raises a whole lot of questions. "We protect our ears from loud noises but what about the baby? No one knows at this point whether prolonged noise can be harmful to the baby. Perhaps, pregnant women need to start wearing T-shirts that read: **Quiet, Baby Under Construction.**"

SLEEP, ACTIVITY AND PLAYING

The unborn child also has a highly individual pattern of sleep and activity that its mother usually becomes aware of. After birth this information can be useful to mothers, although for some reason, mothers tend to forget that this is the same baby they knew so well in the womb.

Even in the womb, the child can socially interact in the form of a game. "I play with my baby," one mother said. "I push with one finger and the baby pushes back."

A question as yet left unexplored is the physical and emotional effect of the baby's thoughts and feelings on the mother.

HOW YOUR FEELINGS AFFECT THE BABY

For their part, mothers have always worried about the effects of their emotional state on the baby. Throughout pregnancy, mothers usually experience emotions ranging from fear, anger, depression, and sadness to hope, joy, and anticipation. None of these feelings damages the fetus.

However, violent rage or grief over death of a loved one may be detrimental to the fetus. If you happen to be experiencing that special kind of intense emotion, some therapists suggest you talk to your baby and explain, for example, that you are not angry at it but at another person or situation.

Inevitably, the great hormonal shifts that occur during pregnancy have a profound effect on your emotions. Your emotions may seem magnified; your reactions, sometimes, out of control. You may not be able to cope the way you used to. You may be more vulnerable to violent and upsetting images on television or in the movies.

This is the time to go easy on yourself and explain your situation to your baby. Accept the validity of your emotions. Work through them the best you can. Remember you may not be able to work through every issue. You may just have to surrender to this heightened state of emotional awareness.

If you want to explore your feelings further, I suggest you use workbooks like **PREGNANT FEELINGS**, or **AN EASIER CHILDBIRTH**, listed below. Relationships are often under stress during pregnancy and major issues may come up. Sometimes, a sympathetic therapist can be very helpful for both partners.

As much as you are able, surround yourself with calm, tranquillity and beauty. Set aside relaxation time every day and during that time talk to the baby, expressing your love, hopes and fears.

Fascinating discoveries are being made into the hitherto secret world of the unborn. This new knowledge ought not to make parents feel guilty or fearful. What really counts most to any child, whether unborn or not, is the warm love and devotion of its parents.

CONNECTING WITH YOUR UNBORN CHILD

1. **BABIES REMEMBER BIRTH, AND OTHER EXTRAORDINARY SCIENTIFIC DISCOVERIES ABOUT THE MIND AND PERSONALITY OF YOUR NEWBORN**, 1988, by Dr. David Chamberlain. This book presents startling new evidence of just how much a newborn knows and feels, and how newborns are actually aware of their birth.

2. **THE SECRET LIFE OF THE UNBORN CHILD**, 1981, by **Dr. Thomas Verny**. This book is written by the psychiatrist who is the founder of the Pre and Perinatal Psychology Association of North America. In it, he demonstrates that the unborn child is deeply influenced by its environment well before birth, and explores the significance of that fact.

3. **NURTURING THE UNBORN CHILD A NINE MONTH PROGRAM FOR SOOTHING, STIMULATING AND COMMUNICATING WITH YOUR UNBORN BABY** by **Dr. Thomas Verny** and **Pamela Weintraub**, 1991. This is a practical guide for couples to encourage the emotional development of their unborn child throughout the pregnancy. Verney has a nine month program of "Womb Harmonics" laid out in a very organized and concise fashion, from which parents can choose what appeals to them.

4. **BONDING BEFORE BIRTH, A GUIDE TO BECOMING A FAMILY**, 1991, by **Leni Schwartz**. Author Jean Houston says of this book, "The clear directives and luminous suggestions... can result in a whole new

way of becoming wise and loving parents." The book gives breathing and relaxation exercises to nurture the child within, to explore the environment and experience of the unborn child and to explore the transformation of birth.

DEALING WITH YOUR EMOTIONS

1. **AN EASIER CHILDBIRTH, A Mother's Workbook for Health and Emotional Well-Being during Pregnancy and Delivery**, by **Gayle Peterson**, 1991. This excellent workbook enables a mother sort out her emotions, beliefs and expectations around birth. It also helps her create a supportive environment as well as a personalized birthing plan.

2. **PREGNANT FEELINGS**, 1986, by **Rahima Baldwin** and **Terra Palmarini**. This is a workbook for pregnant women and their partners to use in exploring the psychological and emotional issues associated with pregnancy, giving birth and being parents.

3. **TRANSFORMATION THROUGH BIRTH**, 1983, by **Claudia Panuthos**, is an unique and readable book that offers great insight into the emotions and psychology of the pregnant woman and how she can create a healthy and rewarding birth experience.

Should Every Pregnant Woman Have An Ultrasound?

From the crude type of ultrasound available in the 1950's, ultrasound (US) has developed into a highly sophisticated diagnostic tool for use during pregnancy. Ultrasound use has grown rapidly to the point where most pregnant women now receive one or more ultrasound exams during their pregnancies. According to 1987 update report on ultrasound by **Health and Welfare Canada**, up to 80 percent of all newborns are exposed to ultrasound.

However, the long-term safety of such exposure for newborns has not yet been proven, and the use of ultrasound for every pregnancy is not officially recommended by experts. Both doctors and women need to take a serious look at whether such widespread use of ultrasound is really beneficial for the baby or the mother.

WHAT IS ULTRASOUND ?

Ultrasound is the name given to sound waves that are much higher in pitch and frequency than can be heard by the human ear. Early in this century, scientists discovered that these high pitched sound waves travelled thorough water, and like audible sound waves, could bounce off objects in their path and return to the sender in the form of an echo. These echoes could then be collected and used to form an electronic picture of objects in the path of these waves. Along with advances in electronics, these discoveries led to the development of ultrasound as a diagnostic tool in many fields of medicine. In fact, one of the main advantages of ultrasound is that it provides information that previously could only be obtained through X-rays or even surgery.

In obstetrics, ultrasound, also called sonography, is the use of an echo sounder to produce a picture of the baby in utero. High frequency low energy sound waves are used to scan the mother's abdomen and reflect the fetus outline on an electronic screen in a series of bright dots.

In order to prepare for an obstetrical ultrasound, a woman must drink approximately six glasses of water about one hour before the exam and not empty her bladder until after the test. A full bladder is necessary to allow a better view of the uterus and the baby.

There is another type of ultrasound used during pregnancy and that is the hand held electronic stethoscope, called the **Doppler Stethoscope**. It is used in the office to listen to the baby's heartbeat early on in pregnancy. This could be usually done just as well using an ordinary fetal stethoscope.

The routine ultrasound exam uses pulsed ultrasound waves at a higher output, for very short periods of time. By contrast, the doppler stethoscope uses continuous low output ultrasound waves for a longer time. The overall ultrasound exposure to the fetus is greater, and it is often repeated at every prenatal visit, starting early on in the pregnancy.

THE DEBATE ON ROUTINE VERSUS SELECTIVE USE OF ULTRASOUND

It is important to be clear on the difference between **routine** ultrasound and **selective** ultrasound.

ROUTINE ultrasound is done for healthy low risk pregnant women whose pregnancy is progressing normally. The exam is usually performed quickly and therefore may be less accurate.

SELECTIVE ULTRASOUND is done for women who are at high risk for complications during their pregnancy or who develop complications during their pregnancy. This ultrasound exam takes longer and may focus on answering specific questions posed by your doctor.

Doctors do not agree on whether ultrasound should be used routinely or not, and scientific proof that routine use is justified is still lacking.

Four studies have been done comparing the outcome for groups of women who had US to groups of women who didn't. Only one study was thought to be supportive of routine US. All four studies had small numbers, even when pooled. Also the studies have been criticized because of varying design quality and outcomes studied.

A larger study has just been completed in the Helsinki area of Finland. It involved about 10,000 women. These were divided into two groups of 5,000 for comparison, one to receive ultrasound, one control group not scheduled for US. However, 75 percent of women in the control group had already received an ultrasound exam before the study started. The study found that there were no differences in birth weights or number of labour inductions in the two groups. There was no statistical difference in the outcome for the babies in the two groups, if babies that were aborted due to major fetal malformations detected during US were subtracted. In other words, the main value of the US shown in this study was to detect major fetal malformations and give the parents the choice of whether to abort.

The **National Institute of Child Health and Human Development** in the U.S. has funded a 12 million dollar landmark study on the value of routine ultrasound, co-ordinated by **Dr. Bernard Ewigman**, **Professor** at the **University of Missouri-Columbia School of Family and Community Medicine**. Over 15,000 women were enroled in this study. One group received two ultrasound exams, one at 18 to 22 weeks and one at 31 to 35 weeks. The other mothers received no routine ultrasound, only selective ultrasound.

In September 1993, the **New England Journal of Medicine** (**NEJM**) published the results of this study. The study found no difference between the two groups for the rate of death or complications in the newborn. The rates of premature delivery and birth weights were nearly identical in the two groups. There were also no difference in outcome for post-date pregnancies, twins and small for dates infants. To date, there is no conclusive evidence that routine ultrasound improves the outcome for the baby.

However, as an editorial in the same issue of the NEJM comments, the principal benefit of routine ultrasound is the detection of birth defects. This might be of psychological benefit to women and may have a favourable effect on the outcome of some pregnancies.

WHAT THE EXPERTS SAY

In 1981, the **Society of Obstetricians and Gynecologists of Canada** stated that, "at the present time data are not yet available to permit the conclusion that diagnostic ultrasound is without any adverse biological effect." It went on to state that the routine use of ultrasound could not be recommended.

The **American Institute of Ultrasound in Medicine** (**AIUT**) and the **American College of Obstetrics and Gynecology** have also recommended ultrasound be used only if problems develop or are suspected during pregnancy.

In Britain, the **Royal College of Obstetricians and Gynecologists** has recommended a single ultrasound in every pregnancy to estimate fetal age. In West Germany, the recommendation was for two ultrasound exams in every pregnancy.

In 1984, the **National Institute of Health** (**N.I.H.**) in the United States sponsored an international conference on the use of ultrasound in pregnancy. Since there was no proof that routine screening made pregnancy safer for either mother or baby, and because of an unproven but possible risk to the fetus, the experts concluded they could not recommend routine screening.

In 1992 the **Canadian Periodic Health Examination Update** concluded there was "fair" evidence to suggest a single routine ultrasound examination during pregnancy.

SELECTIVE USE OF ULTRASOUND

The N.I.H. conference also listed those medical reasons for which ultrasound would be recommended. Some of the main ones are listed below.

1. **Threatened miscarriage, tubal pregnancy and fetal death.**

Ultrasound can tell you whether the baby is still alive or whether a pregnancy is likely to continue after a threatened miscarriage. It can pick up about 90 percent of tubal pregnancies, if combined with vaginal ultrasound.

In the first three months of pregnancy, ultrasound is also necessary to perform special procedures like chorionic villi sampling or placing stitches in the cervix.

Except for the above reasons, ultrasound should **not** be performed in the first three months of pregnancy. If there were any side effects of ultrasound, the baby would be most susceptible at that time.

Dr. Douglas Wilson, Head of Prenatal Diagnosis at **Grace Hospital** in Vancouver puts it this way; "There's very little room for first trimester ultrasound. A lot of patients come in for early dating scans, but there's not much use in that. If someone's having bleeding or a complication, it's reasonable. But in the majority of cases, it's not necessary (**Family Practice**, Nov\89)."

2. To find out how many weeks pregnant you are.

Ultrasound is also used between 15 and 18 weeks pregnancy to date the pregnancy when the dates of the last menstrual period are unknown. At that time, it can predict the date of delivery to within two weeks in 89 percent of pregnancies.

The need for this particular use of ultrasound could usually be eliminated if all women of child-bearing years made it a practice to keep accurate records of their periods. Using menstrual history, the due date can reliably be predicted in between 75 and 85 percent of cases.

3. If your pregnancy has some high risk features, ultrasound can give valuable information.

In high risk pregnancies, such as suspected twins, repeat Cesarean section, abnormal bleeding, diabetes or high blood pressure, elevated alpha fetal protein in the mother's blood (which may indicate a fetal abnormality) or pregnancies where amniocentesis or chorionic villi sampling is required as well as other special situations, the benefits of ultrasound far outweigh the possibility, as yet unproven, of long-term side effects.

Ultrasound is also useful if your doctor thinks you have too much waters or too little waters or if the baby is suspected to be in a position other than the usual head first one.

Dr. Ants Toi, Associate Professor of Radiology at the **University of Toronto**, says, "High fluid, I have not found to be as much a problem as low fluid, which is very serious, especially in early pregnancy." (**SOGC Bulletin**, July\Aug\87) Low fluid is associated with slow growth and fetal abnormalities.

4. To detect abnormalities in the formation of the baby's organs, brain and spine.

The main type of abnormalities that can be detected are **structural defects**. This means that there are problems or defects as the baby forms. Amniocentesis, on the other hand, detects **chromosomal or genetic** problems.

Examples of structural defects are when the skull bone doesn't form over the brain, or the spinal bone only partially forms over the spinal chord, or the intestines form outside the abdomen, or one kidney is missing. After 20 weeks, US can also detect heart problems fairly accurately.

Ultrasound is also very useful for parents who have had a baby with this type of problem in the past and want to see if the problem has repeated itself with this pregnancy.

Successful detection of fetal abnormalities depends on the quality of the equipment, the expertise of the examiner and the reason the exam is done (high risk or normal screening). Not all abnormalities are detected, and there are false positives (ultrasound shows abnormality but the baby is normal) as well as false negatives (ultrasound normal, but baby has abnormality).

Dr. Toi estimates that about 50 to 75 percent of all possible abnormalities can be detected through ultrasound.

5. It may be useful to assess babies who seem to be growing too slowly.

However, if the first US has not be done before 20 weeks, a single measurement at 32 to 36 weeks can be "notoriously inaccurate," according to **Dr. James Youngblood** at the **University of Missouri, Kansas City of Medicine**. (**Journal of Family Practice**, 1989).

Dr. Hunter, Professor of Obstetrics and Gynecology at **McMaster University** in Hamilton, Ontario, says that there is uncertainty about whether the baby's growth can be accurately predicted by a single ultrasound measurement. Furthermore, he says, "Not all small babies are constrained in growth and not all normal weight babies have been able to achieve optimal growth potential (**Journal SOGC**, Jan\91)".

Also, not enough is known about serial measurements of fetal growth and how they affect the outcome for the baby.

6. To examine the placenta and see if it is located in a normal position.

Examination of the placenta is also essential for amniocentesis.

When there is bleeding in later pregnancy, ultrasound is used to locate the position of the placenta. The danger is that the placenta might be lying low in the uterus, blocking the baby's way out or partially separated from the uterine wall which can cause hemorrhaging. A low lying placenta is known as placenta previa and occurs in one in 200 pregnancies.

Early in pregnancy, the placenta often lies low down in the uterus, near the cervical opening. This is commonly reported on the US report as "placenta previa." This causes women considerable unnecessary anxiety and repeat ultrasounds. Actually, the position of the placenta at that early date is usually of no importance, since more than 90 percent of these low lying placentas move into a normal position by the time of birth.

DECIDING ON WHETHER TO HAVE AN ULTRASOUND

The most important thing is to be clear on the reasons you are having the ultrasound, and what information will be gained. You should also be clear on the benefits versus the risks.

Medical ethics specialists, **Drs. Judith** and **Frank Chervenak** and **Dr. Lawrence McCullough**, suggest a prenatal informed consent for US for every pregnant women. They believe the most ethical course is for full information to be provided to the woman including input from her doctor, and that the final decision be left up to her.

SOME QUESTIONS YOU MAY WANT TO ASK YOURSELF

Is a complication suspected by your doctor?

Are you uncertain of the date of your last period?

Are you looking for malformations of the baby?

Would you consider aborting the baby if something showed up?

Is US required as part of another procedure such as amniocentesis or chorionic villi sampling?

What if the US showed an abnormality in the baby that wasn't actually present, as occasionally happens?

The Coalition for Medical Rights of Women in San Francisco recommends that women ask their doctors some or all of the following questions:

1. I'm not sure about the safety of ultrasound and I would like to wait a while. Is there any harm in that?

2. How will the information you get change my care? If it won't then why do it?

3. Are there other things you can do to find out the same thing and are they safer?

Some alternatives to ultrasound suggested by the Coalition include using a fetal stethoscope to hear the baby's heart beat (detectable around 18 to 20 weeks of pregnancy), having the position of the baby felt by an experienced doctor, and waiting until the next prenatal visit to assess the baby's growth.

Dr. Michael Klein, Research Director, Department of Family Medicine, McGill University, in Montreal, helps women in his practice clarify the issues around US. He asks his healthy pregnant women with no suspected complications and who also keep accurate records of their periods, how important is it to you to check for structural problems in the baby and would it make a difference for you to know? Otherwise, he tells them the US is medically unnecessary, but leaves the final decision up to them.

RISKS OF ULTRASOUND

Many doctors, as well as patients, assume that ultrasound is a completely innocuous procedure for the fetus, especially when compared to the known risks of X-rays to the fetus during pregnancy.

Although the best evidence to date indicates no harmful effects of ultrasound exposure to the fetus, no studies have had a long enough follow-up to detect conditions in which there are long latent periods, such as cancer. There still remains the possibility of more subtle side effects that may not show up for ten or 20 years or even until the next generation.

A number of animal studies showed developmental, blood, nervous system, immune and chromosomal effects on fetal animals whose mothers were exposed to ultrasound in pregnancy. However, evidence from animal studies is conflicting and much of it has not been confirmed by other researchers.

At present, there is no good evidence that ultrasound causes harmful genetic effects such as mutation or chromosome breakage. On the other hand, the possibility that ultrasound exposure causes chromosome damage cannot be ruled out.

As **Neilson** and **Grant** say, in their chapter on ultrasound in **EFFECTIVE CARE IN PREGNANCY AND CHILDBIRTH**, (Oxford University Press, 1989), "There has been surprisingly little well organized research to evaluate possible adverse effect of ultrasound exposure on human fetuses." As far as I know, there is little future research planned on this important area.

So far, studies on human children have not verified any harmful effects. However, it is worth noting that research on ultrasound and its safety is on a level similar to where we were before 1950 with the risk of X-rays to newborns.

As Dr. Bernard Ewigman, says in **Journal Of Family Medicine** (Vol 29 Jun\89):

"Following several decades of use, adequately designed studies showed a twofold to threefold increased risk of leukemia in children with fetal X-ray exposure, for an incidence of one in 5,000. No current study of ultrasound exposure has an adequate sample to rule out an adverse consequence of even one in 2,000... The lack of direct evidence linking human fetal ultrasound with adverse outcomes in existing studies, although reassuring, cannot be interpreted to mean there is no risk."

The European Committee for Ultrasound Radiation Safety concluded there were no short term growth defects in children after 20 years of using US.

Two well designed studies checked to see if there was a relationship between ultrasound exposure and childhood cancer. Both showed there was no difference in the cancer rates of children who had been exposed to ultrasound and those that weren't. However, one of the studies showed that children over five dying of leukemia or other cancers were more likely to have been exposed to ultrasound.

To date, there have been only two large scale human studies on the long-term effects of ultrasound on children who have been exposed during pregnancy.

At the **University of Colorado**, 1,600 children whose mothers were exposed to ultrasound and 1,600 children whose mothers were not exposed to ultrasound were studied. From this large group, **Dr. Charles Stark** was able to trace and examine only 425 exposed and 381 unexposed children at seven and 12 years of age. The only difference he noted in the exposed children was an increased incidence of dyslexia, and an increased rate of hospitalizations.

At the **University of Manitoba** in Winnipeg a similar study was carried out with 10,000 exposed children and 5,000 unexposed children. Preliminary reports on this study showed no evidence of increased abnormalities, speech and hearing disorders, cancer or developmental or growth problems in children who were exposed to US while in the womb.

So far only one report on this study has been published. **Dr. Lyons**, the **Director of the Section of Diagnostic Ultrasound** at the University of Manitoba and his colleagues followed 149 pairs of siblings, one of whom had been exposed to ultrasound and the other who had not. There was no difference found in height, weight, or head circumference in the two groups. In March 1992, I spoke to Dr. Lyons and found out there was no further funding to continue analysis of the 15,000 children.

In 1992, Norwegian researchers reported on the results of a eight to nine year follow-up of infants exposed to ultrasound. No differences were noted in reading and writing skills by their teachers. In addition, dyslexia studies on a group of 603 children showed no difference in exposed versus unexposed children.

Most recently, **Dr. James Campbell**, an ear nose and throat specialist and Professor at The **University of Calgary** and **Dr. Wayne Elford**, head of research in family medicine at the same university, studied 72 children who had delayed speech and compared them to children who had no speech problems. Their findings showed that a child with delayed speech is about twice as likely as a child without delayed speech to have been exposed to prenatal ultrasound.

VAGINAL ULTRASOUND

This is a new form of ultrasound, in which a lubricated metal probe is placed in the vagina, and the uterus and tubes scanned. It is said to be more comfortable than the insertion of a speculum or even a pelvic exam. It is particulary useful if a woman is undergoing various fertility treatments or for complications of pregnancy occurring in the first three months.

DANGERS OF DOPPLER ULTRASOUND

Doppler stethoscopes expose the newborn to continuous low output ultrasound early on in the pregnancy. The total exposure is several times greater than routine ultrasound. Although no harmful effects have been demonstrated, the routine use of Doppler stethoscopes cannot be recommended. No studies so far have determined if there is any long-term risk to the baby. For routine use, women can request use of ordinary fetal stethoscopes and thus easily avoid this unnecessary use of ultrasound.

A very advanced type of doppler ultrasound with high power output can be used to study uterine blood flow, umbilical blood flow, and blood flow inside the baby's heart and brain. Although still experimental, advanced doppler may have a role in high risk situations. However, there is absolutely no justification for its routine use during pregnancy. The exposures to the fetus with this type of ultrasound is much higher than for other types of ultrasound and the side effects are simply unknown.

WOMEN'S REACTIONS TO ULTRASOUND IN PREGNANCY

"An ultrasound exam has the potential to be a fascinating and happy experience for prospective parents." Neilson and Grant observe, "But real or mistaken diagnosis of fetal abnormality can lead to psychological devastation."

A study in England showed that unscanned women in a hospital which used ultrasound only selectively were less likely to think they would be more reassured by a scan. An American study found women felt nearly half the value of the scan in an uncomplicated pregnancy was for personal reasons such as knowing the sex of the baby or having an early picture to show their children.

It is important to have the scan interpreted, since "it may look more like the map of the moon," according to **Sheila Kitzinger** in **THE COMPLETE BOOK OF PREGNANCY AND CHILDBIRTH**. Says Kitzinger, "Because it involves sophisticated equipment, ultrasound may seem intimidating; if the picture on the screen is blurred and meaningless, it may be disappointing, but if it is explained to you so that you can actually recognize your baby, it may be the most exciting part of your pregnancy so far."

In fact, studies have shown that women feel far more positive about the ultrasound exam when they have high feedback on the results that if they have poor communications during the exam.

Dr. Klein also points out that the experience of seeing the baby during ultrasound exam has now become part of North American culture, and in many cases, part of a woman bonding with her child.

SUMMARY

The decision on whether to expose your unborn child to ultrasound during an uncomplicated pregnancy remains a personal one, hopefully made with full and careful consideration of all risks versus the benefits. And of course ultrasound can never substitute for the clinical skills and judgment of the attending physician.

FOR FURTHER READING

A GUIDE TO EFFECTIVE CARE IN PREGNANCY AND CHILDBIRTH, by **Iain Chalmers**, **Murray Enkin** and **Marc Keirse** (Oxford University Press, 1989). This is a summary of the effects of care during pregnancy and childbirth, based on over 3,000 studies.

EVERY WOMAN'S GUIDE TO TESTS DURING PREGNANCY, 1986, by the **Coalition for Medical Rights of Women**, 2845 24th St, San Francisco, CA, 94110. 415-826-4401.

ADDENDUM ON ELECTRONIC FETAL MONITORING

The electronic fetal monitor (**EFM**) tracks the fetal heartbeat and records the uterine pressure during contractions. Introduced in the 1970's, EFM was initially used for high risk pregnancies. Before the proper studies had been completed, it became a routine practice in most Canadian and American hospitals. Currently 80 percent of women having babies are exposed to some type of fetal monitoring.

Recent research has shown that EFM, compared to the use of intermittent heart beat checks by a caregiver, does not improve the outcome for the baby. In fact, routine use of EFM increased the C-section rate. This was true even for women in the high risk category.

WHAT IS EFM ?

The external EFM consists of two straps which go around your abdomen. One strap holds a pressure gauge to record contractions and the other strap an ultrasound transmitter to detect the baby's heartbeat. The information provides a continuous printed record of heartbeat and contractions.

With the internal fetal monitor, an electrode is inserted into the baby's scalp and linked to a recording device by a wire inserted though the mother's vagina.

THE DISADVANTAGES OF EFM

Mother confined to bed during labour.

Beeping alarm if mom changes position.

EFM machines frequently break down and malfunction.

Wide variation in EFM interpretation.

False alarms can only be sorted out through taking fetal blood to measure the oxygen level.

Can substitute for regular checking by the care giver.

OTHER OPTIONS OF EFM

Find out when your doctor uses EFM. Request your baby be monitored without EFM, if the staff is available.

Doppler stethoscopes may improve the reliability of fetal monitoring versus the ordinary fetal stethoscope.

Soothing presence, touch, words of caregiver or labour coach can decrease complications.

Testing The Waters - All About Amniocentesis

Over the last decade, amniocentesis has proved a valuable tool for monitoring the progress of women whose pregnancies involve a high degree of risk to their babies. In addition, it is used to detect inherited defects in babies ahead of time, thus giving women the opportunity to abort these fetuses if desired. Thus amniocentesis has ushered in a whole new era of reproductive choice, and brought with it many unanswered questions about the ethics of that choice.

Amniocentesis is a procedure which removes about four teaspoons of fluid ("amniotic fluid") from the bag of waters ("amniotic sac") surrounding the baby. This fluid is removed through a needle placed in the mother's abdomen, and then into the uterus and bag of waters, after the mother's abdomen has been frozen with a local anesthetic. Prior to amniocentesis, an ultrasonic picture of the baby and its bag of waters will determine the best place for the needle to enter. Cells from the amniotic fluid are then grown for chromosomal studies and various chemical tests are performed as well. The results take three to four weeks to complete. The chromosomal studies will also tell you the sex of the baby.

Since amniocentesis is usually performed at 16 weeks of pregnancy, to ensure that there is an adequate amount of fluid formed, the baby is already 20 weeks old by the time its parents must decide its future.

WHO SHOULD CONSIDER AMNIOCENTESIS ?

1. **Women whose family history or those of their partner's includes a child with certain types of genetic problems or birth defects.**

These include a group of **structural** defects resulting from incomplete formation of the spinal chord, or its bony covering, that range from mild to life-threatening. This group of defects includes missing brain, and exposed spinal column, and cause half of all still births. Children who survive with serious cases of exposed spinal chord are usually paralysed, and have severe medical problems. Children with mild defects of the spinal chord that are covered with skin, can lead rich full lives.

Other inherited problems include a range of **genetic** or chromosomal abnormalities. The most common of these is **Down's Syndrome** or **Mongolism**, in which there are usually three instead of two number 21 chromosomes. Down's Syndrome is a major cause of mental retardation worldwide, and people with Down's syndrome are likely to have weak cardiovascular systems, respiratory problems and run a greater risk of childhood leukemia.

2. **Women and their partners who are from certain ethnic communities where there are specific types of inherited diseases.**

Afro-American women, Mediterranean women, or Jewish women who have lived in Eastern Europe, may have a family history of diseases such as Tay Sachs disease, sickle cell anemia, and thalassemia.

3. **Women aged 35 or over.** The incidence of all chromosomal abnormalities increases with age.

However, 95 percent of cases of Down's Syndrome are age-related. At age 30, the incidence of Down's syndrome is one in 885 births; at age 35, it is one in 365 births; and at age 40 the chance of having a Down's child is about one in 109.

In the past, amniocentesis used to be reserved for women 38 or over. With increased demand, its use has been extended to the group between 35 and 38, and even to women younger than 35.

4. **Women known to be carriers of diseases linked with the female or X chromosome**, such as one type of muscular dystrophy and hemophilia. These women then have a chance to abort male fetuses, 50 percent of whom will have these serious conditions.

5. **Women who have fetal abnormalities show up on ultrasound or through other tests.**

Some of these other blood tests include maternal alpha fetal protein, estriol and human chorionic gonadotropin. A new technique is being developed which allows a computer-generated risk to be calculated from the mother's age, pregnancy dates, weight, the results of the above blood tests, and diabetic testing. If the calculated risk is as high as that of a woman 35 or over, amniocentesis will then be offered to a younger woman.

6. **Women who have already given birth to one child with genetic defects or neural tubal defects.**

Remember new evidence shows that taking multivitamins containing folic acid will prevent neural tube defects (but not genetic defects).

7. **Women with a personal or family history of inherited defects in cell metabolism and molecular disorders.**

Over 200 different problems of this type can be diagnosed through amniocentesis.

MEDICAL REASONS

Amniocentesis for medical reasons is done much later in pregnancy.

1. **Women with diabetes and other chronic illnesses.**

In these women, amniocentesis is used in the last months of pregnancy to determine the maturity of the baby's lungs. This information is then used to decide the safest time to deliver the baby.

2. **Women who are RH negative and have formed antibodies to their babies.**

This problem is uncommon now since it is totally preventable. But if for some reason antibodies have formed, then amniocentesis is used to tell how severely the baby is affected and whether the baby will require a transfusion while still in the womb.

WHO SHOULD NOT HAVE AMNIOCENTESIS

Any woman who, for political or religious reasons, does not believe in therapeutic abortion for genetic reasons. However, some women may wish to have an amniocentesis done in order to prepare in advance for the birth of a handicapped child.

Amniocentesis should not be done for such reasons as to assess the damage caused by X-rays performed during pregnancy, or to check for damage from drugs taken by the mother (unless they are known to cause problems) or solely to check for the sex of the baby.

WHAT AMNIOCENTESIS CAN'T TELL YOU

Amniocentesis can detect hundreds of different types of inherited abnormalities. Most of these are rare. Some abnormalities are not detectable through amniocentesis. Keep in mind that at present, the risk having a child with abnormalities with no testing varies between one and three percent.

A new blood test called alpha plus or triple screening may help you decide whether you are at high risk for a child with Down's Syndrome or neural tube defects. If the results show a woman is at low risk for these problems, she may want to reconsider the necessity of amniocentesis. This test enables a woman to get a reasonable estimate of her chance of having an abnormal baby without amniocentesis. (See the next chapter for more details).

As mentioned before, you can lower your risk of neural tube defects through folic acid supplements during pregnancy.

WHAT ARE THE RISKS

One baby in 200 is miscarried as a result of the procedure itself. If you have a tendency to miscarry, this fact must be weighed against the possible benefits of the procedure. Other side effects, such as puncture of the placenta, the baby, or the mother's bladder and infection of the amniotic fluid, are rare.

There is an increased risk of miscarriage, if you have already had bleeding prior to the amniocentesis being done.

In 1978, a British study of amniocentesis showed a possible increase in respiratory problems and hip displacement of newborns who had undergone amniocentesis as compared to those that did not. The British suggested that sometimes enough amniotic fluid was taken, especially in the case of two or more amniocentesis, to restrict the baby's movements.

EARLY AMNIOCENTESIS

This procedure should be considered experimental, as large scale studies on its advantages over routine amniocentesis have not yet taken place. This procedure is done between 11 and 15 weeks.

Miscarriage rates appear to be higher than regular amniocentesis, but lower than chorionic villi sampling.

GENETIC COUNSELLING NECESSARY

Any woman considering amniocentesis should have access to a skilled genetic counsellor, who can assist her and her partner in making the best possible choice for her individual situation.

The most important questions to find out about are:

What are the risks of producing an abnormal child?

What are the risks of the procedure?

Could you or your family and support systems handle raising a handicapped child?

Do the risks of the procedure outweigh the benefits of what you could learn from the testing or vice versa?

WHERE TO HAVE AMNIOCENTESIS

Larger centers with a special prenatal diagnosis unit are the best bet for experienced and skilled doctors. Wherever you choose to have your amniocentesis, make sure your doctor does at least 50 amniocentesis per year.

If abnormal results are found, women should be made aware of all their possible options by the doctor and/or genetic counsellor.

THE DECISION TO TERMINATE

At 20 weeks of pregnancy, the baby is kicking by now, the news may come to you that your baby has a severe handicap. You and your partner then face the painful choice of deciding to end the pregnancy. The shock of a loss of a child and the grieving that follows may come as a surprise to you and your partner who were planning a normal pregnancy. The knowledge that the choice is the right one for your family will not be any consolation. Family and support persons should be sensitive to the fact that you have lost your child and treat you accordingly.

CHORIONIC VILLI SAMPLING

The latest development in prenatal screening is **chorionic villi sampling** (**CVS**). This test can be performed at ten to 12 weeks of pregnancy and results can be obtained in one or two days.

CVS can screen for **genetic abnormalities**, but not for structural abnormalities. After the CVS, screening for this purpose should take place through a blood test known as maternal alpha fetal protein done at 15 to 18 weeks, as well as a detailed ultrasound at 18 weeks.

CVS requires early ultrasound. The long-term safety of this is simply unknown.

The tissue sample can be taken by inserting a catheter through the vagina and into the uterus to remove a small sample of chorionic villi from the placenta. This is called **transcervical chorionic villi sampling** (**TC-CVS**).

A new method of obtaining a chorionic villi sample from the developing placenta is by inserting a needle through the abdomen. Safety and accuracy are believed to be the same as TC-CVS but the cervical technique appears to have a greater risk of spotting or bleeding afterwards (about ten to 20 percent).

Keep in mind that both types of CVS are relatively recent techniques, so there is still less known about their long-term safety and accuracy. Dr. Wilson suggests attending a center where each doctor has done a minimum of 50 CVS per year.

A large American study of the method showed the same rate of fetal loss as for amniocentesis but higher rates of cramping (22 percent), spotting (33 percent) and fluid leakage. However, a large Canadian study showed a higher rate of miscarriage, and possible higher rate of stillbirth following the procedure. For every 200 women having CVS there would be five more miscarriages than with amniocentesis. There is also a higher incidence of uncertain results, and ten percent of the time a woman will have to get an amniocentesis to clarify the results.

In spite of all these drawbacks, Canadian women participating in the study, felt they would opt for CVS in the future. One advantage appears to be that women can be relaxed, and become more attached to their babies six to eight weeks before women who are waiting for their amniocentesis results.

Recent research showed a possible increased risk of fetal limb abnormalities following CVS, especially if the CVS was done before ten weeks of pregnancy. The risk goes from one in 2,000 before CVS to one in a 1,000 after CVS.

AN ETHICAL DILEMMA

Many unanswered questions remain about amniocentesis and chorionic villi sampling:

> Does amniocentesis or CVS give a woman more choice than she wants?

> Does the availability of amniocentesis and CVS conflict with our desire to build a better world for the handicapped?

> What are the effects of early ultrasound on the baby?

> Does amniocentesis or CVS cause any long lasting and subtle physical or psychological damage to the fetus?

> Should only perfect fetuses be saved?

> How can we make late abortions less traumatic for women who choose them?

> How can we educate women on the social as well as the medical facts of what it means to raise a child with Down's Syndrome in this society?

FURTHER READING

THE TENTATIVE PREGNANCY, PRENATAL DIAGNOSIS AND THE FUTURE OF MOTHERHOOD, by **Barbara Rothman** (1986). This book discusses the difficult choice of amniocentesis and the meaning for mothers who choose it or who don't choose it. She also explores mother's feelings about choosing to abort the baby or making the opposite choice.

BIRTH OVER THIRTY (revised 1985), by **Sheila Kitzinger**. This book thoughtfully and reassuringly reviews the joys and challenges facing the older mother.

EVERY WOMAN'S GUIDE TO TESTS DURING PREGNANCY (1986), by the **Coalition for Medical Rights of Women**, 2845 24th St, San Francisco, CA, 94110. 415-826-4401.

The Challenge Of Pregnancy Over Thirty Five

If you are 35 or over and considering pregnancy for the first time, you are joining an ever-growing group of contented older mothers who are rising to the different challenges that motherhood at that age requires. With advances in prenatal care, as well as the increased health awareness of older mothers, pregnancy after 35 is no longer any riskier than pregnancy at an earlier age.

HIGH RISK ?

According to the standard list of risk factors used by your doctor, your age automatically places you in a "high risk" category. This high risk is based on statistics which show a higher rate of complications for both mother and baby in the under 20 group and the over 35 group.

Based on his or her beliefs about your risks and the baby's risks, your doctor will suggest appropriate non-invasive or invasive screening tests. On your part, you must be clear about what questions you need to have answered and the importance of prenatal testing to you personally. You may need gentle but firm persistence to get all your questions answered, and if necessary be referred to a reliable center for genetic counselling and testing. If your doctor insists on treating you like a high risk patient when you feel this is not warranted, you should attempt to find a doctor whose philosophy is more in line with your own.

Keep in mind that the majority of women in your age group experience normal labours and births. When you are likely to have only one or two children, you will only have a couple of chances to give birth your way. Remember, you are not a statistic, so don't let yourself be "psyched out" by them. Remind yourself instead that as a healthy, active woman with a positive attitude toward yourself as a woman and as a mother you can thoroughly enjoy the new and exciting process of pregnancy and birth.

Moreover, a large study (**New England Journal of Medicine**, Mar 8/90) of almost 4,000 women at **Mount Sinai Hospital** in New York showed no increased risks for the babies of older mothers. Women over 35 were no more likely to have a premature baby, or to have babies that were small for their age, or to have babies with low **APGAR** scores at birth (this score measures the vigour of baby at birth). Women over 35 were also no more likely than younger women to have babies die in the womb, or shortly before birth. Women over 34 were slightly more likely to have a low birth weight baby (a baby weighing under five and a half pounds, or two and a half kilograms).

In addition, in this study, although women over 35 had a higher rate of complications during pregnancy and childbirth, younger mothers had a higher rate of cesarean sections and infants who were admitted to the newborn intensive care unit.

These new findings may be partially explained by the fact that you, as an older mother, tend to be in excellent physical shape and receive good prenatal care.

BIRTH DEFECTS AND AGE

The incidence of all chromosomal or genetic abnormalities slowly increases with age. The most common abnormality sought for causes mental retardation and is known as **Down's Syndrome**. Ninety five percent of cases of Down's Syndrome are age-related. At age 30, the incidence of Down's syndrome is about one in 885; at age 35, it is about one in 365 births; and at age 40 the chance of having a Down's child is about one in 109. Chromosomal abnormalities such as Down's syndrome can be ruled out through amniocentesis, keep in mind that two thirds of Down's Syndrome babies are born to women under 35.

However, the good news is that structural defects do not increase with age. Examples of a structural defect are when the skull bone doesn't form over the brain, or the spinal bone only partially forms over the spinal chord, or the intestines form outside the abdomen, or one kidney is missing. At between 15 and 20 weeks of pregnancy, non-invasive tests like ultrasound and the alpha fetal protein blood test can identify 85 to 90 percent of these structural defects. With amniocentesis, the detection rate rises to 95 percent with a one in 200 risk of miscarriage.

Dr. Patricia Baird, professor of medical genetics at the **University of British Columbia**, studied 26,859 children with birth defects. She excluded children with chromosomal abnormalities. She found there was no association between other types of birth defects and the age of the mother.

GET ALL YOUR QUESTIONS ANSWERED BEFORE TESTING

Proper genetic counselling is essential if you are considering prenatal testing like amniocentesis or chorionic villi sampling. As **Dr. R. D Wilson**, **Professor and Chairperson** of the **Genetics Committee at University of British Columbia**, says, "All patients considering prenatal genetic diagnosis should have access to professionals who are knowledgeable in the field and skilled in the procedures."

If you are over 35, you should consider amniocentesis if you feel you could not face raising a child with **Down's Syndrome** or other serious genetic defect, and are prepared to undergo a late abortion at 20 weeks. A newer procedure known as chorionic villi sampling can be done at ten to 12 weeks of pregnancy, with results being available within a week. This newer test does not screen for structural abnormalities, so an alpha fetal protein test will have to be done between 16 and 18 weeks.

Another way to rule out structural defects of the baby and certain heart problems as well, is to consider having an ultrasound examination done. Ultrasound has no known risks to the unborn infant, but the final answer on its long-term safety for infants is not in yet. If the pregnancy is going well, and you are not having an amniocentesis, you might want to wait for a clear-cut reason such as unusual bleeding or suspected twins before having an ultrasound done.

ALPHA FETAL PROTEIN TESTING

A blood test can measure the amount of a special protein known as alpha fetal protein (**AFP**) that is present in the mother's blood. This protein is made by the fetus as it grows, and normally is confined to the baby's circulation. With structural defects, there is a leakage of this protein into the mother's blood, and large amounts of this protein will be found in the amniotic fluid and in the mother's blood. The blood level of alpha fetal protein is best measured between 16 and 18 weeks of pregnancy. At this time in pregnancy, 85 to 90 percent of open spinal tube defects can be detected and 30 to 40 percent of Down's Syndrome.

A positive test does not mean your baby has a defect. It only means that further testing is necessary. Similarly, a normal blood test means you have a higher probability of a normal pregnancy, but does not guarantee a "normal" baby. The AFP test is only a screening test, aimed at only a few of the problems that can occur in pregnancy. False positive results are common, especially if you have miscalculated the dates of your pregnancy. The levels will also be high if you have twins or even due to normal variations in blood levels. Before proceeding to other testing, a repeat test should be done. If the level is still abnormally high, you should consider having a detailed ultrasound. If the ultrasound does not account for the high second reading, you may have to have an amniocentesis done as well.

Of 1,000 women having this test, an estimated 30 will have an abnormally high second reading. Of these 30, eighteen will end up having amniocentesis, and there will be only one to two actual spinal tube defects confirmed at birth. The remaining 16 women will receive high risk care and there is some evidence that these 16 women may be at higher risk from miscarriage, low birth weight, premature delivery and other complications.

Drawbacks of this blood test include the fact that the test will miss about 20 percent of structural defects and has a high rate of false positives, which can cause considerable and unnecessary anxiety.

A low level of alpha fetal protein may suggest but not prove a genetic abnormality such as Down's Syndrome.

ALPHA PLUS OR TRIPLE SCREENING

A new test may help you decide whether you need amniocentesis.

A single blood test can measure three biochemical markers; alpha fetal protein, estriol and human chorionic gonadotropin. The results of these tests as well as a blood test for diabetes, and the mother's age, pregnancy dates, weight, are fed into a computer, which can then print out the calculated risk for Down's Syndrome and other related genetic abnormalities. If the calculated risk is as high as that of a woman 35 or over, amniocentesis will then be offered to a younger woman. If a woman is over 35, she can also get an estimate of how high her risk for these problems is.

In July 1993 the province of Ontario started a province wide screening program to assess the usefulness of this test as part of the prenatal work-up.

Dr. Anne Summers, a clinical geneticist at **North York General Hospital** in Toronto, told the **Medical Post** (Nov 3/93) that the new test will be able to diagnose Down's in 70 percent of the cases overall and in 80 percent of women over 35. It can also pick up about 70 percent of neural tube defects. Dr. Summers feels it gives women over 35 another choice. "If the results show relatively little chance of a Down's Syndrome baby they may decide against amniocentesis."

FOLIC ACID CAN PREVENT STRUCTURAL BIRTH DEFECTS

Defects where the skull bone doesn't form over the spinal chord or brain, (neural tube defect or **NTD**) affect 300,000 to 400,000 infants per year worldwide, with 2,500 to 3,000 per year in the United States, and 800 in Canada. In Canada, the incidence of NTD is about one in 1,000 births. If a woman has already had a child with this problem the incidence is 20 per 1,000. There is now compelling evidence that taking folic acid supplements can reduce the incidence of this serious problem by at least 50 percent.

A 1989 study in Boston, involving 23,000 women, showed that women who took multivitamins containing folic acid during the first six weeks of pregnancy had the lowest risk of delivering a baby with NTD, compared with women who took multivitamins without folic acid, and those starting multivitamins with folic acid after seven weeks of pregnancy.

In 1991, the Lancet medical journal reported on a large well-designed study of 1,195 women at high risk for having an NTD, (because of a previous baby who had the problem) conducted by the **Medical Research Council of Great Britain**, at 33 centers in seven different countries, including Canada and the United States. The study showed that women who took 4mg of folic acid daily for the first 12 weeks of pregnancy were able to prevent 72 percent of neural tube defects, compared to women in the same high risk group who didn't take this supplement.

Most recently, in the December 1992 issue of the **New England Journal of Medicine**, a large, well designed study of 4,000 pregnancies in Hungary provided even more convincing evidence that taking multivitamin supplements containing at least .8mg of folic could prevent NTD in women who did not have a history of a previous problem.

As a result of these and other studies, in March 1993, the **Society of Obstetricians and Gynecologists of Canada (SOGC)**, recommended that doctors advise all women of child bearing age to take supplements containing .4mg of folic acid supplements or the dietary equivalent, according to the food rules. During pregnancy, supplements should contain at least 0.8 to 1.0mg folic acid per tablet.

An alternative approach suggested by the SOGC is for all women of child bearing age to take .4mg folic acid or the dietary equivalent, starting immediately after they stop using birth control, until at least ten to 12 weeks after a missed period.

Women who have already had a baby with NTD and women at high risk for NTD should consider taking 4mg of folic acid daily after discontinuing birth control until ten to 12 weeks after a missed period.

Folic acid is present in dark green leafy vegetables, brewer's yeast, whole grains, legumes and organ meats. Folic acid is very sensitive to heat, light and any type of cooking. Since low doses of folic acid supplements are very safe, it is probably wisest to use supplements as well as diet to get adequate amounts of folic acid.

NUTRITION AND HEALTH

An excellent diet is important for older women, especially if they continue to work throughout their pregnancy. The healthiest diet consists of lots of fresh fruits and vegetables, whole grains and legumes, supplemented by chicken, fish, yogurt, and eggs.

It is not necessary to consume four glasses of milk a day or eat four to six slices of whole grain bread every day. However, if you have no dairy in your diet, it is important to take a calcium magnesium supplement containing 1,000 to 1,200mg of calcium and about half that amount of magnesium. It is important to learn to become aware of what your body is trying to tell you and listen to it. Healthy food cravings should be heeded.

Dr. Lendon Smith, author of the book **FEED YOURSELF RIGHT** (Dell, 1983), believes that especially for women with allergies, it is important to avoid dairy products, to rotate your food, and to space your children at least three years apart. Otherwise he believes that such a mother can predispose her child to having allergies.

Excess dairy products may cause allergic symptoms in the mother as well, such as being constantly stuffed up, having frequent headaches and a runny nose. As long as adequate protein is being taken, along with good calcium magnesium supplement, there is no need to worry that your baby is not getting enough nutrition if you give up cheese and milk.

It is also important to avoid sugar, sugar substitutes, coffee and alcohol. All of these will lower your energy level and have a less than desirable effect on your baby.

GESTATIONAL DIABETES

Some women develop diabetes during pregnancy. This risk of diabetes goes up with age. During pregnancy, you need extra glucose in your blood to help the baby grow. During pregnancy, the insulin doesn't move the glucose out of your blood as quickly as it did when you were not pregnant. This means that blood sugar levels in the last three months are normally higher than non-pregnant levels, and sometimes sugar will even spill over into the urine. All these changes are normal.

However, some women temporarily lose the ability to handle the increased levels of blood sugar in their body. **Henci Goer**, author of a helpful pamphlet entitled **Gestational Diabetes**, says, "It is perhaps unfortunate that this condition is called diabetes. Elevated blood sugar is a concern, but for most women the problem is mild, easily corrected by diet, the pancreas is unimpaired and the risks are much lower than in insulin dependant diabetes."

Gestational diabetes (diabetes that appears for the first time during pregnancy) can only be diagnosed by taking blood and urine samples for three hours after consuming a large amount of sugar.

Some doctors are now doing this test routinely, especially on older women. However, there is controversy about whether there is actual risk to the fetus if the diagnosis is missed, or the treatment is inadequate. There are few well designed studies on this subject. One third of women with gestational diabetes will progress to permanent diabetes within seven years of their affected pregnancy.

If you have been able to keep your blood sugar levels normal through diet alone, and if the baby is growing normally, then your labour should be handled the same as any low risk pregnancy.

COPING WITH FATIGUE

On the one hand, you are emotionally better adjusted and your identity is firmly established by age 35 or older. You are much less likely to resent your children for preventing you from having a career, because you have probably already established a career or done what you wanted with your life.

On the other hand, fatigue may affect you more than a younger mother, and you make take a longer time to recover physically after the birth. Or you may not.

Regular exercise, both stretching and aerobic types, during and after your pregnancy will help your body recover faster after birth, and give you more physical stamina after the baby is born.

Pregnant women over 35 should plan in advance on how to meet their anticipated needs before and after the birth. Try and establish a solid network of friends and family you trust and whom you do not feel embarrassed to call for help.

Of course, this assumes that your partner is your main sustenance and strength and that you are sharing child-caring duties equally if at all possible.

Even with a loving and supportive partner, you may need extra help with housework and preparation of meals as well as encouragement, moral support, and relief from childcare.

A lot of fatigue is the direct result of sleep deprivation. Remind yourself that the way you feel is directly related to the amount of sleep you have missed and not because you are losing your mind.

Hormonal upheavals in the postpartum period and during breast-feeding combined with sleep lack can make you feel a lot more anxious, irritable, impatient, and depressed than your usual self. It is important to have patience with yourself and remember that you will eventually return to your previous hormonal state and getting uninterrupted sleep.

CHANGES IN LIFESTYLE

Adding another person to your household is more of an emotional, physical and psychological adjustment when you are older. Your life will not go on as before, and your old patterns of living will be irrevocably altered. You should avoid inflexible plans about going back to work, as well as a highly scheduled routine in which the baby is fitted into certain hours of the day. You may not be able to predict ahead of time how soon you will want to go back to work.

Another aspect of lifestyle change is the sudden and total loss of privacy. Caring for a young infant may leave you with no time for yourself. It is a demanding 24-hour-a-day job. A co-operative partner or friend can ensure that you have at least an hour a day of uninterrupted time for yourself.

The total loss of private time with your mate may strain a relationship already going through dramatic changes. So try and make sure that you and your partner go out at least once a week without the baby, even for a few hours.

As an older woman, especially with a well-established career, you may be justifiably afraid about how motherhood will affect you as a woman.

Will motherhood obliterate you as a person?

Will you be able to do a good job as a mother?

Will your mind turn to mush?

Will your conversations be limited to baby carriages and diapers?

These questions have no ready answers. But despite these concerns, older mothers are often surprised by the intensity of their positive feelings for their newborn. These feelings make the adjustment to their new roles as mothers smoother and more enjoyable. Older mothers may feel inexperienced, awkward and unskilled, but their maturity and sense of priorities will bail them out in the end.

RESOURCES

BIRTH OVER THIRTY revised 1985, by **Sheila Kitzinger**. Thoughtfully and reassuringly reviews the joys and challenges facing the older mother.

EVERY WOMAN'S GUIDE TO TESTS DURING PREGNANCY, 1986, by the **Coalition for Medical Rights of Women**, 2845 24th St, San Francisco, CA, 94110. 415-826-4401.

GESTATIONAL DIABETES. This booklet is available through **BIRTH AND LIFE BOOKSTORE**, 7001 Alonzo Ave NW, PO Box 70625, Seattle, WA 98107-0625. 206-789-4444.

Keeping Fit While Pregnant Is Good For You And Your Baby

Pregnancy creates a special need for exercise. In fact, pregnancy is a major stress on your body. Fortunately your body is well equipped to handle this stress if you pay attention to its needs and look after it well.

BENEFITS OF EXERCISE

Regular exercise during pregnancy gives you more energy, less fatigue and improved sleep.

It significantly reduces many of the discomforts of pregnancy.

It alleviates constipation, reduces the incidence of backache, leg cramps and varicose veins, relieves breathlessness, and best of all, prevents excessive weight gain.

It also conditions you for the physical exertion of labour and later on, the physical demands of raising a young baby.

As well, aerobic exercise makes the circulatory system, which nourishes your baby, work more efficiently.

Stretching exercises improve posture and strengthen and tone upper and lower back muscles and abdominal muscles, making it easier to carry your baby.

Strengthening pelvic floor muscles makes it easier to carry the weight of the enlarged uterus and improves bladder control. It also makes it easier for these muscles to stretch and accommodate the baby's head, and to go back to their normal shape and function after the birth.

Long-term benefits of pelvic muscle exercises include prevention of dropped uterus and urinary incontinence (losing urine when you cough or sneeze).

Before embarking on a exercise program, discuss your proposed exercise plans with your physician, and make sure no medical reasons exist for you to stop or modify your program like miscarriage, premature labour or anemia.

THE IDEAL PREGNANCY EXERCISE PROGRAM

During pregnancy, you should include in your exercise program:

1. Stretching exercises.
2. Breathing and relaxation practice.
3. Aerobic exercise preceded by warm up exercises and followed by cool down exercise.
4. Specific exercises for childbirth preparation.

This sounds like a lot, but all four can be easily be combined at one session. Numbers 1, 2 and 4 should be practised daily and will take 20 to 30 minutes. This can be broken up into two ten to 15 minute sessions. Aerobic exercises should be performed at least three times a week for a minimum of 15 minutes with one day between each session.

If you are already fit and doing aerobic exercise on a regular basis, whether swimming, cycling, running, jogging, dancing or attending aerobics classes, pregnancy is a good time to maintain your level of fitness.

If you are not already exercising, pregnancy is a good time to design a gentle and regular program of exercise suited to your needs and lifestyle, and one that can easily be continued.

STRETCHING EXERCISES

These will be included in any good prenatal class. Check with your doctor or public health nurse for the location of the nearest classes. It is often easier to stay motivated in a group of pregnant women.

Yoga classes offer excellent stretching exercises, breathing and relaxation practice. In yoga classes, most experts advise avoiding inverted positions, such as the head stand and the plough, and other positions such as the bow or back bend. Your yoga teacher will usually advise you during class.

If there are no stretching or yoga classes in your area, you can easily teach yourself a good stretching routine, using books or videos.

A good stretching routine would include the whole body, with a special emphasis on thigh stretching, abdominal strengthening, and pelvic tilting. The whole set of stretches should be done daily.

AEROBIC EXERCISES

Women just starting vigorous or aerobic exercises should choose one that is enjoyable, practical, easy to do and requires little equipment. Exercising outdoors provides the added benefits of fresh air and sunshine.

Walking is highly recommended for aerobic exercise and can be continued throughout your pregnancy and for the rest of your life. Swimming is also an excellent choice. The water cushions your joints and alleviates the stress of weight bearing. Cycling, dancing, and no-bounce aerobics are also good choices.

During pregnancy, there is a generalized loosening of joints and ligaments in your body. This loosening prepares you for the passage of your baby through the pelvis during birth. However, this fact may also make you more susceptible to injury. To prevent any chance of injury, five minutes of warm up exercises must precede any aerobic exercise and five minutes of cool down exercises must follow it.

Other physical changes due to pregnancy include increased breathlessness because your lungs aren't expanding as efficiently due to an increasingly restricted chest space. Your blood volume also increases by 30 to 50 percent and your heart may beat up to 15 more beats per minute. You will have to adjust your exercise routine to avoid breathlessness or elevation of heart rate.

All women doing aerobic exercises, whether experienced or not, will have to modify their exercises somewhat during pregnancy.

Certain abdominal exercises must be avoided during pregnancy, (especially if the midline abdominal muscles are separated) such as double leg raising, straight leg sit-ups or scissors. Any exercise which exaggerates the hollow of the lower back should also be avoided. If the midline abdominal muscles have separated, special exercises can be done to tone these muscles and to prevent further separation. If in doubt about any particular exercise check with your instructor or doctor.

Whether with strenuous exercise or stretching exercises, it is important to be aware of your body at all times. Pay close attention to what your body is telling you. If it hurts, stop. Pregnancy is no time to push yourself. Go at your own pace and don't compare yourself to anyone else.

Avoid exercising in hot humid weather or when you are sick with a fever. Make sure you drink lots of fluids before and after exercise to prevent dehydration. Also make sure you wear a good exercise bra and well padded running shoes.

Some doctors discourage any sport that jars the body, especially during the first three months, but there is no scientific evidence to support this.

SPECIFIC EXERCISES FOR THE CHILD-BEARING YEARS

These should be done daily and in fact throughout the entire span of your reproductive years.

Top priority are **Kegel** exercises that strengthen the pelvic floor. They are named after **Dr. Arnold Kegel**, an obstetrician who devised these exercises to prevent the need for surgery for urinary incontinence. The pelvic floor is a group of muscles that form a sling across the base of the pelvis, and support everything inside your pelvic cavity, and that includes your uterus, bladder and the lower part of your bowel. Kegel exercises refer to the action of contracting or squeezing this group of muscles on a regular basis.

If you are not aware of these muscles, try starting and stopping a stream of urine. This simple but effective exercise will bring all the pelvic muscles into play and is a useful method of practicing Kegel exercises. You can also practise Kegel exercises during sex. Squeezing the penis and getting feedback from your partner is not only good childbirth preparation, it also improves sexual pleasure for both man and woman.

Pregnant women should get in the habit of doing a series of five Kegels ten to 20 times a day. This means contracting and releasing the whole pelvic area.

Other exercises that should be done on a daily basis are stretches for the thigh area and abdomen. Squatting and sitting frequently in the taylor position, as well as sitting with the heels together and pushed close to the body are good thigh stretchers. Pelvic rocking or tilting (tucking your seat under and flattening the lower back) strengthens the abdominal muscles, prevents backache and improves posture.

Pelvic rocks and Kegels can be done while washing the dishes, waiting for the bus or watching T.V.

Also important for childbirth preparation are gentle exercises to strengthen the abdominal muscles such as abdominal tightening and straight curl ups.

Pregnancy is a good time to pay special attention to your posture whether sitting, standing or lying down. Pregnancy produces changes in the center of gravity which have to be adjusted to. It also puts a great strain on your back and spine.

If you develop back and hip problems during pregnancy it is often a good idea to see a chiropractor experienced in dealing with pregnant women. In fact, I routinely advise pregnant women to see a good chiropractor on a ongoing basis throughout the pregnancy in order to prevent problems from developing.

BREATHING AND RELAXATION

An important aspect of any exercise program is breathing and relaxation exercises. Learning the different types of breathing including deep breathing, chest breathing, the panting breath and the pushing breath, as well as relaxation techniques provide you with an essential tool for labour. These can be learned in prenatal class or from books and tapes. After birth, deep breathing and relaxation practices remain valuable like skills for reducing stress in your life.

Many breathing exercises can be incorporated into your stretches. Generally it is easier to stretch on the out-breath.

SUMMARY

If you experience pain, dizziness, nausea, or spotting during exercise, stop right away and consult your doctor.

If you are already fit, you can maintain your level of fitness during pregnancy and need only introduce specific exercises for childbirth preparation. If they are not already part of your exercise routine, you will also need to introduce breathing, relaxation practice and stretching exercises.

If you are considering pregnancy in the next year or so, now is the time to start an enjoyable exercise program that can be continued easily throughout pregnancy. Remember that it is never too late in the pregnancy to begin a gentle set of exercises.

Perhaps the best advantages of exercising during pregnancy and afterwards are that you recover faster after delivery and that you regain your figure more quickly. However, it is not wise to try and lose those extra pounds until after you have stopped breast-feeding.

FOR FURTHER READING

ESSENTIAL EXERCISES FOR THE CHILD-BEARING YEAR, by **Elizabeth Noble** (third edition, 1988) focuses on the key muscles involved in pregnancy and delivery, and the exercises necessary to tone them, both before and after birth. This book also outlines special exercises for separation of the midline abdominal muscles.

ACTIVE BIRTH, The New Approach to Giving Birth Naturally by **Janet Balaskas**, revised 1992, is an excellent guide to exercise and movement during pregnancy, with an easy to follow program. It helps women develop **all** their bodily resources for labour and birth.

POSITIVE PREGNANCY FITNESS, by **Sylvia Klein Olkin**, is a practical guide that shows women how to get the most out of their pregnancy and birth through a total yoga and relaxation program for mental, physical and spiritual preparation.

FITNESS AND PREGNANCY can be ordered from **Fitness Canada**, 365 Laurier Ave West, Ottawa ON, K1A 0X6.

JOURNEY THROUGH BIRTH, two tape cassettes, a childbirth preparation course by **Sheila Kitzinger**, the renowned childbirth educator.

A BIRTH CLASS, Focus on Labour and Delivery. This 115 minute video, in five segments, shows two childbirth educators teaching four women and their partners the skills they need for labour and birth.

EVERYMOM'S PRENATAL EXERCISE AND RELAXATION VIDEO, by **Tracy Schimdt**. This 70 minute video includes stretching, aerobics, and touch relaxation.

KATHY SMITH'S PREGNANCY WORKOUT. An excellent work-out by a pregnant mom and fitness instructor with lots of practical tips and down to earth advice.

All the above are available by mail order from:

PARENTBOOKS, 201 Harbord St, Toronto, ON, M5S 1HS. 416-537-8334.

BIRTH AND LIFE BOOKSTORE, 7001 Alonzo Ave NW, PO Box 70625, Seattle, WA 98107-0625. 206-789-4444.

Dealing With The Discomforts Of Pregnancy

During pregnancy a woman's body, mind, and emotions go through an amazing transformative process. In the process of this great change, a woman may experience any number of a wide variety of new physical sensations.

If you are experiencing unfamiliar physical sensations during pregnancy, it is important to remember two things.

First of all, pregnancy is an ideal time to become more aware of what your body is saying to you. This will help you figure out the best strategy to deal with the physical discomforts involved. All of the discomforts of pregnancy can be handled through simple natural means, without resort to drugs that can harm the growing fetus.

Secondly, pregnancy is a good time to get out of the habit of taking a pill for every ache, pain, cold or flu. In fact, many drugs (even an aspirin or cold remedy) are not considered safe for use during pregnancy. If in doubt, check with your doctor about the safety of the medication in question.

CONSTIPATION

During pregnancy your body produces a hormone called progesterone. This hormone has the effect of relaxing the smooth muscles of your small and large intestines. Thus food passes through your intestines more slowly. Also your growing uterus may press on and displace the intestines. Another major factor contributing to constipation is taking iron supplements.

1. Drink plenty of fluids. Some suggest six to eight glasses of fluid a day. This fluid should consist of pure water, fruit juice or herbal teas.

2. Eat food that is high in fibre such as fresh fruit, vegetables and whole grains. Cut down or eliminate red meat which is very constipating. Chicken or fish can be eaten instead.

3. One to two tablespoons of unsulphured blackstrap molasses in warm water once or twice a day is a reliable old remedy for constipation. Molasses is also high in iron and trace minerals. (Be sure to brush your teeth well after you take molasses.)

4. Some women find that drinking eight ounces of prune juice daily keeps their bowels moving.

5. A half to one cup of unrefined bran can be taken daily with whole grain cereal.

6. Ground flax seed, two tablespoons in water twice, a day or metamucil (psyllium seed powder) without sugar are two mild laxatives that can be taken safely throughout pregnancy.

7. Discontinue your iron tablets or switch to a less constipating brand or a liquid iron like floradix (available in health food stores). I also have had great success with **NutriChem** iron, which is completely non-constipating. Recent research has shown that iron supplements are not usually necessary during pregnancy. For more information see the chapter on iron.

8. Walk or do some type of physical exercise every day. This promotes regular bowel movements.

9. For some changing their position while sitting may help, i.e. the backless chairs where your knees are lower than your hips.

10. When you are pregnant, the **TIMING** of your bowel movement changes. Never sit on the toilet for long periods of time or strain during bowel movements (this can contribute to the development of hemorrhoids). If the stool is not passing easily, force yourself to get off the toilet and go about your business until you really have to go and the stool will then pass more easily.

HEARTBURN

Heartburn is a burning sensation located in the center of the chest or the upper stomach area. It is caused by progesterone relaxing the muscle that controls the opening at the top of the stomach. This hormone also causes the stomach to empty more slowly. Also the stomach is pressed upwards by the growing baby and as a result, does not function as well. Stress tends to worsen heartburn. Heartburn is usually most noticeable during the last three months of pregnancy, but can occur throughout pregnancy.

1. Avoid foods that are fatty or greasy. Foods that are too acid or too spicy may also bother you. Eliminate from your diet any food that causes discomfort. Stay away from carbonated drinks, processed meats and junk foods.

2. It is crucial to eat slowly and chew your food thoroughly so all the enzymes present in the saliva get a chance to work. Some health experts suggest chewing each bite 50 to 70 times. Then, by the time your food mixed with enzymes reaches the lower part of the stomach, up to 40 percent of your food will be pre-digested.

3. Avoid going a long time between meals. Instead, eat more frequently, at least three meals and three healthy snacks a day. Do not eat after eight at night.

4. Avoid drinking water or other fluids during your meals. It is best to drink fluids between meals. Otherwise the fluids dilute your digestive enzymes and make them less efficient at breaking down your food.

5. Coffee, tea and cigarettes can increase heartburn, and should be avoided as much as possible.

6. Sleep propped up with lots of pillows at night. It may help to elevate the head of the bed using blocks.

7. Do not jump up from the table to serve. Let others do the dishes after supper while you sit and relax.

8. Avoid using antacids that contain aluminum or bicarbonate of soda. These can interfere with absorption of certain nutrients, upset your acid base balance, and possibly harm the fetus.

Calcium in the form of pills, powder or liquid is a natural antacid and can be used in doses of up to 1,200mg per day. Magnesium should always be taken with calcium at about half the dosage of the calcium.

9. One teaspoon of slippery elm bark powder mixed with honey or hot water neutralizes stomach acidity and soothes the stomach.

Also slippery elm powder can be taken in powdered form in OO gelatin capsules, two capsules one to three times a day. Slippery elm throat lozenges sold in most health food stores may also be helpful. These can be sucked on throughout the day.

10. Eat papaya after meals in the form of the fresh fruit, juice, or tablets from the health food store. You can also buy digestive enzymes at the health food store and take them with every meal.

11. When you travel, you can carry raw almonds, and chew on them slowly to help relieve heartburn.

MORNING SICKNESS

In the first three months of your pregnancy, you may experience nausea and sometimes vomiting. By 16 to 20 weeks of pregnancy, the nausea usually begins to taper off.

Pregnant women sometimes worry about the harmful effects of the nausea and vomiting on their baby. Recent studies show that women who are healthy when their baby is conceived, have enough reserves to supply the growing fetus, even if they eat little in the first two or three months of pregnancy. Another study showed that the presence of nausea and vomiting rather than their absence was more likely associated with a favourable outcome of the pregnancy.

Women should not feel guilty because the nausea and vomiting is not abnormal and nor is it a sign of unconscious rejection of the baby as some have claimed.

Karen, a healthy thirty year old mother of two daughters, developed severe nausea and vomiting with her third pregnancy. At one point, she could not even keep water down, and I was about to admit her to hospital and put her on intravenous fluids. As a last resort, I had her try slippery elm gruel and it worked. She got over her vomiting, and went on to have an easy, uncomplicated delivery of her son.

1. There is a strong connection between nausea and low blood sugar levels.

To keep your blood sugar level constant, eat small frequent meals six times a day. These small meals should be high in protein or complex carbohydrates (such as rye crackers or rice cakes) but contain no sugar or sweetener.

2. Take powdered ginger root, available in most health food stores in capsules, three or four a day followed by a glass of water, first thing in the morning. This can be repeated several times as necessary throughout the day.

Fresh ginger tea can be made by adding two tablespoons of grated ginger to four cups of boiling water. You can drink two cups of this tea first thing in the morning and sip on it during the day.

3. Slippery elm is a soothing and strengthening herb for the stomach. It possesses as much nutrition as oatmeal and is so gentle that it can be retained by the most sensitive stomach. It can be taken in powdered form in capsules or made into a gruel.

Slippery elm gruel is made as follows:

-Make a paste with one and a half teaspoons of slippery elm powder mixed with one teaspoon of honey.

-Bring 1/2 pint of milk to a boil and stir in the slippery elm paste as the milk reaches the boiling point.

-Remove from the heat and add a dash of cinnamon or nutmeg.

-The same recipe can be made using water instead of milk.

4. Vitamin-B6, 50 to 100mg a day, is a very effective anti-nauseant. It should be taken as part of a mega-B-50 capsule containing the rest of the B vitamins.

5. Other supplements that may be useful include zinc, 25mg a day and magnesium, 200 to 400mg a day. Brewer's yeast two heaping tablespoons mixed with yogurt and mashed bananas, will help provide extra B vitamins. Stop your iron tablets until the nausea passes.

6. How you get out of bed seems to be very important. Have whole wheat or rye crackers by the bedside. Have someone bring you some raspberry leaf and peppermint tea before you get out of bed and sip on it slowly. Make sure you get out of bed slowly.

7. Other suggestions for morning time include a tea made from dried peach leaves; or one teaspoon of apple cider vinegar in warm water first thing in the morning. You can also try a thermos of warm milk sweetened with honey or molasses by the bedside.

8. Eat small, bland, easily prepared meals.

9. Rest as much as possible. Fresh air and walking a mile a day may also be helpful.

10. Carry raisins, raw almonds, rice cakes or whole wheat crackers with you so that you can always keep your blood sugar up.

11. Keep away from smoky rooms and the smells of cooking. If possible, get someone else to do the cooking. If you are nauseous in the evening, rest in a darkened room and get your mate to prepare the evening meal.

12. Try a mono-diet. Start off with one healthy food say grapes or bananas, and then each day add a new food, brown rice, steamed vegetables, baked fish, etc. After two or three weeks, your nausea will probably subside.

13. Blue green algae, such as spirulina, is very high in protein and very easy to digest. Spirulina powder can be mixed with mashed bananas or other fruit and provides many other nutrients as well.

14. Try to avoid any prescription drugs for your nausea unless it is very severe. Benedictin, in the past prescribed by some doctors for the nausea of pregnancy, has been falsely associated with birth defects such as cleft palate and heart deformities. No association was ever proven and the drug has now been reintroduced into the market in Canada as diclectin (doxylamine 10mg and B-6 10mg).

15. Acupuncture treatments by an experienced practitioner can be very effective for severe and prolonged nausea and vomiting of pregnancy.

STRETCH MARKS

These reddish brown permanent discolorations are related to the amount of weight gain as well as hereditary factors. You can limit your weight gain by eating only healthy food and staying away from desserts, extra bread and potatoes.

To help keep the skin more elastic, I usually recommend 200 to 400 IU of vitamin-E along with 500 to 1,000mg of vitamin-C taken by mouth. I also recommend daily application of vitamin-E oil to the whole abdominal area. Extra trace minerals, especially zinc and silicon, and bioflavonoids have also been suggested as supplements. Vitamin supplementation has not been proven to be effective, but some women claim that they work.

There are creams and lotions on the market that claim to prevent stretch marks but these are unproven.

After childbirth, the stretch marks usually fade and become silvery white over the next year. The sun can either darken or lighten these marks and they may become much more obvious. Half will improve and half will worsen after sun tanning. Some women have had good results with daily application of vitamin-E oil to the stretch marks twice a day for six months to one year after birth.

BACKACHE AND HIP PAIN

To prevent backache strengthen your back and abdominal muscles right from the beginning through gentle stretching exercises and regular aerobic exercise.

Make sure you pay a lot of attention to your posture. Avoid high heeled shoes at all costs as this puts too great a strain on the back.

If you have a persistent backache or hip pain, I feel it is a good idea to see a chiropractor experienced in seeing pregnant women. In fact I advise pregnant women to see a good chiropractor on an ongoing basis from the beginning of the pregnancy. I find this prevents back and hip problems before they happen.

RESOURCES

HEALING YOURSELF DURING PREGNANCY, 1987, by **Joy Gardner**. A clearly written guide to herbs, vitamins and nutrition offering a holistic approach to pregancy from inception to nursing the newborn baby.

ALTERNATIVE MATERNITY, 1989, by **Nicky Wesson**. This book was written by a British woman who was forced to learn about alternative medicine when her two young children were sick and unable to be helped by conventional medicine. This book provides a comprehensive guide to alternative therapies, including acupuncture, homeopathy and herbs.

WISE WOMAN HERBAL FOR THE CHILD-BEARING YEAR, (Ashtree, 1985), by **Susun Weed**. This book emphasizes using simple herbs, ritual and intuition to stay healthy during pregnancy and birth.

NATURAL REMEDIES FOR PREGNANCY DISCOMFORTS, produced by **The Department of Health Services of California**, is an excellent 25 page booklet costing $ 1.95.

All of the above books can be ordered by mail or phone from:

    PARENTBOOKS, 201 Harbord St, Toronto, ON, M5S 1H6. 416-537-8334.

    BIRTH AND LIFE BOOKSTORE, 7001 Alonzo Ave NW, PO Box 70625, Seattle, WA 98107-0625. 206-789-4444.

Section Four:
Satisfying Childbirth

How Painful is Childbirth ? 126

The Unkindest Cut:
Are Episiotomies Really Necessary 130

Once A C-Section, Always? 135

Miscarriage: The Need For Support............................... 139

The Thyroid Gland Acts Up After Pregnancy 141

How Painful is Childbirth ?

For most women in the Western world, childbirth is painful. Most women feel pain during childbirth ranging from mild discomfort to honest-to-goodness pain. Only a few women say they had no pain at all. One mother giving birth to her third child actually laughed throughout her whole labour. But this is uncommon.

In fact, women having their first child may be taken aback by just how painful it is, especially when they have attended prenatal classes or read prenatal books which used euphemisms for pain like "intensity", "discomfort", or "hard work". Women may then feel like failures because they experienced serious pain during labour.

After your first birth, it does not necessarily get easier. However, your labour usually gets shorter, and your coping skills do improve with practice.

"One of the most important duties that a childbirth professional has is to present to women a realistic picture of birth," says author and childbirth expert, **Gayle Peterson**, in her book, **BIRTHING NORMALLY** (Mindbody Press, 1984). "To protect a woman from the concept of pain in childbirth," says Peterson, "is to leave her without preparation for coping."

Peterson believes that women can learn to face their fears about pain, trust their bodies, and yield to the incredible power and strength of the contractions that will birth the baby.

Once a woman comes to terms with the fact that childbirth will be painful, she and her partner can develop a practical plan to cope with the pain and work with it.

WHAT IS THE PAIN LIKE ?

Most women describe labour as starting with mild contractions, like menstrual cramps, and proceeding progressively to the strong and painful contractions of the later part of the first stage and transition. Some women start off right away with strong contractions and never get milder ones.

However, there is not always a direct relationship between how much pain you feel and how fast your labour is progressing. Indeed, the early contractions may feel quite painful, but as you learn to work with the pain, the later contractions may seem easier to handle.

Each woman gives a different description of what the pain actually feels like. Some compare it to an ocean wave slowly gathering momentum from the depths of the ocean, building to its maximum height and force, and then crashing to the shore. Between waves there is stillness and calm.

Childbirth pain, whether sharp or aching, starts slowly, builds to a peak, and then slowly subsides. Between contractions you usually feel no pain. This pause is a good time to take two deep breaths, one for you and one for the baby, and close your eyes and enter into a relaxed state where you can replenish your strength.

ACTIVE LABOUR AND BIRTH

Contractions during the active phase of labour command your full and undivided attention. A woman in active labour has flushed cheeks, and will not talk or laugh during contractions; choosing instead to concentrate on the contractions and her breathing.

The contractions usually slowly build in strength and come more often, and last longer, until the cervix is completely opened up and thinned out. Toward the end of the first stage of labour, there may be a period of time when the contractions seem almost unbearable.

Between the time the cervix is fully opened up and the start of the pushing contractions of the second stage of labour, there may be a pause of between 15 minutes and hour. "Rest and give thanks," advises renowned childbirth educator **Sheila Kitzinger**.

During the second stage of labour, pain may not be as predominant a feature for some women. It can be an immense relief to give into the powerful pushing urges.

As the baby's head starts to emerge, you may feel intense burning and stinging sensations as well as the feeling that you are going to rip apart. Fortunately, the female body is admirably well built to stretch and accommodate the baby's head without tearing.

Postpartum pain usually depends on whether or not an episiotomy was performed. This is a surgical procedure in which a cut is made to enlarge the vaginal opening for the baby's head. Small vaginal tears heal quickly and without pain.

Women who have a "back" labour feel the contractions as an intense aching in the low back area, and may have to take special measures to cope with the pain. Strong pressure on your lower back by your partner and/or frequent changes in your position (a hands and knees position may relieve the pressure best) are often helpful.

TWO ESSENTIAL CHARACTERISTICS

Finally, pain in childbirth has two essential characteristics which make it very different from other types of pain you may have experienced.

Firstly, it is a creative and rewarding kind of pain, in that, whether by vaginal or Cesarean birth, it results in the birth of a child.

Secondly, it lasts for a distinctly limited amount of time, usually not more than 24 hours, with a much shorter period of hard labour.

Moreover, if the question of pain is faced squarely in the prenatal period, you and your partner will be able to develop realistic and positive strategies for dealing with pain.

Just as you plan ahead of time what items to bring in your suitcase for the hospital, so you should select tools or strategies for coping with pain well in advance of labour.

BREATHING

If left on your own during labour, you would naturally adopt a rhythm and style of breathing exactly appropriate to your labour. However, as part of your bag of tricks, you should be familiar with at least three different types of breathing, deep breathing, any pattern of pant-and-blow breathing, and second stage breathing.

These breathing types can be learned in most prenatal classes or through books, audiotapes or videotapes.

However, neither you nor your labour coach should adhere too rigidly to any breathing type. Your partner or labour coach can assist you by breathing with you, and making verbal or non-verbal suggestions as to when to change to a different type of breathing.

Especially important during second stage is to keep your mouth open and relaxed. If your mouth is relaxed, your vagina is automatically relaxed.

RELAXATION

This is the other essential skill needed for labour. The key is learning to relax under pressure. During pregnancy there will be ample opportunities to practice. Specific relaxation techniques are described in the chapter How To Cut Down On Stress.

POSITION

A change in position is often highly useful. Lying on your back is probably the worst position for labour. Studies have shown that if you walk for as long as possible during the first stage of labour, you will speed up the progress of labour due to forces of gravity. While in bed, you can lie on your left side, sit upright or semi-upright, or go on your hands and knees.

VOCALIZATION

Being quiet and keeping a stiff upper lip can be detrimental to the course of your labour. Letting out low-pitched sounds such as "oh" or "ah" during a contraction can relieve muscle tension. Keep your mouth relaxed to provide you with a new focus.

EMOTIONAL EXPRESSION

You should be encouraged to express feelings of love, anger, gratitude, fear, anticipation, or sadness as they come up if this seems appropriate to you. This can sometimes get a "stuck" labour moving again.

SUPPORT SYSTEMS

Very crucial to you as the labouring woman is the loving support and encouragement of your husband, partner, family member or close woman friend. You will find that loving support persons are a much more effective tool for coping with pain than pain-relieving medications.

Support persons can wipe your brow, breathe in rhythm with you, help you relax, suggest a change of position, give you a word or sound to say together, encourage you to express your feelings, and remind you that there is a baby at the end of the labour.

No one, including yourself, should judge your labour like a performance, in terms of good or bad, success or failure.

PAIN RELIEVING MEDICATIONS

These are only other tools in your bag, but ones to be used with great care and discrimination, and without guilt or self-blame. Medications must be used sparingly as they can stay in the baby's bloodstream for days, can affect the baby's breathing, and can cause the baby to be drowsy.

THE BEST LAID PLANS...

Remember that in every labour, there is an element of the unknown. You should be prepared to let go of your image of the "perfect birth" in order to adapt with as much flexibility as possible to whatever happens during your labour and birth.

VISUALIZATION: CAN YOU HANDLE IT ?

The following exercises may provide you with some interesting insights into how you handle pain:

Imagine the sights, sounds and feelings at a time in your life when you handled pain poorly; and one in which you handled it well.

If no examples come to mind, make up some examples in your mind's eye. What was the difference between the two?

Now imagine yourself going through labour fearful and out of control.

Then imagine yourself going through labour calm and experiencing strong painful contractions but coping with well with them.

What resources did you draw on in the second example?

What breathing techniques, positions, sounds and attitudes did you find helpful?

What did support persons say to you that helped?

What did they say that didn't work for you?

What resources came out in this example that you didn't know you had?

NATURAL PAIN RELIEF

Self-hypnosis, acupuncture and acupressure can be very useful. A small portable acupuncture machine known as the **TENS** machine can be rented for use during labour.

Throughout labour, a flower and tree remedy known as rescue remedy can be added to everything that you drink. A herbal mixture of 25 drops of St. John's Wort tincture and 5 drops of Skull Cap tincture can also be added to all drinks and sipped throughout labour.

In addition, 10 to 12 calcium-magnesium tablets taken at the onset of labour can help reduce pain. Homeopathic arnica can be taken throughout labour and continued for at least one week after. It is wonderfully effective at reducing bruising and pain.

In my experience some combination of the above works better than pain killers, which make you drowsy but don't completely take away the pain. In addition, the drugs remain in the baby's blood stream for several days after birth.

IN SUMMARY

Breathing, changes of posture, movement, massage, relaxation, visualization, focused concentration, making sounds, expressing your feelings, the love and support of your partner, family and friends, self-hypnosis, acupuncture and acupressure, are all possible tools for dealing successfully with the real pain of childbirth.

Birth is a journey into the unknown, and should a true emergency arise, modern technology will prove indispensible. Most of the time, however, birth proceeds in a normal natural way, and strengthens and empowers the birthing mother. Remember to make a birth plan and discuss it with your midwife or doctor.

RESOURCES

THE EXPERIENCE OF CHILDBIRTH, by **Sheila Kitzinger** (1986) is written by one of the world's foremost childbirth educators, also a respected anthropologist and mother of five daughters. In her classic book, she integrates the physical, social and psychological aspects of giving birth in a positive, realistic and highly readable style. She also describes the breathing and relaxation exercises that provide such a useful tool during labour and delivery.

AN EASIER CHILDBIRTH, A Mother's Workbook for Health and Emotional Well-Being during Pregnancy and Delivery, by **Gayle Peterson** (1991). This excellent workbook enables a mother sort out her emotions, beliefs and expectations around birth, and create a supportive environment for herself as well as a personalized birthing plan.

MIND OVER LABOUR; USING THE MIND'S POWER TO REDUCE PAIN IN CHILDBIRTH, by **Carl Jones** (1987) is an eight step method using mental imagery to prepare for birth.

EASING LABOUR PAIN, by **Adrienne Lieberman** (revised 1992). This is a comprehensive discussion of bio-feedback, acupressure, breathing, relaxation, hypnosis, labour coaches, medications and all other techniques to make birthing more positive.

JOURNEY THROUGH BIRTH, two tape cassettes, a childbirth preparation course by **Sheila Kitzinger**, the renowned childbirth educator.

A BIRTH CLASS, Focus on Labour and Delivery. This 115 minute video, in five segments, shows two childbirth educators teaching four women and their partners the skills they need for labour and birth.

All the above are available by mail order from:

PARENTBOOKS, 201 Harbord St Toronto, ON, M5S 1HS. 416-537-8334.

BIRTH AND LIFE BOOKSTORE, 7001 Alonzo Ave NW, PO Box 70625, Seattle, WA 98107-0625. 206-789-4444.

The Unkindest Cut: Are Episiotomies Really Necessary

Episiotomy is the most common operation performed on women in Canada and the U.S. without their formal consent. In fact, it is performed in between 40 and 80 percent of all births. An episiotomy is a surgical incision into the area between the vagina and the rectum (the perineum) to enlarge the opening through which the baby will come. After the baby is born, the edges of the cut are approximated, frozen, and sewn back together.

Most doctors consider the episiotomy to be a minor surgical procedure of no importance, and perform it routinely out of habit, without being aware that its use has no scientific basis. In contrast, many women feel it is the most disabling part of childbirth.

The consent for episiotomy is actually covered by the general consent form covering all procedures connected with childbirth that is signed on hospital admission.

HOW THE ROUTINE EPISIOTOMY CAME INTO FASHION

The episiotomy did not come into vogue until the early part of this century. At that time, it was devised to prevent the serious perineal tears that sometimes occurred during childbirth. In order to prevent these tears, the idea was to enlarge the vaginal opening with a straight surgical cut that could easily be repaired afterwards with the woman lying on her back with her feet in stirrups.

In 1871, it was **Dr. William Goodell** who questioned the obstetrician's persistent interference in the natural process. In an article in the **American Journal Of the Medical Sciences**, he asked the question: "Am I to believe that nature, after making such admirable provision, for the earlier stages of labour, bungles matters to such an extent at the end ..? (The) perineum was certainly not created to be torn, unless shored up by the hands of the physician."

In an article in the **Canadian Family Physician Journal**, **Dr. Michael Klein**, **Professor of Family Medicine** at the **University of British Columbia** discusses how in 1920 one prominent American obstetrician was largely responsible for selling the idea of the episiotomy to North American doctors. Dr. **J.B. DeLee** advocated episiotomy as part of his "preventative" forceps delivery, which he considered to be the ideal form of birth.

Dr. DeLee believed that woman's body was badly designed for birth. He compared the stress of delivery to a woman falling on a pitchfork and the effect on the baby to having one's head crushed in a door.

Dr. Klein quotes him as saying: "So frequent are the bad effects (of labour) that I often wonder whether nature did not deliberately intend women to be used up in the process of reproduction, in a matter analogous to that of the salmon, which dies after spawning."

By the 1950's the episiotomy had caught on and become standard obstetrical practice in the majority of deliveries, with or without forceps.

Surprisingly for such a "routine" procedure as the episiotomy came to be, until recently, there had been no scientific studies on whether it was effective in preventing damage either to the mother or infant. There have been a multitude of articles on which position of the episiotomy (midline or lateral) is superior or which suture materials or sewing techniques is optimal. Until 1984 there were no controlled studies comparing the results of normal vaginal delivery with and without an episiotomy.

During their training, few doctors have a chance to witness the incredible ability of a woman's body to stretch to accommodate the largest diameter of the baby's head. "Nature," one Toronto obstetrician told me, when asked about the alternatives to a large episiotomy, epidural and forceps, "would tear the women apart".

On their part, women too readily accepted that medical interventions were always in the best interests of themselves or their babies. Epidurals, for example, can result in the loss of the urge to push, thus necessitating the use of forceps. Forceps, in turn, require the use of a large episiotomy to make enough room to place the blades of the forceps around the baby's head.

THE FIRST NORTH AMERICAN EPISIOTOMY TRIAL

Dr. Michael Klein, has been a pioneer in Canada in raising the whole question of whether routine episiotomies are justified scientifically. The subject was and still is considered too trivial to deserve serious study. Through hard work and persistence, Dr. Klein obtained funding for a proper randomized trial on episiotomy, the first of its kind in North America.

"Far from a trivial matter, episiotomy can involve a woman's sense of mastery or control over her birth," says Dr. Klein,

"and for some it can become a central or symbolic issue."

Dr. Klein's trial was reported in the **Family Practice** journal (Aug/91) and published in the **Online Journal of Current Clinical Trials** in 1992. The trial ran from July 1988 to May 1990 and involved 47 physicians and more than 1,000 women aged 18 to 40. It compared two groups of women, one in which episiotomy was used liberally, and the other in which doctors were asked to try to avoid an episiotomy i.e. to restrict its use. In the liberal or routine use group, episiotomy rates were 81 percent for first babies and 47 percent for subsequent babies, contrasted to 57 percent and 31 percent in the restricted use group.

The trial found that restricting episiotomies increased the length of second stage slightly without harming the baby. Second stage was only increased in women having their first babies by an average of nine minutes. In women having their second or more pregnancy, there was no increase in the length of second stage.

The two groups were followed up for three months after delivery. There was no difference found in pelvic floor functioning. Constipation, pain on moving the bowel, urinary incontinence, and bulging three months after the birth were the same for both groups. Objective measurement of pelvic floor function also showed no differences for the two groups.

Women with no stitches for repair of either a tear or an episiotomy were found to have the least pain and did the best overall (six to seven percent of women having their first babies and 19 to 31 percent of women with second or more babies). In this study, women who had episiotomies compared with women who had tears, experienced the same amount of pain with first babies, but with subsequent babies, tears were less painful.

Severe perineal trauma, with tears that extend into the rectum, "occurs virtually exclusively in the presence of an episiotomy." So much so that Dr. Klein feels that episiotomy should be redefined as being equivalent to a second degree tear, with a 21 percent chance of a tear into the rectum with the first birth and a one percent chance for subsequent births.

Women with severe perineal trauma have the worst outcomes overall: more pain immediately following the birth and for a longer time after discharge from hospital. Women in this group are more likely to describe their pain as being "horrible" or "excruciating." These women also resumed sex later, had more pain during sex and reported less sexual satisfaction, at least in the first three months after birth.

Since the study failed to demonstrate any benefit from routine use of the episiotomy to either mother or baby, Dr. Klein's research team recommended that this practice be abandoned and that episiotomy be used instead only when necessary for the health of mother or baby.

In another arm of the study, Dr. Klein examined the belief systems of participating doctors and how those beliefs impacted on their practice. He found that episiotomy rates depended on the belief system of the individual doctor. Doctors who performed a lot of episiotomies (80 to 90 percent or more for first births) were responsible for most of the severe perineal trauma experienced by women in the study. They also tended to be more interventionist in other ways as well (more Cesarean sections, forceps, epidurals, inductions, etc).

In **England**, a similar trial involving 1,000 women showed that overall there was considerably less trauma to the mother if episiotomies were restricted. The episiotomy rates were ten percent in the restricted group and 51 percent in the liberal use group. Thirty one percent of women having their first babies and 36 percent of those having their second or subsequent baby had no tears or episiotomies. This increased rate of preservation of the perineum was probably due to the use of midwives and nurses to deliver most of the babies. Women in the restricted episiotomy group were more likely to resume sex within a month after delivery. There was a substantial saving in staff time and suture materials in the restricted group.

ALTERNATIVES TO EPISIOTOMIES

In other developed countries, midwives, partially because they were not trained in surgery, became skilled at assisting women to birth their babies without either tears or episiotomies. During their training midwives are specifically instructed in the gentle art of easing the baby into the world without harm to mother or child.

In fact until 1930, similar instructions were also given to doctors on how best to protect the perineum and avoid tears.

On the other hand, the now "routine" episiotomy cuts through skin, vagina, mucosa and three layers of muscle in a sensitive erotic zone. Side effects of episiotomy include pain, bleeding, (especially when the episiotomy is done too soon) breakdown of stitches, and delayed healing. Pain following an episiotomy is often considerable, preventing women from sitting down comfortably for the first week after birth and sometimes for several weeks.

In a small minority of women, painful sex persists for several months after the birth or longer. One of the few studies that has been done on this topic showed an incidence of persistent painful sex after an episiotomy of six percent. Women with episiotomies are more likely to report painful sex than women who have had second degree tears that had to be stitched. A recent Australian study showed that 20 percent of women with episiotomies had painful intercourse for more than six months after the birth, and many in this group had prolonged discomfort even after that time.

The renowned childbirth educator and author **Sheila Kitzinger** points out that, although for some, episiotomy is a minor cut that heals quickly, for many women, it is a wound that leaves them feeling scarred. She believes that the episiotomy can also negatively affect the woman's body image and how she relates to her sexual partner.

PREVENTION DURING THE PUSHING STAGE OF LABOUR

Dr. John Milligan, **Obstetrical Director of the Regional Perinatal Unit** at **Women's College Hospital** in Toronto says most women "do not need an episiotomy, even if it's their first pregnancy, as long as the delivery is controlled and the doctor has the mother's co-operation." He adds that possibly 20 to 25 percent of first time mothers may need an episiotomy or suffer a small tear, "depending on the size and position of the baby."

The prime goal of both mother and doctor is to have the baby's head emerge as slowly as possible, preferably between contractions. To prevent tears or the need of an episiotomy, the pushing stage of labour should be unhurried. And that requires the conscious co-operation of the mother and clear and effective communication between doctor and mother.

Sheila Kitzinger was the first person to describe a natural pause of one half to one hour or more, that occurs during some labours, between the time the cervix is fully opened up and time the urge to push begins. Her advice was to rest and be thankful.

Some research has indicated that prolonged breath holding and strenuous breathing during the pushing stage of labour can interfere with oxygen getting to the baby. It is far better to push for shorter periods of times, only when the urge is overwhelming, and to try to keep the mouth loose and relaxed while doing so.

One British obstetrician, **Dr. C.L. Beynon**, advocates that women not be given any instructions to push whatsoever. He notes that women do not naturally push until the baby's head is right down on the pelvic floor. This also gives more time for the perineum to stretch.

It is naturally much easier to push when you are squatting, semi-upright, lying on your left side or any other comfortable position. Pushing while lying flat on your back goes against the forces of gravity and is usually the most difficult position from which to push a baby out.

Women can learn how to stop pushing when requested to do so by the doctor through controlled breathing (a pant and blow-type of breath like blowing on hot soup in rapid short breaths). With good coaching the baby's head can gradually emerge from the mother while allowing plenty of time for the mother's tissues to gently stretch. After the head is out, the shoulders should be delivered with the same careful slowness.

PREVENTION BEFORE BIRTH

Prenatal preparation is essential. General relaxation, as well as toning and relaxation of the pelvic floor muscles, (**Kegels**) and practice of second stage breathing patterns, are important skills to be learned ahead of time. However, these skills can also be learned right on the spot with the help of a good nurse or labour coach.

Some midwives advocate gently massaging the whole perineal area with olive oil or vitamin-E oil ten to 15 minutes a day for one to three months prior to the birth. This massage can also be done by the woman's partner. Although there is no evidence that it works, it will at the very least make a woman more aware of how to relax that area and promote intimacy between partners. Some midwives also massage the perineum with olive oil during second stage, so the tissues are moist, stretchy and relaxed, and the baby's head can slide out more easily. Again, this technique has not been studied, but the experience of midwives indicates that it may be useful.

THERE IS NO NEED FOR AN EPISIOTOMY IN A NORMAL BIRTH

If asked, most doctors will tell you that they will only perform an episiotomy if necessary. But what they don't tell you is that in their experience, an episiotomy is almost always necessary. From their perspective, they are right. They have never seen any other kind of delivery. A more useful question to pose is what percent of their patients having their first or subsequent child receive episiotomies. They may tell you that women having their first babies usually need an episiotomy. This is not true. In fact in first births, there is usually more than enough time to stretch if adequate time is allowed for second stage pushing. Occasionally in subsequent births, the pushing stage may be rapid and difficult to control.

Obviously certain medical emergencies call for the use of an episiotomy such as when the baby's heart beat suddenly disappears during second pushing, or to facilitate the delivery of a premature or breech baby, and of course when forceps are used. In addition, an episiotomy may be required when the delivery of the baby's head is progressing at a rate or manner which will tear the perineum, or not allow for the normal gentle stretching to occur.

But for the vast majority of normal births there is no medical reason for the performance of a surgical incision of the perineum.

ARROLL'S ADVICE TO DOCTORS

Dr. Bruce Arroll is a **New Zealand** obstetrician. He offers the following suggestions to doctors for low risk women during labour (**Canadian Family Physician**, Nov\84):

FIRST: Give every woman the chance to deliver without an episiotomy.

SECOND: Ask the woman if she has strong feelings about episiotomy. This may help in decision-making although there can be no guarantee an episiotomy won't be necessary.

THIRD: If you're performing episiotomies on more than ten percent of women having their first babies, your episiotomy rate may be too high.

FOURTH: If a tear starts before the largest diameter of the head is out, then an episiotomy may reduce further damage.

Dr. Arroll has called for a consensus conference on what is a medically acceptable episiotomy rate for doctors.

TEARS HEAL QUICKLY

Contrary to what the medical texts say, small tears, if they do occur, heal quickly and with little pain. In my experience with women who have had both, the tears healed faster and with less pain when compared to an episiotomy in a previous birth. This puzzled me at first until I realized that, as any surgeon knows, a straight cut, although easier to repair, takes longer to heal. A small tear goes along tissue lines and takes less time to heal although somewhat harder to repair. Thus a small tear may be preferable to a large and unnecessary episiotomy.

In any case, in an estimated 22 percent of episiotomies, tears still occur as an extension of the original cut; and these tears occur in a more precarious position than ordinary tears with possible extension into the rectum and its attendant complications.

EPISIOTOMY DOES NOT PREVENT LATER PROBLEMS

Some doctors argue that the episiotomy prevents prolapse of the uterus and bladder. Now that a whole generation of women who have had episiotomies has passed, the incidence of uterine and bladder repair has indeed decreased, but the same decline has also been noticed in those countries where episiotomies have not been used routinely.

A few doctors still claim that the episiotomy improves your sex life by making you tight as a "virgin". The return of normal vaginal muscle tone has nothing to do with the performance of the episiotomy. Instead it is dependent on the faithful performance of vaginal muscle contractions ("Kegels") after birth.

In the normal birth, the episiotomy has become an unnecessary and unscientific intrusion. It's time both women and doctors started seriously questioning its routine use.

FOR FURTHER READING

EPISIOTOMY AND THE SECOND STAGE OF LABOUR, by **Sheila Kitzinger** and **Penny Simkin** (revised 1986). This book has an international perspective on how to prevent episiotomy and preserve the health of the baby.

SOME WOMEN'S EXPERIENCES OF EPISIOTOMY (1981) and **EPISIOTOMY, PHYSICAL AND EMOTIONAL ASPECTS** (1981), by **Sheila Kitzinger**, published by the **National Childbirth Trust**, 9 Queensborough Terrace, London, England, W2 3TB.

THE EXPERIENCE OF CHILDBIRTH (1984), by **Sheila Kitzinger**.

SPECIAL DELIVERY, THE COMPLETE GUIDE TO INFORMED BIRTHING (revised 1986), by **Rahima Baldwin**, is a practical guide for couples who want greater responsibility for the birth of their babies, whether at home or in the hospital.

Once A C-Section, Always?

For years doctors have told women who have had Cesarean sections that they would have to deliver all future babies the same way. They based this on a rule postulated in 1916 which said, "Once a Cesarean, always a Cesarean." This policy has caused the C-section rate in the U.S. and Canada to soar dramatically over the last ten years. In Canada, there are about 66,000 Cesareans per year; and almost 970,000 in the U.S. each year. Of these, an estimated 25 percent to 50 percent were clearly unnecessary.

In Canada, the number of Cesarean sections has quadrupled in the last 20 years, as it has in the U.S. Forty percent of these operations were repeat Cesareans. The majority of these repeat sections were not only completely unnecessary, but **two to four times** riskier to the mother compared to vaginal birth.

The July 1991 report of the **Cesarean Birth Planning Committee** of the Ontario Government estimated that between **60 to 70 percent** of the 11,000 repeat Cesareans performed every year in Ontario could have been avoided. The report also said that the need for many first time Cesareans could be reduced, particularly for so called dystocia or failure to progress in labour.

Canada's Cesarean birth rate is one of the highest in the world, fourth after the United States, Puerto Rico, and Brazil. By contrast, European countries that have the same good outcomes for mothers and babies have half the C-section rate.

SIXTY TO SEVENTY PERCENT OF REPEAT CESAREANS ARE UNNECESSARY

In October 1985, a nationwide committee of obstetricians and other experts in Canada met to consider safe ways to reduce the number of Cesareans being performed in this country.

On the basis of convincing data, they concluded that vaginal birth after one Cesarean section could be safely recommended to the majority of women as long as they satisfied certain prerequisites. These prerequisites were that they had a healthy pregnancy, that they had a horizontal and not a vertical cut into their uterus with the previous section, that they are now carrying a single baby in the normal head down position; and, finally, as long as no new reason for a cesarean develops during pregnancy or labour.

The exact same conclusions were reached by the **U.S. Department of Health and Human Services** in 1986, and the **American College of Obstetricians and Gynecologists** in 1985.

REASONS FOR SECTIONS

First time sections are still being done for such vague reasons as prolonged labour or fetal distress, which are subject to a wide variety of interpretations, and which depend more on the doctor's philosophy, convenience, and fear of lawsuits than actual validly defined reasons. In the U.S. especially, Cesareans bring in more money than normal births. The increasing use of fetal monitors, inductions and other interventions have also led to many unnecessary sections.

Most of the reasons a Cesarean section is done the first time do not tend to repeat themselves the second time around.

These include prolonged or difficult labour; failure of the cervix to open up; the baby's heart rate dropping during labour, and even the pelvis being too small for the baby's head (the pelvis gains several centimetres in diameter when a mother squats or assumes an upright position).

For women who have had two or more Cesarean sections, recent studies have shown good success rates with a vaginal birth. Some hospitals now routinely allow a trial of labour for women who have had no more than two repeat Cesareans. Doctors vary on an individual basis as to whether they will allow a trial of labour for three or more Cesareans.

INCISIONS AND SCARS

During a Cesarean operation, the cut into the uterus is usually made in a horizontal direction over the lower portion of the uterus. The outside scar does not necessarily run in the same direction as the incision into the uterus. It is this uterine scar that is of concern. In certain emergency situations, the cut into the uterus is made vertically over the middle or lower portion of the uterus. This vertical type of incision, also called the "classical incision" is considered more unstable than the commonly performed horizontal incision. For this reason doctors usually recommend that women who have had a classical incision have a repeat Cesarean.

The main concern about horizontal uterine scars was whether they would hold up under the strain of labour. In fact, studies to date prove that in the vast majority of cases they do. The risk of separation or even rupture of the horizontal scar is very low, in the range of .05 to 1.0 percent.

If there is serious doubt about the type of scar, it can be examined through a five or ten minute office diagnostic technique known as hysteroscopy before getting pregnant.

ADVANTAGES OF VBAC

Vaginal birth after Cesarean, also called **VBAC** (pronounced **VEE-BACK**) has many distinct advantages over repeat Cesarean.

The major hazards of C-section to the baby relate to the risks of respiratory problems or the risks of prematurity if the pregnancy was dated incorrectly. These hazards would probably be the same with a premature vaginal birth.

The risk of the mother dying from Cesarean birth is very small. However, the maternal death rate associated with Cesarean section is two to four times that associated with a vaginal delivery.

With the aftermath of major surgery as well as the birth of a baby to deal with, a Cesarean mother has to cope with more pain and weakness following delivery.

Having a C-section increases your risk of getting a chronic and disabling pelvic infection six fold, unless preventative antibiotics are given before the surgery.

Moreover, few doctors realize the devastating impact a C-section may have on some women emotionally and psychologically.

As delighted as women are to have their babies safe and sound, they may feel a confusing mixture of shock and deep disappointment.

"Surgical deliveries have profound psychological effects on all women whether the surgery is actually necessary and life-saving or not," says **Claudia Panuthos**, a well-known child birth counsellor. "After the section," she goes on to say, "a woman grieves for her loss of control, her loss of dreams of normal birth, her loss of teamwork with her mate during labour, and the loss of early contact with the baby."

NOT ENOUGH DOCTORS FOLLOW THE GUIDELINES

In spite of the eight year old Canadian guidelines, statistics show that obstetricians have not changed their style of practice very much. Cesareans are still the third most common operation for Canadian women. Most doctors agree with the guidelines, at least in theory, but have been slow to change their practices.

A recent Canadian study (**Canadian Medical Association Journal**, (#142 Jun/90) reviewed C-section births in an Ottawa hospital and found they ranged from 12 to 20 percent. Seventy five percent of these C-sections were done due to failure to progress in labour, a pelvis that was too small, or failed induction of labour. However, the researchers found that C-sections were being done for women with a small pelvis without proper trial of labour, or failure to progress in labour without any sign of the baby in distress. If these practices were modified, the researchers felt the C-section rate could be reduced to about eight percent.

Of the 313 women admitted to a major teaching hospital in Toronto, 71 percent were eligible for a trial of labour. However, only 42 percent of the women were allowed to have one (**Canadian Medical Association Journal**, Aug 15/93).

Provincially, the Cesarean rates in 1988-89 were highest in Newfoundland and British Columbia, and lowest in Manitoba. The C-section rate in Newfoundland was 50 percent greater than in Manitoba. Saskatchewan and Alberta also had lower rates than the other provinces.

A study in a small rural hospital in Alberta showed that by adopting the recommended 1985 guidelines, the C-Section rate was cut by almost 50 percent (CMAJ Dec\91).

Governments in British Columbia, Ontario and Nova Scotia have been calling on doctors to follow the guidelines more closely. The Ontario Cesarean Birth Planning Committee recommended that "labour after a previous Cesarean be the standard of care for women with no identifiable risk." The committee recommended that a healthy woman with a previous section with a transverse incision be placed in the low risk category on prenatal forms. The committee also recommended that doctors should attempt to turn a breech baby in to the head first position before birth, in order to prevent unnecessary Cesareans. Unfortunately, few doctors in North America are being trained in the art of safely delivering a breech baby through the vagina.

According to a 1989 U.S. study, (**New England Journal of Medicine**, Mar 16/89) chances of a C-section depends more on who a woman's doctor is than on any other single factor. In the study the C-section rate ranged from 19 to 42 percent according to the individual doctor's preferences.

Recent research by **Dr. Michael Klein** showed that the degree to which physicians interfere with the birthing process is a function of the setting of the delivery (hospital versus birthing center) and the belief system of the doctor. He believes that tendency to interfere with birth is drilled into doctors early on in their training. He found that doctors who had the highest rates of episiotomy, also had the highest rates of Cesarean sections. Dr. Klein commented that: "Not surprisingly, it turns out that a cutter is a cutter (**Medical Post**, Oct 13/92)." Find out before you deliver if your doctor has that tendency.

GETTING MORE SUPPORT

Cesarean support groups and VBAC groups have sprung up throughout Canada and the U.S. to assist women in sorting out their feelings and to prevent future unnecessary Cesareans. By expressing their feelings to other women with the same experiences, women get a chance to release their feeling of loss, anger, sadness, and disappointment. For most women, the opportunity to have a normal birth after a Cesarean is an enormously gratifying and healing experience.

Dr. Ken Milne, **Professor of Obstetrics** at **Western University** in London, Ontario, and chairperson of the **Ontario Cesarean Planning Committee**, said at a Dec/92 conference in Toronto that VBAC is a philosophy, a different way of seeing the whole birth process. Dr. Milne suggested that hospitals publish their C-section rates, their forceps rates, and their rates of other interventions so that women can make informed choices.

The medical dictum, "Once a Cesarean, always a Cesarean, should be obsolete," said Dr. Milne, "In my opinion, every woman should be given the opportunity to deliver vaginally."

Doctors must educate their patients. Patients and self-help groups must educate their doctors. This joint effort will be the only way to put a halt to the unnecessary surgery being imposed on child-bearing women.

RESOURCES:

BIRTH AFTER CESAREAN: THE MEDICAL FACTS, by **Dr. Bruce Plamm** (General 1992). Dr. Plamm is one of the leading experts on VBAC. He documents all the research, including the five year study he directed, on the safety of VBAC.

THE SILENT KNIFE: CESAREAN PREVENTION AND VAGINAL BIRTH AFTER CESAREAN, by **Cohen** and **Estren**, (1983). This book tells you how to avoid cesareans, how to heal after you have had one, and how to have a vaginal birth the next time around.

OPEN SEASON, A SURVIVAL GUIDE FOR NATURAL CHILDBIRTH AND VBAC IN THE 90'S, by **Cohen** (1991). This book urges child-bearing women to avoid unnecessary Cesareans and tells you exactly how.

BIRTH WITHOUT SURGERY (1988) A GUIDE TO PREVENTING UNNECESSARY CESAREANS, by **Carl Jones** is a step-by-step guide for a safer birth and avoiding unnecessary Cesareans using imagery and non-medical means.

THE VAGINAL BIRTH AFTER THE CESAREAN EXPERIENCE, by **Lynn Baptisti Richards** (1987), contains the first hand accounts of women who went through VBAC as well as the stories of the partners, midwives and physicians that supported them.

ARTEMIS SPEAKS; VBAC STORIES AND NATURAL CHILDBIRTH INFORMATION, by **Nan Koehler** (Koehler, 1989).

HAVING A CESAREAN BABY: The Complete Guide For A Happy And Safe Cesarean Childbirth Experience, 2nd revised edition 1991, by **Richard Hausknecht** and **Joan Rattner-Heilman**. A VBAC positive book designed to provide information and support to couples hopeful of a emotionally fulfilling Cesarean birth.

REBOUNDING FROM CHILDBIRTH: Toward Emotional Recovery, 1994, by **Lynn Madsen**. Recovering emotionally and physiologically from a traumatic experience.

USEFUL ADDRESSES

VBAC CANADA, 8 Gilgorm Rd, Toronto, ON, M5N 2M5.

C/SEC (CESAREAN/SUPPORT/EDUCATION & CONCERN), 22 Forest Rd, Framingham, Mass 01701. 508-877-8266.

C/Sec serves parents and professionals who want information and support in relation to Cesarean childbirth, prevention and VBAC's.

INTERNATIONAL CESAREAN AWARENESS NETWORK, PO Box 152, Syracuse, NY, 13210. 315-424-1942.

This group grew out of necessity from C/SEC. Its goals are to educate women and practitioners in order to decrease the number of women having first Cesareans and to increase the number of women having VBAC's. They publish a feisty newsletter called the **Cesarean Prevention Clarion**.

All the above books can be ordered by mail from:

PARENTBOOKS, 201 Harbord Ave, Toronto, ON, M5S 1H6. 416-537-8334.

BIRTH AND LIFE BOOKSTORE, 7001 Alonzo Ave NW, PO Box 70625, Seattle, WA 98107-0625. 206-789-4444.

Miscarriage: The Need For Support

Approximately one in five women suffer a miscarriage after becoming pregnant. To family, friends, physician, and even to the woman herself, miscarriage may seem like a minor event of no real significance.

But following a miscarriage the mother or father, or both, may be surprised by the intensity of their reaction to their loss, and feel an urgent need for sympathy and understanding from others. At the same time, they may find an uncomfortable silence among family and friends when it comes to discussing the death of a baby so early in pregnancy.

Even though the pregnancy is short-lived, research has shown that a woman still goes through a grieving process similar in every way to women whose babies died much later in pregnancy or in the neonatal period. The only difference is that the grieving process among women who have miscarried does not usually last as long.

Among women who have miscarried, there may be a considerable difference in the length of the grieving process depending on how long the pregnancy lasted (an early miscarriage occurs in the first 12 weeks; a late one from 13 to 20 weeks) and the degree of attachment which the mother and father have formed to the baby.

STAGES OF THE GRIEVING PROCESS

During the grieving process, a woman may experience classical stages of shock and denial, anger, depression, and finally acceptance. But they don't necessarily occur in that order. All the stages may co-exist at once, or feelings may rapidly fluctuate from hour to hour and day to day. Acute pangs of grief can also be brought on by the sight of a baby.

Immediately following the miscarriage, a woman may feel a sense of shock and unreality. Later on, she may be flooded with feelings of anger and sadness. She may feel angry at herself, her partner, her doctor, her religion, and even the baby itself.

Another common feeling following miscarriage is guilt or self-blame.

"If only I hadn't lifted that heavy box..."

"If only I hadn't taken that painkiller..."

"If only I hadn't made love that night I started to spot..."

The sadness women feel following a pregnancy loss ranges from mild depression and irritability to full-blown depression with weeping spells, preoccupation with the loss, insomnia, loss of appetite, and loss of meaning of life. In the case of full blown depression, getting help from your doctor is always a good idea.

Many women experience physical symptoms of grief following miscarriage, which can be incorrectly diagnosed and treated by their physicians. Physical symptoms include headaches, backaches, digestive upsets, fatigue and a whole host of other ailments, all beginning around the time of the miscarriage.

A miscarriage is the death of a potential child, a symbol of hope and new beginnings. Parents may feel a profound sense of failure and loss of confidence and self-esteem. Preoccupation with the events of the miscarriage may continue for many months after the event.

Suppressing natural and valid feelings is the worst thing a woman can do to herself. Absolutely necessary to her recovery is the expression of her emotions as fully as she is able, and the full acknowledgement of what her loss means to her. Only after this work is done can she begin to integrate the loss into her life and create new hope for herself.

GUIDELINES FOR GRIEVING

In her book, **TRANSFORMATION THROUGH BIRTH** (Bergin and Garvey, 1984), **Claudia Panuthos** gives some guidelines for grieving. She stresses that above all, "cast your pride to the wind and allow others to know who you really are and what is truly happening."

She also feels it is important to make yourself a supportable person, find the appropriate support system, and then make your needs clearly known. Furthermore, she feels it is important to find the answers to all the questions you might have surrounding your miscarriage.

Finally, she emphasizes honouring and respecting your body, and feeling the right to remember your baby in any way that seems right to you, including naming the baby.

For friendships and loved ones of the woman who has miscarried, the most helpful stance is to validate her feelings, whatever they may be.

Comments like, "Keep your chin up," "That's life," or "It's nature's way of getting rid of defective fetuses," are not helpful.

The woman has just experienced the loss of her child, however young that child might have been. And that particular child and time can never be replaced.

Similarly, the well-meaning, "you can try again," is also offensive. In fact, trying again is not a good idea. Emotionally it is better to recover from one loss before starting anew, and physically, most doctors recommend waiting between three and six months to allow the body time to return to normal.

After a miscarriage, a woman needs special understanding and caring from her mate. At the same time a woman must keep in mind that her partner may well be experiencing his own feelings of emptiness and loss.

Time and the loving support of family friends and mate will assist you in recovering from a miscarriage. But in the end, letting yourself acknowledge your loss and experience it fully is the kindest thing you can do for yourself.

RECOMMENDED READING

ENDED BEGINNINGS, Healing Child-bearing Losses, by **Claudia Panuthos** and **Catherine Romeo** (Begin and Harvey, 1984).

SURVIVING PREGNANCY LOSS, by **Freidman** and **Gradstein** (Little Brown and Company, 1992). This book deals with physical and emotional aftermath of pregnancy loss, and explores future options.

EMPTY CRADLE, BROKEN HEART, by **Deborah Davis** (Fulcrum 1991). Practical down-to-earth advice as well as a warm understanding for those struggling to cope with pregnancy loss.

MISCARRIAGE by **Anne Oakley**, (Penguin, 1990). This books offers good support and information.

MISCARRIAGE, WOMEN'S EXPERIENCES AND NEEDS, by **Christine Moulder** (Pandora Press, 1990).

PREVENTING MISCARRIAGE: THE GOOD NEWS, by **Jonathan Scher** (Harper and Collins, 1990).

HOW TO PREVENT MISCARRIAGE AND OTHER CRISES OF PREGNANCY, by **Dr. Stefan Semchyshyn** and **Carol Colman** (Collier Books, 1990). This book is full of practical information on preventing miscarriages as well as premature births. Dr. Semchyshyn believes that a woman is an expert on her own body and should not hesitate to follow through on her symptoms, if she feels something is wrong.

GETTING AROUND THE BOULDER IN THE ROAD: USING IMAGERY TO COPE WITH FERTILITY PROBLEMS, by **Aline Zoldbrod** (1990). This can be ordered from Dr. Zoldbrod for $8.00 from 12 Rumford Rd, Lexington, Mass, 02173. The methods in this book can be easily adapted to help deal emotionally with miscarriage.

SHATTERED DREAMS is a newsletter published four times a year to offer "support information, sharing and hope for the future" for women experiencing miscarriage. Write to **Shattered Dreams**, c/o **Debbie Anderson**, 2672 Hickson Cres, Ottawa, ON, K2H 6Y6.

The Thyroid Gland Acts Up After Pregnancy

TRUDI'S STORY

Four months after the birth of her first baby, Trudi felt more tired than she ever remembered feeling before. She often felt depressed and anxious. However, she didn't pay much attention and attributed her symptoms to a combination of the demands of a new baby, postpartum blues and chronic lack of sleep. After another four months, she finally felt like her old self again.

About four months after the birth of her second baby, Trudi again began to feel the same kind of marked fatigue and depression and also noticed a painless swelling in the front of her neck. This time she consulted her physician. He found her thyroid gland to be enlarged and ordered some blood tests. These tests showed that Trudi's thyroid gland was underactive or hypothyroid. He prescribed synthetic thyroid hormone for her, which she took for six months and felt enormously better. One year after her delivery, her thyroid gland was back to normal, and she went off the medication.

POSTPARTUM THYROIDITIS

Trudi had been suffering from a condition only recently recognized by the medical profession called postpartum thyroiditis or transient thyroiditis. This condition is a disturbance of thyroid function where the gland becomes overactive or underactive or both, and then eventually returns to normal.

The thyroid gland is a small, powerful organ located in the neck just below the Adam's apple. It consists of two lobes with a central part between them giving it a butterfly appearance. It weighs a little under an ounce. This gland is the energy regulator of the body. It secretes hormones that determine the rate at which cells burn up food and oxygen to produce energy and body heat. The thyroid hormones also promote growth and development generally.

In a manner of speaking, during pregnancy, the immune system goes on holiday. This is so the mother won't form antibodies to her own baby. So women who have immune disorders will not have them flare up until after the pregnancy is over.

After birth, for reasons still poorly understood, one out of 20 women or more will have a disorder of the immune system and develop antibodies against her own thyroid glands (The immune system is the defense system of the body and forms antibodies against bacteria or viruses or anything foreign to the body). These thyroid antibodies cause some damage to the thyroid gland causing it to temporarily malfunction. The damaged gland then puts out higher than normal levels of thyroid hormone. This period lasts one or two months. Then for a brief period, the gland returns to normal. Then three to six months after delivery, thyroid hormones drop below normal. Finally, usually within a year after delivery, the thyroid gland usually, but not always, returns to normal.

UNDERACTIVE OR OVERACTIVE THYROID ?

When the thyroid gland malfunctions, it usually swells up. This swelling is called a goiter. A goiter may be associated with underactivity (**hypothyroidism**) or overactivity (**hyperthyroidism**).

Early symptoms of underactivity of the gland include:

Fatigue, weakness, nervousness, constipation, intolerance to cold, sluggishness, hoarseness, and menstrual abnormalities. These symptoms are non-specific and may have a lot of other potential causes as well.

Later signs and symptoms include:

Slow speech, modest weight gain, muscular aches and pains, chest pain, puffiness of the face and eyelids, dry skin, thin hair, thinning of the outer third of the eyebrows and slow heart rate.

Overactivity of the gland results in:

Fatigue, restlessness, nervousness, irritability, increased appetite and weight loss, excessive sweating, heat intolerance and fine tremor. Some also notice difficulty in focusing the eyes, diarrhea, and rapid heart rate. These symptoms can have other causes as well.

A TYPICAL CASE

In a typical case of postpartum thyroiditis, a woman has a completely normal pregnancy and delivery. There is usually no history of thyroid disease, either in the past or during the pregnancy. Occasionally, she may have had a small goiter at one time, but no symptoms from it. Sometimes a close relative has thyroid disease.

One to three months after the birth of her child, she may or may not notice symptoms of hyperthyroidism (fatigue, nervousness, irritability, excessive sweating and intolerance to heat). The symptoms may be so mild that she does not even consult her doctor. If more severe, she will be prompted to see her doctor. Blood tests will then show elevated levels of anti-thyroid antibodies. This hyperthyroid state may be severe enough to require the use of anti-thyroid medications which suppress the activity of the thyroid gland.

Next, three to six months after the birth, a woman notices symptoms of an underactive thyroid (marked fatigue, lethargy, depression and cold intolerance). Blood tests then reveal a low level of thyroid in the blood as well as the presence of anti-thyroid hormones in the blood. This hypothyroid state may be so mild as to require no treatment. More often, a woman needs to take daily doses of thyroid hormone in a synthetic form called eltroxin or synthroid.

One year after delivery, the thyroid gland recovers from the temporary damage, and thyroid hormone levels go back to normal. At this point a woman can stop taking thyroid medication. In a very small percentage of cases, the thyroid gland does not recover and long-term use of medication may be required.

Borderline or chronic underactive thyroid can be missed in blood tests. A better way of detecting borderline hypothyroidism is to take the underarm temperature upon waking, before rising, each morning for three to five days or more (see chart). The average basal temperature is determined by the proper functioning of the thyroid gland, and a low body temperature on waking (below 97.8F or 36.55C) may indicate borderline hypothyroidism.

HOW OFTEN DOES THIS OCCUR

Postpartum thyroiditis may occur in anywhere between five and ten percent of all pregnancies. Some researchers suggest routine screening of woman after birth for blood levels of anti-thyroid antibodies. Postpartum thyroiditis can occur with first babies as well as second and third or more. Rarely, it even occurs after miscarriage or abortion. In the past, postpartum thyroiditis was probably often misdiagnosed as postpartum depression. But now it is both easy to diagnose and easy to treat. If a woman has had it once, it is likely to recur after each pregnancy, so both she and her physician will have to be on the look out for it.

Fatigue after childbirth is experienced by most women and is most often due to plain lack of sleep and the demands of new motherhood. Postpartum blues are usually due to a variety of factors including unrealistic expectations, lack of adequate support, and shifting hormone levels after birth. Ninety to 95 percent of women will not experience any difficulties with their thyroid gland after birth. For those who do, treatment is simple and effective.

FOR FURTHER READING

HYPOTHYROIDISM; THE UNSUSPECTED ILLNESS, by B. Barnes (Random House, 1974). This book goes into a lot of detail about undiagnosed thyroid problems, the basal temperature test, and how to treat and monitor problems.

POSTPARTUM DEPRESSION AND ANXIETY (1987) is a practical, self-help guide for helping mothers understand what is happening and what can be done. Available for $5.00 from **Pacific Postpartum Support Society**, 1416 Commercial Dr, Vancouver, BC, V5L 3X9. 604-255-7999.

AFTER THE BABY'S BIRTH, A WOMAN'S GUIDE TO WELLNESS, by **Robin Lim** (1991). Highly recommended, this book helps women and their families have a healthier, saner postpartum experience.

WILSON'S SYNDROME, THE MIRACLE OF FELLING WELL, by **Denis Wilson** (Cornerstone Publishing, 1994, call 1-800-621-7006).

WILSON'S SYNDROME, DOCTOR'S MANUAL, by **Denis Wilson** (Cornerstone Publishing, 1994, call 1-800-621-7006).

TAKING YOUR BASAL TEMPERATURE

Pizzorno and Murray, A Textbook of Natural Medicine, Page 170.

Your body temperature reflects your metabolic rate, which is largely determined by hormones secreted by the thyroid gland. The function of the thyroid gland can be determined by simply measuring your basal body temperature. All that is needed is a thermometer.

Procedure:

1. Shake down the thermometer to below 95F or 35C and place it by your bed before going to sleep at night.

2. On waking, place the thermometer in your armpit for a full ten minutes. It is important to make as little movement as possible. Lying and resting with your eyes closed is best. Do not get up until the ten minute test is completed.

3. After ten minutes, read and record temperature and date.

4. Record the temperature for at least three mornings (preferably at the same time of day) and give the information to your physician. Menstruating women must perform the test on the second, third and fourth days of menstruation. Men and post-menopausal women can perform the test at any time.

Interpretation:

Your basal body temperature should be between 97.6F and 98.2F (36.44C and 36.77C). Low body basal temperatures are quite common and may reflect hypothyroidism.

Common signs and symptoms of hypothyroidism are:

Depression, Difficulty in losing weight, Dry skin, Headaches, Lethargy or Fatigue, Menstrual problems, Recurrent infections and Sensitivity to cold.

High basal temperatures (above 98.6F or 37C) are less common, but may be evidence of hyperthyroidism.

Common signs and symptoms of hyperthyroidism include:

Bulging eyeballs, Fast pulse, Hyperactivity, Inability to gain weight, Insomnia, Irritability, Menstrual problems and Nervousness.

BASAL TEMPERATURE CHART

Month	Day	Temp	Month	Day	Temp	Month	Day	Temp
____	1	988	____	1	____	____	1	____
____	2	____	____	2	____	____	2	____
____	3	____	____	3	____	____	3	____
____	4	____	____	4	____	____	4	____
____	5	____	____	5	____	____	5	____
____	6	____	____	6	____	____	6	____
____	7	____	____	7	____	____	7	____
____	8	____	____	8	____	____	8	____
____	9	____	____	9	____	____	9	____
____	10	____	____	10	____	____	10	____
____	12	____	____	12	____	____	12	____
____	13	____	____	13	____	____	13	____
____	14	____	____	14	____	____	14	____
____	15	____	____	15	____	____	15	____
____	16	____	____	16	____	____	16	____
____	17	____	____	17	____	____	17	____
____	18	____	____	18	____	____	18	____
____	19	____	____	19	____	____	19	____
____	20	____	____	20	____	____	20	____
____	21	____	____	21	____	____	21	____
____	22	____	____	22	____	____	22	____
____	23	____	____	23	____	____	23	____
____	24	____	____	24	____	____	24	____
____	25	____	____	25	____	____	25	____
____	26	____	____	26	____	____	26	____
____	27	____	____	27	____	____	27	____
____	28	____	____	28	____	____	28	____
____	29	____	____	29	____	____	29	____
____	30	____	____	30	____	____	30	____
____	31	____	____	31	____	____	31	____

Section Five:
Specific Women's Problems

PMS - Strength Or Weakness? 146

New Hope For Lumpy Painful Breasts 155

Pelvic Inflammatory Disease 167

Endometriosis - A Disease Of The 90's 173

A New View Of Endometriosis 180

PMS - Strength Or Weakness?

Premenstrual syndrome is a real medical condition that affects about 40 percent of all women in their reproductive years. While the media has made women more aware of the cyclical changes they experience monthly, it has also passed on a lot of negative misinformation.

To add to the confusion, the medical profession itself has lagged behind in recognizing PMS as a real biochemical hormonal disorder that causes both physical and emotional symptoms. The very idea of a physically based problem causing emotional symptoms is still alien to a lot of doctors. Some doctors deny that PMS exists all. Others treat it as a disease and medicate women with tranquilizers, water pills or hormones. Others are just baffled or misinformed about the whole topic.

This is not surprising since nothing was taught in medical school on the subject. And traditionally, women's complaints about the premenstrual time have been viewed as either psychological that is, "all in your head" or part of the biological destiny of women.

Women themselves may have difficulty admitting they have PMS for fear of compromising their struggle for equality in the workplace. But denying symptoms of PMS, which are very real, is no service to women either.

Fortunately, more and more doctors are now educating themselves about PMS. However, more research is needed into both the causes and treatment of PMS.

Nonetheless, there is a lot we do know and a lot that can be done to alleviate or even eliminate the symptoms of PMS.

HOW MANY WOMEN HAVE PMS ?

Unfortunately, women who do not have true PMS have been lumped together with women who have premenstrual symptoms which do not bother them all that much nor affect their day-to-day functioning. In fact, 90 percent of women in the reproductive age group experience premenstrual symptoms of some sort. Ten percent of women will experience no symptoms at all.

Of this 90 percent group, half will experience mild premenstrual symptoms, such as breast tenderness, bloating, food cravings, irritability and mood swings, which alert them that their period is approaching.

In this group of women, premenstrual symptoms are the natural, outward signs of the remarkable fluctuations in hormone levels that a woman undergoes every month when she menstruates (even after a hysterectomy if her ovaries are still in place).

The other half of this group will suffer from PMS symptoms that are serious enough to interfere with their lives. Of this group an estimated five to 12 percent will experience severe, incapacitating PMS.

In modern times, women have had to deal with a lot more periods in their lifetimes than women did in the past. This is because women today spend less time being pregnant. In recent years, women have also experienced a radical change in their diet, environment, stress levels, career and family expectations. It stands to reason that the accumulated effect of all these factors might alter the basic hormonal cycle of women.

WHAT IS PMS ?

True premenstrual syndrome refers to the whole 45 percent group of women whose PMS has a negative impact on their lives. PMS can be defined as that cluster of physical and emotional symptoms that occur one to 14 days before the period, that significantly interfere with a woman's interpersonal relationships and daily activities, and that disappear at or during menstruation.

Symptoms of premenstrual syndrome are diverse and affect almost every body system. The following list, seemingly endless, is only a partial list.

Physical symptoms include:

Breast swelling and tenderness, weight gain and abdominal bloating, constipation or diarrhea.

Headaches, acne or other skin eruptions, eye problems, joint and muscle pain and backache.

Sugar and salt cravings, increased appetite, fatigue, hoarseness, heart pounding, clumsiness and poor co-ordination.

Nausea, menopausal-like hot sweats and chills, shakiness, dizziness, changes in sex drive (either more or less) sensitivity to noise, restlessness, insomnia and even asthma and seizures.

Emotional symptoms include:*PMS*

Sudden mood swings, anxiety, irritability and emotional over-responsiveness.

Anger, rage, loss of control, depression, suicidal thoughts, nightmares, forgetfulness, confusion, decreased concentration, withdrawal, unexplained crying, inward anger, and physical or verbal aggression towards others.

POSITIVE ASPECTS OF PMS

But there is another side to premenstrual symptoms. Some women report increased energy levels, increased sexual drive, and bursts of creativity during this time. Even increased levels of anger and aggression can be viewed as constructive events in a woman's life, empowering her to change untenable situations in her life. Indeed, once a woman has brought troublesome symptoms of PMS under control, she may then be free to realize the positive aspects of this time period.

Other concepts of premenstrual time are emerging. **Dr. Karen Johnson, Assistant Professor of Psychiatry** at the **University of California** and author of, **TRUSTING OURSELVES: the Complete Guide to Emotional Well Being for Women**, sees PMS as a unique opportunity for women. "Women tend to become more assertive," she says in the **East West Journal** (Jan/87), "They are less passive and submissive. They look out for themselves more. They dream of bigger and better things, whether it is to finish a book or degree, or to start a new business." She notes that during this time writers may have their best ideas, artists find inspiration, and scientists become more productive.

Some women use the natural assertive movement of this time period to collect rents or bad debts.

Seemingly irrational outbursts of anger can mask a genuine grievance underneath. Sometimes the problem is not PMS, but a bad marriage or work situation. The answer then lies in addressing the underlying issues. When this is done, symptoms of PMS may lessen or even disappear.

Premenstrual time can also be a reminder for women to take time out of their busy schedules to look after themselves as well as they look after others. It can be a special time where women discover what nourishes them and what drains them, and how to emphasize the nourishing aspects.

HOW OUR CULTURE CONTRIBUTES TO PMS

Marni Jackson, a Toronto journalist, in her article, **HORMONES OR HISTORY**, points out that it is already known scientifically that every thought or image directly affects hormonal activity. For example, the sight or sound of her baby causes a surge of prolactin to be released from the brain of a breast-feeding mother. Jackson speculates that the negative and derogatory values that society places on the biological functions of women communicated through images and sounds on TV and other media might also cause hormonal changes.

In order to remain credible and effective in modern society, Jackson says every woman is being pressured to "cure or suppress whatever changes affect her before her period." She continues, "Happiness and health now seem to be strictly a matter of biochemical fitness. With the right vitamins, a little aerobics and the appropriate hormone therapy, women can be fit as fiddles and as predictable as men. Some of our most intense emotions, from euphoria to rage, can now be dismissed as hormonal hallucinations."

"Still, I think our bodies are trying to tell us something," says Jackson, "and that we have not been listening."

Her theory is that women suffering from the "hormonal imbalance" of PMS are telling a kind of truth about the world we live in. "They are expressing," says Jackson, "in a tangible, physical sense, the degree to which women are still devalued and misunderstood in this culture."

She concludes: "My own prescription for this "social disease" would be to send the whole culture to an Attitude Clinic and to leave the premenstrual patient alone."

DO YOU HAVE PMS ?

To begin with, however, it is important that a woman's experience of her premenstrual time be taken seriously by her family, friends and physician. Most women with PMS are enormously relieved to find out that PMS is actually a physical condition and that it can be successfully treated.

For a woman, finding out that she has PMS can be a revelation. Through charting her symptoms, she becomes more aware of her body and her emotions at various points in the menstrual cycle and how these correlate with events in her life.

Charting, or keeping track of how you feel both physically and emotionally in relationship to your menstrual cycle, is the key to the diagnosis of PMS. There are no blood tests for this condition.

The first thing you should do if you suspect you have PMS is to write down your symptoms every day, rating how severe they are. (for example, on a scale from one to 10) You should do this daily for at least two to three months, noting also the time of your period every month, and major stresses encountered during that month. If all your symptoms are clustered in the two weeks before your period, and seriously affected your life, then you probably have PMS.

On the other hand, if your symptoms stay the same throughout your whole cycle, you may be suffering from another medical or psychological problem and should go to your doctor for a complete assessment.

In treating PMS, the first step is charting and identifying PMS as the problem. The next step is to gain control of your symptoms to your satisfaction, and finally to address the issues that have come up in your family and work life as a result of PMS.

Gaining control of troublesome symptoms requires a multi-faceted approach involving nutrition, vitamins, stress reduction, counselling and support. In severe incapacitating PMS, drugs may occasionally be useful but only as a last resort.

NUTRITION AND VITAMINS

Dr. Carolyn Dean, in her article, on the management of PMS (**Canadian Family Physician** Apr/86), suggests a stepwise approach to PMS. Starting with diet, a woman proceeds along until she finds the right combination that works for her. Each step can be tried for one month or more before the next step is added on. Although these treatments have not been proven in controlled studies, they offer the advantage of being safe methods that a woman can try on her own.

Dr. Dean also stresses that chronic yeast infection can either cause or worsen PMS. According to Dr. Dean, the yeast infection must be treated before other treatments for PMS are attempted. (See chapter on yeast infections).

The first step involves changing your eating patterns. First, sugar, salt, caffeine and alcohol should be reduced or cut out in the two weeks before your period. Secondly, eating small frequent meals seems to help a good deal. This means eating three meals, and three nutritious snacks and not going longer than three hours without eating.

In general, changing slowly to a healthier diet emphasizing grains and beans, fish, chicken, and plenty of fresh fruits and vegetables should be the overall goal. Highly processes food and junk food should be avoided as well as excessive dairy products, fat and red meat.

The second step involves adding the use of vitamin-B6, which improves the overall mood of women with PMS. This can safely be used in doses of between 50 and 200mg either daily throughout the cycle or only for the last two weeks of the cycle. It is advisable to take B6 in a mega-B-50 complex containing all the other B vitamins in equal amounts.

The third step involves the use of the essential fatty acids in the form of evening of primrose oil. Some women find evening primrose oil particularly helpful for symptoms like breast tenderness, depression, irritability, and bloating. The dosage is increased gradually from one or two capsules twice a day during the first two weeks of the cycle to up to six capsules a day in the last two weeks of the cycle.

The fourth step adds the use of vitamin-E in doses of 200 to 800 IU to the above steps. Vitamin-E is relatively non-toxic, even in large doses. All the above mentioned vitamins and supplements should be taken after meals.

Dr. Fred Mandel, **Assistant Professor of Obstetrics and Gynecology** at **The University of Toronto**, suggests adding magnesium 500mg a day plus zinc 10mg a day to this regimen.

Finally, in step five, if none of the above is working, it is wise to consult with a sympathetic doctor.

OTHER NATURAL TREATMENTS FOR PMS

TRYPTOPHAN: Another treatment for PMS which has not been proven, but may well turn out to be useful, is taking the amino acid tryptophan one or two 500mg tablets three times a day between meals with a carbohydrate snack. In the U.S. tryptophan is available by prescription as 5-hydroxy-tryptophan (50mg of 5-hydroxy-tryptophan equals 500mg tryptophan).

Tryptophan is a synthetic version of one of the building blocks of protein and currently available in Canada only by prescription. **JoAnn Cutler Friedrich**, author of **THE PREMENSTRUAL SOLUTION**, has pioneered the use of tryptophan for PMS. She has helped over 100,000 women with PMS. She feels that PMS is basically a sleep disorder caused by a deficiency of one of the neurotransmitters called serotonin (neurotransmitters are the substances that transmit messages in the brain). Tryptophan Increases the level of serotonin in the brain.

Dr. Susan Steinburg, **Assistant Professor of Psychiatry** at **McGill University** in Montreal, is conducting a controlled double blind study comparing 40 women using tryptophan for PMS compared to 40 who are not. The results will ready in October 1993.

DESENSITIZING SHOTS TO PROGESTERONE: Dr. Wayne Konetski, an environmental and allergy specialist from Waukesha, Wisconsin, has found that many women with PMS have developed a hypersensitivity to their own hormones, particularly progesterone. Of the women he has treated, 90 percent also have candida infections, which he treats first. He then treats with desensitizing oral drops of progesterone in the range of 1/100mg to 150mg per month. He has had excellent results when he treats candida first and then prescribes a course of desensitizing drops to the hormone progesterone (similar to allergy shots).

ALLERGIES, CANDIDA AND AMINES: Dr. Robert Wilson specializes in PMS and has authored two books on the subject. He is currently the director of the PMS Clinic at the **Marie Stopes's Well Women Institute** in London England. Dr. Wilson's book, **CONTROLLING PMS** summarizes his treatment regime for mild to moderate PMS as well as for more severe PMS. Dr. Wilson also discusses conditions that can have similar symptoms to PMS and are often missed, namely food allergies and chronic candida or yeast infections.

In cases of severe PMS, Dr. Wilson has found it very useful to limit the intake of amine rich foods. These foods include bananas, avocados, old cheeses, mushrooms, soy sauce, oranges, tomatoes, sour cream and anchovies. He believes that some women lack an enzyme that breaks down the amines, the substances that transmit messages in the brain. Rising levels of amines in the body can aggravate or cause PMS symptoms, such as headaches and mood swings.

LOW THYROID FUNCTION: Dr. Nora Brayshaw of the **Biopsychiatry Institute** in New Jersey found the thyroid gland was mildly underactive in 94 percent of the women with PMS who were tested. Those who took thyroid pills reported complete relief from the symptoms of PMS. Brayshaw said low thyroid may not cause PMS, but two problems could be the result of the same disorder. She believes that virtually everyone with PMS has some kind of thyroid deficiency. See last chapter on The Thyroid Gland And Pregnancy for how to find out if your thyroid gland is mildly underactive.

Other experts say that they doubt that an underactive thyroid contributes to PMS and point out that well designed studies have not yet been done that would prove that thyroid malfunctioning is the cause of PMS.

NATURAL PROGESTERONE SKIN CREAM: The best plant source of natural progesterone is the Mexican wild yam (dioscorea villosa). It is available as (PRO-GEST) cream from **Transitions For Health Inc**, in Portland Oregon. In Canada the product is distributed through **Gahler Enterprises** in Vancouver, BC.

The cream is available without prescription and has no known side effects. Occasionally there is spotting for the first few menstrual cycles, then it disappears. The cream is applied to the skin of the face, neck, back of the wrists, hands, chest or abdomen. The site where it is applied should be rotated daily.

For PMS you begin with 1/4 to 1/2 teaspoon of the cream applied to the skin twice daily, noting the time it takes for the cream to be absorbed. When you observe that the cream is absorbing in less than one minute you increase the amount and the frequency that you apply the cream. Faster absorption means that body requires more progesterone. In the one to two weeks before your period, you will usually require more cream, more often. Some women use up to one to two jars per month. The cream is stopped as soon as the period starts.

It is advisable to continue using the cream every month for three months to a year, then the dosage can be reduced or discontinued.

Dr. Raymond Peat used this progesterone skin cream to treat 200 women with PMS. He found that nearly all of the women, applying the cream themselves, were able to find exactly the right dosage that relieved their symptoms.

REDUCING STRESS AND GETTING SUPPORT

In addition to all of the above, taking practical measures to reduce stress in your life, learning and using relaxation techniques, enlisting the help of family and friends in coping with PMS times, and seeking counselling when necessary are all very important aspects of treating PMS.

One of the messages of PMS may be that you have to pay more attention to your natural rhythms and become less subservient to the needs of others. At times, this may require you to express your anger, clearly communicate your needs, insist others pull their weight in the household, and arrange privacy and quiet time alone.

Larrie Halliday Smith, former director of the **PMS Clinic** at **Women's College Hospital** in Toronto, said that one of the most useful things she provided to her clients was couple counselling, with an emphasis on communication. Marital problems are common in PMS.

Dr. Robert Reid, Professor of Reproductive Endocrinology at **Queen's University** in Kingston and one of the leading PMS researchers in Canada, says that education and reassurance alone help a lot of women. He believes that group or individual counselling by a psychologist experienced in PMS may also be very helpful.

Teenagers and young women in their twenties can get PMS, and the diagnosis is often missed. Dr. Wilson observed that some younger women and teens with PMS had a history of sexual abuse during childhood.

Many women have found great value in joining a PMS support group or starting one of their own. Check the women's center near you for information about the group closest to you.

Regular exercise increases endorphins in the brain, which in turn has a calming effect. Yoga and belly dancing can also be very helpful in reducing PMS symptoms.

The best tool for combating PMS is really educating yourself and those close to you as much as possible.

WHEN SHOULD YOU USE DRUGS FOR PMS ?

Women with severe PMS that does not improve after trying diet, vitamins, stress reduction and counselling for at least three to six months, may want to consider trying some of the drugs used for treating PMS. However, this should never be the initial approach to PMS and is not necessary for the majority of women with PMS.

1. Drugs that lower prostaglandins.

This is a group of fatty acids made naturally in the body that acts in a similar way to hormones. Recent evidence suggests that regular use of these drugs (such as Anaprox, Ponstan, Motrin) for the last seven to ten days of the menstrual cycle can help decrease PMS symptoms in some women. These drugs work best in women who are also experiencing painful periods.

2. Water pills.

Severe troublesome bloating may be helped by occasional use of a type of water pill known as spironolactone, which preserves potassium in the body. Other types of water pills should be avoided. One study showed that taking this drug in the dosage of 25mg four times a day reduced weight gain and psychological symptoms.

3. Drugs that help severe premenstrual breast pain.

A drug called bromocriptine 2.5 twice a day from day ten of the cycle to the beginning of the period is sometimes used for severe premenstrual breast pain. However, this is a powerful drug, not to be used lightly, with side effects of nausea, vomiting and dizziness.

Aqueous diatomic iodine (which has been tested in double blind studies in the U.S.) works just as well but has virtually no side effects. This treatment is being investigated by the **FDA** and may be on the market within a few years (see chapter on fibrocystic breast disease).

4. Natural progesterone suppositories and desensitization.

Some doctors have found natural progesterone in rectal or vaginal suppositories to be useful in treating severe PMS. (These are very different from the synthetic progesterones in the pill). Natural progesterone is inactive when taken in pill form. A nasal spray or gel form of natural progesterone is being developed in England.

Dr. Wilson has had good success using natural progesterone suppositories, started when symptoms begin and ended at menstruation. He says, "Patients rarely require progesterone therapy beyond 12 months. But, if they do, the dosage can be substantially reduced."

The studies done so far do not indicate any advantage of natural progesterone over placebo. However, some women with severe and uncontrollable PMS symptoms have had dramatic relief using natural progesterone.

5. "Hormonal therapy," according to Dr. Mandel, "should be used as a last resort."

Danazol is an expensive synthetic male hormone derivative that shuts down ovarian functions completely and causes a pseudo-menopause. Dr. Wilson suggests that danazol only be used in crisis circumstances such as impending marital or career disaster. Danazol should not be used in women with depression or anxiety states.

The new gonadotropin releasing drugs also create a pseudo-menopause. Sometimes small doses of estrogen and progesterone have to be given as well. However, these drugs are still experimental, extremely expensive and prone to severe side effects (see chapter on endometriosis for more details on these drugs as well as danazol).

6. Antidepressants have not yet been shown to be an effective treatment for PMS.

One study did show that a tranquilizer called alprazolam (xanax) reduced PMS symptoms, especially mood swings, aggressiveness and irritability. However, in general, it is a good idea to steer away from potentially addicting tranquilizers as much as possible.

IN SUMMARY

PMS is real and it is treatable. Up to 40 percent of women have PMS symptoms that impact very negatively on their lives. Dealing with PMS requires women to change their lifestyle. It also requires their care givers to look at the whole environment of women's lives and not just the symptoms.

"PMS," says Dr. Karen Johnson, "should stand for premenstrual strength. In tapping into their cycles, women will find embodied deep within themselves their own unique qualities and their essence, all to be valued, praised and honoured".

Menstrual Symptom Diary

Name: _____ Age:_____ Height: _____ Weight: _____

GRADING OF MENSES
0-none   3-heavy
1-slight   4-heav
2-moderate

GRADING OF SYMPTOMS (COMPLAINTS)
0-none
1-mild-present but does not interferences with activities
2-moderate-present but interferences with activities but not disabling
3-severe-disabling; unable to function

Day of Cycle	1	2	3	4	5	6	7	8	9	10	11	12	13	14	15	16	17	18	19	20	21	22	23	24	25	26	27	28	29	30	31	32	33	34	35	36
Date																																				
Menses																																				

PMT-A

Nervous tension																																				
Mood swings																																				
Irritability																																				
Anxiety																																				

PMT-H

Weight gain																																				
Swelling of extremities																																				
Breast tenderness																																				
Abdominal bloating																																				

PMT-C

Headache																																				
Craving for sweets																																				
Increased appetite																																				
Heart pounding																																				
Fatigue																																				
Dizziness or faintness																																				

PMT-D

Depression																																				
Forgetfulness																																				
Crying																																				
Confusion																																				
Insomnia																																				

Dysmenorrhea-Pain

Cramps																																				
Backache																																				
General aches/pain																																				

Basal weight in lbs.																																				
Basal body temp.																																				

From: Abraham G.E.: Nutritional Factors in the Etiology of the Premenstrual Tension Syndromes. J. Reprod. Med. 28:446-464., 1983
Λ:PMSQu-2

PRISM Calendar

Courtesy of Dr. Robert Reid

Name: _____ Baseline Weight on Day 1: _____ lbs or kg. (circle one)

Bleeding		1	2	3	4	5	6	7	8	9	10	11	12	13	14	15	16	17	18	19	20	21	22	23	24	25	26	27	28	29	30	31	32	33	34	35	36	37	38	39	40	41	42
Days of Cycle																																											
Month: Date:																																											
Weight Change																																											
Symptoms																																											
Irritable																																											
Fatigue																																											
Inward anger																																											
Labile mood (crying)																																											
Depressed																																											
restless																																											
Anxious																																											
Insomnia																																											
Lack of control																																											
Edema or rings tight																																											
Breast tenderness																																											
Abdominal bloating																																											
Bowels: const (c) loose (l)																																											
Appetite: up ↓ down ↑																																											
Sex drive: up ↓ down ↑																																											
Chills (C)/Sweats (S)																																											
Headaches																																											
Crave: sweets, salt																																											
Feel unattractive																																											
Guilty																																											
Unreasonable behaviour																																											
Low self image																																											
Nausea																																											
Menstrual Cramps																																											
Lifestyle Impact																																											
Aggresive physically towards others verbally																																											
Wish to be alone																																											
Neglect housework																																											
Time of work																																											
Disorganized, distractable																																											
Accident prone/clumsy																																											
Uneasy about driving																																											
Suicidal thoughts																																											
Stayed at home																																											
Increased use of alcohol																																											
Life Events																																											
Negative experience																																											
Positive experience																																											
Social activities																																											
Vigorous exercise																																											
Medications																																											

Instructions for Completing this Calendar

1. *On the first day of menstruation prepare the calendar*; Considering the first day of bleeding as day 1 of your menstrual cycle enter the corresponding calendar date for each day in the space provided below. 2. *Each morning:* Take weight after emptying bladder and before breakfast. Record **Weight Change** from baseline. 3. *Each Evening:* At about the same time complete the column for that day as described below.

Bleeding: Indicate if you have had bleeding by shading the box above that days date []; for spotting use an [x]

Symptoms: If you do not experience any symptoms leave the corresponding square blank. If present indicate severity.

Mild:	1 (noticeable but not troublesome)
Moderate:	2 (interferes with normal activity)
Severe:	3 (temporarily incapacitating)

Lifestyle Impact:
If the listed phrase applies to you that day enter an [x]

Life Events:
If you experienced one of these events that day enter an [x]
Experiences: for positive (happy) or negative (sad or disappointing) experiences unrelated to your symptoms specify the nature of the events on the reverse side of this form.
Social Activities: imply events such as a special dinner, show or party etc, involving family or friends.
Vigorous Exercise: implies participation in a sporting event or exercise programme lasting more than 30 minutes.
Medication: In the bottom 3 rows list medications if any and indicate days when taken by entering an [x]

REFERENCES

SELF-HELP FOR PMS, by **Dr. Michelle Harrison**. A good overall book on PMS.

PMS SELF-HELP BOOK, A WOMAN'S GUIDE TO FEELING GOOD ALL MONTH, by **Dr. Susan Lark** (Celestial Arts 1984). Dr. Lark's book describes how to create your own program for PMS using diet, vitamins and minerals, exercise, stress management, massage, acupressure and yoga.

CURING PMS, THE DRUG-FREE WAY, by **Moira Carpenter**. This book is a gem and the best one summarizing natural treatments for PMS, including diet, vitamins, herbs and homeopathy.

THE PREMENSTRUAL SOLUTION: TAMING THE SHREW IN YOU, by **JoAnn Cutler Friedrich**. This book explains the rationale for using tryptophan for PMS and how best to use it.

CONTROLLING PMS, by **Dr. Robert Wilson** (Fitzhenry and Whiteside, 1988). Highly recommended, a very important book for women with PMS.

PMS, A PERSONAL WORKBOOK, by **Dr. Suzanne Trupin**. This book, written by a woman gynecologist, is a very practical tool which helps women gather information, and achieve understanding and control of symptoms using natural methods. Available from **Women's Health Practice**, 301 East Springfield Ave, Champaign, IL, 61820. 217-356-3736.

PMS, A POSITIVE PROGRAM TO GAIN CONTROL, by **S. Degraff Bender** and **K. Kelleher**. This book emphasizes coping with emotions and family life when you have PMS. There is also a whole chapter for men.

BEAT PMS THROUGH DIET, by **Maryon Stewart** (Ebury Press, 1990). This book outlines the four different types of PMS and how to create a unique diet for your particular symptoms. The author also founded the **Women's Nutritional Advisory Service**.

THE PMS SOLUTION, PMS: THE NUTRITIONAL APPROACH, by **Dr. Nazzaro**, **Dr. D. Lombard** and **Dr. D. Horrobin**. This book emphasizes the use of evening of primrose oil for PMS.

PMS, by **Gilda Berger**. Well written book aimed at teenage women who have PMS.

MEDICAL MANAGEMENT OF PMS, by **Dr. Carolyn Dean** and others, **CANADIAN FAMILY PHYSICIAN**, Vol-32, Apr/86.

CYCLES, An American **PMS SUPPORT NEWSLETTER**, PO Box 524, Sharon, MA 02067 (a one year subscription is $18.50) an excellent newsletter published six times a year.

OWNER'S MANUAL, by **Dr. Diane McGibbon**. Dr. McGibbon has designed a convenient and simple tool the size of a cheque book to help women keep an accurate record of their monthly cycle. It evolved out of 16 years of clinical research. Each "Owner's Manual" will last for one year. Write or Fax your order to:

DR. DIANE L. MCGIBBON, 3 Gardenvale Rd, Toronto, ON, M8Z 4B8. 416-239-4644 Fax: 416-239-7428.

Recently, Dr. McGibbon has also published a book **MENSTRUAL REALITIES AND MENSTRUAL MYTHS**. This book is both a handbook and diary for management of menstrual mood disorders.

TRUSTING OURSELVES: the Complete Guide to Emotional Well Being for Women, by **Dr. Karen Johnson** (Atlantic Monthly Press, 1991). An excellent and highly recommended book that should be in every woman's library.

New Hope For Lumpy Painful Breasts

As **Dr. William Ghent**, former **Professor Emeritus of Surgery** at **Queen's University** in Kingston, Ontario, used to say, "premenstrual breast pain and tenderness is not normal. If it's painful, premenstrually, it's sick. I am sure that males would not accept sore testicles for seven to ten days of each month as normal." Dr. Ghent also pointed out that fibrocystic breast disease did not necessarily disappear with menopause, particularly if estrogens were used. Twenty years of research in the field led him to believe that elemental iodine was essential for breast normalcy at any age.

According to the **American Academy of Pathology**, at least 50 percent but as many as 80 percent of North American women suffer from some form of fibrocystic breast disease.(**FCBD**) This condition causes women a lot of pain and discomfort as well as a great deal of anxiety. Although **FCBD** is a benign condition, it can sometimes be difficult for both women and their physicians to distinguish a cystic breast lump from a cancerous one.

WHAT IS FIBROCYSTIC BREAST DISEASE

FCBD is a confusing term. Or, as **Dr. Susan Love, Director of the Breast Cancer Clinic at University of California**, says, "a wastebasket into which doctors throw every breast problem which isn't cancer."

FCBD actually covers a whole spectrum of changes that occur in women during their reproductive years. It refers to a wide variety of non-cancerous conditions of the breast, characterized by painful lumpy breasts, usually on a cyclical basis but can occur throughout the whole cycle, and the formation of breast cysts and scar tissue. The severity of the pain does not necessarily correlate with the amount of lumpiness.

Some women have breast tenderness and enlargement that occur only for a short time in the premenstrual period, and this can be considered within the limits of a normal physiological change.

Other women develop breasts that feel lumpy or irregular to the touch. These women can have considerable breast pain and discomfort often on a daily basis. Every once in while they can feel a larger or more clearly defined cyst. This cyst usually contains clear fluid, and can be drained in the office under local anesthetic. If the cyst does not disappear, then a mammogram and biopsy is usually indicated.

Then there is a significant group of women, as much as 30 percent of women with FCBD, who have an incapacitating problem with frequent formation of breast cysts and scar tissue, accompanied by severe pain that interferes with sleep and normal daily activities.

The constant underlying worry about breast cancer is one of the debilitating aspects of FCBD. In the past, it was thought that women with FCBD had a higher incidence of breast cancer than normal, but further research did not bear out that assumption.

TREATING A PUZZLING DISEASE

Dr. Ghent used to lament that modern treatment for FCBD consisted of "little more than reassurance and the recommendation for a good support bra."

Various researchers have suggested a hormonal imbalance, a decreased ratio of progesterone to estrogen in the second half of the cycle, an abnormality of prolactin regulation, a hypersensitivity to thyroid stimulating hormone and increased estrogen levels.

Dr. Mauvais-Jarvis found that a decreased progesterone to estrogen ratio in patients with mastalgia. His group of French researchers found that breast pain was relieved 95 percent of the time with a natural progesterone gel rubbed into the breasts. This gel is not yet available in North America.

Vitamin supplementation may reduce breast pain and swelling, but studies are inconclusive. Vitamins that have been suggested include vitamin-B6, 100 to 200mg a day throughout the cycle (taken in combination with all the other B vitamins) evening of primrose oil capsules two to six a day, and vitamin-E 400 to 800 IU daily.

One double blind controlled study showed vitamin-E had no effect on breast pain. However, a group of Welsh doctors found evening of primrose oil, taken on a regular basis relieved cyclical breast pain in 20 percent of women.

Avoidance of caffeine has helped some women, although not proven in studies. A low fat diet has been studied and shown to have some effect on breast pain.

American gynecologist **Dr. Christiane Northrup** advises women to follow a diet high in whole grains and fibre and low in fat. She also recommends a three month trial off all dairy products. After the three months period, she recommends adding back low fat dairy food to see if they can be tolerated.

Dr. Northrup also recommends hot castor oil packs applied to the breasts three times a week for one hour for two or three months. (with maintenance afterwards of once a week).

Dr. John Lee, a clinical instructor at the **University of California Department of Family Medicine**, has had success using a two ounce jar of three percent natural progesterone cream for the last two weeks of the cycle for a total of three to six months. Maintenance is half a jar per month. This cream can be made up by any pharmacist.

Danazol has been used to treat women with severe FCBD, unresponsive to any of the above treatments. The effects of prolonged use of danazol are unclear.

All of the above treatments are symptomatic, that is, they deal only with the symptoms of FCBD, but do not reverse the cysts and scars. Elemental iodine is the only treatment so far that is able to get rid of symptoms and heal cysts and scars.

MAKING THE IODINE CONNECTION

Dr. John Myers, a Baltimore gynecologist with a special interest in metabolic disease, was the among the first to recognize the importance of iodine to the breast and ovary. He found that he could completely reverse fibrocystic breast disease using iodine orally and vaginally along with trace mineral elements (still available from 1-800-232-3183) given under the tongue, and magnesium, given intravenously. Cystic breasts would soften quickly under this regimen, sometimes immediately.

Dr. Jonathan Wright, author and medical doctor specializing in nutritional medicine, has had excellent results using an adaptation of the Myer's program. Besides using a program of vitamins and iodine by mouth, Wright paints Lugol's solution onto the vaginal wall of women with FCBD, and three to five minutes later injects 300mg of magnesium into a vein. (Beforehand, he advises checking for iodine sensitivity by painting a small amount of iodine onto the vagina and waiting 2-3 minutes). Treatments are continued until the breasts have returned to normal (on the average of 3 to 5 treatments), and followed by a maintenance program of oral supplements and iodine.

Dr. Bernard Eskin, Professor of Reproductive Endocrinology and Obstetrics and Gynecology at the **Medical College of Pennyslvania** in Philadelphia produced an animal model for FCBD in the rat. In 1970, Dr. Eskin's exhaustive study of the female rat breast and the changes produced by an iodine deficient diet was published in the annals of the **New York Academy of Sciences**. The microscopic changes in the rat breast closely resembled those seen in human breasts.

Eskin and his colleagues had earlier demonstrated the presence of elemental iodine in lobules of rat breast tissue. Strum demonstrated the same distribution in the female human breast.

Research papers between 1910 and 1960 showed an association between both benign and cancerous breast changes with hypothyroidism.

In 1960, two Russian researchers reported a 70 percent improvement in women with FCBD after treatment with sodium iodide. This was the first clinical suggestion in the literature that iodine played a significant role in human breast disease. In the 1970's, Dr. Eskin and Dr. Ghent decided to collaborate on clinical research on the relationship between FCBD and iodine deficiency.

ALL ABOUT IODINE

Iodine is a rare metallic element that can be mined from only one place in the world, Chile. It is also a by-product of the oil industry in many countries of the world. It is a purplish solid with an atomic weight of 126.904.

Iodine is an essential trace element for humans that must be ingested. At least 160 micrograms is required daily. Since 1929 in Canada, and 1924 in the States, potassium iodide has been added to table salt, thereby greatly decreasing the incidence of cretinism and goiter. Seventy-five micrograms is added to each gram of salt.

However, in 1982, the average North American consumed about 8 grams of table salt a day or 600 micrograms. In 1993, the average North American was getting only two grams of salt a day or only 150 micrograms a day. This amount would not meet the needs of a physically active person, or breast-feeding or pregnant woman.

In fact, recent evidence suggests that at least 25 percent of women in North America are iodine deficient at some point in their lives.

Dietary iodine intake depends on the iodine content of the soil and water, and the types of foods consumed. Certain foods are naturally high in iodine such as seafoods and seaweeds. But vegetables and fruits can be deficient in iodine if the soil they were grown on lacked iodine, which is usually the case.

Around the Great Lakes, in a large area known as the goiter belt, there is a little or no iodine in the soil or water. The incidence of both FCBD and breast cancer is higher in these goiter areas. However, most areas in Canada and the U.S. have soils that are deficient in many trace minerals including iodine.

Only small amounts of iodine can be ingested from foods and then the amount absorbed is variable depending on many co-factors. For example, smoking cigarettes and consuming an excess of certain foods such as soybeans, the brassica family eaten raw (cabbage, kale, brussel sprouts, mustard greens, cauliflower and broccoli) peanuts and millet, especially if grown on iodine deficient soil, can block iodine absorption by the thyroid.

GETTING MORE IODINE

Elemental or free iodine, (meaning iodine that is biologically free or available for use by the tissues), is the specific type of iodine that is lacking in breast tissues in FCBD.

This free iodine has a completely different action from the thousands of compounds that contain the element iodine. For example, sodium and potassium iodide mix with water to form a solution that is 95 percent iodide and five percent elemental iodine.

In the past, if more iodine was required, it had to be bound to a salt or a protein. For example, in table salt and in Lugol's solution, it is bound to potassium and in caseinated iodine, it is bound to the milk protein casein.

In 1981, a Canadian scientist and inventor, **Dennis O'Dowd**, discovered and patented a series of methods and devices to control the dissolution of elemental iodine directly into water. O'Dowd now specializes in iodine water purification systems. He found that when 100 parts per billion of iodine is added to drinking water, 60 to 70 percent less chlorine is required. Such systems are now being used in 16 Canadian cities and towns, and may prove useful should future supplementation of iodine be necessary.

GHENT AND ESKIN AT THE NEW FRONTIER

In 1972, when Dr. Ghent first began to study the effects of treating FCBD with iodine, he used Lugol's solution, and subsequently, casein bound iodine in pill form with the brand name iodaminol and finally elemental iodine.

At first, Dr. Ghent used a device invented by Dennis O'Dowd. Drs. Ghent and Eskin subsequently developed their own unique and highly effective method for dissolving the iodine crystals in water and delivering precise dosages of aqueous iodine. Most recently, Dr. Ghent developed an entirely new system of delivery of elemental iodine in the form of gelatin capsules, taken orally, with lactose and cornstarch as fillers.

In the first study, one group of 233 volunteers received Lugol's solution for two years and one group of 588 received iodaminol for five years. The results of this study were intriguing.

In the first group, 70 percent noticed clinical improvement, but the rate of side effects was unacceptably high. Four percent had a change in thyroid indices; three percent developed symptoms of iodism (coryza and enlarged tender lymph nodes) and two percent occurrence of acne (quite apart from the vile taste of Lugol's solution).

In the second group, an excellent response was noted in 40 percent of the patients with 50 percent having marked improvement, and side effects involving 9.5 percent of the women.

In his next research project, Ghent took 145 patients from the first study who had not responded well to iodaminol and found that 74.5 percent of these then improved. Another group of 108 new patients had treatment initiated with elemental iodine, and this group had remarkable success with 98 percent of women having their breasts return to normal.

Next the original series of 233 women were enlarged to 1,365. In this larger group of women, within two years of treatment, 95 percent of women had excellent results with loss of pain and disappearance of cysts and scar tissue and complete return of the breast tissue to normal. This effect is time dependant. That is to say there is greater subjective and objective improvement noted after eighteen months than six months.

Six women fail to respond to any therapy including danazol, bromocriptine, tamoxifen and progesterone, and required subcutaneous mastectomy for definitive treatment. Ghent concluded that there may be a "point of no return", at which time surgery may be the only option.

In Seattle, a prospective double blind study was carried out and supervised by the **FDA** in collaboration with **Dr. Donald Low** and **Dr. Lucius Hill** at the **Department of Surgery at Virginia Mason Clinic**. It involved 23 patients receiving aqueous iodine and 33 receiving an aqueous mixture of brown vegetable dye with quinine added for flavour. The group was followed at two month intervals for an average of six months. The results showed the treatment group had 65 percent subjective and objective improvement and the control group a subjective improvement of 33 percent (the expected placebo response) and an objective worsening of three percent.

In October 1993, the results of Dr. Ghent and his colleagues research was published in the **Canadian Journal of Surgery**.

In an editorial in the same issue entitled **Elemental Iodine- Relief for the Painful Breast? Dr. John MacFarlane**, Chairman of the **Department of Surgery**, at **St. Paul's Hospital** in Vancouver congratulated Dr. Ghent and his colleagues "on an excellent and meaningful study... {which} seems to confirm the validity of the hypothesis that {elemental} iodine can be of significant benefit to patients with fibrocystic breasts. However, Dr. MacFarlane cautioned that although the study is an important one, the findings should be confirmed by another centre before elemental iodine is recommended as standard therapy for symptomatic cystic breast disease.

Although the elemental iodine capsules are still classified as an experimental drug, (approved by HPB in Canada and awaiting FDA approval in the States), it appears to be a very safe and effective treatment for FCBD. Further clinical trials of Dr. Ghent's capsules are in progress and more double blind studies are being organized.

MECHANISM OF ACTION OF ELEMENTAL IODINE

The mechanism of action of elemental iodine is only partially understood, and more research needs to be done in this area.

Eskin's research in rats showed that there was a progressively better resolution of FCBD depending on the type of iodine used. Only elemental iodine corrected the entire disease process. Dr. Ghent's clinical studies paralleled these findings in humans.

When I-2 is replaced, it renders the breast duct cells less sensitive to estrogen, thus acting like a natural anti-estrogen.

In the **Canadian Journal of Surgery**, Ghent and Eskin speculated that the elemental iodine is essential for breast normality, and its absence seems to render the breast ducts more sensitive to estrogen stimulation and subsequent formation of cysts and scar tissue. They theorize that adequate amounts of elemental iodine in breasts tissue makes them less sensitive to circulating estrogens. As such the iodine could be classed as a natural "anti-estrogen", a sort of natural tamoxifen.

SIDE EFFECTS OF ELEMENTAL IODINE TREATMENT

Possible side effects of free iodine include acne in four percent of cases; hair thinning in .4 percent of cases and occasionally increased breast pain at the beginning of treatment. Ghent believes that this period of pain corresponds to a softening of the breast and disappearance of fibrous tissue plaques on clinical examination. Five to ten percent of women reported an increased sense of well-being; and one percent reported an increased sex drive.

At present, this special for of iodine must be taken continuously or the breasts will become cystic again. However, it may be possible after several years to reduce to a maintenance dosage.

MEANWHILE

This unique and beneficial form of iodine is expected to be on the market in Canada and the United States by 1997.

The scientific confirmation of Dr. Ghent's work may take many more years. Until that time, women may want to increase their consumption of seaweeds like kelp and dulse and ocean fish like cod, sea bass, haddock, and perch.

Some physicians including Dr. Wright are using Lugol's solution or SSKI (each drop is 30mg iodine) in doses of 1 to 10 drops a day orally as part of a treatment program for FCBD. Other iodine preparations like colloidal iodine, atomidine, liquid dulse, etc. may also prove useful (the dosage will have to be individually determined).

Treatments should be monitored by an experienced practitioner as you can overdose on iodine causing iodism (see symptoms p.158). However cutting back on the iodine will quickly reverse the symptoms.

IODINE AND BREAST CANCER

An interesting finding that turned up on Dr. Ghent's research on FCBD in 3,200 women for 12,000 women years. The breast cancer rate of women taking elemental iodine was 0.00082 per woman year, while the projected incidence of breast cancer for Ontarian women was .00164 per woman year.

In March 1992, Drs. Ghent and Eskin presented a research paper to the **American Association for Cancer Research**. This controlled study that showed that giving low doses of elemental iodine to rats who had breast cancer chemically induced, reduced tumour volumes, both when given prophylactically before cancer induction and therapeutically after cancer induction. At present, higher doses are also being evaluated. Dr. Eskin will be soon be publishing his further research on the relationship of iodine deficiency to breast cancer.

Dr. Ghent died in July 1993, shortly before his research was published. Throughout his life, he was a tremendous advocate for women's rights. The continuation and confirmation of his work will be the best tribute to his memory.

As Dr. Ghent himself so modestly stated:

> "If this premise is borne out by further animal testing and larger clinical trials, it will be of importance for breast health, normality and longevity."

RESOURCES

Pro-gest cream is available in Canada through **1-800-387-4761**.

In the United States and Canada cream available from:

Transitions For Health Inc, 621 SW Alder #900, Portland OR, 97205-3627. 1-800-888-6814.

Breast Cancer Treatment Center, 275 Bagette St #201, Kingston, ON, K7L 3G4. 613-548-8123.

DENNIS O'DOWD c/o Iomech, 863 Ranch View Rd, Mississauga, ON, L5E 1H1.

Dennis O'Dowd is also a pioneer in water purification systems using iodine.

THE MAMMACARE LEARNING SYSTEM enables women to teach themselves BSE in a way that is much more accurate than the standard type of BSE that is being taught.

The Mammacare kit consists of a lifelike silicone breast with five types of lumps in it, a forty five minute video and a thirty page manual. Women trained in this technique can detect lumps as small as peas, which is approaching the sensitivity of mammogram exam. Mammacare is available for $59.50 plus $4.50 shipping. In the U.S. 1-800-626-2273, in Canada 904-375-0607.

REFERENCES:

CANADIAN JOURNAL OF SURGERY, Vol-36 No-5, Oct/93, pgs 453-459 and 405.

DR. SUSAN LOVE'S BOOK by **Dr. Susan Love** (Addison Wesley, 1990).

NATURAL PROGESTERONE, THE MULTIPLE ROLES OF A REMARKABLE HORMONE by **Dr. John Lee**. BLL Publishing Box 2068, Sebastopol, CA 95473.

Pelvic Inflammatory Disease

Jill Weiss is the co-ordinator of the Canadian PID Society and has done extensive research in the area. She wrote this chapter to make sure women were informed about this important health issue.

INTRODUCTION

Pelvic inflammatory disease (**PID**) is a little known, but common illness that affects many women. Almost 100,000 Canadian women, and over one million women in the United States, contract PID each year. It is estimated that one in four North American women will have had PID by the year 2000. An episode of PID can have a significant impact on a woman's health. PID is the leading cause of preventable infertility and tubal pregnancy. Other long-term health problems and complications such as scarring and adhesion of the pelvic organs, chronic pain, tubal ovarian abscess, chronic infection, spread of infection to the liver capsule, spread of infection to the abdominal cavity and recurring infection are common after only one episode.

Although PID is a common and serious illness, there isn't a lot of public awareness about this disease. As a result, women often have difficulty getting information about treatment and prevention, and women who have PID often feel isolated and stigmatized.

WHAT IS PELVIC INFLAMMATORY DISEASE (PID) ?

Pelvic inflammatory disease (PID) is an infection or inflammation of a woman's reproductive organs (the uterus, fallopian tubes, ovaries and/or the surrounding tissue). Infection can sometimes spread to the abdominal cavity (called peritonitis), to the liver capsule (called perihepatitis), the appendix (periappendicitis), or the sigmoid colon (perisigmoiditis).

WHAT CAUSES PID ?

A woman's reproductive organs are designed to be sterile. That is free of bacteria, viruses etc. A woman's body is specially designed to prevent bacteria from entering these organs. The uterus is shaped like a funnel, and the bottom narrow end of this funnel (the cervix) is usually closed and covered with a mucous that repels bacteria. This cervical "plug" usually prevents bacteria from passing into the reproductive organs.

However, sometimes bacteria can get past the cervix's defences and into the reproductive organs in the following ways.

OPENING OF THE CERVICAL BARRIER: If the cervix is opened, the protective barrier is lost, and vaginal or cervical bacteria can more easily pass into the reproductive organs. Any process or procedure which opens a woman's cervix and allows vaginal or cervical bacteria to pass into the reproductive organs can cause PID. Examples of medical procedures that open the cervix include D-and-C's, abortions, and insertion of IUD's. Women who have IUD's have about a twofold increased risk of developing PID and most of this increased risk is from the opening of the cervix to insert the IUD. Therapeutic abortions also increase the risk of PID because they involve opening the cervix. About three to 13 percent of women will develop PID after an abortion, although rates are higher if the woman already has an infection on her cervix or in her vagina.

Childbirth also opens the cervix and can result in PID. Sometimes pelvic infection after childbirth is called postpartum endometritis, because the infection often starts in the lining of the uterus. About two to five percent of women develop PID after childbirth, but rates are higher if the woman has a cervical or vaginal infection, if the membrane is ruptured for more than six hours, or if labour is prolonged. Women who have cesarean section deliveries have the highest risk of developing PID after childbirth. This is two to five times higher than with a vaginal delivery. (This may happen because the surgical procedure itself may introduce or carry bacteria into the reproductive organs.)

INFECTIONS OF THE CERVICAL BARRIER: The cervix is actually part of the uterus (the lower narrow end), so if a woman has an infection directly on the cervical barrier, this infection can work its way up along the lining of the uterus and into the fallopian tubes. Infections of the cervix are thought to be the most common cause of PID.

Certain bacteria like to grow in cervical tissue and are therefore more likely to pass into the reproductive organs. The most common of these bacteria are chlamydia and gonorrhea (these bacteria will **not** grow in the vagina). These bacteria are called "sexually transmitted" because they can be transferred from one partner to another during oral, anal, or vaginal sex; these bacteria can then attach to the woman's cervix causing a cervical infection. **At this stage, when bacteria have infected the cervix only, the infection is easy to diagnose and treat effectively. A cervical infection which is diagnosed and treated promptly WILL NOT result in PID.**

If chlamydia and gonorrhea are left untreated, they can move up into the reproductive organs and cause PID. It used to be believed that only a small proportion of cervical chlamydial or gonorrheal infections actually resulted in PID. Recent research has shown, however, that up to half of women with cervical chlamydial infections also have infection which has passed into the reproductive organs, even though most of these women did not have any symptoms of infection and therefore did not realize they had an infection.

Most women with cervical infections do not have any symptoms of infection, so unless the woman is especially careful to have regular checks for these bacteria, she may not realize she is infected, increasing the risk that the infection will spread into the reproductive organs. **The lack of symptoms with chlamydial infections is deceptive because "silent" chlamydial infections cause as much or more damage as infections with more obvious symptoms**.

Preventing cervical chlamydial and gonorrheal infections and treating cervical infections promptly BEFORE they progress to PID, are the MOST IMPORTANT STEPS IN PREVENTING PID.

SPERM: Although the cervix is designed to protect the reproductive organs from infection, it is also designed to let sperm pass through so that pregnancy can occur. Researchers have shown that bacteria can attach to sperm, and can then be carried by sperm through the cervix and into the reproductive organs, causing PID (the bacteria that are carried through the cervix on the man's sperm could be bacteria from the man, bacteria from the woman's cervix, or bacteria from the woman's vagina).

Barrier methods of birth control that kill or prevent sperm from crossing the cervix eliminate this risk factor. Women whose partners have had vasectomies rarely develop PID, probably because there is no sperm in the seminal fluid to carry bacteria across the cervix.

VAGINAL INFECTIONS: The cervix actually protrudes into a woman's vagina, so the cervix is in contact with any bacteria or other organisms that may be living there. A healthy woman's vagina usually has bacteria and yeast, living in a complex and balanced ecosystem. Sometimes the balance of the vaginal ecosystem is upset, and bacteria start to multiply quickly in large numbers. If this happens, the large numbers of bacteria may overwhelm the cervix's defences and enter the reproductive organs, causing an episode of PID.

It used to be thought that vaginal infections were not harmful, but recent research has shown that a common vaginal infection (bacterial vaginosis or non-specific vaginitis) can increase a woman's risk for PID especially following Cesarean Section or abortion. However, like cervical infections, vaginal infections are easy to diagnose, so women can reduce their risk by good vaginal health care and regular checkups.

INFECTION FROM SURGICAL OR MEDICAL PROCEDURES: Any surgical or medical procedure that involves touching the reproductive organs with instruments or foreign substances involves the risk of infection. Of course, sterilizing procedures are in place to prevent this, but despite precautions, infections sometimes occur. For example, cesarean section deliveries, which involve an abdominal incision, have a very high rate of pelvic infection (25 to 80 percent), unless an antibiotic is given to reduce this risk. Another procedure which occasionally causes infection is a hysterosalpingogram (a procedure to pass dye through the fallopian tubes to see if they are blocked or open). This is a relatively safe procedure which causes pelvic infection in less than one percent of women having this procedure. However, hysterosalpingograms are a common procedure, and women should be aware that the passage of the dye may introduce bacteria or spread bacteria from an already existing infection. The use of a preventive antibiotic can reduce the risk of this happening.

INFECTION FROM OTHER AREAS: This is believed to be rare (less than one percent of PID), but actually, research is generally lacking on this topic. The idea is that infection of other organs or areas of the body, such as the appendix or bowel, may sometimes spread to the reproductive organs. Also, bowel bacteria, such as E-coli, can be spread to the vagina if a woman wipes from back to front after going to the bathroom. Once in the vagina, these bacteria can then attach to sperm and be transported into the reproductive organs, causing PID.

A little known example of infection spreading from another area of the body into the reproductive organs involves tuberculosis. The tubercular bacteria can infect the reproductive organs, and this sometimes happens when chest X-rays are normal. Tuberculosis is not common in Canada, so this is not a common cause of PID, but rates of tuberculosis are increasing with the AIDS epidemic, and in particular, antibiotic-resistant strains, which are harder to kill, are becoming more common.

HOW DOES PID AFFECT A WOMAN'S REPRODUCTIVE ORGANS ?

PID can cause a significant amount of damage to the reproductive organs. This can be caused by the infection itself and or by the body's own response to infection.

DAMAGE CAUSED BY INFECTION: Infection can cause damage to the lining of the fallopian tube, to the cilia (small hairs which line the tube and move the fertilized egg through the tube), and/or to the ovary. Some bacteria, such as gonorrhea, actually produce a toxin which causes damage to tissue. Chlamydial infections cause a great deal of damage, partly because the chlamydia bacteria lives part of its life inside a person's cells; then at a certain stage in chlamydia's life cycle, it ruptures the host cell and destroys it, causing a significant amount of damage.

DAMAGE CAUSED BY THE BODY'S RESPONSE TO INFECTION: Inflammation occurs in the infected area as the body's defences (neutrophils, lymphocytes, etc,) rush to the area. Chlamydia infections, in particular, cause a lot of inflammation.

In addition, the body produces scar tissue to prevent the pelvic infection from spreading. Unfortunately this scar tissue can partially or completely block the fallopian tubes (causing tubal pregnancy or infertility), can bind organs together (causing pain and mobility restrictions), and can make it more difficult for antibiotics to kill infection (since the antibiotic also has to penetrate the tough scar tissue). **This is one of the most important reasons why it is crucial to treat PID promptly. The body's response to infection happens quickly. Antibiotics can kill the bacteria causing the infection, but they cannot repair damage or remove scar tissue that has already formed**. Chlamydial infections cause extensive scarring, especially with repeated infections, and this is another reason why infection with this bacteria causes so many problems such as infertility and tubal pregnancy.

COMMON COMPLICATIONS AND CONSEQUENCES OF PID

CHRONIC PAIN: About one in five women develops chronic abdominal pain after an episode of PID, although figures are actually higher in North America. Chronic pain after PID is believed to be caused by inflammation, scar tissue, and/or ongoing infection, although chronic pain is usually believed to be caused by scarring. Scarring can cause pain by binding organs together; scar tissue surrounding the ovary can also cause pain because the ovary enlarges during a woman's menstrual cycle, and if scarring restricts this enlargement, significant pain can result.

INFERTILITY: PID is the leading cause of preventable infertility in women. After an episode of PID, one in six women will be infertile. After a second episode, one in three will be infertile. And after three episodes, half will be infertile. Infection can cause infertility by damaging or blocking the fallopian tubes, ovaries, or endometrium; or by damaging the cilia (small hairs which line the fallopian tube and help move the ovum through the tube). The most common cause of infertility is partial or complete blockage of the fallopian tubes by scar tissue formed as part of the body's defense against infection. Scar tissue can also cause the fringed ends of the fallopian tube (fimbria) to stick together, making it difficult for the egg to be picked up by the tube, or scar tissue can cause the cilia lining the fallopian tube to stick together, making it difficult for the fertilized egg to travel through the tube.

ECTOPIC PREGNANCY: PID is the leading cause of ectopic pregnancy. An ectopic pregnancy is a pregnancy which occurs outside of the uterus, usually in the fallopian tube (tubal pregnancy). An ectopic pregnancy is a serious medical emergency because the fallopian tube is not elastic like the uterus and the fallopian tube cannot stretch to accommodate the growth of the embryo. Also, a massive hemorrhage can result because the surface of the tube is not designed to nurture the embryo like the lining of the uterus.

After an episode of PID, ectopic pregnancies result for most of the same reasons as infertility. Conception is successfully completed, but the fertilized egg cannot successfully travel to the uterus because of damage to the hairs lining the fallopian tube or to the surface of the tube, or because passage is partially or completely blocked by scarring or infection. After PID, women have a ten-fold increased risk of ectopic pregnancy. In fact, one in every 63 pregnancies is now ectopic in Canada, a two to three-fold increase mainly due to PID.

RECURRING INFECTION: Recurrences of PID are common, but entirely preventable. After PID, one in four women will have at least one other episode, half within the first year of the first episode.

There are believed to be three reasons for recurrences:

1. Failure to treat the woman's partner (ie the woman is reinfected).

2. Incomplete or inadequate treatment (ie the infection was never really eradicated).

3. An increased vulnerability to infection (some change in the fallopian tubes which may make them more susceptible to future infection).

However, by far the most common cause of recurrence is failure to treat the woman's partner. Both the Canadian and U.S. Guidelines for the Treatment of PID clearly state that partners must always be treated, regardless of whether the partner appears to have infection. In the words of the **U.S. Centers for Disease Control**: **"Treatment for sex partners of women with PID is imperative. The management of women with PID should be considered inadequate unless their sex partners have been appropriately evaluated and treated."** (Centers for Disease Control, **PID Management Guidelines**, 1991, p18) Another PID researcher notes: "If the male partner is not treated, the PID will recur in the woman. In fact, due to the lack of treatment of the male partner, PID is often seen as a recurrent or chronic disease." (**Mohanty**, 1989).

In Sweden, where health authorities have implemented careful follow-up of sex partners since 1977, the rate of repeated episodes of PID has dropped from 22 percent to four percent. Unfortunately, in North America, this practice may not always be followed, resulting in serious health problems for many women.

CHRONIC PID: Chronic PID is a vague term. It usually means an ongoing chronic pelvic infection, but sometimes the term is also used to refer to chronic pain after an episode of PID. Although chronic PID is common (20 to 30 percent of women with PID in Canada and the U.S. are diagnosed with chronic PID), there hasn't been any research on this condition, so basic information about chronic PID and the most effective treatment has not been developed. A woman can develop chronic infection if an episode of PID is never diagnosed or treated, or a woman can develop chronic infection if an episode of PID is not treated thoroughly.

It used to be believed that chronic infection was rare, and that women who appeared to still have PID after treatment really only had adhesions or inflammation. However, recent research has established that chronic pelvic infection is much more frequent than previously believed, especially if chlamydia is involved. Women who have very mild or no symptoms are less likely to have their pelvic infections diagnosed, and may be more likely to develop chronic infection. This is called "**Silent PID**" and is especially likely if chlamydia is involved, as chlamydial infections usually cause very mild or no symptoms.

HOW CAN A WOMAN TELL IF SHE HAS PID ?

This is one of the main problems with PID. PID is extremely difficult to diagnose accurately unless surgery is done. One of the reasons for this is that the reproductive organs lie within the body and can't be seen without surgery. Also, there is no specific blood test or other office test that can be done to show if infection is present in the reproductive organs. Thus if a practitioner tries to diagnose PID without surgery (called a clinical diagnosis), she/he has to rely on indirect information such as general blood tests, symptoms, general signs of infection (eg fever), or tests for infection in other areas of the body (eg the cervix).

Unfortunately, research has shown that these indirect measures do not accurately show if a woman has PID or not. Symptoms of PID vary enormously from woman to woman and do not accurately reflect what's happening internally. Fever is an unreliable indicator of pelvic infection because 60 percent women with PID have **no** fever. If chlamydia is involved, 78 percent have no fever. Blood tests such as the white blood cell count or sedimentation rate are only general indications that the body is fighting infection. One third of women with PID have normal blood tests and cultures from the cervix do **not** have a good correlation with cultures taken directly from the reproductive organs. Also, the symptoms of PID are similar to the symptoms of at least eight other syndromes (such as endometriosis, appendicitis, ovarian cysts, inflammatory bowel disease) and these different conditions are easily confused with each other if diagnosis is based on symptoms. For all these reasons, the clinical diagnosis of PID (ie based on symptoms and signs of infection) is extremely difficult and highly prone to error.

A recent Canadian study by Toronto researcher, **Dr. John Sellors**, compared the clinical diagnosis of PID (without surgery) to diagnosis using the surgical technique of laparoscopy (a procedure that allows the reproductive organs to be directly seen). Even when practitioners were very experienced and used the most careful diagnostic techniques, their clinical diagnosis was no was no more accurate than random chance. A similar result has been found by others studying the diagnosis of PID. Over ten research studies around the world have confirmed that the clinical diagnosis of PID is in error at least 30 to 40 percent of the time.

It is important to remember that the difficulty in diagnosing PID does not occur because the practitioner is not being careful. In fact, no one has been able to develop a reliable way to diagnose PID accurately from symptoms or signs of infection, and unless surgery is done, even the most skilled and careful practitioners will be in error about the diagnosis of PID a significant amount of the time.

The difficulty diagnosing PID is one of the most important reasons to prevent PID. If a laparoscopy is not performed, it is very hard to tell for sure if a woman has PID or not, and as a result, many women aren't treated until significant damage has been done. However, infections of the cervix, which are the most common cause of PID, are easy to diagnose and treat, and prompt treatment will ensure the woman does not develop PID.

TECHNIQUES TO CLINICALLY DIAGNOSE PID

If PID is diagnosed clinically (ie without surgery), the following clinical diagnostic aids or tests can be done. However, keep in mind that none of these tests is definitive, and many diagnostic errors will result.

PELVIC EXAM: This is an essential part of the diagnosis of PID. The doctor will do a gentle bimanual examination in which two fingers are inserted into the woman's vagina while her abdomen is felt with the other hand to see if the uterus, ovaries or fallopian tubes are tender or swollen. Pain or swelling are a strong indication that a woman has PID. These may be the only indications. The doctor can also feel to see if any lumps or masses are present (can be scarring, abscesses), but many masses are not detected this way.

BLOOD TESTS: The two most common tests are the white blood cell count and the erythrocyte sedimentation rate (**ESR**). These are general tests to show if the body is fighting an infection or if inflammation is present, but these tests are not specific. They will not show what kind of infection is present or where the infection is located. The tests should be done because if they are positive they may mean there is an infection somewhere in the woman's body, but it is not possible to know if this infection is PID. Also, about one third of women with PID have normal blood tests, so normal blood tests don't rule out PID.

CERVICAL TESTS: These usually involve tests for chlamydia and gonorrhea. If either of these tests is positive, and if the woman has **any** other signs or symptoms of PID (including tenderness during the pelvic examination), many recommend treating for PID, since the cervical infection has to be treated anyway, and there's a good possibility it may have passed into the reproductive organs.

It's important to remember that a negative cervical test does not rule out the possibility that the woman has PID. The cervix is in a different area of the body than the reproductive organs, and the bacteria living in these two different places may not be the same.

There are several reasons for this:

1. **Chlamydial or gonorrhea may have passed directly into the reproductive organs without infecting the cervix first (ie they may have been carried into the reproductive organs by sperm).**

2. **Chlamydia or gonorrhea may have caused a cervical infection first, but the cervical infection may have been eradicated while infection remains in the fallopian tubes.**

3. **The PID can be caused by other bacteria (ie not chlamydia or gonorrhea).**

Generally, research has shown that there is a poor correlation between bacteria found on the cervix and bacteria found in the fallopian tubes. For these reasons, cervical tests are most useful if they are positive, because they may indicate bacteria which might have caused PID, but a negative result does not rule out PID.

ULTRASOUND: This is a picture created by sound waves. An ultrasound **cannot** show infection (bacteria are too small to be seen), but it can show a thickening or mass, which could be caused by PID. A transvaginal ultrasound (a picture taken through the vagina) is a fairly accurate way to diagnose abscesses. It is important to know if an abscess is there, because this is a serious complication of PID which can cause serious long-term health consequences, and different and longer treatment may be needed. Transvaginal ultrasound, in combination with a serum pregnancy test, can also accurately diagnose ectopic pregnancies, a common and serious complication of PID.

VAGINAL TESTS: These include checking a sample of vaginal fluid for inflammatory cells, for bacterial vaginosis, and to determine the vaginal PH (an acidic PH is healthy). Swedish PID experts believe that if inflammatory cells are present in the vagina, the woman may have PID, but research establishing this as a reliable criteria hasn't been reported. An abnormal vaginal PH or bacterial vaginosis don't indicate if the woman does or doesn't have PID, but they do indicate a condition which might progress to PID (or which may have already done so).

ENDOMETRIAL BIOPSY: This is an office procedure which many believe will improve the accuracy in diagnosing PID without surgery. The basic idea is that a small piece of tissue is removed from the lining of the uterus, stained, and then examined under a microscope for signs that the body is fighting an infection (ie neutrophils, lymphocytes, plasma cells). This procedure has just begun to be tested and initial results are promising. Endometrial biopsy has a good correlation with the results of laparoscopy which is the surgical examination of the reproductive organs which is the most accurate way to diagnose PID.

However, inflammation in the lining of the uterus can be patchy and only a small sample is taken, so endometrial biopsy may miss some inflammation/infection. Also, a woman may have infection in her fallopian tubes, but no infection in the uterus. In this case, the PID would not be detected by an endometrial biopsy, even though pelvic infection was actually there. Thus, while a positive endometrial biopsy does indicate that a woman has PID, a negative endometrial biopsy does not rule out PID.

LAPAROSCOPIC DIAGNOSIS (SURGERY): Laparoscopy allows direct examination of the pelvic organs, so it is the most accurate way to diagnose pelvic infection. During laparoscopy, a general anesthetic is given, a small incision is made below the navel, carbon dioxide gas is used to inflate the abdomen, and a laparoscope (a lighted instrument through which the pelvic organs can be seen) is inserted into the abdomen. Laparoscopy allows the physician to see the state of the pelvic organs, to take cultures, and to take samples of tissue. During laparoscopy, a physician can see if other conditions are present, such as endometriosis or appendicitis, which are easily confused with PID. Another advantage of laparoscopy is that the practitioner can take cultures to indicate what bacteria are involved in the infection so that the most effective treatment can be given. Laparoscopy also allows the physician to see if there are complications such as abscesses, adhesions, or a spread of infection to other organs, so that appropriate treatment can be given.

Most experts recommend the use of laparoscopy to diagnose PID to ensure that all women with PID are promptly and accurately treated. A recent study has shown that laparoscopy is not expensive, because a lot of money is saved when incorrect diagnoses are avoided. In other words, if a clinical diagnosis is used, many women aren't treated until serious damage has occurred, and many women who actually don't have PID are treated unnecessarily for PID. Both of these errors are costly to the health care system and to women. In many European and Scandinavian countries, laparoscopy is routinely given to any women who might possibly have PID. However, in Canada and in North America in general, laparoscopy is less frequently used.

NOTE: If a laparoscopy is performed, it is **essential** that cultures and samples of tissue be examined to check for infection and inflammation which may not be visible to the naked eye. Some pelvic infections do cause obvious signs of infection (pus, redness, inflammation) which can be easily seen through the laparoscope. However, **many pelvic infections do not cause obvious redness or pus, and these infections will be missed if cultures and samples of tissue are not taken.**

For example, a recent Canadian study by Toronto researcher, Dr. John Sellors, compared the results of laparoscopy using visual inspection alone to laparoscopy with cultures and examination of tissue samples under a microscope. This study found that when cultures and microscopic examination of tissue were not used during laparoscopy, **about half of pelvic infections were missed**. This is an important study, because in Canada, laparoscopies are often performed without cultures or samples of tissue being taken, thus not diagnosing about half of pelvic infections.

PROMPTNESS OF DIAGNOSIS AND TREATMENT

A woman who suspects she has PID should try to obtain diagnosis and treatment immediately. Although PID is difficult to diagnose, prompt and accurate diagnosis is very important, because treatment is less effective if it is delayed. Even a short delay can be serious. One study found that most women treated within two days recovered completely, while women whose treatment was delayed for one week had many more serious consequences such as infertility and ectopic pregnancy. For this reason, it is recommended that whatever diagnostic strategy is chosen, treatment must not be delayed due to an uncertain diagnosis.

SYMPTOMS OF PID

It is important to keep in mind that there is no typical pattern of symptoms for PID. In fact, studies have shown that less than five percent of women with PID appear severely ill, and less than 16 percent have three or more of what used to be considered the "typical symptoms" of PID. In fact, most women with PID have only one or two symptoms, and often these are mild. Some women with PID have no symptoms at all. This is called "Silent PID" and is now believed to be far more common than previously thought, especially when chlamydia is involved.

In addition, research has shown that there is no correlation between the severity of a woman's symptoms and the actual severity of pelvic infection. Women who have mild or no symptoms are just as likely to have damage to their reproductive organs as women with more obvious symptoms.

Keeping this in mind, the symptoms of PID are:

Abdominal pain is the most common and often the only symptom. The pain can be mild or severe, occasional or constant. Often the pain is very mild, especially if chlamydia has caused the infection.

1. A feeling of fullness, bloating or pressure in the abdomen.

2. Deep pain during intercourse.

3. Abnormal periods or bleeding between periods.

4. Unusual discharge from the cervix or vagina.

5. Fever or chills.

6. A general feeling of illness or tiredness.

7. Nausea.

8. Lower back pain.

9. Urination that is painful or more frequent than usual.

If a woman has infection which has spread to the liver capsule (perihepatitis), she may also experience pain in the upper right side (near the lungs). This pain is usually, but not always, combined with lower abdominal pain. The pain may be made worse by movement, deep breathing or coughing and may be referred to the shoulder or arm.

TREATMENT OF PID

Successful treatment of PID has three parts. The first is multiple antibiotic treatment to kill the infection. The second is the treatment of the woman's partner to prevent the woman from being re-infected. The third is bed rest to help the pelvic organs heal. All three parts must be combined for treatment to be successful.

MULTIPLE ANTIBIOTICS: The idea with antibiotic treatment is to make sure that the bacteria causing PID are completely eradicated, so more damage does not occur. We don't know why, but most pelvic infections involve many bacteria. For example, the reproductive organs become infected with many different bacteria, even if only one bacterium initially started the infection. This is called polymicrobial infection. For this reason, one antibiotic alone is never recommended for the treatment of PID. Both the Canadian and the U.S. guidelines for the treatment of PID emphasize that multiple antibiotics are essential to insure that all bacteria are eradicated.

Antibiotics for PID can be given orally (by mouth) or intravenously (through a vein, usually this is done in the hospital, but sometimes it can be done on an outpatient basis). Definitive research has not been done, but most experts believe that IV (intravenous) antibiotics are superior because they have better penetration into infected tissues (oral antibiotics must be absorbed through the stomach first), and also because some powerful antibiotics used to treat PID, such as aminoglycosides, cannot be given by mouth. The U.S. Centers for Disease Control states that oral antibiotics may be less effective than IV antibiotics. Both the Canadian and the U.S. guidelines for the treatment of PID recommend IV antibiotics in many cases.

If a woman is given oral antibiotics, the guidelines recommend an injection of ceftriaxone (or a similar cephalosporin antibiotic) plus ten to 14 days of doxycycline (this is effective against many bacteria, including chlamydia). Some experts also recommend the addition of the antibiotic metronidazole (brand name **Flagyl**) to kill anaerobic bacteria. Anaerobic bacteria are bacteria which do not require oxygen to survive. These bacteria are often found in pelvic infection, especially if the infection has gone on for a long time, if an abscess is involved, or if the woman has bacterial vaginosis. The new Canadian guidelines for the treatment of PID recommend that the practitioner consider adding Flagyl if an anaerobic infection is suspected. Anaerobic infections are especially likely if the woman has had repeated bouts of PID, is an older woman, or has had chronic infection. Also, **if a woman is given oral antibiotics, both the Canadian and U.S. guidelines for the treatment of PID recommend that the woman be re-examined within 48 to 72 hours, and if she has not improved by then, hospitalization and evaluation by a specialist are recommended.**

If a woman is given IV antibiotics, there are two recommended options: doxycycline with cefoxitin, or clindamycin with gentamicin.

The Canadian guidelines emphasize the first option as the preferred option and the second as the alternative, but the U.S. guidelines consider both to be equal choices. Both of these IV combinations will kill a wide range of PID-causing bacteria, but neither will kill all of the bacteria that might cause PID. The doxycycline/cefoxitin option is especially effective against chlamydia and a broad range of other bacteria, but it is not the best choice if an anaerobic infection is present. The clindamycin/gentamicin regimen is recommended if anaerobic bacteria or gram-negative bacteria are present. It is important to note that the clindamycin/gentamicin should be used if an abscess is present. Clindamycin is more effective than other antibiotics at penetrating pus, and it is also very effective at killing anaerobic bacteria, which are usually present within abscesses.

All IV antibiotics have to be continued for **at least four days** AND **at least two days after the woman has recovered**. For example, if a woman did not improve until the tenth day, she would need at least twelve days of IV antibiotics. Failure to continue antibiotic treatment for long enough can result in continuing infection and damage to the reproductive organs.

Once a woman has been discharged from hospital, IV antibiotics must be followed by oral antibiotics so that the **combined total of antibiotic treatment is at least ten to 14 days**. Both of the IV antibiotic combinations should be followed by oral doxycycline, to insure that chlamydia is eradicated, but other antibiotics may also be added.

Although these antibiotics are recommended, the recommendations may not always be followed in practice. For example, research in England and the United States shows that most prescriptions given to women with PID do not follow the Center for Disease Control guidelines, and that most prescriptions are not appropriate and would not eradicate most pelvic infections. Similar research has not been done in Canada.

SOME ADDITIONAL POINTS ABOUT ANTIBIOTIC TREATMENT: Single antibiotics, no matter how powerful, are not appropriate for PID. The use of single cephalosporin antibiotics (a large family of antibiotics whose names often begin with "ceph" or "cef") is a special problem. PID researcher **Richard Sweet** has shown that these antibiotics will eradicate chlamydia on the cervix, but NOT in the upper genital tract (i.e. the reproductive organs).

PENICILLIN: Penicillin-type antibiotics (penicillin, amoxicillin, ampicillin) are no longer recommended for the treatment of PID. Many bacteria have become resistant to penicillin (including some strains of gonorrhea), and many bacteria are now able to produce enzymes and other substances which make penicillin ineffective. Also, PID usually involves a buildup of large numbers of bacteria, and penicillin works best with small numbers of bacteria. High treatment failure rates have been reported when penicillin has been used to treat PID. These antibiotics are not on the Canadian or the U.S. recommended guidelines.

TETRACYCLINE: This antibiotic is similar to doxycycline (both are part of the same antibiotic family), but doxycycline has a broader range (it kills more bacteria). Many PID guidelines still list tetracycline as an alternative to doxycycline, but one study reports high treatment failure rates when tetracycline was used to treat PID, so women should be aware that doxycycline may be more effective. Both antibiotics are equally effective, however, at treating cervical chlamydial infections.

TREATMENT OF THE WOMAN'S PARTNER: This is extremely important. A woman and her sexual partner must both be treated if treatment is to be effective. This is essential to prevent the woman from being re-infected and having a recurrence of PID. In Sweden, where health authorities have implemented careful follow-up of sex partners since 1977, the rate of repeated episodes of PID has dropped from 22 percent to four percent.

It is important to remember that most partners of women with PID may not have any symptoms, even though they may be infected. For this reason, **Health and Welfare Canada** strongly recommends that all partners be treated "regardless of the presence or absence of symptoms or signs of infection". (**Laboratory Center for Disease Control, PID Treatment Guidelines**, 1987).

BED REST: Bed rest is an important part of the treatment of PID. It helps to keep the infection from spreading, insures that the fallopian tubes will not be jolted or jarred and inflamed further, and allows the body time to heal. Bed rest means lying in bed and eliminating all activity (including sex). A woman should not resume sexual relations until follow-up has indicated healing is complete and the sex partner(s) are free from infection.

SPECIAL TREATMENT CONSIDERATIONS

TREATMENT OF ABSCESSES: About ten to fifteen percent of women with PID develop abscesses, which is called complicated PID. Women who have abscesses are more likely to experience long-term health problems, and treatment can be difficult and is controversial.

An abscess is a collection of pus which is formed as part of the body's response to infection. If an abscess has formed, this means that the body's defence against infection has been partially successful. Tissue (like that of a healing wound) forms around the site of infection, isolating it from the rest of the body. However, part of the difficulty in treating abscesses is due to the body's own protective response. The formation of an abscess helps to wall off and isolate infection from the rest of the body, but this also makes penetration by antibiotics more difficult. Also, the environment inside the abscess has a low level of oxygen, so anaerobic bacteria multiply rapidly. These bacteria destroy tissue, reduce circulation, and further block the penetration of antibiotics. Very high levels of bacteria build up within abscesses, and these high levels of bacteria can produce enzymes which prevent many antibiotics from working effectively. As a result, it can sometimes be difficult to kill bacteria inside an abscess.

There is a great deal of controversy about the effective treatment of abscesses. Some believe that surgery should be performed immediately to remove pus and damaged organs, while others believe that IV antibiotics, especially with clindamycin involved, are usually effective. A ten year study of women with abscesses in San Francisco, found that women who were treated with clindamycin were twice as likely to recover and much less likely to experience problems later on than women who were treated with other antibiotics. Although abscesses are a common complication of PID, no specific treatment guidelines have been developed. However, the average length of IV antibiotic treatment reported in the medical research for abscesses is 10 to 11 days, or longer.

TREATMENT OF CHRONIC INFECTION: Women can develop chronic infection from PID, either because the infection has gone on for a long time before it was diagnosed, or because the initial treatment was incomplete. This is a common diagnosis, but we really don't know much about the most effective treatment for chronic infection. To our knowledge, no research has been done on this topic. One researcher in France, **Jeanine Henry-Suchet**, suggests very long antibiotic treatment of two to three months for chronic infection, but again, this suggestion is not based on research. We just don't know for sure what would be most effective.

PREVENTION

This is the most important part of this chapter. PID is extremely difficult to diagnose accurately, and much of the damage has already been done to pelvic organs by the time antibiotic treatment has been started. Prevention is the most effective treatment for PID. Here are the basic steps to prevention.

PREVENT CERVICAL STD INFECTIONS: These are the most common cause of PID. The use of condoms or diaphragms with spermicide can protect women from STD's which may lead to PID. These methods are only effective if they are used properly. Research indicates that women who consistently use condoms or diaphragms with spermicide have much lower rates of PID. Women who use condoms or diaphragms also have lower rates of infertility and ectopic pregnancy, common consequences of PID.

STOP CERVICAL INFECTIONS BEFORE THEY PROGRESS TO PID: Preventive measures include regular STD checkups, especially if the woman is not using a barrier method of birth control, if she is very young, if she has a new partner, or if the partner has a new partner. It is also important to watch for symptoms of STD's such as frequent or painful urination, itching or discharge from the vagina, abnormal periods, pain or bleeding during or after sex. However, it is important to remember that many women have cervical or vaginal infections with no symptoms.

REDUCE THE RISK OF PID FROM ANY PROCEDURE OR PROCESS THAT OPENS THE CERVIX: Before undergoing childbirth or any medical procedure which opens the cervix, a woman should see her doctor to insure that she doesn't have a cervical or vaginal infection. If an infection is present, it should be treated beforehand. Also, the use of preventive or prophylactic antibiotics given before the procedure can reduce the risk of infection from insertion of an IUD or from a therapeutic abortion.

After a procedure or process that opens the cervix, nothing should be inserted into the vagina until after the cervix has completely closed (at least six to eight weeks). Also, women should watch for any signs of infection after childbirth or any medical procedure which opens the cervix, and go promptly to a physician if any signs of infection are present.

PREVENT VAGINAL INFECTIONS WHICH CAN LEAD TO PID: Bacteria grow better in warm, moist environments, so it is important to keep the vaginal environment cool and dry (ie loose cotton underwear, etc). Also, recent research indicates that a healthy vagina is acidic, and has lots of helpful bacteria called lactobacilli, which help prevent vaginal infection. Lactobacilli produce substances such as lactic acid and hydrogen peroxide, which make it difficult for other bacteria or yeast to grow. Research on what women can do to keep their vaginas healthy is only just beginning, but some studies have indicated that inserting capsules of lactobacilli or yogurt may be helpful, although it is not clear how long-lasting this effect will be. Women should also be aware that it is easy for a physician to check to see if a woman's vagina is healthy (acidic, with lots of lactobacilli). Therefore, regular checkups are an important part of prevention.

STOP VAGINAL INFECTIONS FROM PROGRESSING TO PID: Bacterial vaginosis, a common vaginal infection which can lead to PID, is easy to diagnose. The physician can check the vaginal PH, can look for signs that lots of bacteria are present (clue cells), can check for the presence or absence of helpful bacteria like lactobacilli, and can check the odour. A fishy odour indicates that bacterial vaginosis may be present. Treatment of bacterial vaginosis is still being studied, but generally clindamycin cream has been found to be effective. Treatment with acidophilus capsules or vinegar douches, although still experimental, has also been found to be successful for some women. Long-term studies have yet to establish the most effective treatment.

PREVENT BOWEL BACTERIA FROM ENTERING THE VAGINA: Bowel bacteria, such as E-coli, can cause PID. These bacteria may be transferred into the vagina if a woman wipes from back to front after going to the bathroom. Prevention involves wiping from front to back after going to the bathroom, and ensuring that vaginal intercourse never follows anal intercourse.

PREVENT COMPLICATIONS OF PID: Be alert for the symptoms and signs of PID. Get medical attention immediately if any symptoms are present. Remember, mild symptoms don't mean a mild infection.

SPECIAL TOPICS

YOUNG WOMEN AND PID: Young women have the highest risk for PID: 75 percent of women with PID are under 25 years of age. Teenagers have the highest risk for PID, two to four times higher than women over 20. In fact, the U.S. Centers for Disease Control estimates that if the current trend continues, half of the women who turned 15 in 1990 will have PID by the year 2000.

The reasons for the higher risk of PID among teenagers are not completely understood, but it is believed that a teenager's immune system may be less developed, especially in response to sexually transmitted diseases, and this may make her more vulnerable to pelvic infection. In fact, the U.S. Centers for Disease Control is now recommending that young women delay the start of intercourse for several years, because of this increased vulnerability and the impact an episode of PID can have on a young woman's health.

Also, teenage women have the highest rate of cervical chlamydial infections in Canada and are therefore more likely to develop PID. Teenagers are also less likely to use barrier methods of birth control. They are more likely to have more sex partners and have cervical mucous that is easier for bacteria to penetrate. In addition, a type of cervical cell called columnar epithelia, is more pronounced on the cervixes of adolescents, and both chlamydia and gonorrhea like to grow in these cells.

BIRTH CONTROL CHOICE: A woman's choice of birth control influences her risk of developing PID. This is a complex subject, and more details can be obtained from the **Canadian PID Society**, but here is a brief outline.

Barrier methods of birth control (condoms, diaphragms) considerably reduce a woman's risk of cervical STD infections, PID, ectopic pregnancy, and infertility. Condoms also offer protection against other serious diseases such as herpes and the AIDS causing HIV virus. Both condoms and diaphragms should be used with a spermicide, and must be used regularly and properly to be effective.

Birth control pills do not offer protection against cervical STD infections. Women who use birth control pills actually have higher rates of cervical chlamydial infections, which is the most common cause of PID. However, there is some evidence that women who use oral contraceptives may have lower rates of diagnosed PID, possibly because the hormones in the pill are thought to thicken the cervical plug and make it harder for bacteria to ascend into the reproductive organs. For this reason, birth control pills are often prescribed for women after an episode of PID.

There is a lot of disagreement about the relationship of birth control pills and PID, and many researchers do not believe that birth control pills really offer protection against PID. This is because oral contraceptives increase the risk of cervical chlamydial infections which are the most common cause of PID. They increase the risk of pelvic infection in animals and they improve the ability of bacteria to attach to fallopian tube tissue in the laboratory. In addition, if birth control pills protect against PID, it would be expected that women who use birth control pills would also have lower rates of ectopic pregnancy and infertility, two of the most common consequences of PID, but this is not the case. For these reasons, many believe birth control pills do not protect against PID.

IUD'S (INTRAUTERINE DEVICES): IUD's increase a woman's risk of PID about two-fold, although the risk for modern IUD's is much lower than for older IUD's. This risk is mainly due to the opening of the cervix to insert the IUD. Some research has also shown that women who use IUD's have higher rates of infertility, although there is much controversy and disagreement about this finding.

VIRUSES AND OTHER MICROORGANISMS: Almost all of the research on pelvic inflammatory disease focuses on pelvic infection caused by bacteria. We really don't know what role viruses, yeast, funguses etc may play in pelvic infection. There are a few studies showing that herpes can cause infection in the lining of the uterus, and one recent study showing that yeast can infect the lining of the abdominal cavity (peritonitis), but basically the possibility that viruses and other organisms can cause PID has not really been explored.

THE HIV VIRUS (AIDS): The rate of HIV infection is increasing faster among women than in any other group. Individuals who are infected with the HIV virus are much more susceptible to any infection, because the HIV virus interferes with the proper functioning of the immune system. For this reason, women who are HIV positive are more susceptible to both cervical and pelvic infections, and may have more difficulty recovering from these infections. The Canadian Center for Disease Control thus recommends that all HIV positive women with PID be hospitalized for most effective treatment.

HYSTERECTOMY: Most experts do not recommend hysterectomy as a treatment for PID. This is because modern antibiotics are usually effective at treating pelvic infection, and even with widespread infections such as peritonitis (spread of infection to the abdominal cavity), treatment with anti-anaerobic antibiotics (such as clindamycin), combined with surgically draining pus and washing the area with antibiotics, has been found to be more successful than hysterectomy.

Despite the fact that hysterectomy is not recommended by medical experts, many women still find that hysterectomy is suggested to them. In fact, in Canada, one in every ten women hospitalised with PID receives a hysterectomy. These figures are even higher in the U.S. where one in four women hospitalised for PID receives a hysterectomy. Because of the seriousness of this procedure and the possibility of complications, women may wish to research this possibility thoroughly and perhaps seek a second medical opinion. The medical research on PID is unanimous that this option should not even be considered until standard treatments have been thoroughly explored.

FOR MORE INFORMATION

Women who want more information about pelvic inflammatory disease or detailed references for this chapter can contact the Canadian Pelvic Inflammatory Disease (PID) Society. The Society offers a free telephone information service on pelvic inflammatory disease; a variety of brochures, booklets, fact sheets and articles; a large resource library with over 2000 articles on pelvic inflammatory disease and related topics; and self-help telephone support networks for women who would like to talk with other women for information and support. The society's highly recommended booklet on PID has recently been completely revised and updated.

CANADIAN PID SOCIETY, PO Box 33804, Stn D, Vancouver, BC. V6J 4L6. 604-684-5704.

Endometriosis - A Disease Of The 90's

This first chapter about endometriosis (endo) discusses what is currently taught in medical schools about endo, and what most doctors still believe. A new section of this chapter has been added to cover the newest drugs used for treatment. Finally, the most recent addition to the first chapter is the latest information on the link between endometriosis and environmental contaminants. Four years ago, I became aware of the intriguing new ideas of Dr. David Redwine which are presented in the second chapter on endo. Out of necessity another section has also been added that outlines a natural approach to treatment.

In 1600 BC Egyptian writings documented possibly the first case of endometriosis ever recorded in history. However, endometriosis is really a 20th century phenomenon. In the past, endometriosis was either rare or undiagnosed, and modern medicine has only recognized it as a disease entity for the last 100 years. During the last century, endometriosis has risen steadily in importance and incidence. It's now a major cause of pain and disability in women and may be linked to infertility. Yet, in spite of over 80 years of research, very little is known about this disease, what causes it or why it does or does not respond to treatment.

For women, it can be a frustrating, chronic, often painful and unpredictable disease, with no ideal treatment and no cure except perhaps menopause. This disease varies markedly in its extent and behaviour. Some women obtain pain relief and fertility enhancement through surgery and/or hormonal treatments. Others do not.

Endo is normal tissue in an abnormal location. It occurs when some of the tissue that normally lines the inside of the uterus, called the endometrium, grows in parts of the body where it doesn't normally grow. This happens most commonly in the pelvic area, ovaries, tubes, ligaments, outside surface of the uterus, lower end of the large bowel, and on the membranes covering the bladder. Occasionally, endometrial tissue spreads to the small intestines, appendix, bladder, ureters, cervix, vagina, old abdominal scars and navel; and very rarely, to the lungs.

In a strange way, endo behaves like a benign tumour. It can spread, invade and distort otherwise normal tissue. In fact, it acts just like normal placental tissues as they burrow their way into the inner wall of the uterus to set up a nourishment system for the fetus.

According to a widely held theory, these abnormally located tissues are just like those that line the uterus and therefore build up and bleed every menstrual period. Since the blood has no way to leave the body as menstrual blood normally does, it can cause internal bleeding, irritation, and inflammation and the formation of cysts and scar tissue.

If you were able to look inside the pelvis of a woman who has endo, you would most likely see endometrial implants on the ovaries, (40-50 percent of implants occur on the ovaries and tubes.) These implants would look like cysts varying from tiny bluish or dark brown blisters to large chocolate cysts (so called because they are filled with dark clotted blood) up to 20 cm or eight inches in diameter.

You might also see tiny blueberry spots or black spots (so called "powder burns") on the back side of the uterus, on the ligaments supporting the uterus, or on the membrane lining the abdominal cavity or on the lower portion of the large bowel. There might also be scarring in the surrounding tissues and the uterus might be fixed and immobile.

SYMPTOMS OF ENDO

In medical school, we were taught that endo begins as increasingly painful periods. The pain was described as a deep seated aching or bearing down or grinding type of pain located in the lower abdomen, vagina and back. The pain was said to be more marked on one side than the other and constant in nature rather than intermittent. According to what we were taught, the pain characteristically started five to seven days before the period, reached a peak at the time of the heaviest flow, and continued with decreasing intensity throughout the whole period and even for a few days afterwards. Then the pain would not reoccur until just before the next period.

However, it is very important to realize there is no one type of pelvic or abdominal pain in women with endo. Women with endo report a wide variety of **types** of pain and **timing** of pain. There is really no "typical" endometriosis pain and it can occur at any time throughout the cycle.

Recent evidence links these painful periods to the increased levels of prostaglandins produced by the inflammatory response that forms around endometrial implants. Prostaglandins are naturally occurring substances in the body and cause contractions of uterine muscle.

Some women with severe endo will have no pain at all. Their endo will be diagnosed either in the course of investigation for infertility, or surgery for other reasons, or even during routine pelvic examination. The location is one important factor determining how much pain and what type of pain will occur. A small endometrial implant in a sensitive area such as on the supporting ligaments of the uterus, or in the pockets between the uterus and the large bowel may cause a lot of pain whereas extensive involvement of the ovaries may cause no pain at all. The depth of the endometrial implant is also a critical factor in determining how much pain will be felt.

Another common symptom of endo is pain during sex or at ovulation. Some women have more pain at ovulation than during their menses. Some women have pain between ovulation and their period. The pain during sex is usually felt deep inside, can be localized to one area of the pelvis; is worse after vigorous or deep thrusting and premenstrually; and often persists for hours after sex.

The type of pain can give you a clue as to where the endometrial implant might be located. If the large bowel is involved, painful bowel movements can occur on a cyclical basis once a month at the time of the period. If the bladder is involved, there may be painful urination and blood in the urine once a month at the time of the period or just before. If the ovaries are extensively involved, there may be spotting between periods, excessive menstrual bleeding or irregular menstrual cycles. Most often, however, even women with severe endo, continue to have regular periods until the periods stop altogether at menopause. If the pelvic ligaments are involved, there may be painful swellings that occur once a month in the groin area.

Rarely, leakage or rupture of large endometrial cysts at or before a period can cause severe abdominal pain that mimics appendicitis. The leaked or spilled blood products can then cause chemical irritation of the lining of the abdominal cavity. This serious emergency usually means immediate surgery to find the source of the pain, and treat it.

Women with endo have a higher rate of miscarriage and pregnancies in the tubes. The rate of miscarriage may be as high as 40 percent of pregnancies with the presence of endo. In fact, sometimes the initial reason that a women sees her doctor is for the investigation of infertility. The infertility can either be the type where the woman has never had a child or the type where a woman has had one child and then no subsequent pregnancies after five or more years without the use of any birth control.

How or why the tissue mis-location occurs in the first place is still a mystery. Many theories have been advanced to explain the cause of endo. One theory proposes that blood and tissue flow backwards out of the fallopian tubes and into the pelvic cavity and onto some organ or ligament. Bleeding from these implants then causes pain and other symptoms.

DIAGNOSING ENDO

A doctor may be alerted to the possibility of endometriosis through a pelvic exam. The doctor may be able to feel a cyst on the ovaries or small lumps or nodules on the ligaments supporting the uterus or just behind the uterus. However, a laparoscopy is necessary to establish a definite diagnosis.

This is a minor operation done under general anesthetic. The doctor inserts a slender light-containing telescope into the abdomen to look at the pelvic organs and sometimes to perform minor surgery. At the time of laparoscopy, a small sample of the endometrial implants is taken and sent to the lab for microscopic examination. This biopsy will confirm the diagnosis.

Ultrasound examination is another useful diagnostic tool but it can not make the diagnosis definitely. It gives an idea of the extent of the endo, or the size of ovarian cysts. It's normally done prior to laparoscopy. However, the appearance of endo on ultrasound pictures is not specific enough to distinguish it from other types of pelvic growths.

TREATMENT OF ENDO

If a woman has no symptoms and does not wish to conceive, then no treatment is necessary, and she need only be seen by her doctor every six months to a year to check on the process of the disease.

Otherwise treatment may be necessary for pain relief or fertility enhancement. Treatment choices are not simple, however, and depend on the age of the woman and her desire to have children.

If a woman has only mild symptoms and infertility is not a factor, simple pain killers like tylenol or tylenol with codeine may be all that is necessary.

For some women with painful periods, drugs which inhibit the production of prostaglandin may be useful to relieve pain. These drugs offer good pain relief for certain women with mild to moderate pain during periods.

For more serious symptoms or those that do not respond to other simpler treatments, and to increase the chance of pregnancy, hormonal treatments may be considered. The aim of these treatments is to stop the ovaries from working and producing estrogen and also to stop the periods.

It has long been believed that pregnancy can improve the condition as well as cause endometrial implants to shrink. This has never been proven. Due to the associated infertility, increased miscarriage rate and possible painful sex, it may be difficult to get pregnant in the first place. Once pregnant, a woman usually experiences relief from pain, at least until the pregnancy is over. Then, the pain and other symptoms may return as before. One study of pregnant women with endometriosis showed multiple discomforts during pregnancy and a higher incidence of difficult labour and postpartum depression. Breast-feeding was found to delay the return of symptoms.

A decade ago, endo was thought to occur mainly in older women in their 30's or 40's and traditionally in white career women of upper middle class status who had delayed marriage and child-bearing. With the widespread use of laparoscopy this has been proven to be only partially true. It also occurs in black women, young women and women who have had early pregnancies. It can even happen in teenagers.

Dr. Donald Goldstein of the **Children's Hospital** in Boston studied 140 teenagers aged 10.5 to 19 years old who had chronic pelvic pain. Thirty five percent turned out to have endometriosis. He believes too often teens are treated for symptoms, without a proper diagnosis being made.

Moreover, there is a very significant hereditary factor. A woman whose mother, sister or daughter has endo may be seven times more likely to develop endometriosis then a woman without such a history. Also, the severity and reoccurrence rate of endo is higher in women whose close relatives have endo.

HORMONAL TREATMENTS

Endo is thought to occur less commonly in women who have been pregnant or who have entered menopause. Based on that assumption, two types of hormonal treatments have been developed, one that mimicked pregnancy, and one that mimicked menopause. Birth control pills and progesterone fall into the first category and danazol and the newer drugs fall into the second.

According to **Dr. David Olive, Director of Reproductive Endocrinology and Infertility** at **Yale University** in New Haven Connecticut, an unbelievable 43 percent of physicians are still using the birth control pill as a treatment for endo. In spite of the fact that no valid studies are available on their usefulness to enhance fertility or relieve pain.

Birth control pills are used in single or double strength. Pills that contain a high progesterone content are preferred. Side effects are numerous and recently smaller doses were found to produce the same results.

Progesterone by itself has also been used to create a pseudo pregnancy. However, breakthrough bleeding, nausea, weight gain and depression are troublesome possible side effects.

Another hormonal treatment that is commonly used to produce a pseudo-menopause is danazol. Firstly, it is very expensive, costing $95.00 to $190.00 per month depending on the dosage. Secondly, it can cause some unpleasant side effects including weight gain, fatigue, depression, oily skin and acne, decreased breast size and development of facial hair. This last side effect does not necessarily reverse after treatment stops.

According to **Dr. John Rock, Professor and Director Division of Reproductive Gynecology** at **John Hopkins University**, with a good exercise regimen, you can avoid most of the side effects of danazol. Danazol can provide pain relief and may improve the immune profile.

Dr. John Collins, Professor of Gynecology and Epidemiology, and his colleagues at **McMaster University** in Hamilton Ontario reviewed only well designed studies and found that neither progesterone nor danazol was better than placebo for the treatment of endometriosis associated infertility.

THE GNRH DRUGS

There are four **GNRH** drugs now available on the market. They were originally only approved for the treatment of prostate cancer in men.

SYNAREL: This is a nasal spray.

LUPRON: This is a monthly or daily injectable at the dose of 3.75mg a month. Too many North American women have been receiving the incorrect and higher dose of 7.5mg a month that is the recommended dose for men with prostrate cancer. This higher dose can cause severe side effects.

ZOLADEX: This drug is a monthly injectable and will be approved for use in endo sometime in 1993 in both Canada and the U.S.

BUSERELIN: This is a nasal spray or daily injectable that is being used in Europe and will soon be approved for use in Canada.

GNRH stands for gonadotropin releasing hormone. This is a hormone released by the hypothalamus in the brain, which triggers other hormones from the pituitary gland in the brain, which in turn triggers the female hormones estrogen and progesterone to be released from the ovaries. These drugs work by exhausting certain areas in the pituitary gland. Lupron is 15 times stronger that the naturally occurring GNRH in the body, and synarel is 200 times more potent.

The net effect of the GNRH drugs is, like danazol, a pseudo-menopause, but much more severe. The major side effect seems to be hot flashes. Other side effects include vaginal dryness, headaches, mood swings, depression, acne, muscle pain and reduction in breast size as well as a decreased sex drive. Another major concern about these drugs is that they cause decreased bone density that can lead to osteoporosis. This effect appears to be more pronounced with synarel than with lupron. The usual maximum course of treatment is six months. A woman should have a bone scan done before she attempts a second course of any of these drugs.

All these drugs are very new, very powerful and very expensive (about $400.00 to $600.00 a month). Too low doses of GNRH may also pose health problems. Researchers found that low doses can trigger hyper-stimulation of the ovaries resulting in high estrogen levels which, in turn, worsen endo. The long-term effects of tampering with the hormonal control areas in a woman's brain will not be known for ten to 20 years. The effect on fertility is dubious. Studies have shown no difference between the synarel and danazol in terms of pain relief (about 80 percent) and fertility enhancement (none).

The latest approach is to "add back" estrogen and progesterone hormones to prevent side effects of bone loss and menopausal symptoms. This adds the complication of the side effects of these two drugs. This concept of total hormonal manipulation is, in my opinion, still experimental and the long-term effects are completely unknown.

AN APPROACH TO USING HORMONAL TREATMENTS

In my opinion, use the least harmful agent first and the one that has been around for the longest time. If possible, use drugs only for crisis management. For example, when the pain becomes unbearable and you want to buy time to think about your options.

It makes sense to start with provera tablets. Dr. Olive suggests 100mg daily by mouth for six months. The rationale is simple. Provera has been proven to be just as good as danazol and the GNRH drugs for the relief of pain and it is very inexpensive.

No drug has been shown to improve pregnancy rates over no treatment at all. All of the drugs have been shown to provide pain relief in 80 to 100 percent of women, and this factor alone make drugs useful for crisis management. You have to carefully weigh the risks of side effects versus the benefits for your particular situation.

If you can't stand the side effects of provera, you might want to try danazol for a short time, say three to six months. Only as an absolute last and desperate resort should you consider the GNRH drugs since so much is unknown about them.

SURGICAL TREATMENTS

So called "conservative" surgery means removing endometrial implants while preserving your ovaries, tubes and uterus as much as possible and thus preserving your child-bearing ability. In the past, major abdominal surgery with a three or four inch bikini incision into the abdomen and removal of endometrial implants and scar tissue through cutting or burning was the main type of surgery available. These days it should be reserved for very large endometrial cysts or masses and deep bowel involvement.

The development of laparoscopic surgery has revolutionized the treatment of endometriosis. A video camera can now be attached to the laparoscope and the picture projected onto a television screen. This allows for excellent visualization and increased precision. Recovery from laparoscopic surgery is faster, and there is less scar tissue formed.

As the **Endometriosis Association** comments: "Operative laparoscopy offers better results than major abdominal surgery. Laparoscopy has been shown to lead to significantly less adhesions."

Another way to remove endometriosis is though using the laser. The laser beam is a high energy light than can be directed and controlled with pin-point accuracy of location and depth. The energy of the beam is absorbed by the water in cells causing them to vaporize.

The Association also says that some experts believe cutting the disease out is better then vaporizing with a laser. They also stress that all disease should be removed, including unusual appearances of endo, and, if possible, all tissue removed should be biopsied.

So called "radical" surgery or the removal of tubes, ovaries, and uterus is rarely necessary. As **Dr. Herbert Goldfarb** says in is book, **THE NO HYSTERECTOMY OPTION** (John Wiley and Sons 1990), "It is extremely rare person in this day and age who should ever need a hysterectomy for endometriosis, no matter how severe the condition."

APPROACH TO SURGICAL TREATMENTS

Surgery can be done for two reasons, to relieve pain or to enhance fertility.

According to Dr. David Olive, research has shown that **surgery for infertility** is most beneficial for women who have severe endometriosis or pelvic organs distorted out of shape, making pregnancy impossible.

If you are planning surgery for pain relief, find out what the track record is for the type of surgery you're getting five, ten and 15 years after surgery.

The experience of the surgeon is the single most important factor in determining the success of the surgery. The surgeon must be highly experienced and highly skilled in the use of the laparoscope and really committed to biopsying and getting rid of all suspicious abnormalities.

Laser has two disadvantages. The diagnosis cannot be checked through biopsy. Secondly, endometriosis has been discovered underneath carbon burns caused by the laser. However, in the hands of a skilled surgeon, laser can be an effective tool.

No one should consider surgery until they have read the Endometriosis Association's excellent and comprehensive guidelines on surgery and how to choose an experienced surgeon.

In 1991 **Dr. David Adamsom, Director of the Fertility and Reproductive Health Unit** in Palo Alto, California, estimated that of the 30,000 gynecologists in the U.S., there are perhaps 50 who have the determination and the skill to remove all of the endometriosis at surgery.

NEW EVIDENCE EMERGES ON ENDO AND THE ENVIRONMENTAL CONNECTION

Thanks to the untiring efforts of **Mary Lou Ballweg**, founder of the Endometriosis Association, convincing evidence on the link between radiation exposure, and organochlorine exposure, and the development of endometriosis have been recently brought to light.

In the mid 1960's, **NASA** began a long-term study on monkeys to find out the effects of ionizing radiation on them. Endometriosis developed in 53 percent of the monkeys after radiation exposure; and in only 26 percent of the monkeys not exposed to radiation. This is a highly significant result.

Researchers **Dr. John Fanton** and **Dr. John G. Golden** from the **Veterinary Science Division** at **Brooks Air Force** base in Texas, conclude their study by saying:

"Endometriosis in our monkey colony was conclusively linked to whole body penetrating energies of ionizing radiation. Women receiving whole body or, in particular, abdominal exposure, to penetrating doses of X-rays should possibly be considered to be at higher risk of developing endometriosis than unexposed women (**Radiation Research**, #126/p141-6/91)."

Meanwhile, the Canadian government had begun a monkey study to determine the effects of adding **PCB**'s and a poison produced by a fungus, to food. Results of the study were reported in 1985. Ballweg reported that the study showed that both substances caused the monkeys to develop endometriosis, which came as quite a surprise to the researchers. **Dr. James Campbell**, one of the researchers, told Ballweg that the PCB part of the study was significant statistically in the **severity** of the endometriosis, but not in the number that developed endometriosis beyond that seen naturally.

Through discussions with Dr. Campbell, Ballweg tracked down another similar study. Since 1977, the **Environmental Protection Agency** funded a long-term study on the effects of adding dioxin to the food of a monkey colony. Researchers noted immune dysfunction in exposed animals as well as difficulty in reproduction. In 1992, the funding for the project had become exhausted, and the animals were to be sold when the Endometriosis Association stepped in and bought the remaining animals. The Association then asked renowned endometriosis experts, **Dr. Dan Martin** and **Dr. Paul Dmowski**, to carry out laparoscopic and immunological studies on the animals. When the codes were broken, the landmark and as yet unpublished results became apparent. The results were published in the **Journal of Fundamental and Applied Toxicology** in Nov/93.

Seventy nine percent of the animals exposed to dioxin in the study developed endometriosis compared to 33 percent in the control group. Most importantly the disease was dose dependant, that is it increased in severity in direct proportion to the amount of dioxin exposure. Immune studies completed so far also indicate depressed immune function in the monkeys exposed to dioxin.

Dr. Paul Wooley is looking at blood from these exposed monkeys to see if there is any evidence of the body producing antibodies against itself as in lupus.

Meanwhile, The **National Institute of Environmental Health Sciences** is carrying out a study to determine the blood levels of dioxin, furan and PCB's in women with endometriosis. PCB's have been linked to endometriosis and thyroiditis in a German study published in 1992. The Environmental Protection Agency is carrying on a study to determine the effects of dioxin in rats who have had endometriosis surgically implanted in their bodies.

Ballweg speculates that based on above studies, "The disease of endometriosis might have been a mild, mostly tolerable disease in the past (except presumably for a few unlucky souls) that has become severe and distinctly intolerable with the additional effects of modern pollutants in our bodies. These studies may help explain why there seems to be an "epidemic" of endometriosis world wide in this century."

HOW TO AVOID EXPOSURE

1. **Avoid exposure to all unnecessary radiation.** Remember all X-ray exposure is cumulative. This means the effect is equal to the sum of all the X-rays you have ever had. For a further discussion on radiation risks, see the chapter on mammograms.

2. **As Greenpeace says, organochlorines like dioxins, furans and PCB's have become some of the most controversial chemicals of modern society.**

Dioxin in particular has been labelled the most toxic chemical ever produced by man. Dioxins are actually a group of 75 chemicals, "which are some of the most persistent and bio-accumulative chemicals released into the environment." These chemicals are used to make PVC plastics, solvents, pesticides, refrigerants, and in the pulp and paper industry. These same chemicals persist in the fat of meat and dairy products.

3. **Women should urgently support the Greenpeace campaign and other environmental action groups to phase out the industrial use of these chemicals, particularly in the pulp and paper industry.**

4. **Women should refuse to use bleached paper products.** This includes toilet paper, sanitary napkins and tampons. Ballweg suggests that before you throw out that last box of napkins/ tampons you call the toll free number of the company and tell them why you're switching.

5. **Support the WEED (Woman and Environments Education and Development Foundation) campaign to phase out organochlorines from sanitary products and disposable diapers.** Two Canadian women wrote a book on the topic entitled **WHITEWASH** (Harper and Collins, 1992).

6. **Avoid fish from the Great Lakes and emphasize whole grains, fresh vegetables and fruits in your diet.** Cut down on fats from milk and meat products. Try to buy organic foods.

ADDRESSES

GREENPEACE, 1017 West Jackson, Chicago, IL, 60607. 312-666-3305.

GREENPEACE, 185 Spadina Ave, Toronto, ON, M5T 2C6. 416-345-8408.

WEED, 736 Bathurst St, Toronto, ON, M5R 2R4. 416-516-2600.

NOTE: ENDOMETRIOSIS ASSOCIATION information and addresses are in the next chapter.

A New View Of Endometriosis

Endometriosis (**endo**) affects an estimated half million women in Canada and five to ten million in the U.S.

To review, endometriosis means that tissue similar to that which normally lines the uterus occurs outside the uterus on ligaments, the bottom most part of the pelvis, bowels, bladder and other tissues in the abdomen and can cause women excruciating pain, chronic disability and infertility.

One of the most frequently mentioned theories originated in 1927. Back then, **Dr. John Sampson** maintained that endometriosis resulted from menstrual blood flowing backward through the uterus and out through the tubes. This endometrial tissue then implanted randomly on various structures in the pelvis and bled every month like the tissue that normally lines the uterus.

Another theory popular today is that endo may be the result of some type of auto-immune disease. This means that the body rejects the abnormal endometrial-like tissue that is located in the pelvis, with both local and generalized effects.

In recent years, it has become evident that the immune system of endometriosis patients is depressed. This includes dysfunction of T-cells, B-cells, and natural killer cells. The cause of this immune disorder is unknown.

However, thanks to the inquiring mind and meticulous research of a gynecologist in a small city in central Oregon, a new and intriguing theory has been advanced that may explain many aspects of endo that have so far been inexplicable. Dr. Redwine has made a major contribution to an understanding of endometriosis, and posed important questions.

This gynecologist has also developed a highly effective method of surgical treatment for endo and has treated over 1,500 patients. Thirty five percent of his patients are Canadians unable to receive comparable treatment in Canada. Many will pay part, if not all, the costs of surgery themselves.

Dr. David Redwine is Director of **The Endometriosis Institute of Oregon** and practices at the **St. Charles Medical Center** in Bend, Oregon.

Between 1979 and 1984, Dr. Redwine studied 143 consecutive patients. What he found surprised him and did not support the common cliches about the illness. Dr. Redwine calls these beliefs cliches because they have been handed down in the textbooks but not backed by scientifically valid studies. However, a lot of doctors still believe them.

"Much of the info we have on endo," says Dr. Redwine, "comes from untested theories. There's been almost no progress with the disease since John Sampson proposed his retrograde menstruation explanation of endo in 1927."

FIVE COMMON CLICHES ABOUT ENDO

1. **"The ovary is the most common site of endometriosis".** In fact three modern studies have refuted that fact.

2. **"Endo can be identified by the classic tiny blueberry spots or black spots known as powder burns or by cysts that are bluish or dark brown in colour."**

In fact, endo can have many different appearances and colours and this can easily be proven by biopsy. Biopsy will show that these "atypical implants" are in fact typical endometriosis tissue. The fact of the myriad and subtle appearances of endo has been confirmed many times by other researchers in the fertility field.

3. **"Pregnancy prevents or cures the disease in women who have never been pregnant."**

Dr. Redwine found that endo was primarily a disease of fertile women.

4. "Endo is a disease that is progressive, and recurrent."

Dr. Redwine believes endo is a static disease that you are born with it as a result of cells left behind during fetal development. In his study, Dr. Redwine found no statistical evidence that the number of areas in the pelvis involved with endo increased with age.

5. "The only cure is menopause."

Again Dr. Redwine says there in no evidence to support the idea that endo tissue evaporates out of the body after menopause. In fact the oldest person diagnosed with endo was 78.

DIAGNOSING ENDO

The diagnosis of endo can be tentatively made through a careful pelvic examination. There is usually exquisite tenderness of the ligaments supporting the uterus. Sometimes small lumps or nodules can be felt on the ligaments or just behind the uterus.

"I keep my eye on the patient's face, if she makes a grimace or arches her back a little bit, this is extremely significant," says Dr. Redwine.

Definitive diagnosis can be made only through surgery, usually through the laparoscope under a general anesthetic.

WHAT ARE THE SYMPTOMS OF ENDO ?

Pelvic pain, not infertility, was the main symptom that caused two-thirds of the women Dr. Redwine studied to seek medical help. "They were fertile women whose main problem was pain," comments Dr. Redwine.

Nancy Petersen, R.N. and **Director of the Endometriosis Treatment Program** in Bend, Oregon, feels women do not make up symptoms of pelvic pain nor do they exaggerate about the severity of pain experienced.

In fact, Petersen says that 75 percent of the women who came to Dr. Redwine's clinic with proven endo had been dismissed in the past by their doctors as being neurotic.

Petersen feels it is logical to expect that anything that causes irritation or inflammation of the peritoneum (the clear saran-wrap-like covering of the abdominal organs) is likely to be extremely painful, as, for example, appendicitis.

She has heard some women describe the pain like "hot lead balls trying to fall out of the pelvis." Dr. Redwine describes the "twisting fist sign." This means that the woman twists her fist towards him or her own body as she describes the intensity of the pain.

The pelvic pain is usually described as sharp, stinging and burning in nature. The pain usually started at ovulation and at times other than during periods. The pain is **not** necessarily associated with periods.

Painful periods occurred in only 45 percent of women, painful sex in 37 percent and infertility in 27 percent. Other symptoms included pain with bowel movements, pain with aerobic exercise or jogging, and pain with posture changes. Twenty percent of women were asymptomatic.

Severe back and leg pain can also be caused by endo. Orthopedic surgeons are usually not aware of this potential cause of back pain. This pain cannot be cured unless the endo is removed from the uterine ligaments.

As Petersen says, "If a man had a disease which caused him to be unable to father a child and unbearable pain during sex and unbearable pain during bowel movements treated by feminizing hormones and surgery, endo would be a national emergency in this country."

WHERE IS ENDO AND WHAT COLOUR IS IT ?

Dr. Redwine felt he had to go back and study the basic assumptions about where endo was found and what it looked like.

To do this, he used the laparoscope to meticulously biopsy anything that didn't look like normal peritoneum. He advanced the tip of the laparoscope up to within one to two centimetres of the pelvic surfaces, which magnified the tissues three to five times. This he named "near contact laparoscopy" as opposed to the more common "panoramic laparoscopy" which views tissues from a greater distance.

Dr. Redwine made a pelvic map for each woman and carefully marked on it where he had taken the biopsy and which biopsies turned out to be endo.

He found that the most common site of endo was the peritoneum, especially behind the uterus in the "cul de sac" or the bottom most part of the pelvis. The ovaries and the fallopian tube were found to be uncommon sites for endo.

When he biopsied all suspicious lesions (abnormalities) in the pelvis, things that didn't look like endo (clear, white, red and yellow in colour called atypical implants) turned out to be endo when examined under the microscope by a pathologist.

Only 36 percent of women had the typical blue or black implants that doctors are always looking for but more 43 percent had atypical implants **only**. These 43 percent of women would have their endo completely missed by a doctor looking only for the blue or black implants.

This was the case with a 26-year-old surgical nurse with severe pelvic pain that was interfering with her work. After a laparoscopic examination of her pelvis, her gynecologist told her she had a normal pelvis and perhaps the pain was in her head. Another one and a half years of pain later and she finally saw Dr. Redwine. He found that the back of her pelvis was riddled with endo that had predominantly a white colour.

Reoccurrences after surgery, he believes, are most often "simply disease the surgeon missed." And the surgeon is likely to miss quite a lot if he or she only removes the classic blue-black abnormalities.

In fact, Dr. Redwine's rule is that "any suspicious area of the pelvic peritoneum is endo until proven otherwise by biopsy." The final diagnosis of endo, he stresses, should by made by the pathologist and not by the gynecologist.

Dr. Redwine also found that endo was hidden in two thirds of peritoneal pockets that he found. These are folds or defects in the peritoneum that must be turned inside out and examined.

In the microscopic study of biopsied tissue, Dr. Redwine found few or no blood or blood vessels. From this he concluded that misplaced endometrial tissue does not bleed in the way he had been taught.

Instead, he believes that the endo tissue secretes a chemical that causes nearby blood vessels to bleed. The blood becomes trapped under the peritoneum and as it ages, turns from clear, white and yellow to red and blue and finally black. He found that women under 30 were more likely to have clear, yellow, or red lesions and women over 30, the characteristic black powder burn lesions.

ENDO DOES NOT PROGRESS

Dr. Redwine found no evidence that the disease is highly recurrent or progressively spreading.

From all these observations, Dr. Redwine concluded that endo is a static disease, persistent but not recurrent, in women of all ages, with pain as the most common problem. It also occurs independent of periods and most of the growths are atypical in appearance.

Dr. Redwine has come up with a theory that explains all of his findings which he calls **Mulleriosis**.

The Mullerian duct system of the fetus gives rise to the cells of the uterus, tubes, ovaries and peritoneum of the adult. Dr. Redwine believes as these Mullerian cells migrate along the back of the pelvic wall, some cells get left behind. If these cells are endometrial cells, endometriosis may result. Other types of cells can be left behind as well. This may explain why ovarian, cervical and tubal cells are found in odd places in the pelvises of some women have endo.

Dr. Redwine believes that drug therapy of endo with danazol or newer drugs like synarel and lupron is expensive, has serious side effects, does not destroy endo and has a high rate of pain reoccurrence as soon as treatment is stopped.

DR. REDWINE'S METHOD OF SURGERY

Dr. Redwine's method of conservative surgery is simple but painstaking. He carefully cuts out all abnormal looking tissue through the laparoscope and this takes anywhere from 2.5 to seven hours.

In 1991, he connected an electrical current to his sessions and in this way was able to reduce time in the operating room by 40 to 60 percent.

"It is," he says, "very tedious surgery, but perhaps the most challenging surgery in gynecology. It takes a while to do... you have to start out each case with a firm commitment in your mind that you're going to get all the disease. In fact, you must dislike this disease to be a good surgeon for the disease."

A woman's best chance of cure is at the first surgery, when there is the least scar tissue present, and the best view of the pelvis is possible.

Many of his patients have had multiple surgeries and drug therapies as well. "Everything was done to them," Dr. Redwine says, "except remove their disease."

He advises surgeons to remove all affected areas of the peritoneum with a wide margin around them, using three or more incisions into the abdomen. The incisions are for the laparoscope, irrigating instruments, and for a rod-like probe that he uses to move the pelvic organs to ensures he identifies and removes all disease. Dr. Redwine has found it is best to leave the peritoneum open and it will regenerate on its own.

Snipping away diseased tissue through a laparoscope equipped with scissors may achieve more precision and less trauma to tissue than laser surgery. It also allows Dr. Redwine to palpate (feel carefully for) all possible growths as well as to see them. The peritoneum is a very flexible membrane and can be pulled up and examined and cut if necessary, thus avoiding underlying structures. There is very little blood loss with this technique. This is an average loss of only 30 cc or two tablespoons.

RESPONSE TO DR. REDWINE'S WORK

To date, Dr. Redwine's surgery has resulted in 80 to 90 percent of women getting relief from their pain. However, some women do not have good results. In the United States there is a small but growing number of doctors using this technique. Dr. Redwine's program, even if expanded, cannot handle all the women who need this type of surgery. Dr. Redwine would like to see many more doctors use this approach.

The first step for interested gynecologists is to start using the near contact lap method and biopsy all suspicious lesions in the peritoneum. In this way, the individual surgeon can see for himself or herself whether Dr. Redwine's theories have any validity.

In fact, several Canadian physicians have visited Dr. Redwine and observed his work. Canadian women from five provinces have been making the trip to Oregon and obtaining excellent results.

In December 1989, Alberta became the first jurisdiction in Canada to approve Dr. Redwine's conservative surgery for use by the province's doctors. While doctors are being trained in his techniques, the government is paying for the expenses of women who go to Oregon.

Dr. John Jarrell, head of obstetrics and gynecology at **Foothills Hospital** in Calgary, said in the **Calgary Herald** that he expects that there will be an initiative from physicians in Alberta soon:

"Aside from Dr. Redwine and a few other doctors, not many doctors have a good data base. There is a growing interest, and I have a sense there will be some changes and the government will be responsive."

"That does not mean people will stop using drugs. It will depend on the needs of patients. A lot of time is spent deciding on one over another and looking at side effects. But there is a ground swell of appreciation that the medicine is nowhere near effective as touted."

CONSUMER POWER

Dr. Redwine believes women should use their consumer power to make sure doctors are aware of the many and varied appearances of endometriosis and the most effective ways of removing and destroying it. He believes women should resist expensive drug treatments that do not destroy the disease nor alter its course.

And finally, before agreeing to any type of surgical or medical therapy, Dr. Redwine suggests women find out whether long-term follow-up studies for pain reoccurrence as well as infertility have been carried out.

ALTERNATIVE TREATMENTS FOR ENDOMETRIOSIS

Dr. Redwine's ideas have been a major breakthrough for women in dispelling the antiquated and unscientific myths about endo perpetrated by the medical profession. However, Dr. Redwine's treatment involves aggressive and highly demanding surgery not easily available in Canada or the United States. Also, Dr. Redwine's surgery is not successful for everyone.

Before resorting to either powerful drugs or major surgery, I would urge women to return to their heritage as wise women and healers and explore the natural alternatives that assist the body in healing itself. If necessary, women can use medical drugs temporarily to buy the time to research and experiment with more natural methods.

There is no doubt that for some women, the symptoms of endometriosis, especially pain, can be alleviated through natural means. However, such approaches require time, patience and commitment. They are not as cut and dry as taking a pill or getting abnormal tissue cut out. There is no single panacea that works for all women with endo.

Some women understandably feel like their body has betrayed them. They do not feel like they can ever get better.

But in the wise woman tradition, according to **Susun Weed**, herbalist and author of **HEALING WISE**, the body is seen as "the perfect vehicle for your unique expression." The illness is seen as a friend, an ally for growth and transformation. Preferred healing methods are unconditional love and nourishment and herbs. The herbs used by the wise woman are simple, familiar, messy and fun.

SPECIFIC NATURAL THERAPIES FOR ENDOMETRIOSIS

In a natural approach to a chronic illness, it is necessary to be patient, to look at all aspects of the problem including emotional and spiritual issues as well as physical and mental aspects of the problem. It will probably be necessary to combine a number of different therapies and to allow sufficient time for them to work. Natural methods do not work as fast or tidily as drugs or surgery.

DIET: Some women have found that the pain completely disappears with a major change in diet. Several cases of remission of symptoms have been reported with a macrobiotic diet. However, it is important to know that long-term adherence to a strict macrobiotic diet can lead to vitamin-B-12 deficiency. For most women, I believe that diet change would only provide part of the solution.

YEAST: According to **Mary Lou Ballweg**, "There is a clear cut relationship between chronic candidiasis and severe endometriosis." That connection is well-detailed in the book **OVERCOMING ENDOMETRIOSIS** which devotes a whole chapter for the endometriosis-candidiasis link. If there is a history suggesting chronic yeast is present, especially prolonged antibiotics and hormone usage, then the yeast infection must be treated as the top priority. Candida is treated through diet, acidophilus and anti-yeast medications (natural or synthetic).

In treating yeast infections, diet is probably the most important element. The diet is a low carbohydrate diet with avoidance of sugars, bread with yeast, dairy, fermented foods, dried fruits, canned, processed and mouldy foods, especially over ripe foods.

Dr. Orian Truss, an internist from Birmingham, Alabama and author of **The Missing Diagnosis**, says, "I think it is very unquestionable that there is a very high association of endometriosis with chronic candidiasis. Naturally we cannot, at this time, be sure whether the yeast is causing the endo or whether some common factor predisposes to both." However, Dr. Truss believes that yeast overgrowth precedes endometriosis. "My own feeling is that the yeast is the cause of endometriosis because it is associated with so much evidence of interference in hormonal function in both men and women."

Dr. Truss has seen dramatic relief of endometriosis symptoms in women who have been treated with diet, anti-yeast medications and yeast desensitization shots.

SUPPLEMENTS: This low carbohydrate diet used for treating yeast infections is the same one suggested by **Dr. Robert Atkins** for endo in his excellent book, **Dr. Atkin's Health Revolution**. Dr. Atkins also suggests the following supplements to help lower the estrogen in the body: choline, methionine, inositol, evening of primrose oil, vitamin-E, vitamin-C and bioflavonoids.

ALLERGIES: Dr. Wayne Konetski, an environmental and allergy specialist from Waukesha, Wisconsin, has found that women with PMS and endo have developed a hypersensitivity to their own hormones, particularly progesterone. Ninety percent of the women he has treated also have candida infections, which must be the first thing treated. He then treats with desensitizing oral drops of natural progesterone in the range of one hundredth of a milligram to 150 milligrams per month. Dr. Konetski has had good results in relieving pain and restoring fertility to women with endo. Of course, his treatment plan must be individualized for each woman.

DIOXIN EXPOSURE: There is a possible link between dioxin exposure and exposure to other organochlorines, and endometriosis, as mentioned in the first chapter on endo. Women with endo should use only unbleached tampons and sanitary napkins, and make every effort to avoid such exposure in meat, dairy and fish.

HERBS: Western herbs as well as Chinese herbs have been useful in the treatment of endo. Herbal therapy as well as nutritional therapy is best done under the supervision of an experienced naturopath or medical doctor.

ACUPUNCTURE: Some women have found acupuncture treatments very helpful. A minimum of six treatments is required before a woman can see whether this treatment modality holds promise for her. It would be preferable to find a highly experienced acupuncturist, preferably one who is experienced in the treatment of endo. The **TENS** machine, a small hand-held machine that stimulates acupuncture points electrically has been a useful adjunct for the treatment of the pain for some women.

HOMEOPATHY: Homeopathy has a lot to offer a woman with endo. With very minute doses of natural substances, it can stimulate the body's healing. Again, it is necessary to find and work closely with an experienced homeopath. Due to the complex knowledge required, it is difficult to self-prescribe homeopathic remedies for a chronic illness.

CONCLUSION

It is important not to overlook the emotional issues caused by having a disabling disease and preceding the development of endo. Visualization, affirmations and relaxation are essential and very practical tools that I recommend to anyone dealing with a chronic illness.

The new age attitude that we create our own reality, while it has some merit, has resulted in people beating up on themselves or others who have chronic illness. The implication is that women with endo have done something wrong in their physical or emotional life that caused the illness. All such attitudes prevent healing.

The will to get well and determination to do it whatever it takes is the key to turning around any major illness.

For a challenging illness like endo, it requires courage, stamina and persistence to face and overcome a disease with so many unknowns in it. I believe that women have the natural strength and resiliency to do so.

USEFUL RESOURCES

THE ENDOMETRIOSIS NETWORK OF TORONTO (TENT), PO Box 3125, Markham Industrial Park, Markham, ON, L3R 6G5. 416-591-3963.

TENT is an independent volunteer self-help group that offers telephone and written support as well as support groups and educational public meetings.

THE ONTARIO NETWORK FOR ENDOMETRIOSIS, City Center Place, 25 Peele Center Dr, #133, Brampton, ON, L6T 3R5.

This is a non-profit volunteer group that shares info and support with groups throughout Ontario.

ENDOMETRIOSIS ASSOCIATION, U.S. and Canada Headquarters, 8585 North 76th Place, Milwaukee, WI, 53223. 1-800-426-2END.

Canadian branches of the **ENDOMETRIOSIS ASSOCIATION** are found in most provinces. Call the toll free number to get a list of branches near you.

The Endometriosis Association was founded in U.S. and provides support and information to women with endo, conducts research, and educates doctors and the public. The Association also publishes an excellent newsletter six times a year.

Nancy Petersen, C/O **St. Charles Medical Center**, Endometriosis Treatment Program, 2500 NE Neff Rd, Bend OR 97701-6015. Toll free number: 1-800-446-2177.

The St. Charles Medical Center has a waiting period of 2.5 to three months. Surgical, pathology reports and the woman's written history must be mailed (not faxed) to Dr. Redwine for review beforehand. The average cost of surgery is $4,000 to $5,000 U.S. Please address letters and inquires to the above address. Interested physicians can find out about training programs, and the scientific basis of this work by writing directly to Dr. Redwine at the above address.

THE MOST USEFUL BOOKS

THE ENDOMETRIOSIS SOURCEBOOK, by **Mary Lou Ballweg** and the **Endometriosis Association** (Contemporary Books, 1995). Written for women by women, this book is the most comprehensive resource available on endometriosis, a chronic, debilitating, and very confusing disease. An indispensable compilation of current information and more, this sourcebook provides you with everything you need to know: the most up to date research, new treatments, both surgical and medical, alternative treatments, including nutrition, common myths about the disease, pregnancy, labour, and postpartum experiences of women with endo. It also includes advice for coping with endo both physically and emotionally citing personal case histories of women sharing their struggles and successes.

OVERCOMING ENDOMETRIOSIS, NEW HELP FROM THE ENDOMETRIOSIS ASSOCIATION (1987) is an invaluable book that gathers together the latest research and treatment information.

An American woman has written an excellent book entitled, **LIVING WITH ENDOMETRIOSIS; How to Cope with the Physical and Emotional Challenges**, (Addison-Wesley, 1987), by **Kate Weinstein**. Many women have found this book very useful.

THE ENDOMETRIOSIS ANSWER BOOK; NEW HOPE NEW HELP, by **Laurson**, **Niels** and **Constance De Swann** (1987) includes the endometriosis diet that promotes healing. Recommended although sometimes a patronizing attitude.

OTHER BOOKS ON ENDOMETRIOSIS

COPING WITH ENDOMETRIOSIS, by **Dr. Breitkopf Lyle** and **Mation Gordan Bakoulis** (Prentice Hall, 1989).

ENDOMETRIOSIS AND INFERTILITY AND TRADITIONAL CHINESE MEDICINE, A LAYWOMAN'S GUIDE, by **Bob Flaws** (Boulder Colorado, Blue Poppy Press, 1989).

UNDERSTANDING ENDOMETRIOSIS, by **Caroline Hawkridge** (Macdonald Optima, 1989).

ENDOMETRIOSIS, by **Suzie Hayman** (Penguin Press, 1991).

ENDOMETRIOSIS, by **Julia Older** (New York Charles Scribner, 1984).

ENDOMETRIOSIS AND YOU, by **Gail Papke** and others (Budlong, 1988).

Section Six:
Growing Older Getting Better

The Major Milestone Of Menopause 188

Preventing And Treating Bone Loss 205

How To Save Your Uterus 218

The Great Debate
Over Breast Cancer Screening 227

The Major Milestone Of Menopause

Menopause is a process of change and transition as a woman's body sheds its child-bearing potential and adjusts to lower levels of hormones. Menopause usually starts around the late forties, when periods start to get more irregular and finally stop altogether. The average age at which periods stop is around fifty, but it can occur earlier, particularly in black and non-European women.

Like childbirth, menopause is a complex topic that women only recently have begun to explore in depth. And like childbirth, the truths about menopause have been obscured by myths and fallacies. Unlike childbirth, every woman will experience menopause either naturally, or surgically induced through the removal of the uterus, with or without the ovaries being left in place. Some women may experience an earlier menopause following a tubal ligation. Earlier menopause may also be induced by chemotherapy or radiation therapy.

In the past, medical descriptions of menopause have been intimidating. Phrases that referred to the menopause as "deterioration," "deficiency disease," "estrogen starvation," "living decay" or "partial death" projected to women an image of irreversible and inevitable physical and mental decline.

In addition, our culture has created a negative stereotype of the menopausal woman. Added to this is the fact that a lot has been attributed to menopause that has nothing to do with it. Although sometimes difficult, it is worth trying to distinguish the normal healthy changes of menopause from the normal healthy changes of aging.

In spite of the negative press, studies show that women feel positive or neutral about menopause and that most are relieved by the end of their fertility. The post-menopausal years can be energetic ones. As **Margaret Mead** once said, "the most creative force in the world is the post-menopausal woman with zest."

While the physical and emotional changes of the menopausal period may be numerous, only three physical symptoms are said to be directly attributed to the hormonal shifts that occur during menopause. They are menstrual changes, hot flashes and vaginal changes. However, the medical profession's understanding of menopause is still growing.

MENSTRUAL CHANGES

The first symptoms that a woman notices, usually in her mid-forties, is that her periods start to change. Some women menstruate more frequently, others skip periods altogether, and others find their periods are more widely spaced. The amount of bleeding varies from the same to lighter or heavier. Her periods may last for a longer or shorter time. The timing of her periods may become unpredictable. Occasionally there is only spotting at the time of the expected period. Eventually, around the average age of 50, the periods stop altogether. There are no hard and fast rules about the age at which periods become irregular or the age at which the periods stop.

Normally, a woman's ovary releases one egg every month and secretes into the bloodstream the female hormones estrogen and progesterone. In the first half of the cycle estrogen predominates; and then after the egg is released at ovulation, progesterone predominates with estrogen still present. Later in the cycle, barring pregnancy, both estrogen and progesterone reach their low points and the period begins.

Around the time of menopause, ovulation becomes irregular and some cycles don't occur at all. With no ovulation, estrogen remains high and progesterone low. Since progesterone is necessary to shed the uterine lining, there is no period or only scant spotting. Sometimes the weight of the menstrual material causes it to slough off in late and very heavy flow.

Eventually at menopause the ovaries stop producing eggs altogether, and the levels of estrogen and progesterone go way down. But long before the ovaries slow down, the body develops other sources of estrogen. These are located in the fatty tissues of the body and in the adrenal glands. The ovaries themselves continue to secrete small amounts of estrogen for ten years or longer after the periods stop. In addition, the ovaries and the adrenal glands continue to produce androgens. Androgens are like male hormones but they very much belong in a female body. Androgens are responsible for a sense of well being and for maintaining muscle strength and sex drive. Androgens can also be converted into estrogens.

According to **Dr. Sadja Greenwood**, a leading menopause expert and author of the book, **MENOPAUSE NATURALLY**, "the best menopausal body is one that is a little plump." This is because the fat cells can convert androgens into estrogen. This extra estrogen cushions women against the extremes of menopausal symptoms. At the same time the extra estrogen may cause erratic or heavier bleeding.

Heavy menstrual bleeding can be a frightening and sometimes debilitating experience. Heavy bleeding is usually the result of hormonal imbalance (fluctuating levels of estrogen with not enough progesterone). In a small percentage of cases, the bleeding is due to uterine fibroids, an overgrowth of the uterine lining, cancer of the cervix or cancer of the uterus. After these other causes have been ruled out, becoming anemic may be the only risk. Iron supplements may be needed (See chapter on Iron).

HOT FLASHES

The second well known symptom of menopause is hot flashes. Although these occur in the majority of women in North America, Japanese women, for example, do not get hot flashes and some women, especially overweight women, have no hot flashes at all.

A hot flash is described as sudden reddening of the skin over the head, neck and chest or even the entire body, accompanied by a feeling of intense body heat. The hot flash may last from several seconds to several minutes, rarely up to an hour. The frequency of hot flashes varies from rare to occurring every half hour. They are sometimes more frequent at night. Some women sweat profusely; others just a little, or not at all. Hot flashes are usually preceded or followed by chills. Within two years after the last period, hot flashes will subside completely for the most part. However, one third of women may continue well after that.

Hot flashes may be visible to others, but not usually. They can also be triggered by hot drinks, spicy food, alcohol, emotional stress hot weather or overheated rooms. The key to handling hot flashes is to keep cool, dress in layers, carry a portable fan, avoid the triggering factors, and keep a sense of humour. Hot flashes have been likened to teenage acne. Some women find hot flashes enjoyable. More importantly, hot flashes are absolutely harmless.

A small number of women are incapacitated with hot flashes. They interfere with their sleep or work. Some women wake up drenched in sweat and have to change their nightgown and sheets three to four times a night. These women may want to consider taking low doses of estrogen, after a careful discussion of the risks versus benefits with their doctor. Estrogen usually stops hot flashes immediately. It does not prevent wrinkles or other signs of aging or treat psychological problems. Estrogen is usually prescribed in combination with a progesterone. (See below for a discussion on the pros and cons of hormones).

VAGINAL DRYNESS

The third symptom of menopause is vaginal soreness and dryness. This dryness can sometimes cause painful sex.

As you age, the lining of the vagina becomes thinner, the walls of the vagina become smoother, and the colour changes from deep pink to lighter pink. The cervix no longer secretes as much mucous for lubrication as it once did.

Fortunately, this problem is one that is easily remedied. Simple lubricants such as vegetable oils or water soluble jellies like **Lubrafax** or **KY Jelly** may be all that is needed. **Astroglide** and **Replens** are special products designed specifically as lubricants for menopause. Slower sex with more foreplay may also be very helpful. Regular sex, through intercourse or masturbation, increases the amount of vaginal lubrication.

Finally, if necessary, estrogen cream applied to the vaginal area will alleviate the problem within a few weeks. Estrogen taken this way is absorbed directly into the blood stream, bypassing both the digestive track and the liver. However, circulating levels of estrogen after vaginal administration are only one quarter of those seen with equivalent doses orally. Usually about one eighth of an inch of an applicator is all that is needed once or twice a week for maintenance. At that low dose, there is no increase in blood levels of estrogen and it may not be necessary to take a progesterone.

With larger vaginal doses on a regular basis (greater than .3mg premarin or an eighth of an applicator) you will still need to take a progesterone for at least ten days three or four times a year, or to get an endometrial biopsy of the uterine lining done once a year.

A new estrogen releasing vaginal ring is being developed and one study showed that Swedish women preferred it over creams.

OTHER SYMPTOMS OF MENOPAUSE

If you have other symptoms of menopause, your doctor may not believe they are related to menopause, but they could be.

More than 50 percent of women experience joint pain at some time during menopause. Migraine headaches may start for the first time or worsen around menopause.

According to **Janine O'Leary Cobb**, author of **UNDERSTANDING MENOPAUSE**, and editor of **A FRIEND INDEED** newsletter, up to 20 percent of post-menopausal women may experience a bothersome condition called burning mouth syndrome, which consists of a very dry and burning mouth.

There may be changes in the skin and hair. Underarm hair, pubic hair and scalp hair may thin out and change texture. Unwanted facial hair may also appear.

Many women experience bloating, indigestion and gas. Some women temporarily experience unusual changes in one or more of their five senses.

Changes in sleep patterns are very common. Insomnia may be very debilitating for women and make other problems seem worse.

MENTAL AND EMOTIONAL CHANGES

Emotional and psychological changes of menopause are probably related both to shifting hormone levels as well as to the diverse ways in which women handle major change in their lives, and the quality of women's support systems, family, friends and community.

Many women report depression, irritability, mood swings and emotional over-reaction. Women also note increased forgetfulness, memory loss, disorientation, and lack of concentration. Hormonal levels are probably at least partially responsible for these symptoms.

Hormonal changes particularly affect women who have premenstrual symptoms. During menopause these symptoms may be exaggerated. This is due again to high levels of estrogen without the opposing progesterone.

Levels of satisfaction with yourself, your work, your mate, family and friends also has a lot to do with mental and emotional states; as does attitudes to the visible signs of aging that occur around the same time as menopause, like wrinkles, weight gain, grey hair, and the need for reading glasses.

At this time of life, women may also find themselves "sandwiched" between looking after the needs of aging and ill parents, and dealing with the increased demands and difficulties of teenaged children.

There is no peak of mental illness at menopause but there is the added stress of major physical and emotional changes added to already existing problems.

This time around menopause is an ideal time to cut back on commitments to family, friends, community and career, in order to create more space to really look after your needs, improve your level of health, and celebrate this important transition.

DEPRESSION, SELF-ESTEEM AND UNREWARDING ROLES

Depression may be a realistic response of a woman to her restrictive role in the family, at least in this culture. This is the view of **Dr. Beverly Burnside**, **Research Associate** at the **University of British Columbia**. She has developed **SHOP (Social Health Outreach Program)**, a grass roots program to help women deal with depression and other problems of aging.

According to Dr. Burnside, "In most cases, female depression is an emotional and physiological response to constricted and unrewarding social roles, and is best understood as **demoralization**."

The SHOP program offers a woman concrete ways to develop her self-esteem, to expand her role in society, to meet new friends, to work outside the home and to develop better support networks. Dr. Burnside found that women who had already expanded their circle of friends and interests outside the family suffered a lot less depression after menopause.

The SHOP program has been proven highly effective in treating depressed older women without drugs or therapy. A one-year follow-up study has shown that SHOP's positive effects are lasting.

IS MENOPAUSE A DISEASE ?

Menopause is known to be associated with decreasing estrogen levels, but what is not known is whether these decreased levels of estrogen do in fact cause all the symptoms of menopause. There is no direct proof that estrogen lack causes bone loss, heart disease or other ailments associated with the menopause.

Germaine Greer puts it more succinctly in her book, **The Change**:

"The proponents of **HRT** [hormone replacement therapy]... have never proved that there was an estrogen deficiency, nor have they explained the mechanism by which the therapy of choice effected its miracles. They had taken the improper course of defining a disease from its therapy..."

Dr. Jerilynn Prior, researcher and **Professor of Endocrinology** at the **University of British Columbia**, agrees. In an article in the A Friend Indeed newsletter (Jan/92), she puts it this way:

"Linking the menopausal change in reproductive capability with aging, and making menopause a point in time rather than a process, and labelling it an estrogen deficiency disease, are all reflections of non-scientific, if you will, prejudicial thinking by the medical profession."

Dr. Prior says that no study proving the relationship between estrogen deficiency and menopausal symptoms and related diseases has yet been done. "Instead," says Dr. Prior, "a notion has been put forward that since estrogen levels go down, this is the most important change and explains all the things that may or may not be related to menopause. So estrogen treatment at this stage of our understanding is premature. This is kind of backwards science. It leads to ridiculous ideas like calling a headache an aspirin deficiency disease."

Since it is commonly assumed that menopausal symptoms were due to estrogen deficiency, in many studies, progesterone levels were not even measured. Both Dr. Prior and **Dr. John Lee**, a clinical instructor at the **University of California Medical School, Department of Family Medicine**, believe that menopausal symptoms including bone loss are mainly caused by a deficiency of progesterone.

Dr. Prior found she could reverse bone loss by giving 10mg of synthetic progesterone (Provera) alone daily for ten days a month. In fact, Dr. Prior points out that during menopause progesterone decreases 1,200 percent from its baseline while estrogen only decreases 50 to 100 percent from its baseline. Dr. Lee found he could reverse bone loss and, furthermore, could control hot flashes and other menopausal symptoms using a natural form of progesterone in a skin cream with no apparent side effects.

SHOULD I OR SHOULDN'T I TAKE HORMONES ?

Doctors disagree about whether all menopausal women should be on hormones, which hormones and whether hormones should be reserved for the use of women with severe hot flashes, severe vaginal dryness, or women at high risk for bone loss or heart attacks. There is no agreement as to how many years hormones should be taken. Increasingly, doctors believe that all menopausal women should be on both estrogen and progesterone until death.

There are two ways in which hormones are being prescribed. Hormone replacement therapy or **HRT** means taking both estrogen and progesterone together. Estrogen replacement therapy or **ERT** means taking estrogen alone.

Women who take HRT, or ERT, according to Germaine Greer, may be taking more than five times the amount of estrogen that they had in their bloodstream before menopause. Older women seem to adapt to levels of estrogen at a fifth of their previous levels derived from the ovaries, adrenals, and fatty tissues. Taking HRT may cause the body to stop producing its own estrogen.

Greer poses the following question: "What if those female bodies that fight menopause by flooding themselves with FSH and keeping up estrogen secretion, are robbing other vital functions in the process, so that the organism has to go short of endorphins and cortico-steroids?"

The use of commonly prescribed estrogen (ERT) is associated with a three to four times increased incidence of uterine cancer. However, as Germaine Greer points out, the incidence of endometrial cancer is still rare, and it rose by only ten percent in the 20 years that estrogen was taken by itself. Many other factors could have accounted for the increased rate; during the same period, the incidence of all cancers rose.

Then, as Greer says, based on the scant evidence of two small studies, all women were advised to go on synthetic progesterones or progestins. The studies showed that estrogen did not adversely affect the uterine lining in 90 percent of women, but for the ten percent of women who did develop an overgrowth of the uterine lining, adding progestin did prevent cancer. Greer feels it would make more sense to screen women for uterine changes, and then treat the ten percent who develop significant changes of the uterine lining (which is usually easily treated).

Instead, it is now recommended that all women who have not had their uteruses removed take synthetic progesterone or progestins (Provera, Norlutate or Micronor) as well as estrogens (Premarin, Estrace, Estinyl, C.E.S., Ogen, by mouth; or the Estraderm patch; which slowly releases estrogen through the skin). Most doctors advise women who have had hysterectomies that they can safely take estrogen by itself.

Overweight women, women with liver disease and women with polycystic ovarian disease are also at increased risk for uterine cancer and may be advised to consider progestin alone therapy. Progestin alone does provide some relief of menopausal symptoms, including hot flashes.

In any case, taking progestins for 10 to 14 days out of every cycle means that a woman will continue to bleed every month after menopause, although this bleeding apparently decreases in time and becomes more like spotting.

Side effects of Provera appear to be related to the dose. New ways of giving Provera are being developed, such as giving 2.5mg or 5mg of Provera along with .625mg of premarin every day of the month. The safety of these combinations has not yet been established.

After six months of hormones at this lower dose, which is often recommended for women in their 60's and 70's, bleeding should stop altogether. However, the beneficial effects of estrogen on blood lipids may be somewhat reduced by continuous Provera and cancelled by Norlutate.

A new combination estrogen-progestin skin patch is being developed and is now on the market. It is called **Estracomb**.

THE DOWN SIDE OF SYNTHETIC PROGESTERONE

"This would not be a problem," says Germaine Greer," if taking progestins was fun, but progestins make many women feel sicker than menopause ever did."

Not surprisingly, some women do not like to bleed every month after going through the menopause. Some women prefer to take progestin intermittently. At least every three to six months is recommended to counter the risk of uterine cancer. However, bleeding could be heavier at that point.

An acceptable alternative approved by many experts is to get a biopsy of the uterine lining done every year as an alternative to taking progestin for 10 to 14 days every month. This endometrial biopsy can be done in a gynecologist's office without a local anesthetic. This procedure can be uncomfortable even with new flexible sampling systems.

Some women come in and say they will never take progestins because of the associated mood swings and depression. In fact, the addition of progestin to estrogen is known in the medical literature to produce marked premenstrual symptoms.

Gail Sheehy reports in her book, **THE SILENT PASSAGE**, that many doctors hear common complaints about progestin: "Whenever I take Provera, I have migraines, bloating, breast tenderness, the blues: I feel awful and want to die."

Dr. Prior does not believe Provera causes these side effects. She points to two double blind studies which showed no increase in PMS symptoms with the addition of Provera to estrogen.

THE BENEFITS OF NATURAL PROGESTERONES

Provera is a synthetic or man-made form of progesterone. Natural progesterone has the same structure as the one normally found in the female body. Natural progesterone appears to be safe and have far fewer effects than its distant synthetic relative.

Since natural progesterone taken by mouth is broken down in the stomach, it has to be taken in special micronized oral form or by rectal or vaginal suppository or skin cream.

According to Gail Sheehy, some experts believe "that oral micronized progesterone (**OMP**) is the wave of the future." **Dr. Joel Hargrove** did a small study on the effect of taking a daily combination of natural oral micronized progesterone (200 to 300mg per day) and natural estrogen in the form of estriol. Women on this regimen felt well, had a better blood lipid readings and the uterus was still protected.

Dr. Malcolm Whitehead, Chairperson of the British Menopause Council, says that OMP in adequate doses causes sleepiness and drowsiness. He says he would recommend taking the natural progesterone by vaginal or rectal suppository instead. Natural progesterone is better absorbed through this route, thus lower doses can be used.

Through his research, Dr. Whitehead has found that at least 300mg of Utrogestan (a type of OMP made by a French company and soon now available in Canada as **Prometrium**) for 10 to 14 days a month is necessary to fully protect the uterus. Dr. Whitehead also uses Duphaston (another form of natural progesterone that is made in Holland but not available in North America).

Dr. Don Gambrell, Professor of Gynecology, Physiology and Endocrinology in Atlanta, recommends 25 to 50mg of natural progesterone twice daily in a vaginal suppository form; or in a capsule form taken by mouth: 100mg in the morning and 200mg at bedtime. Both these doses will protect the uterus from cancer.

OMP is currently available through specialized pharmacies by prescription only.

Dr. John Lee believes that most menopausal symptoms, including prevention of bone loss, can be best handled through a natural progesterone cream that is applied to the skin. One to one half jars of the progesterone cream is used per month and each two ounce jar contains 900mg of natural progesterone. The chapter on osteoporosis gives details on how the cream is applied.

HORMONES AND THE HEART: THE PROS

Although well designed studies have yet to be done, experts point out that the studies to date, although of mixed quality, show a positive effect of estrogen on the heart and perhaps as high as a 50 percent reduction in the rate of heart disease.

The protective effect of estrogen was originally thought to be due to its favourable effect on cholesterol levels in the blood.

Estrogens decrease total cholesterol, increasing the good cholesterol (**HDL**) and decreasing the bad cholesterol (**LDL**). They also increase levels of one of the "bad fats" in the blood, known as triglycerides. When estrogen skin patches are used, HDL levels do not increase. Some forms of synthetic progestin may cancel out many of the beneficial effects of the estrogen. In contrast, natural progesterone has a positive effect on HDL.

According to **Dr. Pierre Fugere**, from the **University of Montreal Menopause Clinic**, "This action [of estrogen] on the lipid profile would explain between 25 percent and 50 percent of the reduction of risks. Thus 50 to 75 percent of the risks must be explained by a direct action of estrogen on the coronary blood vessels."

Estrogens also appear to have a positive effect on blood vessels throughout the body. In addition, estrogen appears to decrease fibrinogen levels, which cause the blood to become thicker. Higher fibrinogen levels are associated with higher levels of heart disease.

ARE YOU AT HIGH RISK FOR HEART DISEASE ?

Even after a woman has proven heart disease that shows up on a coronary arteriogram, some studies have shown that estrogen is beneficial.

However, in spite of strong evidence suggesting that estrogen by itself reduces heart disease, experts **Dr. Elizabeth Barrett-Connor** and **Dr. Trudy Bush** recommend prescribing estrogen only to women who are at high risk for heart attacks until there are proper studies completed that support the widespread use of this drug for disease prevention (**Journal of the American Medical Association**, Apr 10/91).

Women with the following risk factors may be at high risk for heart attacks:

1. Already proven hardening of the arteries of the heart (arteriosclerosis).
2. Both ovaries removed.
3. Cigarette smoking.
4. High blood pressure.
5. High cholesterol or triglycerides.
6. Diabetes or pre-diabetes.

Most of these risk factors can be substantially altered through lifestyle and dietary changes. **Dr. Dean Ornish** has written a comprehensive book outlining one such program entitled, **DR. DEAN ORNISH'S PROGRAM FOR REVERSING HEART DISEASE** (Random House, 1990).

Interestingly enough, when **Meir Stampfer**, **Associate Professor of Epidemiology** at the **Harvard School of Public Health**, analyzed the Nurses' Study, he found that those who took 100IU or greater of vitamin-E for 2 years or longer, had **sixty percent less risk of major heart disease**. However, in the case of an inexpensive vitamin with few side effects, this is not considered good enough evidence. Stampfer maintains that public policy recommendations should await randomized trials. However, at a recent meeting in Toronto, he did allow that it was "not unreasonable" to take vitamin E to prevent heart disease.

HORMONES AND THE HEART: THE CONS

Dr. Prior points out that the approval of menopausal hormone therapy as a drug for the prevention of heart disease is premature. No other heart drug (for example like a new beta blocker) would be approved based on the quality of evidence now available.

The present evidence, Prior says, is based on cross sectional, cohort and prospective studies. The largest of these was the Nurses' Study, began in 1976, which sent out thousands of questionnaires, including, among others, a question about whether the women were taking estrogen. The questionnaires were sent out every two years, with a ten year follow up to date.

The results showed that women taking estrogen had 50 percent fewer heart attacks. However, the nurses taking estrogen were healthier, had a higher economic or educational status, exercised more and smoked less, and were also less likely to suffer from hypertension, diabetes, or obesity.

Dr. Stampfer's sub-analysis of the nurse's study using data from healthy low risk women, found that estrogen users still showed a fifty per cent reduction in heart disease.

Nonetheless, Prior maintains that without a proper double blind controlled study, accurate estimates of the heart attack risk for estrogen users cannot be made.

In the Friend Indeed article (Jan/92), Prior expressed her other concerns, saying:

"There are no convincing data showing that menopausal women [matched by age and all risk factors] have more heart attacks because of their menopausal state... I believe that, for some women, estrogen treatment may increase the risk of heart attack. Estrogen has a known potential to raise blood pressure, to increase the level of triglycerides in the blood and to increase blood clotting....The strongest concern is that a properly controlled, blinded study was performed in which men were given estrogen treatment to prevent a second heart attack. This study had to be stopped after 18 months (instead of the 60 months planned) because the men on estrogen had more heart attacks."

Critics point out that high doses of estrogen were used in the men's study (5.0mg premarin for one group and 2.5mg for the other); Prior counters by saying higher doses of estrogen were also used in the Nurses' study. (1.25 mg to 2.5 mg.)

HORMONES AND BONE LOSS

Estrogen hormone therapy has been widely used to prevent bone loss in menopausal women and to reduce the incidence of fractures. Therapy for at least eight to ten years is usually recommended. Stopping estrogen therapy, even after four years of treatment, can cause rapid acceleration of bone loss. Estrogen, in standard doses, does not appear to increase bone mass.

Most bone loss occurs in the first three to six years after menopause. Smaller amounts of bone loss occur for up to 20 years after menopause. Thus, many experts are now recommending that ERT be started at the onset of menopause.

A recent editorial in the **New England Journal of Medicine** (Aug 27/92) puts it this way: "If begun soon after menopause, estrogen therapy prevents the early phase of bone loss and decreases the incidence of subsequent osteoporosis related fractures."

However, there is no agreement among doctors as to how long hormones should be continued to prevent bone loss, although many doctors now recommend taking HRT indefinitely.

"When estrogen therapy is begun," continues the same editorial, "it is unclear how long it must be continued to maintain the benefit, because its discontinuation leads to a phase of accelerated bone loss, like that which follows natural menopause, and protection against fractures may therefore be lost five or more years after estrogen therapy is discontinued. Thus, although it is widely believed that five to ten years of estrogen therapy is sufficient to lower the frequency of osteoporosis related fractures, much longer treatment, possibly 20 years or more, is required."

Certain groups of women are at high risk for bone loss and fractures. The details of risk and prevention are outlined in the chapter on osteoporosis. Women at high risk should carefully consider the pros and cons of HRT.

There is a good alternative to taking synthetic hormones for the rest of your life. Dr. John Lee has studied the use of a natural progesterone cream which is applied to the skin, and found it will prevent bone loss even without the addition of estrogen. Other forms of progesterone in oral micronized form or vaginal suppository may also prevent bone loss.

HORMONES AND BREAST CANCER

Hormone replacement therapy after menopause is probably linked to an increased risk of breast cancer, but most researchers think this risk is small, especially when weighed against possible benefits.

Dr. Sidney Wolfe, editor of the **Public Citizen Health Research Group Health Letter**, disagrees. He testified at the United States **Senate Subcommittee on Aging** in April 1991, and commented on a recent review of studies on estrogen and breast cancer. (**Journal of the American Medical Association** Apr 17\91).

"If a woman used estrogen pills for 15 years, she had a 30 percent excess rate of breast cancer. If used for 25 years, a "goal" toward which many doctors are pushing their patients, there would be a 50 percent increased risk of breast cancer... When just the five high quality studies were analyzed, the 15 year risk was an increase of 60 percent in breast cancer and the 25 year risk would be 100 percent or a doubling in the amount of breast cancer. The authors [of the study] estimate that, based on an increased risk of 30 percent, the excess number of breast cancer which would be caused by the use of estrogens by three million women would be 4,708 new cases of breast cancer and 1,468 breast cancer deaths. If the excess risk is 60 percent, as found in the high quality studies, there would be about 10,000 new cases of breast cancer and 3,000 deaths per year."

Women have now been exposed to both long-term hormone treatment in the form of the birth control pill and long-term hormone treatment in the form of estrogen replacement.

No one really knows what the combined effect might be on the intricate workings of the female reproductive system. There are several ongoing studies to evaluate that specific interaction, but results are not yet available.

In Britain, the **Imperial Cancer Research Fund** is to carry out a large study of the birth control pill and hormone replacement therapy. The study will look at the results of 40 previous studies involving more than 60,000 British women. It will compare 30,000 women with breast cancer to 30,000 women who are free of the disease.

Post-menopausal women who are moderately overweight may have a slightly higher risk of breast cancer because of the increased amount of estrogen hormone produced by fat tissues.

Women exposed to **DES** during pregnancy have an increased risk of breast cancer 20 years after exposure.

WEIGHING THE RISKS VERSUS THE BENEFITS

So far, there have been no long-term studies on the effects of estrogen and progesterone on healthy post-menopausal women without low bone mass or coronary risk factors.

The first three year study on the effects of HRT on healthy women was completed in 1995. Known as **PEPI** or **Progestin-Estrogen Prevention Intervention**, the study looked at the effect of HRT on blood lipids, blood pressure, and insulin of healthy post-menopausal women.

According to the study results published in the **Journal of the American Medical Association** (Jan/95), there were 875 women studied between the ages of 45 and 64. The women were divided into five groups, no treatment, .625mg premarin alone, .625mg premarin plus 10mg Provera for 12 days, .625mg premarin plus 2.5mg Provera daily and .625mg premarin plus 2.5mg OMP for 12 days.

Systolic blood pressure increased slightly in all groups. Insulin levels tended to decrease for all groups. Estrogen alone had the most positive effect on blood lipids, but one third of women developed pre-cancerous changes of the uterus. Those on Provera regimens showed a slight increase in HDL, but OMP had the most positive effect on HDL. In all groups, except those women receiving no treatment, triglycerides increased 20 to 25 percent above baseline.

However, woman on no treatment showed an average of a ten percent increase in fibrinogen, a risk factor for heart disease, while women in the treatment groups showed little change. Longer and more detailed studies involving large numbers of women are now underway.

One of them, a large ten year clinical trail involving 140,000 women, known as the **Women's Health Initiative** was authorized by the **National Institute of Health** in the United States. Among other issues, it will study the effects of estrogen therapy on the rate of heart attacks, breast cancer, fractures and death.

The long-term effects of taking estrogen are unknown. The risk of breast cancer is still an unsettled and unsettling question.

Recently, a long-term U.S. study published in the **New England Journal of Medicine** (Jun/95), showed that women receiving HRT or ERT for 6 or more years beyond menopause had a 40 percent increase in breast cancer risk. Commented the principal author of the study, **Dr. Graham Colditz**: "If a woman uses [hormones] long-term and stops, within two years, the risk goes back to that of a woman who never used the hormones."

Another alarming statistic recently came to light in 1995. A study of 240,000 women sponsored by the **American Cancer Society** found that those who took estrogen for at least six years had a 40 percent increased risk of fatal ovarian cancer.

Some doctors believe that the increased risk for uterine, ovarian and breast cancer caused by taking estrogen could be offset by decreasing deaths due to bone fractures and heart disease.

Gail Sheehy, puts it this way: "Is it even conceivable that millions of men over 50, those at the highest levels of the power structure, would be herded by physicians toward chemical dependence on powerful hormones at suspicion for causing testicular cancer?"

She goes on to quote public health expert, **Dr. Lewis Kuller**, who says that HRT is the largest uncontrolled clinical trial in the history of medicine.

FIFTY SOMETHING IN THE NINETIES

Every woman will have to decide for herself whether the risks outweigh the benefits. As **Dr. John Collins**, **Professor of Obstetrics and Gynecology** at **McMaster University** in Hamilton, says: "You must make the choice that suits you. There are numerous issues and no outsider can tailor these to the way you live your life."

FIFTY SOMETHING IN THE NINETIES is the title of a thoughtful article by Dr. Collins on the whole question of HRT. Dr. Collins says that at age 50 a woman faces a 32 percent lifetime risk of a spinal fracture. Estrogen use might decrease this to a 26 percent risk and for hip fractures, from a 16 percent lifetime risk to a 13 percent risk. At age 50 there is a 31 percent risk of dying from coronary heart disease. Estrogen would reduce this risk by 20 to 25 percent. Breast cancer risk would rise slightly from 2.8 percent to 3.3 percent. Risk of uterine cancer would also rise from .7 percent to .8 percent (see chart).

Concludes Dr. Collins: "Estrogen forever was a theme in the 1940's and again in the 1960's and it is now frequently recommended in the 1990's. Women who are fifty something in the 1990's face an interesting challenge. Given the promise of longer life and taller stature, women who take risks will want to take estrogen; more cautious women may prefer to wait for better evidence."

At the **University of California, Dr. Deborah Grady** and her colleagues did an extensive review of all relevant research on HRT published since 1970. They summarized risks and benefits of hormone therapy for healthy post-menopausal women considering long-term therapy to prevent disease or to prolong life. Women with a uterus on hormone replacement therapy increased their life expectancy by only one year. For women without a uterus, the increased life expectancy was 1.1 years (see chart).

The authors concluded that, "There is evidence that estrogen therapy decreases the risk for heart disease and for hip fracture, but long-term estrogen therapy increases the risk for endometrial cancer and may be associated with a small increase in risk for breast cancer. The increase in endometrial cancer risk can probably be avoided by adding a progestin to the estrogen regimen for women who have a uterus, but the effects of combination hormones on risks for other diseases has not been adequately studied."

They conclude that "HRT should probably be recommended for women who have had a hysterectomy and those with coronary heart disease or at high risk for coronary heart disease. For other women, the best course of action is unclear."

A NEW WAY OF LOOKING AT MENOPAUSE

Menopause is better viewed as the gateway to a second adulthood. Gail Sheehy suggests that, "If 45 is the old age of youth, 50 is the youth of this second adulthood... The life expectancy of a woman fortunate enough to live to age 50 is now 81. So from the time she reaches peri-menopause, the average woman has 33 more years."

She proposes four demarcations of this second adulthood:

PERI-MENOPAUSE: The start of the transition (40's).

MENOPAUSE: The completion of the ovarian transition (50's).

COALESCENCE: In which women can tap into new vitality (60's).

MATURESCENCE: The passage to full maturity in the seventies (70's).

NATURAL ALTERNATIVES TO HORMONES

1. Natural Progesterone.

The oral form has been widely used in Europe for many years with good results. One brand will soon be available in Canada under the trade name prometrium. Meanwhile, women who have their drugs covered by insurance can get a prescription from their family doctor for the oral capsules or vaginal suppositories, which can be made up by specialized pharmacies.

The skin cream, known by the brand name of Pro-Gest, and available without a prescription, may prevent bone loss and protect the uterus from cancer. **Dr. John Lee**, a clinical instructor at the **University of California Medical School**, found he could reverse bone loss and, furthermore, could control hot flashes and other menopausal symptoms using this cream alone. The cream may also improve sex drive and if applied vaginally, may help dry vagina. More studies on this cream are needed.

2. Natural Estrogen.

These are estrogens derived from plant sources such as soybeans and licorice root extract.

Some contain a higher ratio of estriol or estriol alone. Estriol is a form of estrogen that is thought to be more protective of breast cancer than other forms of estrogen. Natural estrogen is available in capsule form, vaginal cream and skin cream through specialized pharmacies. Some experts advise that natural progesterone should be taken along with these estrogens. Natural estrogens may be helpful for women with severe hot flashes or vaginal dryness that does not respond to other natural treatments. It may also be important for premature menopause or women who experience surgical menopause.

3. Acupuncture and Chinese Medicine.

The twelve energy pathways of the body are balanced with acupuncture needles, and herbs. Many women have had excellent relief of menopausal symptoms when they receive acupuncture and Chinese herbal treatments from an experienced practitioner.

4. Female Tonics.

VITEX AGNUS CASTUS: Also known has chaste tree, this slow acting tonic for the female system reduces hot flashes and dizziness, strengthens vaginal tissues, and decreases nervousness. The usual dosage is twenty drops of the tincture twice a day for three to six months at a time.

DONG QUAI: This root is famed in Chinese medicine for its affinity for the female constitution. It contains many natural plant estrogens and balances the amount of estrogen in the body. Take two capsules two or three times a day with meals. As a herbal tincture, use ten drops in one-quarter cup of water three times a day. Herbalist **Susun Weed** author of **MENOPAUSAL YEARS; THE WISE WOMAN WAY**, suggests taking dong quai for four weeks, followed by ginseng for two weeks and repeating this cycle for two years or as long as necessary.

GINSENG: Panax ginseng, either Oriental or North American, will increase energy levels and metabolic rate, stimulate the immune system, and help normalize body functions. It goes well with vitamin-E. It works well for hot flashes, as well as stress, and mental and physical fatigue. Try to find high quality ginseng in capsule or liquid form. It is not recommended for those who are anxious, or have insomnia or high blood pressure. Siberian ginseng, which belongs to a different family, also stimulates the immune system and protects against aging effects.

HOMEOPATHY: There are several excellent homeopathic combination remedies for menopause, available at pharmacies and health food stores. If possible, obtain specific individualized remedies from a homeopathic doctor.

GLANDULARS: Often women go into menopause with their adrenal glands very stressed. In such cases, adrenal glandular extracts can be very helpful. In addition ovarian and uterine glandulars can help support the reproductive system through this transition.

HEALTHY LIFESTYLE: Avoid smoking and excess alcohol, which not only worsen menopausal symptoms, but also accelerate aging. Avoid caffeine, sugar, sugar substitutes, and junk food. Sugar and sugar substitutes send blood sugar levels up and when they come down you may feel irritable, moody, depressed, dizzy, headachy or weak.

Experiment until you find out which foods are most optimal for your energy requirements

MENOPAUSE SPECIFICS: HOT FLASHES

VITAMIN-E: Vitamin-E enhances the effect of estrogen in the body. Start with 400 IU (international units) daily. You can increase up to 1,600 IU a day, if necessary. Take it at whatever time of day suits you. Don't use vitamin-E in high doses if you have high blood pressure, or if you are on drugs that decrease blood clotting.

VITAMIN-C AND BIOFLAVONOIDS: One controlled study of 94 women showed that women who received 200mg of vitamin-C combined with 200mg of bioflavonoids six times a day for hot flashes, 67 percent reported complete relief and 21 percent reported partial relief.

EVENING OF PRIMROSE OIL: Take two capsules a day, after meals. Work up to six or eight a day. A possible side effect is diarrhea. If this occurs, cut back on the dose, or take the capsules with meals.

BEE POLLEN: Start with two capsules or chewable tablets a day. Work up to as many as 12 or more until the hot flashes stop. Take it throughout the day, whenever it suits you. Make sure you aren't allergic to bee pollen.

MENOPAUSE SPECIFICS: MOOD SWINGS, IRRITABILITY AND INSOMNIA

MEGA B-50 CAPSULES: Take one or two with breakfast and one or two more with lunch, depending on how stressed you feel. Never take Mega B-50 at bedtime. It may keep you awake.

CALCIUM-MAGNESIUM CAPSULES: Take 600 to 1,200mg calcium and 300 to 600mg magnesium at bedtime on an empty stomach. Take the low-end dose if your diet is excellent and not too high in protein. If your diet is poor or high in protein, take the high-end dose. The capsules have a calming effect and will help you sleep.

TRYPTOPHAN: Tryptophan is an amino acid, one of the building blocks of protein and is available only by prescription. In doses of 2,000 to 4,000mg it helps you to sleep without a hangover effect. It is not yet officially approved for this usage. In the U.S. tryptophan is available by prescription as 5-hydroxy-tryptophan (50mg of 5-hydroxy-tryptophan equals 500mg of tryptophan).

VITAMIN-C: Take a capsule of 500 to 1,000mg three times a day. It is best to take a natural vitamin-C supplement containing bioflavonoids.

VAGINAL DRYNESS

VITAMIN-E: Use the same dose as suggested for hot flashes (don't double the dose for the two symptoms).

VITAMIN-C: 500 to 1,000 IU three times daily.

VITAMIN-E OIL OR CASTOR OIL AND VITAMIN-E OIL MIXED: Insert these oils into the vagina with an eye dropper or cotton tip applicator or rub into the area by hand.

REGULAR SEX OR MASTURBATION: Regular sexual activity increases the tone and lubrication of the vaginal tissues.

REJUVENATING METHODS

To remain energetic and vigourous after menopause:

Drink lots of pure water.

Eat fresh whole organic fruits and vegies as well as whole grains and beans, supplemented by chicken, fish and low fat dairy if necessary.

Practice some form of stretching such as Yoga or Tai-Chi.

Walk at least 30 minutes three times a week.

Train with weights three to five times a week to maintain muscle mass in arms and legs.

Jump five to ten minutes a day on the minitrampoline to tone the lymph system.

For ten to twenty minute periods daily, pray, meditate or practise relaxation.

One day a week eat only fruits and vegetables.

Two to four times a year eat only fruit, vegies and brown rice for one week along with a good herbal cleansing program.

Once or twice a year, retreat or vacation away from your family, work, and usual duties.

Keep reading and learning new skills.

Get involved in activities and projects outside your family.

Take a high quality multimineral and vitamin every day.

Take good quality digestive enzymes with every large meal.

Take a good calcium-magnesium supplement every night.

Take antioxidants every day to slow aging and to prevent cancer and heart disease. Minimum daily dose: Vitamin-E 400 IU, betacarotene 25,000 IU and vitamin-C 500mg.

Take a supergreen food supplement to increase energy and counter the effects of aging and polluted food, air and water.

Always seek out new ways to keep silliness and fun in your life.

In her book, **THE AGELESS BODY**, **Chris Griscom** says: "The Ageless Body is not a body that is forever pickled in the wrinkle-less fat-less mannequin of youth... If you aspire to be ageless, you must learn to joke and play with your body and become actual friends with it."

Concludes Sheehy: "Despite the trial and error state of medical care, a woman at 50 now has a second chance. To use it she must make an alliance with her body and negotiate with her vanity. Today's healthy active pace-setters will become the pioneers mapping out a whole new territory for potent living and wisdom sharing from one's fifties to one's eighties and even beyond."

Menopause is a powerful and sometimes tumultuous transition time for women as they enter into the creative and zestful period of post-menopause. It is also a wake up call to abandon unhealthy habits of mind and body, and embrace the full rich life of the wise woman and grandmother.

LIFETIME RISKS OF DEATH FOR 50 YEAR OLD WOMEN

Dr. John Collins in The **Journal of Obstetricians and Gynecologists of Canada** (Sept/91) calculated the risk of dying from certain medical conditions and the effect of estrogen use in modifying these risks.

CORONARY HEART DISEASE:
Lifetime Risk: .... 31 percent.
Effect of Estrogen Use: .... 0.8 percent.
Altered Lifetime Risk: .... **25 percent.**

HIP FRACTURE:
Lifetime Risk: .... 2.8 percent.
Effect of Estrogen Use: .... 0.8 percent.
Altered Lifetime Risk: .... **2.2 percent.**

BREAST CANCER:
Lifetime Risk: .... 2.8 percent.
Effect of Estrogen Use: .... 1.1 percent.
Altered Lifetime Risk: .... **3.3 percent.**

ENDOMETRIAL CANCER:
Lifetime Risk: .... 0.7 percent.
Effect of Estrogen Use: .... 1.05 percent.
Altered Lifetime Risk: .... **0.8 percent.**

RELATIVE RISK OF SELECTED CONDITIONS FOR A 50 YEAR OLD WHITE WOMAN TREATED WITH LONG-TERM HORMONE REPLACEMENT:

Women with a Uterus:

Condition	No Treatment	Estrogen	Estrogen & Progestin
Heart Disease	46.1%	34.2%	34.4%
Stroke	19.8%	20.2%	20.3%
Hip Fracture	15.3%	12.7%	12.8%
Breast Cancer	10.2%	13.0%	13.0%
Endometrial Cancer	2.6%	19.7%	2.6%
Life Expectancy	**82.8 yrs**	**83.7 yrs**	**83.8 yrs**

Women without a Uterus:

Condition	No Treatment	Estrogen Treated
Heart Disease	46.2%	34.4%
Stroke	19.8%	20.4%
Hip Fracture	15.3%	12.8%
Breast Cancer	10.2%	13.0%
Endometrial Cancer	0.0%	0.0%
Life Expectancy	**82.8 yrs**	**83.9 yrs**

Dr. Deborah Grady et al., Annals of Internal Medicine, December 15, 1992.

HIGHLY RECOMMENDED:

A FRIEND INDEED, is a lively and informative newsletter about women's experience of menopause and midlife (available in French as, Une Veritable Amie).

A FRIEND INDEED, PO Box 515 Place du Parc Stn. Montreal, PQ. H2W 2P1.

UNDERSTANDING MENOPAUSE, by **Janine O'Leary Cobb** (Key Porter revised 1993), is an excellent book on all aspects of menopause, including women's first hand experiences of the symptoms of menopause. **Janine O'Leary Cobb** is the founder and editor of **A FRIEND INDEED**.

MENOPAUSE NATURALLY, by **Dr. Sadja Greenwood** (Volcano Press, revised 1992) is a practical, down-to-earth guide through menopause, highly recommended.

THE MENOPAUSE INDUSTRY, HOW THE MEDICAL ESTABLISHMENT EXPLOITS WOMEN, by **Sandra Cowey** (Hunter Press, 1994). This book explores midlife health and the truth about HRT and related issues. An outstanding book by a well known New Zealand writer which examines the pros and cons of HRT.

MENOPAUSE AND MIDLIFE HEALTH by **Dr. Morris Notelovitz** and **Diana Tonnessen** (St. Martin's Press, 1993) Dr. Notelovitz is one of the leading clinicians and researchers in women's mid-life health. In this book, he offers his comprehensive program of preventive medicine and offers solid information and advice, along with plentiful illustrations and charts.

NATURAL MENOPAUSE, by **Dr. Katherine O'Hanlan** and **Susan Perry** (Addison Wesley, 1992). This is practical and balanced view point by a Stanford University professor and gynecologist.

WISE WOMAN WAYS-MENOPAUSAL YEARS, by **Susun Weed** (Ash Tree Publishing, PO Box 64, Woodstock, NY 12498). More than just a book about a wide range of herbs and natural remedies to soothe the passage of menopause, this book provides ways to celebrate and prepare for this important passage.

MENOPAUSE: TIME FOR A CHANGE, by **Merri Lu Park** (Changing Woman Press) is one of the best books to describe natural alternatives to taking hormones. 604-598-3538 for information.

MENOPAUSE WITHOUT MEDICINE, by **Linda Ojeda** (Hunter House, revised 1995). This book describes natural remedies for menopausal symptoms.

SUPER NUTRITION FOR MENOPAUSE, by **Louise Gitlleman** (Simon and Shuster, 1993). An excellent, clearly written book by a nutritionist.

MENOPAUSE, How You Can Benefit From Diet, Vitamins, Exercise and Other Methods, by **Dr. Michael Murray** (Prima Publishing, 1994).

SECOND SPRING, by **Honora Lee Wolfe** (Blue Poppy Press, 1990). This is a complete guide to healthy menopause through traditional Chinese medicine.

THE WISE WOMAN, A NATURAL APPROACH TO MENOPAUSE, by **Judy Hall** and **Dr. Robert Jacobs** (Element Books, 1992). This is a wonderful book offering a truly holistic approach combining the best of natural medicine and Western Medicine. Judy Hall also covers such topics as the menopause journal, overcoming the past, female sexuality and rites of passage.

THE MENOPAUSE SELF-HELP BOOK, by **Dr. Susan Lark** (Celestial Arts, 1990) Subtitled, **A WOMAN'S GUIDE TO FEELING WONDERFUL IN THE SECOND HALF OF HER LIFE**. This is a practical guide for relieving and preventing menopausal symptoms using diet, vitamins, exercise, yoga and acupressure.

AGELESS AGING, The Natural Way To Stay Young, by **Leslie Kenton** (Arrow, 1987). An excellent book that outlines a comprehensive anti-aging program based on exercise, good nutrition, vitamins and herbs.

THE AGELESS BODY, by **Chris Griscom** (Light Institute Press, 1992). A fascinating and useful book on how to stay vibrant that deals with emotional and sexual aspects of aging as well as the physical ones.

MENOPAUSE AND EMOTIONS: Making Sense of Your Feelings When Your Feelings Make No Sense, by **Lafern Page** (Primavera Press, 1993).

MANAGING YOUR MENOPAUSE, by **Dr. Wulf Utian** and **Ruth Jacobovitz** (Prentice Hall, 1990). Dr. Utian is a leading expert in menopause and founder of **The North American Menopause Society**. He offers his 12 step program for the menopause and some excellent information, but is strongly in favour of hormone replacement therapy. Ruth Jacobovitz has just brought out her own book, **150 MOST ASKED QUESTIONS ABOUT MENOPAUSE: WHAT WOMEN REALLY WANT TO KNOW**. This book has a more balanced view about hormone replacement therapy.

THE SILENT PASSAGE, by **Gail Sheehy**, (Random House, 1991). Now in paperback, this book provides unique information on hormones and new concepts of menopause. Sheehy leans strongly towards hormones. Most of the 153 page book was contained in the Oct/91 issue of **Vanity Fair**.

LOVE AND SEX AFTER 60, by **Dr. Robert Butler** and **Myrna Lewis** (Harper and Rowe, revised, 1988). This is one of the few books available on this topic. It deals with sexuality in a practical and straightforward manner.

IS IT HOT IN HERE OR IS IT ME?, **Gayle Sand** (Harper and Collins, 1993). This down to earth book is subtitled **A Personal Look at Facts Fallacies and Feelings of Menopause**.

LAMBDA GREY, by **Adelman** (Newcastle Publishing, 1993). A practical emotional and spiritual guide for gays and lesbians who are growing older.

HORMONE REPLACEMENT THERAPY, by **Betty Kamen**. This copiously illustrated book provides an alternative look at the HRT question, with emphasis on the use of natural progesterone cream.

ESTROGEN: IS IT RIGHT FOR YOU?, by **Paula Dranov** (Fireside Books, 1993). This book provides a thorough factual guide to help you decide.

TAKING HORMONES, CHOICES, RISKS, BENEFITS, (1989) available for $7.50 US from:

THE NATIONAL WOMEN'S HEALTH NETWORK, 1325 G St, North West, Washington, DC, 2005.

This booklet presents a balanced viewpoint on both sides of this complex issue.

THE MONTREAL HEALTH PRESS has just brought out a comprehensive and informative 54 page booklet entitled, **A BOOK ABOUT MENOPAUSE**, which contains basic and clearly explained health information on all aspects of menopause. It is available in French and English, from **Second Story Press** in Toronto or can be obtained by sending $4.00 (which includes postage and handling) to:

> **THE MONTREAL HEALTH PRESS**, PO Box 1000, Stn Place du Parc, Montreal, PQ, H2W 2N1. 514-272-5441.

HOT FLASH: A NEWSLETTER FOR MIDLIFE AND OLDER WOMEN, is available from:

> **THE NATIONAL ACTION FORUM FOR MIDLIFE AND OLDER WOMEN**, Box 816, Stony Brook, NY, 11790-0609.

It contains articles and news about health and social issues.

THE FIRST MATURE WOMEN'S NETWORK SOCIETY, offers support, information and referrals to women age 45 and over. The Network has published two highly recommended manuals, the first describes how you can set up the SHOP program in your community, **THE LEADER'S MANUAL FOR THE SHOP** and the highly readable book, **DEPRESSION IS A FEMINIST ISSUE** is also available. The manuals cost $12.00 each and are available from:

> **THE MATURE WOMEN'S NETWORK**, 411 Dunsmuir St, Vancouver, BC, V6B 1X4.

MENOPAUSE SUPPORT GROUPS

To see if a menopause support group exists in your area of Canada or the United States, call or write:

> **AMERICAN SELF-HELP CLEARING HOUSE**, St. Clares Riverside Medical Center, Denville, NJ, 07834. 201-625-7101.

SUPPLIERS OF NATURAL HORMONES AND VITAMIN SUPPLEMENTS

KRIPP'S PHARMACY, 994 Granville St, Vancouver, BC, V6Z 1L2. 604-687-2564.

SMITH'S PHARMACY, 3463 Yonge St, Toronto, ON, M4N 2A3. 416-488-2600 or 1-800-361-6624.

SUPPLEMENTS PLUS, 451 Church St, Toronto, ON, M4Y 2C5. 416-962-8269 Canada wide mail order: 1-800-387-4761.

This excellent supplement store carries all the above supplements as well as Pro-Gest skin cream. It also carries a combination of natural estrogens (derived from soybean and licorice) and natural progesterone in the form of a skin cream, a vaginal cream and sublingual tablets, known as **Ostaderm**. These products are made by **Bezwecken Transdermal Systems Inc.** 12525 SW 3rd St, Beaverton, OR, 97005. 503-644-7800 or 1-800-243-2256 (in the U.S. only).

WOMEN'S INTERNATIONAL PHARMACY, 5708 Monona Dr, Madison, WI, 53716-3152. 608-221-7800, or 1-800-279-5708 in the United States.

TRANSITIONS FOR HEALTH INC, 621 SW Alder #900, Portland OR, 97205-3627. 1-800-888-6814.

This company makes Pro-Gest cream and publishes a wonderful catalogue called, **TRANSITIONS FOR HEALTH** with a excellent selection of women's health products. Call 1-800-888-6814 for a copy.

PHILLIPS NUTRITIONALS, 27071 Cabot Rd #122, Laguna Hills, CA 92653. 1-800-514-5115.

This company makes a complete line of women's health products including vitamins, minerals, herbs and cosmetics. One product of note is called yamcon and contains a combination of herbs and wild yam extract. Yamcon is helpful for reliving menopausal symptoms and comes in the form of skin cream, vaginal cream, vaginal lubricant, oral tablets and sublingual drops. Preliminary studies in Scandanavia showed that Yamcon could help reverse menopausal bone loss.

Preventing And Treating Bone Loss

Bone is a living tissue which is always changing. New bone is constantly being made and old bone is constantly being taken up or reabsorbed. These two processes are coupled together and normally balance each other out so that there is no net bone loss.

Osteoporosis occurs when this balance is altered and the bone thins out, although the mineral content remains the same. This means that osteoporotic bone is much more susceptible to fractures, especially of the vertebrae in the spine, the wrist bone and the hip bone.

Osteoporosis is an enormous and very costly health problem. In the U.S. approximately 25 million people are affected and one million people develop osteoporosis-related fractures every year. By age 70, over 40 percent of women have evidence of at least one fracture. By age 90, more than a third of women suffer hip fractures.

In the U.S., the latest estimate for the cost of treating fractures caused by osteoporosis is ten billion dollars per year.

In Canada, 800,000 Canadians are now suffering from fractures and another 2.5 million are seriously at risk for these osteoporosis-related fractures.

As **Dr. Robert Josse**, **Chief of Endocrinology and Metabolism** at **Saint Michael's Hospital** in Toronto told a symposium in Ottawa:

"Something in the order of 25 percent of post-menopausal Caucasian [white] North American women have this disease. More than 20 percent of elderly patients may die within three months of a fracture, and 15 to 20 percent of individuals are institutionalized within one year of the event."

Dr. Josse estimates that the cost of treating all fractures associated with osteoporosis "would tally between $250 to $300 million for the year 1989."

Dr. Josse distinguishes between two types of osteoporosis. The first type affects mainly women between the ages of 51 and 70 and consists of loss of the spongy inner part of bone (called trabecular bone). Loss of this type of bone occurs most rapidly in the first five years after menopause. Weakening of this type of bone leads primarily to fractures of the spinal column and the wrist.

The second type of osteoporosis occurs in both men and women aged 70 or over, and consists of loss of both the trabecular bone as well as the hard outer part of the bone known as cortical bone. This commonly causes fractures of both the hip and the spinal column.

Osteoporosis is mainly a problem of the Western world. As **Janine O'Leary Cobb** notes in her excellent book, **UNDERSTANDING MENOPAUSE** (Key Porter, revised 1993).

"Osteoporosis is not a worldwide, female only problem. It is more common in affluent, northern countries. Women who have had multiple pregnancies, who eat red meat infrequently, who do strenuous physical labour, and who are overweight [by our standards] are not likely to develop osteoporosis. These are the characteristics of the majority of the women in the world." Moreover, black women rarely suffer from osteoporosis since their bones are genetically denser than those of white women. Orientals are, however, vulnerable, presumably because they tend to be small-boned and slim; because their genetic bone structure is not dense."

PREVENTING OSTEOPOROSIS

WEIGHT BEARING EXERCISE: A sedentary lifestyle can definitely contribute to the development of osteoporosis. Exercise should be begun as soon as possible, but certainly by age 30 to build up peak bone mass. However, hereditary and racial factors may be the most important determinants of peak bone mass.

Experts recommend brisk walking for a minimum of 45 minutes three times a week. Aerobic exercise or dancing will accomplish the same thing. Ideally arms as well as legs should be exercised to maintain strong bones.

Recent studies suggest that women who exercise, even if they start well after menopause, can still improve their bone mass.

One study showed that women in a nursing home (average age 80) who exercised their arms and legs for 30 minutes a day while sitting in their chairs, were able to increase their bone mass.

An Australian study compared three groups of menopausal women, and found that bone loss was slowed or prevented by exercise when combined with either calcium or hormones.

STRENGTH TRAINING: The most important factor affecting the quality of life as you age may be loss of lean body mass or muscle mass. Optimal health may depend on just the right combination of muscle, bone and fat in your body.

In the 80's or 90's there can be up to an 80 percent loss of muscle mass causing muscle weakness, fatigue, and inability to lift a grocery bag, or pot of water, with resultant loss of independence. A recent study showed that women in their 90's, after eight weeks of resistance training with weights, had an increase in muscle mass of ten to 15 percent, and a doubling or tripling of the muscle strength of their legs.

After a ten week strength training program in which you train five times a week, you can maintain your strength by exercising just four times a week.

With strength training, you break down your muscle tissue before you build it up. Research shows that anti-oxidants like vitamin-C, vitamin-E and betacarotene protect muscle from excessive breakdown and encourage muscle repair.

Dr. Jeffrey Blumberg, Senior Scientist, anti-oxidants Lab, USDA Human Nutrition Research Center on Aging, Tufts University, in Boston, says that both vitamin-D and magnesium are critical players in the ability to gain muscle mass as you age. As women age, they are often lacking in both those nutrients.

Research is in progress to determine whether weight training may also increase bone mass as well.

DIET: Menopause is one of the few times in a woman's life where it is advantageous to be ten to 15 percent overweight because it has a protective effect against osteoporosis and other menopausal symptoms.

Getting enough calcium in your diet is important. But much more important is the total composition of your diet and how well calcium is absorbed into your body.

For example, a diet high in caffeine, sugar, soft drinks, alcohol, and dairy products can result in a calcium deficiency.

A long-term study of 85,000 nurses showed that women who drank the most coffee (four or more cups per day) had almost three times the incidence of hip fractures when compared to women who drank little or no coffee.

It is a myth to think you need to drink milk in order to get enough calcium in your diet.

Even if you don't eat any dairy products, you can still get enough calcium. Vegetarian dietary sources of calcium include deep green vegetables, tahini, dulse, kelp, lime processed tortillas, tofu made with calcium sulphate, and mashed sunflower and sesame seeds.

High protein diets can cause a negative calcium balance by increasing calcium loss through the urine. In fact, studies of ethnic groups have shown that the higher the average intake of protein, the higher the rate of osteoporosis.

For example, Eskimos consume a very high protein fish based diet and take in more that 2,000mg of calcium every day. They appear to have the highest rate of osteoporosis in the world.

In contrast, the Bantu tribes of central Africa have low protein, vegetable and grain diets and take in only 300mg of calcium a day. Osteoporosis is unknown among the Bantu, even in old age.

Japanese women who have a low protein diet with only 300mg of calcium a day, have a lower rate of osteoporosis than their American counterparts who take in an average of 800mg of calcium a day.

This ties in with the statistic that the average measurable bone loss of female meat-eaters at age 65 is 35 percent; versus the average measurable bone loss of female vegetarians at age 65 at 18 percent.

In any case, if you cut down on red meat and excessive diary products and move toward a low fat diet of fresh fruits, vegetables and whole grains, chicken and fish, you will also be following current recommendations for the prevention of both heart disease and cancer.

And if you are eating a low protein vegetable diet you will need a lot less calcium in your diet.

CALCIUM SUPPLEMENTS

Women with high protein diets should take 1,200 to 1,500mg of calcium a day combined with about half that amount of magnesium. I prefer to use liquid calcium-magnesium, or the powder or capsule form, as I think they are better absorbed. Calcium-magnesium supplements are best taken at bedtime, when they help you get a better sleep, and prevent the extra loss of calcium that can occur during the night.

It is also important to have adequate vitamin-D to make sure that the calcium is well absorbed. Unless you get lots of sunshine you should take at least 400 to 800 IU of vitamin-D along with the calcium. Two recent studies showed that women without adequate vitamin-D lost more bone, especially in the winter months.

A good source of trace minerals including boron, zinc, manganese and other minerals is also important for bone health.

Women on pure vegetarian diets (no meat or dairy) can probably take lesser amounts of calcium and magnesium; about 1,000mg of calcium and 500 or 600mg of magnesium.

High quality calcium-magnesium supplements include **Natural Factors'** calcium-magnesium citrate capsules. **Nu-life's Framework**, **Karuna's Osteonex**, **Osteoguard**, Dr. Alan Gaby's **OsteoPrime**, **Biotics Research's Osteo-B-Plus**, **P.H.P.'s Pro-Osteo** and **Osseous Complex**, **Klaire Lab's Osteo-Balance** and **Vitaplex Natural's** calcium-magnesium boron effervescent powder. Mint flavoured calcium-magnesium liquid is also available.

Another calcium supplement called microcrystalline hydroxypatite is a high quality bone food that provides calcium in a readily available form. Several studies have shown that it may help increase bone mass as well.

In addition, especially for women having difficulty with calcium absorption, I recommend a high quality silica. This is an extract of horsetail that is very well absorbed, and which contains large amounts of the trace mineral silicon. It is claimed that the body naturally changes silica into calcium in a very efficient manner. Homeopathic calcium carbonate may also help increase the absorption of calcium.

Women who have weak digestion may have considerable difficulty absorbing calcium. For these women, good quality enzymes taken with each meal may substantially increase calcium absorption (see below). A supplement by **Natur-pharm** known as **Cal-plex** contains not only calcium but magnesium, boron, vitamin-C and hydrochloric acid (HCL).

CALCIUM SUPPLEMENTS USEFUL EVEN AFTER MENOPAUSE

In the first five years following menopause, women can lose up to one to three percent of their bone mass per year. This initial loss of bone usually does not respond to calcium supplementation.

However, five years or more after the menopause, a new study has showed that the addition of 800mg of calcium citrate maleate (available in Canada as **Calcium Citramate** capsules from **Thorne Research Canada**) in the diets of women with low calcium intake helped prevent bone loss in the hip, wrist and spine. Calcium in the form of citrates or aspartates are the best absorbed of the calciums. Calcium carbonate, on the other hand, maintained bone mass at the hip and wrist, but not at the spine.

The best absorbable forms of magnesium are also the citrates or the aspartates.

BORON ALSO IS ONE OF THE KEY MINERALS FOR BONE

Recent animal and human research into the trace mineral, boron, suggests that this little known element may play a key role in the prevention of osteoporosis.

Dr. Forrest Nielsen, a biochemist who is the head of the **Human Nutrition Research Center** in Grand Forks, North Dakota, has completed detailed studies of the effect of adding boron to the diets of over 40 people.

In the first study of post-menopausal women, Dr. Nielsen noted that within a week of going on a supplement containing 3mg of boron, the women lost 40 percent less calcium, one third less magnesium and slightly less phosphorus through their urine.

His other studies have confirmed that boron has a positive effect on calcium metabolism.

However, Dr. Nielsen does not recommend boron supplements until more studies have been done. He notes that boron can be toxic if ingested in excessive amounts.

"It is best", says Nielsen, "to get boron through a balanced diet containing an abundance of non-citrus fruits (apples, grapes, pears, cherries, etc.), leafy green vegetables (spinach, parsley, cabbage, broccoli, beet greens etc.), nuts and legumes (dried beans, peas, lentils, etc.) A diet containing an abundance of these items is likely to supply 2 to 6mg of boron daily. This is a safe intake of boron."

To really make a difference, Nielsen believes that boron has to be at the 3 to 5mg level in the diet.

Interestingly enough, meat, fish, milk products and highly processed foods have a low boron content.

EATING WELL AND NOT ABSORBING WHAT YOU NEED ?

The most important factor that determines exactly how many nutrients you can absorb from your food and vitamins is the amount of acid produced by your stomach. Acid or HCL production declines with age. **In fact, 25 percent of 60 year olds and 80 percent of 80 years olds do not produce enough HCL for proper digestion.** As you age, there may be less of the other digestive enzymes as well.

Thus it is important to eat slowly, chew well and not drink too much at meal time. Drinking more than four ounces of fluid with meals dilutes the acid and digestive enzymes, and may cause gas and bloating. It is also important to take high quality enzymes with meals and if necessary, with the calcium-magnesium supplements. In cases where there is no history of ulcer, you can also take HCL capsules under the supervision of a doctor.

Dr. Elson Haas, author of the excellent book, **STAYING HEALTHY WITH NUTRITION** (Celestial Arts, 1992), suggests as an alternative to HCl tablets, that you drink the juice of half a lemon squeezed in water, or a teaspoon of apple cider vinegar in a glass of warm water, twenty minutes before meals.

A nutritional survey of older people conducted in Boston showed that most were deficient in not just one, but many nutrients. **In the 60 to 69 year group, 65 percent were deficient in vitamin-D, 70 percent in folic acid, 70 percent in vitamin B-12, 35 percent in calcium and 65 percent in zinc. All of these nutrients are essential to good bone health.**

In particular, women were receiving less than two thirds of the minimal daily requirement of many vitamins and minerals. A high quality multivitamin and mineral would compensate for most of these deficiencies.

FOLIC ACID, HOMOCYSTEINE AND BONE

Methione is one of the eight essential amino acids. It can be converted in part to a toxin known as homocysteine. According to **Dr. Jonathan Wright** and **Dr. Alan Gaby**, individuals with high levels of homocysteine due to a genetic disorder develop severe osteoporosis at an early age. After menopause, women seem to lose their efficiency at converting homocysteine to less toxic compounds. This loss of efficiency can be partly corrected through taking folic acid supplements.

ARE YOU AT HIGH RISK FOR BONE LOSS ?

Although it is best to start building your bone mass before age 35, it is never too late to start improving your diet and exercise level. Take the test at the end of the article to find out what risk category you are in. Women who are at high risk for osteoporosis will have to carefully weigh the pros and cons of taking hormone replacement therapy (**HRT**). Currently HRT is the favoured treatment for both the prevention and the treatment of osteoporosis.

Remember that finding out your risk category by analyzing your risk factors will only pick up about 70 percent of women at high risk. Having a bone scan is the most accurate way to access whether you are losing bone or not. If you feel you are at risk for bone loss, and are trying to decide about HRT, then a bone scan may aid you in your decision. If you are going to take HRT, there is no need for a bone scan.

A new screening method for osteoporosis is being tested. It involves an ultrasound of the heel, which would be a quick and inexpensive test. In addition, a urine test will soon be available from **Ostex International** of Seattle. This urine test will show whether a person is losing more bone than normal.

WOMEN WHO DON'T HAVE REGULAR PERIODS AT RISK FOR BONE LOSS

Dr. Jerilynn Prior, a Vancouver endocrinologist and **University of British Columbia** researcher, says: "A woman who has a late onset of menarche [the first period] and intermittent ammenorrhea [no periods] and anovulation [failure to ovulate] is at risk for fracture by the time she reaches menopause." This risk can occur even if a woman is having regular periods but is not ovulating, and this happens more often as a woman moves toward menopause.

If you want to know whether you are ovulating, you can check your cervical mucous and basal temperature, and observe your symptoms (see chapter Know Your Body's Cycles). Dr. Prior has also made up specific charts for women to use in order to determine if they are ovulating, and has kindly allowed us to include them in this chapter.

Dr. Prior suggests that doctors ask: "Can you tell by the way you feel, that your period is coming?" Woman have probably ovulated if they answer that their breasts become tender along the sides, especially with fluid retention or bloating in the week before the flow. Women who notice only mood changes in the week before they menstruate are unlikely to have ovulated. If a woman says,"Sometimes I get breast tenderness and sometimes, I don't," then it is likely that the woman is ovulating off and on.

Dr. Prior corrects the problem by giving women Provera for ten days of the month until ovulatory cycles are re-established.

ESTROGEN AND PROGESTERONE - WHICH ONE IS MOST IMPORTANT FOR BONE HEALTH ?

Dr. Prior believes that it is progesterone which is the important bone-saving hormone. Only a small number of doctors agree with her despite some compelling evidence.

Instead, doctors have been promoting estrogen as the most important hormone to reduce bone loss. In fact, estrogen hormone therapy has been widely used to prevent further bone loss in menopausal women and to reduce the incidence of fractures. Estrogen alone, in standard doses, does not appear to increase bone mass.

Once begun, estrogen therapy should be continued for at least eight to ten years, or longer. Stopping estrogen therapy, even after four years of treatment, may cause a rapid acceleration of bone loss.

However, some experts are now saying that bone health is still improved, even after estrogen is discontinued. British menopause experts, **Dr. John Stevenson** and **Dr. Malcolm Whitehead**, refer to studies which show that the effect of estrogen on bone is not lost after estrogen is stopped and that protection may persist into old age.

However, one study showed that 14 percent of women failed to improve their bone mass, even with adequate replacement of both estrogen and progesterone.

Many doctors now suggest that estrogen therapy be started at the onset of menopause. According to an editorial in the **New England Journal of Medicine** (Aug 27/92) by **Dr. Riggs** and **Dr. Melton**, from the **Endocrinology Department** at the **Mayo Clinic**: "If begun soon after menopause, estrogen therapy prevents the early phase of bone loss and decreases the incidence of subsequent osteoporosis related fractures."

However, there is no agreement among doctors as to how long hormones should be continued to prevent bone loss, although many doctors are now recommending taking HRT indefinitely.

"When estrogen therapy is begun," continues the same editorial, "it is unclear how long it must be continued to maintain the benefit, because its discontinuation leads to a phase of accelerated bone loss like that which follows natural menopause and protection against fractures may therefore be lost five or more years after estrogen therapy is discontinued. Thus, although it is widely believed that five to ten years of estrogen therapy is sufficient to lower the frequency of osteoporosis related fractures, much longer treatment, possibly 20 years or more is required."

More recently, researchers analyzed the data on 670 women in the Framingham study. Of these, only 212 had taken estrogen replacement therapy. Only one third took the estrogen for seven years or longer. Among women under 75, **Dr. David Felson** and his colleagues at the **Boston Arthritic Center** found that bone density was higher in women treated with estrogen.

"Unfortunately, the effect of estrogen does not persist long after the discontinuation of therapy. In women over 75, even 10 years of past estrogen use did not have a significant effect on bone density."

In an accompanying editorial, **Dr. Bruce Ettinger** and **Dr. Deborah Grady** argue that one alternative to lifelong HRT for prevention of osteoporosis might be to start HRT at age 70. Based on his own research, Ettinger, has shown that half the usual estrogen dosage plus 1500mg calcium daily prevents bone loss and may produce fewer long term effects for women.

Meanwhile, Prior asks, should all menopausal women be given menopausal hormone therapy when only 20 to 25 percent are at high risk for bone loss?

Estrogen skin patches also preserve bone just as well as the oral forms and the patch was approved for treatment of osteoporosis in 1992. The 50 microgram patch has been shown to stop the loss of bone. The 100 microgram patch combined with exercise and adequate calcium will apparently build new bone. Studies at the **Mayo Clinic** using an experimental estrogen-progesterone patch have shown that the patch increases bone in the hip and the spine.

All women who have not had their uteruses removed will need to take progesterone as well as estrogen, to minimize the risk of uterine cancer. This means that a woman will continue to bleed every month after menopause, as long as she is on the hormone replacement.

An editorial in the **Lancet** (Apr 6/91) commented: "Since the long-term safety of hormone replacement has not yet been fully elucidated, there is need for other effective therapies for the prevention and treatment of osteoporosis."

OTHER DRUGS FOR OSTEOPOROSIS

A new drug on the market called editronate belongs to a family of compounds called biphosphonates. Biphosphonates are absorbed to bone crystals. When these biphosphonate bone crystal complexes are taken up by the bone cells that resorb bone, these cells stop resorbing bone. This allows bone mass to be preserved.

Biphosphonates also impair mineralization of new bone and thus can only be taken for 14 days at a time. This is followed by a rest period of between 11 and 13 weeks and repeated four times a year. Treatment regimens are complicated and expensive.

Two well designed studies on one of the biphosphonates, editronate disodium, have now been reported in the medical literature.

American researchers studied 429 post-menopausal women with osteoporosis in seven different centers. Results showed a significant increase in the bone mineral density of the spine within one year of treatment and a significant decrease in the rate of new fractures of the spine. Similar results had been reported earlier in a single center study in Copenhagen involving 66 women with proven osteoporosis.

Etridonate is available both in the U.S. and Canada, but has not yet been approved for use in osteoporosis. However, problems are emerging with long-term use. In one study, by the third year of treatment, fracture rates increased in the treatment group compared to the controls. Other problems are the fact that decreasing bone resorption may cause reduced bone formation, the unresolved question of increasing hip fracture incidence and the uncertainty about long-term safety.

Another biphosphonate, alendronate, is being studied, and the quality of bone formed appears normal. At the three year mark, double blind studies show a decreased fracture rate, an increased bone mass and normal bone quality. Other biphosphonate drugs are also being developed. Alendronate is now available in Canada.

Estrogen and calcitrol have a similar mechanism as the biphosphonates in that they block the resorption of bone. Calcitrol is an active form of vitamin-D called vitamin-D3. Some studies showed that calcitrol does increase calcium absorption, improves calcium balance and reduces bone loss. Other studies showed conflicting results. Problems with vitamin-D3 include the high cost and the risk of elevated blood calcium levels. An editorial in the New England Journal of Medicine (Feb 6/92) says that this form of vitamin-D is still an experimental treatment that warrants close follow-up with monitoring of blood and urine calcium levels and kidney function.

How the effect of estrogen and calcitrol on the bone compares to the biphosphonates has yet to be studied.

Calcitonin was discovered in the early 1960's in Canada by **Dr. D. H. Copps**. Calcitonin is a hormone secreted by the thyroid gland of mammals, birds and fish. It acts to inhibit bone reabsorption. It must be given by intramuscular injection or nasal spray. Calcitonin reduces early bone loss during menopause and is also very useful to reduce pain and to increase mobility after fractures have occurred.

Currently the only agent that simulates bone formation of the spinal bones is sodium fluoride. However, there is controversy about whether the fluoride-treated bone has normal strength.

NEW RESEARCH ON PROGESTERONE ALONE PREVENTING BONE LOSS

As mentioned before, bone loss in menopause occurs most rapidly in the first five years after menopause and then slows down. New York physician **Dr. Carolyn Dean** calls this period "bone-pause" and says that during that time the body temporarily rejects calcium and thus bone loss increases. However, after this initial period of time, she believes that bone loss seems to stabilize, especially with an optimal diet, supplements and exercise program.

Recent evidence from Dr. Prior and **Dr. John Lee** indicate that it may be the progesterone, and not the estrogen, that is the most positive hormone for the bone. In many recent studies on the effect of estrogen on bone loss, progesterone was given as well. So it is not possible to know which hormone was responsible for the improvement in the bone or how the two hormones interact together.

Dr. John Lee is an internationally recognized authority on fluoride and osteoporosis, and a clinical instructor at the **University of California Medical School**, **Department of Family Medicine**. For over ten years, he has been studying the effects of natural progesterone on bone loss. "Natural progesterone," explains Dr. Lee, "...declines to a lower rate than estrogen does with menopause, and it is the key hormone in causing these bones to regain their normal activity for strength and long life."

Dr. Prior made a detailed study of 66 women (New England Journal of Medicine, Nov 1/90). Twenty nine percent of these women were not ovulating even though they were having regular periods. These same women had low serum progesterone levels and were losing two percent of bone annually. If this holds true for the general population, says Dr. Prior, then many women are losing bone before menopause. Dr. Prior found she could reverse the bone loss by giving 10mg of Provera (a synthetic progesterone) daily for ten days a month.

Although one study showed there were no significant side effects if Provera or synthetic progesterone was given with continuous use of the estrogen skin patch, many users of Provera report troublesome side effects. On the other hand, natural progesterone, which is identical to the body's own progesterone, has few side effects except drowsiness. However, it is difficult to take by mouth because it is destroyed by stomach acid. It must be made into special preparations to be absorbed (oral micronized, vaginal and rectal suppositories or topical creams).

In a report published in the **Lancet** (Nov 24/90) of 100 women applying a natural progesterone cream to their skin, Dr Lee documented bone scan increases in bone density over three years ranging as high as 22 percent. The amount of bone increase was proportional to the bone loss before treatment. This means that patients with the lowest bone density before treatment would gain the greatest amount of bone during treatment.

Dr. Lee has also published an excellent article on his work entitled, **OSTEOPOROSIS REVERSAL, THE ROLE OF PROGESTERONE (Intern Clin Nutr Rev pgs-384-391/90)**, as well as a more comprehensive book on natural progesterone entitled, **NATURAL PROGESTERONE, THE MULTIPLE ROLES OF A REMARKABLE HORMONE.**

In the 1950's it was discovered that the wild yam contains plant estrogens and diosgenin. Diosgenin can be made into natural progesterone through a relatively simple chemical process.

The cream is available without prescription and has no known side effects. One-quarter to one-half of a teaspoon is applied to the thin skin of soft tissue areas such as the face, neck, back of the wrists, inner arms, breast, hands, chest, abdomen and inner thighs on a rotating basis for 12 days a month. The site where it is applied should be rotated daily, so the fat tissue does not become saturated. The same amount of cream can also be applied in smaller doses spread out through the whole month.

The brand used by Dr. Lee known as Pro-Gest cream contains 900mg of progesterone per two ounce jar. Dr. Lee says about 80 percent of the cream is absorbed.

Dr. Lee recommends starting with at least one two-ounce jar per month for the first three to six months. This amounts to 900mg of natural progesterone spread over the whole month. Maintenance dosage of progesterone suggested by Dr. Lee is 500 to 1,000mg per month. Dr. Lee determines the correct dose by measuring the improvement in the bone scan every three to six months.

Compounding pharmacists can make up 3 to 6 percent natural progesterone skin creams or provide natural progesterone in the form of pills or vaginal suppositories.

A confusing number of wild yam creams are on the market all claiming to contain natural progesterone but without concrete information to support that claim. Make sure if you are using any of these creams you know how many milligrams of natural progesterone is contained in each jar.

Aeron Life Cycle and **Diagnostechs** now offer a way to test the effectiveness of your progesterone cream by measuring salivary progesterone levels.

Dr. Alan Gaby author of the highly recommended book, **PREVENTING AND REVERSING OSTEOPOROSIS**, stresses a comprehensive holistic program that includes diet, lifestyle, a broad range of nutritional supplements, a more physiological natural approach to hormone replacement therapy and avoidance of certain environmental toxins. He believes this approach is heralding a new area in the treatment and prevention of osteoporosis, one that truly offers hope for both men and women.

RESOURCES:

PREVENTING AND REVERSING OSTEOPOROSIS, by **Dr. Alan Gaby** (Prima Publishing, 1994, PO Box 1260 BK Rockin CA 95677, 916-786-0426) Written by one of the foremost authorities in nutritional and natural medicine, this book offers practical advice on all aspects of bone health including vitamins, minerals, diet, digestion, hormones, and natural remedies.

NATURAL PROGESTERONE, THE MULTIPLE ROLES OF A REMARKABLE HORMONE, by **Dr. John R. Lee**, B.LL. Publishing, PO Box 2068, Sebastolpol, CA 95473. $12.00 US postage included. 101 pages.

Watch for **Dr. Lee's** book entitled, **WHAT YOUR DOCTOR MAY NOT TELL YOU ABOUT MENOPAUSE, The Breakthrough Book on Natural Progesterone** (Warner, 1996).

OSTEOPOROSIS: THE LONG ROAD BACK, by **Pamela Horner**. This excellent book tells the story of how a BC women learned to cope with severe osteoporosis.

STAND TALL, THE INFORMED WOMEN'S GUIDE TO PREVENTING OSTEOPOROSIS, by **Dr. M. Notelovitz** (Triad, 1982).

OSTEOPOROSIS, YOUR HEAD START ON THE PREVENTION AND TREATMENT OF BRITTLE BONES, by **Dr. D.F. Fardon** (Body Press, 1987).

HEALTHY BONES- WHAT YOU SHOULD KNOW ABOUT OSTEOPOROSIS, by **Nancy Appleton** (Avery Publishing, 1991), Subtitled, **Towards Preventing And Overcoming Osteoporosis Through Simple Body Chemistry Balance**. This book looks at why calcium is drawn from the bones in the first place, and how a holistic approach to diet will prevent the problem.

THE CALCIUM BIBLE, HOW TO HAVE BETTER BONES IN YOUR LIFE, by **Patricia Hausman** (Rawson, 1985).

OSTOP OTTAWA, C\O Good Companions Center, 670 Albert St, Ottawa, ON, K1R 6L2. 613-236-0428.

Ostop groups are also active in Vancouver and Victoria, BC. Ostop is a self-help group for osteoporosis founded by the indomitable **Lindy Fraser**, who suffered for osteoporosis for decades. You can also start a self-help group in your own area.

OSTEOPOROSIS SOCIETY OF CANADA, 33 Laird Dr, Toronto, ON, M4G 3F9. 416-696-2663.

THE NATIONAL OSTEOPOROSIS FOUNDATION, 1150-17th St, #500, Washington, DC, 20036.

These societies provides info to the public as well as to physicians. Educational videos are also available.

THE UNIVERSITY OF TORONTO BONE AND MINERAL GROUP, 38 Shuter St #212, Toronto, ON, M5B 1A6.

PRODUCTS

KRIPP'S PHARMACY, 994 Granville St, Vancouver, BC, V6Z 1L2. 604-687-2564.

SMITH'S PHARMACY, 3463 Yonge St, Toronto, ON, M4N 2A3. 416-488-2600 or 1-800-361-6624.

SUPPLEMENTS PLUS, 451 Church St Toronto, ON, M4Y 2C5. 416-962-8269, Canada wide mail order: 1-800-387-4761.

Supplements Plus sells all the vitamin and mineral supplements listed in the article as well as Pro-Gest cream.

WOMEN'S INTERNATIONAL PHARMACY, 5708 Monona Dr, Madison, WI, 53716-3152. 608-221-7800, or 1-800-279-5708 in the United States.

TRANSITIONS FOR HEALTH INC, 621 SW Alder #900, Portland OR, 97205-3627. 1-800-888-6814.

Transitions for Health makes Pro-Gest cream and publishes a wonderful catalogue called, **TRANSITIONS FOR HEALTH** with a excellent selection of women's health products. Call 1-800-888-6814 for a copy.

PHILLIPS NUTRITIONALS, 27071 Cabot Rd #122, Laguna Hills, CA 92653. 1-800-514-5115.

This company makes a complete line of women's health products including vitamins, minerals, herbs and cosmetics. One product of note is called yamcon and contains a combination of herbs and wild yam extract. Yamcon is helpful for reliving menopausal symptoms and comes in the form of skin cream, vaginal cream, vaginal lubricant, oral tablets and sublingual drops. Preliminary studies in Scandanavia showed that Yamcon could help reverse menopausal bone loss.

BIOTICS, PO Box 36888, Houston, TX, 77236. 1-800-231-5777.

KLAIRE LABORATORIES, 1-800-533-7255.

PROFESSIONAL HEALTH PRODUCTS (**PHP**), PO Box 80085, Portland, OR, 97280-1085. 1-800-952-2219.

LABORATORIES

AERON LIFE CYCLE SALIVARY TEST KIT, 1-800-866-9085.

DIAGNOSTECHS, 1-800-878-3787.

Both these labs offer quick and reliable tests of progesterone levels, so you can test the effectiveness of a product.

THE DAILY PERIMENOPAUSE DIARY:

Copyright 1991, Dr. Jerilynn Prior.

This form will help you become aware of the way your body responds to the menopausal changes in your life and to any treatments. Although this form is mostly self-explanatory, I have provided additional information so your record-keeping can best help you (and your physician, if you choose to share it). Please take a minute before you go to bed each night to record the information about your day. The scale at the top goes from 0 to 4, zero represents something you did not experience and four represents the worst it has ever been for you. The scale at the bottom uses letters to indicate if feelings or body symptoms go up or down from your usual "(U)" or normal state. Please start filling in the form on the first day of your menstrual flow.

MENSTRUAL FLOW: You are requested to evaluate the amount of your flow on that day. Use the number scale 0-4 provided on your Diary Form to indicate the intensity of flow. A "1" would be spotting and "4" is changing pads or tampons every 2 hours or having clots. If you have no flow or no longer have your uterus, ignore this line.

BREAST TENDERNESS: You are being asked to note both front and/or side breast soreness. Touch firmly with the palm of your hand to determine if you have breast tenderness there. There may be very little soreness, but the pressure will feel different, for example, from the same pressure on your leg.

FLUID RETENTION: This means feeling bloated or puffy, with water weight gain and getting up to urinate at night.

HOT FLUSHES: Record the **actual number** of hot flushes you experience in the rows labelled "# Flushes-day" and "# Flushes-night". Please record the **intensity** of or how strong the hot flush was in the other box using 0-4 scale above. A "1" would be a feeling of slight heat and a "4" would be dripping wet all over.

MUCOUS SECRETIONS: The mouth of the uterus (cervix) makes a clear stretchy fluid when estrogen levels are high. If mucous can be stretched out 6-8 cm (3-4") between two fingers or pieces of tissue, this is an estrogen effect.

STRESS AND FEELINGS: you are asked to record how you **feel** each day and to evaluate the amount of stress that is part of your life. These two things are not the same. Record feelings on the numbered scale and outside stresses on the bottom scale (with letters). For example, on a given day you may not feel anxious. At the same time you may judge the stresses in your life to be a little more than usual because of a work deadline you had to meet. Please write your comments at the bottom of the column. This may include any particular event which influenced how you felt that day (for example, report if you are ill, have a job promotion, win a major prize, have an argument with your partner). Additional comments or explanations may be noted on the back of the form.

This form is designed to help you better understand the changes you are experiencing. It will also help us to understand. Eventually, through data-gathering like this, a large body of understanding will accumulate so our daughters will be more prepared than we are for their "menopausal years".

Perimenopausal Menstrual Cycle Symptom Diary Form

Name: _____ Month: _____ Year: _____

Cycle Day	1	2	3	4	5	6	7	8	9	10	11	12	13	14	15	16	17	18	19	20	21	22	23	24	25	26	27	28	29	30	
Date																															
# tampons/pads/day																															

Record 0 = none, 1 = minimal, 2 = moderate, 3 = moderately intense, 4 = very intense

Amount flow																															
Breast tenderness: side																															
Breast tenderness: front																															
Fluid retention																															
Hot flushes - day																															
# of flushes - day																															
Hot flushes - night																															
# of flushes - night																															
Mucous secretions																															
Constipation																															
Headache																															
Sleep problems																															
Feeling anger/frustration																															
Feeling depressed																															
Feeling anxious																															

Record M = much less, L = a little less, U = usual, Y = a little Increased, Z = much increased

Appetite																															
Breast size																															
Interest in sex *=activity																															
Feeling of energy																															
Feeling of self-worth																															
Stress - work, home, etc.																															
Basal temperature																															
Comments: (cramps, illness, temperature taken late, etc)																															

OSTEOPOROSIS RISK PROFILE

This chart, created by **Diana Palmason** for **FITNESS LEADER**, (Oct/1984), is intended to help you assess the extent to which you are at risk for spontaneous fractures of the spine, hip and wrist that occur in persons with post-menopausal osteoporosis. Listed below are a number of factors that affect your risk profile, including those that can affect through your lifestyle ("**takens**"), as well as those that are genetically determined ("**givens**"). Beside each factor, find the statement that best applies to you, note the number beside that statement, and write the number down in the right-hand column.

GIVENS

Age:

Female - under 35	1
Female 35 - 50	3
Female 51 - 65	7
Female Over 65	12
Male - under 50	1
Male 51 - 65	2
Male 66 - 80	3
Male Over 80	4

Heritage:

Black	1
Oriental	2
Mediterranean or Middle Eastern	3
Nordic or Anglo-Saxon	5

Complexion:

Dark	1
Ruddy/Olive	2
Fair/Pale	5

Heredity:

No known bone problems in family	1
Relative over 60 with bone disease	3
Parent with bone disease	4
Relative under 60 with bone disease	5

Wrist Size:

Over 6-3/4" (17cm)	1
6" to 6-1/4" (15cm)	2
5-3/4" to 6" (14cm)	3
Under 5-3/4" or 14cm	4

Height:

Over 5'8" (1.7m)	1
5'5"-5'8" (1.6-1.7m).............................	2
5'2"-5'5" (1.5-1.6m).............................	3
Under 5'2" or 1.5m	4

Body Type:

Mesomorphic (high muscle, low fat)	1
Endomorphic (high fat, low muscle)	6
Ectomorphic (low fat, low muscle)	6

Gynecological Status:

Still menstruating or post-menopausal after age 50	1
Menopausal or post-menopausal between ages 46 and 50	3
Early menopause** at age 45 or under .	5
Surgically menopaused before age 45 ...	7

**Deduct 5 points if estrogen therapy was started within one year after surgery or early menopause, 3 points if started more than three years after surgery or early menopause.

TOTAL OF "GIVENS" _____

TAKENS

Exercise:

Total body exercise 4 or more times wkly.	0
Total body exercise 1 to 3 times wkly.	3
Total body exercise 3 times monthly	6
Tend to avoid any physical activity	12

Eating Habits:

(a) Calcium intake:***

4 or more servings of low-fat dairy products daily	0
More than two servings of dairy products daily	3
Two servings or less of dairy products daily	6
Do not eat dairy products if at all possible	12

***Subtract **3** points if you take a daily calcium supplement that provides from 500 mg to 1500 mg of calcium.

(b) Protein intake:

Avoid red meat altogether	0
Seafood and white meat of poultry only	1
Meat 3 times wkly or less	3
Meat 4 times wkly or more.....................	6

Drinking Habits:

(a) Caffeine intake:

Avoid caffeine and tannin beverages	0
Decaffeinated drinks and/or tea only	2
Three cups or less of coffee or tea daily	3
Four cups or more of coffee daily	6

(b) Alcohol intake:

Wkly average: less that 2 beers, 8 oz. wine or 3 oz. spirits	0
Wkly average: 2 to 4 beers, 8-16 oz. wine or 3-6 oz. spirits	2
Daily average: up to 2 beers or 8 oz. wine or 3 oz. spirits.	4
Daily average: more than 4 beers, 16 oz. wine or 6 oz. spirits.	8

Tobacco use:

Non-user	0
Occasional cigarette, less than 14 wkly .	2
Daily smoker but less than 10 daily	5
Ten cigarettes or more daily	8

Total Of "Takens" _____

Add "Givens" _____

FINAL TOTAL _____

ASSESS YOUR RISK ACCORDING TO THE FOLLOWING:

8 to 25 is a well below average risk.

26 to 48 is a below average risk.

49 to 59 is a generally average risk.

60 to 82 is a Moderate risk.

83 to 100 is a Considerable risk.

Note: This chart is not intended to diagnose whether you are or will be osteoporotic. It is simply an indication of the extent to which you are similar to women who have been found to have osteoporosis. For an accurate diagnosis, it is necessary to have a bone scan.

How To Save Your Uterus

Hysterectomy is the most common major surgery performed in North America today. In both Canada and the U.S. you have a 30 to 50 percent chance of having your uterus surgically removed by the time you are 65 years old. In contrast, if you live in Sweden or any of six other European countries, your chance of having a hysterectomy is only ten percent by that age.

The modern hysterectomy (or surgical removal of the uterus) was developed in the late 1800's. Initially, it was very risky and was reserved for life threatening situations. Over the last 50 years, the hysterectomy has become a much safer operation. In fact, from only 15 hysterectomies performed in the United States 67 years ago, there has been a million fold increase to over half a million hysterectomies every year. The annual cost in the U.S. is about three billion dollars annually. In Canada, about 60,000 hysterectomies are performed annually.

The number of hysterectomies in both countries has not increased over the last ten years. What has changed is that women are much more aware of the serious consequences of hysterectomies and the fact that any where between 30 and 50 percent of hysterectomies are clearly unnecessary.

Only about ten percent of hysterectomies are done for life threatening emergencies. The remainder are done electively, that means by choice through prior arrangement between a woman and her doctor. That means a woman has plenty of time to get a second opinion on whether the surgery is really necessary.

An estimated 63 percent of hysterectomies are done on women under age 45. **The vast majority of hysterectomies are done on women between the ages of 20 and 49.** Unfortunately, it is estimated that half the women over 40 who are having hysterectomies are also convinced to have both ovaries removed at the same time, although there is rarely a medical reason to do so. This is creating a whole new generation of women who are going into surgical menopause, with its increased risk of heart disease and bone loss. Removal of both ovaries may necessitate taking hormone replacement therapy for the rest of your life.

In fact, the percentage of hysterectomies where both ovaries are removed has increased from 25 to 41 percent between 1965 and 1984, especially in older women between age 35 to 64. Removal of both ovaries may necessitate taking hormones for the rest of your life.

HYSTERECTOMY RATES VARY ACROSS THE COUNTRY

Hysterectomy rates very much depend on where you live, your socio-economic status and type of medical coverage. Hysterectomy rates in Atlantic Canada are much higher than in the rest of Canada. In fact, as **Zelda Abramson** says in her well researched article on hysterectomy. "If you live in Newfoundland, you have a 61 percent greater chance of having a hysterectomy than a woman living in Saskatchewan (**Healthsharing**, summer/90)."

In the U.S., women in the south and central parts of the country have two to three times the hysterectomy rate as women in the northeast and west coast. One study showed that the more education a woman had, the lower her chance of having a hysterectomy.

Also, in the U.S. women with health insurance had twice as many hysterectomies as those who do not have insurance. There are higher hysterectomy rates in countries where doctors are paid per operation than in those where they are paid by salary.

An interesting Swiss study showed that female gynecologists performed 50 percent fewer hysterectomies than male gynecologists.

When a study of unnecessary surgery was announced in Saskatchewan in 1971, the hysterectomy rate in the period following the announcement dropped sharply. The study showed that the number of unnecessary hysterectomies ranged from 17 to 59 percent in five different hospitals.

Another Canadian study showed that there was a five-fold variation in hysterectomy rates across hospital areas in one province. The highest rate occurred when the woman's primary doctor was a gynecologist or surgeon, as compared to a general practitioner or internist.

UNNECESSARY HYSTERECTOMIES

As you may have guessed by now, there are a lot of unnecessary hysterectomies being done. In fact, several studies estimate **that between 30 and 50 percent of hysterectomies performed are clearly unnecessary**. Another ten to 20 percent could be possibly avoided by using alternative approaches.

Educating yourself about hysterectomies is the best protection. A recent European study showed that rates of hysterectomy fell 25 percent after there was a program to educate the community about hysterectomy compared to a one percent increase in another town where no information was given to the public.

MYTHS ABOUT HYSTERECTOMY

1. If your ovaries are left in, your hormone levels are not affected.

In the words of Californian gynecologist, **Dr. Vicki Hufnagel**, "In more than a third of the cases the ovaries simply die following hysterectomy and menopausal symptoms ensue." It appears that the blood supply to the ovary may be damaged during the surgery (**No More Hysterectomies**, 1988).

Unfortunately, doctors may dismiss real symptoms of menopause (such as hot flashes, menstrual irregularities, vaginal dryness, depression, irritability, and mood swings) as being psychological in origin, since the ovaries are still in place, and therefore miss the diagnosis altogether.

Dr. Winnifred Cutler says that on the average, premenopausal women who lose their uterus but still have their ovaries go into menopause five years earlier than women who keep their uterus. She estimates that 50 percent of women who had their uteruses out **with ovaries left in** will eventually suffer from a premature lack of ovarian hormones. However, this effect may not show up until two years after surgery (**Hysterectomy, Before and After**, 1988).

"Following hysterectomy," says **Janine O'Leary Cobb** (**A Friend Indeed**, Feb/92), "ovaries may produce estrogen at levels ranging from adequate to nil. In some cases, ovaries may falter for weeks or months and then rally to produce enough estrogen. In a significant proportion of cases, ovarian functions gradually ebbs and menopausal symptoms ensue."

On a practical level, earlier menopause means earlier aging, increased risk of bone loss, and risk of coronary heart disease. Dr. Cutler concluded that "hysterectomy, with or without the ovaries removed, increases the risk of atherosclerosis and coronary heart disease three to seven-fold over age matched women who have not had the surgery."

2. There will be no change in your sex life.

One thing is certain, there will be a change in your experience of sex. Some women find their sex life improved due to lack of pain, bleeding or fear of pregnancy. However, many more women find their sex life altered in a negative way.

Orgasm can result from stimulation of the clitoris or uterus or both. Pressure on the cervix, uterus and its surrounding ligaments and membranes causes highly pleasurable sensations. This is known as the uterine orgasm, and is not possible to achieve after hysterectomy. For women whose orgasms center in the deep uterine contractions produced during that type of orgasm, this loss may be great indeed. Some women experience primarily clitoral orgasms and these women may not notice too much difference in their experience of orgasm after hysterectomy.

If the ovaries fail or have been removed, you may lack the androgen hormones (male type hormones naturally found in a woman's body) 50 percent of which are produced by the ovaries and which are necessary for sexual responsiveness and sexual drive. **Dr. Barbara Sherwin**, **Associate Professor of Psychology** at **McGill University** in Montreal, has been researching the relationship of sexual drive to the level of testosterone for 15 years. She believes that testosterone is the androgen hormone necessary for sexual motivation. After a hysterectomy, this loss of motivation can occur suddenly right after surgery or within several years of surgery, when a woman finds she is no longer interested in sex.

Treatment is usually estrogen pills with injections of testosterone or a vaginal cream made of estrogen and testosterone. In the United States, a product known as **ESTRATEST** is widely available. It is a pill taken by mouth that contains both estrogen and testosterone. Side effects of testosterone include masculinizing effects such as facial hair, deepening of the voice and enlarged clitoris. These side effects may be mostly reversed if the dose is adjusted. The long-term side effects are unknown.

Vaginal lubrication usually tends to lessen after hysterectomy. Also if the vagina has been shortened, or scar tissue forms in the vagina or pelvis, painful sex may then result.

3. You are safer because you no longer have to worry about uterine and/or ovarian cancer.

Deaths from uterine cancer are the same as deaths from unnecessary hysterectomies. There is no justification for routine hysterectomy for the prevention of uterine cancer.

Ovarian cancers occurs in one in 100 women over 40 with cure rates of only ten to 20 percent This is the reason that so many gynecologists recommend taking out the ovaries out as a preventative measure. However, the question is highly controversial and it is far from clear that risks of routine removal of the ovaries outweighs the benefits. It is estimated that **two hundred normal ovaries have to be cut out to prevent one woman from getting ovarian cancer.**

Some studies show that the actual risk for developing ovarian cancer after a hysterectomy with the ovaries left in place is very small, around one in a 1,000.

Furthermore, removal of the ovaries may necessitate taking hormone replacement with estrogen and progesterone for the rest of your life or facing bone loss, immediate menopause and increased likelihood of cardiac disease.

After menopause, the ovaries continue to secrete hormones for ten to 20 years later. Some of these hormones support the well-being and health of the older women and also protect against bone loss. Artificially administered hormones can never replace the complex interrelationships between the ovaries, uterus and brain, as yet imperfectly understood.

4. Complication rates and recovery period after hysterectomy is the same as after other major surgery.

Hysterectomy is followed by two to three times the incidence of post-op depression compared to other elective surgery such as gallbladder surgery. Hysterectomy patients also have a much longer recovery period, an average of 11.9 months compared to three months for other types of surgery. Thus before you have a hysterectomy, you should arrange for extra help and plan to go easy on yourself for the 12 months following your hysterectomy. This recovery period may be dramatically shortened as laparoscopic hysterectomy becomes more available (see below).

The risk of dying from hysterectomy is very low, about one per thousand. In real numbers this adds up to 600 women per year in the U.S. dying from complications of hysterectomy, and 60 a year in Canada.

Forty to 50 percent of women have surgical complications following hysterectomy. These include post-op infections, urinary tract complications, and hemorrhage (more than one in ten woman will require a blood transfusion).

Other less common complications include damage to the bowels during surgery (2 percent of women with hysterectomies will later require further bowel surgery to remove scar tissues) blood clots, complications from anesthesia and formation of scar tissue in the abdomen.

Since the uterus holds many of the internal organs, **Dr. Vicki Hufnagel** has noted that after hysterectomy, other organs may cave in or collapse causing pelvic pain, sexual problems and pressure on bowel and bladder.

After hysterectomy, there is an increased incidence of urinary incontinence or the inability to hold your urine.

5. The uterus has no function except reproduction.

The uterus and its surrounding ligaments serve as a vital support structure helping to keep your female organs separate from your intestines and allowing the bladder and rectum to maintain their correct position. Removal of the uterus can subsequently cause constipation, bloating, painful sex, and inability to hold urine.

As mentioned earlier, the uterus is also a sexual organ and many women miss the deep orgasm that its presence enables.

In myth and custom, the uterus is seen as an essential and vital organ, the source of a woman's creativity, power, and dreaming.

Recent research has proven that the uterine wall also secretes hormonal and other active substances with a vital role in women's health that has not been fully explored yet.

LAPAROSCOPIC HYSTERECTOMY

A promising new technique is being developed where the uterus can be removed through a laparoscope. The first American total laparoscopic hysterectomy was performed in 1992 in Philadelphia.

The laparoscope is a slender telescope like instrument that is attached to a TV monitor. The surgery requires great skill, because the surgical instruments must be manipulated through two or three tiny incisions one quarter to half an inch long and the uterus must be carefully removed. According to **Dr. Ivan D'Souza**, one of a small number of gynecologists in Canada that is highly experienced in this technique, a laparoscopic hysterectomy (abdominal extraction only), requires longer operating time, more equipment and greater skill.

Dr. D'Souza and his partner, **Dr. Anthony Lopez**, prefer to use a laparoscopically assisted vaginal hysterectomy, where the uterus is freed from its ligaments from above and the rest of the surgery completed through the vagina. In this procedure, the uterus is removed through the vagina. This procedure has the shortest operating time. Some laparoscopic skills are required but more vaginal skills are involved. Skilled surgeons can do this operation in under two hours on most occasions (this surgery is anywhere between 30 and 90 minutes longer than the standard type of hysterectomy).

As with gallbladders removed this way, your hospital stay is greatly reduced to about two and a half days. With the smaller incision, post-operative pain is much less. You may be able to return to work within four to five weeks. However, there is no doubt that without the larger incision, there is much less pain and much faster recovery with this type of surgery.

Two potential problems exist. The first is the possibility of an unskilled surgeon doing the operation. It is essential to know the experience and training of any surgeon doing this operation. At present, this surgery is not widely available in Canada. If your surgeon is going to be learning on you, you had better give your consent ahead of time. Secondly, the quick recovery period for this surgery makes it more tempting for surgeons to remove the uterus unnecessarily.

REGRETS AFTER A HYSTERECTOMY

It is important to realize that many women have had their health and well-being immeasurably improved by the performance of a necessary hysterectomy.

If you have already had a hysterectomy for any reason, you should never berate yourself about it. Because given the information you had at the time, and perhaps considering the pain or bleeding that you were enduring, and your lack of access to alternative choices, you undoubtedly made the best decision you could have under the circumstances. If you feel dissatisfied or angry at what happened to you, you can use that anger to demand changes in unacceptable medical practices and help educate other women about their choices. You can also take the opportunity to improve and maximize your own health, even after a hysterectomy.

VALID REASONS FOR A HYSTERECTOMY

Uterine cancer or cervical cancer that is invading the uterus, but not cervical cancer that is in situ or confined to the cervix.

Rare but serious complications of childbirth, such as rupture of the uterus.

A very large fibroid which is pressing on other organs or cause debilitating bleeding.

Massive blood loss every month and persistent anemia. A new alternative is a procedure called "endometrial ablation" which consists of scraping off the lining of the uterus, which results in permanent sterility. It may be useful for some women in well selected cases. This procedure is not yet widely available (More on this later).

POSSIBLE CONDITIONS THAT MAY IN SOME SITUATIONS WARRANT A HYSTERECTOMY

Excessive growth of the lining of the uterus. This can often be bette*Hysterectomy*r handled through hormonal therapy using natural or synthetic progesterone. Progesterone causes the excess lining of the uterus to shed itself.

Uterine prolapse. Women can also do Kegel exercises (see prenatal exercise chapter) or use pessaries to hold the organs in place. Sometimes small amounts of estrogen may be used vaginally to strengthen tissues. If symptoms are severe, the best course of action may be a surgical repair and/or reconstruction of the uterus, bladder, rectum and their supporting structures. Sometimes, a severely prolapsed uterus may have to be removed.

Stress incontinence or leaking of urine when you cough or sneeze. There is no evidence that hysterectomy will help this problem, in fact it may make it worse.

Chronic PID can benefit from complete bed rest and prompt and adequate treatment of flare-ups. Even for acute PID with infection of the whole abdominal cavity, intravenous antibiotics and drainage is safer than hysterectomy. All this as well as commentary on other forms of treatment such as acupuncture are contained in the excellent booklet put out by the **PID Society** in Vancouver. Be sure to read the chapter on PID before making your final decision.

Severe Endometriosis. The number of hysterectomies done for endometriosis has increased steadily over the years and only recently seems to be levelling off. Unfortunately too many women recover from hysterectomy to discover that their pain is still there. Endometriosis can have many appearances and occur in many places in the pelvis. Therefore, hysterectomy does not solve the problem, and may add many new problems. As **Dr. Herbert Goldfarb** says in is book, **THE NO HYSTERECTOMY OPTION** (John Wiley and Sons 1990), "It is extremely rare person in this day and age who should ever need a hysterectomy for endometriosis, no matter how severe the condition."

Before making any final decision, please consult the two chapters on endometriosis in this book, especially the work of **Dr. David Redwine. The Endometriosis Association** has the latest information about surgery and drugs as well as information about what all your alternatives are. You can also buy time by taking medications for a short time while you do your reading and research.

Chronic pelvic pain not due to any of the above conditions. In this case, there is little proof that a hysterectomy would help.

Dr. R.C. Reiter studied chronic pelvic pain in women who had normal laparoscopies. At leat 50 percent of these women had sources for their pain that were missed, like bowel or bladder problems. Of course if your doctor didn't know how to look for endometriosis, he may have missed unusual appearances of endometriosis on the bowel or bladder.

Fifty percent of the women were found to have their pain related to stress, depression and especially common was the history of sexual abuse or trauma. In the latter case, "The last thing a woman needs," says Reiter, "is to have another assault on her sexual organs."

Uterine fibroids are the cause of about **one third** of hysterectomies. Fibroids are non-cancerous growths on or in the uterus. They are harmless in themselves, but sometimes cause bleeding, pain or pressure symptoms.

Moderate vaginal bleeding. This can be due to many causes including fibroids and hormonal imbalance. Other solutions should definitely be explored first including hormonal medications.

WHAT TO DO ABOUT FIBROIDS

Fibroids which are causing no symptoms and which are growing slowly can be left alone. Fibroids larger than the size of a grapefruit that are causing pressure symptoms or severe bleeding can be better handled through myomectomy which means removal of the fibroid tumour with preservation, and if necessary, reconstruction of the uterus. These operations can be more complicated, require a longer time, and cause more blood loss than hysterectomies. Usually it will take some research and input from women's groups to find a gynecologist who is skilled at removing fibroids, even in a large city.

Small fibroids under one or two cm in size or that have a stalk or that are protruding into the uterine cavity can be easily removed through the hysteroscope. Fibroids between 2.5 cm and five cm can be removed the same way after they have been shrunk through medication (GNRH drugs, see chapter on endometriosis for more details). Fibroids larger than five cm must be shrunk medically, and then removed in two steps.

In the case of removal of small fibroids causing bleeding, 50 to 87 percent of women return to normal menstruation after the hysteroscopic operation. If the uterus is larger than a 14-week pregnancy size (about the size of a grapefruit), than hysteroscopic removal cannot be done.

Some fibroids can be removed through the laparoscope. In addition, women with disabling bleeding from fibroids may be possible candidates for endometrial ablation.

There is at least a ten percent chance that the fibroids may grow back enough to necessitate surgery. If you are planning to have a myomectomy, you should make sure your iron stores are built up before the operation.

Fibroids will also grow larger if you are taking the hormone estrogen. Fibroids will also shrink after menopause. So if you are approaching menopause, the best course may be to leave them alone until that time.

MORE ABOUT MODERATE TO HEAVY BLEEDING

This is a common reason for hysterectomy. When a woman is having periods that are debilitating or interfering with her life, a hysterectomy can seem like an appealing option. However there are many things a woman can do before resorting to the hysterectomy as a last resort.

1. Sometimes simple over the counter medications such as anti-inflammatory and pain reliever drugs for painful periods, such as as motrin, or anti-histamines, such as chlortripolon, will bring the bleeding under control. Avoid anti-histamines like seldane or hismanal.

2. Make sure you have your blood level of iron and iron stores checked.

If you are anemic, you should work aggressively on keeping your iron levels high (see chapter on iron). Some studies indicate that chronic iron deficiency may itself be a cause of heavy bleeding.

3. Make sure your thyroid function has been checked. Even a slightly lowered thyroid function can cause menstrual disturbances including heavy bleeding. Also make sure that you check your basal temperature. (See the chart at the end of the chapter on The Thyroid Gland And Pregnancy).

4. Consider going on a hormonal regime using natural progesterone capsules or cream to regulate the bleeding and make it more predictable.

5. If you are significantly overweight, your fat tissues will produce extra estrogen, which can increase bleeding.

6. Always find out the cause of the bleeding. This can be done through a simple office procedure called endometrial biopsy. A small sample of the lining of the uterus is taken and cancer can be ruled out. If the lining of the uterus is overgrown, short term treatment with Provera will solve the problem.

A D-and-C is sometimes useful and may help the bleeding. However, an office procedure called hysteroscopy, where a lighted tube is introduced through the cervix is a much more sensitive and accurate procedure than a D-and-C for both diagnosis and treatment.

7. Consider seeking natural solutions for your bleeding problems. Consider seeing a skilled acupuncturists who will give Chinese herbs as well as acupuncture to bring the body into balance. The Chinese herb dong quai is the foremost of female tonics and can help regulate periods and reduce bleeding.

A skilled homeopath may also be very helpful. The Queen of England has her own homeopathic physician as well as the regular kind. A naturopath experienced in women's health problems may be able to provide a combination of diet, vitamins and herbs to bring the bleeding under control.

8. Look at any emotional factors in your life that may be overwhelming you and try to reduce their impact. Seek professional counselling if necessary.

9. Although its long-term side effects are unknown, some women may want to consider a new procedure known as **endometrial ablation**. This is an operation which permanently removes the lining of the uterus and leads to immediate sterility. However the rest of the uterus is left intact.

The procedure only eliminates bleeding in 40 to 50 percent of cases and reduces it in 40 to 50 percent with a ten percent failure rate. There have rarely been serious side effects including "isolated fatal cases and near fatal cases". (**JOURNAL SOGC**, Mar/Apr/92). So, overall, there are substantial risks to this procedure including at least a ten percent chance it will not help at all. However, it may be suitable for a small group of well selected women who understand all the risks.

A WORD ABOUT SUBTOTAL HYSTERECTOMY

Since 1975, according to American gynecologist, **Dr. Thomas Lyons** of Atlanta, ninety five percent of hysterectomies have been total meaning the whole uterus is removed.

However, at the 1993 **World Congress of Gynecologic Endoscopy**, Dr. Lyons and **Dr. Kurt Semm** argued in favour of a return to the subtotal hysterectomy, where the lower part of the uterus, the cervix, is left intact, leaving the cervix in place may improve sexual pleasure for some women.

Dr. Lyons says regular PAP tests are the best tools for preventing cervical cancer, not routinely removing the cervix.

Studies are now going to compare the results of subtotal hysterectomies with total hysterectomies.

NEVER HAVE A HYSTERECTOMY FOR THE FOLLOWING REASONS

1. **SMALL FIBROIDS THAT ARE CAUSING NO SYMPTOMS.**
2. **STERILIZATION.** Hysterectomy has ten to 20 times the complication rate of tubal ligation.
3. **CHRONIC CERVICITIS** (chronic inflammation and infection of the cervix).
4. **CERVICAL CANCER THAT IS CONFINED TO THE CERVIX.**
5. **PREMENSTRUAL SYNDROME.** Symptoms will continue with or without the uterus if the ovaries are still present.
6. **MILD VAGINAL BLEEDING.**

WHAT YOU CAN DO TO SAVE YOUR UTERUS

EDUCATE YOURSELF: This is the single most important thing that you can do for yourself. Knowledge of the reasons for, complications of, and alternatives to hysterectomy will enable you to make an intelligent and careful decision of what is best for you.

TAKE YOUR TIME: An elective hysterectomy means you usually have the time to consider carefully the pros and cons of hysterectomy and make a wise decision based on your individual problems and needs. It also gives you time to properly prepare for a hysterectomy thereby minimizing your chances of complications.

DO NOT MAKE YOUR DOCTOR THE ULTIMATE AUTHORITY: Take charge of your own body and don't allow your vital organs to be removed needlessly. The uterus has no equivalent in the male body and its function is as yet imperfectly understood. The ovaries are equivalent to the male testes. Both the uterus and the ovaries have complex and important functions in a woman's body long after her child-bearing years are over.

TWO STORIES

After a routine Pap smear, Judy, 35, was told that she had cervical cancer that had not spread past the cervix. Her doctor recommended a hysterectomy. The word cancer threw her into a panic state. Although she had three kids, she was still thinking about having a fourth. The stress of thinking about cancer, plus the recent death of her father, made her feel confused and uncertain. Her gynecologist was putting a lot of pressure on her to have the hysterectomy. He said it would also cure her endometriosis, which had been severely painful for so long. When Judy came to her senses, she had lost her uterus for no good reason, and within two weeks her endometriosis pain came back, worse than before.

On the other hand, Deborah, 45, felt that "something funny was happening inside of her." She visited her gynecologist and he ordered a pelvic ultrasound. Visibly alarmed, her doctor told her there was a large black shadow over one ovary which he thought could be cancer. He suggested an immediate hysterectomy.

Deborah went into a state of shock. She thought she was going to die. After she recovered from the shock, she went straight to the library to read about hysterectomies and cancer. She asked her family doctor to arrange for a second opinion. She talked to other women about their experiences with hysterectomies.

The second gynecologist said he thought the shadow was probably a fibroid, but he would have to operate to find out for sure. Deborah agreed to surgery with one condition, that if it wasn't cancer she wanted her uterus and ovaries to be left in.

"I didn't want to have anything removed that's not diseased." she said.

Fortunately, the shadow turned out to be a single large fibroid, which her doctor was able to remove while leaving her uterus intact.

"Medical doctors do not have the answer to everything," she told me, although, "they often act like they do."

REMEMBER:

1. It is OK to panic but it is not OK to have major surgery done without getting all the facts and a second opinion.

2. Doctors do not know everything and even the most experienced one can still make mistakes.

3. Doctors have feelings and can get over concerned and fearful about missing cancer in their patients.

4. Most of the time you can take the extra few weeks, even months, to make a proper well informed decision that you can live with.

5. If you are having a lot of bleeding or pain and are confused about whether to take medications for these symptoms, go ahead and take them for three to six months. This buys you enough time to read and explore the alternatives.

RESOURCES:

Make sure that your library carries these books or order them through your local bookstore.

NO HYSTERECTOMY; YOUR BODY YOUR CHOICE, by **Dr. Herbert Goldfarb** and **Judy Greif** (Wiley and Sons, 1990). I highly recommend this book which is written by a sensitive and sympathetic gynecologist. It is clear and offers many options to women including well designed checklists for yourself and your doctor.

YOU DON'T NEED A HYSTERECTOMY: New and Effective Ways of Avoiding Major Surgery, by **Dr. Ivan Strausz** (Addison and Wesley, 1993). This is a new book which **Janine O'Leary Cobb** says is "both informative and enormously supportive to women," although he is too accepting of the practice of removing the ovaries of women over 45 or 50.

HOW TO AVOID A HYSTERECTOMY, by **Lynn Payer** (Pantheon Books, 1987). This book is subtitled. "An indispensable guide to exploring all your options before you consent to a hysterectomy," and is the official **National Women's Health Network Guide**. It has an excellent section on fibroids and myomectomies.

COPING WITH A HYSTERECTOMY, by **Dr. Susanne Morgan** (Doubleday, revised 1985). This book presents a well balanced overview of the whole question and a discussion of alternatives.

NO MORE HYSTERECTOMIES, by **Dr. Vicki Hufnagel** (NAL Books, 1988). This book is easy to read, well formulated book which gives details of surgical and hormonal alternatives to hysterectomy. The author definitely favours complicated and long surgical treatment.

HYSTERECTOMY BEFORE AND AFTER, by **Dr. Winnifred Cutler** (Harper and Rowe, 1988) is a comprehensive guide to preventing, preparing for, and maximizing health after hysterectomy. The author is strongly biased in favour of hormones.

THE CASTRATED WOMAN, by **Naomi Miller Stokes** (Franklin Watts, 1986). As a result of the serious aftereffects of her own hysterectomy, Ms. Stokes researched the whole question and offers concrete answers to women.

ESSENTIAL ADDRESSES:

U.S.-CANADIAN ENDOMETRIOSIS ASSOCIATION, Headquarters Office, PO Box 92187, Milwaukee, WI, 53202. 1-800-426-2END.

HERS - HYSTERECTOMY EDUCATIONAL RESOURCES AND SERVICES, 422 Bryn Mawr Ave, Bala-Cynwyd, PA, 19004. 215-667-7757.

This foundation was founded by **Nora Coffey** in 1982 to ensure that no woman is hysterectomized and/or castrated without prior knowledge of the alternative and lifelong consequences of these surgeries. For women suffering from the after effects of surgery, HERS offers coping techniques as well as validation of symptoms. HERS also publishes a newsletter on hysterectomy, and its possible side effects, and sponsors conferences on the topic. It offers a 24-hour answering service and a telephone counselling service at the above number between 9 am and 5 pm EST. There is no charge for the counselling.

THE CANADIAN PID SOCIETY, PO Box 33804, Stn D, Vancouver, BC, V67 4L6. 604-684-5704.

Their highly recommended booklet entitled, **PELVIC INFLAMMATORY DISEASE**, was written to provide information for women who have PID, their families, and health care professionals. PID is the leading cause of infertility and hysterectomy in young women, yet it is preventable.

TORONTO WOMEN'S BOOKSTORE, 73 Harbord St, Toronto, ON, M5S 1G4. 416-922-8744.

Any of the above books may be ordered by mail through this bookstore.

VANCOUVER WOMEN'S HEALTH COLLECTIVE, 302-1720 Grant St, Vancouver, BC, V5L 2Y7. 604-736-5262.

BOSTON WOMEN'S HEALTH BOOK COLLECTIVE, PO Box 192, West Somerville, MA, 02144. 617-625-0271.

This well known public information center contains national and international publications concerning women's health and other issues pertaining to women. All of their books are recommended, especially the newly revised **OUR BODIES OURSELVES** (revised 1992).

NATIONAL WOMEN'S HEALTH NETWORK, 1325 G St NW, Washington, DC, 200003. 202-347-1140.

This is a national organization devoted exclusively to women and health. It publishes a newsletter as well as special news alerts concerning issues requiring immediate attention.

The Great Debate Over Breast Cancer Screening

Fear of breast cancer strikes terror into the heart of many women. One in nine or ten women will develop breast cancer in the course of her life time. According to recent estimates, 70 to 75 percent of these women will survive five years after diagnosis. Ten years later, only 60 to 63 percent will be alive. This is an improvement of only two to three percent over 1950 survival rates.

However terror is not a good basis for a sound judgment about the best way for an individual woman to detect early breast cancer.

In fact, the best strategy for women is to do all they can to prevent breast cancer before it happens.

"According to some breast cancer experts," writes medical journalist, **Ruth Spear** in, **Women's Health**, 1986, "fear of breast cancer is more epidemic than the disease itself... Fear of the disease and its consequences immobilize many women to the point where they avoid breast examinations or delay medical treatment. Fear can be best remedied by concrete knowledge about detection and prevention."

SCREENING FOR BREAST CANCER

Although 25 percent of the women who get breast cancer fall into a predictable high risk category, the remainder cannot easily be predicted.

One thing is known for sure and that is that the incidence of breast cancer increases with age. Seventy to 80 percent of breast cancer occurs after age 50.

For many years, doctors have been trying to find a screening method that can detect breast cancer early enough and often enough to reduce deaths from breast cancer.

The majority of doctors and researchers are convinced that regular mammography or X-ray examination of breast tissue is that screening method, at least for women 50 years of age and older.

However, that belief may be only partially true. Good physical exam and well taught self exam may be equally important, and may reduce the annual death rate from breast cancer as much as having mammograms every two years, even in the over 50 age group.

A few years ago, **Dr. Charles Wright**, **professor of health care and epidemiology** at the **University of British Columbia**, predicted that although early studies showed some benefit of screening mammograms, later studies would show less and less benefit. He was right.

Dr. Wright believes that the motivation of doctors promoting screening mammography is good. They want desperately to do something to reduce the toll from breast cancer. But he remains unconvinced that screening mammography will accomplish that goal.

HOW USEFUL ARE SCREENING MAMMOGRAMS ?

The best evidence to date shows no reduction in breast cancer death rates from screening mammograms in women aged 40 to 49. For women 50 and older, screening mammograms every two or three years will reduce the annual death rate by a small amount. This varies between 20 percent (or less) and 40 percent.

Skilled physical exam by a physician is an essential component of any breast cancer screening program. The results of the **Canadian National Breast Screening Study** (**NBSS**) showed that for women 50 and over regular examination of the breasts by a skilled practitioner **alone** reduced the annual death rate from breast cancer as much as mammogram exam combined with physical exam.

Both mammograms and breast exam must be of high quality to be any use at all. A mammogram must be performed on specialized equipment and interpreted by an experienced radiologist. **The Canadian and American Associations of Radiologists** have put in place a program to accredit mammogram centers, but many centers have not been approved yet. There is no nationwide co-ordination to monitor mammogram quality, equipment, interpretation, management and follow-up in either country.

Likewise, doctors have not been trained adequately in the art of skilful breast exam. Breast exams may be haphazard or sloppily performed. Thus, most experts still recommend that all women 50 or over get a screening mammogram every two years, as well as an annual physical exam of the breasts.

Dr. Anthony Miller, director of the NBSS study, testifying before a status of women committee on breast cancer said, "I think our study demonstrated that [physical examination of the breasts] is rarely performed well by physicians... [They] just do not take the time, they do not know what they are looking for... I personally believe... that we need to set up a professional education program in this country (**C.M.A. Journal**, Jan/93)."

NOT ALL MAMMOGRAMS ARE CREATED EQUAL

When you go for a mammogram, the procedure may be stressful and may likely hurt. After you strip to the waist, your breast will be flattened between two plates positioned above and below the breast while X-ray pictures are taken of each breast separately. If possible, schedule your mammogram during or soon after your period when the breasts are the least tender.

Screening for breast cancer with mammography is of no value unless the mammogram is done correctly and interpreted by an experienced radiologist.

Dr. Cornelia Baines, **Department of Preventative Medicine and Biostatistics**, **University of Toronto** and **Deputy Director of the National Breast Screening Study**, said recently that screening for breast cancer is only effective if certain criteria are met.

These criteria are:

- The picture of the breast on the X-ray film must be of the highest quality. The machine should be used for mammograms only (a dedicated X-ray machine).

- The technician and the radiologist should be specially trained in mammography.

- There is maximum compression of the breast (it may hurt).

- Very careful quality control procedures are followed.

- A physical examination of the breasts accompanies the mammogram.

The safest bet for a reliable mammogram is a center that specializes in mammograms and does at least 20 to 30 mammograms a day. **Dr. Howard Seiden** (**Toronto Star**, Dec.17/92) suggests that you pay extra to have your mammogram interpreted by a second radiologist. He maintains that approximately 15 percent of cancers missed by the first doctor will be picked up by the second.

The **U.S. Preventative Services Task Force** found that the quality of a mammograph varied greatly from place to place. Of the 11,000 mammography units in the U.S., only 3,500 have been accredited by the **American College of Radiology**. In Canada, as in the U.S., there are no nationwide standards being enforced. In the U.S. women can call the **National Cancer Institute** at 1-800-4-CANCER or the state chapter of the **American Cancer Society** to find out where to get quality mammograms.

MAMMOGRAPHY CAN BE USED FOR TWO PURPOSES

1. To check a suspicious breast lump found by the doctor or the woman on self exam (diagnostic mammogram).

2. To screen for breast cancer in healthy woman with no breast lumps or other breast symptoms. This chapter focuses on the screening type of mammogram.

HOW OFTEN SHOULD I HAVE A SCREENING MAMMOGRAM ?

Only 20 percent of breast cancer occurs before age 50, 40 percent of breast cancer is found in women between 50 and 65, and 40 percent in women over 65.

Canadian guidelines for breast screening recommend that women over 50 have screening mammograms done every two years. This is based on the favourable studies mentioned below and other studies indicating that the death rates from breast cancer may be reduced by 20 to 40 percent by such screening.

The American College of Physicians and **The American College of Obstetricians and Gynecologists** follow these guidelines and there are similar guidelines in Sweden, Holland, Italy and England. In 1993, the U.S. National Cancer Institute issued new guidelines suggesting screening mammograms begin at age 50.

Other American groups disagree. **The American Medical Association**, The National Cancer Institute, and **The American Cancer Society**, suggest that women begin the screening process as early as age 40, with a physical exam and mammography every one to two years, or as recommended by their doctor. After age 50 these groups recommend a yearly mammogram.

WHAT OTHER SCREENING TECHNIQUES ARE AVAILABLE ?

PHYSICAL EXAMINATION: The most important other screening technique involves a woman having her breast examined by a experienced doctor or nurse practitioner to check for lumps or other abnormalities. One study of 80 physicians at a university medical center showed that their ability to detect breast lumps in a silicon breast model was only fair averaging 44 percent of lumps detected. (**Journal of the A.M.A.** 1985, #253).

The same study showed that 71 percent of doctors felt that their medical school or residency training had been inadequate. Eighty four percent felt at least some need to improve their abilities in breast lump detection.

The Canadian study is the only study so far to evaluate the value of a mammogram over and above physical exam in women 50 years or older. The researchers found that although more cancers were detected in the mammogram group, the breast cancer death rate was no higher in the group that only received a yearly breast exam from a trained nurse or doctor, with no mammogram being done.

BREAST SELF EXAMINATION (BSE): Between 50 and 60 percent of breast cancers are discovered by women themselves either accidentally or through purposeful BSE. To be worth doing, BSE must be taught well and performed well. A new learning method called the **MAMMACARE LEARNING SYSTEM** enables women to teach themselves BSE in a way that is much more accurate than the usual type of BSE that is being taught.

TRANSILLUMINATION: Low intensity red or near infra-red light is shone through the breasts. The shadows and reflections of the light are then fed into a computer and made into a composite picture. This method is not as accurate as a mammogram in detecting small cancers, but is very safe and has no side effects.

The light exam may be useful for women with dense breasts, especially younger women, women with lumpy breasts and pregnant women.

The light exam can also be a useful adjunct to a good physical exam, either by itself or with a mammogram.

NEW TECHNIQUES

The August 1992 newsletter of the **Breast Cancer Action** group in San Francisco provided much of the information on new diagnostic tests for breast cancer contained in this section.

1. **THE BIOCHRON: Barry Hirschowitz** has invented the Biochron, a kind of electrocardiogram of the breast.

Electrodes are placed on the breast and the electrical charges of breast cells are measured. Eventually he wants to develop a cheap device for home use. The whole procedure is painless and the skin is never punctured.

2. **BLOOD TESTS FOR ANTIBODIES - THE AMAS: Dr. Samuel Bogosh** developed a method of screening for active breast cancer by testing the blood for antibodies.

The test is known as AMAS (anti-malignant antibody in serum). More than 4,000 double blind studies of the accuracy of this test have shown that it has a 99 percent sensitivity. In England, the **National Health Service** has purchased the test to use as a screening tool for women who have abnormal mammograms as a possible alternative to a breast biopsy.

3. **PESTICIDE CONCENTRATION IN FATTY TISSUES:** It may be that we should be measuring concentrations of organochlorines in fatty tissues to predict who will be at risk for breast cancer.

A 1987 pilot study of 50 women in **Connecticut** showed that concentrations of PCB, DDE and other pesticides were 50 to 60 percent higher in the fatty tissues of women with breast cancer. (**Archives of Environmental Health**, Mar/Apr/92).

Dr. Mary Wolff, an epidemiologist at the **Mount Sinai Medical Center** in New York who led the study, told **NOW** reporter **Megan Williams** that the results of the study surprised her.

"This is the first new evidence that could be a clue about the rising breast cancer rates," she says, "I've been a sceptic all along about the environmental concerns, but I keep getting proven wrong (NOW, Dec 2/92)."

When levels of DDT, lindane and BHC in Israeli dairy products (previously 100 to 800 percent greater than in U.S. dairy products) were reduced, the breast cancer death rate also fell dramatically by an estimated 20 percent.

Starting in 1994, the **National Institute for Environmental Health Sciences** in the U.S. will fund a much larger study measuring levels of DDT and its metabolites in the blood samples of 15,000 women, and try to correlate them with breast cancer rates.

SO WHAT DO THE STUDIES SHOW SO FAR ?

Even for doctors, there is a confusing maze of studies, all with varying interpretations. Some doctors believe this information is difficult for women to understand. However, I believe that a woman can make a more informed decision about routine mammograms if she understands fully the complexity of the issues involved.

FAVOURABLE STUDIES

THE HIP STUDY: In 1963 **The Health Insurance Plan of New York** (**HIP**) and The National Cancer Institute launched the first large scale study of breast cancer screening. It involved two groups of women of 30,000 each. The study group received physical exams plus annual mammograms for four years and the control group, their usual medical care only. The follow-up on all these women continued for 23 years until 1986.

This is one of the major studies in the field, along with a Swedish study, and both are considered scientifically valid because they have the proper control group to compare the results of the study group to (known as a randomized study).

The HIP study showed a 30 percent reduction in the breast cancer death rate in women aged 40 to 64 in the first ten years of the study. Eighteen years into the study, the reduction in breast cancer death rate dropped to 25 percent. The reduction in death rate was greatest for women over 50 years of age.

The HIP study was not designed to study various age groups, only the overall effect of mammography and physical exam on the death rate from breast cancer. Nonetheless, many interpretations of this study have been made. The value of screening mammography for women under 50 was little, but a small decrease in the death rate from breast cancer occurred 18 years after the study.

In this large study, not only mammography but breast examination by a trained medical practitioner contributed to the detection of breast cancer. In fact, 33 percent of breast cancers were only seen on mammography, and 45 percent found only through breast examination.

Another important finding of the study was that breast cancer found in the study group was at an earlier stage and had less incidence of spread to the lymph glands under the arm than in the control group.

BCDDP TRIAL: Between 1973 and 1981, a large screening project called **The Breast Cancer Detection Demonstration Project** (**BCDDP**) was begun in the U.S. The project involved 283,222 women in 29 centers. Women in the project received physical exams and five annual mammograms (only 51 percent of the women completed all five mammograms).

The project was not intended as a research study and did not include a control group of women who did not receive mammography for comparison.

Furthermore, in the midst of the project, controversy arose over the harmful effects of the X-ray exposure from the mammograms. Mammograms used in both HIP and **BCDDP** are considered primitive by today's standards and the dose of radiation to the breast was about 20 times more than that used today.

At the height of the **BCDDP** study, in 1976-7, several doctors including **Dr. John Bailar III**, editor of the **Journal of the National Cancer Institute** at that time, and now **Professor of Biostatistics and Epidemiology** at **McGill University School of Medicine**, raised the possibility that the radiation from mammograms was causing as many cancer deaths as it was preventing. As a result of these concerns, women under age 50 were dropped from the mammogram part of the project, unless they were in a high risk group. However, women in this age group did return every year for a physical exam.

However, the BCDDP did demonstrate the ability of mammography to pick up small cancers. Fifty nine percent of very early cancers were detected by mammography alone compared with six percent with physical exam alone.

THE SWEDISH TWO COUNTY STUDY: This randomized study was begun in 1977 and ended in 1984, and involved 77,000 screened women and 56,000 women in the control group. Mammograms (a single view of each breast) were done every two years for women aged 40 to 49; and every three years for women over 50.

As of December 31, 1990 the study showed an overall reduction in breast cancer death rate of 30 percent, especially in the over 50 group.

But for women aged 40 to 49, more breast cancer deaths occurred in the screened group and 50 percent of breast cancers were detected in the intervals between screenings. One third of breast cancer deaths occurred in women who did not attend screening, especially those over age 70 years.

Three other studies, although not randomized, showed between 30 to 50 percent reduction in annual breast cancer death rate in screened women over the age of 50. Two of the studies took place in Holland and one in Italy.

WHAT DOES A 30 PERCENT REDUCTION IN BREAST CANCER DEATH RATE REALLY MEAN ?

Dr. Peter Skrabenek is an outspoken critic of screenin*Breast Cancer Screening*g mammography and lectures on community medicine in Dublin. He says that to put this figure into its proper perspective, a 30 percent death rate reduction does **not** mean that one in three women with breast cancer is saved, it means that for each 15,000 women screened, there will be one less death from breast cancer each year.

Another way of looking at this, according to Dr. Baines, is that for every ten women who would die of breast cancer without breast screening, seven will still die even with breast screening.

UNFAVOURABLE STUDIES

Malmo, Sweden was the site of another large study, involving 21,000 women in the study group who had mammograms every 18 to 24 months, and 21,000 women in the control group. This study showed that "deaths from breast cancer were reduced by 20 percent in women over 55 or older despite a lower participation in this group."

However, **women younger than 55 in the study group showed a 29 percent higher death rate from breast cancer.** "Although this could be a random phenomenon," the researchers say, "negative results of a screening mammogram may have falsely reassured some patients and led to a deleterious delay in diagnosis."

The Malmo study has been criticized for its design, and also for the fact that women in the control group had mammograms that led to the detection of 20 percent of cancer in that group.

In Edinburgh, 45,000 women were entered into a randomized trail of breast cancer screening by mammography and clinical examination. After seven years of follow up the death rate was reduced by 17 percent, but in women over fifty this rose to 20 percent. This is still not considered to be a statistically significant reduction in the death rate.

The researchers concluded that, "The Edinburgh mortality data lack statistical power and are consistent either with no reduction in mortality or a reduction of over 30 percent. Longer follow up is required to establish which, and we will report further after 12 years of follow up."

Between 1979 to 1981 a non-randomized trail was started on women age 45 to 64 living in eight different locations in the United Kingdom. Nine years into the study, the reduction in breast cancer death rate was about 20 percent, falling just short of statistical significance.

THE NATIONAL BREAST SCREENING STUDY IN CANADA

For 12 years, leading breast cancer experts have been waiting for the outcome of a large well designed Canadian study that began in 1980. The National Breast Screening Study studied 89,000 women in 15 centers across Canada. The study was designed to definitively answer questions about whether physical exam plus mammography decreases the death rate from breast cancer in women 40 to 49 years and whether mammography contributes over and above physical examination to the detection of breast cancer in women age 50 to 59 years.

The NBSS is the largest individually randomized study to date evaluating breast screening among women aged 40 to 49 years. The researchers found that although the combination of yearly mammography and physical exam detected more and smaller breast cancers than in the unscreened group, there was no impact on the annual breast cancer death rate at the seven year mark. In fact, there were more deaths in the screened group than in the unscreened group (38 versus 28), although this was not statistically significant.

The NBSS study is the only study so far to evaluate the value of mammography, over and above physical exam in women 50 years or older. The researchers found that although more cancers were detected in the group getting mammograms and physical exams, the breast cancer death rate was the same for both groups. This may mean mammography detects non-fatal cancers, or it may mean it is too soon to see any benefit from mammography screening.

Some radiologists, and some physicians involved in the **British Columbia Cancer Control Agency**'s project to screen women aged 40 to 49 in that province, maintain that NBSS results are invalid because the quality of mammography early on was less than desirable. Some of the radiologists criticising the study were among the fifty who were reading mammograms for the NBSS.

Dr. Anthony Miller, has countered the accusations saying (**CBC** radio, Nov.21/92), "we used what was available in Canada at the time. We used the experts that we could find. If they regarded their training as being inadequate, they certainly never told us so."

In fact, as Dr. Anthony Miller and Dr. Cornelia Baines, told The **Medical Post** (Jan.5/93), "All NBSS radiologists were certified and based in either teaching hospitals or provincial cancer centers; were expert diagnostic mammographers; received feedback from the reference radiologist, and had an opportunity for upgrading their skills at meetings."

Dr. Antoni Basinski, from the Institute for **Clinical Evaluative Sciences** at **Sunnybrook Hospital** in Toronto, states in his article in the **CMAJ** (Nov 15/92). "Suboptimal quality (of mammograms) may be expected to diminish the size of a potential effect but not abolish it... The NBSS investigators appropriately addressed internal quality control and took measures to improve quality where necessary."

Moreover, as Dr.Cornelia Baines points out the mammograms done in the first two years of the study, when there was the most problem with mammogram quality, only comprise 2.5 percent of the total mammograms done.

Dr. Vivien Basco, chairman of the **Policy Advisory Group to the NBSS**, and ironically an outspoken critic of the study, said in a CBC radio interview(Nov/92). "The quality of the mammograms in NBSS was almost certainly as good as the ordinary mammography being done in the country at the time, or for that matter in the U.S. but not up to the standards of expert mammography clinics."

Dr. Charles Wright, told the **Globe and Mail** reporter **Paul Taylor** (Nov 14, 1992). "What we are going to see here is a massive attempt to discredit this study. And the attack is going to come from the huge multi-billion industry that has developed around screening, which includes the manufacturers, the radiologists, and the technicians."

THE ADVANTAGES OF ROUTINE MAMMOGRAPHY

1. It may detect small breast cancers before they can be felt and before they have spread to the lymph glands. The outlook for breast cancer is better if the cancer has not spread to the lymph glands.

2. It may reduce the death rate from breast cancer by 20 to 40 percent in women over 50 years old.

THE DISADVANTAGES OF MAMMOGRAMS

1. **RADIATION:** Most experts believe that the risk from radiation induced breast cancer is very small and nothing to worry about. Estimates of the amount of radiation-induced cancers range from one to 42 per million women screened.

Of much greater concern is the fact that radiation exposure varies from one place to another and there is no real regulation of radiation levels. A U.S. government study showed that the amount of radiation exposure could vary as much as 100 times from one facility to another.

In the U.S., mammograms are being done much more frequently than in Canada, and mammograms are a big money maker for some radiologists. **The American Geriatric Society** is concerned that, "If a woman had her first mammogram at the age of 35 and follow-up annual studies after the age of 50 and she would live to 100, she would have undergone over sixty mammograms... the cumulative effects of 30, 40 or 50 mammograms are essentially unknown. Furthermore, the number of facilities that perform mammograms with outdated high dose radiation equipment is unknown."

As an individual, you should be aware that your radiation risk is equal to the additive effect of all the X-rays you have ever had, and heed the following advice of The National Cancer Institute (NCI).

In 1980, **The National Cancer Institute of Canada Support and Advocacy Division** made the following recommendations to the **Toronto Board of Health** concerning the radiation risk for women participating in The Canadian National Breast Screening Study:

"While we conclude that the level of radiation to be used in the study offers small risk, we are concerned at the incalculable nature of the risk from the addition of other sources of radiation, especially chest or dental X-rays. We note that, according to OHIP records, in Ontario, in the last year 1.7 million chest X-rays were given or one for every five persons in the province.

The Board, therefore, should recommend that previous X-ray history be discussed with all potential participants before they join the study. Then, those women with high X-ray exposure should be informed explicitly that the risk to them is entirely unknown if they participate in the study... Specifically each woman should be told: (A) The possible risk to her is small. (B) The possible benefit to her is small. (C) There is a completely unknown risk from accumulated radiation from different sources."

Dr. Rosalie Bertell, author of **NO IMMEDIATE DANGER** (Women's Press, Toronto, 1985) and **Director of the International Institute of Concern for Public Health**, believes the radiation risk from mammograms has been underestimated (see her comments below on the Ontario screening program).

2. **FALSE POSITIVES AND UNNECESSARY SURGERY:** A false positive means that something shows up in your mammogram that suggests cancer, but when a breast biopsy is done, no evidence of cancer is found. False positives can occur in up to ten percent or more of mammograms.

In the National Breast Cancer Screening Study in Canada, at the beginning of the study, there were ten false positives showing up on mammograms for every true positive proven by biopsy. Later, in the study, the ratio dropped to five false positives to every true positive.

Researchers for the Swedish Two County study noted that in North America only one in every six to ten breast biopsies would be positive for cancer. The rate of false positives is much higher in North America than in Europe. In Sweden for example, if you have a breast biopsy, there is a 50 to 75 percent chance it will be cancer, whereas in North America, there is about ten to 20 percent chance it will be cancer.

3. **FALSE NEGATIVES:** This means your mammogram shows up no sign of cancer, but there is a cancer. Women are thus falsely reassured and may delay seeking treatment. The percentage of false negatives is not known, but may be as high as ten to 15 percent, particularly in younger women.

Paradoxically, according to Dr. Baines, a false negative is more likely to occur with larger cancers.

In younger women, cancers can occur in the intervals between screenings, and these are usually fast growing cancers (about 20 percent of breast cancers). Mammograms are unlikely to be able to detect these kinds of cancer, which can sometimes double in size in 21 days.

4. **OVERDIAGNOSIS OF CANCER: Dr. Philip Prorok, Chief of The Screening Section of the National Cancer Institute**, has stated that mass screening tends to detect mainly cancer in the dormant stage ("in situ" or "non invasive"). These cancers, he says, are known to be slow growing and have a better prognosis, screening or no screening. This means, according to Dr. Prorok, that screening programs have a built in bias to look as though they improve survival rates.

Fast growing breast cancers, which can double in size rapidly, are the ones most likely to be missed by screening, especially for women in the 40 to 49 age group.

Mammograms can detect cancers as small as one half centimetre (1/4 of a inch) Regular self exam can detect lumps at about one centimetre size (1/2 of a inch) But, says Prorok, "When a mammogram uncovers a very tiny tumour... it's not possible to know if it would have gone onto be a killing cancer, never surfaced, or even surfaced as a kind of cancer that could have even treated very well even at that point."

WHAT ARE THE CRITICS OF ROUTINE MAMMOGRAPHY SAYING ?

"If it should turn out that the **type** of cancer (fast or slow growing) is more important that the **when** it is diagnosed," says the **Boston Women's Health Collective**, "we will need to rethink our whole approach to cancer detection and treatment."

Dr. John Bailar III says that "virtually all experts conclude that an asymptomatic woman who is at least 50 years old will benefit from regular breast cancer screening by a combination of mammography and careful physical examination."

However, Dr. Bailar is opposed to screening for women under 50. Costs of screening, he says, "include not only the monetary costs, but also the anxiety, unnecessary biopsies, grave diagnostic delays from false negative reports, loss of faith in future screening examinations (and perhaps other medical care) resulting from the frequent false positive reports, and vigorous treatment of lesions that look bad under a microscope but are not life threatening, and would have been left alone in the absence of screening (**JAMA**, Mar.11/88)."

Dr. Charles Wright said in an article in the Medical Post (Feb.6/90). "Women are clamouring for mammograms because of the hype created around the benefits of mammography." He estimated that the Saskatchewan screening mammogram program would save the lives of five women per year at the cost of about 1.25 million dollars a year per life saved.

Dr. Wright wrote in **Surgery** (Oct/86) magazine. "On the positive side of the balance sheet there is a marginal reduction in deaths from breast cancer in older women... Negative factors include the false positive results leading to unnecessary operations, the false negative results that lead to an inappropriate reassurance, the raised level of anxiety in the female population and the tiny but real risk of radiation induced cancers."

At the 1988 annual meeting of **The Irish College of General Practitioners**, **Dr. Skrabenek** caused a furore when he claimed that screening had become a vast and profitable industry for radiologists.

Dr. Skrabenek said in article on medical ethics in **The Lancet Medical Journal** (May 21/88). "If individual "guinea pigs" must be protected from excessive research zeal by having to be informed about the inherent risks, the same imperative should apply with even greater force when whole populations of healthy people are put at risk by screening."

Dr. Maureen Roberts was the clinical director of **The Edinburgh Breast Screening Project** from 1979 until her death from breast cancer in June 1989. Her letter appeared in **The British Medical Journal** after her death.

She poses the question: "What can screening actually achieve? Two randomized trials, The Health Insurance Plan and the Swedish two county trail, showed a reduction in mortality [death rate] of 30 percent in women offered screening. Other trials such as the Malmo, United Kingdom and Edinburgh trails found a non-significant reduction in mortality. We cannot ignore them and it is not enough to say that our techniques were not good enough a few years ago but are adequate now. We all know that mammography is an unsuitable screening test, it is technologically difficult to perform, the pictures are difficult to interpret, it has a high false positive rate, and we don't know how often to carry it out. We can no longer ignore the possibility that screening may not reduce mortality in women of any age, however disappointing that may be."

Dr. Roberts suggests that the final decision should be left to women and that:

"A truthful account of the facts be made available to the public and the individual patient. It will not be what they want to hear. They should be told that the test is to detect breast cancer while it is still small; that we don't know how much it can influence mortality, but there is a 30 percent chance (though maybe much less) that it may prolong life; that the test does not detect all cancers, some of which may appear between screenings, and that it cannot predict whether breast cancer will develop in the future. In addition, we do not know how to treat breast cancer. There is no successful treatment; different surgeons will carry out different procedures... (Those with normal mammograms) can feel suitably reassured except that they must remember that they can develop the disease at any time; screening is not prevention."

ANOTHER VIEW

Dr. Robert's colleague **Dr. Jocelyn Chamberlain** in a response to her letter says:

"During the next 20 years, I, in my late 50's stand a one in forty chance of dying from breast cancer. If screened from age 50 onward I may be able to reduce this risk to one in 55. To me this reduction is worth the slight inconvenience of going for a mammography every few years; of having a one in 14 chance of being referred and a one in 170 chance of having a benign biopsy (both of which have happened to me and were more irritating than alarming); and even of artificially increasing my chance of breast cancer diagnosis. On what evidence do you base your claim that "women will not want to hear" these facts and, by implication, will not want to avail themselves of the protection which screening offers? To me it seems a mildly inconvenient but sensible precaution in the same league, albeit at a greater cost, as a cholera or typhoid immunisation before a foreign trip. In summary, therefore, I believe that breast screening is good for women, though perhaps not for the taxpayer."

THE LARGE SCREENING PROGRAM IN ONTARIO

In Ontario, a 15 million dollar program for screening women over age 50 was started in August 1990. The objective of the program is to screen 70 percent of women aged 50 to 64 every two years until their 70th birthday. This project will involve an estimated 300,000 women per year.

Advocates of this program point out that 300 lives per year might be saved based on the studies mentioned above.

Dr. Aileen Clarke, Cancer Co-ordinator for the province of Ontario and chief of epidemiology at the **Ontario Cancer Treatment and Research Foundation**, points out in a July 1990 letter that:

"In the absence of an organized province wide program, women who will not benefit from mammography will receive mammography, possibly of a questionable quality, and women who would benefit from mammography (older and less likely to request screening) will not necessarily be aware of its value."

The number of mammograms done in Ontario, Dr. Clarke says, had risen from 70,000 in 1983 to 243,000 in 1989 at a cost of more than 12 million dollars. "More than half of these mammograms were performed in women under the age of 50, for which there is questionable evidence as to whether screening mammography is effective in reducing mortality... Unless an organized program for breast screening for women age 50 to 60 years is implemented in Ontario, it is estimated that only 30 percent of women who will benefit from screening will be screened and that reduction in mortality will be in the order of 80 lives saved per year as opposed to 300."

Dr. Rosalie Bertell is against this screening program. By 1995, she calculates that X-ray exposure from this program will result in between 15 and 40 cancers, of which seven to 18 will be fatal. Most of these cancers will not appear until after age 70 years, when the women are no longer in the screening program. She claims the other cancers would be detected by a physician or the woman herself.

Dr. Bertell suggests that women who start in the program should complete it so that these radiation induced cancers won't be missed.

In addition, Dr. Bertell estimates that 10,000 women will have false positives and have to be retested, and about 163 women will have unnecessary surgery due to the program. True, she says, 307 will not die of breast cancer but less than three percent (eight or nine women) would be due exclusively to the program. The other breast cancers would be detected by a physician or the woman herself.

She is also concerned that X-ray exposure is known to promote or accelerate cancers which are hereditary and are caused by other environmental or life style carcinogens. "How many tumours are promoted or accelerated will be learned from the experiment on Canadian women," says Dr. Bertell.

"Since the Hippocratic oath demands that physicians at least "do no harm," says Dr. Bertell, "I assume the breast mammography program had considered the serious problem of increasing breast cancer incidence rate by X-ray exposure as a method of reducing the overall breast cancer death rate."

"As a woman, I am not ready to trade off lives in order to improve fatality records. Every breast cancer and every surgery is tragic. Every life is precious and I do not believe physicians can justify killing some women to "save" other women."

British Columbia is the only province that is screening women 40 to 49 years with yearly mammograms. Alberta and Saskatchewan have screening programs for women age 50 and over, accompanied by physical exams.

THE POLITICS OF BREAST CANCER RESEARCH

In the U.S. research for AIDS has received 1.28 billion dollars while research on breast cancer only 90.2 million. **Virginia Soffer**, founder of the **Breast Cancer Action** group in Burlington, Vermont, puts it this way, "This is a major feminist issue, and people haven't caught onto that. If one in nine men had testicle cancer and their testicles were being cut off, there would be an outcry, you can be sure, and something would be done (**Insight**, Feb/92)."

Many cancer research dollars are spent on researching new drugs for treatment and not on prevention. **Dr. Susan Love**, **Director of the Breast Clinic** at the **University of California School of Medicine**, called for more research into the possible promoters of breast cancer such as diet, birth control pills and hormones. "We need to invest our dollars in promising new leads in genetics and immunology, not just in new ways of giving chemotherapy." Love also maintains that women with breast cancer need to be included in the development of study design and decisions about which trials should be funded.

Important environmental causes of breast cancer are just beginning to be studied. **Pat Kelly**, founder of the Breast Cancer Action group in Canada, says it's not surprising that so little is known about the environmental co-factors. The total research budget for breast cancer research in Canada in 1991-2 was less than four million dollars.

Fortunately, women are organizing themselves at a grass roots level in groups such as Breast Cancer Action, to educate themselves about cancer prevention, detection and treatments and to lobby politicians about funding cancer research and future directions.

WHAT'S A WOMEN TO DO ?

1. **HIGH RISK GROUPS:** If you are in a high risk group, you may want to consider having regular mammograms, especially after age 50. The U.S. **Preventive Services Task Force** suggests that so called high risk women start mammograms at age 35 despite the absence of good evidence.

The major risk factors for breast cancer are if you have a positive family history (a mother or sister who had breast cancer before menopause) or if you have already had breast cancer, or if you are over 50.

Other minor risk factors, such as no children or late childbirth, early onset of periods, or late menopause etc. are not of great significance, since 75 percent of women who get breast cancer do not have these risk factors nor do they have a positive family history.

A detailed study of 2,000 women is going on in three major centers in the U.S. and may give more information about specific risk factors.

2. **THYROID FUNCTION AND IODINE:** Rates of breast cancer are high in developed countries with the exception of Japan. Since breast cancer is known to be higher in countries where iodine content of soil and water is low, some believe the high level of iodine in seaweeds consumed by Japanese women may have a protective feature, but this has not yet been proven.

Breast cancer is often associated with low levels of thyroid hormones, or hypothyroidism. However, thyroid hormone blood levels may be normal, but functioning at suboptimal levels. Basal body temperature below 97.6F on a regular basis combined with symptoms of low metabolism may indicate the thyroid is not functioning well (see chart for information on how to take the basal body temperature correctly).

In his twenty years of research into fibrocystic breast disease, **Dr. William Ghent**, professor of surgery at **Queen's University** in Kingston, Ontario, has found that a special form of non-toxic diatomic iodine reduces the incidence of breast cancer in women who take this preparation on a regular basis. His results will be published in the **Canadian Journal of Surgery** in Oct/93 (see chapter on cystic breast disease).

3. **DIET AND BREAST CANCER:** A diet high in animal fats and dairy products is associated with an elevated risk of breast cancer.

The countries with the highest breast cancer rates are those with the highest rate of fat consumption. A large scale study sponsored by The National Cancer Institute is studying 15,000 women on normal diets and 15,000 women on a 20 percent fat diet and will compare their rates of breast cancer. The results will be ready between 1995 and 97.

Many women's groups feel that although the low fat diet has not been conclusively proven, it makes sense to reduce fat for other health reasons as well.

The first **National Conference on Diet and Breast Cancer** called for government and industry to lower the fat content of food. The conference said that medical doctors are not trained in nutrition, and their attitude towards diet and breast cancer is often one of "passive neglect."

There is much you can do to improve your diet right now. The best cancer preventive diet is one that emphasizes fresh fruits and vegetables, whole grains and fish and poultry and avoids sugar, excess fat, dairy and red meat.

There is evidence to suggest that eating foods high in vitamins A, C, E, and selenium lowers cancer risk. As well, research indicates that taking extra betacarotene and vitamin-C help protect against cancer.

Women should limit alcohol consumption, since women who drink two glasses of alcohol a day have a higher rate of breast cancer than non-drinkers.

4. **ENVIRONMENT AND BREAST CANCER:** As mentioned earlier, several studies have indicated that women with breast cancer tend to have higher levels of organochlorines in their breast tissues than women who do not have breast cancer.

Greenpeace has just published a report (Nov/92) entitled, **Breast Cancer and the Environment: The Chlorine Connection**.

Organochlorines are highly persistent and toxic substances, like DDT, PCP and dioxin plus literally thousands of other chemicals whose effects have not yet been studied. These chemicals are used to make PVC plastics, solvents, pesticides, refrigerants, and in the pulp and paper industry. These same chemicals persist in meat and dairy products. This may be the real reason that high fat diets lead to increased breast cancer risk.

"The Cancer Establishment has trivialized evidence that links increasing rates of cancer, including breast cancer, with exposure to cancer causing industrial chemicals and radiation that now permeate our environment, food, water, air and workplace." says **Dr. Samuel Epstein**, professor of occupational and environmental medicine at the **University of Illinois School of Public Health** and author of **THE POLITICS OF CANCER**, in his introduction to the Greenpeace report.

Dr. Epstein says that the U.S. National Cancer Institute has adopted a blame the victim mentality (concentrating too much on personal habits like dietary fat and too little on the avoidable carcinogens that accumulate in fat) and that preventive research is being neglected in favour of a futile and lucrative quest for cures (**International Journal of Health Services**, vol 22-3/92).

Dr. Epstein believes that the pesticides in foods, and estrogens in meat, not their fat content, are responsible for the higher rates of cancer. "Our diets are laden with a wide variety of carcinogens," says Epstein, "many of which have been shown to induce breast cancer in experimental animals."

Greenpeace researcher **Joe Thornton** says that "stopping organochlorine pollution of the environment and our bodies should be a priority of breast cancer prevention strategies."

Women should urgently support the movement to phase out chlorine as well as to buy only unbleached paper products and tampons.

5. **RADIATION AND BREAST CANCER:** In 1987, researcher Nancy Wertheimer reported finding an association between exposure to extremely low frequency electromagnetic fields (ELF) and breast cancer.

Exposure to ELF comes from computers, water beds, electric blankets. See the chapter on health hazards of computers to find out how to protect yourself from ELF.

Another important type of radiation exposure comes from X-rays and nuclear fallout pollution such as Chernobyl.

In 1945, the first atomic bomb was exploded in New Mexico, and the second and third were dropped on Hiroshima and Nagasaki. Women born around that time, (now in their 50's) were also exposed to repeated fallout from nuclear weapons testing. Between 1946 and 1958, 109 nuclear weapons were detonated over the Pacific Islands.

As Dr. Rosalie Bertell points out, "women who were in their 20's at the time of this testing comprise the largest group of today's breast cancer victims... If the root of today's breast cancer epidemic lies in above ground nuclear testing, a source of further exposure to radiation may only intensify the problem."

Dr. Bertell also points out that between 1951 and 1963, 214 bombs were detonated in the Nevada desert. "Radioactive debris from these tests drifted eastward; and measurable amounts of radioactivity were found in food sources in the U.S. and Canada. Women born in 1951 are just now approaching their 40's and will soon be approaching a high risk age (**Mothering**, summer/92)."

"Certainly," says Dr. Bertell, "since babies born in the 40's and 50's have become a generation of men and women at risk for many diseases such as AIDS, toxic shock syndrome, and chronic fatigue, the password ought to be **CAUTION.**

Women should avoid all unnecessary X-rays and consider carefully the risk of adding more radiation from mammograms, especially if you have had a lot of X-ray exposure in the past.

6. **HORMONES AND BREAST CANCER:** Four well designed studies have shown a link between the birth control pill and breast cancer, especially for women who used the higher dose pills and for women who used the pill longer than eight years or eight years before their first pregnancy. Other studies do not confirm this connection.

Hormone replacement therapy (HRT) after menopause is probably linked to an increased risk of breast cancer, but most researchers think this is small, especially when weighed against possible benefits. However, some doctors feel that the risks of breast cancer are being underestimated. They feel that HRT is one of the main reasons that the breast cancer rate for women over 50 is on the rise.

Recently, a long-term U.S. study published in the **New England Journal of Medicine** (Jun/95), showed that women receiving HRT or ERT for 6 or more years beyond menopause had a 40 percent increase in breast cancer risk. Commented the principal author of the study, **Dr. Graham Colditz**: "If a woman uses [hormones] long-term and stops, within two years, the risk goes back to that of a woman who never used the hormones."

Women have now been exposed to both long-term hormone treatment in the form of the birth control pill and long-term hormone treatment in the form of estrogen replacement. No one really knows what the combined effect might be on the intricate workings of the female reproductive system. There are several ongoing studies to evaluate that specific interaction. The results won't be available for ten to 20 years.

Post-menopausal women who are moderately overweight may have a slightly higher risk of breast cancer because of the increased amount of estrogen hormone produced by fat tissues.

Women exposed to DES during pregnancy have an increased risk of breast cancer 20 years after exposure.

SPECIAL NOTE, TAMOXIFEN IS NOT PREVENTION: With much fanfare, on April 29, 1992, the U.S. National Cancer Institute launched a study that will enrol 16,000 women over the course of the next two years in the U.S. and Canada. Eligible women will include those at high risk defined as age 60 or over, or age 35 with a positive family history. Only half the women will receive tamoxifen, the other half will receive a placebo.

Tamoxifen is an anti-cancer, anti-estrogen drug. Side effects such as hot flashes, nausea, and vomiting occur in 25 percent of women taking tamoxifen. Swollen ankles, irregular bleeding, vaginal discharge and skin rash occur less commonly. There can also be changes in the eye and liver enzymes.

In fact, in England, there have been **five deaths** from liver disease linked to tamoxifen. These deaths prompted Britain's **Medical Research Council** to refuse to back the tamoxifen trial. Four cases of liver failure have been linked to the drug, three of which were fatal. Five women developed hepatitis and one of these has died. Eleven other women suffered from liver complications and 15 more had abnormalities of their blood cells. These potential side effects are not mentioned in the information sheet for women participating in the trial.

Clearly this is not a drug to be given lightly to healthy women and clearly it has nothing to do with prevention whatsoever. **Dr. Adriane Fugh-Berman**, Director of **The National Women's Health Network**, and **Dr. Samuel Epstein** feel the side effects of tamoxifen are too toxic for a healthy population (The Lancet, 1992). **They pose the question: "is this disease prevention or disease substitution?"**

7. **BREAST SELF EXAM (BSE):** "Very few women examine themselves and that includes women physicians," says Dr. Susan Love, "The reason is they're scared to find a lump."

The attitude with which you perform **BSE** is important. A study by a woman psychologist revealed that women who admitted they were afraid of discovering breast cancer, **believing it was beyond their control anyway**, were much less successful in detecting lumps than women with positive attitudes.

Dr. Baines says that women should only do BSE regularly but only from age 40 onwards:

A. If they want to.

B. If they have been taught well by a doctor or nurse.

C. If they have these instructions repeated every year.

Dr. Baines believes it is not good enough to hand a woman a pamphlet on BSE and expect her to learn competent BSE from it. She feels that no BSE is better than sloppily done BSE.

Dr. Baines emphasizes that BSE in women under age 40 is unwarranted because too many lumps are found and too many unnecessary biopsies may result.

Dr. Love believes that BSE has been wrongly presented to women. "The accent," she says, "should be on **not** finding anything. The idea is not to look for lumps but to familiarize yourself with your breasts in their normal state so you'll notice anything different."

8. **LEARN HOW TO ACCURATELY EXAMINE YOUR OWN BREASTS USING THE MAMMACARE LEARNING SYSTEM:** The biggest obstacle to women is that they don't know what they are feeling for when they do a breast self exam. This kit addresses this problem head on. It is the result of a seven year research project at the **University of Florida**, partially funded by the U.S. National Cancer Institute.

Reasoned researcher **Dr. Pennypacker**, "If you could teach fingers to read braille, you could teach fingers to detect lumps smaller than golf balls."

In fact, women can easily learn to feel lumps as small as peas. The Mammacare kit consists of a lifelike silicone breast with five types of lumps in it, a 45 minute video, and a 30 page manual. It is designed to teach you the life long skill of good breast exam. Learning this skill may be one of the most valuable investments you make in your health.

Untrained woman can detect lumps that are one and half inches in diameter, (4 cm) women trained in the usual BSE can detect lumps three quarters of an inch (2 cm) in diameter and woman trained in this technique can detect lumps between one quarter and three eights in diameter (between .3 cm and one cm). In fact, women trained in this method are capable of developing a greater sensitivity than doctors in detecting lumps. One study showed the women's sensitivity to be 59 percent versus 44 percent for the doctors.

9. **ANNUAL PHYSICAL EXAM OF THE BREAST:** This cannot be stressed enough. Have your breasts thoroughly examined once a year by a doctor or nurse that has been competently trained in breast examination.

Mammacare has also developed a kit to train physicians in correct breast exam, a skill that is often not taught adequately in medical school.

10. **EMOTIONAL DEFENSE:** The best defense is to learn to express your emotions, especially anger and to avoid investing all your energy in one person or one project. It is also important to learn how to overcome depression and negative emotions.

In general, I have noticed that breast cancer patients are "too nice." They sacrifice their own needs and even their own health to look after everyone else's needs. They nourish everyone, except themselves. Writer **Susan Gibson** feels that breast cancer gave her an unparalleled opportunity to break out of a self-defeating life pattern and begin anew. She feels that women have been socially and culturally trained to serve others and that this "servers' disease syndrome" is one of the root causes of breast cancer.

Dr. Lawrence Le Shan, a psychologist who has worked with cancer patients for over 35 years (author of two highly recommended books, **YOU CAN FIGHT FOR YOUR LIFE; EMOTIONAL FACTORS IN THE TREATMENT OF CANCER** and **CANCER AS A TURNING POINT**) has studied the emotional and mental attitudes of cancer patients and found:

A: A loss of a sense of purpose of life had occurred.

B: The individual had difficulty expressing anger and tended to suppress hostile feelings.

C: There were unresolved feelings around the death of a parent.

D: The person was not involved in meaningful work that excited them or inspired them.

FUTURE TRENDS

Although controlled trials have not proven the benefit of self exam, women aged 40 or over should be taught good self exam using the Mammacare model. Learning occurs best in small groups, independent from cancer societies, in an educational context that reduces fears around both breast self exam and breast cancer, provides information about cancer prevention and empowers women in getting to know their own bodies. One such project, the **Burlington Breast Cancer Support Group**, successfully trained 800 women, and was unable to meet the demand. Similar types of projects are recommended by the **Status of Women** report, **Breast Cancer, The Unanswered Questions**. As Pat Kelly, breast cancer activist, commented. "Too many doctors assume that breast self exam is just this feeble silly thing that women are doing." Instead family doctors could be promoting competent breast self exam both as a screening and educational tool.

Only 25 percent of women have predictable breast cancer risk factors. A more important risk factor may be increasing age. A bigger risk factor may be chemical residues in our fatty tissues, accumulating over time as well as chronic exposure to low levels of radioactivity both from nuclear testing and nuclear spills.

"Screening mammography is not the answer," says Dr. John Bailar, "After 40 years and countless billions of dollars, we have made progress, but not much. We must stop, re-examine and start in a new direction. It's time to get serious about the prevention of cancer.

SUGGESTED READING

Dr. Lawrence Le Shan, is the author of two highly recommended books, **YOU CAN FIGHT FOR YOUR LIFE; EMOTIONAL FACTORS IN THE TREATMENT OF CANCER** and **CANCER AS A TURNING POINT**.

DR. SUSAN LOVE'S BREAST BOOK, by **Dr. Susan Love** (Addison Wesley 1990). This is a warm compassionate book on all aspects of breast related concerns from size and sensitivity to lumps and cancer. **Esther Rome**, of the Boston Women's Health Collective disagrees with Dr. Love's attitude toward plastic surgery but says, "...There is no other lay book that explains breast problems, cancer and treatments with such clarity and detail." (Women's Review of Books).

BREAST CANCER, BREAST HEALTH, The Wise Woman Way, by **Susun Weed** (Ashtree Publishing, 1996). This book focuses on our inherent wisdom and resiliency as woman and in the true prevention of environmental and lifestyle risks. A truly revolutionary book that challenges the victim consciousness surrounding breast cancer prevention, diagnosis and treatment.

A GUIDE TO UNCONVENTIONAL CANCER THERAPIES, by **The Ontario Breast Cancer Exchange Program**, is an excellent compendium of alternative breast cancer therapies. 905-727-3300.

BREAST CANCER, What You Should Know (But May Not Be Told), by **Steven Austin** and **Cathy Hitchcock** (Prima Publishing, 1994). Written by a naturopathic physician and his wife who had breast cancer, this book looks at all your options both natural and conventional.

HOW TO PREVENT BREAST CANCER, by **Ross** and **Taffy Pelton** and **Vinton Vint** (Fireside, 1995). A lifestyle guide for the prevention of breast cancer and its reoccurence.

YOU CAN PREVENT BREAST CANCER, by **Harvey Diamond** (Promotion, 1996). This book emphasizes diet and lymphatic drainage.

THE BREAST BOOK: The Essential Guide to Breast Care and Breast Health, by **Dr. Miriam Stoppard** (Random House, 1996).

RELATIVE RISK LIVING WITH A FAMILY HISTORY OF BREAST CANCER, by **Nancy C. Baker**. This book explains what to do if your mother or sister or aunt has breast cancer.

MAMMOGRAPHY SCREENING: A DECISION MAKING GUIDE, by **Mary Ann Napoli** (1990) is available for $5.00 from **Center for Medical Consumers** This is an excellent 12 page booklet reviewing the pros and cons of screening and how to choose a mammogram facility with high standards.

THE CENTER FOR MEDICAL CONSUMERS, 237 Thompson St, New York, NY, 10012.

The center is a non-profit public interest organization that houses the first medical library specifically designed for lay person and supports itself with a monthly newsletter called **HEALTH FACTS**, that reviews health issues. The cost is $21.00 U.S. a year. Back issues are also available.

MAMMACARE, Box 15748, Gainesville, FL, 32602.

Mammacare is available for $59.50 plus $4.50 shipping. In the U.S. 1-800-626-2273, in Canada 904-375-0607.

BREAST CANCER ACTION PO Box 4332, Stn E, Ottawa, ON. 613-232-3117 or Fax: 613-788-4378.

The group can tell you where to obtain the Status of Women report entitled, **Breast Cancer: Unanswered Questions.** The parent group is located in the U.S. at PO Box 460185, San Francisco, CA, 94146. 415-922-8279.

GREENPEACE, 185 Spadina, Toronto, ON, M5T 2C6. 416-345-8408.

Greenpeace can send you their report (Nov/92) entitled, **Breast Cancer and the Environment: The Chlorine Connection**. The U.S. address is, 1017 West Jackson, Chicago, IL, 60607. 312-666-3305.

BREAST CANCER: WHAT ARE THE RISKS ?

You've heard or read the numbers: A woman has a one in nine chance of developing breast cancer.

A statistic that has driven fear into the hearts of many women. The problem is you probably don't have the full story. When we talk about a one in nine risk, we're talking about the risk a woman has of developing cancer at the end of her lifetime.

In other words, at different ages women have different risks for developing breast cancer. As age increases, the risk for developing breast cancer rises. To further clarify matters, a recent study in the **Journal of the National Cancer Institute** (June 2/93) breaks down the numbers, specifying the varying risks for varying ages.

Age of a Healthy, Cancer Free Woman	Risk of Breast Cancer
20	1 in 2,500
30	1 in 233
40	1 in 63
50	1 in 41
60	1 in 28
70	1 in 24
80	1 in 16
95	1 in 8

As you can see, the risk of developing breast cancer is far from negligible. But in the absence of other factors, your risk rises to a significant level only as you get up in years, Also, despite what you read elsewhere, remember that the risk of dying of of breast cancer hasn't increased by a great deal in the last 20 years. In 1970 the risk of dying of breast cancer in the course of one's lifetime was 1 in 30. Today it is 1 in 28.

Taken from the **People's Medical Society** newsletter, October, 1993.

Section Seven:
Vital Women's Problems

Life Can Be A Drag Without Enough Iron 244

Exploring The Inside Of Your Uterus............................. 249

Those Annoying Varicose Veins.. 254

Beauty With Conscience.. 258

The Good News About Gallstones And Women 261

Lesbian Health Care.. 267

Life Can Be A Drag Without Enough Iron

Kathy, a 31-year-old mother of two preschool children, felt tired all the time. She wondered if something was wrong with her. She started swimming three times a week, but only felt worse. At first, her doctor told her that her fatigue was inevitable with two young kids. At her insistence, her doctor finally did blood tests, and found her to be anemic due to low iron levels in her blood. She began to pay special attention to the sources of iron in her diet, and took iron supplements for six months. Within three weeks, she felt much better, and within six weeks her energy level had returned to what it had been before the two pregnancies. She was astonished at the difference that iron had made in her life.

This is not an unusual story. In fact, an estimated **one in three** women are anemic due to iron deficiency.

Iron is the real workhorse of your body. It transports oxygen from your lungs to each and every cell of your body. Iron is one element your body cannot make on its own. All the iron you need has to be ingested through food or supplements.

Iron is used to make the hemoglobin molecule, which is the main constituent of red blood cells. Hemoglobin is composed of an iron containing compound (heme), which gives red blood cells their colour; and a protein (globin). Three hundred million hemoglobin molecules make up every red blood cell, and are incessantly at work picking up oxygen from your lungs and carrying it to all the tissues and organs of your body.

In spite of the tremendous importance of iron to your sense of well-being, you don't die from a lack of iron. Even with only 20 percent of your normal hemoglobin, you can still walk, although you may be literally dragging yourself around due to lack of oxygen in your tissues.

HOW IRON IS TAKEN INTO THE BODY AND STORED

Of the iron that you take in through food, only five to ten percent is absorbed. This iron is absorbed in the upper part of your small intestine. If you are low in iron, the percentage of iron absorbed goes up. Iron is relatively difficult to absorb, because your body protects itself from the harmful effects of absorbing too much iron.

After the iron is absorbed, it is bound to a protein in your blood, and transported to your bone marrow to be used in making red blood cells. Your body conserves iron carefully and reuses most of the iron from the breakdown of red blood cells to make new ones. Since the life of a red blood cell is about 120 days, two hundred thousand million new red blood cells have to be made every day.

A reserve of iron is stored in your bone marrow, liver and spleen. This stored iron is like a spare tire. It functions as an emergency reservoir for when you need extra iron.

SYMPTOMS OF IRON DEFICIENCY OR ANEMIA

If you have too little iron in your body and your iron reserves are used up, you can develop anemia or "poor blood". The red blood cells become thin and pale and poorly filled with hemoglobin. The number of red blood cells in your blood goes down. The hemoglobin, which normally makes up between 120 and 160 grams per 1,000 cc of blood also decreases.

Symptoms of iron deficiency can affect every body system. However, they usually develop slowly over time and may be hard to pinpoint. The most common symptoms you might experience are fatigue, weakness, drowsiness, palpitations and light-headedness.

Other symptoms include depression and irritability, headache, ringing in the ears, black spots before the eyes, shortness of breath, chest pain, rapid heart rate, swelling of the ankles, muscle weakness, numbness and tingling in the hands or feet, increased sensitivity to cold, and decreased tolerance to exercise.

Gastrointestinal complaints can include loss of appetite, heartburn, nausea, painful swallowing, and constipation. Menstrual disturbances are also very common with iron deficiency anemias. Your periods can become heavy, irregular or stop altogether.

Rarely you can experience bizarre food cravings for substances such as ice, clay or cornstarch.

In severe anemia (hemoglobin less than 70 grams per litre of blood) the inside of the lower eyelid is a pearly white colour, and there is no colour in the creases in the palm of the hand. The hair and nails are brittle, the tongue smooth, the nails spoon shaped and the corners of the mouth cracked.

REASONS FOR IRON DEFICIENCY

Anemia due to low iron can result from any or all of the following factors that cause either not enough iron to go into your body or too much iron to leave your body.

1. **What you eat is low in iron.**

2. **You have problems absorbing iron from your food.**

Causes of poor absorption include dietary factors, poor digestion, chronic diarrhea, malabsorption syndrome and following a partial or complete gastrectomy.

3. **You lose too much blood.**

Women are particularly vulnerable to increased blood loss, because they bleed every month at their period. In addition to losing about one-tenth of a cup of blood per period, they lose anywhere from one-half to one cup of blood at childbirth. If they are having heavy periods, the blood loss can be as high as a half cup per period. Women can also become anemic around menopause if they have repeated heavy or prolonged periods.

Blood loss can also come from the stomach or intestines, as for example with bleeding ulcers or bleeding hemorrhoids. This bleeding can either be obvious (vomiting blood or passing black, tarry stools) or hidden (only found on microscopic examination of the stool).

The blood loss from all these causes can add up, and produce an iron deficiency that develops slowly over months or years.

Alternatively, anemia can quickly develop if you lose a lot of blood over a short period of time.

NOT ALL ANEMIAS ARE CAUSED BY LOW IRON

Not all anemias are caused by low iron. Low hemoglobin levels can be caused by a lack of certain vitamins such as B-12 or folic acid. Deficiencies of B-6 or zinc can also lead to an anemia which mimics iron deficiency anemia.

Afro-Americans normally have a hemoglobin which is 100 grams lower than Caucasians, and thus may be needlessly treated for anemia.

Inherited abnormalities of the hemoglobin molecule itself can also cause anemia. Sickle cell anemia, which occurs mainly among Afro-Americans, may produce different kinds of anemia including iron deficiency anemia. Thalassemia minor causes anemia and is due to a defect in making hemoglobin. It was originally thought to be present mainly in Mediterranean people, but can occur in any race.

THE NORMAL "ANEMIA" OF PREGNANCY

In medical school, I was taught that pregnant women have increased iron requirements and should be taking iron supplements throughout their pregnancy.

In a well-nourished pregnant woman, there will normally be a doubling of her blood volume, resulting in a low hemoglobin, and a low blood iron. The blood iron binding capacity will normally rise during pregnancy. It now appears that these blood changes are a natural part of normal pregnancy and do not have to be treated.

In fact, the larger circulating blood volume may enable women to better withstand blood loss during childbirth.

Treatment of a low hemoglobin in a well-nourished pregnant woman is usually unnecessary, unless there is other evidence of iron deficiency such as a low iron stores (ferritin) or a decreased mean cell volume of the red blood cells.

Two well-designed studies showed a possible association between higher hemoglobins and an increased incidence of premature delivery and low birth weight babies.

TESTS FOR IRON DEFICIENCY ANEMIA

To find out whether you are anemic, the first screening test is usually the amount of hemoglobin present in your blood. To perform this test, blood is usually taken from a vein in your arm. Hemoglobin can also be determined, although with less accuracy, with blood taken by pinprick from your finger.

The hematocrit is another blood test which shows the percentage of cells, mostly red blood cells, that make up the total blood volume. This test is more accurate after you hemorrhage, because the hemoglobin will not change right away, and this test takes into account the blood volume lost. Some doctors feel it is a better screening test than hemoglobin.

These days the complete blood count is often done routinely. This includes the hemoglobin, the hematocrit, the white blood count and the red blood count, and other computer-calculated ratios of red blood cell volumes and concentrations.

A decrease in the ratio known as the mean red blood cell volume is also a very accurate indicator of anemia. If it falls, it means that the red cells have become smaller.

A blood smear, which involves looking at the red and white blood cells under the microscope, can also give a lot of information. In iron deficiency anemia, the red blood cells will appear paler, thinner and smaller. Their shapes can also be distorted.

If the hemoglobin or hematocrit is found to be low, the next step is to find the cause. It should not be assumed that every anemia is due to iron deficiency, although this is by far the most common cause in women. If an iron deficiency is suspected, blood iron levels as well as the iron binding capacity of the blood should be done. In iron deficiency anemia, the blood iron level is decreased and the iron binding capacity of the blood is increased.

Another very important test is that of the blood ferritin levels which is a measure of the amount of iron reserves in the body.

Some women have normal or low normal hemoglobins with lower than normal iron stores. In such cases, I advise increasing the iron in the diet, and the use of a natural iron supplement once or twice a day for six months.

If iron lack is found to be the cause of the anemia, it is still important to discuss with your doctor what caused the iron deficiency in the first place, and what you can do to prevent a reoccurrence of the problem.

Pregnant women should have a complete blood count at their first prenatal visit and monthly starting at about six months. The blood count should also be checked at the six week visit after the birth, especially if there was prolonged bleeding at or after the birth. Any women with chronic fatigue or prolonged or heavy periods should also have her complete blood count measured.

Iron deficiency anemias are usually treated with an iron rich diet combined with iron supplements.

DIETARY SOURCES OF IRON

Iron can be obtained in food through dark green leafy vegetables such as spinach, chard, turnip greens, kale, lamb's quarters, dandelion greens, broccoli, and alfalfa sprouts. The rule of thumb is that the darker green the colour of the vegetable, the higher in chlorophyll and thus in iron.

Beets, and fruits such as black cherries, blackberries, blueberries, apricots and bananas are also good sources of iron. Sunflower seeds, black beans, sesame seeds, whole grains and egg yolks are also excellent ways to increase the iron in your diet. Seaweeds such as dulse and nori (used to wrap sushi in) are also high in iron.

However, the iron found in red meat, poultry and fish is in a form that is easier to absorb than iron found in other foods. All red meats contain iron in high quantities, especially kidney, heart, liver and bone marrow.

Unfortunately, since liver concentrates the antibiotic and chemical residues used in raising livestock, it cannot be recommended. Bone marrow can be contaminated with lead and strontium 90. And of course, excessive consumption of red meat contributes to a higher risk of heart disease and cancer. A better choice would be poultry or seafood, which are excellent sources of iron (although not as high as beef), especially clams, oysters, sardines, and shrimp.

The iron added to processed white breads and cereals is difficult to absorb. It is best to eat 100 percent whole wheat bread, sugar free cereals and other whole grains.

The iron in your food can be increased by cooking in cast iron cookware. More iron can also be added to your diet by adding liquid chlorophyll to your drinking water.

Moreover, iron absorption is increased by the use of vitamin-C and hydrochloric acid taken with food. Gastric analysis of people with iron deficiency anemia showed that two-thirds of them had little or no hydrochloric acid being produced in the stomach to help digest food. It is not known whether the low HCL in the stomach is the cause of the iron deficiency anemia or the result of it.

A poor diet means less iron is absorbed. The tannic acid in tea interferes with iron absorption, so do the phosphates in soft drinks and some food preservatives such as EDTA. Excess calcium carbonate, certain antacids, and excess zinc are thought to interfere with iron absorption. Trace minerals such as copper and manganese appear to enhance the absorption of iron.

OTHER NATURAL SOURCES OF IRON

I have had good results treating anemia in women who can't take iron supplements with unrefined black strap molasses, one tablespoon in warm water daily. Women using molasses must brush their teeth carefully afterwards.

Blue green sea algae such as spirulina are high in iron, chlorophyll, B-12 and folic acid. Spirulina has been used in Japan to successfully treat iron deficiency anemias. It was most beneficial in cases related to long-term inadequate dietary intake of iron, but it also helped speed recovery from blood loss anemias. The blue green algae can be taken in the form of powder to be mixed with water or juice, or in tablet or capsule form.

Tea made from red raspberry leaves is high in iron. Another iron rich drink is made by blending turnip tops, beet greens, spinach, chard, kale, nettles, chickweed, dandelion leaves, etc. with water or juice.

NATURAL IRON SUPPLEMENTS

Floradix and **Fera** are two excellent liquid iron supplements that are derived from fruits and vegetables in a yeast base. These supplements are easy to take and they do not cause constipation.

Chelated natural iron supplements are available from many health food stores and do not usually cause constipation or heartburn. Chelation encloses the iron molecule in a large protein molecule to enhance absorption. Iron in this form appears to be well absorbed.

In Ottawa, **Kent McCloud**, biochemist and pharmacist, has developed a form of natural iron in capsules that is extremely well absorbed and non-constipating. It is very effective at building up the hemoglobin and I highly recommend it.

SYNTHETIC IRON SUPPLEMENTS

Synthetic iron is combined with various forms of iron salts. Any of the following iron salts can be prescribed:

1. **Ferrous fumarate** 200mg of this compound is equivalent to 65mg of elemental iron.

2. **Ferrous gluconate** 300mg is equivalent to 35mg of iron.

3. **Ferrous sulphate** 300mg equals 60mg of iron.

4. **Ferrous ascorbate** 225mg equals 33mg of iron.

5. **Ferrous succinate** 100mg equals 35mg of iron.

In my experience, I have found that ferrous sulphate is constipating and can cause stomach upset. Ferrous fumarate and ferrous gluconate are less constipating.

Iron supplements should also be taken with vitamin-C 500 to 1,000mg, or a glass of orange juice, at least once a day. Taking the iron with a good enzyme tablet or capsule (available at any health food store) will also increase the absorption of iron.

Vitamin-E should be taken six to 12 hours apart from the iron salts.

Iron is also available by injection, and this can be effective in exceptional cases of severe anemia. However, iron supplements taken by mouth will work just as well, only slower. The injections have many serious side effects, such as severe allergic reactions, and phlebitis. Leakage of the injection fluid will stain the skin permanently brown.

Some women experience nausea, heartburn, or constipation while taking iron supplements. This is why it is better to take the iron with meals, although the iron is best absorbed on an empty stomach. All synthetic iron supplements will turn the stools a pitch black colour.

THE DANGERS OF TOO MUCH IRON

Generally speaking, iron supplements should not be taken for longer than six months unless there is continued vaginal bleeding or repeated pregnancies. Excess iron can be harmful to your body. It is not usually possible to overdose on iron from food and natural sources.

In September 1992, Finnish researchers reported on a study that linked heart disease with the build-up of excess iron in the body. The research director, **Dr. Juuka Salonen**, advised men to cut down on their consumption of red meat and to consider giving blood several times a year.

Researcher **Dr. Jerome Sullivan** believes that the sex differences in heart disease (women rarely get heart disease before menopause) can be explained by the fact that menstruating women have lower iron stores due to the regular blood loss. Thus he advises most adult men and post-menopausal women to donate blood several times a year, and to avoid taking iron supplements. Premenopausal women should **not** donate blood, as this can cause anemia.

Excessive iron storage is also strongly associated with diabetes. Toronto physician **Dr. Paul Cutler** found that lowering iron stores by precipitating out the iron, through a series of intravenous injections known as **Chelation Therapy**, resulted in a dramatic improvement in the diabetes.

CONCLUSION

Since the iron in hemoglobin is the primary carrier of oxygen in your body, you should make sure that eating iron rich foods becomes an integral and enjoyable part of your lifestyle during the reproductive years. After menopause, you have less need for iron and usually no need for iron supplements.

Being ironclad means you retain vitality, and sparkle and literally the colour in your cheeks.

RESOURCES:

KENT MACLEOD, C/O NUTRICHEM PHARMACY, 1303 Richmond Rd, Ottawa, ON, K2B 7Y4. 1-800-363-6327 Fax: 1-800-465-2965. In the U.S. call: 613-820-4200.

Exploring The Inside Of Your Uterus

D-and-C is an abbreviation for one of the most common operations performed on women of all ages. The initials stand for dilatation and curettage, and refer to a short surgical operation usually done under general anesthesia, although it can be done under local anesthesia too. During this operation, the mouth of your womb, or cervix, is opened up or dilated to about the size of your thumb, and the lining of your womb is then scooped out with a spoon-like instrument called the curette. The D-and-C is usually used as a diagnostic tool. But it can also be used as a treatment.

A newer procedure known as **HYSTEROSCOPY** may eventually replace many of the uses of the D-and-C. Hysteroscopy refers to an operation in which a small lighted instrument (scope) is used to look inside your uterus (hystero). The hysteroscope is inserted through your vagina and cervix into your womb. A side connection to the scope allows a salt or sugar solution or carbon dioxide gas to flow into the uterus, expanding it and making it easier to see inside.

The advantage over the D-and-C is that the doctor can see the entire lining of the uterus. Since the cervix doesn't have to be opened up in hysteroscopy for diagnostic purposes, it can be done in the office, using no anesthetic or a local anesthetic. The hysteroscope can also be used for treating many conditions. For simple operations, little or no anesthesia is required. For longer and more complex operations, a general anesthetic is definitely required.

"Perhaps the most exciting advance in the field," says **Dr. Patrick Taylor**, a professor at the **University of British Columbia** who trains physicians in the use of the hysteroscope and who has co-authored a book on the subject, "is the ability to perform both minor and more complex operative procedures by hysteroscopic means." The use of a video camera attached to the hysteroscope allows the doctor to be guided by watching the picture of the inside of the uterus on a television screen during surgery, thus allowing even greater accuracy.

Currently, there is a shortage of physicians trained in this procedure in both Canada and the U.S. Many centers in both countries lack the necessary equipment.

Dr. Taylor adds that "No [doctor] should embark on a new surgical approach until they are trained and comfortable with both the technique and the management of any complications that may arise."

FOR DIAGNOSIS

ABNORMAL VAGINAL BLEEDING: Both hysteroscopy and D-and-C are commonly used to find the cause of excessive or irregular uterine bleeding.

This bleeding can occur at the time of your period or between periods. The bleeding can be caused by hormonal imbalance, overgrowth of the lining of the uterus (endometrial hyperplasia), polyps, fibroids or uncommonly, by cancer of the cervix or uterus.

If your doctor suspects a hormonal imbalance as the cause of your bleeding, he or she will try to time the D-and-C after the mid-point or ovulation phase of your cycle, in order to best analyze the influence of your hormones on the uterine lining. The hysteroscope exam is usually best performed earlier in the cycle before ovulation has occurred.

According to Dr. Patrick Taylor, the hysteroscope should replace the D-and-C as the best means to detect the cause of abnormal bleeding, since the D-and-C will miss up to 25 percent of the causes of abnormal bleeding.

UTERINE FIBROIDS AND POLYPS: Both the hysteroscope and the D-and-C can be used to diagnose uterine fibroids (benign tumours that grow outside, inside, or within the wall of the uterus) and to diagnose uterine and cervical polyps (tube-like protuberances from the uterine wall or cervix, also benign).

UTERINE CANCER AND ENDOMETRIAL HYPERPLASIA: The D-and-C is one definitive method for diagnosing uterine cancer or endometrial hyperplasia. The hysteroscope also allows biopsy of suspicious abnormalities of the uterine lining, but under direct visualization, contrasted to the "blind" D-and-C.

Thus either a D-and-C or hysteroscopy is recommended for menopausal women who have started to bleed after their periods have stopped, in order to rule out cancer of the uterus. Some are now advocating that hysteroscopy and directed biopsy replace the D-and-C altogether for the most accurate diagnosis.

Recently, a simple screening test for uterine cancer has now become widely available and can quickly be done in the office without any special instruments. This is known as endometrial aspiration and consists of taking a small piece of the uterine lining to send to the lab, using a tiny tube that is inserted through the cervix. If done with an instrument known as the pipelle, it can be painless. This screening test is particularly useful for post-menopausal women who are taking estrogen alone with their uterus intact.

INFERTILITY: As part of the infertility investigation, the hysteroscope is a valuable test that can confirm the nature of any problems with the structure of the uterus that were detected by X-ray.

CERVICAL ABNORMALITIES: The microcolpohysteroscope is a complex instrument that has the properties of both the telescope and the microscope. Suspicious areas in the cervix can be visualized and biopsied.

New data suggests that the use of this instrument may be as accurate as a Pap smear to detect abnormalities and early cancer of the cervix. It has the advantage over the colposcope of being able to see further up the cervical canal, and could save women from the need to undergo a cone biopsy. At present, this instrument is still in developmental stages.

UTERINE SCARS AND UTERINE SURGERY: Investigation of a uterine scar is sometimes necessary prior to vaginal birth following C-Section. Also, the amount of scarring in the uterine cavity following surgery can also be determined. Both can only be done through the hysteroscope.

TO FIND A MISPLACED IUD: The hysteroscope is the best procedure for this as through it the doctor can see if the IUD is embedded in the uterine wall. The D-and-C can also be used for this purpose, but the location and depth of the IUD cannot be seen.

FOR TREATMENT

PREGNANCY AND CHILDBIRTH COMPLICATIONS: The D-and-C can be used as an emergency treatment to stop excessive uterine bleeding.

After the birth of a baby, a D-and-C may be necessary to remove either part or the whole placenta (afterbirth) if it doesn't come out on its own. After an incomplete miscarriage, the D-and-C is also used to clean out the uterus and prevent infection or further bleeding.

THERAPEUTIC ABORTION: Usually a D-and-C is performed using a vacurette instead of a curette. A vacurette is a plastic or metal hollow tube with one or more holes near the tip. The vacurette is passed through the cervix after it has been dilated. The vacurette is connected to a suction machine. The machine is turned on as the vacurette is moved back and forth in the uterus. The suction makes a vibrating noise lasting for one minute. When the fetal material has all been removed, the vacurette is removed. Some doctors will then check with a curette to make sure the uterus is empty.

UTERINE CANCER: Hysteroscopy can also be used to detect, treat and monitor cancerous and precancerous conditions of the uterus as well as endometrial hyperplasia. This can be done with no cervical dilation and without local anesthesia most of the time. Therefore hysteroscopy is being advocated to replace D-and-C as a simpler, safer, and more accurate technique.

REMOVAL OF CERVICAL POLYPS AND SMALL UTERINE FIBROIDS: Hysteroscopy is more sensitive and accurate than D-and-C for removal of polyps and fibroids.

In a 1985 study, **Dr. Goldrath** and **Dr. Sherman** found that large numbers of polyps and fibroids were missed at the time of a blind D-and-C because "less than half of the uterine cavity had been curetted in 60 percent of the patients and less than a fourth of the cavity in 16 percent."

Dr. Herbert Goldfarb studied 300 women who had a D-and-C using the hysteroscope. He found that most patients still had their polyps after D-and-C.

Small fibroids under one or two cm in size or that have a stalk or that are protruding into the uterine cavity can be easily removed through the hysteroscope. Fibroids between 2.5 cm and five cm can be removed the same way after they have been shrunk through the use of medication (see GNRH drugs). Fibroids larger than five cm must be shrunk medically, and then removed in two steps.

In the case of removal of small fibroids causing bleeding, 50 to 87 percent of women return to normal menstruation after the hysteroscopic operation. If the uterus is larger than a 14-week pregnancy size, than hysteroscopic removal cannot be done.

ENDOMETRIAL ABLATION: This means destroying the uterine lining permanently. This treatment is sometimes used as a last resort for severe bleeding problems (see details in chapter on hysterectomy).

TO REMOVE A MISPLACED IUD: Both D-and-C and hysteroscope can be used to perform this job, but again the hysteroscope is more accurate.

PREPARATION FOR A DIAGNOSTIC OR SIMPLE OPERATIVE HYSTEROSCOPY WITH NO OR LOCAL ANESTHETIC

If the procedure is done in the office or in the out-patient department, a woman may be given a pain killer (like motrin) one hour before the exam to reduce cramping afterwards. There is usually no need for an anesthetic, since the cervix is not being dilated, but should a woman feel uncomfortable, the doctor should have available a local anesthetic which can be injected into the cervical area. A local anesthetic is only required about five percent of the time.

Before beginning the procedure, Dr. Taylor suggests that the doctor should have all "in readiness" before placing the woman in the awkward position required for the hysteroscopic exam. The whole procedure usually takes only between five and 15 minutes to perform. Once the procedure is completed, there may be mild cramping or light bleeding afterwards.

For simple operative procedures, no or a local anesthetic may be all that is required. These procedures last about twenty minutes. Longer procedures will usually require a general anesthetic.

PREPARATION FOR AN OPERATIVE HYSTEROSCOPE OR A D-and-C UNDER GENERAL ANESTHETIC

First of all make sure you are clear about why the procedure is being done and what the doctor plans to examine, remove or treat. The night before you may shower or bath in your usual way. No douching or extra cleansing of the genital area is required. There is also no need to shave your pubic hair. And of course, a good night's sleep is recommended. After midnight the night before your operation, you should eat no food of any kind, nor drink any fluids, not even water, to minimize the risks of throwing up while under anesthetic. However, in the case of an emergency D-and-C, you may not have the chance to fast before hand, and the anesthetist will take this into account.

These days, the history, physical and blood and urine tests are often done before admission. Procedures vary at different hospitals so be sure to check with your doctor and find out exactly what preparations are necessary at your hospital.

AT THE HOSPITAL

After the usual admitting procedures, you will be taken to your room. There a nurse will take a brief medical history with special emphasis on any allergies to medications or adverse effects of previous anesthetics. The nurse will also arrange for you to give urine and blood samples. Usually a complete blood test is done, including the amount of iron in your blood, as well as a fasting blood sugar. Your urine will be tested for a sugar, protein, and bacteria.

At some point, you will change into a hospital gown. A nurse may give you a shot in either the arm or leg. This shot usually consists of two or three drugs. One is to dry up saliva and stomach and lung secretions, one is a pain killer, and the third (optional) is an anti-nauseant. These drugs make up the routine preparation for any general anesthetic. These drugs are only given if requested by your doctor.

IN THE OPERATING ROOM

Most often, you are wheeled to the operating room on a bed, and then transferred directly onto the operating table. Once in the operating room, you will notice everyone wearing masks, gowns, hats and slippers. If the anesthetist hasn't already visited you, he or she will check your medical history again. The anesthetist will then put a needle into your vein, in the wrist area, and run through it a solution containing sugar and water or electrolytes and water. Putting this needle in can cause some discomfort but it is short-lived. Using this same intravenous line, the anesthetist will inject a drug that acts quickly to produce sleep. In fact, by the time you have counted to 10, you will be out.

After this, the anesthetist places a mask over your face and turns on the gases that will keep you asleep throughout the entire operation. In an emergency D-and-C, the anesthetist will also put a tube down your throat and into your lungs to prevent any of the stomach's contents from getting into your lungs and to monitor your breathing better. During the operation, the anesthetist will carefully monitor your pulse, blood pressure and breathing.

THE OPERATION

The general practitioner or gynecologist places your feet in stirrups, and then does an ordinary pelvic exam to feel the size of your uterus and its position in the pelvis. He or she will also examine your ovaries and tubes on each side.

Next, the doctor places a metal speculum into your vagina, and washes off the vagina and cervix with an antiseptic solution. Then the doctor puts a clamp on the cervix and passes a uterine sound through the cervix as far as it will go. This sound measures the length of your uterus, and shows the direction of your cervical canal.

Following this, your cervix is gradually opened up using a series of metal rods or dilators starting with one the size of a straw and working up to one the size of your thumb. Here the two operations differ.

D-and-C: The lining of your uterus is then carefully removed using curettes. The curette is a spoon-like instrument with a long handle and sharp edges that can scrape the inner walls of the uterus. These scrapings are then sent to the lab for further studies. The whole operation takes only five to 15 minutes on average.

HYSTEROSCOPY: The special lighted instrument needed to perform the specific operation (with its video camera attached) is then inserted through the cervix. The vaginal speculum is removed. Then the liquid or gas used to expand the uterine cavity is allowed to flow into the uterus through a tube connected to the lighted instrument. While viewing the inside of the uterus on a television screen, the surgeon then proceeds to perform the surgery. It could be the removal of fibroids or the uterine lining or any of the possibilities listed above.

During the surgery, the surgeon must pay close attention to the amount of fluid going in and out of the uterus. Once the surgery is completed, the inside of the uterus is examined one last time to check for any bleeding. This operation will take anywhere from 30 minutes to a few hours, with the average length of surgery being about one hour.

AFTER SURGERY

Just before you wake up, the doctor checks for bleeding, lifts your feet out of the stirrups, and puts a sanitary napkin in place.

However you won't wake up until the recovery room. A first you will feel drowsy and everything will look blurry. When you are more awake, you will go back to your room.

D-and-C: Once fully awake, you can go home unless there has been some complication. You can expect to feel some cramps and soreness that day and perhaps the day after. Spotting can continue for a few weeks after a D-and-C. Until your bleeding has stopped, it is a good idea to shower instead of bathing to prevent infection as your cervix is still open at first. Your periods may return at any time, usually within three to six weeks. Any excessive bleeding should be immediately reported to your doctor, i.e. soaking through your pad.

HYSTEROSCOPY: Since the procedure is longer, you will take longer to wake up from the anesthetic, depending on what was done. Most procedures are done at day care or short stay units. There will usually be more spotting. In the case of endometrial ablation, there may be considerable discharge of tissue over days or weeks.

At your follow-up visit with your doctor, discuss the findings from the hysteroscope or D-and-C and what they mean, if these procedures were done for diagnostic purposes. If you are using birth control you will need to continue it as usual, right away. However, it is probably a good idea to avoid sex until your bleeding has stopped.

COMPLICATIONS

D-and-C: If you experience fever, abdominal cramps or pain, and a foul smelling vaginal discharge, you should be checked right away for a possible infection. Other potential complications are uncommon and include hemorrhage, perforation of the uterus or surrounding internal organs, injury to the cervix, scar tissue forming inside the uterus and reactions to the anesthesia.

Overall D-and-C is a very safe operation, with a low rate of complications and with a death rate of .4 per 100,000.

However, according to **Jill Weiss** of the **Canadian PID Society**, a serious pelvic infection (**PID**) may follow anywhere between three and 13 percent of abortions. This problem is most marked in younger women. At an abortion clinic, women under 20 had a 28 to 40 percent chance of developing PID after abortion and women over 20, a 15 to 18 percent chance.

HYSTEROSCOPY: Complications unique to hysteroscopy include reactions to the liquid or gas mediums used to expand the uterine cavity. The most common complication is uterine perforation.

Carbon dioxide may cause shoulder tip pain. There is also the small risk of gas embolism (blockage of a blood vessel by gas travelling in the bloodstream) and very rarely death from that cause. Occasionally, there are also irregular heart rhythms that develop as a result of the carbon dioxide.

The fluid mediums like sugar and salt solutions can uncommonly cause fluid overload and heart failure. Severe allergic and lung reactions to a thick medium called dextran can also occur.

Other late onset complications of hysteroscopy include PID (rarely) and formation of scar tissue inside the uterine cavity.

Complications after hysteroscopy are greater than for D-and-C, especially when a general anesthetic is used. The overall risk of major complications is high at three percent compared to hysterectomy which is one to 2.5 percent. This rate includes longer operative procedures under general anesthesia as well as five minute office hysteroscopy. The complication rate from diagnostic hysteroscopy is very low. A 1986 study found a risk of serious complications of .012 percent. The death rate with hysteroscopy is very low at 2.4 per 100,000 compare to two per 1,000 women for hysterectomy.

Both these operations are invasive procedures. So, the benefit-risk ratio has to be carefully considered for each woman and for each situation. However, hysteroscopy has become an indispensable gynecological tool both for diagnosis and treatment. And, in most situations, it offers women a lot of advantages over the traditional blind D-and-C.

Those Annoying Varicose Veins

Most doctors find the whole topic of varicose veins boring. In fact, many doctors do not know a lot about them. The whole topic has been neglected because it is just another one of those annoying problems that mainly affects women. Approximately 40 percent of women have varicose veins, and the amount of suffering and disability from aching, swollen and painful veins is considerable.

The circulation of the blood to and through all the tissues of the body is an incredible feat of engineering. Approximately 60,000 miles of blood vessels carry oxygen and nutrient rich blood from the heart and return it there carrying waste products and carbon dioxide. The arteries carry the blood away from the heart to the tissues and the veins return the blood back to the heart. Because the veins have to return blood to the heart against the forces of gravity, almost all veins have a system of valves. These valves prevent the backward flow of the blood.

The veins in the legs have many valves because they have to return the blood the longest distance and against the forces of gravity. Two forces help the blood return, the squeezing action of the calf muscles and the pulsing pressure exerted on some veins by the arteries that lie right beside them.

WHAT ARE VARICOSE VEINS ?

Varicose veins usually means swollen, elongated surface veins that become twisted and bunched, usually in the lower leg. **Dr. Guylaine Lanctôt**, a specialist in the field, defines them as "veins that are permanently dilated and unable to carry blood back to the heart."

By definition, varicose veins are **superficial**, which means limited to the surface of the leg, or directly under the skin. This is why diagnosis is best made by a thorough inspection and palpation of the superficial veins by a physician. Complicated diagnostic tools are completely unnecessary.

On the other hand, **deep** vein problems, involving the deeper veins, cannot be treated. If both legs appear normal in shape and contour, it is very unlikely that the deep veins are involved. If one leg is more swollen than the other, it is possible that the deep veins are involved. The deep veins are rarely affected in women who have varicose veins, except indirectly, when inflammation of the deep veins leads to a secondary problem with the surface veins.

The cause of "primary" varicose veins is unknown. For some reason, the valves in the leg veins become altered and don't function properly. As a result, not all the blood is returned to the heart. Instead, some remains and pools in the veins and tissues surrounding them. Some believe that there is an inherited weakness in the vein wall or the vein valve.

Other factors are known to predispose you to varicose veins. This includes jobs that involve prolonged standing or heavy lifting, constricting clothing, or being markedly overweight. Women are affected almost twice as frequently as men, and the chance of developing varicose veins rises with each pregnancy. The pressure of the pregnant uterus on the pelvic veins appears to interfere with return of blood from the leg veins to the heart.

"Secondary" varicose veins develop secondary to another cause and account for only a small percentage of varicose veins. Usually that cause is phlebitis or inflammation of the deep veins of the legs, which then damages the vein or causes blockages in the superficial veins. This condition is known as post-phlebitis syndrome.

"Spider veins" are relatively harmless, but unsightly in appearance. They have been called broken capillaries and are small bluish blotches found on the sides and back of the leg as well as the feet.

DIET AND VARICOSE VEINS

In contrast to the Western world, varicose veins are rarely seen in parts of the world where high fibre and whole unrefined foods are consumed. A high fibre diet also prevents constipation and straining during a bowel movement which is thought to put increased pressure on the leg veins.

Although not all doctors agree that low fibre diets high in refined foods are a causative factor in varicose veins, it is much healthier to avoid such a diet and emphasize fresh fruit, vegetables, whole grains and legumes in your diet.

SYMPTOMS OF VARICOSE VEINS

The commonest symptoms are aching, swelling, heaviness, cramps, or itching in the legs. Women may also be bothered by the ugly appearance of swollen, twisted veins or surface spider vines. The aching is usually described as a dull, heavy bursting sensation, particularly after prolonged periods of standing, and before the periods. Symptoms tend to be worse toward the end of the day and are relieved by elevating the legs. Swelling is usually confined to the ankles and feet.

Symptoms of post-phlebitis syndrome are usually more severe. Itching, and skin changes including dermatitis and dark coloration, as well as ankle ulcers may occur in long-standing conditions of this type. Swelling of the legs also tends to be more extensive.

VITAMINS AND VARICOSE VEINS

The Canadian researchers, **Drs. Evan** and **Wilfred Shute**, reported that varicose veins improve on Vitamin-E in doses of 400 to 800 IU a day. Please note that if you have high blood pressure, you should reduce the dosage to 100 IU a day.

Rutin (found in buckwheat) and bioflavonoids (the white material in orange and grapefruit rinds) may help strengthen the veins in dosages of 500 to 1,000mg per day. These supplements can be found in any good health food store. It is also important to combine the above supplements with at least 1,000mg or more of Vitamin-C, as well a good mega B complex vitamin containing 50mg of all the B vitamins. In addition at least 10,000 units of vitamin-A and 25 to 50mg of zinc should be taken daily.

Vitamin-E oil and vitamin-A ointment may also be applied to the veins directly.

SELF-HELP FOR VARICOSE VEINS

Water therapy may be useful to stimulate circulation and relieve aching. Alternating hot and cold towels on the legs, always ending with cold, may reduce swelling and discomfort. Cold running water on the legs for one minute at a time can also be useful. This cold treatment should be repeated five or six times at a session.

Lemon oil has a tonic effect on the veins. You can add six drops to your bath and rub three drops of lemon mixed with 1/4 cup of almond oil on the affected areas every day.

Witch hazel is one of the oldest remedies for varicose veins. You could apply compresses made by soaking cloths or towels in distilled witch hazel (which can be found in any drug store) and take a glass of water with two or three drops of the extract at each meal.

You can also apply apple cider vinegar to the swollen veins morning and night, allowing the vinegar to dry on the skin.

Another old remedy is to use the leaves of Savoy cabbage after you have softened them and flattened them with a bottle or rolling pin. You then place the leaves flat on the veins and hold them in place overnight with bandages.

Hot castor oil packs can also be applied at night for pain and swelling relief. They are highly effective.

CONSTIPATION AND VARICOSE VEINS

Naturopaths believe that constipation is a very important factor in causing varicose veins. They say that the lower bowel puts pressure on the veins of the pelvis. It is important to have at least one bowel movement a day, preferably three, one after each meal. Metamucil powder without sugar can be safely taken every day if necessary.

CONSERVATIVE TREATMENT

Conservative non-surgical treatment is usually limited to those women with a post-phlebitis problem. The mainstay of treatment is elastic stockings, which compress the veins and tissues of the lower leg to assist the blood in returning to the heart.

Elastic stockings come in light, medium, strong and extra strong varieties, are prescribed by a physician, and are covered by some medical plans. Remember that it's better to get a lighter pair of nylon support hose and wear them regularly, than to let a heavier pair of elastic stockings prescribed by your doctor sit unused in the drawer.

If you have difficulty putting on heavy elastic stockings, you can put on two lighter pairs of support hose instead.

Walking at least a mile a day to promote the blood return through the pumping action of the muscles is highly recommended.

For severe varicose veins, elastic stockings worn while walking doubles the compression efficiency in returning the blood to the heart.

All women with varicose veins should follow the old advice and keep their legs up whenever they are sitting as much as possible. I also suggest placing your legs against the back of a wall or couch and allowing them to drain completely each night before bed. A slant board may also be used for this purpose (available through health food stores).

Another very useful aid is to raise the foot of your bed, using blocks or books by about nine inches. This greatly aids the veins in draining and helps relieve symptoms. However, you should check with your doctor to make sure you don't have any medical reason to prevent you from using this method.

It is also advisable to wear low heels or negative heels. Some women have found that the German Birkenstock sandal or shoe helps alleviate swelling.

SURGERY AND SCLEROTHERAPY

Fortunately, a Canadian woman physician has been a pioneer in the diagnosis and treatment of varicose veins. Dr. Guylaine Lanctôt has successfully treated over 80,000 patients for varicose veins, with excellent results. She has also trained doctors in her method of diagnosis and treatment. She emphasizes the use of "low tech" diagnostic tools, namely the physicians's hands, over expensive "high tech" diagnostic machines which are usually unnecessary.

Varicose veins involving the large veins of the legs usually require surgery. Medium and smaller sized veins can usually be treated with a non-surgical technique known as sclerotherapy.

Dr. Lanctôt has classified large varicose veins according to the degree of incompetence of the largest superficial vein of the leg (the long saphenous vein).

1. **CERTAIN:** The long vein of the leg is swollen bulging and twisted (tortuous).

2. **PROBABLE:** The long vein resembles hose pipe, swollen but not bulging.

3. **POSSIBLE:** The long vein looks normal despite the symptoms and varicosities of other superficial veins.

For treatment of the first two categories, the best results are obtained with a combination of stripping and sclerotherapy. The third category is best treated with support stockings and observed carefully over time to see if any signs of larger vein involvement appear.

The type of stripping operation that Dr. Lanctôt recommends is a short 30-minute operation (to remove the upper part of the problem vein) that can be done under a local anesthetic. There are only two small incisions required for this operation. After part of the vein is removed, other veins take over in that same area to return the blood to the heart.

Do not confuse this surgery with the old and complicated surgery under general anesthetic that used to be done. This type of surgery involves multiple incisions, and does not yield any better results.

Sclerotherapy consists of tiny injections of a chemical agent into affected veins that cause the walls of the veins to glue together permanently. As Dr. Lanctôt adds, "This technique leaves no marks, although slight skin discoloration may occur in rare instances." Sclerotherapy can get rid of most of the ugly looking spider veins as well as smaller and medium sized veins.

Usually, sclerotherapy is done over about eight to ten sessions, with 25 to 30 injections of the sclerosing agent being given at each session. Scelerotherapy should start with the larger veins first, with the spiders being done at the very end. Usually there is little pain, described as being like a pin prick, and less than for electrolysis. However, local anesthetic may be added to each injection if necessary.

Treating spider veins is considered a cosmetic procedure and this will not be covered by medical plans. However, treatment of veins causing significant symptoms and involving the large veins will usually be covered.

What you can expect after surgical and/or sclerotherapy treatment is almost always relief of symptoms as well as a pleasing cosmetic result. Varicose veins may reoccur after surgery, especially if attention is not given to the preventative steps outlined in this chapter.

PREVENTION OF VARICOSE VEINS

1. Get regular exercise especially walking, cycling or swimming.

2. Eat a high fibre diet emphasizing fresh fruits and vegetables, whole grains and beans. Cut down or eliminate red meat and excess fat. Drink plenty of water.

3. Avoid being constipated and straining during bowel movements.

4. Use the vitamin supplements mentioned above to prevent or modify the tendency to varicose veins.

5. Good support hose should be worn during all jobs that require a lot of standing or heavy lifting, especially during pregnancy. Nowadays, fashionable sheer nylon support hose are easily available.

FURTHER INFO

VARICOSE VEINS SELF-HELP, by **Dr. Leon Chaitow** (Thorsons, 1986). This helpful book on natural treatments for varicose veins can be obtained through your health food store or by mail order from **Alive Books**, Box 80055, Burnaby, BC, V5H 3X5. 1-800-663-6513. In the U.S. from **Keat's Publishing**, 27 Pine St, New Canaan, CT, 06840-0876.

HOW TO HAVE GREAT LEGS AT ANY AGE, A Woman Doctor's Personal Program for Strong, Healthy and Attractive Legs, by **Dr. Guylaine Lanctôt** (New Chapter Press, 1988). Dr. Lanctôt has established clinics for treatment of varicose veins in Quebec, Ontario and Florida and has trained many physicians in her methods.

Beauty With Conscience

The new ecological awareness of the 1990's has made women increasingly aware of their power and responsibility as consumers. Today, consumers, the majority of them women, spend well over two billion dollars on beauty and cosmetic products every year in Canada and 200 billion in the U.S.

Up until recently, most cosmetics and household products have been tested on millions of animals, mainly using two outdated and barbaric tests: the **Draize Eye Irritancy Test** and the **Lethal Dose Fifty Percent Test**.

No accurate figures are available, but somewhere between two and ten million animals in North America are subjected to painful procedures and killed in order to test the new products that consumers purchase. Moreover, most of the tests are of dubious value for evaluating human safety.

What is surprising to many people is that animal testing is not required by law either in the U.S. or Canada. These cruel and unscientific tests continue for many reasons. These include government and industry inertia, industry's belief that these tests will protect them from law suits, and lack of public awareness.

THE DRAIZE EYE IRRITANCY TEST

The draize eye irritancy test is a method used for assessing the degree to which a substance or chemical mixture irritates the eyes. The usual subjects are young albino rabbits which are tightly restrained for a number of days after a test substance (like deodorant, mascara or detergent) has been dropped onto one of the animal's eyes. The other eye serves as a control. Rabbits' eyes are most often used because their corneas are more sensitive than humans'. The damage to the eye is graded according to the size of the area damaged, the degree of swelling and the amount of pus and irritation. Blindness, ulceration and hemorrhage of the eye may occur. The results are considered valid if at least six rabbits survive the test for each substance.

The Draize test is a crude test for determining irritancy as it can do so only on a pass/fail basis.

Moreover, due to the many anatomical and physiological differences between the rabbit and human eye, the Draize test may correlate poorly with actual human experience. **Dr. Stephen Kaufman** of the **New York University Department of Opthalmology** maintains that the Draize test is scientifically unsound and inapplicable to clinical situations. "Reliance on the test is in fact dangerous because the animal data cannot be reliably extrapolated to men. Substances proven safe in the lab animals may in fact be dangerous to people".

In fact, histamine and selenium are examples of two chemicals that produce severe reactions in the human eye but not in the rabbit eye.

As **Dr. Murray Cohen** of the **Mount Sinai Medical Center** in Toronto says, "I consider the Draize test archaic, cruel, irrational and dangerous and the rationale for its use has nothing to do with human welfare."

DERMAL IRRITANCY TEST

Another common test is the **Dermal Irritancy Test**. This test involves applying the test substance directly to the shaved skin of an immobilized animal for a period of time. After examination of the resulting rashes, burns or blisters, the animal is either recycled into another test or destroyed.

Fortunately, safe alternatives to such testing already exist. Test tube cultures of both rabbit and human corneal tissue have been successfully utilized to observe the effects of chemical irritants by means of their direct action on cells. These cell culture tests can produce more accurate results than those provided by the Draize test.

THE LETHAL DOSE FIFTY PERCENT TEST

The other objectionable test is **The Lethal Dose Fifty Percent Test** or **LD-50**. LD-50 refers to the amount of a substance which when administered in a single dose (this can be through food, stomach tube, injection, inhalation or direct application to the skin) will kill 50 percent of a test group of animals within a specified time. The lower the LD-50, the more toxic the substance. A standard LD-50 test involves three groups of ten or more animals, one group for each dose level. All surviving animals are killed and autopsied.

Common signs of poisoning include moaning and crying out, tears, diarrhea, discharge, bleeding from the eyes or mouth and convulsions.

Even with large numbers of animals being tested, there are considerable variations in test results, due to the influence of factors such as the type of animal species used, age, sex, diet and cage conditions, etc.

"Results of the LD-50 vary dramatically from laboratory to laboratory, between strain, age, sex, and species of animals, and extrapolation to humans is questionable," says **Dr. Gil Langley** in the **New Scientist** magazine in 1985.

A report from the **U.S. Office of Technology Assessment** mentions that, "The results of the LD-50 vary greatly both among and within species... and are difficult to extrapolate to humans because there are so many mechanisms by which death can occur." However, the report does go on to conclude that animal testing, although imperfect, is still useful.

"As a board-certified emergency medicine physician who has been practising for ten years," claims American physician **Dr. Neill S. Barber**, "I have never found data from LD-50 or eye irritancy test on animals to be useful in treating patients. I would not rely on these data to treat patients and I know of no physician who does."

Others maintain that the LD-50 test and the Draize test are misleading to the consumer. They are used to issue certificates of safety to household products and cosmetics, which in the U.S. still cause 200,000 hospital recorded poisonings every year.

Chronic toxicity tests are carried out on rabbits and dogs, typically beagles, to see if small amounts of the test substance become toxic over long-term exposure. The substance is mixed with food or administered through a stomach tube. The test continues for two years, and afterwards the remaining animals are killed and examined.

As mentioned before, many alternative testing methods already exist which do not include the use of live animals, and at the same time do not compromise safety. These include tissue and cell cultures, bacterial and protozoal studies, bird embryos and eggs, mathematical and computer models and various assay techniques.

Some companies eliminate the need for animal testing by using natural food ingredients such as avocado and almond oil. Other ingredients are deemed to be safe because they have been on the market for 20 or 30 years and their safety record is well established.

Beauty Without Cruelty in Britain was one of the first companies to devote itself to cruelty free products made from natural ingredients. This company reports no incidence of injury or death in their 27-year history.

Approximately 200,000 animals are used for product testing in Canada. Fifteen of the 23 commercial lab facilities in Canada are located in the province of Ontario. However, it is important to remember that many Canadian companies are involved in animal testing, but it is performed in U.S. labs.

In Ontario, MPP **Bill Wildman** had introduced **Bill 190** in order "to prohibit the use of animals in non-medical experimentation involving the Draize Eye Irritancy Test or the Classical LD-50 Acute Toxicity Test and similar tests." However, in spite of growing public support, the bill is unlikely to pass.

Eight states in the U.S. have legislation pending that would limit or ban animal testing of products.

The **Food and Drug Administration** in the U. S. has recently announced that it was assembling information to eliminate duplicative testing. This would allow cosmetic companies to find out an ingredient's safety history without repeating all the tests.

Recently, eleven of the largest cosmetic firms (including three of the top four: **Avon**, **Revlon** and **Faberge**) have announced permanent bans on animal testing of their finished products. Other companies include **Amway**, **Bonne Bell**, **Christian Dior**, **Clinique**, **Estee Lauder**, and **Shaklee**.

WHAT YOU CAN DO:

EDUCATE YOURSELF AND USE CONSUMER POWER: Purchase only cruelty free products that do not use animal testing and encourage stores and hair dressers to stock cruelty free alternatives. Contact the **Humane Society** in your area for information and what you can do.

RESOURCES:

Write to or call:

THE TORONTO HUMANE SOCIETY, 11 River St, Toronto, ON, M5A 4C2. 416-392-2273 Fax: 416-392-9978.

THE HUMANE SOCIETY OF THE U.S., 2100 L St NW, Washington, DC, 20037. 202-452-1100.

They provide a free list of cruelty free cosmetics and household products as well as further information on testing and its alternatives and what you can do to help.

THE CARING CONSUMER'S CRUELTY FREE SHOPPING GUIDE, by **People For The Ethical Treatment Of Animals** (**PETA**), PO Box 42516, Washington, DC, 20015. 301-770-PETA.

A free catalogue and excellent mail order service is provided by the following companies:

BEAUTY WITHOUT CRUELTY, 26 Day St, Cambridge, ON, N1S 3P9. 519-621-5986.

THE BODY SHOP, Mail Order Department, 15 Andrew Place, Don Mills, ON, M3C 2H2. 416-441-3202.

The Body Shop also offers biodegradable products, recycled paper and even offers a refill service. As part of their philosophy, the Body Shop is also actively committed to environmental and community issues.

The Good News About Gallstones And Women

Fifteen to 20 percent of all North Americans have gallstones, and gallbladder surgery is the most commonly performed abdominal surgery in both Canada and the United States. More than 50,000 gallbladders are removed annually in Canada and about 500,000 in the U.S. The good news is that gallstones is probably another health problem related to the excesses of the Western diet, and there is much that a woman can do to prevent their occurrence.

Women are three times more likely to develop gallstones than men. North American native women have the highest gallstone incidence in the world. The incidence of gallstones also increases with age. Recent studies reviewed in the **Lancet** medical journal (January 1990), have shown that "women not only have more gallstones, but also more often complain of symptoms and are more often aware of their condition than men."

WHAT DOES YOUR GALLBLADDER DO ?

Your liver is constantly making bile and delivering it to your gallbladder, which is a small muscular sac located under the liver. Your gallbladder concentrates bile five to ten times and then stores it until it is needed after you eat a meal containing fat. The purpose of bile is to remove waste products from the liver and to carry the bile salts which digest fat. Bile salts are essential to break down and absorb fats and the fat soluble vitamins A, D, E, and K.

As soon as your food arrives in the first part of the small intestine from the stomach, your gallbladder contracts and empties its contents of bile. The bile travels through a special passageway called the common bile duct and is released into the intestine.

Remarkably, **one half to one-and-a-half litres** (32 to 48 ounces) of bile are secreted by the liver every day, and concentrated in a gallbladder that can only hold **40 to 70 cc of bile** (roughly one to two ounces) at a time. Ninety percent of the bile salts are reabsorbed from the intestine and are used about ten times before being lost through the stool.

WHAT GALLSTONES ARE MADE OF

Gallstones can be round or oval, smooth or lumpy. They can be one to ten or more stones ranging in size from one to 25 mm across (up to about an inch in diameter). Eighty-five to 90 percent of gallstones are made predominantly of cholesterol. The remaining ten to 15 percent of stones are made predominantly of calcium. Calcium stones are much more common in the Orient than in Western countries.

Cholesterol will not dissolve in water, and thus certain substances made in the liver (the bile salts) keep the cholesterol dissolved. If the amount of cholesterol in the bile increases, or if anything happens to reduce the concentration of these bile salts, then the cholesterol can precipitate out and form gallstones.

For example, increased secretion of cholesterol can be caused by obesity, pregnancy, birth control pills, a diet high in saturated fats and rapid weight loss (either surgically or through dieting or fasting). Increased loss of bile salts can occur when the last part of the small intestine is inflamed (as in Crohn's disease) and cannot absorb back the bile salts.

The incidence of cholesterol gallstones is highest in the Native population, lower in Caucasians, and lowest among those of African and Oriental descent.

WHAT ARE TRUE SYMPTOMS OF GALLBLADDER PROBLEMS ?

Fortunately, 80 percent of those with gallstones will never develop symptoms and thus need no treatment.

Most people think that bloating, heartburn, intolerance of fatty food, and vague right upper abdominal pain are sure signs of a gallbladder problem. These symptoms, however, have been found to be unrelated to gallbladder disease and would be better treated by careful attention to diet and lifestyle.

It used to be said that the typical gallbladder patient was "forty, female, fertile, and fat." However, this is not true for many people who have gallstones. The sex difference becomes progressively less after the age of 50.

The 20 percent of women and men who have true symptoms from gallbladder disease usually know it. True gallbladder pain or biliary colic, as it is called, is intense and unforgettable. **Sir Walter Scott**, when he experienced gallbladder pain, turned away from his family and prepared to dictate his last will and testament. As **Dr. Noel Williams**, **Head of Gastroenterogy** at **Dalhousie University** in Halifax, says in his article in the **Canadian Journal of Diagnosis** (May/91), "Patients often mention that their biliary pain is the most severe they have experienced, more severe than that suffered with the passing of a kidney stone, perforation of an intestine or childbirth."

Gallbladder pain, known as biliary colic, is usually caused when the gallbladder repeatedly tries to expel the stone or stones which have temporarily been stuck in one of the ducts leading from the gallbladder. This pain is typically steady and severe and characteristically located in the right upper section of the abdomen. The pain lasts more than one hour, but not usually past 12 hours. The pain commonly occurs in the middle of the night and causes a marked restlessness, causing the person to "walk the floor." The pain may also radiate into the right shoulder tip or to the area between the shoulder blades, and be accompanied by nausea and vomiting. Pain usually subsides when the stone passes through the duct, but there may be residual soreness or achiness in the area for about 24 hours.

SERIOUS COMPLICATIONS OF GALLSTONES

According to **Dr. Eldon Shaffer**, Chairman, **Department of Medicine University of Calgary**, in May 1991 **Diagnosis**, if the severe pain lasts for more than 12 to 17 hours, or is accompanied by fever and chills, you may have developed inflammation of the gallbladder (known as acute cholecystitis) or inflammation of the pancreas (known as acute pancreatitis). This means you should go to the emergency right away, and be prepared to be admitted into the hospital.

With acute cholecystis, what happens is that trapped bile irritates and inflames the gallbladder wall. Seventy-five percent of the time the acute inflammation subsides with medical treatment alone. Of those 75 percent, 25 percent will have a reoccurrence within one year and 60 percent within six years.

The other 25 percent will develop serious complications necessitating immediate surgery. Surgery becomes necessary when the gallbladder becomes infected and full of pus, or when a gallstone causes the intestine to be blocked off or when the blood supply to the gallbladder is cut off. Occasionally, an infected gallbladder bursts, and the pus is localized to the area around the gallbladder. Rarely the pus spreads throughout the whole abdomen, which is a life threatening situation.

With acute pancreatitis, what happens is that the bile backs up into the pancreas where it causes it to become inflamed. This condition is usually treated with pain killers and intravenous fluids. If the pancreas is severely damaged, it can cause low blood pressure, heart failure, kidney failure, respiratory failure, accumulation of fluid in the abdomen and formation of cysts and abscesses in the damaged gland.

Serious complications of gallbladder disease such as jaundice (yellow skin and eyes) from the stone blocking the common bile duct, cholecystitis or pancreatitis occur in about one percent of people with gallstones and are just as common in those who have never had any prior abdominal pain. Once any of these complications has developed, surgery is absolutely necessary.

HOW TO DIAGNOSE GALLSTONES

The usual method for diagnosing gallstones is a sound wave picture of your gallbladder, known as gallbladder ultrasound, which is a simple and painless procedure.

If gallstones show up, and if there are no symptoms, no treatment is necessary.

If you have even one attack of biliary colic or cholecystitis, or any other complication of gallstones, treatment is advised.

CUTTING OUT THE GALLBLADDER, THE OLD WAY

There are several treatment possibilities. Traditional cholecystectomy (removal of the gallbladder) is major abdominal surgery requiring a general anesthetic and involving an incision that is six to eight inches long. The operation lasts between one-half to two hours, depending on the surgeon and his approach. The incision is generally painful for at least two weeks. The usual hospital stay following the operation is between four and six days.

The rate of complications reported ranges from 6 to 21 percent. The death rate from the operation ranges from 1 in 1,000 to 3 in a 100. It may be as high as six to eight per 100 for persons over 65 presenting with acute gallbladder inflammation.

Traditional cholecystectomy requires a recovery period of six to 12 weeks. This operation is still considered the most definitive treatment for symptomatic gallbladder disease.

CUTTING OUT THE GALLBLADDER, THE NEW WAY

A better option is a new operation that removes the gallbladder through three or four small incisions, O.5 cm to 1.O cm long (less than half an inch). There is no cutting of the muscles of the abdominal wall, and there is much less pain from the small incisions. In fact, surgeons have been surprised at the extent to which pain and disability following surgery were due to the large incision.

Surgical instruments as well as a lighted instrument known as the laparoscope are inserted through these incisions. The gallbladder is cut away from the liver and removed through one of the small incisions. The surgeon views the entire procedure on a television screen.

This operation, known as laparoscopic cholecystectomy, is longer (1.5 to two hours) but there is a much faster post-operative recovery. Patients can eat the same evening and go home the day after surgery. Eighty percent of patients can return to work within two weeks.

Five to ten percent of the time, due to technical problems in removing the gallbladder through the small incisions, the incision must be enlarged to six to eight inches and thus converted into the traditional cholecystectomy. Accidental injury to the common bile duct or the intestines also requires conversion to the longer incision.

Laparoscopic cholecystectomy is rapidly becoming a popular method for removing the gallbladder in the United States and Europe, according to an analysis of the method that appeared in the April 1991 issue of the **New England Journal of Medicine**. This article reviewed 1,518 such operations and found that the complication rate was comparable to the more traditional type of cholecystectomy.

In Canada, at present an estimated two thirds of hospitals offer or will soon offer this type of surgery. Skilled surgeons can learn how to do this procedure quickly. However, the operation should only be performed by qualified surgeons who have completed a certified course. Ideally, such a course would require that 60 to 70 cholecystectomies be performed under direct supervision before certification, especially for surgeons with no previous laparoscopic experience.

Dr. Eldon cautions against "improperly trained individuals performing an excess of laparoscopic cholecystectomies on minimally symptomatic patients."

Long-term studies on the safety and long-term effects of this type of surgery have not yet been done. One recent series of 381 patients reported two cases of intestinal injury that resulted in death. The much larger series of 1,518 mentioned previously had only one death, four intestinal injuries and seven injuries to the ducts, all of which were successfully repaired. The 1991 government report concluded that "this has raised considerable concern about the rate of common bile duct and intestinal injury."

With this surgery, there is a greater risk that surrounding structures could be damaged. The risk appears to depend on the experience of the surgeon. A 1992 study at **McGill University** in Montreal and the **Toronto Hospital** compared the outcome of traditional cholecystectomies with laparoscopic ones. The study found that patients who had laparoscopic cholecystectomies fared much better. They returned to full diet earlier, needed less pain killers and went back to full activities sooner.

NON-SURGICAL TREATMENTS

Nonsurgical treatment alternatives include the use of medicines that dissolve gallstones or lithotripsy (high intensity shock waves that break up the stones). With both types of treatments, there is a 50 percent chance that stones will reoccur in the following five years. However, the chance of reoccurrence would probably decrease a lot more if you significantly improved your diet after the stones were dissolved.

DISSOLVING THE STONES

Medicines that dissolve the stones like ursodeoxycholic acid (UDCA) are taken by mouth either at bedtime or with meals for six months to two years. These medicines are especially suitable for persons who are too high risk to consider surgery, who are unwilling to consider surgery, or who have lost weight too quickly. The gallstones must also be less than 1.5 cm in size, made of cholesterol and the gallbladder must still be able to function. Only about 30 percent of people with symptomatic gallstones will meet these requirements, and of those only 30 to 50 percent will be successful at dissolving the stones. This therapy is continued until two ultrasounds of the gallbladder spaced three to six months apart show no evidence of stones.

Currently, these drugs require your doctor to get prior approval from the **Health Protection Branch** of the Canadian Government.

UDCA has one main side effect, which is diarrhea, which can be easily remedied by decreasing the dosage of the medication.

SHATTERING THE STONES

Lithotripsy for gallstones is not yet widely available and is currently undergoing evaluation. It can only be used when there are three or fewer cholesterol type stones with maximum stone size less than two cm. This amounts to about 15 to 20 percent of all symptomatic gallstone patients. Lithotripsy must also be followed by oral medicines for six weeks to dissolve the tiny fragments of stones that are left.

Patients undergoing this treatment must wear hearing protectors and receive an injection of a sedative, says **Dr. Paul Whelan**, **Director of the Hamilton Stone Clinic** in Ontario. In a September 1990 article in the **Globe and Mail**, he says that these precautions are necessary because of the aggravating sensation experienced during lithotripsy "like being slapped on your side 15,000 times." Notwithstanding, according to a 1991 government report on gallstone therapies, compared to both types of surgery, this is the least invasive and least painful procedure.

The Hamilton clinic is one of three centers in North America selected to study the value of lithotripsy. The study was started in September 1990 and was completed in March 1992. A study comparing lithotripsy to other methods of treatment is currently under way in Montreal.

Lithotripsy can be done on an outpatient basis and no anesthetic is required. The procedure lasts 45 minutes and requires only one to two sessions. The recovery time is one to two days.

Afterwards, about 20 percent develop biliary colic requiring pain killers but this usually clears up within hours. Many develop blood in the urine after the procedure, but this also clears up within 48 hours. One to three percent of all patients will develop pancreatic inflammation, and in the same percentage fragments of stones will block the gallbladder ducts requiring surgical removal.

"More than 15,000 patients have been successfully treated in Europe," says Dr. Whelan, "and we hope our study will pave the way for a new treatment option for North American patients."

Unfortunately, lithotripsy for gallstones was opposed by the **FDA** and by a lobby group of American surgeons. So, lithotripsy for gallstones is no longer available in the United States or Canada. Lithotripsy for kidney stones is a well established procedure with minimal complications.

LOSING WEIGHT TOO QUICKLY ?

Dr. Noel Williams recently completed a study of severely overweight women, who underwent surgery for weight reduction. Half the women were put on UDCA and the other half were not. There was a dramatically reduced incidence of gallstones in the group that received the preventative treatment.

In fact, Dr. Williams recommends that women who are planning to lose large amounts of weight over a short period of time (30 or 40 pounds over three months or less) take UDCA to prevent gallstones from developing.

Women who have already developed gallstones as a result of rapid weight loss, says Dr. Noel Williams in the **Canadian Journal of Diagnosis** (May/91), are not at risk for further gallstone formation once their weight is stable. These women, says Dr. Williams, are ideal candidates for UDCA therapy to dissolve the gallstones. After the stones are dissolved, "the treatment can be discontinued with the expectation of no reoccurrence of the gallstones."

HORMONES AND GALLSTONES

The higher dose pill did increase the risk of gallstone formation. Women on both the high and lower dose pill have a greater risk than non-users of having gallbladder stones requiring surgery. Most cases of painful and symptomatic gallbladder disease occur in the first one to three years of pill use.

Pregnancy, especially multiple pregnancies, may also predispose to gallstone formation, especially when combined with being overweight.

Since women have a higher incidence of gallstones in any case, says Dr. Williams, it is difficult to separate this tendency from the effects of natural or artificial hormones alone.

At a 1990 conference on gallstone disease held in Rome, Italy, the issue of whether or not the pill or hormones used for menopause caused gallstones, was hotly debated. It was concluded that neither low dose birth control pills or hormone replacement were important factors in gallstone formation.

However after hormone replacement, women are more likely to have gallbladder surgery. One study suggests that the risk of gallbladder disease in estrogen users persists after the drug is discontinued. Also, according to the Lancet report on the conference, women with gallstones who take the pill are operated on earlier and more frequently.

In fact estrogen receptor sites have been found in the gallbladder, suggesting that hormones act by affecting the gallbladder secretions directly.

SIDE EFFECTS OF GALLBLADDER SURGERY

Some have reported a "post cholecystectomy syndrome" with food intolerance, indigestion, heartburn or diarrhea and abdominal cramps.

In addition, there have been several studies which suggested an association between gallbladder removal and an increased incidence of right sided colon cancer in women. This is thought to be due to the possible cancer causing effect of increased amounts of bile salts circulating in the bowels. About 50 percent of studies have shown this association and 50 percent have not. To date, the connection between having the gallbladder removed and the increase in colon cancer is unclear.

It remains to be seen whether the removal of the gallbladder could cause long-term health effects.

DIET AND GALLSTONES

Gallstones are probably another example of a disease induced by the Western diet. It is unknown in cultures where there is a high fibre, low meat and low fat diet. That's probably why vegetarians have been observed to have half the gallstone incidence of meat eaters.

Gallstones are likely to be present in more than half of patients who are twice their ideal body weight. Elevated triglyceride levels in the blood are associated with gallstones, but ironically, elevated blood cholesterol levels are not. There is also a link between pre-diabetes and diabetes and gallstones.

PREVENTION OF GALLSTONES

In a presentation he made at an international workshop on gallstone disease, Dr. Williams suggested the following measures for prevention:

> Maintain ideal body weight.

> Avoid repetitive prolonged fasting.

> Use a birth control pill of low estrogen content or an alternative method of birth control.

> Reduce the concentration of cholesterol in bile by diet changes.

Diet changes alone may be useful as a preventative in people who are at high risk for gallstones, according to Dr. Williams. Diet is particularly useful for patients whose gallstones have been dissolved by medication. If the diet and normal body weight can be maintained, the gallstones are not likely to reoccur.

Dr. William's recommended diet to prevent gallstones or aid in their reduction is high fibre (30 grams or more), low protein (20 to 25 percent of calories) low fat (30 to 35 percent of calories) and high complex carbohydrates (40 to 50 percent of calories). He advises regular meals with a bedtime snack of fat or protein to contract and empty the gallbladder (at about ten or 11 pm).

In other words, plenty of fresh fruits and vegetables, low fat dairy products, 100 percent whole wheat or rye bread and pastas, brown rice, millet and other whole grains, along with moderate amounts of chicken and fish. This is the same diet that also prevents heart disease and cancer.

And as the Lancet says, "One can only reinforce the currently fashionable counsel for the healthy lifestyle which attempts to keep us slim and avoid very large families."

Lesbian Health Care

No book on women's health would be complete without addressing the health concerns of lesbians. **Dr. Ruth Simkin** has moved to British Columbia from Calgary, Alberta where she was **Associate Professor In Family Practice** at the **University of Calgary**. For many years, she has written and taught about lesbian health care issues, and has graciously agreed to contribute this chapter.

Women often ask me why we need to speak about lesbian health care. After all, aren't lesbians women, and isn't all women's health care the same? Many studies have shown that lesbians do not get adequate health care a good deal of the time. As well, there are some very specific differences in terms of health risks.

It is presently thought that five to 20 percent of women are lesbians, although we can be an invisible group and difficult to quantify. What exactly is a lesbian? Trying to define a lesbian is akin to trying to define a heterosexual. Like heterosexuals, lesbians can be celibate, promiscuous and everything in between.

One definition: A lesbian is a woman who shows affectional preference for women, who is woman-identified and who, if sexually active with others at the present time, is sexually exclusive with women. However, the continuum of what defines a lesbian has a wide range.

Mary Hunt, a theologian from Washington, DC says: "Being a lesbian is very hard to quantify. From our various experiences of being a lesbian, we share the fact that we transgress fundamental cultural norms for love and we consider that transgression healthy, natural and holy."

Martha Barrett, in her book **INVISIBLE LIVES**, says: "Being a lesbian is a twenty-four-hour-a-day role. It's not just having sex. You are your sexual identity, perhaps unconsciously. It covers everything, your personal relationships, your job, your plans for the future, the way you deal with people, what you talk about."

Lesbianism is an identity, not an activity. It is not a lifestyle, but rather the way in which we live our lives, affecting every aspect of our thoughts and actions and feelings. To take a whole world and call it a "lifestyle" is a belittling and demeaning way to treat a person and is one way we experience homophobia.

Suzanne Pharr, from her excellent book **HOMOPHOBIA: A WEAPON OF SEXISM**, states: "Homosexuality is simply a matter of sexual identity, which along with heterosexual identity, is formed in ways that no one conclusively understands. **The American Psychological Association** has said that it is no more abnormal to be homosexual than to be left-handed. It is simply that a certain percentage of the population is."

GENERAL QUALITY OF HEALTH CARE

Most books on general health care say nothing about lesbians. One recent book on the Canadian health care system had no listing under "lesbian" and most articles and books assume the male imperative. There is very little research done on lesbians; we need only to rely on ourselves for information on our own health. If you look up "lesbianism" in the **Index Medicus**, you are directed to "homosexuality." Medical researchers assume that because we're all lumped together as homosexuals, that lesbians and gay men have similar concerns, although we know that lesbians differ from gay men in the same way heterosexual women differ from heterosexual men.

Society's assumption of heterosexuality is so strong that lesbians almost always have to volunteer information about our homosexuality to doctors. In one study, only 25 percent of heterosexuals in the U.S. reported knowing a homosexual. Many physicians claim they have never seen a lesbian. It's highly unlikely that any physician who treats females has not treated a lesbian, yet of 110 gynecologists surveyed in a Florida study, 50 percent said they had never seen a patient who they thought was a lesbian.

A 1981 study revealed that less than one percent of the lesbians surveyed had been questioned about their sexual preferences by doctors; one study released in 1985 found that 9.3 percent of lesbians had been asked.

One study looked at professionals' reactions when told by their patients that they were lesbian. Eighty nine percent of all professionals' reactions were negative, 12 percent were cool to the news, 30 percent acted embarrassed, 25 percent responded in an inappropriate way ranging from mental health referrals to voyeuristic questions, and 22 percent rejected their lesbian clients overtly by leaving the examination room and having their nurses finish the health histories.

It is clear that homophobia (irrational fear of homosexuals) and heterosexism (believing that heterosexuality is the **only** way to be) are problems affecting the health care of lesbians. The heath care risk for lesbians in this context is that we avoid the system.

HOW TO INCREASE YOUR CHANCES OF GETTING BETTER HEALTH CARE

1. Spend some time and effort finding a doctor you trust.

If you don't know where to start, then call the **Status of Women** office in the nearest city, or the **Lesbian Information Lines**, if there is one. Most cities have a womens' health collective as well. Usually, these numbers are available from directory assistance and the alternative press.

2. Don't be afraid to interview your doctor to make sure you feel comfortable with her (him, if there are no other choices).

3. Educate your physician about what your needs are; be clear and concise.

4. If you do not trust a physician and you feel that the patient-physician relationship is not respected, then leave and find other heath care.

HEALTH DIFFERENCES BETWEEN LESBIAN AND HETEROSEXUAL WOMEN

1. Lesbians are at the lowest risk for contracting AIDS than any other group including children.

2. Lesbians have fewer gynecological problems than heterosexual women.

3. Lesbians are generally healthier than heterosexual women.

4. There are no medical problems specific to lesbians.

DIFFERENCES IN EXPERIENCING THE HEALTH CARE SYSTEM

The most significant health risk for lesbians is the fact that we avoid seeking routine health care. Forty percent of lesbians surveyed reported they feared that if they told their doctor they were lesbians, they would receive inferior care. Eighty four percent of lesbians surveyed had experienced a general reluctance to seek health care, finding it non-empathic. And ninety-six percent of lesbians "anticipated situations in which it could be harmful to them if their health care provider knew they were lesbians."

The implications of lesbians avoiding the health care system can be serious. Lesbians may not receive early warning of abnormal pap smears, endometrial cancer or breast cancer. All of these can be screened for easily, but women who feel ill served by a heterosexist system may not seek that screening. A 1981 study in the US showed the average time between pap smears for heterosexual women was eight months and for lesbians, 21 months.

The result of all this is that lesbians are more likely to orient health care around a specific crisis rather than a routine evaluation. One study showed that 58 percent of lesbians sought gyne care only when a problem occurred.

Lesbian health issues have been left to the attention of lesbians ourselves. A woman called her local women's health clinic to ask about lesbian services and was told that "the woman who deals with that stuff" was away. She asked: "Shouldn't everyone there deal with it?" Another lesbian went to **Planned Parenthood** to investigate a suspicious lump in her breast and was told that choosing some type of birth control method was a mandatory part of the visit. Yet another woman's experience: "After I knew for sure that I was a lesbian, I went to a doctor to get my IUD taken out. He told me I was just going through a phase and refused to take it out."

SPECIFIC WAYS LESBIANS GET SUB-OPTIMAL HEALTH CARE

HOSPITAL ACCESS: Lesbians are often denied access to their partners in emergency or ICU because we are not considered "family." Make sure you and your partner have all the appropriate legal documents giving you power of attorney. A power of attorney authorizes one person to make decisions for the other. This does not hold in cases of mental incapacity. So what we need is an **Enduring Power of Attorney** which continues to function in case of incapacity and terminates only with death. You can also make a **Nomination of Committee** in writing which allows the nominee to act on your behalf only when you are incapacitated. The court must declare you mentally incapable and then appoints as your Committee the person(s) you mentioned. You do not need a lifetime partner to do this; if there is someone you trust with your life, you can insure your best interests by taking legal precautions before they become necessary. Discuss the best options for you with your lawyer. Do not allow the hospital to dictate arbitrary rules to you. If the nurse will not listen to you, ask to speak to the supervisor, or the hospital administrator if necessary.

DEATH: Along the same lines, make sure you have a legal will expressing your wishes. If you do not specify what you want, your next of kin will automatically inherit your belongings, even if you wanted them to go to your partner or friends. Your lover or friends may have no involvement with your funeral or plans after your death.

In Canada, at the present time, lesbian couples do not qualify as "family" for bereavement leave. This issue has been before the courts and hopefully in the near future lesbians will have all the same rights as heterosexuals.

PARENTING

MAKING A DECISION: It is difficult for any woman to make a decision to have a child. For a lesbian, there are some extra considerations. Parts of society do not think that lesbians make good parents. This is compounded by the fact that we think in order to have a child, we need to be superhuman. We need to be very healthy emotionally and sure of ourselves to overcome all the criticism we will be sure to hear about being a lesbian having a child.

DECIDING THE METHOD: There are different ways for a lesbian to become pregnant. She must decide whether or not to have sexual intercourse, or use alternative insemination (**AI**). If she chooses the latter, she then needs to decide whether she wants to use fresh or frozen sperm or have a known or unknown donor. Many AI clinics limit their services to heterosexual couples, making it difficult for lesbians to access the system. In many large Canadian cities, there is an AI underground and the local lesbian association will usually know about it.

The parent-to-be can also decide to adopt or become a foster parent and then needs to make the decision as to whether or not to come out to social services. If she comes out, she may forfeit getting the child; however, it is important to keep in mind that by not coming out in this context, she is condemning herself to a life of lying and secrecy, not a healthy outlook, and also is not serving as a very good role model for her child in terms of self-love and respect.

The whole issue of parenthood is huge and the decisions are life-changing. Before you make any decisions in this area, read all you can find, talk to other lesbians who have become parents or decided not to, and give yourself adequate time to consider all your options.

OTHER ASPECTS: There is also the legal issue of adopting one's partner's child. Maternity benefits for the non-biological mother may be impossible to come by. The non-legal connection of the non-biological co-parent may prove difficult at times in the relationship, as she has no legal influence or community recognition.

Cheri Pies has written an excellent workbook called **CONSIDERING PARENTHOOD, A WORKBOOK FOR LESBIANS**.

SEXUALITY: There are many misunderstandings and misperceptions about lesbian sexuality. There have been studies done comparing lesbian lovemaking with that of gay men and heterosexual couples. These studies state that lesbians have repressed and minimal sex lives and that heterosexuals do "it" more often. These studies think it is irrelevant that lesbians spend hours pleasuring and loving one another without penetration, because that is not "it", i.e. intercourse. So a thirty second or three minute or thirty minute heterosexual penetration becomes more meaningful to researchers in defining our sexuality than hours upon hours of nurturing, loving, sexual interactions between two women.

Lesbian sex is anything two women do together in a sexual context and is not dependent upon heterosexual definitions. We must learn to be more open about our sexuality by reading, discussing, going to groups, and in general, becoming at ease with our bodies and their natural expressions.

JoAnn Loulan has written many excellent books, e.g. **LESBIAN SEX**, and also has cassette tapes out on many subjects relevant to lesbians.

SEXUALLY TRANSMITTED DISEASES: Lesbians are at much less risk for contacting STD's than heterosexual women. **The Kinsey Institute** found that the incidence of venereal disease in lesbians was less than one percent. Lesbians can get the same STD's as heterosexual women, but the fact is that most STD's are not easily transmitted from one woman to another. In fact, it is so rare for a lesbian to have syphilis or gonorrhea that sex with a man is immediately considered.

Some STD's require a certain type of sexual activity to be spread, for example, one kind of hepatitis. Hepatitis type A virus lives in feces, so lesbians doing oral-anal sex without precautions may pass the virus during lesbian sex.

Monilia (yeast, candidiasis), trichomonas, and gardnerella are all vaginal infections that can be transmitted by vulva to vulva contact, fingers to vagina, sharing sexual toys without proper cleaning or using barriers, or through sharing towels and washcloths. Usually none of these are spread to the mouth and throat unless the woman has a compromised immune system.

Bladder infections or cystitis are uncommon in lesbians. However, a lesbian can still develop cystitis when her resistance is lowered, when she is fatigued and generally unwell and when she is sexually vigorous. Cystitis should be treated quickly.

Lesbians, like anyone else, can spread Herpes Simplex types 1 and 2. Herpes Simplex 1 is on lips and mouth 95 percent of the time and on genitals five percent of the time. The reverse it true for Herpes Simplex 2. Lesbians should not have sex when the virus is active and should avoid contact with the virus on mucous membranes for at least ten days or until the lesions are completely healed.

Another virus that is spread by vulva contact is venereal warts. They may not show up for one to three months after contact. If you know you may have them, you must be responsible in getting them treated and informing your partner.

Just a quick word about lesbians and AIDS. It is very rare for one woman to transmit the AIDS virus to another woman. Each lesbian needs to inform herself on all aspects of safe sex and make her own decisions in that regard. The one important thing to remember is that we need to keep in mind that lesbians are not homogeneous. We are sex trade workers, married, IV drug users, and many other things that put us at high risk for contracting the AIDS virus. It is imperative to be informed, know your partner and practice safe sex whenever it is remotely indicated.

VIOLENCE: Lesbian battering is a very real entity. A woman does not have to be battered by a man to be considered a battered person. The lesbian community has been loathe to recognize this aspect of our lives, but lately there has been more support for both the battered lesbian and her batterer. To get specific information in your area, try the local lesbian organization if there is one, a rape crisis center or a battered women's shelter. Not all heterosexual institutions will be supportive, but many of them will.

Lesbians also risk violence on the street, especially if they are clearly identified as lesbians. The incidence of "gay bashing" has been on the increase, and many communities have responded with patrolling groups of lesbians and gay men who offer protection to the community. Violence against lesbians does not have to be strictly physical. Verbal harassment is also a violent act against a lesbian.

EMOTIONAL ASPECTS

One of the biggest health issues affecting lesbians is our emotional well-being. We all know that emotional health is an integral part of general health. Even if our body functions routinely, we are not considered healthy unless our emotional side is also functioning healthily. It is important that we talk about and increase our awareness of lesbians. It is a contradiction to tell us that it is okay to be a lesbian but not to talk about it. It is not healthy to have to pretend that you are not as you are.

Most lesbians live in a world where nothing fits into reality. Almost every magazine we look at, every television show or movie, every advertising image, novels, mainstream music, etc., constantly shows a way of life that is not ours. Some of us live decades with another woman and are not able to share with her families' celebrations. Some of us have become experts at genderless pronouns or we change pronouns or lie to protect our jobs, our homes, our children and our lives. The effect on our emotional health can be devastating. Living in such a homophobic world, there has to be some self-doubt in all but the strongest women. If the community does not validate a person or a relationship, then the individuals involved don't either, or if they are able to validate themselves, they do so at great emotional cost. This is really brought home when the **American Medical Association** advises practitioners to at least mention to patients the fact that therapies for "reversals" do exist. Of course, nowhere does it say to tell the patients that these therapies don't work. There is no cure for lesbianism because there is no illness.

Lesbian culture or community is necessary for self-esteem. It is evidence that we are viable human beings. Our identity becomes tangible, more than just an idea. **Jewel Gomez**, a writer, says: "It's very hard to want to be something and not have a reflection for it." If a community doesn't validate the relationship then the individuals don't either.

A lesbian couple, patients of mine, had been living together for years and it did not occur to them to bequest personal belongings to their partner in their wills, only to their families of origin, because they have never heard of two women doing that before. We need to begin to open up options for lesbians living in a heterosexual world.

The question of choice comes up often. Some people feel that lesbians have the choice of not being lesbians. In other words, they say that we don't have to act out our sexual identities. If we put this in the context of heterosexuals not acting out their sexual identity, we can see how absurd this concept really is. Choice is involved in the degree of openness in which a lesbian can live her life, not in being a lesbian which is inherent.

Doctors have the exclusive right to define disease and order treatment. Too often this is done without considering minority health differences, cultural, religious, class or social contexts, or the invisibly disadvantaged. When any person is denied her right to decide what is best for her, she can end up feeling vulnerable and powerless. What we need to do is educate ourselves, read books on lesbian health care, and women's health care that are considerate of lesbians. Ask questions. Write letters. And above all, we must feel free to demand all the rights and considerations that are ours as citizens in a democratic society.

If a lesbian tells her doctor she is a lesbian and the doctor responds that it doesn't matter, then the doctor has missed the point. It does matter or it would not have been brought up. Suzanne Pharr, in her excellent book **HOMOPHOBIA: A WEAPON OF SEXISM**, states: "To say that lesbianism is just a bedroom issue is to deny the wholeness of sexual identity and its social expression, and it denies the presence and effects of homophobia."

It is important for health care pro*Lesbian Health Care*viders not to assume we are heterosexual. It can be as simple as asking us whether we are lesbians or inquiring whether we need birth control and accepting our response. Instead of asking if we are married, we can be asked what support systems we have and with whom we live. A patient's partners and friends can be included in medical discussions and recovery.

Lesbians function in families of lovers, children, house-mates and friends. When one of our family members, albeit extended family, has a medical emergency or otherwise enters the health care system, we must be recognized as family and allowed to participate in the recovery of those we love.

Until society has learned to treat lesbians with the same respect and caring as other valued members of society, then our heath care must involve some activism as well. We need to be aware of our medical and legal rights, and if the medical profession is not, we need to help educate them. Read books on lesbian health, read alternative newspapers, make contact with lesbian organizations and status of women organizations, know who represents you in government who is supportive of your views. And don't be afraid to ask for whatever it is that you need.

RESOURCES

ALIVE AND WELL, A Lesbian Health Guide, by **Cuca Hepburn** with **Bonnie Gutierrez** (Crossing Press, 1988).

CONSIDERING PARENTHOOD, A Workbook for Lesbians, by **Cheri Pies** (Spinsters Ink, 1985).

INVISIBLE LIVES, The Truth About Millions of Women-Loving Women, by **Martha Barron Barrett** (William Morrow, 1989).

LESBIAN CONNECTION. This is an international forum of news and ideas for, by and about lesbians. It is published six times a year and is free to lesbians with a suggested donation. Write to **EPI**, PO Box 811, E Lansing, MI, 48826. 517-371-5257.

LESBIAN HEALTH MATTERS! by **Mary O'Donnell, Val Leoffler, Kater Pollock, Ziesel Saunders** (1979). This book can be ordered from **The Santa Cruz Women's Health Center**, 250 Locust St, Santa Cruz, CA, 95060.

LESBIAN PASSION, Loving Ourselves and Each Other by **JoAnn Loulan** (Spinsters/Aunt Lute, 1987).

LESBIAN SEX, by **JoAnn Loulan** (Spinsters Ink, 1984).

LESBIAN AT MIDLIFE: The Creative Transition, editors **Barbara Sang, Joyce Warshow and Adrienne J. Smith** (Spinsters Ink, 1991).

LESBIANS IN CANADA, edited by **Sharon Dale Stone** (Between the Lines, 1990).

HOMOPHOBIA: A WEAPON OF SEXISM, by **Suzanne Pharr** (Chardon Press, 1988).

THE LAVENDER COUCH, A Consumer's Guide to Psychotherapy for Lesbians and Gay Men, by **Dr. Marny Hall** (Alyson Publications, 1985).

   MOMAZONS, PO Box 02069, Columbus, OH. 43202.

MOMAZONS is a national organization that provides an opportunity for lesbians and our friends to explore options in bearing, adopting, raising or being involved with children.

HERBS AND NATURAL HEALING

ENCYCLOPEDIA OF NATURAL HEALING, for the public, by **Pizzorno** and **Murray**, (Prima Publishing, 1991).

A TEXTBOOK OF NATURAL MEDICINE, by **Pizzorno** and **Murray**, for the professional, (John Bastyr College, 144 NE 54th St, Seattle WA, 98105, 206-523-9585.

BETTER HEALTH THROUGH NATURAL HEALING, by **Dr. Ross Trattler**.

HEALING YOUR BODY NATURALLY, by **Gary Null** (A Four Walls Eight Windows First Edition, 1992).

HEALING WISE, by **Susun Weed**.

HOW TO GET WELL, by **Paavo Airola**.

NATURAL HEALING IN GYNECOLOGY, by **Rina Nissim**.

NATURAL MEDICINE FOR WOMEN, by **Julian and Susan Scott**, (Avon, 1991).

SCHOOL OF NATURAL HEALING, by **Dr. John R. Christopher**.

THE HOLISTIC HERBAL, by **David Hoffman**.

THE NEW HEALING YOURSELF, by **Joy Gardner**.

WHAT YOUR DOCTOR WON'T TELL YOU, by **Jane Heimlich**.

ALTERNATIVE MEDICINE: THE DEFINITIVE GUIDE, by **Burton Gulberg Group**, (Future Medicine Publishing, 1993).

COMPLEMENTARY NATURAL PRESCRIPTION FOR COMMON ALIMENTS, by **Dr. Carolyn Dean** (Keats, 1994).

RETURN TO JOY OF HEALTH- NATURAL MEDICINE AND ALTERNATIVE TREATMENTS FOR ALL YOUR HEALTH COMPLAINTS, by **Zoltan Rona**, (Alive, 1995).

CHILDHOOD DISEASES

HOW TO RAISE HEALTHY CHILDREN IN SPITE OF YOUR DOCTOR, by **Robert Mendelsohn**.

NATURAL CHILDCARE, by **Maribeth Riggs**.

IMMUNIZATION; THE REALITY BEHIND THE MYTH, by **Walene James**.

DIET

DETECTING YOUR HIDDEN ALLERGIES, by **Dr. William Crook**.

DIET FOR A NEW AMERICA, by **John Robbins**.

DON'T DRINK YOUR MILK, by **Dr. Frank Oski**.

EATING ALIVE, by **Dr. John Matsen**.

FIT FOR LIFE, by **Harvey And Marilyn Diamond**.

FOOD AND THE GUT REACTION, or, **BREAKING THE VICIOUS CYCLE** (Revised, 1995), by **Elaine Gotschall**.

STAYING HEALTHY WITH NUTRITION, by **Elsan Haas**.

THE D'ADAMO DIET, by **Dr. James D'Adamo**.

THE NUTRITIONAL CHALLENGE FOR WOMEN, by **Louise Lambert-Lagace**.

TRADITIONAL FOODS ARE YOUR BEST MEDICINE, by **Ronald Schmidt**.

HOMEOPATHY

THE WOMEN'S GUIDE TO HOMEOPATHY, by **Dr. Andrew Lockie** and **Dr. Nicola Geddes**.

A WOMAN'S GUIDE TO HOMEOPATHY, by **Dr. Trevor Smith**.

EVERY DAY HOMEOPATHY, by **Dr. David Gemmell**.

EVERYBODY'S GUIDE TO HOMEOPATHY, by **Cummings** and **Ulman**.

HOMEOPATHIC MEDICINE AT HOME, by **Panos-Heimlich**.

HOMEOPATHIC MEDICINE FOR CHILDREN AND INFANTS, by **Dara Ullman**.

THE FAMILY GUIDE TO HOMEOPATHY, by **Dr. Andrew Lockie**.

VITAMINS AND NUTRITION

FEED YOURSELF RIGHT, by **Lendon Smith**.

HOW TO GET WELL, by **Paavo Airola**.

PRESCRIPTION FOR NUTRITIONAL HEALING, by **Dr. James Balch**.

STAYING HEALTHY WITH NUTRITION, by **Elson Haas**.

THE CHEMISTRY OF MAN, by **Dr. Bernard Jensen**.

EMOTIONAL AND SPIRITUAL

AT A JOURNAL WORKSHOP, by **Ira Progoff**.

HOW SHALL I LIVE, by **Richard Moss**.

LOVE AND FORGIVENESS, by **Leonard Shaw**. Send $12.00 US to International Psychotherapy Institution Of Love And Well Being, 702-11th Ave East, Scattle WA 98102, 902-322-5785.

MAPS OF ECSTASY, by **Gabrielle Roth**.

THE PICTURE OF HEALTH, by **Lucia Capacchione**.

THE DANCE OF ANGER AND THE DANCE OF INTIMACY, by **Harriet Goldhor Lerner**.

THE HEALING OF EMOTION, by **Chris Griscom**.

THE AGELESS BODY, by **Chris Griscom**.

EXERCISE

TRAGER MENTASTICS, by **Milton Trager**.

RELAXERCISE, by **D. and K. Zerach-Bersin** And **Mark Resse**.

MASTER LEVEL EXERCISE - PSYCHOCALISTHENICS, by **Oscar Ichazo** (Available In Book, Tape And Video From Sequoia Press Inc, 150 Fifth Avenue, New York, NY, 10011).

THE HANDBOOK OF SELF-HEALING- YOUR PERSONAL PROGRAM FOR BETTER HEALTH AND INCREASED VITALITY, by **Meir Schneider**, (Penguin, 1994).

ATTITUDINAL

AFFIRMATIONS, by **Stuart Wilde**.

FEELING GOOD: THE NEW MOOD THERAPY, with workbook, by **David Burns**, (Avon, 1992).

LIFE 101, by **Peter McWilliams** and **John Roger** (To Order Call 1-800-LIFE-101 Or Write To Prelude Press.

LOVING RELATIONSHIPS, by **Sondra Ray**.

THE WILL TO BE WELL, by **Neville Hodgkinson**.

YOU CAN'T AFFORD THE LUXURY OF A NEGATIVE THOUGHT, by **Peter McWilliams** and **John Roger** (To Order Call 1-800-874-6569 Or 800 U-r-In-Joy, Or Send $14.95 Plus Postage To Prelude Press, 8165 Mannix Drive, Los Angeles, CA, 90046).

YOU CAN HEAL YOUR LIFE and **LOVE YOURSELF, HEAL YOUR LIFE WORKBOOK**, by **Louise Hay**.

CANCER

CANCER AS A TURNING POINT, by **Lawrence Leshan**.

GOD I THOUGHT YOU DIED, by **Claude Dosdall**.

CANCER THERAPY - THE INDEPENDENT CONSUMER'S GUIDE TO NON-TOXIC TREATMENT AND PREVENTION, by **Ralph Moss**.

THE CANCER INDUSTRY, by **Ralph Moss**.

BEATING CANCER THROUGH NUTRITION, by **Patrick Quillan**.

THIRD OPINION, by **John M. Fink**.

QUESTIONING CHEMOTHERAPY, by **Ralph Moss**, (Equinox Press, 1-800-929-WELL).

HEALING CHOICES: CANCER REPORT SERVICE

Your Healing Choices report from acclaimed medical writer Ralph W. Moss, Ph.D. will provide you with objective, detailed information on the most promising alternative methods and practitioners for your particular type of cancer. The reports usually range from 30 to 50 pages. Call, write, or fax, Healing Choices, 144 St John's Place, New York NY, 11217. Tel: 718-636-4433, Fax: 718-636-0186 to request a Healing Choices packet, which contains a detailed questionaire. Phone consultations with Dr. Moss are also available at no extra cost.

THE HEALTH RESOURCE

An individual comprehensive research report on your medical condition can be obtained from **The Health Resource**, 209 Katherine Drive, Conway, AR, 72032, 501-329-5272. Fax: 501-329-8700. This 50 to 150 page report includes the computer print out plus copies of articles from medical journals and consumer magazines and books. It also includes information on treatment options - both conventional and alternative. The cost is $125 for this comprehensive report, or $68 for a "mini-report" of 20 to 25 pages.

THE WORLD RESEARCH FOUNDATION

The World Research Foundation, 15300 Ventura Blvd, #405, Sherman Oaks CA, 91403, 818-907-5483, is an non-profit health and environmental information network with an extensive library system containing books dating to the 1600's. In addition to books and periodicals, the Foundation is linked to over 500 computer databases which gives access to important medical, scientific and environmental information from over 100 countries. The library is open 9:30am to 5:30pm, Monday through Friday. Two different types of searches are available for a nominal fee, A Computer Search and/or a Library Search. Library searches tend to contain complementary, alternative, non-traditional and natural therapeutics. Computer searches contain the latest and most up-to-date allopathic, ie, pharmaceutical and surgical, information. The basic fee for a library or computer search is $40 plus $7 postage in US funds for Canadian residents.

Organizations

A FRIEND INDEED, PO Box 515 Place du Parc Stn. Montreal, PQ. H2W 2P1.

AERON LIFE CYCLE SALIVARY TEST KIT, 1-800-866-9085.

AMERICAN SELF-HELP CLEARING HOUSE, St. Clares Riverside Medical Center, Denville, NJ, 07834. 201-625-7101.

BEAUTY WITHOUT CRUELTY, 26 Day St, Cambridge, ON, N1S 3P9. 519-621-5986.

BEREAVED FAMILIES OF ONTARIO, 214 Merton St, #204, Toronto, ON, M4S 1A1. 416-440-0290.

BEREAVEMENT SERVICES AND COMMUNITY EDUCATION, 1403 Bayview Ave, Toronto, ON, M4G 3A8. 416-485-6415. Toll free number 1-800-268-2787.

BIOTICS, PO Box 36888, Houston, TX, 77236. 1-800-231-5777.

BIRTH AND LIFE BOOKSTORE, 7001 Alonzo Ave NW, PO Box 70625, Seattle, WA 98107-0625. 206-789-4444.

BOSTON WOMEN'S HEALTH BOOK COLLECTIVE, PO Box 192, West Somerville, MA, 02144. 617-625-0271.

Breast Cancer Treatment Center, 275 Bagette St #201, Kingston, ON, K7L 3G4. 613-548-8123.

BREAST CANCER ACTION PO Box 4332, Stn E, Ottawa, ON. 613-232-3117 or Fax: 613-788-4378.

C/SEC (CESAREAN/SUPPORT/ EDUCATION & CONCERN), 22 Forest Rd, Framingham, Mass 01701. 508-877-8266.

CANADIAN PID SOCIETY, PO Box 33804, Stn D, Vancouver, BC. V6J 4L6. 604-684-5704.

CANDIDA RESEARCH AND INFORMATION FOUNDATION, PO Box 2719, Castro Valley, CA. 94546.

CANDIDA RESEARCH AND INFORMATION FOUNDATION (CRIF), C/O The Canadian Schizophrenic Foundation, 17 Florence Ave, Toronto, ON, M2N 1E9. 416-733-2117. Fax: 416-733-2352.

CANDIDA RESEARCH INFORMATION SERVICE (CRIS), 41 Green Valley Court, Kleinburg, ON, L0J 1C0. 416-832-0789.

CFIDS ROCHESTER RESEARCH PROJECT, 1200 Edgewood Ave, Rochester NY, 14618.

COMPASSIONATE FRIENDS, 685 William Ave, Winnipeg, MB, R3E 0Z2. 204-787-2460.

COPA (Community Older Persons Alcohol Project) C\O **Dr. Sarah Saunders**, **Addiction Research Foundation**, 33 Russell St, Toronto, ON, Canada, M5S 2S1. 416-595-6106.

DCAHS, Doctors Concerned About Human Sterilization, c/o Dr. John Cattanach, 37 Vista St, Bulleen, Vic 3105, Melbourne, Australia. 03-852-0644. Fax: 03-852-0096.

DENNIS O'DOWD c/o Iomech, 863 Ranch View Rd, Mississauga, ON, L5E 1H1.

DIAGNOSTECHS, 1-800-878-3787.

DR. DIANE L. MCGIBBON, 3 Gardenvale Rd, Toronto, ON, M8Z 4B8. 416-239-4644 Fax: 416 239 7428.

DR. ORIAN TRUSS, CRITICAL ILLNESS RESEARCH FOUNDATION, 2614 Highland Ave, Birmingham, AL. 35205. 205-326-0642.

DR. PAUL CHENEY, 10620 Park Rd #234, Charlotte, NC, 28210. 704-542-7444.

DR. PAUL FUGAZZOTO, Director Urinary Research Center, 624 6th St, Rapid City, SD, 57701. 605-343-9495.

DR. TORI HUDSON, Portland Naturopathic Clinic, The Teaching Clinic of The College of Naturopathic Medicine, 11231 SE Market St, Portland, OR, 97216. 503-255-7355.

DYING WITH DIGNITY, 600 Eglinton Ave East, #401, Toronto, ON, M4P 1P3. 416-486-3998.

EFAMOL RESEARCH INSTITUTE, PO Box 818, Kentville, NS, B4N 4H8. 902-678-3001.

ENDOMETRIOSIS ASSOCIATION, U.S. and Canada Headquarters, 8585 North 76th Place, Milwaukee, WI, 53223. 1-800-426-2END.

FERTILITY AWARENESS NETWORK, PO Box 1190, New York, NY, 1009.

FERTILITY AWARENESS SERVICES, PO Box 986, Corvalis, OR. 97339.

FIBROMYALGIA ASSOCIATION OF BC, PO Box 15455, Vancouver, BC, V6B 5B2.

FIBROMYALGIA NETWORK, PO Box 31750, Tuscon, AZ, 85751-1750. 520-290-5508 Fax: 520-290-5550.

GREENPEACE, 1017 West Jackson, Chicago, IL, 60607. 312-666-3305.

GREENPEACE, 185 Spadina, Toronto, ON, M5T 2C6. 416-345-8408.

HALTON HAMILTON WENTWORTH SUPPORT GROUP, 762 Upper James St, Box 143, Hamilton, ON, L9C 3A2. 416-383-4431.

HEALTH AND WELFARE CANADA, Publications, Health and Welfare, Brook-Claxton Buildings, Tunney's Pasture, Ottawa, ON, K1A OK9.

HERS - HYSTERECTOMY EDUCATIONAL RESOURCES AND SERVICES, 422 Bryn Mawr Ave, Bala-Cynwyd, PA, 19004. 215-667-7757.

IDEAL COMPUTER ENVIRONMENTS, 306-584-2262.

INFERTILITY AWARENESS ASSOCIATION OF CANADA, 104-1785 Alta Vista Dr, Ottawa, ON, K1G 3Y6. 613-738-8968.

INTERNATIONAL CESAREAN AWARENESS NETWORK, PO Box 152, Syracuse, NY, 13210. 315-424-1942.

INTERNATIONAL HEALTH FOUNDATION, PO Box 3494, Jackson, TN 38303. 901-427-8100.

KENT MACLEOD, C/O NUTRICHEM PHARMACY, 1303 Richmond Rd, Ottawa, ON, K2B 7Y4. 1-800-363-6327 Fax: 1-800-465-2965.

KLAIRE LABORATORIES, 1-800-533-7255.

KRIPP'S PHARMACY, 994 Granville St, Vancouver, BC, V6Z 1L2. 604-687-2564.

MAMMACARE, Box 15748, Gainesville, FL, 32602. 1-800-626-2273 or 904-375-0607.

MOMAZONS, PO Box 02069, Columbus, OH. 43202.

NATIONAL INSTITUTES OF HEALTH BACKGROUNDER ON FIBROMYALGIA. 301-494-4484.

NATIONAL ME/FM ACTION NETWORK, 3836 Carling Ave, Hwy 17B, Nepean, ON, K2H 7V2. 613-829-6667.

NATIONAL WOMEN'S HEALTH NETWORK, 1325 G St NW, Washington, DC, 200003. 202-347-1140.

NATURAL ENERGY WORKS, PO Box 864, El Cerrito, CA. 94530. 510-526-5978.

NEW CONCEPTS, 6710 Embassy Blvd, #204, Port Richey, FL, 43668. 813-845-7544.

NEW DIMENSIONS, 416-488-6330 or 514-426-2590.

NORAD CORPORATION, 1549 11th St, Santa Monica, CA 90401. 313-345-0800.

NUTRITIONAL UPDATE, 1-800-528-0559.

ONTARIO FIBROSITIS ASSOCIATION, c/o The Arthritis Society, 250 Bloor St East, #410, Toronto, ON, M4W 3P2. 416-967-1414.

ONTARIO MINISTRY OF LABOUR c/o **Radiation Protection Branch**, 81 Resources Rd, Weston, ON, M9P 3T4. 416-235-5922, Fax: 416-235-5926.

OSTEOPOROSIS SOCIETY OF CANADA, 33 Laird Dr, Toronto, ON, M4G 3F9. 416-696-2663.

OSTOP OTTAWA, c\o Good Companions Center, 670 Albert St, Ottawa, ON, K1R 6L2. 613-236-0428.

OVULATION METHOD TEACHER'S ASSOCIATION, PO Box 101780, Anchorage, Alaska. 99510-1780.

PARENTBOOKS, 201 Harbord St Toronto, ON, M5S 1HS. 416-537-8334. Fax: 416-537-9499.

PATIENT INFORMATION ON CHRONIC ILLNESS (**PICI**), 575 Avenue Rd #601, Toronto, ON, M4V 2K2.

PHILLIPS NUTRITIONALS, 27071 Cabot Rd #122, Laguna Hills, CA 92653. 1-800-514-5115.

PHYSICAL MEDICINE RESEARCH FOUNDATION, 510-207 West Hastings St, Vancouver, BC, V6B 1H7. 604-684-4148 or 604-684-5345.

PROFESSIONAL HEALTH PRODUCTS, PO Box 80085, Portland, OR, 97280-1085. 1-800-952-2219.

RECOVERY INC, Self-help for Nervous Symptoms and Fears, 802 North Dearborn St, Chicago, IL, 60610. 312-337-5661 Fax: 312-337-5756.

SMITH'S PHARMACY, 3463 Yonge St, Toronto, ON, M4N 2A3. 416-488-2600.

ST. CHARLES MEDICAL CENTER, Nancy Petersen, Endometriosis Treatment Program, 2500 NE Neff Rd, Bend OR 97701-6015. Toll free number: 1-800-446-2177.

SUPPLEMENTS PLUS, 451 Church St, Toronto, ON, M4Y 2C5. 1-800-387-4761.

THE BODY SHOP, 15 Andrew Place, Don Mills, ON, M3C 2H2. 416-441-3202.

THE CANADIAN ASSOCIATION FOR CHILDREN OF ALCOHOLICS 102 Wychcrest, Toronto, ON. 416-533-6293.

THE CANADIAN CENTER FOR OCCUPATIONAL HEALTH AND SAFETY, (**CCOHS**), 250 Main St East, Hamilton, ON, L8N 1H6. Toll free 1-800-263-8276 or Fax: 416-572-2206.

THE CANADIAN PID SOCIETY, PO Box 33804, Stn D, Vancouver, BC, V67 4L6. 604-684-5704.

THE CANADIAN PID SOCIETY, PO Box 33804, Stn D, Vancouver, BC, V67 4L6. 604-684-5704.

THE CFIDS ASSOCIATION, PO Box 220398, Charlotte, NC, 28222-0398. Phone (Canada): 704-362-2343 Fax: 704-365-9755. In the U.S. 1-800-442-3437 or 1-900-988-2343.

THE COMPUTER SHIELD GROUP, 416-971-4242.

THE ENDOMETRIOSIS NETWORK OF TORONTO (TENT), PO Box 3125, Markham Industrial Park, Markham, ON, L3R 6G5. 416-591-3963.

THE HUMANE SOCIETY OF THE U.S., 2100 L St NW, Washington, DC, 20037. 202-452-1100.

THE INTERSTITIAL CYSTITIS ASSOCIATION: PO Box 5814, Stn A, Toronto, ON, M5W 1P2.

THE INTERSTITIAL CYSTITIS ASSOCIATION OF B.C., 1204-2024 Fullerton Ave, North Vancouver, BC, V7P 3G4.

THE INTERSTITIAL CYSTITIS FOUNDATION, 120 South Spalding Dr, #210, Beverley Hills, CA, 90212.

THE INTERSTITIAL CYSTITIS ASSOCIATION (ICA), PO Box 1553, Madison Square Stn, New York, NY, 10159.

THE JUSTISSE GROUP, PO Box 441, Stn P, Toronto, ON, M5S 2S9. 416-656-7659.

THE M.E. ASSOCIATION OF CANADA, 400-246 Queen St, Ottawa, ON, K1P 5E4. 613-563-1565.

THE MATURE WOMEN'S NETWORK, 411 Dunsmuir St, Vancouver, BC, V6B 1X4.

THE MONTREAL HEALTH PRESS, PO Box 1000, Stn Place du Parc, Montreal, PQ, H2W 2N1. 514-272-5441.

THE MYALGIC ENCEPHALOMYEL-ITIS ASSC. OF ONTARIO, 90 Sheppard ave. East, #108, North York, ON, M2N 3A1. 416-222-8820 Fax: 416-224-2181.

THE NATIONAL ACTION FORUM FOR MIDLIFE AND OLDER WOMEN, Box 816, Stony Brook, NY, 11790-0609.

THE NATIONAL OSTEOPOROSIS FOUNDATION, 1150-17th St, #500, Washington, DC, 20036.

THE NIGHTINGALE RESEARCH FOUNDATION (**NFR**), 383 Danforth Ave, Ottawa, ON, K2A 0E1. 613-729-9643.

THE ONTARIO NETWORK FOR ENDOMETRIOSIS, City Center Place, 25 Peele Center Dr, #133, Brampton, ON, L6T 3R5.

THE PLANETARY ASSOCIATION FOR CLEAN ENERGY, 100 Bronson Ave, #10001, Ottawa, ON, K1R 6G8. 613-238-4437.

THE TORONTO HUMANE SOCIETY, 11 River St, Toronto, ON, M5A 4C2. 416-392-2273 Fax: 416-392-9978.

THE UNIVERSITY OF TORONTO BONE AND MINERAL GROUP, 38 Shuter St #212, Toronto, ON, M5B 1A6.

TORONTO WOMEN'S BOOKSTORE, 73 Harbord St, Toronto, ON, M5S 1G4. 416-922-8744.

TRA INSTRUMENTS in Salt Lake City, Utah. 1-800-582-3537.

TRANSITIONS FOR HEALTH INC, 621 SW Alder #900, Portland OR, 97205-3627. 1-800-888-6814.

U.S.-CANADIAN ENDOMETRIOSIS ASSOCIATION, Headquarters Office, PO Box 92187, Milwaukee, WI, 53202. 1-800-426-2END.

VANCOUVER WOMEN'S HEALTH COLLECTIVE, 302-1720 Grant St, Vancouver, BC, V5L 2Y7. 604-736-5262.

VDT NEWS: The VDT Health and Safety Report, PO Box 1799 Grand Central Stn, New York, NY, 10163. 212-517-2800.

VBAC CANADA, 8 Gilgorm Rd, Toronto, ON, M5N 2M5.

WEED, 736 Bathurst St, Toronto, ON, M5R 2R4. 416-516-2600.

WOMEN AND WORK RESEARCH AND EDUCATION SOCIETY, 4340 Carson St, Burnaby, BC, V5J 2X9. 604-430-0458.

WOMEN FOR SOBRIETY, PO Box 618, Quakertown, PA, 18951. 1-800-333-1606.

WOMEN'S INTERNATIONAL PHARMACY, 5708 Monona Dr, Madison, WI, 53716-3152. 608-221-7800, or 1-800-279-5708 in the United States.

YEAST CONSULTING SERVICES, PO Box 11157, Torrance, CA. 905010. 310-375-1073.

Index

A:

0-3-4-12 RULE: 25
150 MOST ASKED QUESTIONS ABOUT MENOPAUSE: 203
5-hydroxy-tryptophan 7, 149, 199
A BIRTH CLASS 120, 129
A BOOK ABOUT BIRTH CONTROL 55
A BOOK ABOUT MENOPAUSE 203
A BOOK ABOUT SEXUALLY TRANSMITTED DISEASES 92
A Consumer's Guide to Psychotherapy 272
A Friend Indeed 190, 191, 202, 219
A GUIDE TO EFFECTIVE CARE IN PREGNANCY AN CHILD-BIRTH 107
A GUIDE TO PREVENTING UNNECESSARY 137
A GUIDE TO UNCONVENTIONAL CANCER THERAPIES 241
A LAYWOMAN'S GUIDE 186
A Mother's Workbook for Health and Emotional Well-Being 96, 100, 129
A NATURAL APPROACH TO MENOPAUSE 202
A New View Of Endometriosis 180
A PHYSICIAN'S GUIDE TO MYALGIC ENCEPHALOMYELITIS 10
A WOMAN'S GUIDE TO FEELING WONDERFUL IN THE SECOND HALF 202
AA 23-27
Abbey, Dr. Susan 8
abdomen 33, 61, 62, 101, 103, 108, 110, 113, 119, 150, 165-167, 173, 174, 177, 180, 183, 212, 220, 262
abdomen, fluid in 262
abdomen, lower 173
abdomen, pressure in 167
abdomen, upper section 262
abdominal and perineal problems, prevention 96
abdominal area 124
abdominal bloating 147
abdominal cavity 161, 171-174, 222
abdominal cramps 253, 265
abdominal exercises 118
abdominal extraction 221
abdominal incision 162
abdominal muscles 117-120, 124
abdominal muscles, midline 118, 120
abdominal pain, chronic 163
abdominal pain, lower 89, 167
abdominal pain, recurrent 62
abdominal pain, right upper 90, 262
abdominal pain, severe 174
abdominal pain, upper 89, 90, 262
abdominal pains, low 87
abdominal scars 173
abdominal strengthening 118

abdominal surgery 59, 61, 177, 261, 263
abdominal swelling 89
abdominal tightening 119
ABLATION 222-224, 251, 253
abortion 54, 56, 60, 61, 89, 109, 111, 113, 142, 161, 162, 170, 250, 253
abortion clinic 253
abortion, Legal 56
abortion, therapeutic 60, 109, 161, 170, 250
Abortion, Illegal 56
abortions, late 111, 113
Abramson, Zelda 218
abscesses 161, 166, 165, 166, 168, 169, 262
abscesses, diagnose 166
ABSCESSES:, TREATMENT OF 169
abuse 13, 23, 24, 41, 150, 222
Academy Award Recovery 39
aching, deep seated 173
aching, intense 127
acid base balance 70, 122
acidophilus 70, 76, 77, 81-83, 91, 170, 184
acidophilus capsules 91, 170
acidophilus powder 83
acidophilus suppositories 82, 83
ACIDOPHILUS: 76
acne 6, 52, 53, 70, 73, 74, 147, 158, 159, 175, 176, 189
acne, pre-existing 53
acne, teenage 189
ACTIVE BIRTH 96, 120
acupressure 129, 154, 202
acupuncture 9, 25, 36, 66, 84, 85, 95, 123, 129, 185, 198, 222, 223
acupuncture needles 36, 198
acupuncture points 84, 185
acupuncture treatments 123, 185
Acupuncture and Chinese Medicine 198
ACUPUNCTURE: 185
acupuncturist, experienced 185
acupuncturists 223
Acute Toxicity Test 259
Adam's apple 141
Adamsom, Dr. David 177
addiction, drug 4, 14
addiction, physical 25
addiction, psychological 25
Addiction Research Foundation 24, 27
Addison-Wesley 21, 186, 202
adenovirus 5
adhesions 62, 164, 166, 177
adolescents 6, 50, 73, 171
adolescents, cervixes of 171
adopting, legal issue 269
adrenal function tests 50
adrenal glands 6, 7, 9, 188, 198
adrenal glands very stressed 198
adrenal glandular extracts 198
ADRENAL 6, 7, 9, 50, 188, 198
adrenals 192

aerobic exercise 117, 118, 124, 181, 206
aerobic training, submaximal 7
aerobics, no-bounce 118
Aeron Life Cycle salivary test kit 213
affirmations 27, 185
AFP 113
Afro-American 108, 245
AFTER SUICIDE 43
AFTER THE BABY'S BIRTH, A WOMAN'S GUIDE TO WELLNESS 97, 143
AGELESS AGING, The Natural Way To Stay Young 202
aging, accelerate 198
aging, biomarker for 6
aging effects 198
aging, healthy changes 188
aging, premature 3
aging, sexual aspects 202
aging, signs of 189, 190
aging, slow 200
AI clinics 269
AIDS 7, 13, 36, 50, 54, 66, 87, 88, 163, 165, 171, 172, 236, 238, 256, 268, 270
AIDS, panic about 87
air, Fresh 118, 123
air, indoor 33, 81
air pollutants 33
air quality 33
air, quality of 28
air traffic controllers 29
airline reservation agents 29
AIUT 102
albino 258
alcohol 2-4, 13, 15, 22-25, 27, 38, 41, 65, 115, 148, 189, 198, 206, 217, 237
alcohol, abuse of 24
alcohol, cravings for 25
alcohol, excess 198
alcohol free life 27
alcohol intake, excessive 65
alcoholic drinkers 25
ALCOHOLICS ANONYMOUS 23, 26, 27
ALCOHOLISM - THE BIOCHEMICAL CONNECTION 27
alendronate 211
Alexander 17, 31
alfalfa sprouts 246
algae, blue green 123, 247
Ali, Dr. Majid 8, 9
Alive Books 257
ALIVE AND WELL, A Lesbian Health Guide 272
allergic reactions 71-74, 248
allergies 3, 4, 7-9, 80, 84, 85, 115, 149, 185, 251
allergies, food 4, 7, 84, 85, 149
allergies to medications 251
ALLERGIES, CANDIDA AND AMINES: 149
ALLERGIES: 185
allergy 9, 54, 149, 185

allergy shots 149
allergy specialist 149, 185
almond oil 255, 259
almonds, raw 122, 123
alpha fetal protein, elevated 103
ALPHA FETAL PROTEIN TESTING 113
ALPHA PLUS OR TRIPLE SCREENING 109, 114
alprazolam 151
Altered Lifetime Risk 201
ALTERNATIVES TO EPISIOTOMIES 132
AMAS 229, 230
American Academy of Pathology 155
American Association for Cancer Research 159
American Cancer Society 196, 228, 229
American College of Obstetricians and Gynecologists 102, 135, 229
American College of Physicians 229
American College of Radiology 228
American Geriatric Society 233
American Institute of Ultrasound in Medicine 102
American Journal Of the Medical Sciences 130
American Medical Association 194-196, 229, 271
American Psychological Association 267
AMERICAN SELF-HELP CLEARING HOUSE 203
amines, levels of 149
amino acids 7, 25, 41, 80, 149, 199, 208
aminoglycosides 168
amitriptyline 8
ammenorrhea, intermittent 209
amniocentesis 103, 104, 108-114
amniocentesis, availability of 111
amniocentesis, necessity of 109
amniocentesis, routine 110
AMNIOCENTESIS, EARLY 110
amniotic fluid 108-110, 113
amniotic sac 108
amoxicillin 83, 169
ampicillin 83, 169
Ampligen 7
Amway 260
AN EASIER CHILDBIRTH 96, 99, 100, 129
Anaerobic 7, 168, 169, 172
Anaerobic training 7
anal 162, 171, 270
Anaprox 150
anchovies 149
Anderson, Debbie 140
androgen activity 52
androgen hormones 219
androgen receptors 52
androgens 52, 189
anemia, indicator of 246
anemia, persistent 222
anemia, severe 245, 248

Anemia *4, 52, 71, 74, 108, 117, 222, 244-248*
anemias *22, 245-247*
anemias, blood loss *247*
anesthesia *61, 220, 249, 250, 253*
anesthesia, complications from *220*
anesthetic charges *59*
anesthetic, general *61, 83, 84, 166, 174, 181, 249, 251-253, 257, 263*
anesthetic, local *59, 83, 84, 108, 155, 192, 249-251, 257*
anesthetic, no *249, 264*
anesthetist *59, 251, 252*
anger *15, 21, 23, 40, 81, 99, 128, 137, 139, 147, 150, 221, 240*
anger, difficulty expressing *240*
anger, express your *150*
anger, feelings of *139*
anger, increased levels *147*
anger, inward *147*
anger, outbursts of *15, 147*
angina *29*
angiostat *84*
animal testing *159, 258-260*
ankles *51, 239, 244, 255*
ankles, swelling of *51, 244*
ankles, Swollen *239*
ankles, ulcers *255*
ANNUAL VDT PRODUCT DIRECTORY *36*
Annals of Internal Medicine *5*
anorexia *13, 73*
anovulation *209*
antacids *122, 247*
anthropologist *38, 94, 129*
anti-aging program *202*
anti-anaerobic *172*
anti-cancer *71, 239*
anti-chlamydial *90*
anti-chlamydial treatment *90*
anti-depressant *6, 84*
anti-depressant medication *84*
anti-estrogen drug *239*
anti-inflammatory *84, 223*
anti-inflammatory agent *84*
anti-malignant *230*
anti-nauseant *123, 252*
anti-thyroid *142*
anti-yeast *6, 71, 74-77, 81, 91, 184*
anti-yeast preparations *76, 77, 81*
Anti-Estrogen *158, 239*
ANTI-YEAST MEDICATIONS: *76*
antibiotic-resistant strains *163*
antibiotic treatment *81, 168-170*
antibiotic treatment, multiple *168*
ANTIBIOTIC USAGE *80*
antibiotics, anti-anaerobic *172*
antibiotics, intravenous *222*
antibiotics, IV *168, 169*
antibiotics, long-term *80*
antibiotics, modern *172*
antibiotics, oral *168*
antibiotics, overexposed to *73*
antibiotics, overuse of *5, 8*
antibiotics, penetration by *169*
antibiotics, preventative *136*
antibiotics, prolonged *184*
antibiotics, prophylactic *170*
antibiotics, repeated courses *70, 79*
antibiotics, unnecessary *71*
ANTIBIOTICS, PROLONGED OR REPEATED USE *70*
ANTIBIOTICS:, MULTIPLE *168*

antibodies, anti-thyroid *142*
antibodies, Monoclonal *67, 68*
antibodies, thyroid *141, 142*
antibody *67, 80, 88, 230*
antibody in serum, anti-malignant *230*
Antidepressants *151*
ANTIHISTAMINES: *84*
antioxidant vitamins *7*
antioxidants *200*
antiseptic *61, 72, 252*
antiseptic soap *61*
antiseptic solution *252*
Antiviral regimen *7*
anxiety attacks *6*
anxiety states *151*
anxiety, unnecessary *104, 113*
APGAR *112*
appendicitis *165, 166, 174, 181*
appendix *161, 163, 173*
appetite changes *52*
appetite, increased *142, 147*
appetite, loss of *15, 29, 139, 245*
apple *123, 141, 208, 255*
Appleton, Nancy *212*
apricots *246*
arches *181*
Archives of Environmental Health *230*
arnica *129*
arms *19, 47, 200, 206, 212*
arms, inner *212*
Arroll, Dr. Bruce *133*
ARTEMIS SPEAKS *138*
arteries *47, 80, 194, 254*
arteries, hardening of the *47, 194*
arteriogram, coronary *194*
arthritic symptoms *51*
Arthritis *4, 10, 41, 52, 73, 80, 90*
artificial sweeteners *84*
AS YOU EAT, SO YOUR BABY GROWS *95*
ascorbate *247*
aspartame *84*
aspartates *207*
aspirin *121, 191*
assertiveness training course *17*
asthma *20, 52, 73, 80, 147*
astralagus *7*
Astroglide *189*
atherosclerosis, risk of *219*
Atkins, Dr. Robert *185*
Atkinson, Dr. Holly *2, 9*
atomidine *159*
Attitude Clinic *148*
Austin, Steven *241*
autism *73*
auto-immune diseases *74, 80, 180*
avocados *79, 149, 259*
Avon *85, 260*
Azbug, Bella *38*

B:

B-1 *22*
B-12 *6, 7, 10, 184, 208, 245, 247*
B-12, Injectable *7*
B-50 *17, 25, 123, 148, 199*
B-50 CAPSULES:, MEGA *199*
B-6 *123, 245*
B-cells *180*
B-lymphocytes *7*
B vitamins *51, 123, 148, 156, 255*

babies, first *131-133, 142*
babies, inherited defects *108*
babies, normal weight *104*
babies, small *104*
babies, subsequent *131*
BABIES REMEMBER BIRTH, AND OTHER EXTRAORDINARY SCIENTIFIC *99*
baby, abnormal *109*
baby, abnormality *104*
baby carriages *116*
baby, demands of a new *141*
baby, malformations *104*
baby massage *95*
baby, premature *40, 112*
baby, sex of *106, 108, 109*
baby's bloodstream *128*
baby's breathing *128*
baby's circulation *113*
baby's growth *104*
baby's head *79, 117, 127, 130-133, 135*
baby's heart *104, 106, 133, 135*
baby's heartbeat *101*
baby's lungs *109*
back bend *118*
back, low *41, 62, 81, 127*
back, lower *89, 117-119, 127, 167*
back muscles *29, 36, 117*
back pain *29, 36-38, 41, 81, 89, 167, 181*
back pain, lower *89, 167*
BACK PAIN:, LOW *81*
BACK TO HEALTH *74*
backache *15, 29, 117, 119, 124, 139, 147*
backache, incidence of *117*
backache, persistent *124*
BACKACHE AND HIP PAIN *124*
bacteria, anaerobic *168, 169*
bacteria, good *70, 82*
bacteria, gram-negative *168*
bacteria, harmful *70*
bacteria, helpful *82, 170*
bacteria multiply, anaerobic *169*
bacteria, PID-causing *168*
bacteria, tubercular *163*
bacteria, vaginal *75*
Bailar, Dr. John *231, 234, 241*
Baines, Dr. Cornelia *228, 232, 234, 239*
Baird, Dr. Patricia *113*
Baker, Nancy C. *241*
baking soda *72, 83*
Bakoulis, Mation Gordan *186*
Balaskas, Janet *95, 96, 120*
Baldwin, Rahima *97, 100, 134*
Ballweg, Mary Lou *178, 179, 184, 186*
bananas *79, 123, 149, 246*
Bantu tribes *206*
Barber, Dr. Neill S. *259*
Barrett-Connor, Dr. Elizabeth *194*
Barrett, Martha *194, 267, 272*
basal temperature *142-144, 209, 223*
Basco, Dr. Vivien *232*
Basinski, Dr. Antoni *232*
baths, warm water *7, 72*
BBT *65, 66*
BCDDP TRIAL: *231*
beans *6, 148, 200, 208, 246, 257*
beans, black *246*
beans, dried *208*

bearing down *173*
BEAT PMS THROUGH DIET *154*
Beatty, Paul *10*
Beauty Without Cruelty *259, 260*
Becker, Dr. Samuel *30*
Beckman, Linda *23*
Bed rest *91, 168, 169, 222*
BED REST: *169*
BEE POLLEN: *199*
beef *247*
beers *217*
beets *208, 246, 247*
BEGINNINGS, A BOOK FOR WIDOWS *43*
behaviour changes *31, 35*
belief system *131, 137*
Bell, Bonne *260*
Bell Canada *29*
belly button *61*
Bender, Degraff *154*
Benedictin *123*
BEREAVED FAMILIES OF ONTARIO *43*
bereavement leave *269*
Bereavement Clinic *41*
BEREAVEMENT SERVICES AND COMMUNITY EDUCATION *43*
Berger, Gilda *154*
Berman, Sallee *95, 239*
Bertell, Dr. Rosalie *35, 37, 233, 236, 238*
Bested, Dr. Alison *8*
beta blocker *194*
betacarotene *6, 7, 200, 206, 237*
betadine douche or suppository *72*
Beynon, Dr. C.L. *132*
BEYOND WIDOWHOOD *43*
Bezwecken Transdermal Systems Inc *204*
BHC *230*
bi-phasic or tri-phasic pill formulations *52*
bikini incision *177*
bile duct, common *261-264*
bile, purpose of *261*
bile salts *261, 265*
bile salts, loss *265*
biliary colic *262-264*
Bill 190 *259*
biochemical changes *33*
biochemical fitness *147*
biochemical markers *114*
BIOCHRON *229*
biofeedback *17*
bioflavonoids *124, 185, 199, 255*
Bioniche Inc *86*
biopsies, breast *230, 233, 234*
biopsies, unnecessary *234, 239*
biopsy *49, 68, 80, 83, 155, 166, 174, 177, 180-183, 190, 192, 223, 230, 233-235, 239, 250*
biopsy, uterine *68*
Biopsychiatry Institute *149*
biorhythms *35*
Bioself *65, 67*
biostatistics *228, 231*
Biotics Research's *207*
biphosphonate bone crystal complexes *210*
Birkenstock sandal or shoe *256*
birth control, barrier methods *51, 54, 57, 162, 171*
birth control method *11, 57, 89, 268*

birth control, natural methods *62*
birth control, no *51, 88, 89*
birth control, non-barrier *89*
birth control, permanent *59*
birth control pills *46-56, 70, 73, 74, 81, 171, 175, 196, 236, 238, 239, 261, 265, 266*
birth control pills and PID *171*
birth defects *31, 50, 102, 108, 112-114, 123*
birth defects, chromosomal *50*
birth defects, limb *50*
birth, expectations around *96, 100, 129*
birth, premature vaginal *136*
birth process *95, 137*
birth, psychological aspects of *94, 129*
birth, realistic picture *126*
birth, shifting hormone levels after *142*
birth, transformation of *100*
birth, vaginal *135-138, 250*
birth weight babies, low *246*
birth weight, low *112, 113, 246*
BIRTH AFTER CESAREAN: THE MEDICAL FACTS *137*
BIRTH AND INFANCY *95*
BIRTH AND LIFE BOOKSTORE *97, 110, 120, 124, 129, 138*
BIRTH CONTROL, NATURAL *65*
BIRTH CONTROL, OTHER MEANS OF *54*
BIRTH CONTROL: *54, 59, 82, 171*
BIRTH DEFECTS AND AGE *112*
BIRTH OVER THIRTY *95, 111, 116*
BIRTH REBORN *94*
BIRTH WITHOUT SURGERY *137*
birthing alternatives *94*
birthing plan, personalized *96, 100, 129*
BIRTHING NORMALLY *96, 126*
births, premature *140*
black women *175, 205*
bladder attack *84*
bladder augmentation *85*
bladder control *117*
bladder defences *81*
bladder, full *101*
bladder infection, simple *83*
bladder infections *79, 81-83, 270*
bladder infections, acute *82*
bladder infections, chronic *82*
bladder infections, repeated *79, 81, 83*
bladder, inflammation *78*
bladder irritation *89*
bladder muscle *78*
bladder pain *78-80*
bladder problems, chronic *78, 85*
bladder problems, repeated episodes *78*
bladder-proof recipes *85*
bladder tissue *80, 81, 83, 85*
bladder, training the *85*
bladder, ulcerated *78*
bladder wall *79, 80, 83, 84*
BLADDER DISTENTION: *84*
BLADDER RETRAINING: *85*
bleed, prone to *60*
bleeding, abnormal *103, 249*
bleeding, breakthrough *51, 53, 54, 88, 175*

bleeding, debilitating *222*
bleeding, excessive *253*
bleeding, heavy *61, 189, 223*
bleeding, internal *48, 173*
bleeding, light *251*
bleeding, pinpoint *83*
bleeding problems, severe *251*
bleeding, prolonged *246*
bleeding, unusual *113*
bleeding, vaginal *89, 222, 224, 248, 249*
blindness, sudden *51*
Blindness *51, 90, 258*
blisters *75, 173, 258*
blisters, brown *173*
blisters, painful clear *75*
bloating *73, 146, 147, 149, 151, 167, 190, 193, 208, 209, 221, 262*
blockage *81, 89, 163, 253, 254*
blockers, H1 and H2 *84*
blood changes *245*
blood chemistry *31, 41*
blood chemistry abnormalities *41*
blood clots, risks *47*
blood, clotted *173*
blood clotting, decreases *84*
blood clotting, increase *195*
blood count *4, 83, 246*
blood count, red *246*
blood count, white *246*
blood flow *6, 106*
blood flow, umbilical *106*
blood flow, uterine *106*
blood iron, low *245*
blood levels *53, 62, 67, 113, 142, 178, 189, 237*
blood levels, hormonal *62*
blood levels of estrogen *189*
blood loss *4, 183, 222, 223, 245, 247, 248*
blood loss during childbirth *245*
blood loss, regular *248*
blood, mother's *103, 113*
blood, nutrient rich *254*
blood pressure *3, 15, 20, 29, 31, 41, 47, 50, 103, 194-196, 198, 199, 252, 255, 262*
blood pressure, high *3, 15, 20, 29, 41, 47, 103, 194, 198, 199, 255*
blood pressure, low *262*
blood pressure, raise *195*
blood, protein in *244*
blood sugar, Elevated *115*
blood sugar, fasting *50, 251*
blood sugar, fluctuations *84*
blood sugar levels *50, 53, 84, 115, 123, 199*
blood sugar, low *74, 123*
blood supply *29, 62, 63, 219, 262*
blood, Systolic *196*
blood tests *6, 50, 68, 74, 75, 89, 109, 110, 113, 114, 141, 142, 148, 164, 165, 229, 244, 246, 251*
blood tests, hormonal *68*
blood tests, normal *165*
blood vessels *47, 51, 62, 80, 83, 84, 182, 193, 194, 253, 254*
blood vessels, coronary *193*
blood volume *118, 245, 246*
BLOOD CLOTS, HEART ATTACKS AND STROKES *46*
BLOOD TESTS FOR ANTIBODIES - THE AMAS: *229*

bloodstream *128, 188, 191, 253*
blotches, bluish *254*
Blue green sea algae *247*
blues *78, 141, 142, 193*
Blumberg, Dr. Jeffrey *206*
body heat *141, 189*
body temperature *64, 65, 142, 143, 237*
Body Shop *260*
Body Type *216*
Bogosh, Dr. Samuel *229*
BONDING BEFORE BIRTH, A GUIDE TO BECOMING A FAMILY *99*
bone, cortical *205*
bone crystals *210*
bone density *176, 210, 211*
bone, fluoride-treated *211*
bone formation *210, 211*
bone fractures *196*
bone health *207-209, 212*
bone loss, accelerated *195, 210*
bone loss, acceleration *195, 209*
bone loss, early *211*
bone loss, prevent *195, 198, 207, 209*
bone loss, prevention *193*
bone loss, reverse *191, 198*
bone loss, risk *219*
bone mass *52, 195, 196, 205-211*
bone mass, low *190*
bone mass, peak *205*
bone mineral density *210*
bone reabsorption *210, 211*
bone scan *176, 209, 211, 212, 217*
bone, spinal *103, 113*
Bone marrow *244, 246, 247*
bones *64, 68, 205, 206, 211, 212*
bones, spinal *211*
Boric acid *72, 73*
Boroditsky, Dr. Richard *88*
boron, safe intake *208*
boron supplements *208*
BORON *207, 208*
Boston Arthritic Center *210*
Boston Women's Health Collective *49, 50, 55, 66, 226, 234, 241*
bowel bacteria *163, 170*
bowel, deep *177*
bowel, large *173, 174*
bowel, lower *256*
bowel movement *121, 255, 256*
bowel movement, straining *255, 257*
bowel movements, pain during *181*
bowel movements, painful *174*
bowel movements, regular *121*
bowel, pressure on *220*
bowel problems *6*
bowel surgery *220*
bowel syndrome, irritable *62*
Bowie, Dr. William *87, 90, 91*
bra, support *155*
Bracken, Dr. *50*
braille *240*
brain *5, 6, 8, 17, 31, 32, 47, 64, 76, 80, 81, 103, 106, 108, 113, 114, 147, 149, 150, 176, 220*
brain fog *76*
brain function *6*
brain, missing *108*
brain scans *6*
brain waves *8*
brain, woman's *64, 176*
bran, unrefined *121*

brassica *157*
brassica family *157*
Brat, Dr. Theo *53*
Brayshaw, Dr. Nora *149*
bread *72, 73, 76, 84, 115, 124, 184, 247, 266*
bread dough *72*
bread, rye *266*
bread, whole grain *115*
bread, whole wheat *247*
bread, yeasted *84*
breads, white *247*
breakfast *6, 199*
breast biopsy, alternative *230*
breast cancer, chance of developing *242*
breast cancer death rate *229-232, 236*
breast cancer, detection *230, 232*
breast cancer, developing *49, 242*
breast cancer, family history *49, 241*
breast cancer, fear *227*
breast cancer, incidence *49, 155, 159, 227, 237*
breast cancer, risk of dying *242*
breast cancer, root causes *240*
breast cancer, worry about *155*
breast cancers, fast growing *234*
breast cancers, small *233*
breast check-ups *49*
breast disease, cystic *49, 52, 158, 237*
breast, electrocardiogram *229*
breast exam *228, 229, 230, 240*
breast-feeding *50, 96, 116, 119, 147, 157, 175*
breast-feeding mothers *50, 96, 147*
breast lump, cystic *155*
breast lump detection *229*
breast lumps *155, 228, 229*
breast milk *50*
breast, non-cancerous conditions *155*
breast pain *151, 155, 156, 159*
breast pain, cyclical *156*
breast pain, premenstrual *151, 155*
breast screening, guidelines *229*
breast self exam *239, 240*
breast size, decreased *74, 175*
breast size, reduction *176*
breast tenderness *146, 149, 155, 193, 209, 214*
breast tissue *62, 156, 158, 227*
breast vcancer, death rates *229*
Breast cancer risk *49, 54, 196, 197, 237, 240*
Breast Cancer and the Environment: The Chlorine Connection *237, 241*
Breast Cancer Clinic at University of California *155*
Breast Cancer Detection Demonstration Project *231*
Breast Cancer Treatment Center *159*
Breast Cancer: Unanswered Questions *240, 241*
Breast self examination *49, 229*
Breast swelling *147*
BREAST CANCER ACTION *229, 236, 241*
BREAST CANCER, BREAST HEALTH, The Wise Woman Way *241*

BREAST CANCER, What You Should Know (But May Not Be Told) 241
BREAST CANCER: WHAT ARE THE RISKS ? 242
BREAST-FEEDING, SUCCESSFUL 96
BREAST-FEEDING YOUR BABY 96
BREAST SELF EXAM 239, 240
BREAST SELF EXAMINATION 49, 229
breasts, dense 229
breasts, lumpy 155, 229
breasts, normal 96
breasts, painful lumpy 155
BREASTS, ANNUAL PHYSICAL EXAM 228, 240
breath, blow-type of 133
breath, panting 119
breath, prolonged 132
breath, pushing 119
breath, shortness of 244
breathing, deep 90, 119, 127, 167
breathing, pant-and-blow 127
breathing, strenuous 132
breathing techniques 128
BREATHING AND RELAXATION 94, 100, 117-119, 129
breathlessness, increased 118
breech baby 133, 137
Brewer's yeast 114, 123
Brief Michigan alcohol screening test: 25
British Columbia Cancer Control Agency 232
British Medical Journal 6, 235
broccoli 157, 208, 246
Brodeur, Paul 30, 32
bromocriptine 151, 158
bronchitis 70
Brooks Air Force 178
Brown, Dr. Stanley 47
Bruce, Dr. Andrew 82
brussel sprouts 157
BSE 160, 229, 239, 240
buckwheat 255
Bureau of Radiation and Medical Devices 31
Burlington Breast Cancer Support Group 240
burning 28, 61, 62, 73, 75, 78, 80, 83, 84, 91, 121, 127, 177, 181, 190
burning, intense 127
burning mouth syndrome 190
burning sensation 78, 84, 121
burns 8, 12, 33, 85, 141, 173, 177, 180, 182, 258
burns, carbon 177
burns, eye 33
burns, powder 173, 180
Burns, Dr. David 46
Burnside, Dr. Beverly 190, 191
bursting 255
Burston, Maggie 77, 85, 86
BUSERELIN: 176
Bush, Dr. Trudy 194
Butler, Dr. Robert 203

C:

C/SEC (CESAREAN/SUPPORT/ EDUCATION & CONCERN) 138

C-Section 13, 135-137, 250
cabbage 157, 208, 255
cabbage, Savoy 255
CADNA MEDICAL DIAGNOSTIC INC 67
caffeine, Avoidance of 156
Caffeine 14, 24, 41, 148, 156, 198, 206, 217
Cal-plex 207
Calcitonin 211
calcitrol 211
calcium absorption 207, 211
calcium balance 206, 211
calcium balance, negative 206
calcium carbonate, Homeopathic 207
calcium citrate maleate 207
calcium deficiency 206
calcium in your diet 206, 207
calcium intake, low 207
calcium levels, blood 211
calcium levels, urine 211
calcium loss 206
calcium-magnesium 17, 25, 115, 199, 200, 207, 208
calcium-magnesium boron effervescent powder 207
calcium-magnesium citrate capsules 207
calcium-magnesium, liquid 207
calcium-magnesium liquid 207
calcium-magnesium supplements 200, 207, 208
calcium sulphate 206
calcium, vegetarian dietary sources 206
Calcium carbonate 207, 247
Calcium Citramate 207
Calcium stones 261
CALCIUM-MAGNESIUM CAPSULES: 199
CALCIUM SUPPLEMENTS 207
calendar rhythm method 67
Calgary Herald 183
Campbell, Dr. James 106, 178
Canadian Advisory Council on the Status of Women 16
Canadian and American Associations of Radiologists 228
Canadian Association for Children of Alcoholics 27
Canadian Cancer Society 57
Canadian Center for Occupational Health and Safety 33, 36
Canadian Family Physician 130, 133, 148, 154
Canadian Journal of Diagnosis 262, 265
Canadian Journal of Surgery 158, 160, 237
Canadian Labour Congress Report 28
Canadian Labour Law 34
Canadian Medical Association Journal 136
Canadian National Breast Screening Study 227, 233
Canadian PID Society 51, 89, 91, 92, 161, 171, 172, 226, 253
cancer and the pill 48
cancer, brain 32
cancer centers, provincial 232
cancer, childhood 33, 105

cancer, colon 265
cancer detection 231, 234
cancer, developing 242
cancer, early cervical 48
cancer-ELF link 34
cancer, endometrial 192, 197, 201, 268
cancer epidemic, breast 238
cancer experts, breast 227, 232
cancer, fatal ovarian 196
cancer, killing 234
cancer of the cervix 48, 189, 249, 250
cancer of the uterus 189, 250
cancer, ovarian 48, 52, 196, 220
cancer, prevent 192, 200
cancer, prevention of 241
cancer, prostate 176
cancer screening, breast 227, 230, 232-234
cancer, skin 49
cancer, thyroid 49
cancer, urinary tract 49
cancer, uterine 52, 192, 197, 210, 220, 221, 250
Cancer and Steroid Hormone Study 49
CANCER AS A TURNING POINT 240, 241
CANCER:, OVERDIAGNOSIS OF 234
CANCER:, UTERINE 250
cancerous growths 48, 51, 222
cancers, detecting small 229
cancers, early 231
cancers, fast growing 234
cancers, fatal 232
cancers, radiation induced 234, 236
cancers, small 229, 231
CANCERS, OTHER 49, 105, 236
candida and parasites, overgrowth 8
candida antibodies 75
candida, chronic 50, 75, 76, 149, 184
candida diagnosis 74, 76
candida infections 77, 149, 185
candida, overgrowth of 8
candida research 75-77, 86
Candida albicans 70
Candida overgrowth 73
CANDIDA 8, 9, 50, 70, 73-77, 86, 149, 184, 185
CANDIDA RESEARCH AND INFORMATION 76, 77
CANDIDA RESEARCH INFORMATION SERVICE 77, 86
CANDIDIASIS 184, 270
canesten 72, 73
capillaries, broken 254
caprylic acid 76, 77
carbohydrates 123, 149, 184-185, 266
Carbon dioxide 166, 249, 253, 254
carcinogenic potential 46
carcinogens 30, 236, 238
cardiac disease 220
cardiovascular system 31
cardiovascular systems, weak 108
Carlton University 24
Carnegie Mellon University 31
Carpal tunnel syndrome 29
Carpenter, Moira 154
CARTER PRODUCTS 67
Cassals 69
castor bean oil 76

castor oil packs 156, 255
cat's claw 7, 76
CATARACTS 32, 33, 51
catecholamines 29
catheter 84, 85, 110
Cattanach, Dr. John 62, 63
Caucasian 205, 245, 261
cauliflower 157
CCOHS 33, 36
cefoxitin 91, 168
ceftriaxone 168
cell culture tests 258
cell growth 30
cell, host 163
cells, bladder 81
cells, blood 239, 244, 246
cells, bone 210
cells, breast 229
cells, breast duct 158
cells, clue 170
cells, endometrial 182
cells, fat 189
cells, helper 6
cells, inflammatory 166
cells, killer 6, 180
cells, plasma 166
cells, pus 82, 89
cells, red blood 244, 246
cells, suppressor 6
cells, tubal 182
cells, water in 177
cells, white blood 246
cells, yeast 70, 73
Center for Disease Control 49, 168, 169, 172
Center for Medical Consumers 241
cephalosporin 83, 168, 169
cervical area 251
cervical bacteria 161
cervical barrier 161, 162
cervical canal 250, 252
cervical cancer 48, 54, 56, 57, 221, 224, 225
cervical cancer, preventing 224
cervical cap 54, 57, 58, 65, 88
cervical cells 89, 171
cervical chlamydial infections, risk 171
cervical infection 58, 90, 162, 165, 166, 170
cervical mucous 51, 55, 64, 66, 68, 171, 209
cervical mucous, poor quality 66
cervical plug 161, 171
cervical secretions 58, 70, 71
cervical STD infections, risk 171
cervical test, negative 165
cervical tests 165, 166
CERVICAL ABNORMALITIES: 250
CERVICAL BARRIER 161, 162
CERVICAL CANCER THAT IS CONFINED TO THE CERVIX 224
CERVICAL INFECTIONS 58, 90, 162, 170
CERVICAL STD INFECTIONS 170, 171
CERVICAL TESTS: 165
CERVICITIS, CHRONIC 224

cervix *48, 51, 54, 57, 58, 62, 64, 70, 75, 88, 89, 91, 103, 126, 132, 135, 161, 162, 164-167, 169-171, 173, 189, 214, 219, 221, 223, 224, 225, 249-253*
CERVIX: 48, 170
Cesarean *60, 94, 96, 103, 112, 127, 131, 135-138, 161, 162*
Cesarean Birth Planning Committee 135, 137
Cesarean births 94
Cesarean Prevention Clarion 138
Cesarean section 60, 103, 135, 136, 161, 162
Cesarean section, reasons 135
Cesarean section, repeat 103
CESAREAN PREVENTION AND VAGINAL BIRTH AFTER CESAREAN 137
Cesareans, first time 135
Cesareans, prevent unnecessary 137
Cesareans, repeat 135
CFIDS ASSOCIATION 9
CFIDS CHRONICLE 9
CFIDS Rochester Research Project 9
CFIDS, sleeping problems 7
CFIDS, specific marker 8
CFIDS- Chronic Fatigue and Immune System Dysfunction Syndrome 5-10, 80
Chairperson of the British Menopause Council 193
Chaitow, Dr. Leon 257
Chalker, Rebecca 58, 85
Chalmers, Iain 107
Chamberlain, Dr. David 98, 99
Chamberlain, Dr. Jocelyn 235
chard *246, 247*
Charron, David 31
Charting 65-67, 148
chaste tree 198
Cheek, Dr. David 98
cheeks *33, 126, 248*
cheese, cottage *71, 72*
cheeses, old *149*
Chelated natural iron supplements 247
chelation therapy *248*
chemical irritation *174*
chemical mixture *258*
chemical residues *240, 247*
chemical sensitivities *73*
chemical tests *108*
chemicals, bio-accumulative *179*
chemicals, industrial *80, 238*
chemicals, toxic *8*
chemotherapy *188, 236*
Cheney, Dr. Paul *6-9*
Chernobyl *238*
cherries *208, 246*
cherries, black *246*
Cherry, Frank *38-40, 42*
Chervenak, Frank *104*
chest *19, 29, 38, 118, 119, 121, 141, 150, 163, 189, 212, 233, 244*
chest breathing *119*
chest pain *29, 141, 244*
chest space, restricted *118*
chicken *6, 17, 25, 115, 121, 148, 200, 207, 266*
chicken pox *51*
chickweed *247*
child, abnormal *110*

child-bearing ability *177*
child-bearing potential *3, 188*
child-bearing years *103, 118, 224*
child-caring duties *116*
child custody *12, 15*
child, Death of *13, 40*
child development *94*
child, loss of *110*
childbirth *4, 60, 61, 79, 94-97, 99, 100, 105-107, 112, 117, 119, 120, 124, 126, 127, 129, 130, 132, 134, 137, 138, 142, 161, 170, 188, 222, 237, 245, 250, 262*
childbirth, Before undergoing 170
childbirth, infection after *161, 170*
childbirth is painful *126*
childbirth preparation *94, 117, 119, 120, 129*
childbirth preparation, good *119*
childbirth professional *126*
childcare, relief from *116*
childhood leukemia *33, 34, 108*
children, lymphoma in *34*
children, unexposed *105, 106*
Children's Hospital 175
chills *147, 167, 189, 262*
Chinese medicine *85, 186, 198, 202*
Chiropractic adjustments *85*
chiropractor *85, 119, 124*
chlamydia bacteria *163*
chlamydia, complication of *89*
chlamydia culture, negative *89*
chlamydia epidemic *92*
chlamydia, incubation period of *91*
chlamydia, infected with *87*
chlamydia infection *87, 88, 90*
chlamydia infection, unrecognized *87*
chlamydia is very difficult to culture 87
chlamydia pneumonia *90*
chlamydia, risk for *88*
chlamydia testing *87*
chlamydia, treatment for *90*
Chlamydia cultures *75, 88*
CHLAMYDIA AND PREGNANCY 90
CHLAMYDIA, TREATING 90
CHLAMYDIA, WHAT IS 87
chlamydia's life cycle *163*
chlamydial cell wall *88*
chlamydial infections *50, 51, 87, 89, 90, 162-164, 169, 171*
chlamydial infections, cervical *162, 169, 171*
chlamydial infections, silent *162*
chlamydial or gonorrheal infections *162*
CHLAMYDIAL INFECTIONS, SYMPTOMS AND COMPLICA-TIONS 89
chlorine *157, 237, 238, 241*
chlorophyll *246, 247*
chlortripolon *223*
chocolate *79, 173*
CHOICE IN CHILDBIRTH 94
cholecystectomies, laparoscopic *263, 264*
cholecystectomy *263, 265*
cholecystectomy syndrome, post *265*
cholecystis, acute *262*
cholecystitis *262, 263*
cholesterol, bad *53, 193*

cholesterol, concentration of *266*
cholesterol, elevated blood *266*
cholesterol, good *53, 193*
cholesterol, HDL *53*
cholesterol, High *47, 194*
cholesterol in the bile *261*
cholesterol levels *193, 266*
cholesterol, secretion of *261*
cholesterol type *264*
cholesterol type stones *264*
choline *6, 185*
choline citrate *6*
chores, household *3, 17, 60*
chorionic gonadotropin *109, 114*
chorionic villi *103, 104, 110, 111, 113*
Christian Dior 260
chromosomal effects *105*
chromosomal studies *108*
Chromosomal abnormalities 108, 112, 113
chromosome *105, 108*
chromosome breakage *105*
chromosome damage *105*
chronic cystitis, infective type of *81*
chronic fatigue *2-5, 7-10, 13, 15, 75, 80, 238, 246*
chronic fatigue cases, unexplained *5*
chronic fatigue patients *8*
Chronic Fatigue Syndrome 4, 5, 7, 9, 10, 13, 75
Chronic illness 5, 13, 77, 81, 86, 184, 185
CHRONIC CYSTITIS, SYMPTOMS 78
CHRONIC CYSTITIS - THE INFECTIVE TYPE 81
CHRONIC FATIGUE SYNDROME AND THE YEAST CONNECTION 7, 9
cigarettes *4, 121, 157, 194, 217*
cilia lining the fallopian tube *163*
cinnamon *123*
circulation *113, 169, 254, 255*
cirrhosis of the liver *22*
Citramate *207*
citrate *6, 7, 83, 207*
citrus *208*
Clarke, Dr. Aileen *235*
Classical LD-50 Acute Toxicity Test 259
cleaners, household *81*
CLEARPLAN 67
cleft palate *123*
clindamycin *168-170, 172*
Clinical Evaluative Sciences 232
clitoral area *79*
clitoral orgasms *219*
clitoris *80, 219, 220*
clonazepam-doxepin *8*
Clonazepam 8
clothes, synthetic *33*
clothing, constricting *254*
CLOTHING, TIGHT 71
clotrimazole *72*
clots, Blood *46, 47, 220*
clotting, blood *46, 47, 51, 53, 84, 195, 199*
clotting complications *46*
CMAJ 137, 232
co-enzyme *6, 7, 10*
co-ordination *147, 228*
coaching, good *133*
COALESCENCE 197

Coalition for Medical Rights of Women 104, 107, 111, 116
Cobb, Janine O'Leary 63, 190, 202, 205, 219, 225
coconut oil *76*
cod *6, 159*
cod liver oil *6*
coffee *2, 4, 25, 26, 115, 121, 206, 217*
Coffey, Nora 226
Cognitive behavioural therapy 8
Cohen and White 36
Cohen, Dr. Michael 54
Cohen, Dr. Murray 258
cold, intolerance to *141*
cold medicines *80*
cold remedy *121*
cold, sensitivity to *143, 244*
cold treatment *255*
Colditz, Dr. Graham 196, 239
colic *262-264*
College of Family Physicians of Canada 25
Collinge, Dr. William 9
Collins, Dr. John 21, 53, 97, 140, 176, 179, 197, 201, 203
Colman, Carol 140
colon *76, 161, 265*
colon, sigmoid *161*
colposcope *250*
Columbia University 8
COMFORTING THOSE WHO GRIEVE 42
COMPASSIONATE FRIENDS 43
Comprehensive Therapy 22
COMPU-LENZ 34
computer-generated *109*
computer-generated risk *109*
computer hazards, public awareness 36
computer, lap top *34*
computer models *259*
computer, older *35*
computer work stations *3, 28*
Computer Shield Group 35
computers *3, 14, 28-37, 65, 67, 36, 37, 109, 114, 229, 238, 246, 259*
computers, cheap *33*
computers, health hazards *3, 238*
CONCEIVE 50, 67, 68, 175
concentration, decreased *147*
concentration, focused *129*
concentration, lack of *5, 35, 190*
CONCORD FEMINIST HEALTH CENTER 58
condoms *54, 57, 58, 60, 65, 71, 88, 89, 170, 171*
condoms, Ultrathin *54*
cone biopsy *250*
confidence, loss of *139*
conflicts, unresolved *3*
conjunctivitis *90*
CONNECTING WITH YOUR UNBORN CHILD 99
CONSIDERING PARENTHOOD, A WORKBOOK FOR LESBIANS 269, 272
constipation, alleviate *117*
CONSTIPATION 35, 73, 117, 121, 131, 141, 147, 221, 245, 247, 248, 255, 256
CONSTIPATION AND VARICOSE VEINS 256

CONSUMER POWER 183, 260
contact lens prescriptions 51
contraceptives, oral 46, 55, 56, 171
contractions 19, 126-128, 132, 134, 174, 219
contractions, early 126
contractions, mild 126
contractions, painful 126, 128
contractions, pushing 126
conventional medicine 95, 124
convulsions 259
cooking 20, 114, 123, 247
cookware, cast iron 247
coordination, loss of 5
COPA 27
coping skills 8, 126
COPING WITH A HYSTEREC-TOMY 226
COPING WITH ENDOMETRIOSIS 186
COPING WITH FATIGUE 115
COPING WITH YOUR ALLERGIES 9
copper 247
Copps, Dr. D. H. 211
corneal 258
corneas 258
Cornell University 33
cornstarch 72, 157, 245
coronary heart disease, risk 219
coronary risk factors 196
cortico-steroids 192
cortisols, low serum 7
cortisone 5, 71
corynebacterium vaginale 75
coryza 158
cosmetic procedure 257
cosmetics 258-260
cotton 71, 170, 199
cough syrups 80
coughing 90, 167
counselling, couple 150
counselling, individual 150
counselling, Psychological 9
couples 11, 42, 61, 66, 68, 99, 134, 138, 269
couples, older 42, 66
Covey, Stephen 21
Cowey, Sandra 202
coxsackie B virus 5
cramping 62, 111, 251
cramping, mild 251
cramps 117, 126, 253, 255, 265
Crandall, Dr. Margorie 77
cravings, food 115, 146, 245
cravings, salt 147
creativity, bursts of 147
CRIF 77
CRIS 77
crisis management 176, 177
Critical Illness Research Foundation 75, 76
Crohn's disease 74, 261
Crook, Dr. William 7, 9, 74-76
CROSSCURRENTS; THE PERILS OF ELECTROPOLLUTION 30
crying, unexplained 147
cul de sac 182
cultures, cell 31, 259
curette 249, 250, 252
CURING PMS, THE DRUG-FREE WAY 154
curl ups, straight 119

CURRENTS OF DEATH: Power Lines, Computer Terminals 30
Cutler, Dr. Paul 149, 154, 248
Cutler, Dr. Winnifred 219, 226
cyclamates 84
cycles, Irregular 64, 65, 68
cycling 7, 117, 118, 257
CYLCEN 52
Cystistat 86
cystitis, chronic 78, 81, 82, 85, 86
cystitis symptoms 81
CYSTITIS 8, 74, 78, 80-86, 270
cystoscope 83
cystoscopy 83
cystoscopy examination 83
cysts 48, 52, 155, 156, 158, 165, 173, 174, 177, 180, 262
cysts, breast 155
cysts, disappearance of 158
cysts, formation of 158, 173, 262
cysts, large chocolate 173
cysts, large endometrial 174, 177
cysts, ovarian 48, 52, 165, 174
cytomegalovirus 5

D:

D-and-C 62, 78, 89, 161, 223, 249-253
D-and-C, blind 250, 253
D-and-C, emergency 251, 252
D'Souza, Dr. Ivan 221
Diamond, Harvey 241
dairy, excess 73, 115
dairy food, low fat 156, 266
dairy free acidophilus powder 83
dairy, low fat 156, 200, 266
dairy products 115, 148, 156, 179, 206, 217, 230, 237, 266
dairy products, Excess 115
dairy products, Israeli 230
dairy products, U.S. 230
Dalhousie University 262
Dana, Bill 21, 96
danazol 151, 156, 158, 175-177, 182
danazol, prolonged use 156
dancing 20, 117, 118, 150, 206
dancing, belly 150
dandelion 246, 247
data entry 14, 28, 29
Davidson, Dr. Glen 41, 42
Davis, Deborah 140
Davis, Elizabeth 95
Dayger, Kendra 9
DCAHS, Doctors Concerned About Human Sterilization 63
DDT 30, 230, 237
De Shepper, Dr. Luc 74
De Swann, Constance 186
DEALING WITH SUICIDE 43
Dean, Dr. Carolyn 25, 49, 75, 76, 148, 154, 211
Decaffeinated 217
DeCherney, Dr. Alan 53
decision making 12, 241
defects, growth 105
deficiency disease 188, 191
deformities 123
dehydration 118
dehydroepiandrosterone 6
Deits, Bob 39-42
DeLee, J.B. 130
delirium tremens 25

deliveries, cesarean section 161, 162
deliveries, Surgical 136
delivery, date of 103
delivery, normal vaginal 130
delivery, premature 102, 113, 246
delivery, Traumatic 13
delivery, uncomplicated 123
DeMatteo, Bob 29, 31, 36
DeMeo, Dr. James 35
denial syndrome 24
deodorant 258
deodorants, Vaginal 71
DEODORANTS AND SPRAYS 71
Department Of Health Services of California 124
depression, female 191
depression, full-blown 139
depression, mild 139
depression, pill and 51
depression, post-op 220
Depression 15, 20, 22-25, 29, 35, 41, 51, 73, 74, 81, 97, 99, 139, 141, 142, 143, 147, 149, 151, 175, 176, 190-192, 203, 219, 220, 222, 240, 244
DEPRESSION IS A FEMINIST ISSUE 203
DEPRESSION, SELF-ESTEEM AND UNREWARDING ROLES 190
Dermal Irritancy Test 258
dermatitis 255
DES 49, 196, 239
desensitization 151, 184
desogestrel 52, 53
DETECTING YOUR HIDDEN ALLERGIES 9
dextran 253
DFA 88
DHEA 6, 7
diabetes 4, 41, 47, 71, 103, 109, 114-116, 194, 248, 266
diabetes, gestational 115, 116
diabetes, insulin dependant 115
diabetes, risk of 115
DIABETES, dramatic improvement 248
diabetic testing 109
DIAGNOSTECHS 212, 213
diapers 116, 179
diaphragm 54, 57, 58, 60, 65, 82, 88, 89, 170, 171
diaphragm fitting 57
diarrhea 35, 73, 84, 142, 147, 199, 245, 259, 264, 265
diarrhea, chronic 245
diatomic 151, 237
diet, attention to 8, 262
diet, cancer preventive 237
diet, elimination 7, 84
diet, endometriosis 186
diet, high fibre 255, 257
diet high in animal fats 237
diet high in saturated fats 261
diet, holistic approach 212
diet, iodine deficient 156
diet, iron rich 246
diet, low carbohydrate 184, 185
diet, low fat 156, 207, 237, 266
diet, low protein 206
diet, low protein vegetable 207
diet, macrobiotic 184
diet pills 80
diet, poor 2, 5, 14, 71, 76, 247

diet, recommended 266
diet, restricted 84
diet, short-term 84
diet, sugar free 6
diet, Western 261, 266
Diet change 48, 184
Diet changes 266
DIET AND BREAST CANCER 237
DIET AND VARICOSE VEINS 255
dieting 2, 13, 261
diets 4, 206-208, 237, 238, 255
diets, high fat 237
diets, High protein 206, 207
diets, low fibre 255
diflucan 76
digestion 207, 208, 212, 245
digestion, poor 245
digestion, weak 207
digestive enzymes 7, 121, 122, 200, 208
digestive track 70, 81, 189
digestive upsets 139
Digestive difficulties 73
Digital Equipment Corp 32
DiGiulio, Robert 43
dilatation and curettage 249
dilation, cervical 250
dilators 252
DIMETHYL SULFOXIDE (DMSO): 84
dioscorea villosa 150
diosgenin 212
dioxin and food 178
dioxin exposure 178, 185
dioxins 178, 179, 185, 237
disability, chronic 180
disappointment, deep 136
discharge 24, 65, 71, 75, 89, 91, 131, 167, 170, 239, 253, 259
discharge, Unusual 167
discoloration 257
DISCOVERIES ABOUT THE MIND AND PERSONALITY OF YOUR NEWBORN 99
discrimination 3, 11, 13, 14, 128
disorders, molecular 109
diurnal rhythm 7
dizziness 15, 29, 33, 35, 52, 119, 147, 151, 198, 199
Dmowski, Dr. Paul 178
DMSO 84
DNA fragments 81, 81, 88
Doctors Concerned About Human Sterilization 63
Dodds, Dr. Charles 46
domestic violence 24
Dominque, Dr. Gerald 81
dong quai 198, 223
doppler stethoscope 101, 106
DOPPLER ULTRASOUND, DANGERS 106
douches, vinegar 71, 75, 170
douching 71, 251
Down's Syndrome 108, 109, 111-114
doxycycline 90, 91, 168, 169
Dr. Atkin's Health Revolution 185
DR. DEAN ORNISH'S PROGRAM FOR REVERSING HEART DISEASE 194
draize eye irritancy test 258, 259
Dranov, Paula 203
dreams 3, 38, 136, 140, 147

drinkers, casual 22
drinkers, low risk 25
drinkers, Problem 25
drinking problem 24
Drinking Habits 217
DRINKING GUIDELINES:, SAFE 25
drinks, carbonated 121
drinks, hot 189
drinks, soft 4, 206, 247
drowsiness 3, 41, 193, 211, 244
drowsy 128, 252
drug abuse 41
drug therapies 183
drug therapy 182
drugs, over-reliance on 76
drunk driving 25
dryers, blow 30
dryness 176, 189, 191, 198, 199, 219
ducts, breast 158
dulse 159, 206, 246
duphaston 193
dye 82, 89, 158, 162
DYING WITH DIGNITY 43
dyslexia 105, 106
dystrophy 108

E:

E-coli 163, 170
ear infections 70, 90
Easier Childbirth 96, 99, 100, 129
EASING LABOUR PAIN 129
East West Journal 147
eating disorders 2, 20
eating habits 14, 217
EATING WELL AND NOT ABSORBING WHAT YOU NEED 208
EB's 87, 88
EBV 83
echinacea 7
echo sounder 101
econazole 72
ecostatin 72, 73
ecosystem 70, 162
Ectomorphic 216
ectopic pregnancy, lower rates 171
eczema 51
Ed Leeper, Monitor Industries 35
Edinburgh Breast Screening Project 235
editronate disodium 210
EDTA 247
EFAMOL RESEARCH INSTITUTE 10
EFFECTIVE CARE IN PREG-NANCY AND CHILDBIRTH 105
egg, fertilized 163, 164
egg yolks 246
Eiger, Marvin 96
Eisenberg, Arlene 94, 95
ejaculation, abstain from 67
elastic stockings 256
elavil 84
elbow rest 34
electric heat 30
electric shocks 79, 80
Electric blankets 30, 37, 238
Electric fields 35
ELECTRIC AND MAGNETIC FIELDS FROM 60 HERTZ ELECTRIC POWER 37

electrical stimulation 84
Electricite de France 30
electricity, static 35
electrocardiogram 229
electrocautery 63
Electrodes 229
electrolysis 257
electrolytes 252
electromagnetic fields 30-32, 35, 36, 238
electromagnetic waves 30, 31
ELECTROMAGNETIC RADIA-TION AND ITS EFFECTS 30
ELECTROMEDICINE 30
electromyography 36
electronics, advances in 101
ELECTROSTATIC CHARGES 33
Elemental Iodine- Relief for the Painful Breast? 158
ELF PROTECH 35
ELF WAVES 30, 32-34
Elford, Dr. Wayne 106
Elkins, Valmai 94
Elliot, Rose 95
Ellis, Dr. Albert 8
ELMIRON 84
eltroxin 142
embolism 253
embolus 47
embryo 31, 164, 259
embryo, nurture the 164
embryos, bird 259
embryos, chick 31
EMF RESOURCE DIRECTORY 36
emotional awareness 99
emotional development 99
emotional health 270, 271
emotional illnesses 73
emotional issues 97, 100, 185
emotional over-responsiveness 147
emotional reactions, repetitive 8
emotional states 190
emotional symptoms 146, 147
emotional trauma 41
emotional upheaval 96
emotional well-being 96, 100, 129, 270
EMOTIONAL CONFLICTS 3
EMOTIONAL DEFENSE: 240
EMOTIONAL EXPRESSION 128
EMOTIONAL FACTORS IN THE TREATMENT OF CANCER 240, 241
emotions, intense 99, 147
emotions, Negative 26, 81, 240
emphysema, chronic 4
EMPTY CRADLE, BROKEN HEART 140
Encephalitis 5
ENCEPHALOMYELITIS 10
ENDED BEGINNINGS 43, 140
endo, surgical treatment for 180
endo, treatment for 175, 180, 185
ENDO, DIAGNOSING 174, 181
ENDO, SYMPTOMS OF 173, 181
endocrinologist 64, 209
endocrinology 150, 156, 175, 191, 193, 205, 209
endometrial ablation 222-224, 251, 253
endometrial biopsy 166, 190, 192, 223
endometrial biopsy, negative 166

endometrial biopsy, positive 166
endometrial-like tissue, abnormal 180
endometrial tissue 173, 180, 182
endometrial tissue, misplaced 182
ENDOMETRIAL CANCER: 201
endometriosis 66, 74, 151, 165, 166, 173-186, 222, 223, 225, 226
endometriosis pain 174, 225
endometriosis, unusual appearances 177, 222
Endometriosis Association 177-179, 186, 222, 226
Endometriosis Institute of Oregon 180
Endometriosis, Severe 177, 184, 222
ENDOMETRIOSIS, ALTERNA-TIVE TREATMENTS 184
ENDOMETRIOSIS AND INFER-TILITY AND TRADITIONAL CHINESE MEDICINE 186
ENDOMETRIOSIS AND YOU 186
ENDOMETRIOSIS NETWORK OF TORONTO (TENT) 185
endometrium 163, 173
endorphins 150, 192
energy levels, increase 6, 147, 198
Enkin, Murray 107
enterococcus 80
enteroviruses 5
ENVIRONMENT AND BREAST CANCER: 237
environmental causes of breast cancer 236
environmental factors 81, 85, 236
environmental pollution 81
environmental stresses 76
Environmental Protection Agency 30, 178
enzymes 6-8, 10, 48, 51, 88, 121, 122, 149, 169, 200, 207, 208, 239, 248
EPA 30
EPI 272
epidemiology 50, 53, 176, 194, 227, 231, 235
Epidurals 130, 131
epilepsy 52
epileptic seizure 33
episiotomies, routine 131
EPISIOTOMIES 130-134
episiotomy 127, 130-134, 137
episiotomy, alternatives to a large 130
episiotomy, consent for 130
episiotomy, large 130, 131
episiotomy, position 130
episiotomy, restricted 131, 132
episiotomy, unnecessary 134
EPISIOTOMY AND THE SECOND STAGE OF LABOUR 134
EPISIOTOMY DOES NOT PREVENT LATER PROBLEMS 134
EPISIOTOMY, PHYSICAL AND EMOTIONAL ASPECTS 134
epithelia, columnar 171
epsom salts 72
Epstein Barr virus 5, 9, 80
Epstein, Dr. Samuel 238, 239
ergonomics 28, 32, 36
ERGONOMICS FOR WORK-PLACES WITH VDT'S 36
ERT 191, 192, 195, 196, 238

erythematosus 80
erythrocyte 165
erythromycin 80, 83, 90, 91
Eskimos 206
Eskin, Dr. Bernard 156-159
ESR 165
Essentia Communications Inc 35
ESSENTIAL EXERCISES FOR THE CHILD-BEARING YEAR 96, 120
Estee Lauder 260
Ester-C 7
Esther Rome 241
estinyl 192
estrace 192
ESTRACOMB 192
estraderm 192
ESTRATEST 220
Estren 137
estriol 109, 114, 193, 198
estrogen content 46, 52, 266
estrogen content, low 266
estrogen cream 189
estrogen deficiency 62, 191
estrogen deficiency, early 62
estrogen lack 191
estrogen levels, increased 155
estrogen, low doses 189
estrogen pills 195, 220
estrogen-progesterone 210
estrogen-progesterone patch 210
estrogen receptor sites 265
estrogen replacement therapy 191, 210
estrogen secretion 192
estrogen starvation 188
estrogen stimulation 158
Estrogen skin patches 193, 210, 211
ESTROGEN AND PROGESTER-ONE - WHICH ONE IS MOST IMPORTANT 209
ESTROGEN: IS IT RIGHT FOR YOU? 203
estrogens 155, 158, 189, 192-194, 196, 198, 204, 212, 238
estrogens derived from plant sources 198
estrogens, natural plant 198
estrogens, Natural 193, 198, 204
estrogens, plant 198, 212
ethics specialists, Medical 104
Etridonate 210
Ettinger, Dr. Bruce 210
euphemisms 126
European Committee for Ultrasound 105
evening of primrose oil 6, 10, 149, 154, 156, 185, 199
EVERY WOMAN'S GUIDE TO TESTS DURING PREGNANCY 107, 111, 116
EVERYMOM'S PRENATAL EXERCISE AND RELAXATION VIDEO 120
Ewigman, Dr. Bernard 102, 105
exercise, cool down 117
exercise, need for 117
exercise program 8, 117, 119, 211
exercise, Regular 2, 41, 115, 117, 150, 257
exercise, strenuous 118
exercise, sustained 8
EXERCISE AND YOGA 96

EXERCISE, BENEFITS OF 117
EXERCISE REGULARLY 17
EXERCISE, WEIGHT BEARING 205
exercises, pelvic muscle 117
exercises, relaxation 17, 94, 100, 119, 129
exercises, stretching 117-119, 124
EXPECTANT PARENTS 94
expectations, unspoken 16
EXPLAINING DEATH TO CHILDREN 43
eye complaints 28
eye exam 36
eye injury 32
eye irritancy test 258, 259
eye irritation 33
eye problems 28, 36, 147
Eye-Guard 35
Eye-Guard Radiation Shield 35
EYE CHANGES 51
eyeballs, Bulging 143
eyebrows 141
eyelid, lower 245
eyelids 18, 28, 141, 245
eyelids, twitching 28
eyes, irritated 28
EYESTRAIN 28

F:

F.D.A. 49, 57
Faberge 260
face, puffiness 141
Fallon 78
fallopian tubes 59, 64, 161-166, 169, 171, 174, 182
fallopian tubes, blockage 163
false negatives 88, 103, 234
false positives 88, 103, 113, 233, 234, 236
family violence 15
Family Practice 103, 131, 267
FAMILY LIFE; NOT ENOUGH MONEY, TOO MUCH STRESS 12
Fanton, Dr. John 178
Fardon, Dr. D.F. 212
fasting 50, 251, 261, 266
fasting, prolonged 266
fat 8, 47, 50, 53, 148, 156, 179, 189, 193, 196, 200, 206, 207, 212, 216, 217, 223, 237-239, 257, 261, 262, 266
fat consumption 237
fat, excess 237, 257
fat tissues 196, 212, 223, 239
fatal 196, 224, 232, 236, 239
fatality 236
fatigue 2-10, 13, 15, 29, 33, 38, 71, 73, 75, 80, 89, 115-117, 139, 141, 142, 143, 147, 175, 198, 206, 238, 244, 246
fatigue, generalized 29
fatigue, less 117
fatigue, Long-term 2
fatigue, marked 141, 142
fatigue, physical 198
fatigue, pre-dated the 5
fats, bad 193
fatty acids, essential 149
fatty substances 47, 53
fatty tissues 188, 192, 230, 240
FCBD 155-159

FCBD, modern treatment 155
FDA 7, 151, 158, 265
feces 270
FEED YOURSELF RIGHT 115
FEEDING YOUR BABY IN THE 90'S: From conception to age two 95
Feeley, Dr. Helen 28, 36
feeling of fullness 167
feeling of loss 137
FEELING GOOD AGAIN HANDBOOK 8
FEELING GOOD AGAIN: THE NEW MOOD THERAPY 8
feelings, hostile 240
feelings, unresolved 240
feelings, valid 139
feet 18, 19, 34, 64, 98, 130, 244, 252, 254, 255
Feldenkrais, Dr. Moshe 17, 21
Felible, Roma 21
Felson, Dr. David 210
feminist 23, 38, 58, 203, 236
Fera 247
fermentum 82
ferritin levels, blood 246
ferrous sulphate 247, 248
Ferrous ascorbate 247
Ferrous fumarate 247, 248
Ferrous gluconate 247, 248
Ferrous succinate 247
fertile days 55, 65, 67
fertile mucous 65
fertility awareness 54, 55, 68, 69
fertility awareness books 69
fertility awareness methods 54, 69
fertility awareness teachers 69
fertility clinic 65
fertility drugs 68
fertility, effect on 176
fertility enhancement 68, 173, 175, 176
fertility, probable times of 65
fertility, restoring 185
fertility tester, PG-53 65
fertility treatments 106
FERTILITY AWARENESS NETWORK 69
FERTILITY AWARENESS SERVICES 69
FERTILITY CONTROL, THE NATURAL APPROACH 69
FERTILITY PROBLEMS 69, 140
fetal abnormalities 103, 106, 109
fetal death 102
fetal development 181
fetal distress 135
fetal growth 30, 104
fetal limb abnormalities 111
fetal loss 111
fetal malformations, major 102
fetal monitoring 89, 107, 135
fetal stethoscopes 101, 104, 106
fetal X-ray exposure 105
fetus 33, 34, 99, 101, 102, 105, 106, 108, 111, 113, 115, 121, 140, 122, 173, 182
fetus, growing 121, 122
fetus, harm the 122
fetus, risks of x-rays 105
fetuses, defective 140
fetuses, male 108
fetuses, perfect 111

fever 89, 118, 164, 165, 167, 253, 262
fibre 8, 121, 156, 255, 257, 266
fibre, high 255, 257, 266
fibrinogen levels 194, 196
fibrocystic breast disease, reverse 156
Fibrocystic breast disease 151, 155, 156, 237
FIBROCYSTIC 151, 155, 156, 158, 237
fibroid, large 222, 225
fibroids, removal of 252
fibroids, Small 223, 224, 251
fibroids, uterine 52, 189, 222, 249, 250
FIBROMYALGIA 6, 10, 80
FIBROMYALGIA ASSOCIATION OF BC 10
FIBROMYALGIA NETWORK 10
FIBROSITIS 10
FIFTY SOMETHING IN THE NINETIES 197
fimbria 163
FIRST MATURE WOMEN'S NETWORK SOCIETY 203
FIRST NORTH AMERICAN EPISIOTOMY TRIAL 131
FIRST RESPONSE OVULATION PREDICTOR TEST 67
fish 6, 17, 25, 115, 121, 123, 148, 159, 179, 185, 200, 206-208, 211, 237, 246, 266
fish, baked 123
fish from the Great Lakes 179
Fishal, Ruth 27
fishy 75, 170
FISONS CORPORATION 67
Fitness Canada 96, 120
FITNESS AND PREGNANCY 96, 120
FITNESS LEADER 216
Flagyl 168
flashes, hot 16, 176, 188, 189, 191, 192, 198, 199, 219, 239
Flaws, Bob 186
flax seed 7, 121
Floradix 121, 247
fluconazole 6, 73, 75, 76
fluid retention 209, 214
fluorescent antibody test 88
fluoride 211
flushes, hot 214
Focus on Labour and Delivery 120, 129
focusing, difficulty 28
folic acid 22, 48, 109, 114, 208, 245, 247
FOLIC ACID CAN PREVENT STRUCTURAL BIRTH DEFECTS 114
FOLIC ACID, HOMOCYSTEINE AND BONE 208
food, fast 17
food, fried 41
food, intolerance of fatty 262
food, junk 2, 4, 14, 17, 41, 121, 148, 198
food, polluted 200
food related problems 95
food, rotate your 115
food rules 114
food, spicy 189

Food and Drug Administration 49, 259
foods, acidic 79, 83
foods, amine rich 149
foods, fermented 76, 184
foods, iron rich 248
foods, mouldy 76, 184
foods, organic 179
foods, refined 25, 71, 255
foods, unrefined 255
Foote, Dr. E.B. 57
Foothills Hospital 183
for estrogen, precursor 6
forceps 130, 131, 133, 137
Ford Motor Company 36
foreplay 189
formaldehyde 30
fracture rates 210
fractures 64, 65, 195-197, 205, 206, 201, 209-211, 216
fractures, incidence of 195, 209
fractures, mobility after 211
fractures of the spinal column 205
Framingham study 210
FRANKLIN DIAGNOSTICS 67
Fraser, Lindy 213
Friedrich, JoAnn Cutler 149, 154
fruit 84, 121-123, 200, 255
fruits and vegies, organic 200
fruits, dried 76, 184
fruits, fresh 4, 6, 17, 115, 148, 207, 121, 122, 237, 255, 257, 266
fruits, non-citrus 208
fruits, over-ripe 76
Frulen, Dr. Hakow 31
FSH 192
Fugazzoto, Dr. Paul 80, 81, 86
Fugere, Dr. Pierre 193
Fugh-Berman, Dr. Adriane 239
FULL OF LIFE 9
fumarate 247, 248
funeral home 40, 42
fungal 8
funguses 171

G:

Gaby, Dr. Alan 207, 208, 212
Gahler Enterprises 150
gallbladder disease 48, 221, 262, 263, 265
gallbladder ducts 264
gallbladder, infected 262
gallbladder inflammation 263
gallbladder patient 262
gallbladder, removal 263, 265
gallbladder removal 265
gallbladder secretions 265
gallbladder surgery 220, 261, 265
gallbladder wall 262
Gallbladder pain 262
gallstone disease 265, 266
gallstone formation, factors 265
gallstone incidence 261, 266
gallstone patients 264
gallstones, cholesterol 261
gallstones, diagnosing 263
gallstones, incidence of 261, 265
gallstones, people with 262
gallstones, reoccurrence 265
gallstones, symptomatic 264
GALLSTONES, DIET AND 266

GALLSTONES, PREVENTION OF 266
Gambrell, Dr. Don 193
Gardner, Joy 95, 124
gardnerella 72, 75, 270
gardnerella vaginalis 75
garlic 72, 76, 84
garlic-like odour 84
gas embolism 253
gastrectomy 245
gastritis 62
Gastrointestinal complaints 84, 245
Gates, Donna 74
gay bashing 270
gay men 267, 269, 270, 272
gelatin capsules 72, 83, 122, 157
genetic abnormalities 110, 112, 114
genetic counselling 110, 112, 113
genetic defect, serious 113
genetic defects 109
genetic disorder 208
genetic effects, harmful 105
genetic predisposition 8
genetic problems 103, 108
GENETIC COUNSELLING NECESSARY 110
geneticist, clinical 114
genetics 24, 27, 113, 236
genital area, itching 71
genital tract, upper 169
gentamicin 168
Gentian violet 72
Geriatric 233
gestodene 52
GETTING AROUND THE BOULDER IN THE ROAD 69, 140
Ghent, Dr. William 155-159, 237
Gibson, Mary 21
Gibson, Susan 240
Gillespie, Dr. Larrain 78-81, 83-85
ginger 123
GINSENG: 198
Gitleman, Louise 202
glands 6, 7, 9, 54, 141-143, 149, 176, 188, 198, 211, 223, 230, 233, 262
glandular abnormalities 74
glare screen 34
Glasburn, Vicki 74
glasses 33, 101, 115, 121, 190, 237
glasses, reading 190
Globe and Mail 12, 36, 55, 64, 82, 233, 264
gluconate 247, 248
glucose 115
glutamine 25
GNRH 176, 177, 223, 251
Goer, Henci 115
goiter 141, 142, 157
Golbitz, Frances 9
Goldbach, Nikki 95
Golden, Dr. John G. 178
Goldfarb, Dr. Herbert 177, 222, 225, 251
Goldhaber, Dr. Marilyn 31
Goldrath, Dr. 250
Goldstein, Dr. Donald 175
Golos, Natalie 9
Gomez, Jewel 271
gonadotropin 109, 114, 151, 176
gonadotropin releasing hormone 176
gonorrhea 54, 57, 66, 75, 88-91, 162, 163, 165, 166, 169, 171, 270

Good Housekeeping 17
GOODBYE HANGOVERS, HELLO LIFE 23, 27
Goodell, Dr. William 130
Graafian follicle 46
Grace Hospital 103
Grady, Dr. Deborah 197, 201, 210
grain cereal 121
grains, whole 4, 6, 17, 114, 115, 121, 156, 179, 200, 207, 237, 246, 247, 255, 257, 266
grapefruit 6, 75-77, 223, 255
grapes 123, 208
gravis 74
gravity, forces of 127, 132, 254
Great Lakes 157, 179
GREENPEACE 179, 237, 238, 241
greens 157, 208, 246, 247
Greenwood, Dr. Sadja 189, 202
Greer, Germaine 191, 192
Greif, Judy 225
grief 3, 12, 24, 38-43, 99, 139
grief counselling 41
grief, pangs of 139
grief reaction 12
grieving process 41, 139
GRIEVING 3, 38-42, 94, 110, 139, 140
GRIEVING, GUIDELINES FOR 40, 140
Griscom, Chris 200, 202
groin 174
Grollman, Earl 43
growth inhibition 50
growths, non-cancerous 51, 222
guinea pigs 34, 234
GUM DISEASE 51
Gutierrez, Bonnie 272
Gynecological Status 216
gynecologist, sympathetic 225
gynecologists 50, 59, 75, 88, 102, 114, 135, 154, 156, 177, 180-183, 202, 201, 219, 218, 220-225, 229, 252, 267
gynecologists, female 218
gynecologists, male 218
Gynecology 47, 53, 87, 98, 102, 104, 149, 156, 176, 183, 193, 197

H:

Haas, Dr. Elson 208
haddock 159
hair dryer 28, 72
hair dryer, electric 28
hair, facial 175, 190, 220
hair, grey 190
hair growth 51, 53
hair loss 51
hair, loss of 52
hair, pubic 190, 251
hair, scalp 190
hair, thin 141
hair thinning 159
hair, Underarm 190
hairdressers 30
hairdressers who use blow dryers 30
Hall, Dr. Marny 272
Hall, Dr. Philip 98, 87, 91
Hall, Judy 186, 202, 203
hallucinations, hormonal 147

HALTON HAMILTON WENTWORTH SUPPORT GROUP 10
handicapped child 109, 110
Handsfield, Dr. H. Hunter 89
hangover 7, 27, 199
Hanna, Thomas 21
Hansen, Dr. Peter 16
harassment 3, 11, 14, 270
Hargrove, Dr. Joel 193
Harris, Frann 64
Harrison, Dr. Michelle 154
Harvard School of Public Health 194
Hausknecht, Richard 138
Hausman, Patricia 212
HAVING A CESAREAN BABY: The Complete Guide 138
Hawkridge, Caroline 186
Hayman, Suzie 186
HCL 207, 208, 247
HDL 53, 54, 193, 196
headaches 5, 6, 15, 29, 33, 35, 38, 41, 115, 139, 143, 147, 149, 176, 190, 191, 244
headaches, frequent 115
headaches, migraine 41, 190
Healing Child-bearing Losses 43, 140
HEALING INTO LIFE AND DEATH 39, 42
HEALING WISE 184
HEALING YOURSELF DURING PREGNANCY 95, 124
health food stores 17, 70, 83, 121-123, 198, 247, 248, 255-257
health insurance 218, 230, 235
Health and Welfare Canada 31, 55, 101, 169
Health Insurance Plan of New York 230
Health Protection Branch 264
HEALTH FACTS 241
Healthsharing 23, 218
HEALTHY BONES- WHAT YOU SHOULD KNOW ABOUT OSTEOPOROSIS 212
hearing 35, 105, 264
hearing protectors 264
heart attack risk 194
heart beat, baby's 104, 133
heart deformities 123
heart disease 15, 29, 41, 47, 52-54, 191, 193, 194, 196, 197, 200, 201, 207, 218, 219, 247, 248, 266
heart disease, coronary 197, 201, 219
heart disease prevention 194
heart disease, risk factor 196
heart drug 194
heart failure 253, 262
heart pounding 147
heart problems 6, 103, 113
heart rate, rapid 142, 244
heart rate, slow 141
heart rhythms, irregular 253
HEART AND HANDS 95
HEART ATTACKS 46, 47, 191, 194-196
heartburn 15, 29, 121, 122, 245, 247, 248, 262, 265
heartburn, relieve 122
heat intolerance 142
Hedge, Dr. Alan 33

heels, low 256
heels, negative 256
height 105, 126, 216, 231
HELPING CHILDREN COPE WITH SEPARATION AND LOSS 43
HELPING CHILDREN COPE WITH DEATH 43
hematocrit 246
hemoglobin levels, Low 245
hemoglobin, low 245, 246
hemoglobin molecule, abnormalities 245
hemoglobin molecules 244, 245
hemoglobin, normal 244
hemoglobins, higher 246
hemoglobins, low normal 246
hemophilia 108
hemophilus 75
hemorrhage 164, 220, 246, 253, 258
hemorrhage, massive 164
hemorrhoids 29, 121, 245
Henry-Suchet, Jeanine 170
heparin 84
hepatitis 5, 51, 239, 270
Hepburn, Cuca 272
herbal cleansing program 200
herbal tincture 198
herbal treatment 48, 56
Herbal therapy 185
HERBAL TREATMENT FOR CERVICAL CANCER AND ABNORMAL PAP SMEARS 56
herbalist 184, 198
herbs 7, 9, 68, 85, 95, 124, 154, 184, 185, 198, 202, 223, 224
herbs, Chinese 185, 223
herbs, Western 185
hereditary 124, 175, 205, 236
hereditary factors 124, 175
Heredity 216
Heritage 184, 216
herpes 5, 9, 54, 58, 75, 88, 171, 270
herpes 6 virus 5
Herpes Simplex types 1 and 2 270
HERS - HYSTERECTOMY EDUCATIONAL RESOURCES AND SERVICES 226
heterosexist system 268
heterosexual couples 269
heterosexual definitions 270
heterosexual identity 267
heterosexual penetration 269
heterosexuality 267, 268
heterosexuals 267, 269, 271
Hewett, John 43
Hietanen, Dr. Maila 32
Higa, B.W. 74
Hill, Dr. Lucius 158
hip bone 205
hip displacement of newborns 110
hip fractures 197, 201, 205, 206, 210
hip pain 124
hip problems 119, 124
HIP FRACTURE: 201
HIP STUDY: 230
Hippocratic 236
Hirschowitz, Barry 229
hirsutism 53
hismanal 223
histamine 84, 258
Hitchcock, Cathy 241
HIV infection, rate 172

HIV positive 172
HIV positive women with PID 172
HIV virus 171, 172
hoarseness 141, 147
Holmes, Dr. King 90
HOMEBIRTH 95
homeopath, experienced 185
homeopathic 85, 185, 198, 207, 224
homeopathic doctor 198
homeopathic physician 224
homeopathic remedies 85, 185
homeopathic remedies, self-prescribe 185
Homeopathy 9, 66, 95, 124, 154, 185, 198
homocysteine, levels of 208
homophobia, effects of 271
homophobia, experience 267
HOMOPHOBIA 267, 268, 271, 272
HOMOPHOBIA: A WEAPON OF SEXISM 267, 271, 272
homosexuals 267, 268
homosexuals, irrational fear of 268
honey 122, 123
hormonal activity 147
hormonal changes 70, 71, 147, 190
hormonal control 176
hormonal cycle, basic 146
hormonal disorder, biochemical 146
hormonal disturbances 74
hormonal functions 74
hormonal imbalance 148, 155, 189, 222, 249
hormonal influences 79
hormonal intervention 50
hormonal manipulation 176
hormonal medications 222
hormonal shifts 99, 188
Hormonal levels 4, 190
Hormonal upheavals 11, 116
HORMONAL FACTORS 81
HORMONAL TREATMENTS 173, 175, 176
hormone, bone-saving 209
hormone, growth 51
hormone horror 55
hormone levels 15, 62, 63, 142, 146, 190, 219
hormone levels, lowered 63
hormone levels, shifting 142, 190
hormone, luteinizing 64, 66
hormone progesterone, lack 64
hormone regulation 70
hormone replacement therapy 191, 195-197, 203, 208, 212, 218, 238
hormone secretions 61
hormone, steroid 6, 49
hormone, synthetic male 151
hormone, synthetic thyroid 141
hormone therapy, appropriate 147
hormone therapy, estrogen 195, 209
hormone therapy, menopausal 194, 210
hormone treatment, long-term 196, 239
hormone usage 184
hormones, anti-thyroid 142
hormones, artificial 265
hormones, female 22, 176, 188
hormones, male 52, 151, 189, 219
hormones, mother of all 6
hormones, stress 29
hormones, synthetic 195

hormones, thyroid 71, 141, 142, 237
HORMONES AND BONE LOSS 195
HORMONES AND BREAST CANCER: 238
HORMONES AND GALLSTONES 265
HORMONES OR HISTORY 147
Horner, Pamela 212
Horrobin, Dr. David 10, 154
horsetail, extract of 207
hose, support 256, 257
HOSPITAL ACCESS: 269
hospitalization 61, 62, 90, 168
hot castor oil packs 156, 255
hot flashes, control 191, 198
hot flashes, frequency 189
hot flashes, reduces 198
hot flashes, severe 191, 198
hot sweats, menopausal-like 147
HOT FLASH: A NEWSLETTER FOR MIDLIFE AND OLDER WOMEN 203
housework 2, 42, 116
HOW TO AVOID A HYSTEREC-TOMY 225
HOW TO HAVE GREAT LEGS AT ANY AGE 257
HOW TO PREVENT MISCAR-RIAGE AND OTHER CRISES OF PREGNANCY 140
HRT 191, 192, 195-197, 202, 203, 208-210, 238
Hudson, Dr. Tori 48, 56
Hufnagel, Dr. Vicki 219, 220, 226
Huggins, Kathleen 96
human chorionic gonadotropin 109, 114
human corneal tissue 258
human immune virus 87
Human Nutrition Research Center 206, 208
Human Nutrition Research Center on Aging 206
Humane Society 260
humour 20, 21, 41, 189
Hunt, Mary 267
Hunter, Dr. Marlene 21, 89, 104, 202
Hyde, Dr. Bryon 5, 6, 9
Hydro-Quebec 30
hydrochloric acid 207, 247
hydrogen peroxide 170
Hydrotherapy 7
hydroxypatite 207
hyper-irritability 74
hyperactivity 73, 74, 143
hyperplasia, endometrial 249, 250
hypersensitivity 149, 155, 185
hypertension 4, 194
hyperthyroidism, symptoms of 141-143
HYPNOSIS 17, 18, 21, 81, 98, 129
hypnotherapy 25
hypnotist 98
hypoallergenic 7
hypochondriac 73
hypoglycemia 4
hypothalamus 176
hypothyroid 141, 142
hypothyroidism, borderline 142
HYPOTHYROIDISM 141-143, 156, 237

HYPOTHYROIDISM; THE UNSUSPECTED ILLNESS 142
hysterectomies, consequences of 218
hysterectomies, deaths from unnecessary 220
hysterectomies, total 224
hysterectomies, unnecessary 218-220
HYSTERECTOMIES 192, 218-220, 222-226
hysterectomy, immediate 225
hysterectomy, laparoscopic 220, 221
hysterectomy, modern 218
hysterectomy, necessary 221
hysterectomy rates, higher 218
hysterectomy, rates of 219
hysterectomy, risk of dying 220
hysterectomy, routine 220
hysterectomy, standard type 221
hysterectomy, subtotal 224
hysterectomy, vaginal 221
Hysterectomy, Before and After 219
HYSTERECTOMY BEFORE AND AFTER 226
hysterosalpingogram 162
hysteroscope 62, 223, 249-251, 253
hysteroscopic exam 249, 251
hysteroscopic operation 223, 251
hysteroscopy, complications of 253
HYSTEROSCOPY 136, 223, 249-253

I:

IBM 31, 32, 36
IC 78-86
ICA 78, 85, 86
Ideal Computer Environments 35
imagery 19, 69, 81, 95, 129, 137, 140
imagery, mental 95, 129
imidazole drugs 72
immune defence system 80
immune disorders 141
immune enhancing properties 7
immune function, depressed 178
immune status, altered 8
immune stimulating herbs 7
immune system 2, 5, 6, 9, 32, 33, 41, 80, 141, 171, 172, 180, 198, 270
immune system, compromised 270
immune system dysfunction 5, 80
immune system, weakened 8
immunisation, typhoid 235
IMMUNITY, PEAK 9
immunization 5
Immuno-depressive 9
immunoabsorbent assay, enzyme-linked 88
immunoglobulins 6
immunological studies 178
immunology 81, 236
Imperial Cancer Research Fund 196
implants, atypical 180, 182
implants, black 182
implants, endometrial 173-175, 177
impotence 69
IMPRINTS 97
in utero 101
in vitro fertilization 68
incest 23, 24
incision, large 263
incision, lower 61
incision, surgical 130, 133
incision, transverse 137

incision, upper 61
incisions, multiple 257
incisions, small 257, 263
INCISIONS AND SCARS 136
incontinence, Stress 222
incontinence, urinary 117, 118, 131, 220
Index Medicus 267
Indiana University Center 90
indigestion 73, 190, 265
infection, polymicrobial 168
INFECTION:, RECURRING 164
infections, Anaerobic 168
infections, bacterial 78-80
infections, cervical STD 170, 171
infections, chlamydia cervical 90
infections, gonorrheal 162
infections, parasitic 74
infections, post-op 220
infections, Recurrent 38, 143
infections, repeated 78, 81-83, 163
infections, repeated bacterial 78
infections, urinary 8, 82
infections, vaginal 15, 70-73, 75, 83, 161, 162, 170, 270
INFECTIONS, HIDDEN BACTE-RIAL 80
INFECTIONS:, VAGINAL 162
infertility 11, 14, 20, 49, 50, 65, 66, 68, 69, 73, 89, 90, 92, 161, 163, 164, 167, 170, 171, 173-177, 180, 181, 184, 186, 226, 250
infertility, cause of 90, 92, 163, 226
infertility clinics 68
infertility, higher rates 171
infertility investigations 66, 68, 174, 250
infertility, lower rates 170
infertility, permanent 89
infertility, preventable 161, 163
infertility problems 68
infertility, surgery for 177
Infertility due to male causes 66
INFERTILITY AFTER THE PILL 49
INFERTILITY AWARENESS 69
INFERTILITY AWARENESS ASSOCIATION OF CANADA 69
INFERTILITY, DIAGNOSING 68
INFERTILITY - PROBLEMS GETTING PREGNANT 68
inflammation, acute 262
inflammation, low grade 87
inflammation, pancreatic 264
inflammatory bowel disease 8, 165
influenza virus 5
infrared light 30, 33
inhalation 259
inherited abnormalities 109, 245
Inherited 24, 81, 108, 109, 245, 254
injection, intramuscular 211
injections 6, 7, 91, 168, 211, 220, 248, 257, 259, 264
injections, intravenous 248
inositol 185
insemination, alternative 269
insemination, artificial 68, 90
insomnia 8, 29, 41, 139, 143, 147, 190, 198, 199
Institute of Occupational Health 32
insulin 51, 115, 196
intercourse 132, 167, 171, 189, 269
intercourse, anal 171

intercourse, delay the start 171
intercourse, pain during 167
intercourse, painful 132
intercourse, vaginal 171
Intern Clin Nutr Rev 211
internal organs 220, 253
International Health Foundation 75, 76
International Journal of Health Services 238
INTERNATIONAL CESAREAN AWARENESS NETWORK 138
internist 74, 184, 219
interstitial cystitis 8, 78, 80, 81, 83-86
Interstitial Cystitis Association 78, 81, 83, 85-86
interstitium, inflammation 78
intestinal injury 263, 264
intestine, perforation of 262
intestine, small 244, 261, 173
intestines 76, 103, 113, 121, 173, 221, 244, 245, 261-263
intestines, large 121
intolerance, cold 142
intolerance, food 265
intramuscular 6, 211
INTRAUTERINE DEVICES 171
intravenous fluids 123, 262
intravenous supplements 8
INVISIBLE LIVES 267, 272
iodaminol 157, 158
iodine absorption, block 157
iodine absorption by the thyroid 157
iodine and seaweeds 237
iodine, aqueous 157, 158
iodine, Aqueous diatomic 151
iodine, beneficial form 159
iodine by mouth 156
iodine, casein bound 157
iodine, caseinated 157
iodine, colloidal 159
iodine content 157, 237
iodine content of the soil and water 157
iodine crystals 157
iodine deficiency 156, 159
iodine deficient 156, 157
iodine, Dietary 157
iodine dye 82
iodine, elemental 155-159
iodine, free 157, 159
iodine onto the vagina 156
iodine orally 156
iodine, overdose on 159
iodine preparations 159
iodine sensitivity 156
iodine solution, antiseptic 72
iodine, specific type 157
IODINE, ALL ABOUT 157
IODINE AND BREAST CANCER 159
IODINE CONNECTION 156
IODINE, GETTING MORE 157
iodism 158, 159
Iomech 159
ionizing radiation 178
Irish College of General Practitioners 234
iron, absorbing 245
iron absorption 247
iron binding capacity 245, 246
iron, blood level 223
iron deficiency 4, 223, 244-247

iron deficiency anemia 4, 245-247
iron deficiency anemias 245-247
iron, elemental 247
iron, Excess 248
iron, good sources 246
iron in hemoglobin 248
iron levels 4, 223, 244, 246
iron, liquid 121, 247
iron, low 244-246
iron molecule 247
iron, natural 246, 247
iron, NutriChem 121
iron requirements 245
iron reserves 244, 246
iron salts 247, 248
iron, sources of 244, 246, 247
iron storage, Excessive 248
iron stores 4, 223, 246, 248
iron stores, low 246, 248
Iron supplements 121, 189, 244-248
IRON DEFICIENCY OR ANEMIA, SYMPTOMS 244
IRON DEFICIENCY, REASONS 245
IRON, DIETARY SOURCES 246
IRON, OTHER NATURAL SOURCES 247
IRON SUPPLEMENTS, NATURAL 247
irritability 15, 62, 116, 74, 139, 142, 143, 146, 147, 149, 151, 190, 199, 219, 244
IS IT HOT IN HERE OR IS IT ME? 203
IS MENOPAUSE A DISEASE 191
itching 33, 70-72, 75, 170, 255
itching, vaginal 70
itraconazole 73, 76
IUD 54, 56, 57, 60, 89, 91, 161, 170, 171, 250, 251, 268
IUD fitting 89
IUD, insertion 91, 170
IUD's, modern 171
IUD's, older 171
IUD'S (INTRAUTERINE DEVICES): 171
IV 168, 169, 270
IV antibiotic treatment, length 169
IV drug users 270
IVF 90
IVP 81, 82

J:

Jackson, Marni 9, 76, 147, 148, 179, 241
Jacobovitz, Ruth 203
Jacobs, Dr. Robert 202
JAMA 234
James and Cherry 38-40
James, John W. 42
Japanese women 189, 206, 237
Jarrell, Dr. John 183
jaundice 51, 262
jaundice, yellow 51
jellies, water soluble 189
Jessop, Dr. Carol 6, 7, 75, 76
Jewelt, Claudia 43
Jewish women 108
jogging 117, 181
John Hopkins University 30, 176
Johnson, Ben 55
Johnson, Dr. Karen 147, 151, 154

Johnson, Sonia 23, 24
joint pains 38
joint swelling 5
joints 5, 38, 80, 118, 137, 147, 190
joints, loosening of 118
Jones, Carl 95, 129, 137
Jones, Dr. Robert 90
Josse, Dr. Robert 205
Journal of Family Practice 103
Journal of Obstetricians and Gynecologists 201
Journal of the American Medical Association 229, 194-196
Journal of the National Cancer Institute 231, 242
Journal Of Family Medicine 105
Journal SOGC 53, 104, 224
JOURNEY THROUGH BIRTH 120, 129
joys 95, 111, 116
juice 121, 122, 208, 247, 248
juice, fruit 121
juice, orange 248
juice, prune 121
JUSTISSE GROUP 68
JUSTISSE METHOD FOR FERTILITY MANAGEMENT 64, 68
JVC 32

K:

Kaiser Clinic 31
kale 157, 246, 247
Kamen, Betty 203
Kansas City of Medicine 103
Karuna's Osteonex 207
KATHY SMITH'S PREGNANCY WORKOUT 120
Kaufman, Dr. Stephen 258
Kegel, Dr. Arnold 118
Kegel exercises 118, 119, 133, 134, 222
Keirse, Marc 107
Kelleher, K. 154
Kelly, Pat 236, 240
kelp 159, 206
Kenton, Leslie 202
ketoconazole 6, 75, 76
kidney failure 262
kidney function 81, 211
kidney stones 262, 265
kidneys 13, 52, 79, 81-83, 103, 113, 211, 246, 262, 265
Kilmartin, Angela 86
Kinsey Institute 270
Kirkpatrick, Dr. Jean 23, 24, 27
Kitzinger, Sheila 94-97, 106, 111, 116, 120, 126, 129, 132, 134
KLAIRE LABORATORIES 213
Klein, Dr. Michael 96, 104, 106, 120, 130, 131, 137
Koehler, Nan 138
Konetski, Dr. Wayne 149, 185
KRIPP'S PHARMACY 77, 204, 213
Kritz, Ruth 81
Kuller, Dr. Lewis 197
KY Jelly 189

L:

L.I.F.T. 43
La Leche League 96

labia 72, 75
labour, active phase 126
labour coach 127, 133
labour, failed induction 136
labour, failure to progress 135, 136
labour fearful and out of control 128
labour, first stage 126, 127
labour inductions 102
labour like a performance 128
labour, physical 205
labour, premature 117
labour, progress of 127
labour, prolonged 135
labour, pushing stage 132
labour, second stage 126, 127, 134
labour, serious pain during 126
labour, strain of 136
labour, trial of 135, 136
labour, worst position 127
labours, normal 112
LACTATION 50
lactic acid 170
lactobacilli, normal growth 82
lactobacilli, poor population 82
lactobacilli, protective 70
lactobacillus 70, 75, 76, 82
lactobacillus acidophilus 70, 76
lactobacillus casei 82
lactobacillus fermentum 82
lactobacillus powder 70, 73
lactose 157
lamb's quarters 246
LAMBDA GREY 203
Lambert-Lagace, Louise 95
Lancet Medical Journal 6, 114, 210, 211, 234, 239, 261, 265, 266
Lanctot, Dr. Guylaine 254, 256, 257
Langley, Dr. Gil 259
laparoscope 59, 61, 166, 167, 177, 181, 183, 221, 223, 263
laparoscopic experience 263
laparoscopic skills 221
laparoscopic surgery, Recovery 177
LAPAROSCOPIC DIAGNOSIS 166
laparoscopies, normal 222
laparoscopy 165-167, 174, 175, 177, 182, 222
laparoscopy, near contact 182
laparoscopy, Operative 177
laparoscopy, panoramic 182
laparotomy 62
Lark, Dr. Susan 154, 202
Larkin, Maureen 37
laser 84, 177, 183
laser surgery 183
LASER TREATMENT: 84
latex rubber 54
LAUGH A LOT 20
Laurson 186
LAVENDER 272
laxatives 121
LCD 36
LD-50 259
LDL 53, 54, 193
LDL levels, decrease 53
Le Shan, Dr. Lawrence 240, 241
lead aprons 33
learning disabilities 73
LEARNING TO SAY GOODBYE 43
Lee, Dr. John 156, 160, 191, 193, 195, 198, 211, 212
Lee, Dr. Matthew 85
Leeper 35

left-handed 267
leg, back of 254
leg cramps 117
leg raising, double 118
leg veins to the heart 254
legs 19, 29, 47, 117, 118, 181, 200, 206, 214, 252, 254-256
legs, itching 255
legumes 114, 115, 208, 255
lemon 208, 255
Lemon oil 255
lentils 208
Leoffler, Val 272
Leon 53, 257
Lerner, Harriet Goldhor 21
lesbian, battered 270
lesbian couples 11, 269, 271
lesbian, define a 267
lesbian having a child 269
lesbian lovemaking 269
lesbian organizations 270, 271
lesbian services 268
Lesbian battering 270
Lesbian culture 271
Lesbian Information Lines 268
LESBIAN AT MIDLIFE: The Creative Transition 272
LESBIAN CONNECTION 272
LESBIAN HEALTH MATTERS! 272
LESBIAN PASSION, Loving Ourselves and Each Other 272
LESBIAN SEX 270, 272
lesbians and AIDS 270
lesbians, awareness of 270
lesbians, medical problems specific to 268
Lesbians and Gay Men 267, 270, 272
LESBIANS IN CANADA 272
LeShan, Eda 43
lesions 182, 183, 234, 270
lesions, suspicious 182, 183
Lethal Dose Fifty Percent Test 258, 259
LETHAL 87, 258, 259
lethargy 3, 142, 143
leukemia 30-34, 105, 108
Levine, Stephen 39, 42
Lewis, Myrna 197, 203
LH DETECTION 67
LH in the urine 67
LH surge 64, 67, 68
libido, absent 74
libido, loss of 62
licorice 198, 204
Lieberman, Adrienne 129
life expectancy 12, 197, 201
LIFE 101 16
LIFE AFTER LOSS 39, 40, 42
lifestyle change 74, 116
lifestyle, sedentary 205
LIFESTYLE, CHANGES IN 116
LIFETIME RISKS OF DEATH FOR 50 YEAR OLD WOMEN 201
lifting, heavy 61, 254, 257
ligaments 118, 173, 174, 180, 181, 219, 221
ligaments, uterine 181
light-headedness 244
LIGHTING, OFFICE 28
Lim, Robin 97, 143
Limbo and Wheeler 43
lindane 230

lining of the abdominal cavity 171, 174
lining of the fallopian tube 163
lining of the uterus 89, 161, 162, 164, 166, 171, 222-224, 249
lining of your womb 249
lipid effects 53
lipid levels, blood 48
lipid profile 47, 53, 193
lipid readings, blood 193
lipids, blood 47, 48, 50, 192, 193, 196
liquid crystal display 34, 35
lithotripsy for gallstones 264, 265
Lithotripsy 264, 265
liver 6, 7, 9, 22, 31, 48, 51, 76, 90, 161, 167, 189, 192, 239, 244, 246, 247, 261, 263
liver capsule 90, 161, 167
liver complications 239
liver disease 192, 239
liver enzymes 51, 239
liver function 51, 76
liver tumours 48
liver tumours, benign 48
LIVER AND GALLBLADDER PROBLEMS 48
Living is For Today 43
LIVING THOUGH MOURNING 42
LIVING WITH ENDOMETRIOSIS; 186
Lombard, Dr. D. 154
Lopez, Dr. Anthony 221
loss of dreams of normal birth 136
loss of early contact with the baby 136
loss of her child 140
loss of lean body mass 206
loss of meaning of life 139
loss of private time 116
loss of teamwork with her mate 136
Loulan, JoAnn 270, 272
love, unconditional 184
Love, Dr. Susan 155, 160, 236, 239, 241
LOVE AND SEX AFTER 60 203
lovemaking 269
Low, Dr. Donald 158
Lowe, Graham 12
lozenges 7, 122
Lu Park, Merri 202
Lubrafax 189
lubricants 189
Lugol's solution 156-159
lumbar spine 62
lumbar vertebrae 85
lump, suspicious 268
lumps 155, 160, 165, 174, 181, 228, 229, 234, 239-241, 268
lumpy 155, 229, 261
Lundy, Dr. Colette 24
lung reactions 253
lung secretions 252
lungs 13, 31, 47, 80, 109, 118, 167, 173, 244, 252, 253
Lupron 176, 182
lupus 51, 74, 80, 178
luteinizing hormone (LH) surge 66
lymph glands 230, 233
lymph nodes, tender 5, 158
lymphatic flow, improve 7
lymphocytes 7, 163, 166
lymphoma 32, 34

Lyons, Dr. Thomas 105, 106, 224

M:

M.E. ASSOCIATION OF CANADA 10, 21
MacFarlane, Dr. John 158
MACLEOD 77, 248
Madsen, Lynn 138
magnesium 6, 7, 10, 17, 25, 115, 122, 123, 149, 156, 199, 200, 206-208
magnesium, given intravenously 156
magnesium sulphate 6
Magnesium citrate liquid 7
magnetic fields 31-35, 37
MAKING PREGNANCY DECISIONS AND BIRTH PLANS 94
malabsorption syndrome 245
malaise, generalized 5
malaise, post-exertional 5
maleate 207
Malmo study 231, 235
Mammacare 160, 229, 239-241
MAMMACARE LEARNING SYSTEM 160, 229, 239
mammogram quality 228, 232
mammogram, reliable 228
mammogram, screening 227-229, 231, 234
MAMMOGRAM 14, 155, 160, 227-229, 231-234, 241
mammograms, abnormal 230
mammograms, annual 230, 231
mammograms, quality 228
mammograms, radiation from 231, 238
mammograms, routine 230
mammographers, expert diagnostic 232
mammography, quality of 232
mammography, regular 227
mammography, screening 227, 230, 231, 235, 241
MAMMOGRAPHY CAN BE USED FOR TWO PURPOSES 228
MAMMOGRAPHY SCREENING: A DECISION MAKING GUIDE 241
MANAGING IC 85
Mandel, Dr. Fred 149, 151
Mandeville, Dr. Rosemonde 31
manganese 207, 247
Manning, Doug 42
mapping 8, 200
Marha, Dr. 31
marital problems 12, 15, 150
Marital reconciliation 14
marriage breakdown 12, 16, 78
marrow 244, 246, 247
Martin, Dr. Alexander 30, 31, 38
Martin, Dr. Dan 178
Martin, Pamela Sue 78
MARVELON 52
mascara 258
mask 50, 147, 252
massage 6, 17, 25, 36, 41, 95, 129, 133, 154
mastectomy 13, 158
masturbation 189, 199
maternal alpha fetal protein 109, 110
maternity wards 31
MATERNITY, ALTERNATIVE 95, 124

Matthews-Larsens, Joan 27
MATURE WOMEN'S NETWORK 203
MATURESCENCE 197
Mauvais-Jarvis, Dr. 155
Mayo Clinic 209, 210
McCloud, Kent 77, 247, 248
McCullough, Dr. Lawrence 104
McDonald, Dr. Alison 31
McGibbon, Dr. Diane 154
McGill University 30, 104, 149, 219, 231, 264
McKendree, Diana 42
McKenzie, Robyn 55
McMaster University 53, 84, 104, 176, 197
McSherry, Dr. James 88
McWilliams 16
Mead, Margaret 38, 188
meals, regular 266
meals, small frequent 123, 148
meat 114, 121, 148, 179, 185, 205, 207, 208, 217, 237, 238, 246-248, 257, 266
meat eaters 266
meat-eaters, female 207
meat, red 121, 148, 205, 207, 217, 237, 246-248, 257
meats, organ 114
meats, processed 121
median nerve 29
Medical College of Pennsylvania 156
Medical Journal of Australia 62
Medical Post 54, 62, 114, 137, 232, 234
Medical Research Council of Great Britain 114, 239
MEDICAL MANAGEMENT OF PMS 154
medications, anti-thyroid 142
medications, anti-yeast 6, 71, 74, 76, 91, 184
medicine, modern 46, 173
medicine, preventative 41, 228
meditation 9, 17, 27
Mediterranean people 245
Mediterranean women 108
mega-B-50 123, 148
melanoma, malignant 49
Melton, Dr. 209
memory 5, 35, 74, 159, 190
memory loss 5, 35, 190
memory, loss of 74
memory, short term 5
menarche 209
menopausal change 191
menopausal period 188
menopausal symptoms 81, 176, 189, 191-193, 198, 202, 206, 219
menopausal woman, negative stereotype 188
menopausal woman with zest 188
MENOPAUSAL YEARS 188, 198, 202, 214
MENOPAUSAL YEARS; THE WISE WOMAN WAY 198
menopause, anemic around 245
menopause, beginning of 50
menopause, difficult 13
menopause, earlier 188, 219
menopause, healthy changes 188
menopause, immediate 220
menopause, medical descriptions 188

menopause, medical profession's understanding of 188
menopause, mimicked 175
menopause, natural 195, 202, 210
menopause, premature 61-63, 198
menopause, surgical 198, 218
menopause, symptoms of 190, 191, 202, 219
MENOPAUSE AND EMOTIONS: Making Sense of Your Feelings When Your Feelings Make No Sense 202
MENOPAUSE AND MIDLIFE HEALTH 202
MENOPAUSE, How You Can Benefit From Diet, Vitamins, Exercise 202
MENOPAUSE NATURALLY 189, 202
MENOPAUSE SPECIFICS: 199
MENOPAUSE SUPPORT GROUPS 203
MENOPAUSE WITHOUT MEDICINE 202
MENOPAUSE: TIME FOR A CHANGE 202
menstrual abnormalities 141
menstrual bleeding, excessive 52, 174
menstrual bleeding, Heavy 62, 189
menstrual blood 58, 71, 173, 180
menstrual changes 188
menstrual complications 62
menstrual cycle 58, 67, 70, 74, 148, 150, 163, 215
menstrual cycles, irregular 174
menstrual difficulties 15
menstrual flow 62, 214
menstrual history 103
menstrual irregularities 50, 219
menstrual pain 52, 62
menstrual pain, increased 62
menstrual periods, heavier 62
Menstrual disturbances 223, 245
Menstrual problems 73, 143
MENSTRUAL REALITIES AND MENSTRUAL MYTHS 154
menstruation 50, 58, 71, 73, 143, 146, 151, 180, 223, 251
menstruation explanation, retrograde 180
menstruation, normal 223, 251
mental deterioration 22
mental health 12, 27, 268
mental health, community 27
mental health referrals 268
mental hospitals 24
mental illness 190
mental incapacity 269
MENTASTICS 21
metabolic disease 156
metabolic rate 143, 198
METABOLIC CHANGES 51
metabolism 24, 109, 205, 208, 237
metabolism, low 237
metabolites 230
metals, heavy 8
Metamucil 76, 121, 256
Metcalf, C.W. 21
Methione 208
methionine 185
methylcellulose 7
metronidazole 168

miconazole 72
microcolpohysteroscope 250
microcrystalline hydroxypatite 207
micronized 193, 195, 211
micronor 192
microorganisms 171
microsurgery 59
MICROWAVE NEWS 30, 33, 36
midwives 95, 132, 133, 138
Migraine 41, 52, 80, 190, 193
milk 50, 115, 123, 157, 179, 206, 208
milk protein casein 157
Millar, Dr. Diane 50
Miller, Dr. Anthony 226, 228, 232
millet 157, 266
Milligan, Dr. John 132
Milne, Dr. Ken 137
MIND OVER LABOUR; USING THE MIND'S POWER 95, 129
mineralization of new bone 210
minerals, trace 121, 124, 157, 207, 247
minilaparotomy 62
minitrampoline 200
miracles 191
miscarriage, early 139
miscarriage, grief following 139
miscarriage, incomplete 250
miscarriage, threatened 102, 103
MISCARRIAGE 13, 30-32, 38, 50, 102, 103, 110, 111, 113, 117, 139, 140, 142, 174, 175, 250
MISCARRIAGE, WOMEN'S EXPERIENCES AND NEEDS 140
miscarriages, preventing 140
Miscarriages 40, 74, 109, 111, 139, 140
miscarry, tendency to 109
MISSED CONCEPTIONS 68
Molasses 121, 123, 247
MOMAZONS 272
money 3, 12, 37, 67, 135, 166, 233
Mongolism 108
monistat 72, 73
monitors, field 35
monkeys 178
MONTREAL HEALTH PRESS 55, 92, 203
mood changes 209
mood disorders 154
mood swings 15, 41, 53, 73, 146, 147, 149, 151, 176, 190, 192, 199, 219
MOOD-ALTERING DRUGS: 84
MOOD SWINGS, IRRITABILITY AND INSOMNIA 199
Morgan, Dr. Susanne 226
Morgan, M. Granger 31, 37
morning sickness 122, 123
mortality, reduction in 232, 235, 236
Mossman, Caroline 23
motherhood 7, 11, 15, 94, 97, 111, 112, 116, 142
Mothering 60, 238
mothers, older 112, 116
mothers, younger 112
motivation 219, 220, 227
Motrin 150, 223, 251
Moulder, Christine 140
mouldy 76, 184
Mount Sinai Medical Center 41, 112, 230, 258
mouth, burning 190

Ms. Magazine 38
MU metal 32
mucous charts 67
mucous membranes 270
mucous observations 66, 68
mucous pattern 65
mucous plug 64
mucous readings 65
mucous secretions 70, 214
mucous, stretchy 65, 67
mucous symptoms 67
mucous, transparent 65
MUCOUS: 65
Mullens, Anne 68
Mullerian duct system 182
Mulleriosis 182
multiple sclerosis 74
multivitamins 7, 25, 109, 114, 208
Murray, Michael 202
muscle aches 8
muscle contractions 19, 134
muscle mass 200, 206
muscle pain 5, 147, 176
muscle re-education 36
muscle strength 189, 206
muscle weakness 5, 206, 244
muscles, calf 254
muscles, eye 28
muscles of the abdominal wall 263
muscular aches 33, 141
muscular contraction 29
muscular dystrophy 108
muscular sac 261
muscular tension, chronic 17
muscular weakness 6
MUSCULOSKELETAL PROB-LEMS 29
mushrooms 149
music 8, 20, 98, 271
mustard greens 157
Myalgic Encephalitis 5
MYALGIC ENCEPHALOMYELITIS ASSC. OF ONTARIO 10
myasthenia gravis 74
mycelia 70
mycocidin 76
mycostatin 72, 91
Myer's program 156
Myers, Dr. John 156
myomectomy 223, 225
MYTHS ABOUT HYSTERECTOMY 219

N:

N.I.H. 102
nails, brittle 245
nails, spoon shaped 245
NALMEFENE 84
Namka, Lynne 27
Napoli, Mary Ann 241
NASA 178
nasal spray 151, 176, 211
National Cancer Institute 228-231, 233, 234, 237-239, 242
National Childbirth Trust 134
National Conference on Diet and Breast Cancer 237
National Health Service 230
National Institute of Child Health and Human Development 49, 102

National Institute of Environmental Health Sciences 178, 230
National Institute of Health 10, 102, 196
National Selected Morticians 42
National Women's Health Network 55, 203, 225, 226, 239
NATIONAL ACTION FORUM FOR MIDLIFE AND OLDER WOMEN 203
NATIONAL BREAST SCREENING STUDY IN CANADA 232
NATIONAL INSTITUTES OF HEALTH BACKGROUNDER ON FIBROMYALGIA 10
NATIONAL ME/FM ACTION NETWORK 10
NATIONAL OSTEOPOROSIS FOUNDATION 213
native women 261
Natur-pharm 207
Natural Energy Works 35, 36
Natural Factors 207
Naturopaths 48, 185, 224, 256
nausea 33, 51, 55, 119, 122, 123, 147, 151, 167, 175, 239, 245, 248, 262
nausea, prolonged 123
nausea, severe 122
navel 166, 173
Nazzaro, Dr. 154
NBSS 227, 228, 232
NCI 233
near contact lap method 183
neck 15, 29, 33, 36, 37, 82, 141, 150, 189, 212
negative ions 33
Neilson, Lydia 10
neonatal 139
nervous system 30, 31, 35, 105
nervous system, autonomic 31
nervousness 52, 141-143, 198
nettles 247
neural tube defects 109, 114
neuromyasthenia, post-infectious 5
Neurophychophysiologist 8
neurotherapy 8
neurotic 181
neurotoxic free radicals 7
neurotransmitters 80, 149
neutrophils 163, 166
New Concepts 34, 203
New Dimensions 35
New England Journal of Medicine 32, 102, 112, 114, 137, 195, 196, 209, 211, 238, 263
New Scientist 259
New York Academy of Sciences 156
New York Telephone Company 30
New York University 258
NEW OUR BODIES OUR SELVES 66
NEW YORKER 30
newborn, complications in 102
newborn intensive care unit 112
newborns 94, 95, 99, 102, 101, 105, 106, 110, 112, 116, 124
newborns, risk of X-rays 105
newspapers, alternative 271
NFR 9, 10
niacinamide 25
nicotine 24
Nielsen, Dr. Forrest 208

NIGHTINGALE RESEARCH
  FOUNDATION 9
nightmares 147
NIOSH 29, 32
nitrofurantoin 80, 83
nizoral 76
NO HYSTERECTOMY; YOUR
  BODY YOUR CHOICE 225
NO IMMEDIATE DANGER 37, 233
NO MORE HYSTERECTOMIES
  219, 226
Noble, Elizabeth 96, 120
nodules 174, 181
noise, sensitivity to 147
Nomination of Committee 269
non-drinkers 237
non-pill-users 47
Norad Corporation 35
norepinephrine 80
norgestimate 52
norlutate 192
Norsigian, Judy 49
North American Menopause Society
  203
North American women 155, 161,
  176, 205
North York General Hospital 114
Northrup, Dr. Christiane 156
nose, runny 115
Notelovitz, Dr. Morris 202, 212
Nourse, Dr. Alan E. 27
NTD 114
Nu-life's Framework 207
nuclear testing 238, 240
NU-FOCUS 69
numbness 29, 244
nurse-midwife 95
Nurses' Study 194, 195
nursing women 34
NURSING 15, 34, 95, 96, 124, 206
nurturing 7, 99, 269
NURTURING THE UNBORN
  CHILD 99
nutmeg 123
nutrasweet 84
NUTRICHEM 77, 121, 248
NUTRICHEM PHARMACY 77, 248
Nutridophilus Rx 77
Nutrition 4, 24, 26, 27, 66, 95, 115,
  123, 124, 148, 202, 206, 208, 237
NUTRITION AND HEALTH 115
NUTRITION AND VITAMINS 148
NUTRITION FOR MOTHER AND
  CHILD 95
nuts 79, 208
nylon support hose 256, 257
nystatin 72, 73, 76, 77

O:

O'Donnell, Mary 272
O'Dowd, Dennis 157, 159
O'Hanlan, Dr. Katherine 202
Oakley, Anne 140
oatmeal 123
obesity 194, 261
obstetrician, persistent interference
  130
Obstetricians 98, 118, 102, 114, 130,
  132, 133, 135, 136, 201, 229
Odent, Michael 94
OHIP 233
Ojeda, Linda 202

Older, Julia 186
Olds, Sally 96, 208
olive oil 133
Olive, Dr. David 175-177
Olkin, Sylvia Klein 96, 120
OMP 193, 196
Online Journal of Current Clinical
  Trials 131
Ontario Breast Cancer Exchange
  Program 241
Ontario Cancer Treatment and
  Research Foundation 235
Ontario Cesarean Planning
  Committee 137
Ontario Hydro 30-32
Ontario Medicine 50, 52
Ontario Ministry of Labour 35
Ontario screening program 233
ONTARIO FIBROSITIS ASSO-
  CIATION 10
ONTARIO NETWORK FOR
  ENDOMETRIOSIS 185
OPEN SEASON, A SURVIVAL
  GUIDE FOR NATURAL
  CHILDBIRTH 137
operating room 59, 183, 252
operations, unnecessary 234
Opthalmology 258
Optima 186
oral drops, desensitizing 149, 185
oranges 149
organochlorines 178, 179, 185, 230,
  237, 238
orgasm, uterine 219
orgasms 219, 221
ORGONE 35
Oriental 198, 205, 216, 261
Ornish, Dr. Dean 194
ORTHO Pharmaceutical 55
ORTHOCEPT 52
Orthopedic surgeons 181
Osseous Complex 207
Ostaderm 204
Osteo-B-Plus 207
Osteo-Balance 207
Osteoguard 207
osteoporosis, new screening method
  209
osteoporosis, post-menopausal 216
osteoporosis related fractures 195,
  209, 210
osteoporosis-related fractures 205
osteoporosis, severe 208, 212
osteoporosis, treatment of 208, 210
OSTEOPOROSIS, OTHER DRUGS
  FOR 210
OSTEOPOROSIS, PREVENTING
  205, 212
OSTEOPOROSIS REVERSAL, THE
  ROLE OF PROGESTERONE 211
OSTEOPOROSIS RISK PROFILE
  216
OSTEOPOROSIS SOCIETY OF
  CANADA 213
OSTEOPOROSIS, YOUR HEAD
  START 212
OSTEOPOROSIS: THE LONG
  ROAD BACK 212
OsteoPrime 207
OSTOP OTTAWA 213
Our Bodies Ourselves 26, 55, 56, 226
outbursts 15, 147
Outreach 190

ovarian abscess, tubal 161
ovarian cysts, size 174
ovarian disease, polycystic 192
ovarian functions 151, 219
ovarian hormones, premature lack of
  219
ovarian transition 197
ovaries 48, 59, 62-64, 66, 146, 156,
  161, 163, 165, 173-177, 180, 182,
  188, 192, 194, 218, 219, 220, 224,
  225, 252
ovaries removed 194, 218, 219, 220
OVERCOMING BLADDER
  DISORDERS 80, 83, 85
OVERCOMING ENDOMETRIOSIS
  184, 186
overdose 159, 248
overweight 189, 192, 196, 205, 206,
  223, 239, 254, 265
overweight women 189, 192, 265
ovral 55
OVUDATE 65, 67, 68
OVUDATE-BBT 65
OVUDATE LH KIT 67, 68
ovulation detection 69
ovulation, induce 66
ovulation inhibition rate 54
ovulation, irregular 188
ovulation phase 249
ovulation, predict 64
ovulation, predicting 67
ovulation prediction 66-68
ovulation prediction kits 67, 68
ovulation, recording 64
ovulation test kits 67
ovulation, time of 22, 65-67
Ovulation prediction home test kits
  66, 67
Ovulation prediction tests 66
OVULATION METHOD
  TEACHER'S ASSOCIATION 69
ovulations, irregular 66
ovulator 67
ovulatory cycles 209
OVUQUICK SELF TEST FOR
  OVULATION PREDICTION 67
OWNER'S MANUAL 154
Oxford Program: 26
oxidants 30, 206
oxidative injury, accelerated 8
oxygen 75, 132, 141, 168, 169, 244,
  248, 254
oysters 247
OZONE TREATMENTS: 85

P:

Pacific Postpartum Support Society
  97, 142
pacing 8, 12
pain, chronic 4, 10, 13, 161, 163, 164
pain killers 175, 251, 252, 262, 264
Page, Lafern 202
Pakes, Dr. Edward 41
Palmarini, Terra 97, 100
Palmason, Diana 216
palpitations 244, 254
Panax ginseng 198
pancreas 22, 115, 262
pancreatitis, acute 262
pantothenic acid 7
pants, Tight-fitting 71
panty-hose, nylon 71

Panuthos, Claudia 43, 97, 100, 136,
  140
pap smears, abnormal 48, 56, 58,
  268
Pap smear, routine 225
PAP smears 14, 48, 56, 58, 89, 90,
  225, 250, 268
PAP tests, regular 224
papaya 122
papillomavirus, human 48
Papke, Gail 186
parasite, pear-shaped 75
parasites 8, 4, 8, 74-76, 87
parasites, intestinal 4
parent, foster 269
Parentbooks 43, 97, 120, 124, 129,
  138
parenthood 58, 268, 269, 272
PARENTING 12, 97, 269
parents, good 269
parents, loving 100
parsley 208
pastas 266
pathologist, hematological 8
pathology 8, 155, 186
Patient Information on Chronic
  Illness 86
Payer, Lynn 225
PC-2000 FERTILITY TESTER 69
PCB's 178, 179, 230
PCP 237
peach leaves 123
peanuts 157
pears 208
peas 160, 208, 240
Pellegrino, Charles 9
Pelton, Ross and Taffy 241
pelvic area 62, 119, 173
pelvic cavity 119, 174
pelvic exam 75, 83, 106, 165, 174,
  252
pelvic examination 165, 174, 181
pelvic examination, routine 174
pelvic floor 117, 118, 131-133
pelvic growths 174
pelvic infection, chronic 89, 164
pelvic infection, diagnose 166
pelvic infections 4, 51, 54, 66, 87, 89,
  90, 136, 161-168, 171, 172, 253
pelvic infections, silent 51, 90
pelvic organs 161, 166, 168, 170,
  174, 177, 183
pelvic organs, adhesion 161
pelvic pain 78, 89, 91, 175, 181, 182,
  220, 222
pelvic pain, bilateral 89
pelvic pain, chronic 78, 175, 222
pelvic tilting 118
Pelvic Inflammatory Disease 51, 52,
  75, 92, 161, 171, 172, 226
Pelvic rocking 119
PELVIC EXAM: 165
PELVIC SURGERY: 82
pelvis 47, 118, 135, 136, 173, 174,
  180-183, 220, 222, 252, 256
pelvis, normal 182
pelvis, small 136
penicillin, resistant to 169
PENICILLIN: 169
Pennypacker, Dr. 240
pentosanpolysulfate 84
People For The Ethical Treatment Of
  Animals 260

People's Medical Society 242
PEPI 196
peppermint tea 123
pepsid 84
Perez-Marrero, Dr. Ramon 84
periappendicitis 161
perihepatitis 90, 161, 167
PERIMENOPAUSE 197, 214
perinatal 98, 99, 132
perinatal psychology 98, 99
perineal tears 130
perineal trauma 131
perineum 79, 130, 132, 133
period, last 104, 189
period, neonatal 139
period, premenstrual 22, 155
period, recovery 59, 61, 62, 220, 221, 263
periods, abnormal 167, 170
periods, absent 65
periods, bleeding between 167
periods, heavy 62, 245, 246
periods, irregular 49, 64, 188
periods, lighter 62
periods, longer 62
periods, menstrual 22, 61, 62, 103, 173
periods, painful 62, 89, 150, 173, 175, 181, 223
periods, painful disabling 89
periods, predictable 52
periods, prolonged 245, 255
periods, regular 174, 209, 211
perisigmoiditis 161
peritoneal pockets 182
peritoneum 181-183
peritonitis 161, 171, 172
Perry, Susan 202
PESTICIDE CONCENTRATION IN FATTY TISSUES: 230
pesticides 81, 179, 230, 237, 238
PETA 260
Peter, Dr. Lawrence 21
Petersen, Nancy 181, 186
Peterson, Gayle 96, 100, 126, 129
PG-53 65
PH, acidic 166
pharmacies, specialized 193, 198
pharmacists 68, 156, 212, 247
PHARMASCIENCE 67
Pharr, Suzanne 267, 271, 272
Phelan, Dr. Jeffery 98
Phelps, Dr. Janice 24, 25, 27
phlebitis 29, 248, 254-256
PHILLIPS NUTRITIONALS 204, 213
phorbol esters 80
phosphates 247
phosphorus 208
photochemical oxidants 30
photosensitivity 91
PHYSICAL MEDICINE RE-
SEARCH FOUNDATION 10
PICI 85, 86
PID 51, 89-92, 161-172, 222, 226, 253
PID, accuracy in diagnosing 166
PID, Antibiotics for 168
PID caused by chlamydia 91
PID, chronic 164, 222
PID, Chronic pain after 163
PID, clinical diagnosis 165
PID, complicated 169

PID, diagnose without surgery 164
PID experts, Swedish 166
PID Management Guidelines 164
PID, recurrence of 169
PID, repeated episodes 164, 169
PID, serious complication 166
PID, Silent 164, 167
PID, symptoms for 167
PID, SYMPTOMS OF 89, 165, 167
PID Treatment Guidelines 169
PID, TREATMENT OF 164, 168, 169
PID, WHAT CAUSES 161
PID, women hospitalised with 172
Pierson, Dr. Roger 64
Pies, Cheri 269, 272
pigs 34, 234
pill, high dose 47, 48, 52
pill, lower dose 47, 265
pill users, long-term 51
PILL, ADVANTAGES 52
PILL DEVELOPMENTS, NEW 52
pineal gland 54
pituitary gland 64, 176
Pizzorno and Murray 143
placebo 82, 151, 158, 176, 239
placenta 104, 109, 110, 250
placenta, low lying 104
placenta, position 104
placenta previa 104
placenta, puncture of 109
placental tissues 173
Plamm, Dr. Bruce 137
Planetary Association for Clean
Energy 36
Planned Parenthood 58, 268
PLAYING WITH OUR HEALTH:
HAZARDS IN THE AUTOMATED
OFFICE 36
PMS 13, 146-151, 154, 185, 193
PMS, A PERSONAL WORKBOOK 154
PMS, A POSITIVE PROGRAM TO
GAIN CONTROL 154
PMS Clinic 149, 150
PMS, CONTROLLING 149, 154
PMS, diagnosis of 148
PMS, identifying 148
PMS, mood of women with 148
PMS, OTHER NATURAL
TREATMENTS 149
PMS, POSITIVE ASPECTS 147
PMS SELF-HELP BOOK, A
WOMAN'S GUIDE TO FEELING
GOOD ALL MONTH 154
PMS SUPPORT NEWSLETTER 154
PMS symptoms, uncontrollable 151
PMS, teens with 150
PMS, treatment of 146
PMS, WHAT IS 146
pneumonia among infants 90
poisoning, signs of 259
poisonings, recorded 259
Policy Advisory Group to the NBSS 232
poliomyelitis 5
poliovirus 5
POLITICS 236, 238
Pollock, Kater 272
pollutants 33, 35, 178
pollution 81, 238
polyarteritis 80

polycystic 192
polymicrobial 168
polyps 249-251
Ponstan 150
positive ions 33
POSITIVE PREGNANCY
FITNESS 96, 120
post-menopausal women 143, 190, 196, 197, 208, 210, 239, 248, 250
post-menopausal women, healthy 196, 197
post-menopausal women with
osteoporosis 210
post-menopausal years 188
post-phlebitis 254-256
postnatal 98
postpartum blues 141, 142
postpartum depression 97, 142, 175
postpartum endometritis 161
postpartum experience 97, 143
postpartum period 116
postpartum thyroiditis 141, 142
Postpartum pain 127
POSTPARTUM DEPRESSION
AND ANXIETY 97, 142
postural problems 33
posture 3, 21, 117, 119, 124, 129, 181
potassium citrate 83
potassium iodide 157
Poultry 217, 237, 246, 247
power lines 30, 33, 34
pre-diabetes 194, 266
Pre and Perinatal Psychology
Association 99
precancerous 48, 49, 250
pregnancies, diagnose ectopic 166
pregnancies, high risk 94, 103
pregnancies, multiple 205, 265
pregnancies, post-date 102
pregnancies, repeated 74, 248
pregnancies, tubal 52, 87, 89, 103
pregnancy, Complicated 13
pregnancy dates 109, 114
pregnancy, discomforts of 117, 121
pregnancy, early 103
pregnancy, ectopic 89, 164, 166, 167, 170, 171
pregnancy, fear of 219
pregnancy, holistic approach 95, 124
pregnancy impossible 177
pregnancy loss 94, 139, 140
pregnancy loss, aftermath 140
pregnancy, low risk 115
pregnancy, mimicked 175
pregnancy, movement during 96, 120
pregnancy, normal 110, 113, 142, 245
pregnancy, nutrition in 95
pregnancy, prevent 54
pregnancy, preventing 54, 57
pregnancy, pseudo 175
pregnancy test, serum 166
pregnancy, tubal 50, 59, 61, 89, 102, 161, 163, 164
pregnancy, uncomplicated 106, 107
pregnancy, unwanted 60
Pregnancy, Terminating 56
PREGNANCY AND CHILDBIRTH
COMPLICATIONS: 250
PREGNANCY AND CHILDBIRTH
PREPARATION 94
PREGNANCY, CHILDBIRTH AND
THE NEWBORN 94

PREGNANCY, LACTATION AND
THE PILL 50
PREGNANCY:, ECTOPIC 164
pregnant woman, well-nourished 245, 246
PREGNANT FEELINGS 97, 99, 100
premarin 190, 192, 195, 196
premature delivery, rates 102
prematurity, risks of 136
premenopausal 219, 248
Premenopausal women 219, 248
premenstrual strength 151
premenstrual symptoms 61, 146, 147, 190, 192
premenstrual syndrome 20, 73, 146, 147, 224
premenstrual tension, severe 74
Premenstrually 4, 155, 174
prenatal and postnatal life 98
prenatal books 126
prenatal care, good 112
prenatal class 118, 119
prenatal classes 126, 127
prenatal diagnosis 103, 110, 111
prenatal exercise 120, 222
prenatal forms 137
prenatal genetic diagnosis 113
prenatal informed consent 104
prenatal nutrition 95
prenatal testing 112, 113
prenatal visit 89, 101, 104, 246
prenatal work-up 91, 114
Prenatal preparation 133
preschool 2, 244
prescription, Abuse of 13
Prescription drugs 3, 13, 72, 123
preservatives, food 247
Preston, Dr. Myra 8
Preventative Services Task Force 228
PREVENTING AND REVERSING
OSTEOPOROSIS 212
PREVENTION BEFORE BIRTH 133
Preventive Services Task Force 236
Prior, Dr. Jerilynn 64, 191, 209, 214
privacy, loss of 116
Pro-Osteo 207
PRO-GEST cream 150, 159, 198, 204, 212, 213
PROFESSIONAL HEALTH
PRODUCTS 213
PROFILES OF WOMEN UNDER
STRESS 15
progesterone content, high 175
progesterone cream, natural 156, 193, 195, 203, 211
progesterone, deficiency of 191
progesterone-estrogen combinations 81
progesterone gel, natural 155
progesterone levels, reliable tests 213
progesterone levels, salivary 212
progesterone levels, serum 211
progesterone, natural 150, 151, 155, 160, 185, 195, 198, 204, 212
progesterone, oral micronized 193
progesterone receptors 52
progesterone skin cream 150
progesterone suppositories, Natural 151
progesterone therapy 62, 151
progesterones, new 52, 53

progesterones, old *52, 53*
progesterones, synthetic *151, 191, 192, 211, 222*
progestin, synthetic *193*
progestin type pills, old *53*
Progestin-Estrogen *196*
Progestin-Estrogen Prevention Intervention *196*
progestins *52-54, 192, 197, 201*
progestins, new *52-54*
progestins, new class of *52*
prolactin regulation, abnormality *155*
prolactin, surge of *147*
prometrium *193, 198*
Prorok, Dr. Philip *234*
prostaglandin, production of *175*
prostaglandins *150, 174, 175*
protein, low *206, 207, 266*
protein molecule *247*
protozoal *259*
Provera *176, 177, 191-193, 196, 209, 211, 223*
pseudo-menopause *151, 175, 176*
PSYCH YOURSELF IN *21*
psychiatric help *79*
psychiatrist *5, 7, 8, 41, 74, 78, 99*
Psychiatry *23, 147, 149*
psychological problems *41, 62, 148, 189*
Psychology *97-100, 219*
PSYCHONEUROIMMUNOLGY *81*
psychosomatic illness *74*
Psychotherapy *272*
psyllium seed powder *76, 121*
pubic *61, 190, 251*
pubic bone *61*
Public Citizen Health Research Group Health Letter *195*
pulmonary embolus *47*
pulse *143, 252*
pus *82, 89, 167-169, 172, 258, 262*
pushing, second stage *133*
pushing urges, powerful *127*
PVC plastics *179, 237*

Q:

Q-10, Co-enzyme *6, 7, 10*
Queen's University *150, 155, 237*
Quiet, Baby Under Construction *98*
quinine *158*

R:

R.W. Johnson Pharmaceutical Research Institute *53*
rabbits *258, 259*
radiation, accumulated *233*
radiation, electromagnetic *30, 32, 33, 35, 37*
radiation exposure *178, 233, 238*
radiation, invisible *28, 30*
radiation levels *31, 233*
radiation meters *36*
radiation risks *179*
radiation therapy *188*
radiation, unnecessary *179*
Radiation Protection Branch *35*
Radiation Research *178*
RADIATION AND BREAST CANCER: *238*
RADIATION, SHIELDING FOR *32*

RADIATION: *233*
Radioactive debris *238*
radioactivity *238, 240*
radiologist, experienced *228*
radiologist, reference *232*
radiologists *228, 232-234*
Radiology *103, 228*
rages, uncontrollable *15*
rape *13, 23, 270*
rashes *33, 51, 258*
raspberry leaf *123, 247*
Ratner, Dr. Vicki *78, 86*
Rattner-Heilman, Joan *138*
reactions, bad *91*
reactions, inflammatory *84*
REBOUNDING FROM CHILD-BIRTH: Toward Emotional Recovery *138*
RECOVERY INC, Self-help for Nervous Symptoms and Fears *27*
rectal *65, 151, 193, 211*
rectum *71, 78, 79, 130, 131, 134, 221, 222*
red meat, consumption *247, 248*
redness *5, 72, 167*
Redwine, Dr. David *173, 180-184, 186, 222*
refrigerants *179, 237*
Reid, Dr. Gregor *82*
Reid, Dr. Robert *150*
Reiter, Dr. R.C. *222*
relaxation, touch *120*
RELAXATION *5, 9, 17, 19, 20, 42, 94, 96, 99, 100, 117-120, 127, 129, 133, 150, 185, 200*
RELAXERCISE *21, 37*
Remington, Dr. D.W. *74*
remission *85, 184*
repetitive strain injury (RPI) *36*
Replens *189*
REPORT ON ORAL CONTRACEP-TIVES *46, 55, 56*
reproduction *46, 130, 178, 221*
reproduction, difficulty in *178*
reproduction, process of *130*
reproductive age *146*
reproductive capability *191*
reproductive choice *108*
reproductive cycle, female *46*
reproductive health *32, 87, 177*
reproductive organs *31, 161-169, 171*
reproductive potential *60*
reproductive system *22, 196, 198, 239*
reproductive years *118, 146, 155, 248*
Reproductive Biology Research Unit *64*
respiratory complications, long-term *90*
respiratory failure *262*
respiratory illnesses *73*
respiratory problems *108, 110, 136*
rescue remedy *129*
Resse, Mark *21, 37*
restlessness, marked *262*
Restoration Plus *82*
retardation, mental *108, 112*
REVIEW OF MAINSTREAM CFIDS LITERATURE *9*
Revlon *260*
RH negative *109*
rheumatoid arthritis *4, 52, 80*
rhinitis, allergic *80*
rice, brown *123, 200, 266*

rice cakes *123*
Richards, Lynn Baptisti *138*
Riggs, Dr. *209*
ringing in the ears *244*
RNA *7*
Roberts, Dr. Maureen *235*
Robinson, Rita *43*
Rock, Dr. John *176*
Rogers, Dr. Sherry A. *9*
Romeo, Catherine *43, 140*
Rona, Dr. Zoltan *69*
Rothman, Barbara *111*
Rotterdam University *54*
Royal College of General Practice *49*
Royal College of Obstetricians and Gynecologists *102*
RPI *36*
rye *123, 266*

S:

Safe Computing Company *35, 36*
Saint Michael's Hospital *205*
saliva testing *69*
Salonen, Dr. Juuka *248*
salpingography *89*
salt *35, 72, 147, 148, 157, 247-249, 253, 261, 265*
salt, table *157*
Sampson, Dr. John *180*
Samuels, Nancy *95*
San Francisco Blue Cross *29*
Sand, Gayle *203*
Sang, Barbara *272*
sanitary napkins *72, 82, 179, 185, 252*
Santa Cruz Women's Health Center *272*
sardines *247*
Satt, Dr. *98*
saunas *7*
Saunders, Dr. Sarah *24, 27*
Saunders, Ziesel *272*
scalp *190*
scans *6, 101, 103, 106, 176, 209, 211, 212, 217*
scans, early dating *103*
scar, horizontal *136*
scar tissue *62, 155, 158, 163, 173, 177, 183, 220, 253*
scar tissue in the abdomen *220*
scar tissue inside the uterine cavity *253*
scar, uterine *136, 250*
scarring *66, 87, 90, 161, 163-165, 173, 250*
scarring, extensive *163*
scarring in the uterine cavity *250*
scarring of the tubes *66*
scarring, tubal *90*
scars *61, 136, 156, 173, 250*
Scelerotherapy *257*
Schaeff, Anne Wilson *27*
Scher, Jonathan *140*
Schiff, Harriet *42, 43*
Schimdt, Tracy *120*
schizophrenia *74, 77*
Schneider, Meir *37*
Schwartz, Leni *99*
Scientific American *25*
sclerosing agent, injections *257*
sclerotherapy treatment *257*

SCLEROTHERAPY *256, 257*
Scott, Sir Walter *262*
screened group *231, 232*
screening for active breast cancer *229*
screening mammogram, negative results *231*
screening, normal *103*
screening, risk by *235*
screening, routine *102, 142*
screening tests *25, 71, 88, 89, 112, 113, 235, 246, 250*
screening, triple *109, 114*
Screening Section of the National Cancer Institute *234*
SCREENING FOR BREAST CANCER *227, 228*
screenings, intervals between *231, 234*
seafood *157, 217, 247*
Seattle King Department of Public Health *89*
Seattle's Harbour View Medical Center *90*
seaweeds *157, 159, 237, 246*
SECOND SPRING *202*
sedatives *2, 264*
sedimentation rate, erythrocyte *165*
Seiden, Dr. Howard *228*
seizures *147*
seldane *223*
selenium *237, 258*
self-esteem *23, 139, 190, 191, 271*
SELF HEALING BODY MOVE-MENT *36*
SELF-HELP FOR PMS *154*
SELF-HELP FOR VARICOSE VEINS *255*
SELF-HYPNOSIS:, EASY *18*
Sellors, Dr. John *165, 167*
Selye, Dr. Hans *11, 16*
Semchyshyn, Dr. Stefan *140*
seminal fluid *162*
Semm, Dr. Kurt *224*
Senate Subcommittee on Aging *195*
Serotonin *80, 149*
servers' disease syndrome *240*
sesame seeds *206, 246*
sex, after *68, 82, 170, 174*
sex, bleeding during or after *170*
sex drive, changes *147*
sex drive, decreased *176*
sex drive, improve *198*
sex drive, increased *147, 159*
sex drive, lowered *55*
sex, healthy *12*
sex life, change *219*
sex life, enhanced *61*
sex lives, minimal *269*
sex, oral *82*
sex, oral-anal *270*
sex, Oral-genital *71*
sex, pain during *131, 174, 181*
sex, painful *72, 89, 132, 175, 181, 189, 220, 221*
sex, refrain from *91*
sex, Regular *189, 199*
sex, resume *132*
sex, safe *270*
sex, satisfying *12*
sex, Slower *189*
sex, timing of *66*
sex, too little *82*

sex, Too much 82
sex, unprotected 55
sex, vaginal 162
SEX, MEN AND 71
SEXISM 267, 271, 272
sexual abuse 13, 23, 24, 150, 222
sexual activity 86, 199, 270
sexual assault 55, 92
sexual discrimination 3
sexual identity 267, 271
sexual interactions between two
 women 269
sexual lifestyle 58
sexual motivation 219
sexual orientation 13
sexual partner 66, 88, 89, 91, 132,
 169
sexual pleasure 119, 224
sexual practices 48, 82
sexual preferences 13, 267
sexual problems 23, 29, 220
sexual relations, resume 169
sexual responsiveness 219
sexual satisfaction 131
sexual toys, sharing 270
Sexual difficulties 14, 73
Sexual harassment 3, 11, 14
sexuality, lesbian 269
sexually abused 23
sexually active women 75, 88, 89
sexually transmitted diseases 50, 54,
 55, 57, 87, 88, 90, 92, 171, 270
Shaffer, Dr. Eldon 262
shakiness 147
Shaklee 260
Shallenberger, Dr. Frank 85
shamans 46
Shattered Dreams 140
Sheehy, Gail 193, 197, 200, 203
shelter, battered women's 270
Sherman, Dr. 250
Sherwin, Dr. Barbara 219
shock therapy 24
shoes, high heeled 124
shoes, running 118
shoulder blades 262
shoulder pain 36
shoulder tip 253, 262
shrimp 247
Shute, Wilfred 255
Siberian ginseng 198
sick building syndrome 33
sickle cell anemia 108, 245
silicone breast 160, 240
silver nitrate 85
Simkin, Dr. Ruth 267
Simkin, Penny 94, 134
Simpson, Elizabeth 27
sinusitis, chronic 8
sit-ups, straight leg 118
skin cream, anti-yeast 71
skin deterioration 62
skin discoloration 257
skin, dry 74, 141, 143
skin eruptions 147
skin, oily 175
skin patch, estrogen-progestin 192
skin problems 41, 51, 73
skin rashes 51
skip periods 188
Skrabenek, Dr. Peter 231, 234
Skull Cap 129
Skuy, Mr. Percy 55

sleep deprivation 15, 116
sleep disorder 149
sleep disturbances 5
sleep, improved 117
sleep lack 13, 116
sleep lack, Chronic 13
sleep, lack of 4, 71, 141, 142
sleep problems 15, 38
sleep, uninterrupted 116
sleep, unrefreshing 5
sleepiness 193
sleeping, difficulty 15
sleeping habits 14
sleeping pills 3
Slesin, Dr. Louis 30, 32, 34-36
slippery elm 122, 123
Smith, Adrienne J. 272
Smith, Dr. Lendon 115
Smith, Larrie Halliday 150
SMITH'S PHARMACY 10, 77, 204,
 213
smoking 2, 15, 47, 54, 56, 157, 194,
 198, 217
snack, carbohydrate 149
snacks 121, 148, 149, 266
Social Health Outreach Program
 190
Society of Obstetricians and
 Gynecologists of Canada 102, 114
sodium bicarbonate 84
sodium fluoride 211
sodium iodide 156
sodium pentosanpolysulfate 84
Soffer, Virginia 236
soft drinks, phosphates in 247
SOGC 53, 103, 104, 114, 224
soil, iodine deficient 157
solvents 80, 179, 237
SOMATICS 17, 21
sonography 101
soreness 189, 214, 253, 262
sound waves 101, 166
sour cream 149
soy sauce 149
soybeans 157, 198, 204
Spear, Ruth 227
SPECIAL DELIVERY, THE
 COMPLETE GUIDE TO
 INFORMED BIRTHING 134
speculum 106, 252
speech and hearing disorders 105
speech, delayed 106
speech, Slow 141
speech, slurred 5
sperm 57, 59, 64, 66-68, 90, 162,
 163, 166, 269
sperm, conserve 67
sperm count, reduced 66
sperm, frozen 269
sperm, motility of 66
spermicidal jelly 54, 57
spermicides 54, 57, 82, 89, 170, 171
Speroff, Dr. Leon 53
sphincter 79
spider veins, Treating 257
spiderworts 35
spinach 208, 246, 247
spinal chord 103, 108, 113, 114
spinal column 108, 205
spinal tube defects 113
spine 62, 103, 119, 205, 207, 210,
 216
spironolactone 151

Spirulina 123, 247
spleen 244
spots 6, 19, 173, 180, 244
spots, black 173, 180, 244
spots, blueberry 173, 180
spotting between periods 174
spotting during exercise 119
spotting, scant 188
Spotting 110, 111, 119, 150, 174, 188,
 192, 214, 253
sprouts 157, 246
SSKI 159
St. Boniface Hospital 87
St. Charles Medical Center 180, 186
St. John's Wort 129
St. Michael's Hospital 47
St. Paul's Hospital 158
stamina 7, 115, 185
stamina, physical 115
Stampfer 194
standing, prolonged 254, 255
Stark, Dr. Charles 105
stature, taller 197
Status of Women 16, 228, 240, 241,
 268, 271
STAYING HEALTHY WITH
 NUTRITION 208
STD checkups 170
STD's 170, 270
Steinberg, Dr. Wilfred 47, 50, 52
Steinburg, Dr. Susan 149
sterility 50, 87, 90, 91, 222, 224
sterility, immediate 224
sterility in men 90
sterility in women 87
sterility, permanent 222
sterility, risk of 91
sterilization 56, 59, 61-63, 224
sterilization, female 59
sterilization, laparoscopic 61, 62
STEROID 6, 49, 55, 71
steroids 8, 74, 84, 192
stethoscope 101, 104, 106
Stevenson, Dr. John 209
Stewart, Maryon 43, 154
stiffness, morning 6
stillbirth 40, 90, 111
stillbirth, higher rate 111
STIMULATING AND COMMUNI-
 CATING WITH YOUR UNBORN
 BABY 99
stirrups 130, 252
stitches 61, 103, 131, 132
Stochly, Dr. Maria 31
stockings, support 256
Stoff, Dr. Jesse 9
Stokes, Naomi Miller 226
stomach 22, 90, 91, 121-123, 168,
 193, 199, 208, 211, 245, 247, 248,
 252, 259, 261
stomach acid 211
stomach acidity 122
stomach, sensitive 123
stomach tube 259
stomach ulcers 22
stomach, upper 121
stomach upset 91, 248
Stone, Sharon Dale 272
STONES, DISSOLVING THE 264
stool samples, fresh 8
stools 8, 121, 245, 248, 261
stools a pitch black colour 248
stools, tarry 245

Stoppard, Dr. Miriam 241
strain injuries, repetitive 29, 36
strain on the back 124
strains 28, 29, 36, 82, 116, 119, 121,
 124, 136, 163, 169, 259
Strausz, Dr. Ivan 225
STRENGTH TRAINING: 206
stress, chronic 17
stress, economic 12
stress, emotional 81, 85, 189
stress, financial 40
stress levels 28, 29, 146
stress, major 5, 14, 117
stress management 8, 9, 154
stress reduction 4, 148, 150
stress-related diseases 16
stress relief 15
STRESS, MONEY 12
STRESS, REDUCING 21, 119, 150
STRESSES, LIFE 12
STRESSES, RELATIONSHIP AND
 FAMILY 11
STRESSES, WORK 12
stretch marks 124
stretching 118, 119, 124, 133
stroke 47, 55, 201
STROKES 46, 47
strontium 90, 247
suction 57, 58, 250
suction machine 250
sugar 2, 4, 6, 8, 14, 24-27, 41, 50, 51,
 53, 70-76, 84, 115, 121, 123, 147,
 148, 184, 198, 199, 206, 237, 247,
 249, 251-253, 256
sugar addiction 6
sugar cravings 84
sugar free cereals 247
sugar metabolism 24
sugar solution 249
sugar substitutes 4, 115, 198
sugars, avoidance of 184
suicidal thoughts 147
suicidally depressed 73
suicide 13, 22, 43, 78, 147
Sulfa drugs 83
sulfamethoxazole 91
SULFOXIDE 84
Sullivan, Dr. Jerome 248
sulphate 6, 206, 247, 248
Summers, Dr. Anne 114
Sunflower seeds 206, 246
sunlight sensitivity 51
Sunnybrook Hospital 232
sunshine 118, 207
SUPER NUTRITION FOR
 MENOPAUSE 202
supergreen food supplement 200
supplementation 24, 48, 66, 69, 124,
 156, 157, 207
SUPPLEMENTS PLUS 10, 77, 204,
 213
support network 20, 60
Support and Advocacy Division 233
suppositories, vaginal 73, 82, 151,
 193, 195, 198, 212
suppository, rectal 193
surgeries, multiple 183
surgery, aftermath 136
surgery, corrective 66
surgery, elective 220
surgery, immediate 61, 174, 262
surgery, laparoscopic 177

surgery, unnecessary 137, 218, 233, 236
SURVIVING PREGNANCY LOSS 140
SURVIVORS OF SUICIDE 43
SUSAN LOVE'S BREAST BOOK 241
sushi 246
swallowing, painful 245
sweat, drenched in 189
sweating, excessive 142
Swedish study 30, 49, 230
Swedish Two County study 231, 234
Sweet, Richard 169
swelling 5, 51, 72, 89, 141, 147, 156, 165, 244, 255, 256, 258
swelling, painless 141
swimming 7, 117, 118, 244, 257
sympathy, need for 139
SYNAREL: 176, 182
synthroid 142
syphilis 270

T:

T-cell function 6
T-cells 180
T-helper lymphocytes 7
tahini 206
Tai-Chi 200
TAKING CONTROL OF YOUR FUTURE 36
TAKING HORMONES, CHOICES, RISKS, BENEFITS 203
tamoxifen 158, 239
tampons 71, 72, 82, 179, 185, 214, 238
tampons, Perfumed 71
tampons, unbleached 82, 185
Tannelbit 76
tannic acid 247
tannins 76, 217
Tay Sachs disease 108
taylor position 119
Taylor, Dr. Patrick 249, 251
Taylor, Paul 36, 233
TBM's, abnormal 8
TC-CVS 110
tea 2, 4, 25, 121, 123, 217, 247
tear, second degree 131
tear, small 132, 134
tears, avoid 132
teas, herbal 121
teenage women 50, 154, 171
teenager's immune system 171
Teenagers 50, 91, 150, 171, 175
TEENAGERS AND THE PILL 50
teeth 121, 247
telephone operators 29
temperature charting 67
tenderness 51, 146, 147, 149, 155, 165, 181, 193, 209, 214
tenderness of the breasts 51
tenderness of the ligaments 181
tendonitis 29
TENS UNIT: 84, 129, 185
TENT 185
terconazole 73
TERMINAL SHOCK 29, 36
Tesslar Watch 35
testes 90, 224
testicles 59, 155, 236

testicular cancer 197, 236
testicular size 55
testosterone 6, 219, 220
testosterone, injections of 220
testosterone, level of 219
tetracycline 70, 73, 80, 83, 90, 91, 169
tetracycline, side effects 91
TETRACYCLINE: 169
TEXTBOOK OF NATURAL MEDICINE 143
Thalassemia minor 245
thalidomide 123
The AC Field Cancellation System 35
The CAGE Test: 27
The Change 191
The Complete Guide to Emotional Well Being for Women 147, 154
The Missing Diagnosis 74, 184
THE ADVANTAGES OF ROUTINE MAMMOGRAPHY 233
THE AGELESS BODY 200, 202
THE BENEFITS OF NATURAL PROGESTERONES 193
THE BEREAVED PARENT 43
THE BIRTH Center 95
THE BIRTH PARTNER: Everything You Need To Know 94
THE BODY ECOLOGY DIET: Recovering Your Health And Rebuilding 74
THE BREAST BOOK: The Essential Guide to Breast Care and Breast Health 241
THE CALCIUM BIBLE, HOW TO HAVE BETTER BONES IN YOUR LIFE 212
THE CANARY AND CHRONIC FATIGUE 9
THE CARING CONSUMER'S CRUELTY FREE SHOPPING GUIDE 260
THE CASTRATED WOMAN 226
THE CLEAR PLAN 68
THE CLINICAL AND SCIENTIFIC BASIS OF ME/CFS 10
THE COMPLETE BOOK OF BREAST-FEEDING 96
THE COMPLETE BOOK OF PREGNANCY AND CHILDBIRTH 94, 106
THE COMPLETE CERVICAL CAP GUIDE 58
THE DANCE OF ANGER 21
THE DOORMAT SYNDROME 27
THE DRAIZE EYE IRRITANCY TEST 258, 259
THE ENDOMETRIOSIS ANSWER BOOK; NEW HOPE NEW HELP 186
THE ENDOMETRIOSIS SOURCEBOOK 186
THE ESSENTIAL GUIDE TO GIVING BIRTH OUTSIDE THE HOSPITAL 95
THE EXPERIENCE OF CHILD-BIRTH 94, 95, 129, 134
THE FEMALE STRESS SYN-DROME 16, 21
THE GRIEF RECOVERY HANDBOOK 39, 40, 42

THE HANDBOOK OF SELF-HEALING 37
THE HANDBOOK ON VDT HAZARDS 36
THE HIDDEN ADDICTION AND HOW TO GET FREE 24, 27
THE IDEAL PREGNANCY EXERCISE PROGRAM 117
THE INFORMED WOMEN'S GUIDE TO PREVENTING OSTEOPOROSIS 212
THE JOURNEY WITHIN 27
THE JOY OF STRESS 16
THE LAUGHTER PRESCRIPTION 21
THE LAVENDER COUCH 272
THE LEADER'S MANUAL FOR THE SHOP 203
THE MENOPAUSE INDUSTRY, HOW THE MEDICAL ESTAB-LISHMENT EXPLOITS 202
THE MENOPAUSE SELF-HELP BOOK 202
THE MESSENGER 10
THE NEW MOOD THERAPY 8
THE NEW OUR BODIES OURSELVES 55, 56
THE NEW PROGESTERONES-HOPE AND HYPE 52
THE NO HYSTERECTOMY OPTION 177, 222
THE NURSING MOTHER'S COMPANION 96
THE NURSING MOTHER'S GUIDE TO WEANING 96
THE NUTRITION CHALLENGE FOR WOMEN 95
THE ORGONE ACCUMULATOR HANDBOOK 35
THE OVERALL STATE OF YOUR HEALTH 71
THE PILL AND WOMEN OVER 35 50
THE PMS SOLUTION, PMS: THE NUTRITIONAL APPROACH 154
THE POLITICS OF BREAST CANCER RESEARCH 236
THE POLITICS OF CANCER 238
THE PREMENSTRUAL SOLU-TION: TAMING THE SHREW IN YOU 154
THE PREVENTION AND TREATMENT OF BRITTLE BONES 212
THE RIGHTS OF THE PREG-NANT PARENT 94
THE SECRET LIFE OF THE UNBORN CHILD 99
THE SEVEN HABITS OF HIGHLY EFFECTIVE PEOPLE 21
THE SILENT KNIFE 137
THE SILENT PASSAGE 193, 203
THE SPIRAL OF GRIEF 42
THE TEN COMMANDMENTS FOR REDUCING STRESS 21
THE TENTATIVE PREGNANCY, PRENATAL DIAGNOSIS 111
THE THORNY QUESTION OF CANCER 48
THE VAGINAL BIRTH AFTER THE CESAREAN EXPERIENCE 138

THE VDT OPERATOR'S PROBLEM SOLVER 36
THE WELL PREGNANCY BOOK 95
THE WISE WOMAN 184, 198, 200, 202, 241
THE WOMANLY ART OF BREAST-FEEDING 96
THE YEAR AFTER CHILDBIRTH 97
THE YEAST CONNECTION 7, 9, 74, 75
THE YEAST CONNECTION AND THE WOMAN 74
THE YEAST SYNDROME 74
THERE IS NO NEED FOR AN EPISIOTOMY IN A NORMAL BIRTH 133
theta waves 8
thighs 118, 119, 212
Thorne Research Canada 207
Thornton, Joe 238
thought patterns, repetitive 8
throat 5, 6, 106, 122, 252, 270
thumb 246, 249, 252
thyroid disease 41, 52, 142
thyroid function 50, 74, 83, 141, 149, 223, 237
thyroid function blood tests 50
thyroid function, low 74, 149
thyroid function test 83
thyroid gland 141-143, 149, 211, 223
thyroid hormone blood levels 237
thyroid hormone in a synthetic form 142
thyroid, low 74, 149
thyroid, underactive 4, 142, 149
THYROID AND ADRENAL EFFECTS 50
THYROID FUNCTION AND IODINE: 237
THYROID FUNCTION:, LOW 149
thyroiditis, transient 141
THYROIDITIS 141, 142, 178
TIRED OR TOXIC 9
Tobacco use 217
tofu 206
Toi, Dr. Ants 103
toilet paper 71, 179
Toilet habits 71
tomatoes 149
tongue 156, 245
Tonics, Female 198, 223
Topographic Brain Mapping 8
Toronto Board of Health 233
Toronto General Hospital 82
Toronto Hospital 264
Toronto Star 52, 82, 228
TORONTO HUMANE SOCIETY 260
TORONTO WOMEN'S BOOK-STORE 226
tortillas, lime processed 206
TOWARDS PREVENTING AND OVERCOMING OSTEOPOROSIS 212
towels 75, 255, 270
toxic response 31
toxic shock syndrome 238
toxins 3, 79, 212, 163, 208
TRA INSTRUMENTS 35
trabecular bone 205
trace element, essential 157

Trager, Dr. Milton 21
TRAGER MENTASTICS 21
transcervical chorionic villi sampling
110
Transcutaneous electrical nerve
stimulation 84
TRANSFORMATION THROUGH
BIRTH 97, 100, 140
transfusion 109, 220
TRANSILLUMINATION 229
TRANSITIONS FOR HEALTH
INC 150, 159, 204, 213
traumas, major psychological 8
Treating The Female Patient 47
tremor, fine 142
trials, clinical 53, 131, 158, 159
triazoles 73
TRICHOMONAS 72, 75, 83, 270
TRICYLCEN 52
triglycerides 47, 193-196, 266
Trowbridge, Dr. J.P. 74
Trupin, Dr. Suzanne 154
Truss, Dr. Orian 74, 76, 184
TRUST YOUR BODY BEFORE
THE EXPERTS 35
TRUSTING OURSELVES: 147, 154
TRYPTOPHAN 7, 8, 25, 41, 80, 84,
149, 154, 199
tubal ligation 56, 59-63, 188, 224
tubal ligation, Laparoscopic 56
tubal reconstructions 59
TUBAL LIGATION AND
PREMATURE MENOPAUSE 62
Tuberculosis 163
Tufts University 206
Tulane University 81
tumour, fibroid 223
tumours 48, 159, 173, 223, 234, 236,
249
tumours, benign 173, 249
TUMS 83
turnip 246, 247
twins 94, 102, 103, 113
tylenol 175
typhoid 235
tyramine 80
tyrosine 80, 84

U:

U.S. Bureau of Labour Statistics 29
U.S. Centers for Disease Control
164, 168, 171
U.S. Department of Health and
Human Services 135
U.S. National Institute of Occupational Safety and Health 29
U.S. Office of Technology Assessment
259
U.S. Preventative Services Task Force
228
UBC Division of Infectious Diseases
87
UCLA 23
UDCA therapy 264-265
ulcer, history of 208
ulcer, peptic 52
ulcers 15, 20, 22, 29, 51, 52, 83-85,
208, 245, 255
ulcers, bleeding 245
ulcers in the mouth 51
ultrasound, alternatives to 104
ultrasound, detailed 110, 113

ultrasound, diagnostic 102, 105
ultrasound, doppler 106
ultrasound, early 110, 111
ultrasound exams 101, 102
ultrasound exposure 101, 105
ultrasound exposure to the fetus
101, 105
ultrasound, fetal 105
ultrasound, first trimester 103
ultrasound, gallbladder 263
ultrasound, infants exposed to 106
ultrasound measurement 104
ultrasound, obstetrical 101
ultrasound of the heel 209
ultrasound, pelvic 225
ultrasound pictures 174
ultrasound, report on 101
ultrasound, routine 101, 102, 106
ultrasound, safety of 104
ultrasound, selective 101, 102
ultrasound, transvaginal 166
ultrasound, vaginal 64, 68, 103, 106
ultrasound waves, pulsed 101
ultrasound, widespread use 101
ULTRASOUND, RISKS OF 105
ULTRASOUND, SELECTIVE USE
101, 102
ULTRASOUND, WHAT IS 101
ultrasounds of the gallbladder 264
ultrasounds, repeat 104
Ultrathin 54
ULTRAVIOLET, INFRARED AND
VISIBLE LIGHT 33
unborn child 98-100, 107
Underarm 142, 190
Understanding Menopause 63, 190,
202, 205
UNDERSTANDING CYSTITIS, A
Complete Guide to Overcoming
Thrush 86
UNDERSTANDING
ENDOMETRIOSIS 186
UNDERSTANDING MOURNING
42
underwear, cotton 71, 170
underwear, synthetic 71
University of Bologna 29
University of British Columbia 113,
130, 190, 191, 209, 227, 249
University of Brussels 53
University of Calgary 106, 262, 267
University of California 6, 75, 147,
155, 156, 191, 197, 198, 211, 236
University of Colorado 105
University of Florida 239
University of Illinois 238
University of Manitoba 105
University of Missouri 102, 103
University of Montreal Menopause
Clinic 193
University of Pennsylvania 80
University of Saskatchewan 64
University of Southern California 98
University of Toronto 31, 103, 149,
213, 228
UNIVERSITY OF TORONTO
BONE AND MINERAL GROUP
213
Upmalis, Dr. David 53
Urban Institute of Washington 78
urethra 72, 78-80, 82, 85
urethra, irritation 72
urethral dilations 78, 79, 85

urinalysis 89
urinary frequency 78, 79, 85
urinary infections, chronic 8
urinary kit to detect ovulation 67
urinary temperature 65, 67
urinary testing, new approach 88
urinary tract 49, 51, 74, 78, 79, 81,
82, 220
urinary tract complications 220
urinary tract infections 51
urination, burning on 91
urination, frequency of 85
urination, frequent 80
urination, pain on 89
urination, painful 72, 75, 90, 170,
174
urination, timing of 79
Urination that is painful 167
urine, blood in 174, 264
urine cultures 78, 83, 87
urine dipsticks 82
urine, inability to hold 221
urine, leaking of 222
urine screening test 71
urine, stream of 79, 119
urodynamic studies 83
urologists 78, 79, 83
Urology 80, 82
ursodeoxycholic acid 264
USC 98
USDA 206
USING HERBS, HOMEOPATHY
AND NUTRITION WISELY
DURING PREGNANCY 95
uterine bleeding, abnormal 62
uterine bleeding, excessive 250
uterine bleeding, irregular 249
uterine cancer, prevention 220
uterine cavity 64, 223, 250-253
uterine contractions 219
uterine lining 188-190, 192, 249-252
uterine perforation 253
uterine wall 104, 221, 249, 250
Uterine prolapse 222
UTERINE CANCER AND
ENDOMETRIAL HYPERPLASIA:
250
UTERINE FIBROIDS AND
POLYPS: 249
UTERINE SCARS AND UTERINE
SURGERY: 250
uterus, dropped 117
uterus, enlarged 117
uterus, inflammation in the lining
166
uterus, pregnant 254
uterus, prolapsed 222
uterus, protect the 193, 198
uterus, reconstruction 222, 223
uterus surgically removed 218
UTERUS AND OVARIES 48, 225
Utian, Dr. Wulf 203

V:

vacurette 250
vagina, dry 198
vagina, early atrophic 62
vagina, help dry 198
vagina, irritation 75
vaginal bleeding, irregular 89
vaginal cell walls 70

vaginal discharge 71, 75, 89, 91,
239, 253
vaginal dryness 176, 189, 191, 198,
199, 219
vaginal environment 70, 170
vaginal fluid 166
vaginal infection, common 162, 170
vaginal infections with no
symptoms 170
vaginal lubrication 189, 220
vaginal opening 127, 130
vaginal PH 166, 170
vaginal secretions 70, 72
vaginal soreness 189
vaginal tablets 72, 73
vaginal tissues, strengthens 198
vaginal walls 70, 72
Vaginal birth after Cesarean 136,
137
Vaginal cuts 71
VAGINAL BLEEDING, MILD 224
VAGINAL BLEEDING:, ABNOR-
MAL 249
VAGINAL TESTS: 166
vaginalis, hemophilus 75
vaginitis, non-specific 162
vaginosis, bacterial 75, 162, 166,
168, 170
Vancouver Women's Health
Collective 68, 226
Vanity Fair 203
varicose veins 29, 47, 117, 254-257
varicose veins, large 256
varicose veins, primary 254
varicose veins, Secondary 254
VARICOSE VEINS, PREVENTION
257
VARICOSE VEINS SELF-HELP
257
VARICOSE VEINS, SYMPTOMS
255
vas deferens 59
vasectomy 56, 59-61, 162
VASECTOMY OR TUBAL
LIGATION 59
VBAC 136-138
VBAC CANADA 138
VBAC STORIES AND NATURAL
CHILDBIRTH INFORMATION
138
VDT monitoring 29
VDT NEWS 29, 32, 33, 35, 36
VDT operators 29, 32
VDT screen 28, 30, 33
VDT SCREEN DESIGN 28
VDT workers 29, 31, 32, 36, 37
VDT's 28-37
vegetable dye 158
vegetable oils 189
vegetables 4, 6, 17, 25, 72, 114, 115,
121, 123, 148, 157, 179, 189, 200,
206-208, 237, 246, 247, 255, 257,
266
vegetables, leafy green 208
vegetables, steamed 123
Vegetarian 206, 207, 266
vegetarians, female 207
vein, long saphenous 256
vein, problem 254, 257
vein, superficial 256
veins, blockages in the superficial
254
veins, deep 254

veins, inflammation of the deep 254
veins, leg 254, 255
veins, painful 254
veins, pelvic 254
veins, smaller sized 256
veins, spider 254, 257
veins, surface 254
veins, twisted 255
venereal 88, 270
venereal disease in lesbians 270
ventilation 3, 35
Verny, Dr. Thomas 99
Veterinary Science Division 178
video camera 62, 177, 249, 252
video display terminal 28
video games 33, 34
villosa 150
vinegar 71, 72, 75, 123, 170, 208, 255
Vint, Vinton 241
VIOLENCE 15, 24, 270
viral illness 5
viral infections 5, 51, 74, 80
Virginia Mason Clinic 158
viruses 5, 9, 37, 48, 79, 80, 83, 87, 141, 161, 171, 172, 270
VIRUSES AND OTHER MICROOR-GANISMS: 171
vision, blurred 28
vision, double 28
vision problems, uncorrected 28
visualization, direct 250
Visualization 9, 27, 96, 128, 129, 177, 185, 250
vitamin-B6 deficiency 51
vitamin-C 6, 7, 17, 25, 51, 83, 124, 185, 199, 200, 206, 207, 237, 247, 248, 255
vitamin-D 6, 206-208, 211
vitamin-D3 211
vitamin-E oil 124, 133, 199, 255
vitamin protocols, intravenous 8
VITAMIN-C AND BIOFLAVONOIDS: 199
VITAMIN-E 6, 7, 51, 124, 133, 149, 156, 185, 194, 198-200, 206, 248, 255
VITAMIN-E OIL OR CASTOR OIL AND VITAMIN-E OIL MIXED: 199
vitamins, fat soluble 261
VITAMINS AND VARICOSE VEINS 255
Vitaplex Natural's 207
VLF WAVES 31
VOCALIZATION 128
voltage, high 30, 33, 34
vomiting 51, 55, 122, 123, 151, 239, 245, 262
vulva to vulva contact 270

W:

waist 228
Walker, M. 74
Walsh, Dr. M. L. 32
Warshow, Joyce 272
warts 48, 88, 270
warts, venereal 88, 270
Washington State Department of Labour and Industries 29
water beds 30, 37, 238
water, Cold running 255

water, drinking 121, 157, 247
water, pure 121, 200
water purification systems 157, 159
Water pills 146, 151
WATERBIRTH, THE CONCISE GUIDE TO USING WATER DURING PREGNANCY 95
waters, bag 108
waters, too little 103
waters, too much 103
Weed, Susun 124, 179, 184, 198, 202, 241
weeping spells 139
weight, Difficulty in losing 143
weight gain 51, 53, 95, 117, 124, 141, 147, 151, 175, 190, 214
weight gain, excessive 117
weight gain, modest 141
weight gain, reduced 151
weight, ideal body 266
weight, Inability to gain 143
weight loss 142, 261, 265
weight, normal body 266
weights 102, 200, 206
Weinstein, Kate 186
Weinstein, Merryl 68
Weintraub, Pamela 99
Weiss, Jill 51, 161, 253
Wesson, Nicky 95, 124
Western University 31, 47, 137
WHAT TO EAT WHEN YOU'RE EXPECTING 95
WHAT TO EXPECT WHEN YOU'RE EXPECTING 94
WHAT YOUR DOCTOR MAY NOT TELL YOU ABOUT MENOPAUSE 212
wheat, whole 123, 247, 266
Whelan, Dr. Paul 264, 265
WHEN A BABY DIES 43
WHEN A CHILD OR BABY DIES 43
WHEN A PARENT IS VERY SICK 43
WHEN SOCIETY BECOMES AN ADDICT 27
Whitehead, Dr. Malcolm 193, 209
WHITEWASH 179
Whitmore, Kristene 78, 80, 83-85
WHO KILLED CANDIDA? 74
WIDOWS 43
wife, perfect 20
Wilde, Dr. Adolphe 57
Wildman, Bill 259
Wiley, Dr. Michael 31, 177, 222, 225
will, legal 269
Williams, Dr. Noel 262, 265, 266
Williams, Megan 230
wills, living 43
Wilson, Denis 143
Wilson, Dr. Douglas 103
Wilson, Dr. Robert 111, 113, 149-151, 154
WILSON'S SYNDROME, DOCTOR'S MANUAL 143
WILSON'S SYNDROME, THE MIRACLE OF FELLING WELL 143
wine 22, 79, 217
wise woman tradition 184
WISE WOMAN HERBAL FOR THE CHILD-BEARING YEAR 124
WISE WOMAN WAYS 202

witch hazel 72, 255
Witkin-Lanoil, Dr. Georgia 15, 16, 21
Wolfe, Dr. Sidney 195
Wolfe, Honora Lee 202
Wolff, Dr. Mary 230
Woman and Environments Education and Development Foundation 179
womb 48, 49, 55, 87, 98, 99, 105, 109, 112, 249
Womb Harmonics 99
women, non-European 188
women, older 24, 42, 50, 115, 175, 191, 203, 218, 220, 234
women, white 205
women, young 54, 62, 87, 92, 150, 171, 175, 226
Women And Work Research and Education Society 36
WOMEN CENTRED STRESS TEST 13
WOMEN FOR SOBRIETY 23, 26, 27
WOMEN FOR SOBRIETY ACCEPTANCE PROGRAM 26
WOMEN PAID/UNPAID WORK AND STRESS 12, 16
Women's College Hospital 132, 150
Women's Health Initiative 196
Women's Health Practice 154
Women's Nutritional Advisory Service 154
WOMEN'S INTERNATIONAL PHARMACY 204, 213
Wooley, Dr. Paul 178
word processing 28, 37
work environment 28, 33, 36
work habits 36
work regimens 28
Work stations 3, 28, 29, 34
workers, sex trade 270
working conditions 2, 14, 28, 29
WORKING WOMAN'S GUIDE TO BREAST-FEEDING 96
Workman's Compensation Board 32
workplace 10, 13, 36, 37, 146, 238
World Congress of Gynecologic Endoscopy 224
World Health Organization 50
Wright, Dr. Charles 227, 233, 234
Wright, Dr. Jonathan 156, 159, 208
wrinkles 189, 190
wrist area 252
wrist bone 205
wrist muscles 29
wrist pain 29, 36
wrist tendons 29
Wrist Size 216
wrists 29, 36, 150, 205, 207, 212, 216, 252
Wylie, Betty Jane 43

X, Y, Z:

X chromosome 108
X-ray examination 227
X-ray exposure 105, 179, 231, 233, 236, 238
X-ray history 233
X-ray, kidney 81
X-ray machine, dedicated 228
X-rays, chest 163, 233

X-rays, unnecessary 238
xanax 151
Yale University 175
Yamcon 204, 213
yam creams, wild 150, 212
yeast, Chronic 4-6, 13, 70, 73-76, 79, 81, 84-86, 91, 148, 184
yeast desensitization shots 184
yeast growth is predominate in the intestines 76
yeast infection, full-blown 72
yeast infections 4, 5, 6, 50, 70-77, 79, 84-86, 91, 148, 149, 184, 185
yeast infections, recurrent 70, 71, 73
yeast infections, severe 75
yeast infections, simple 71, 72
yeast infections, Vaginal 70
yeast overgrowth 73, 76, 184
yeast smell, fermenting 72
YEAST CONSULTING SERVICES 77
YEAST INFECTION, SYMPTOMS 71
YEAST INFECTIONS, PERSIS-TENT REOCCURRING 73
yoga 96, 118, 120, 150, 154, 200, 202
yogurt 79, 115, 123, 170
York, Geoffrey 12
YOU CAN FIGHT FOR YOUR LIFE 240, 241
YOU CAN PREVENT BREAST CANCER 241
YOU DON'T HAVE TO LIVE WITH CYSTITIS 85
YOU DON'T NEED A HYSTER-ECTOMY: 225
YOUNG WOMEN AND PID: 171
Youngblood, Dr. James 103
YOUR BABY, YOUR WAY: 94
YOUR FERTILITY SIGNALS 68
yuppie flu 5
zantac 84
Zerach-Bersin, D. and K. 21, 37
Ziedrich, Linda 96
zinc 6, 25, 51, 76, 123, 124, 149, 207, 208, 245, 247, 255
zinc, chelated 51
zinc, excess 247
ZOLADEX: 176
Zoldbrod, Aline 69, 140